EDMUND WILSON

LITERARY ESSAYS AND REVIEWS OF THE 1920s & 30s

The Shores of Light
Axel's Castle
Uncollected Reviews

THE LIBRARY OF AMERICA

The paper used in this publication meets the
minimum requirements of the American National Standard for
Information Sciences—Permanence of Paper for Printed
Library Materials, ANSI Z39.48—1984.

Distributed to the trade
in the United States by Penguin Putnam Inc.
and in Canada by Penguin Books Canada Ltd.

Library of Congress Control Number: 2007928898
ISBN 978-1-59853-013-1

First Printing
The Library of America—176

Manufactured in the United States of America

Edmund Wilson's
Literary Essays and Reviews of the 1920s & 30s
is published with support from

THE GEOFFREY C. HUGHES FOUNDATION

and will be kept in print by its gift to
the Guardians of American Letters Fund,
established by The Library of America
to ensure that every volume in the series
will be permanently available.

Contents

THE SHORES OF LIGHT

*A Literary Chronicle
of the Twenties and Thirties*

CONTENTS

THIS BOOK was originally planned as a companion volume to my *Classics and Commercials: A Literary Chronicle of the Forties*: a similar selection from my literary articles published during the twenties and thirties; but it has turned into something rather different. I have aimed in the present collection to present a kind of panorama of the books and the ideas, the movements and the literary life, of a period that was very much livelier and had a much more exciting development than the war-darkened years of the forties. I have therefore included some youthful stuff that can only, if at all, be of interest from an historical point of view—in showing how it looked to a contemporary; and I have not confined myself, as in the earlier volume, to essays and reviews, but have admitted dialogues, jeux d'esprit, satires, short sketches and personal letters. I have even put in a few pieces that do not deal with writing at all, but these, too, are intended to contribute to a general picture of the culture of a recklessly unspecialized era, when minds and imaginations were exploring in all directions. I have suppressed the worst of my aberrations, and I have thoroughly revised almost everything, sometimes trimming and toning down what I originally wrote and sometimes expanding it with material taken from my old notes. In the case of some articles that had been hastily written, I have found it a satisfaction to get them into better shape, even after twenty or thirty years. In this volume, I have not arranged the pieces in strictly chronological order, but have sometimes grouped them in such a way as to put together pieces on the same subject or to bring out some special aspect of the period.

The reader may find here, as I have done, attitudes that surprise or amuse him; but I have generally refrained from comment and leave him to do his own discounting. The self-assertive approach of the twenties, which seems rather brash today, I have not always been able to eliminate. We had grown up on the journalism of Shaw and Chesterton, Belloc and Max

Beerbohm, and later, in the United States, of the Mencken and Nathan of the *Smart Set* and the Woollcott and Broun of the *World*. All these writers were everlastingly saying "I": the exploitation of personality had become an integral part of criticism. It all stemmed, I suppose, from Oscar Wilde, who had a genius for self-dramatization and who was imitated in this respect by Bernard Shaw. In the twenties a young man who was still nobody made a point of saying "I"—"I don't like so-and-so," "I can't read so-and-so," "I have always thought so-and-so,"—in the hope of being taken for somebody. Now the habit has gone out of fashion. Aside from this personal emphasis, however, I have not reprinted here very much that I disapprove of, as of the date when it was first written—though, of course, I see some things today in a somewhat different perspective: in the light of the author's subsequent work or of my own better information. I have sometimes had to leave in passages that are more or less duplicated in my other books, but I do not suppose that this will worry anybody. I apologize for printing documents in which other writers pay me compliments, but this is part of this ancient history, too, and I have offset them by putting in others in which I am taken to task. I have added a few pieces of later date, whose presence explains itself.

Of these ninety-seven pieces, seventy-three first appeared in the *New Republic*. *Christian Gauss as a Teacher of Literature* was first printed in the *American Scholar*; *The Literary Worker's Polonius* in the *Atlantic Monthly*; *F. Scott Fitzgerald* in the *Bookman*; *Marxism at the End of the Thirties* in the New York *Call*; *The Classics on the Soviet Stage* in the Moscow *Daily News*; *Mr. E. A. Robinson's Moonlight*, *"A Lost Lady,"* *Byron and His Biographers*, *Late Violets from the Nineties*, *Sherwood Anderson's "Many Marriages,"* *Ring Lardner's American Characters*, *Mr. Hemingway's Dry-Points* and *"The Seven Lively Arts"* in the *Dial*; *The Pleasures of Literature* and *Edna St. Vincent Millay* in the *Nation*; *"The Great Audience," "Things As They Are," Dream Poetry* and the second article, of which part is given under *Talking United States*, in the *New Yorker*; *The New Byron Letters* in the New York *Tribune*; and *"One of Ours"* and *Eugene O'Neill as Prose Writer* in *Vanity Fair*. The following pieces were included, after their first periodical publication, in collections of essays by various hands: *F. Scott Fitzgerald* in *The Literary Spotlight*, published by George H. Doran in 1924; *The All-Star Literary Vaudeville* in *American Criticism*, published by Harcourt, Brace in 1926; and *Notes on Babbitt and More* in *The Critique of Humanism*, published by Brewer & Warren in 1930. *The Satire of Samuel Butler* appeared in my book *The Triple Thinkers*, published by Harcourt, Brace in 1938, but was removed in a later edition to make room for new material. The two *Imaginary Dialogues* are reprinted from a book of mine, *Discordant Encounters*, published by Albert & Charles Boni in 1926.

I have to thank Mr. Ernest Hemingway, Mr. Henry Miller, M. André Malraux and Mr. John Crowe Ransom for permission to print their letters; Mr. Leonard Woolf for permission to reprint a letter of Virginia Woolf; Miss Norma Millay for permission to print two letters of Edna St. Vincent Millay; Mr. Harold R. Medina for permission to reprint his tribute to Christian Gauss from the Princeton *Alumni Weekly*; Brandt & Brandt for permission to include *To Love Impuissant* from *A Few Figs From Thistles*, published by Harper & Brothers, copyright 1920, 1948, by Edna St. Vincent Millay, and *Portrait* from *The Buck in the Snow*, published by Harper & Brothers, copyright 1928 by Edna St. Vincent Millay; and Mr. Philip Horton for permission to include a quotation from a letter of Hart Crane included in his biography *Hart Crane*. The words and music of *Wedding Joy* are reprinted by permission from the *Botsford Collection of Folk Songs*, copyright 1929 by G. Schirmer, Inc.

Prologue, 1952

Christian Gauss as a Teacher of Literature

WHEN Christian Gauss of Princeton died on November 1, 1951, I was asked by the Princeton *Alumni Weekly* to write something for a set of tributes that were to appear in the issue of December 7. I sent the editor, who wanted a column, only part of what I had written in response to this request, and even this was much cut before it was printed. I have now further elaborated my original memoir, and I am including it here to serve as a sort of prologue, for it indicates to some extent the point of view from which I started off in my criticism of the twenties.

I have been asked to write about Christian Gauss as an influence on my generation at Princeton. Since we knew him as a teacher of literature only—I was in the class of 1916, and he did not become dean of the college till 1925—I shall speak mainly of this side of his activity.

As a professor of French and Italian, then, one of the qualities that distinguished Gauss was the unusual fluidity of mind that he preserved through his whole career. A teacher like Irving Babbitt was a dogmatist who either imposed his dogma or provoked a strong opposition. Christian Gauss was a teacher of a different kind—the kind who starts trains of thought that he does not himself guide to conclusions but leaves in the hands of his students to be carried on by themselves. The student might develop, extend them, transpose them into different terms, build out of them constructions of his own. Gauss never imposed, he suggested; and his own ideas on any subject were always taking new turns: the light in which he saw it would be shifted, it would range itself in some new context. It bored him, in his course on French Romanticism, to teach the same texts year after year; and with the writers that he could not get away from, he would vary the works read. With the less indispensable ones, he would change the repertory altogether. If Alfred de Vigny, for example, had been featured in the course

when you took it, you might come back a few years later and
find that he had been pushed into the background by Stendhal. Christian would have been reading up Stendhal, and his
interest in him would seem almost as fresh as if he had never
read him before. He would have some new insights about him,
and he would pass these on to you when you came to see him,
as he was doing to his students in class. I know from my own
experience how the lightly dropped seeds from his lectures
could take root and unfold in another's mind; and, while occupied in writing this memoir, I have happened to find striking
evidence of the persistence of this vital gift in the testimony of
a student of Romance languages who sat under Gauss twenty
years later, and who has told me that, in preparing his doctor's
thesis, he had at first been exhilarated by an illusion of developing original ideas, only to find the whole thing in germ in
his old notes on Gauss's lectures. But though his influence
on his students was so penetrating, Gauss founded no school
of teaching—not even, I suppose, an academic tradition—
because, as one of his colleagues pointed out to me, he had no
communicable body of doctrine and no pedagogical method
that other teachers could learn to apply. If one went back to
Princeton to see him, as I more or less regularly did, after one
had got out of college, one's memory of his old preceptorials
(relatively informal discussions with groups of five or six students) would seem prolonged, without interruptions, into
one's more recent conversations, as if it had all been a long
conversation that had extended, off and on, through the years:
a commentary that, on Christian's part, never seemed to be
trying to prove anything in any overwhelming way, a voyage
of speculation that aimed rather to survey the world than to fix
a convincing vision. In his role of the least didactic of sages,
the most accessible of talkers, he seemed a part of that good
eighteenth-century Princeton which has always managed to
flourish between the pressures of a narrow Presbyterianism
and a rich man's suburbanism. It is probable that Christian was
at home in Princeton as he would not have been anywhere
else. He was delightful in the days of his deanship, in the solid
and compact and ample yellow-and-white Joseph Henry house,
built in 1837, where there was always, during the weekends, a
constant going and coming of visitors, who could pick up with

him any topic, literary, historical or collegiate, and pursue it till someone else came and the thread was left suspended. Though by this time so important a local figure, he seemed always, also, international. He had been born of German parents in Michigan, and German had been his first language. In his youth he had spent a good deal of time in France. He had no foreign accent in English, and, so far as I was able to judge, spoke all his languages correctly and fluently; but French, Italian and English, at any rate, with a deliberate articulation, never running the words together, as if they were not native to him. One did not learn a bad accent from him, but one did not learn to speak the Romance languages as they are spoken in their own countries. On the other hand, the very uniformity of his candid tone, his unhurried pace and his scrupulous precision, with his slightly drawling intonations, made a kind of neutral medium in which everything in the world seemed soluble. I have never known anyone like him in any academic community. He gave the impression of keeping in touch, without the slightest effort—he must have examined all the printed matter that came into the university library—with everything that was going on everywhere, as well as everything that had ever gone on. It used to amuse me sometimes to try him out on unlikely subjects. If one asked him a question about the Middle Ages, one absolutely got the impression that he had lived in Europe then and knew it at firsthand.

This extreme flexibility and enormous range were, of course, a feature of his lectures. He was able to explain and appreciate almost any kind of work of literature from almost any period. He would show you what the author was aiming at and the methods he had adopted to achieve his ends. He was wonderful at comparative literature, for his reading had covered the whole of the West, ancient, medieval and modern, and his memory was truly Macaulayan (an adjective sometimes assigned too cheaply). He seemed to be able to summon almost anything he wanted in prose or verse, as if he were taking down the book from the shelf. (He told me once that, in his younger days, he had set out to write something about Rabelais and had presently begun to grow suspicious of what he saw coming out. On looking up Taine's essay on Rabelais, he found that he had been transcribing whole paragraphs from it,

his unconscious doing the work of translation.) He was brilliant at revealing the assumptions, social, aesthetic and moral,
implicit in, say, a scene from a romantic play as contrasted with
a scene from a Greek tragedy, or in the significance of a character in Dante as distinguished from the significance of a
character in Shakespeare. I remember his later quoting with
approval A. N. Whitehead's statement, in *Science and the Modern World*, that, "when you are criticizing the philosophy of an
epoch," you should "not chiefly direct your attention to those
intellectual positions which its exponents feel it necessary explicitly to defend. There will be some fundamental assumptions which adherents of all the variant systems within the
epoch unconsciously presuppose. Such assumptions appear so
obvious that people do not know what they are assuming
because no other way of putting things has ever occurred to
them." Gauss had always had a special sense of this. But he was
interested also in individuals and liked to bring out the traits of
a literary personality. His commentary on a poem of Victor
Hugo's—*Le Mendiant* from *Les Contemplations*—would run
along something like this: "A poor man is passing in the frost
and rain, and Victor Hugo asks him in. He opens the door
'd'une façon civile'—he is always democratic, of course. *'Entrez,
brave homme,'* he says, and he tells the man to warm himself
and have a bowl of milk brought him—as anybody, of course,
would do. He makes him take off his cloak—*'tout mangé des
vers, et jadis bleu'*—and he hangs it on a nail, where the fire
shines through its holes, so that it looks like a night illumined
by stars.

> Et, pendant qu'il séchait ce haillon désolé
> D'où ruisselaient la pluie et l'eau des fondrières,
> Je songeais que cet homme était plein de prières.
> Et je regardais, sourd à ce que nous disions,
> Sa bure où je voyais des constellations.

"This sounds impressive, but what does it mean? Not a thing.
We have not been told anything that would indicate that the
old man is full of prayers. It is a gratuitous assumption on the
part of Hugo. That the cloak with its holes reminded him of a
heaven with constellations has no moral significance whatever.
Yet with his mastery of verse and his rhetoric, Victor Hugo

manages to carry it off. —I don't mean," he would add, "that he was insincere. Rather than live under Louis Napoleon, he went into voluntary exile—at considerable personal inconvenience—for almost twenty years. He lived up to his democratic principles, but he was always a bit theatrical, and he was not very profound."

I include such reminiscences of the classroom in the hope that they may be of interest in putting on record Gauss's methods as a teacher, for the work of a great teacher who is not, as Gauss was not, a great writer is almost as likely to be irrecoverable as the work of a great actor. Not that Christian was ever in the least histrionic, as some of the popular professors of the time were. On the contrary, for all the friendliness of one's relations with him outside class when one eventually got to know him, his tone was sober and quiet, his attitude detached and impersonal. This was partly due to shyness, no doubt; but the impression he made was formidable. He would come into the classroom without looking at us, and immediately begin to lecture, with his eyes dropped to his notes, presenting a mask that was almost Dantesque and levelling on us only occasionally the clear gaze that came through his eyeglasses. When he made us recite in Dante, he would sometimes pace to and fro between the desk and the window, with his hands behind his back, rarely consulting the text, which he apparently knew by heart. In the case of some appalling error, he would turn with a stare of ironic amazement and remonstrate in a tone of mock grief: "You thought that barretry was the same as banditry? O-o-oh, Mr. X, that's too-oo ba-a-ad!" This last exclamation, drawled out, was his only way of indicating disapproval. His voice was always low and even, except at those moments when he became aware that the class was falling asleep, when he would turn on another voice, loud, nasal, declamatory and pitilessly distinct, which would be likely to begin in the middle of a sentence for the sake of the shock-value, I think, and in order to dissociate this special effect from whatever he happened to be saying—which might be something no more blood-curdling than a statement that André Chénier had brought to the classical forms a nuance of romantic feeling. When this voice would be heard in the class next door—for it penetrated the partition like a fire-siren—it always made people laugh; but for the students in Gauss's own room, it seemed to saw right through the base of the spine and made them sit forward intently. When it had had this effect, it would cease. He was never sarcastic and never bullied; but the discipline he maintained was perfect. Any signs of disorder were silenced by one straight and stern look.

Nevertheless, though Christian's methods were nondramatic, he had a knack of fixing in one's mind key passages and key facts. His handling of Rousseau, for example, was most effective in building up the importance of a writer whom we might otherwise find boring. (In this case, he *has* left something that can be used by his successors in his volume of *Selections* from Rousseau, published by the Princeton University Press—though, as usual with Gauss's writing, the introduction and notes have little of the peculiar effectiveness of his lecture-room presentation.) He would start off by planting, as it were, in our vision of the panorama of history that critical moment of Rousseau's life which, since he did not include it in the *Confessions*, having already described it in the first of his letters to M. de Malesherbes, is likely to be overlooked or insufficiently emphasized (compare Saintsbury's slurring-over of this incident and its consequences for Western thought, in his *Encyclopedia Britannica* article): the moment, almost as momentous as that of Paul's conversion on the road to Damascus, when Jean-Jacques, then thirty-seven, was walking from Paris to Vincennes, where he was going to see Diderot in prison, and happened to read the announcement that the Academy of Dijon was offering a prize for the best essay on the question, "Has the progress of the arts and sciences contributed to corrupt or to purify society?" Such an incident Gauss made memorable, invested with reverberating significance, by a series of incisive strokes that involved no embroidery or dramatics. It was, in fact, as if the glamor of legend, the grandeur of history, had evaporated and left him exposed to our passing gaze, the dusty and sunstruck Jean-Jacques—the clockmaker's son of Geneva, the ill-used apprentice, the thieving lackey, the vagabond of the roads—sinking down under a tree and dazzled by the revelation that all the shames and misfortunes of his life had been the fault of the society that had bred him—that "man is naturally good and that it is only through institutions that men have become wicked." In the same way, he made us feel the pathos and the psychological importance of the moment when the sixteen-year-old apprentice, returning from a walk in the country, found for the third time the gates of Geneva locked against him, and decided that he would never go back.

Christian admired the romantics and expounded them with the liveliest appreciation; but the romantic ideal in literature was not his own ideal. In spite of his imaginative gift for entering into other people's points of view, he was devoted to a certain conception of art that inevitably asserted itself and that had a tremendous influence on the students with literary interests who were exposed to Gauss's teaching. Let me try to define this ideal. Christian had first known Europe at firsthand as a foreign correspondent in the Paris of the late nineties, and he had always kept a certain loyalty to the "aestheticism" of the end of the century. There was a legend that seemed almost incredible of a young Christian Gauss with long yellow hair—in our time he was almost completely bald—who had worn a green velvet jacket;* and he would surprise you from time to time by telling you of some conversation he had had with Oscar Wilde or describing some such bohemian character as Bibi-La-Purée. It was rumored—though I never dared ask him about this—that he had once set out to experiment one by one with all the drugs mentioned in Baudelaire's *Les Paradis Artificiels*. He rather admired Wilde, with whom he had talked in cafés, where the latter was sitting alone and running up high piles of saucers. He had given Christian copies of his books, inscribed; and Christian used to tell me, with evident respect, that Wilde in his last days had kept only three volumes: a copy of Walter Pater's *The Renaissance* that had been given him by Pater, Flaubert's *La Tentation de Saint Antoine* and Swinburne's *Atalanta in Calydon*. And it was always Gauss's great advantage over the school of Babbitt and More that he understood the artist's morality as something that expressed itself in different terms than the churchgoer's or the citizen's morality; the fidelity to a kind of truth that is rendered by the discipline

*I learn from Mrs. Gauss, who has shown me a photograph, that the realities behind this legend were a head of blond bushy hair and a jacket which, though green, was not velvet.

of aesthetic form, as distinct from that of the professional moralist: the explicit communication of a "message." But there was nothing in his attitude of the truculent pose, the defiance of the bourgeoisie, that had been characteristic of the fin de siècle and that that other professor of the Romance languages, Gauss's near-contemporary, Ezra Pound, was to sustain through his whole career. How fundamental to his point of view, how much a thing to be taken for granted, this attitude had become, was shown clearly in a conversation I had with him, on some occasion when I had come back after college, when, in reply to some antinomian attitude of mine, or one that he imputed to me, he said, "But you were saying just now that you would have to rewrite something before it could be published. That implies a moral obligation." And his sense of the world and the scope of art was, of course, something very much bigger than was common among the aesthetes and the symbolists.

Partly perhaps as a heritage from the age of Wilde but, more deeply, as a logical consequence of his continental origin and culture, he showed a pronounced though discreet parti pris against the literature of the Anglo-Saxon countries. In our time, he carried on a continual feud—partly humorous, yet basically serious—with the canons of the English department. I remember his telling me, with sly satisfaction, about a visiting French professor, who had asked, when it was explained to him that someone was an authority on Chaucer, *"Il est intelligent tout de même?"* Certain classical English writers he patronized—in some cases, rightly, I think. Robert Browning, in particular, he abominated. The author of *Pippa Passes* was one of the very few writers about whom I thought his opinions intemperate. "That Philistine beef-eating Englishman," he would bait his colleagues in English, "—what did he know about art? He writes lines like 'Irks care the crop-full bird? Frets doubt the maw-crammed beast?'" When I tried to find out once why Browning moved Christian to such special indignation, he told me, a little darkly, that he had greatly admired him in boyhood and had learned from him "a lot of bad doctrine." He said that the irregular love affairs in Browning were made to seem too jolly and simple, and insisted that the situation of the self-frustrated lovers of *The Statue and the Bust* had never been faced by Browning: If "the end in sight was a vice," the poet should not have wanted to have them get together; if he wanted them to get together, he ought not to have described it as a vice, but, on the other hand, he ought to have foreseen a mess. "He is one of the most immoral poets because he makes moral problems seem easy. He tells you that the good is sure to triumph." He would suggest to you an embarrassing picture of a Browning offensively hearty—"not robust," he would say slily, "but robustious"—bouncing and booming in Italy, while the shades of Leopardi and Dante looked on, as Boccaccio said of the latter, "*con isdegnoso occhio.*" The kind of thing he especially hated was such a poem as the one, in *James Lee's Wife*, that begins, "O good gigantic smile o' the brown old earth." . . . Of Byron—though Byron's writing was certainly more careless than Browning's—he had a much better opinion, because, no doubt, of Byron's fondness for the Continent as well as his freer intelligence and his experience of the ills of the world. He accepted Byron's love affairs—he had nothing of the prig or the Puritan—because Byron knew what he was doing and was not misleading about it. As for Shakespeare, though Christian was, of course, very far from the point of view of Voltaire, there was always just a suggestion of something of the kind in the background. He knew Shakespeare well and quoted him often, but Shakespeare was not one of the authors whom Christian had lived in or on; and he always made us feel that that sort of thing could never come up to literature that was polished and carefully planned and that knew how to make its points and the meaning of the points it was making. He was certainly unfair to Shakespeare in insisting that the Shakespearean characters all talk the same language, whereas Dante's all express themselves differently. For Christian, the great poet was Dante, and he gradually convinced you of this in his remarkable Dante course. He made us see the objectivity of Dante and the significance of his every stroke, so that even the geographical references have a moral and emotional force (the Po that finds peace with its tributaries in the Paolo and Francesca episode, the mountain in the Ugolino canto that prevents the Pisans from seeing their neighbors of Lucca); the vividness of the scenes and the characters (he liked to point out how

Farinata's arrogant poise was thrown into dramatic relief by the passionate interruption of Cavalcanti); and the tremendous intellectual power by which all sorts of men and women exhibiting all sorts of passions have been organized in an orderly vision that implies, also, a reasoned morality. No Englishman, he made us feel, could ever have achieved this; it would never have occurred to Shakespeare. Nor could any English novelist have even attempted what Gustave Flaubert had achieved—a personal conception of the world, put together, without a visible seam, from apparently impersonal descriptions, in which, as in Dante, not a stroke was wasted. He admired the Russians, also, for their sober art of implication. I remember his calling our attention to one of the church scenes in Tolstoy's *Resurrection*, in which, as he pointed out, Tolstoy made no overt comment, yet caused you to loathe the whole thing by describing the ceremony step by step. This non-English, this classical and Latin ideal, became indissolubly associated in our minds with the summits of literature. We got from Gauss a good many things, but the most important things we got were probably Flaubert and Dante. John Peale Bishop, who came to Princeton intoxicated with Swinburne and Shelley, was concentrating, by the time he graduated, on hard images and pregnant phrases. Ezra Pound and the imagists, to be sure, had a good deal to do with this, but Gauss's courses were important, too, and such an early poem of Bishop's as *Losses*, which contrasts Verlaine with Dante, was directly inspired by them. Less directly, perhaps, but no less certainly, the development of F. Scott Fitzgerald from *This Side of Paradise* to *The Great Gatsby*, from a loose and subjective conception of the novel to an organized impersonal one, was also due to Christian's influence. He made us all want to write something in which every word, every cadence, every detail, should perform a definite function in producing an intense effect.

Gauss's special understanding of the techniques of art was combined, as is not always the case, with a highly developed sense of history, as well as a sense of morality (he admirably prepared us for Joyce and Proust). If he played down—as I shall show in a moment—the Thomist side of Dante to make us see him as a great artist, he brought out in Flaubert the moralist and the bitter critic of history. And so much, at that period, was all his thought pervaded by the *Divine Comedy* that even his own version of history had at moments a Dantesque touch. It would not have been difficult, for example, to transpose such a presentation as the one of Rousseau that I have mentioned above into the sharp concise self-description of a character in the *Divina Commedia*: "I am the clockmaker's son of Geneva who said that man has made man perverse. When for the third time the cruel captain closed the gates, I made the sky my roof, and found in Annecy the love Geneva had denied" . . .

With this sense of history of Christian's was involved another strain in his nature that had nothing to do with the aestheticism of the nineties and yet that lived in his mind with it quite comfortably. His father, who came from Baden—he was a relative of the physicist Karl Friedrich Gauss—had taken part in the unsuccessful German revolution of 1848 and come to the United States with the emigration that followed it. The spirit of '48 was still alive in Christian, and at the time of the first World War an hereditary hatred of the Prussians roused him to a passionate championship of the anti-German cause even before the United States declared war. Later on, when Prohibition was imposed on the nation, the elder Gauss, as Christian told me, was so much infuriated by what he regarded as an interference nothing short of Prussian with the rights of a free people that he could not talk calmly about it, and, even when dean of the college and obliged to uphold the law, the American-born Christian continued in public to advocate its repeal, which required a certain courage in Presbyterian Princeton. It was this old-fashioned devotion to liberty that led him to admire Hugo for his refusal to live under the Second Empire, and Byron for his willingness to fight for Italian and Greek liberation. "Everywhere he goes in Europe," Christian would say of Byron, "it is the places, such as the prison of Chillon, where men have been oppressed, that arouse him." When he lectured on Anatole France, he would point out the stimulating contrast between the early France of *Sylvestre Bonnard*, who always wrote, as he said, like a kindly and bookish old man, and the France who defended Dreyfus, made a tour of the provinces to speak for him and remained for the rest of his life a social satirist and a radical publicist. In the years when

I was first at Princeton, Gauss called himself, I believe, a socialist; and during the years of depression in the thirties, he gravitated again toward the Left and, in *A Primer for Tomorrow*
(1934), he made some serious attempt to criticize the financial-
industrial system. In an inscription in the copy he sent me, he
said that my stimulation had counted for something in his
writing the book. But I was never able to persuade him to read
Marx and Engels at firsthand: he read Werner Sombart instead; and I noted this, like the similar reluctance of Maynard
Keynes to look into Marx, as a curious confirmation of the
theory of the Marxists that the "bourgeois intellectuals" instinctively shy away from Marxist thought to the extent of
even refusing to find out what it really is. Yet Christian had
read Spengler with excitement—it was from him that I first
heard of *The Decline of the West*—immediately after the war;
and he never, in these later years, hesitated, in conversation, to
indulge the boldest speculations as to the destiny of contemporary society.

He was a member of the National Committee of the American Civil Liberties Union, and he made a point, after the second war, of speaking to Negro audiences in the South. On
my last visit to Princeton when I saw him, in the spring of 1951,
he talked to me at length about his adventures in the color-
discrimination states—how the representatives of some Negro
organization under whose auspices he had been speaking had
been unable to come to see him in his white hotel, and how, as
he told me with pride, he had succeeded, for the first time in
the history of Richmond, in assembling—in a white church, to
which, however, he found the Negroes were only admitted on
condition of their sitting in the back pews—a mixed black and
white audience. As he grew older, he became more interna-
tionalist. He foresaw, and he often insisted, at the end of the
first World War, that nothing but trouble could come of creating more small European states, and, at the end of the second
war, he was bitterly opposed to what he regarded as the development of American nationalism. He complained much, in this
connection, of the intensive cultivation, in the colleges, of
American literature, which had been carried on since sometime in the middle thirties with a zeal that he thought more

and more menacing to sound international values. I did not, on the whole, agree with him in disapproving of the growth of American studies; but I could see that, with his relative indifference to English literature, he must have conceived, at the end of the century, an extremely low opinion of American. He took no interest in Henry James and not very much in Walt Whitman. He told me once that Henry Ford had said, "Cut your own wood and it will warm you twice," not knowing that Ford had been quoting Thoreau. For Christian, the level of American writing was more or less represented by William Dean Howells, the presiding spirit of the years of his youth, for whom he felt hardly the barest respect. It was absolutely incredible to him—and in this I did agree with him—that *The Rise of Silas Lapham* should ever have been thought an important novel. "It wasn't much of a rise," he would say. Yet the "renaissance" of the twenties—unlike Paul Elmer More—he followed with sympathetic, if critical, interest.

Christian Gauss was complex personality as well as a subtle mind, and one finds it in some ways difficult to sort out one's impressions of him. I want to try to deal now with the moral qualities which, combined with his unusual intellectual powers, gave him something of the stature of greatness. In some sense, he was a moral teacher as well as a literary one; but his teaching, in the same way as his criticism, was conveyed by throwing out suggestions and dropping incidental comments. In this connection, I want to quote here the tribute of Mr. Harold R. Medina, the distinguished federal judge, from the symposium in the *Alumni Weekly*. It expresses a good deal better than anything I was able to write myself, when I drafted this memoir for the first time, the penetrating quality of Gauss's power, and is interesting to me in describing an experience that closely parallels my own on the part of an alumnus of an earlier class—1909—who was to work in a different field yet who had known Christian Gauss, as I had, not as dean of the college, but as teacher of literature.

"Of all the men whom I have met," Mr. Medina writes, "only four have significantly influenced my life. Dean Gauss was the second of these; the first, my father. From freshman year on I had many courses and precepts with Dean Gauss and during my senior year I was with him almost daily. He attracted me as he did everyone else; and I sensed that he had something to impart which was of infinitely greater importance than the mere content of the courses in French Literature. It was many years after I left Princeton before I realized that it was he who first taught me how to think. How strange it is that so many people have the notion that they are thinking when they are merely repeating the thoughts of others. He dealt in ideas without seeming to do so; he led and guided with so gentle a touch that one began to think almost despite oneself. The process once started, he continued in such fashion as to instil into my very soul the determination to be a seeker after truth, the elusive, perhaps never to be attained, complete and utter truth, no matter where it led or whom it hurt. How he did it I shall never know; but that it was he I have not the slightest doubt. His own intellectual integrity was a constant example for me to follow. And to this precious element he added another. He gave me the vision of language and literature as something representing the continuous and never-ending flow of man's struggle to think the thoughts which, when put into action, constitute in the aggregate the advance of civilization. Whatever I may be today or may ever hope to be is largely the result of the germination of the seeds he planted. The phenomena of cause and effect are not to be denied. With Dean Gauss there were so many hundreds of persons, like myself, whom he influenced and whose innate talents he developed that the ripples he started in motion were multiplied again and again. In critical times I always wondered whether he approved or would approve of things I said and did. And this went on for over forty years."

"To instil into my very soul the determination to be a seeker after truth . . . no matter where it led or whom it hurt." I remember my own thrilled response when, in taking us through the seventeenth canto of the *Paradiso*, Christian read without special emphasis yet in a way that brought out their conviction some lines that remained from that moment engraved, as they say, on my mind:

E s'io al vero son timido amico,
  Temo di perder viver tra coloro
  Che questo tempo chiameranno antico.

—"If to the truth I prove a timid friend, I fear to lose my life
[to fail of survival] among those who will call this time ancient." The truth about which Dante is speaking is his opinion
of certain powerful persons, who will, as he has just been fore-
warned in Heaven, retaliate by sending him into exile—a truth
which, as Heaven approves, he will not be deterred from uttering. Another moment in the classroom comes back to me
from one of Christian's preceptorials. He had put up to us the
issue created by the self-assertive type of romantic, who followed his own impulse in defiance of conventional morality and
with indifference to social consequences; and he called upon
me to supply him with an instance of moral conflict between
social or personal duty and the duty of self-realization. I gave
him the case of a problem with which I had had lately to deal
as editor of the *Nassau Lit*, when I had not been able to bring
myself to tell a friend who had set his heart upon contributing
that the manuscripts he brought me were hopeless. "That's
not an impulse," said Christian, "to do a humane thing: it's a
temptation to do a weak thing." I was struck also by what
seemed to me the unusual line that he took one day in class
when one of his students complained that he hadn't been able
to find out the meaning of a word. "What did you call it?" asked
Christian. "Didn't you call it something?" The boy confessed
that he hadn't. "That's bad intellectual form," said Christian.
"Like going out in the morning with your face unwashed. In
reading a foreign language, you must never leave a gap or a
blur. If you can't find out what something means, make the
best supposition you can. If it's wrong, the chances are that
the context will show it in a moment or that you'll see, when
the word occurs again, that it couldn't have meant that." This
made such an impression on me that—just as Mr. Medina says
he has been asking himself all his life whether Christian would
approve of his actions—I still make an effort to live up to it.

I love to remember, too, how Christian began one of his lectures as follows: "There are several fundamental philosophies
that one can bring to one's life in the world—or rather, there

are several ways of taking life. One of these ways of taking the
world is not to have any philosophy at all—that is the way that
most people take it. Another is to regard the world as unreal
and God as the only reality; Buddhism is an example of this.
Another may be summed up in the words *Sic transit gloria
mundi*—that is the point of view you find in Shakespeare." He
then went on to an explanation of the eighteenth-century philosophy which assumed that the world was real and that we
ourselves may find some sense in it and make ourselves happy
in it. On another occasion, in preceptorial, Christian asked me,
"Where do you think our ideals come from—justice, righteousness, beauty and so on?" I replied, "Out of the imaginations of
men"; and he surprised me by answering, "That is correct."
This made an impression on me, because he usually confined
himself to a purely Socratic questioning, in which he did not
often allow himself to express his own opinions. I felt that I had
caught him off guard: what he had evidently been expecting to
elicit was either Platonic idealism or Christian revelation.

It was only outside class and at secondhand that I learned
that he said of himself at this time that his only religion was
Dante; yet it could not escape us in the long run that the Dante
we were studying was a secular Dante—or rather, perhaps, a
Dante of the Reformation—the validity of whose art and morality did not in the least depend on one's acceptance or non-
acceptance of the faith of the Catholic Church. Christian would
remind us from time to time of Dante's statement, in his letter
to Can Grande, that his poem, though it purported to describe
a journey to the other world, really dealt with men's life in
this, and we were shown that the conditions of the souls in
Hell, Purgatory and Heaven were metaphors for our moral situation here. The principle of salvation that we learned from
Dante was not the Catholic surrender to Jesus—who plays in
the *Divine Comedy* so significantly small a role—but the vigilant cultivation of *"il ben del intelletto."*

Some of those who had known Christian Gauss in his great
days as a teacher of literature were sorry, after the war, to see
him becoming involved in the administrative side of the University. I remember his saying to me one day, in the early stages
of this, "I've just sent off a lot of letters, and I said to myself as

I mailed them, 'There are seventeen letters to people who don't interest me in the least.'" But the job of the Dean's office did interest him—though it seemed to us that it did not take a Gauss to rule on remiss or refractory students. He had never liked repeating routine, and I suppose that his department was coming to bore him. He made, by all accounts, a remarkable dean—for his card-catalogue memory kept all names and faces on file even for decades after the students had left, and the sensitive feeling for character that had been hidden behind his classroom mask must have equipped him with a special tact in dealing with the difficult cases. His genius for moral values had also a new field now in which it could exercise itself in an immediate and practical way, and the responsibilities of his office—especially in the years just after the war, when students were committing suicide and getting into all sorts of messes— sometimes put upon him an obvious strain. Looking back since his death, it has seemed to me that the Gauss who was dean of Princeton must have differed almost as much from the Gauss with whom I read French and Italian as this austere teacher had done from the young correspondent in Paris, who had paid for Oscar Wilde's drinks. The Gauss I had known in my student days, with his pale cheeks and shuttered gaze, his old raincoat and soft flat hat, and a shabby mongrel dog named Baudelaire which had been left with him by the Jesse Lynch Williamses and which sometimes accompanied him into class —the Gauss who would pass one on the campus without speaking, unless you attracted his attention, in an abstraction like that of Dante in Hell and who seemed to meet the academic world with a slightly constrained self-consciousness at not having much in common with it—this figure warmed up and filled out, became recognizably Princetonian in his neckties and shirts and a touch of that tone that combines a country-club self-assurance with a boyish country-town homeliness. He now met the college world, unscreened, with his humorous and lucid green eyes. He wore golf stockings and even played golf. He interested himself in the football team and made speeches at alumni banquets. Though I know that his influence as dean was exerted in favor of scholarships, higher admission requirements and the salvaging of the Humanities—I cannot do justice here to this whole important phase of his career—the only moments of our long friendship when I was ever at all out of sympathy with him occurred during these years of officialdom; for I felt that he had picked up a little the conventional local prejudices when I would find him protesting against the advent in Princeton of the Institute for Advanced Study or, on one occasion, censoring the *Lit* for publishing a "blasphemous" story. One was always impressed, however, by the way in which he seemed to have absorbed the whole business of the University.

We used to hope that he would eventually be president; but, with the domination of business in the boards of trustees of the larger American colleges, it was almost as improbable that Christian would be asked to be president of Princeton as it would have been that Santayana should be asked to be president of Harvard. Not, of course, that it would ever have occurred to anyone to propose such a post for Santayana, but it was somehow characteristic of Christian's career that the idea should have entered the minds of his friends and that nothing should ever have come of it. There appeared in the whole line of Christian's life a certain diversion of purpose, an unpredictable ambiguity of aim, that corresponded to the fluid indeterminate element in his teaching and conversation. He had originally been a newspaper correspondent and a writer of reviews for the literary journals, who hoped to become a poet. He was later a college professor who had developed into a brilliant critic—by far the best, so far as I know, in our academic world of that period—and who still looked forward to writing books; I once found him, in one of his rare moments of leisure, beginning an historical novel. Then, as dean, in the late twenties and thirties, he came to occupy a position of intercollegiate distinction rather incongruous with that usually prosaic office. Was he a "power" in American education? I do not believe he was. That kind of role is possible only for a theorist like John Dewey or an administrator like Charles W. Eliot. Though he was offered the presidency of another college, he continued at Princeton as dean and simply awaited the age of retirement. When that came, he seemed at first depressed, but later readjusted himself. I enjoyed him in these post-official years. He was no longer overworked and he no longer had to worry about the alumni. He returned to literature and started

an autobiography, with which, however, he said he was unsatisfied. In October of 1951, he had been writing an introduction
for a new edition of Machiavelli's *Prince*, and he was pleased
with it when he had finished. He took Mrs. Gauss for a drive in
the car, and they talked about a trip to Florida. He had seemed
in good spirits and health, though he had complained the Saturday before, after going to the Cornell game, where he had
climbed to one of the top tiers of seats, that he was feeling the
effects of age—he was now seventy-three. The day after finishing his introduction, he took the manuscript to his publisher
in New York and attended there a memorial service for the
Austrian novelist Hermann Broch, whom he had known when
the latter lived in Princeton. While waiting outside the gates
for the train to take him back to Princeton, with the evening
paper in his pocket, his heart failed and he suddenly fell dead.

One had always still expected something further from Christian, had hoped that his character and talents would arrive at
some final fruition. But—what seems to one still incredible—
one's long conversation with him was simply forever suspended. And one sees now that the career was complete, the
achievement is all there. He has left no solid body of writing;
he did not remake Princeton (as Woodrow Wilson in some
sense was able to do); he was not really a public man. He was a
spiritual and intellectual force—one does not know how else
to put it—of a kind that it may be possible for a man to do any
of those other things without in the least becoming. His great
work in his generation was unorganized and unobtrusive; and
Who's Who will tell you nothing about it; but his influence was
vital for those who felt it.

> Chè in la mente m'è fitta, ed or m'accora,
>   La cara e buona imagine paterna
>   Di voi, quando nel mondo ad ora ad ora
> M'insegnavate come l'uom s'eterna. . . .

F. Scott Fitzgerald

I T HAS been said by a celebrated person* that to meet F. Scott Fitzgerald is to think of a stupid old woman with whom someone has left a diamond; she is extremely proud of the diamond and shows it to everyone who comes by, and everyone is surprised that such an ignorant old woman should possess so valuable a jewel; for in nothing does she appear so inept as in the remarks she makes about the diamond.

The person who invented this simile did not know Fitzgerald very well and can only have seen him, I think, in his more diffident or uninspired moods. The reader must not suppose that there is any literal truth in the image. Scott Fitzgerald is, in fact, no old woman, but a very good-looking young man, nor is he in the least stupid, but, on the contrary, exhilaratingly clever. Yet there *is* a symbolic truth in the description quoted above: it is true that Fitzgerald has been left with a jewel which he doesn't know quite what to do with. For he has been given imagination without intellectual control of it; he has been given the desire for beauty without an aesthetic ideal; and he has been given a gift for expression without very many ideas to express.

Consider, for example, the novel—*This Side of Paradise*—with which he founded his reputation. It has almost every fault and deficiency that a novel can possibly have. It is not only highly imitative but it imitates an inferior model. Fitzgerald, when he wrote the book, was drunk with Compton Mackenzie, and it sounds like an American attempt to rewrite *Sinister Street*. Now, Mackenzie, in spite of his gift for picturesque and comic invention and the capacity for pretty writing that he says he learned from Keats, lacks both the intellectual force and the emotional imagination to give body and outline to the material which he secretes in such enormous abundance. With the seeds he took from Keats's garden, one of the best-arranged gardens in England, he exfloreated so profusely that he blotted out the path of his own. Michael Fane, the hero of *Sinister*

*This was Edna St. Vincent Millay, who met Scott Fitzgerald in Paris in the spring of 1921.

30

Street, was swamped in the forest of description; he was smothered by creepers and columbine. From the time he went up to Oxford, his personality began to grow dimmer, and, when he last turned up (in Belgrade) he seemed quite to have lost his identity. As a consequence, Amory Blaine, the hero of *This Side of Paradise*, had a very poor chance of coherence: Fitzgerald did endow him, to be sure, with a certain emotional life which the phantom Michael Fane lacks; but he was quite as much a wavering quantity in a phantasmagoria of incident that had no dominating intention to endow it with unity and force. In short, one of the chief weaknesses of *This Side of Paradise* is that it is really not *about* anything: its intellectual and moral content amounts to little more than a gesture—a gesture of indefinite revolt. The story itself, furthermore, is very immaturely imagined: it is always just verging on the ludicrous. And, finally, *This Side of Paradise* is one of the most illiterate books of any merit ever published (a fault which the publisher's proofreader seems to have made no effort to remedy). Not only is it ornamented with bogus ideas and faked literary references, but it is full of literary words tossed about with the most reckless inaccuracy.

I have said that *This Side of Paradise* commits almost every sin that a novel can possibly commit: but it does not commit the unpardonable sin: it does not fail to live. The whole preposterous farrago is animated with life. It is rather a fluttering and mercurial life: its emotions do not move you profoundly; its drama does not make you hold your breath; but its gaiety and color and movement did make it come as something exciting after the realistic heaviness and dinginess of so much serious American fiction. If one recalls the sort of flavorless fodder of which Ernest Poole's *The Harbor* was an example, one can understand the wild enthusiasm with which *This Side of Paradise* was hailed. The novel was also well-written—well-written in spite of its illiteracies. It is true, as I have said above, that Fitzgerald mishandles words; his works are full of malapropisms of the most disconcerting kind. You will find: "Whatever your flare [sic] proves to be—religion, architecture, literature"; "the Juvenalia of my collected editions"; "There were nice things in it [the room] . . . offsprings of a vicarious [vagarious] impatient taste"; "a mind like his, lucrative in intelligence,

intuition and lightning decision"; etc., etc. It reminds one
rather of:

> Agib, who could readily, at sight,
> Strum a march upon the loud Theodolite.
> He would diligently play
> On the Zoetrope all day,
> And blow the gay Pantechnicon all night.

It is true that Scott Fitzgerald plays the language entirely by
ear. But his instrument, for all that, is no mean one. He has an
instinct for graceful and vivid prose that some of his more pretentious fellows might envy.

In regard to the man himself, there are perhaps two things
worth knowing, for the influence they have had on his work.
In the first place, he comes from the Middle West—from St.
Paul, Minnesota. Fitzgerald is as much of the Middle West of
large cities and country clubs as Sinclair Lewis is of the Middle
West of the prairies and little towns. What we find in him is
much what we find in the more prosperous strata of these cities:
sensitivity and eagerness for life without a sound base of culture and taste; a structure of millionaire residences, brilliant
expensive hotels and exhilarating social activities built not on
the eighteenth century but simply on the flat Western land.
And it seems to me rather a pity that he has not written more
of the West: it is perhaps the only milieu that he thoroughly
understands. When Fitzgerald approaches the East, he brings
to it the standards of the wealthy West—the preoccupation
with display, the appetite for visible magnificence and audible
jamboree, the vigorous social atmosphere of amiable flappers
and youths comparatively untainted as yet by the snobbery of
the East. In *The Beautiful and Damned*, for example, we feel
that he is moving in a vacuum; the characters have no real connection with the background to which they have been assigned; they are not part of the organism of New York as the
characters in, say, the short story *Bernice Bobs Her Hair* are a
part of the organism of St. Paul. Surely F. Scott Fitzgerald
should some day do for Summit Avenue what Lewis has done
for Main Street.

But you are not to suppose from all this that the author of
This Side of Paradise is merely a typical well-to-do Middle

Westerner, with correct clothes and clear skin, who has been sent to the East for college. The second thing one should know about him is that Fitzgerald is partly Irish and that he brings both to life and to fiction certain qualities that are not Anglo-Saxon. For, like the Irish, Fitzgerald is romantic, but also cynical about romance; he is bitter as well as ecstatic; astringent as well as lyrical. He casts himself in the role of playboy, yet at the playboy he incessantly mocks. He is vain, a little malicious, of quick intelligence and wit, and has an Irish gift for turning language into something iridescent and surprising. He often reminds one, in fact, of the description that a great Irishman, Bernard Shaw, has written of the Irish: "An Irishman's imagination never lets him alone, never convinces him, never satisfies him; but it makes him that he can't face reality nor deal with it nor handle it nor conquer it: he can only sneer at them that do . . . and imagination's such a torture that you can't bear it without whisky. . . . And all the while there goes on a horrible, senseless, mischievous laughter."

For the rest, F. Scott Fitzgerald is a rather childlike fellow, very much wrapped up in his dream of himself and his projection of it on paper. For a person of his mental agility, he is extraordinarily little occupied with the general affairs of the world: like a woman, he is not much given to abstract or impersonal thought. Conversations about politics or general ideas have a way of snapping back to Fitzgerald. But this seldom becomes annoying; he is never pretentious or boring. He is quite devoid of affectation and takes the curse off his relentless egoism by his readiness to laugh at himself and his boyish uncertainty of his talent. And he exhibits, in his personality as well as in his writings, a quality rare today among even the youngest American writers: he is almost the only one among them who is capable of lighthearted high spirits. Where a satirist like Sinclair Lewis would stew "the Problem of Salesmanship" in acrid rancorous fumes, Fitzgerald, in *The Beautiful and Damned*, has made of it hilarious farce. His characters—and he—are actors in an elfin harlequinade; they are as nimble, as gay and as lovely —and as hardhearted—as fairies: Columbine elopes with Harlequin on a rope ladder dropped from the Ritz and both go morris-dancing amuck on a case of bootleg liquor; Pantaloon is pinked with an epigram that withers him up like a leaf; the

Policeman is tripped by Harlequin and falls into the Pulitzer Fountain. Just before the curtain falls, Harlequin puts on false whiskers and pretends to be Bernard Shaw; he gives reporters an elaborate interview on politics, religion and history; a hundred thousand readers see it and are more or less impressed; Columbine nearly dies laughing; Harlequin sends out for a case of gin.

Let me quote a characteristic incident in connection with *The Beautiful and Damned*. Since writing *This Side of Paradise* —on the inspiration of Wells and Mackenzie—Fitzgerald has become acquainted with a different school of fiction: the ironical-pessimistic. In college, he had supposed that the thing to do was to write biographical novels with a burst of ideas toward the close; since his advent in the literary world, he has discovered that another genre has recently come into favor: the kind which makes much of the tragedy and what Mencken has called "the meaninglessness of life." Fitzgerald had imagined, hitherto, that the thing to do in a novel was to bring out a meaning in life; but he now set bravely about it to contrive a shattering tragedy that should be, also, a hundred-percent meaningless. As a result of this determination, the first version of *The Beautiful and Damned* culminated in an orgy of horror for which the reader was imperfectly prepared. Fitzgerald destroyed his characters with a succession of catastrophes so arbitrary that, beside them, the perversities of Hardy seemed the working of natural laws. The heroine was to lose her beauty at a prematurely early age, and her character was to go to pieces with it; Richard Carmel, a writer of promise, was to lose his artistic ideals and prostitute himself to the popular taste; and the wealthy Anthony Patch was not only to lose his money but, finding himself unable to make a living, abjectly to succumb to drink and eventually to go insane. But the bitterest moment of the story was to come at the very end, when Anthony was to be wandering the streets of New York in an attempt to borrow some money. After several humiliating failures, he finally approaches an old friend whom he sees with an elegant lady just getting into a cab. This is the brilliant Maury Noble, a cynic, an intellectual and a man of genuine parts. Maury cuts Anthony dead and drives away in the taxi. "But," the author explains, "he really had not seen Anthony. For

Maury had indulged his appetite for alcoholic beverage once too often: he was now stone-blind!" But the point of my story is this: though Fitzgerald had been perfectly serious in writing this bathetic passage, he did not hesitate, when he heard people laugh at it, to laugh about it himself, and with as much surprise and delight as if he had just come across it in Max Beerbohm. He at once improvised a burlesque: "It seemed to Anthony that Maury's eyes had a fixed glassy stare; his legs moved stiffly as he walked and when he spoke his voice was lifeless. When Anthony came nearer, he saw that Maury was dead."

To conclude, it would be quite unfair to subject Scott Fitzgerald, who is still in his twenties and has presumably most of his work before him, to a rigorous overhauling. His restless imagination may yet produce something durable. For the present, however, this imagination is certainly not seen to the best advantage: it suffers badly from lack of discipline and poverty of aesthetic ideas. Fitzgerald is a dazzling extemporizer, but his stories have a way of petering out: he seems never to have planned them completely or to have thought out his themes from the beginning. This is true even of some of his most successful fantasies, such as *The Diamond as Big as the Ritz* or his comedy, *The Vegetable*. On the other hand, *The Beautiful and Damned*, imperfect though it is, marks an advance over *This Side of Paradise*: the style is more nearly mature and the subject more solidly unified, and there are scenes that are more convincing than any in his previous fiction.

But, in any case, even the work that Fitzgerald has done up to date has a certain moral importance. In his very expression of the anarchy by which he finds himself bewildered, of his revolt which cannot fix on an object, he is typical of the war generation—the generation so memorably described on the last page of *This Side of Paradise* as "grown up to find all gods dead, all wars fought, all faiths in men shaken." There is a moral in *The Beautiful and Damned* that the author did not perhaps intend to point. The hero and the heroine of this giddy book are creatures without method or purpose: they give themselves up to wild debaucheries and do not, from beginning to end, perform a single serious act; yet somehow you get the impression that, in spite of their fantastic behavior, Anthony and Gloria Patch are the most rational people in the book. Wherever they come in contact with institutions, with the serious life of their time, these are made to appear ridiculous, they are subjects for scorn or mirth. We see the army, finance and business successively and casually exposed as completely without point or dignity. The inference we are led to draw is that, in such a civilization as this, the sanest and most honorable course is to escape from organized society and live for the excitement of the moment. It cannot be merely a special reaction to a personal situation which gives rise to the paradoxes of such a book. It may be that we cannot demand too high a degree of moral balance from young men, however able or brilliant, who write books in the year 1921: we must remember that they have had to grow up in, that they have had to derive their chief stimulus from the wars, the society and the commerce of the Age of Confusion itself.

March, 1922

Mr. E. A. Robinson's Moonlight

*T*he *Poetry of Edwin Arlington Robinson*, by Mr. Lloyd Morris, "was written to commemorate an award" and "attempts to express the appreciative attitude of the Authors' Club toward Mr. Robinson's work." It is, therefore, rather like a speech at a birthday dinner: except for an interesting and valuable chapter on Robinson's philosophic sources, it has little importance as criticism, and one should not perhaps expect too much of it. Yet one cannot but boggle at the wholesale way in which Mr. Morris has swallowed his subject. There is no word of the poet's limitations; no candid effort to gauge his stature. To read Mr. Morris's monograph, you would think that all Robinson's poems had achieved an equally consummate success.

That this is very far from the case is indicated all too clearly by *Roman Bartholow*, Mr. Robinson's new long poem. This is one of the most arid products of a mind which has always run much into the sands. I will admit, à la rigueur, that the novel in verse is a practicable form—I suppose that *The Ring and the Book* has still some claims to distinction. And I will grant that Mr. Robinson's shadowy world has an authentic relation to the real one: with the examples of Hawthorne and Henry James, we cannot refuse credence to shadows. It seems to he characteristic of the genius of the New England writers that their shrewdness is combined with shyness—that they are occupied with casuistry rather than with action and prefer ghosts to carnal men. To appreciate the fiction of New England, it is necessary to accept this world of phantoms. But what I cannot forgive Robinson the poet is the absence in *Roman Bartholow* of poetry. Surely a poem should be beautiful as well as interesting: it is beauty which makes it a poem. But *Roman Bartholow*, though it sometimes interests, almost never rises to beauty.

Yet Edwin Arlington Robinson began as a real poet—and a poet of a very rare sort. He was the last, and probably the greatest, of the line of the New England poets. To the countryside and the coast of Longfellow, Lowell and Whittier, the lone farm houses and sea-scoured towns, the thin air of the northern hills and the blackness of the northern nights, he brought a more sophisticated point of view and a far greater artistic seriousness. Luke Havergal and Aaron Stark are even better than Floyd Ireson. And the moral ideas of *The Man Against the Sky* are a marked advance on *The Psalm of Life*.

But Robinson, even in youth, was a poet of regrets and failures. He was preoccupied with New England in decay. In the moonlight of an eternal autumn, he sat brooding on the poor ghosts of men—but in sadness rather than grief, for time has calmed that passion like the others. Through a long contemplation of life, he has learned to what end are doomed our loves and our worldly ambitions. One can only fix one's eye on "the gleam," which drifts faintly on the weedy dunes—pale green like an *ignis fatuus*—and which must surely be the most spectral and unluminous beacon that has ever kept a poet from despairing. We can hardly be warmed by this gleam, but the landscape itself may enchant us. When the red western gates have been locked, the moonlight strips the world to white bones, and among them dim forms of the dead move faintly in unfinished gestures.

Mr. Robinson began with the autumn, and he has never had his rightful spring. He was old in spirit from the very first; and now that he is old in years, not merely are his branches bare: they are blurred by the moon's waning. As he told us in his poems of the nineties, he arrived on the poetic scene to find Amaryllis "grown old" and the flutes of Arcady "broken"; and though he has written of their ruin with poignance, he has not brought them back to their prime. He himself has felt the pinch of sterility. Even his poignance has lately been failing. I do not say that his later long poems—*Avenel Gray* and *Avon's Harvest*—have no fine lines or moving moments; but I cannot, like Mr. Morris, accept the Arthurian series as Robinson's crowning glories. Except for an occasional passage, they seem to me among the flattest of latter-day blank-verse deserts. The earlier blank-verse idylls that dealt with New England subjects had far more flavor and life. And when it comes to *Roman Bartholow* and the later historical monologues, the old charm has been quite left behind. In *Roman Bartholow*, for example, we, as usual, hear much of moonlight: the culmination of the poem is enveloped in it. But this is not the moonlight we used to know. It no longer possesses radiance. It leaves glamorless the situation, sufficiently unpleasing in itself, that the poet intends it to bathe. That situation, understood subtly and skillfully presented though it is, never undergoes the transmutation that can make an idea into a work of art.

Yet one ought not to complain too much of the dreariness of the later Robinson. He has already given us enough to put us forever in his debt. He is one of the few first-rate artists of the older generation, and even his artistic failures could only have been produced by a distinguished and original mind.

May, 1923

Two Novels of Willa Cather

I. *One of Ours*

C AN H. L. Mencken have been mistaken when he decided
  that Willa Cather was a great novelist? I have not read *My
Ántonia*—which is said to be her best book—but I have not
been able to find anything in her last two that seemed to bear
out this description. Miss Cather's new novel—*One of Ours*—
seems to me a pretty flat failure. She has taken what might, if
it had been better handled, have provided a very interesting
theme—the career of an imaginative Nebraska boy, who,
though charged with the energy for great achievements, is
balked and imprisoned first by the necessity of running his
father's farm, and then by his marriage with a pious and prosaic Prohibition worker; but whose noble and romantic impulses are finally freed by the war. The publishers hint that
Claude Wheeler is a symbol of the national character, and one
can see that Miss Cather has aimed to make her people American types: the money-making farmer father, jocular and lacking
in intelligence; the sympathetic religious mother; the son made
wretched by passions which are outlawed among his neighbors
and for which he can find no fit objects, which he is finally
obliged to extinguish in the dubious crusade of the war. And
this theme might indeed have served for a tragedy of national
significance. But I feel, in the case of this book as I did with
her collection of short stories, *Youth and the Bright Medusa*,
that it has cost Miss Cather too much effort to summon her
people from the void and that, even when she has got them
before us, they appear less like human beings, or even the
phantoms of human beings, than like pale unfeatured silhouettes, pasted on cardboard backs and, skillfully but a little mechanically, put through the paces of puppets. Even in incidents
that might be convincing—as in the first night of Claude
Wheeler's wedding trip, when his new bride coldly tells him
she is ill and requests him not to share her state-room—the
emotions of the hero are not created: we do not *experience* the
frustration of Claude when his wife will not return his love,

and in the latter part of the book, where Miss Cather has imposed on herself the special handicap of having to imagine her hero in relation to the ordeal of the war, we feel that she has told us with commendable accuracy almost everything about the engagements she describes except the thing that is vital to the novel—what they did to the soul of Claude.

Admirers of Willa Cather will declare that this kind of criticism is based on a misunderstanding; that her method is not to get inside her characters—as Dostoevsky does, for example—and depict their emotions directly, but rather, in the manner of Turgenev, to tell you how people behave and to let the inner blaze of their glory or grief shine through the simple recital. But the reader, in either case, must demand that the characters come to life. In this novel, they never do. Flaubert, by a single phrase—a notation of some commonplace object—can convey all the poignance of human desire, the pathos of human defeat; his description of some homely scene will close with a dying fall that reminds one of great verse or music. But Miss Cather never finds this phrase.

Let it be counted to her for righteousness, however, that, like Flaubert, she has devoted her life to her art; that—even though her colors are faint and the characters she animates shadowy—she understands how fine work should be done. She knows that in a decent novel every word should be in its place and every figure in its right perspective, that every incident should be presented with its appropriate economy of detail. If *One of Ours* only had more vitality, it might figure as a standard and a stimulus, as, for the limited number of people who have read it, James Joyce's *Ulysses* has done. It might serve to shame the "younger novelists" from their sloppiness and their facility; but, as it is, they can evade the moral of Willa Cather's example by complaining that her books are dull. And, unfortunately, one cannot deny it.

October, 1922

II. *A Lost Lady*

Willa Cather's new novel—*A Lost Lady*—does something to atone for *One of Ours*. Miss Cather seems to suffer from a disability like that of Henry James: it is almost impossible for her to describe an emotion or an action except at secondhand. When Henry James, in *The Wings of the Dove*, wants to present his heroine, Milly Theale, who is supposed to be dying for lack of love, he abandons the direct record of her psychological processes as soon as the situation becomes acute, and allows the reader to watch her only through the eyes of the fortune-hunter Merton Densher, and when the relation between Milly and Densher begins to be really dramatic, he sidesteps it altogether and passes on the culmination of the tragedy to the insight of a second observer who talks with Densher after Milly's death. I am aware of the aesthetic advantages on which Henry James insisted in favor of this use of reflectors, but I am inclined to believe he arrived at it by way of his limitations. It had always been his tendency to admit us to only so much of the drama of his more daring and sophisticated protagonists as might have been observed or guessed at by some timid or inexperienced person who happened to be looking on. If the most satisfactory of James's novels is perhaps *What Maisie Knew*, it is because here the person who is looking on and whose consciousness is to be laid before us is not even a grown-up person, but merely a little girl, who in consequence makes a minimum demand for experience or adult emotion on the part of the author himself. *One of Ours*, for a converse reason, was one of Miss Cather's least satisfactory performances: she had to deal directly with the problem of rendering not only the cramping of the passions and aspirations of a young Middle Westerner on a farm, but also his eventual self-realization as a soldier in the war.

In *A Lost Lady*, however, Miss Cather falls back on the indirect method of James—who was a great artist, as novelists go, for all his not infrequent incapacity to fill in with adequate color the beautiful line and composition of his pictures; and she achieves something of James's success. Here her problem is to present the vicissitudes of a young and attractive woman, with a vigorous capacity for life, in the course of her marriage, during the pioneering period after the Civil War, with an elderly contractor of the "railroad aristocracy," who has brought her from California to live somewhere between Omaha and Denver. For this purpose, she invents another of those limpid and sensitive young men to whom she has always been rather ad-

dicted and makes him the Jamesian glass through which we are
to look at her heroine. It is significant that on the only two important occasions when the author tries to show us something
that was not directly witnessed by young Niel Herbert, she
strikes, in the first case—the brief scene between the lady and
her lover that takes place in the house at night—perhaps the
only false melodramatic note to be found in the whole story
("'Be careful,' she murmured as she approached him, 'I have a
distinct impression that there is someone on the enclosed stair-
way. . . . Ah, but kittens have claws, these days!'"); and in
the second—the expedition in the sleigh—is able to save the
situation only by introducing a subsidiary limpid young man
whose function is to witness phenomena unmanageable for the
first.

In any case, *A Lost Lady* is a charming sketch performed
with exceptional skill. Willa Cather is, in fact, one of the only
writers who has been able to bring any real distinction to the
life of the Middle West. Other writers have more enthusiasm
or animation or color or humor, but Miss Cather is perhaps
unique in her art of imposing a patina on that meager and
sprawling scene. There are exquisite pages of landscape in *A
Lost Lady*, and the portrait of the veteran railroad man is surely
one of the most sensitive and accurate that has ever been put
into a novel of the best type of old-fashioned American of the
post-Civil War period—a type greatly preferable, I grant Miss
Cather, in its straightness and simplicity and honor, for all its
cultural limitations, to the sharpers who superseded it.

Not, however, that Willa Cather sentimentalizes the Middle
West or represents it as spiritually richer than it is—as Mr.
Vachel Lindsay, for example, seems to do. There run through
Miss Cather's work two currents of profound feeling—one for
the beauty of those lives lived out between the sky and the
prairie; the other—most touchingly in *A Wagner Concert*, my
favorite among her short stories, and now in certain scenes of
A Lost Lady—for the pathos of the human spirit making the effort to send down its roots and to flower in that barren soil.

January, 1924

Ezra Pound's Patchwork

EZRA POUND'S new book of poems—*Poems 1918–21*—is as unsatisfactory as his previous ones. He still spends two-thirds of his time translating or quoting other poets, and a good deal of the rest of it in imitating them (where it used to be Browning and Yeats, it now seems to be T. S. Eliot*), and he has not even yet, in his original work, really mastered his own style, which still remains patchy and uneven and acutely self-conscious. The failure of Pound as a poet is a curious literary phenomenon. Ezra Pound's aesthetic ideal is probably one of the highest in contemporary poetry in English. Indifferent to public approval, he has labored conscientiously and fiercely to reduce the vague substance of words to a sharp hard residuum of beauty which should have nothing in common with the comparatively loose rhetoric of even such a good poet as Masefield. From Catullus to Yeats, his masters (with the possible exception of Browning) have been the severest and the most durable in the whole range of poetry. And for a line or two at a time he has sometimes crystallized this beauty. In his newest book—which, nonetheless, has far fewer fine things in it than *Lustra*, his best collection up to date—we find: "Dawn, to our waking, drifts in the green cool light"; "But to-day, Garonne is thick like paint, beyond Dorada"; "That he may free her—who sheds such light in the air." Such isolated lines as these have certainly an authentic ring; but the trouble is that all his lines are isolated lines. His poems do not hang together. His eye for a general effect is poor. It is as if he could not fix any picture squarely in his imagination and reproduce it for the reader, but could only try to piece it out with separate details and aspects, conceived and perhaps jotted down without proper regard for the whole. It is all like a pile of fragments from a collection of objets d'art: there are the foot of a Chinese jade god, the hand of a Tanagra statuette, a green, gold and blue initial from a medieval book and a pale nearly perfect

---

*I did not know at that time that both Eliot and Yeats had been influenced by Pound.

amethyst engraved with a Renaissance Apollo. None of them is complete, and they do not go together.

There is a strange discrepancy between Pound's ideals and his ability to embody them in his work. It is as if his conception of style had matured while his taste had remained immature: not only has he never learned to deal with large problems, he has never been able to outgrow a certain beguilement with preciosity and mystification. For, in spite of the parade of cultures and the pontifical pretenses which have terrified the more naïve of the American intelligentsia, Ezra Pound is really at heart a very boyish fellow and an incurable provincial. It is true that he was driven to Europe by a thirst for romance and color that he could scarcely have satisfied in America, but he took to Europe the simple faith and the pure enthusiasms of his native Idaho. And he took, also, the fresh cavalier spirit which remains his greatest charm. His early poems were full of gallant and simply felt emotions; but they were already tainted with an obsession which has cursed him all his life: the frantic desire to flee as far from Idaho as possible, the itching to prove to Main Street that he has extirpated it from his soul. That he has remained unsuccessful to this day is sufficiently attested by the fact that he still spends so much time insulting the United States. He seeks refuge in bawdiness, in obscurity, in recondite erudition, in the most extravagant of the modern movements, such as dadaism and vorticism, but he can never slough off his self-consciousness at having settled in the Sacred Grove. "Look at me!" he says in effect to his compatriots at home. "See how cultured and cosmopolitan I have become since I've left America—how different from you over there! I'll bet there's not a man among you who knows about Pratinas and Gaudier-Brzeska. I can read half a dozen languages! I am a friend of Francis Picabia!" But his sophistication is still juvenile, his ironies are still clumsy and obvious; when he ridicules Americans in Europe not very much simpler than himself, he reveals the callowness of the hunter by the pettiness of the game he pursues.

One fears that Ezra Pound has repeated the recurrent and oft-told tragedy of the artistic American fled to Europe. What the American flees to in Europe is the Europe he has read about, and unfortunately it is all too often exclusively the

Europe of books in which he finds himself forced to continue to live. I take this as a way of accounting for Ezra Pound's peculiar deficiencies of experience and feeling. His contacts seem still to remain almost exclusively literary contacts. Consider, for example, the long poem of which he has now published seven cantos. The first six cantos of this work are occupied with literary reminiscences; it is apparently a cross-section of the poet's mind; odds and ends of old reading seem to float in and out—the Latin poets, Homer, a Latin translation of Homer, fragments of Chinese poetry, tags from the annals of Provence. At last, with the seventh canto, he seems to arrive at something that has been part of his own life: he remembers a girl called Eleanor, but the name immediately recalls to him the Aeschylean puns about Helen; and from this point on, in the first twenty-four lines, we have quotations from five languages and have presently lost our way altogether. Toward the end, we seem to get our bearings and find ourselves in a classroom of some sort; but the poet is bored with the class, and his mind begins to run on Lorenzaccio and Dante. So everything in life only serves to remind him of something in literature.

There exist without doubt in Ezra Pound some of the elements of a bold personality, a first-rate modern poet; but, for some reason, champion and poet have never quite rounded themselves out or stood on their own feet. One of the symptoms of his incompleteness is his continual recourse to translation: he tries to realize his own personality by putting on the costumes of other poets with whom he seems to himself to have some kinship. As Propertius, as Arnaut Daniel, as Guido Cavalcanti, he tries to attain his full stature. But even with the material they give him to supplement his defective experience and the solid and clear-cut personalities that they lend him to prop up his own, he still reveals his fatal inadequacy in the lameness of his rendering of them. In his hands they somehow become (with the possible exception of the Chinese poets) uncertain and unsatisfactory like Ezra Pound himself.

The truth about Ezra Pound is no doubt, as I have already suggested, that he merely presents a new instance of the now familiar dilemma of the clever and sensitive man in the United States of his day: his case has something in common with that of Henry James. America could not supply Pound with the society and the tradition he needed to develop a very special and very delicate talent; but Europe, of which he has never been part, cannot supply him with it either. He is a case for Mr. Van Wyck Brooks, that expert in American artistic failures. But let us, at least, do him honor for having failed in so high a cause.

April 19, 1922

Wallace Stevens and E. E. Cummings

THE poems of Mr. Wallace Stevens have now been collected in a volume, with the title *Harmonium*. Mr. Stevens is the master of a style: that is the most remarkable thing about him. His gift for combining words is baffling and fantastic but sure: even when you do not know what he is saying, you know that he is saying it well. He derives plainly from several French sources of the last fifty years, but—except for an occasional fleeting phrase—he never really sounds like any of them. You could not mistake even a title by Wallace Stevens for a title by anyone else: *Invective Against Swans*; *Hibiscus on the Sleeping Shores*; *A High-Toned Old Christian Woman*; *The Emperor of Ice-Cream*; *Exposition of the Contents of a Cab*; *The Bird with the Coppery Keen Claws*; *Two Figures in Dense Violet Night*; *Hymn from a Watermelon Pavilion*; and *Frogs Eat Butterflies. Snakes Eat Frogs. Hogs Eat Snakes. Men Eat Hogs.*

These titles also represent Mr. Stevens's curious ironic imagination at its very best. The poems themselves—ingenious, charming and sometimes beautiful though they are—do not always quite satisfy the expectations aroused by the titles. If you read only a few poems by Mr. Stevens, you get the impression from the richness of his verbal imagination that he is a poet of rich personality, but when you come to read the whole volume through, you are struck by a sort of aridity. Mr. Stevens, who is so observant and displays so distinguished a fancy, seems to possess emotion neither in abundance nor in intensity. He is ironic a little in Mr. Eliot's manner; but not poignantly, not tragically ironic. Emotion seems to emerge only furtively in the cryptic images of his poetry, as if it had been driven, as he seems to hint, into the remotest crannies of sleep or disposed of by being dexterously converted into exquisite amusing words. Nothing could be more perfect in its tone and nothing by itself could be more satisfactory than such a thing as *Last Looks at the Lilacs*. But when we have gone all through Mr. Stevens, we find ourselves putting to him the same question that he himself, in the last poem of his book, puts *To a Roaring Wind*:

> What syllable are you seeking,
> Vocallissimus,
> In the distances of sleep?
> Speak it.

Mr. E. E. Cummings, on the other hand, in his volume *Tulips and Chimneys*, does not show himself, like Mr. Stevens, a master in a peculiar vein; a master is precisely, as yet, what Mr. Cummings is not. Cummings's style is an eternal adolescent, as fresh and often as winning but as half-baked as boyhood. A poet with a real gift for language, for a melting music a little like Shelley's, which rhapsodizes and sighs in soft vowels disembarrassed of their baggage of consonants, he strikes often on ethereal measures of a singular purity and charm—his best poems seem to dissolve on the mind like the flakes of a lyric dew; but he never seems to know when he is writing badly and when he is writing well. He has apparently no faculty for self-criticism. One imagines him giving off his poems as spontaneously as perspiration and with as little application of the intellect. One imagines him chuckling with the delight of a schoolboy when he has invented an adverb like "sayingly" or hit upon the idea of writing capitals in the middles of words instead of at the beginnings. One imagines him just as proud to have written:

> last   we
> on the groaning flame of neat huge
> trudging kiss moistly climbing hideously with
> large
> minute
> hips, O
>   .press

as:

> on such a night the sea through her blind miles
> of crumbling silence

or the sonnet about the little dancer:

> abslatively posolutely dead,
> like Coney Island in winter

And there is really, it seems to me, a certain amateurishness about even the better of these specimens as well as about the worse. Just as, in the first example, he takes one of the lines of least resistance with a complex and difficult sensation by setting down indiscriminately all the ideas it suggests to him without focussing it for the reader, so he succumbs, in the second, to an overindulgence in the beautiful English long *i* which, from Shelley's "I arise from dreams of thee" to Mr. T. S. Eliot's nightingale filling "all the desert with inviolable voice," has been reserved for effects of especial brightness or clearness. Mr. Cummings has cheapened it a little by too much reiteration. One or two of these *i*'s, rightly placed and combined with other long vowels, is enough to illuminate a passage, but Mr. Cummings cannot resist them, and he likes to turn them on all over till his poems are lit up like Christmas trees.

Mr. Cummings's eccentric punctuation is, also, I believe, a symptom of his immaturity as an artist. It is not here merely a question of an unconventional usage: unconventional punctuation may very well gain its effect. But though the methods of Mr. Cummings have been explained to me by one of his friends and though I have made a sincere effort to appreciate them, I still feel that his punctuation does not gain the effects he intends. It is, I learn, Mr. Cummings's theory that punctuation marks, capitalization and arrangement of words on the page should not be used by the poet as conventional indications of structure that make it easier for the reader to follow the meaning of the words themselves but as instruments of expression, susceptible, like the words, of infinite variation. Thus he refuses to make use of capitals for the purposes for which they were invented—to announce the beginnings of sentences and the occurrence of proper names—but presses them into service for purposes of special emphasis; and he even demotes the first person singular of the pronoun by writing it with a small *i*, only restoring its stature as a capital when he desires to give it salience—not, apparently, aware of the fact that, since the reader is accustomed to the capital, the poet makes it more instead of less conspicuous by writing it with a dot. But the really serious case against Mr. Cummings's punctuation is that the results which it yields are ugly. His poems on the page are hideous. He insists upon breaking up even the least unconventional of his verses, which would be more appropriately printed as neat little blocks of type like the prose poems of Logan Pearsall Smith, into systems of exploded fragments, and this, so far from making the cadences plainer, only involves us in a jigsaw puzzle of putting the lines together again. I think it may be said that a writer is obliged to depend on the words themselves, through the order in which they are written, to carry his cadence and emphasis. The extent to which punctuation and typography can supplement this is certainly very limited.

Behind this barrier of strange punctuation and deliberate disorganization, for which Mr. Cummings seems, unfortunately, so far to have achieved most celebrity, his emotions are familiar and simple. They occasionally even verge on the banal. You find the adoration of young love and the excitement of the coming of spring, and you find the reflection that all flesh must die and all "roses" turn to "ashes." But this is perhaps precisely where E. E. Cummings has the advantage over Wallace Stevens. Whatever Mr. Cummings is, he is not insulated or chilled; he is not indifferent to life. Eagerly and unconstrainedly, he takes what the world has to offer. His poetry is the expression of a temperament of a kind very rare in America —of a being who desires and enjoys, who reacts to everything that touches him with a tenderness or a mockery quite free from the inhibitions from which so much American writing is merely the anguish to escape. E. E. Cummings is, I suppose, one of the only American writers living who is not reacting against something. And for this—for the fact that, though not yet fully grown, he is a genuine lyric poet at a time when there is a great deal of writing of verse and very little poetic feeling— Mr. Cummings deserves well of the public.

March 19, 1924

This review in its original version was to have been called *Two American Symbolists*, and it began with the following paragraph, in which I tried to relate Stevens and Cummings to the French symbolist school. I saw, however, that this was too large a subject to be treated in a review of this kind, and I did not deal fully with the influence of symbolism till, in 1929 and 1930, I came to write the studies that were later brought together in my book *Axel's Castle*.

*

Both Mr. E. E. Cummings and Mr. Wallace Stevens have reputations as innovators; and the only questions usually raised in connection with their work are based on the assumption that their technique is unconventional. So it is, perhaps, in America; but there is little in their work that is new. They are merely the latest representatives in English of a belated development of French symbolism, and what they are trying to do is, in general, as old as Mallarmé.

Nor should it be possible for symbolism in itself to inspire terror and consternation, as it seems to do in the case of so many Anglo-Saxon critics—even if one has never heard of a literary movement which is already about forty years old. Symbolism consisted, by definition, of substituting symbols for things—but it was by no means so different from any other kind of poetry as you might have thought to hear the outcry raised years ago in France over Verlaine's *Sagesse* or only the other day in New York over T. S. Eliot's *The Waste Land*. All metaphors are symbols that stand for things; and what symbolism did was merely to cut the metaphors loose from their moorings. The tendency was to present the metaphors without mentioning the subject that inspired them, to suggest it to the reader, to make him guess, without letting him know precisely what it was. Symbolism, at its most successful, contrives to communicate emotions by images whose connection with the subject and whose relevance to one another we may not always understand. Who can tell, for example, to take two fairly easy instances, precisely what Verlaine is referring to, in the poem that begins, *"L'espoir luit comme un brin de paille dans l'étable,"* when he writes *"Que crains-tu de la guêpe, ivre de son vol fou?,"* or precisely what Eliot means, in *The Waste Land*, when he suddenly begins talking about "Phlebas the Phoenician, a fortnight dead"? But who can fail to feel the effectiveness of these strange lines? We respond to their magic emotionally before our minds have propounded the riddle. In one case, we get the impression of something troublesome and rather sinister from which the poet is trying to escape; in the other, of a longing for peace, of an assuagement, if even by death, of some torturing thirst of the spirit. These images could probably have been conveyed in a perfectly conventional manner—as Dante, describing a state of mind surely not less unusual and difficult, would write in the *Paradiso* of the fading from his memory of the divine vision, "so the snow is unsealed by the sun, so the light leaves of the Sybil's message are scattered by the wind." But the method of symbolism was to cut away the links that indicated how the images grew out of the subject—even sometimes, so far as was possible, to suppress the subject itself. Along with this isolation of metaphors, there appeared also a general addiction to hiatuses of all sorts. The point was not that the emotions of, say, Jules Laforgue were necessarily more complicated than those of, say, Catullus in his sequence of poems about Lesbia, but rather that the symbolist poet— instead of disentangling a complex emotion into a series of varying moods or at least, when the mood of a single poem is allowed to change abruptly (as in Catullus's *Illa Lesbia* . . .), of subduing the disordered feeling to the logic of consecutive statement—is in the habit of telescoping the whole thing by a few stenographic strokes. Nor are his feelings necessarily more difficult to render than those, say, of Wordsworth in the most mysterious of his visions of the natural world; but the symbolist —instead of attempting to reduce an unearthly elusive sensation to the lucidity of simple language—invents for it a vocabulary and a syntax as unfamiliar as the sensation itself.

In considering the work of such American poets as Stevens and E. E. Cummings, their technique should no longer be made an issue. They should be judged by their greater or less success in a tradition that can already boast its masterpieces. It is a question, not at all of method, but of the good artist or the bad. The good artist, in this as in any other style, is one who can create a work that has completeness and significance outside himself, that is not merely a literary ectoplasm imperfectly disengaged from his drift of consciousness. Such good artists of this symbolist school, Verlaine and Eliot certainly are in the poems I have quoted above, and Laforgue in his *Derniers Vers*. Mallarmé, for all his labor and integrity, seems to me not quite to have succeeded, and Tristan Tzara, at the other end of the line but essentially attempting the same sort of thing, seems to me, so far as I have read him, not to have succeeded at all. In the first class, the logic of the images, the association of ideas is never quite out of reach of the reader; in the second, we are incapable of enjoying the poems—or at least this reader is—because the key to this association is buried in the poet's mind. The emotion, if there was an emotion, has not really been captured and fixed; the words that the poet combines do not bring it before the reader.

Byron in the Twenties

I. The New Byron Letters

I CANNOT accept the opinion of Mr. Maurice Hewlett and others who have asserted that the new collection of Byron letters, *Lord Byron's Correspondence* (a supplement to the six volumes of *Letters and Journals* published at the beginning of the century) only supply more conclusive evidence that Byron was a "blackguard" and a "cad." This is to simplify the matter too much. It is to assume that when Byron writes "Maid of Athens, ere we part, Give oh give me back my heart!" in one breath and in the next tells Hobhouse that "the old woman, Theresa's mother, was mad enough to imagine I was going to marry the girl, but I have better amusement," and when he sneers at his wife in his private correspondence, not long after having written, "even though unforgiving, never 'Gainst thee shall my heart rebel," he is sincere in his cynicism but not in his warmth of emotion. It is to assume that one cannot take a personal relation with cynicism and seriousness at the same time—that Childe Harold and Manfred did not represent realities of Byron's experience as well as Don Juan. The truth is that Byron was a man of picturesque and violent moods, who reacted to life with extraordinary vividness, but without discipline or order. He never knew where he stood nor what he really wanted. He was a force of enormous energy, running amuck through a world in which he could not find peace. His compromises with civilized society were doomed to disaster from the beginning, though in them he was surely sincere in seeking tranquillity or discipline. To say, as Mr. Hewlett does, that he cold-bloodedly seduced Lady Frances Webster seems to me to melodramatize the situation. Even if Lady Frances had not been all of a flutter from the moment Byron came into the house and in a mood of violent reaction against the clumsy and stupid husband who had boasted that she was as passionless "as Jesus Christ," these letters seem amply to prove that Byron believed himself in love with her and was ready at any moment to drop everything and run away with her.

55

The fact that he was an old hand at lovemaking and was amused by the humors of the situation and dramatized the whole affair in almost daily bulletins to Lady Melbourne does not prove him to have been much more of a popinjay than the average imaginative person. In a similar fashion, it is certainly true that he was honestly seeking happiness in his marriage; he wanted, he said, some one to "govern" him—which was unquestionably what he needed. The trouble was that Annabella Milbanke was a quite unsuitable wife for Byron. He had qualms at the last moment and was ready to give the whole thing up; but Lady Melbourne, who had been "governing" him lately and in whose judgment he seems to have trusted absolutely, had arranged the marriage herself and urged it upon him as a panacea. The relationship was impossible from the start. It is clear that Byron behaved abominably, but, then, he was by nature and fortune a spoiled and refractory child, while poor little Miss Milbanke was a correct jeune fille, charmless and unsophisticated, who went in for mathematics and was a little priggish about it. With the best intentions on both sides, the situation could hardly have turned out differently. "Disease or not," says Lady Byron, speaking of Byron's supposed madness, "all my recollections and reflections tend to convince me that the irritability is inseparably connected with me in a greater degree than with any other object, that my presence has been uniformly oppressive to him from the hour we married —if not before, and in his best moods he has always wished to be away from me . . . had we continued together, he *would* have gone mad."

It is, therefore, a great pity that Byron was ever persuaded to marry Miss Milbanke. He had already a sharp sense of his unfitness to play a role in English society. When Miss Milbanke finally came to accept him, he had been fully prepared to go back to the East; *there* were fighting and adventure—gaiety, color and sun; *there* was no boring politics or business; women were not taken seriously; *there* he would be able to find something like the kind of life he understood. His genius has its happiest expression in his letters to Hobhouse from the Continent and in the harlequinade of *Beppo* and *Don Juan*.

For Byron's gift was for living rather than for literature. He had neither the intensity nor the fineness to fuse, for per-durable brilliants, the shifting moods of the soul. Don Juan, after all, was always more real than Childe Harold. The windy storms of passion that were blown off in *Childe Harold* and the tragedies were never the most solid realities of that deeply sensuous life. If he had only not tried to live in England, if the women only hadn't set their hearts on him, what an amiable figure he might have been! There is nothing more exhilarating in literature than Byron's first trip to Greece—his duels and skirmishings with bandits, his heroic swimming of the Helle-spont, his reception by Vely Pasha and his delight at the Pasha's present of "a very pretty horse," his defense of the Temple of Athena against the depredations of Lord Elgin and his row with the authorities at Constantinople because they would not allow him, as a Peer of the Realm, to take first place in a Turkish official reception. To read Byron is to watch a panorama of the Europe of the early nineteenth century—the morrow of the French Revolution and of the victory of Napoleon seen through the eyes of a sophisticated man who is as much alive to how people are feeling and to what sort of struggles they are waging as to how they are drinking and making love. How amusing he makes Milan and Geneva and Venice!—that Venice of which Stendhal wrote that it constituted "a distinct world, of which the gloomy society of the rest of Europe can form no conception; care is there a subject of mockery." Here as yet was neither Burbank with his Baedeker nor Bleistein with his cigar, but balconies to which one looked up to encounter romantic black eyes peeping out from behind long blinds; covered gondolas gliding at night through narrow canals of wavering water; the dancing, the delirious wines and the masqued flirtations of the Carnival; the revolutionary young countess Guiccioli with her aged and complacent husband and her English *cavalier servente*, the scandalous witty Lord Byron.

Yet this record, as we follow it further, produces an effect of depression that at last becomes almost unbearable. For one thing, life had played poor Byron not the least annoying of its tricks: by the time he had acquired enough judgment not to make any further disastrous mistakes and to be sure in what manner of life his hope for happiness lay, he had already hurt others and himself so grievously in the process of learning that both his peaceful pursuits and his pleasures were forever impaired by the wounds. Among the motley baggage of his soul, there was a sort of Calvinistic conscience (supposed to have been implanted by his early education in Edinburgh) which gnawed its nails and gnashed its teeth amid the very laughter of Venice. "It must be admitted," says Stendahl, writing of Byron at this period, "that during nearly a third of the time we passed in the poet's society he appeared to us like one laboring under an access of folly, often approaching to madness. . . . One evening, among others, the conversation turned upon a handsome Milanese female who had eagerly desired to venture her person in single combat with a lover by whom she had been abandoned; the discussion afterward changed to the story of a prince who in cold blood had murdered his mistress for an act of infidelity. Byron was instantly silent, endeavored to restrain his feelings, but, unequal to the effort, soon afterward indignantly quitted the box."

Then, Byron had by this time another remorse to stave off by champagne. Jane Claremont, a connection of the Shelleys and a romantic foolish young girl, mad to give herself to a poet, had laid violent siege to Byron and had finally nagged him into gratifying her. They had parted in Switzerland, Byron refusing implacably ever to see her again, and when Jane with the Shelleys had returned to England, she bore Byron a daughter. The new documents published here in elucidation of this affair take glamor from both Byron and Shelley. They reveal the dismal underside of that stimulating lyric revolt. One is chilled to find the price these poets paid—and that other people paid—not only in pain and grief, but in sordidness and raw distress. How much good life was plowed under in the triumph of that noble defiance! And how messy the triumph itself appears when looked at in the process of its making.

Well, art has its origin in the need to pretend that human life is something other than it is, and, in a sense, by pretending this, it succeeds to some extent in transforming it. What we see when we turn back our eyes to the age of Shelley and Byron is not the ignominy of mute broken hearts, of hurriedly muffled-up births, but a blaze of divine white light and the smoky torches of rebellion. And yet, poor Jane Claremont, to have set her heart on a love affair with a poet! Poor Annabella Milbanke, to have been so naïve and misguided as to marry an inspired rake! Poor Shelley and poor Byron, to have carried in their hearts the consciousness of such guilt as no wine could for long disguise, no songs could forever relieve. Poor male and female human beings, who, understanding life in different fashions and unfitted to live together, yet cannot leave each other alone! For a moment, as we read these letters, the very splendors of *Childe Harold* and *Prometheus* seem dwindled and insubstantial, like witch-fires above a bog.

July 2, 1922

II. Byron and His Biographers

The Political Career of Lord Byron by Dora Neill Raymond is an interesting, though not very penetrating, book, written from the point of view of the conventional admiring biographer. For Miss Raymond, all of Byron's political lampoons and parliamentary speeches, as well as his revolutionary activities in Italy and Greece, are the results of wise and well-considered opinions. Byron's motives are invariably generous, disinterested and straightforward; and the question of his complex and unsteady character does not arise at all. In discussing Byron's hatred of the radicals, to take a single example, Miss Raymond describes the squib that he wrote about Hobhouse's relations with them as "a rollicking and somewhat sarcastic ballad"—whereas it will perhaps seem more likely to a reader of the ballad in question and of the poet's letters dealing with this period that he had merely given vent to his own irritation at the aimlessness of his life in Italy and his envy of his friend's achievements at home by an outburst less rollicking and sarcastic than jeering and ill-natured. Furthermore, it seems clear that Byron's hatred of oppression and the readiness of his sympathy with the unfortunate were somehow bound up with what would be nowadays called a sort of "inferiority complex." But it never occurs to Miss Raymond to question either the soundness of Byron's character or the exaltedness of his position, so she quite fails to understand either his personal or his social situation.

Mr. Harold Nicolson, on the other hand, in *Byron: The Last Journey*, understands these matters only too well. Mr. Nicolson is a pupil of the school of Strachey, and he has picked up the whole technique of emphasizing the idiosyncrasies and the personal imperfections that, ignored by the contemporary public, fix the shape of spectacular public careers. This enables him, if not to rival the consummate successes of the Master, at least to write such a passage as the following, which comes nearer to arriving at the truth about Byron than a biography in Miss Raymond's vein can do: "It must be realized that the life of Byron is not, as has often been imagined, a series of wasted opportunities; rather is it a catalogue of false positions. His brain was male, his character was feminine. He had genius, but it was misunderstood and misdirected; he had beauty, but it was branded by deformity; he had rank, but no position; fortune, but it came too late; fame, but it blazed for him too early. From his childhood the foreground of his life had been out of focus with the background; throughout his career this error of focus marred the sincerity, the completeness and even the meaning of the whole."

Yet this formula of Strachey's has its penalties as well as its dazzling rewards. One of these is the use or the excessive use of irony where irony is not really in order. The irony of Strachey himself always serves to convey some criticism: as Mr. Clive Bell has said, Strachey's attitude toward the Victorian Age implies a judgment derived from a study of the history of society. We do not find Lytton Strachey writing about Madame du Deffand or Racine in the same vein as about Florence Nightingale, Cardinal Manning or Dr. Arnold. Even in *Eminent Victorians*, where he is most cruel, perhaps most unfair, all his efforts are directed toward compelling us to accept a certain definite point of view. But his followers are always in danger of taking over the mocking tone without understanding this point of view. The worst offender in this regard is perhaps Mr. Philip Guedalla. The biographical writing of Mr. Guedalla is full of details and inflections that have an invidious mocking sound but which, when one comes to examine them, seem to lack any real significance. And Mr. Nicolson, in writing of Byron, is not entirely free from this vice. "'Our visit was a long one,' records Lady Blessington. It was. They sat in the large, cool room," etc. Now, what is there ridiculous about the fact that this visit to Byron was rather long? Why does Mr. Nicolson write "It was" in such a sly knowing way? For no other reason on earth than that he has caught the tone from Lytton Strachey. There is certainly some place for irony in a biography of a figure like Byron, whose romantic reputation has been swollen by so much nonsense; but, except in his preface, Mr. Nicolson has surely leaned a little too far over backward in his endeavor to avoid the legend. For the legend, after all, was a reality as much as Byron's effeminate voice, which Mr. Nicolson is so unwilling to have us forget.

Here is a typical passage: "That in this sudden ferment of unexpected adulation Byron should have been manoeuvred into adopting the postures which were expected of him was perhaps inevitable. . . . [The provoking specter of Childe Harold] thrust upon him the exacting function of being a very dangerous and enterprising man. His slightest civility was interpreted as a seduction; his chance encounters became assignations. They persisted, all of them, in taking him at his word. For a man who, although kindly and sentimental, was only adequately sexed, all this became extremely exhausting." But, after all, it was Byron himself who had created Childe Harold and his postures. He had certainly more than half believed in them, and he succeeded in making others believe in them, and they thus became actual values, which Mr. Nicolson should have brought on the stage. "Kindly and sentimental" is a quite inadequate description of Byron in his relations with women: on the contrary, he seems always to have been ready to flare up, if only momentarily, into a fever of eager devotion, and in even the most unpromising of his love affairs, to have been able to work up at least a mood or two of something like passionate conviction. Even from the half-humorous bulletins that he sent off to Lady Melbourne, it is plain that he pursued his mistresses with an energy and an anxiety considerably more than "kindly and sentimental." Mr. Nicolson, in writing about Byron with Childe Harold left out, has illustrated the unhumanistic point of view to which Stracheyism is likely to lead. If a biographer be too wary of taking the figures of history and the heroes of literature at their own valuation and that of their contemporaries, he is likely to miss the point altogether. Every age has its complacent failures of intelligence, and we have learned in our own time to laugh at the "reasonable" point of view that was fashionable in the eighteenth century and the moral point of view of the nineteenth, but it looks as if this new sort of ironic belittlement were likely to become characteristic of our own. What should be most interesting at any time is to find out to what actuality of human ideals and adventures a creation like Childe Harold corresponded.

For the rest, Miss Raymond's book is a readable and useful one, and Mr. Nicolson's a vivid and amusing one, which has a great deal more of his own in it than his preceding biography of Tennyson, in which one found him paraphrasing, as if for a literary exercise, the whole last page of Strachey's *Queen Victoria*. Confining itself, as Mr. Nicolson's book does, to the last year of Byron's life, it cannot be expected to supply a satisfactory full-length portrait of Byron. Mr. Nicolson presupposes on the part of the reader a knowledge of most of what has gone before and concentrates on Byron's last year, of which he makes an absorbing narrative. Mr. Nicolson has unpublished documents and a firsthand knowledge of Greece, and both these books are of the picture-filling-in sort particularly valuable in connection with Byron. For Byron, in literature, presents a peculiar case: he was not a great literary artist, and it is only by familiarizing ourselves with his life as well as with his work that we come to appreciate his merits and understand why it was possible for Arnold to speak, as he did, in one breath, of "Goethe's sage mind and Byron's force." What we come to do justice to then—and both Miss Raymond's and Mr. Nicolson's books help us to do justice—is the knowledge of Europe and the world, the consciousness of the stage upon which he was playing, that make Byron so remarkable among nineteenth-century Englishmen; the generous ideas and impulses which counterbalance his faults and his errors; and the inexhaustible capacity for experience that is so satisfactory today in its contrast with the limitations of the typical literary man who agreeably diverts the hours of a safe and regular life by turning out novels or poems.

June, 1925

Late Violets from the Nineties

M R. CARL VAN VECHTEN, in *The Blind Bow-Boy*, has tried his hand at a kind of burlesque fiction of which we have had all too little in America: the satiric iridescent novel of the type of *Zuleika Dobson* and *La Révolte des Anges*; and, though at times a little less fantastic, a little less surprising than one could wish, he gets away with it, on the whole, very well. You must remember that he has had the hardihood to go to New York for his rococo *Satyricon*; and you may imagine whether New York is recalcitrant. The result, in spite of all the green orchids and the rose-jade cysts for cosmetics that the author finds in East Nineteenth Street, may come closer to the pro- saic reality—or conventional reality of fiction—than Mr. Van Vechten perhaps intended. The marriage of the hero, Harold, with the rich, boring, well-bred Alice Blake might almost have taken place in the New York of Edith Wharton. It is rather the figure of Campaspe Lorillard who exists on a high comic plane, and I am inclined to believe that the book should have cen- tered about her rather than Harold. Campaspe craves no other activity than the luxurious enjoyment of her mind, thoughts and sensations, the play of an exquisite taste and the exercise of a ruthless intelligence; she snubs her husband with a regal kindness, yet declines any other attachment, and sees as little of her children as possible, thereby trebling their interest in her. The only member of her family who interests *her* is her mother, whom she calls by her first name. She is Mr. Van Vechten's most successful achievement.

It is not, of course, in comparison with current American novels that I call Mr. Van Vechten prosaic. Beside Floyd Dell and Willa Cather, he is Ariel, Till Eulenspiegel. But I have been reading *The Flower Beneath the Foot* by the Englishman Ronald Firbank, a writer for whom Mr. Van Vechten has ex- pressed immense admiration and with whom he will not, I am sure, consider it inappropriate to compare him; and I am struck by how much further Mr. Firbank has got beyond the world of our commonplace fiction than even Mr. Van Vechten's Cam- paspe. From the first pages of *The Flower Beneath the Foot*, you find yourself closed about by a new and more vivid world, and a world so complete in itself that, for all its artificiality, one feels sure it must somewhere exist. You are moving through the high-windowed rooms of the Winter Palace of Pisuerga: silk swishes and gossip tinkles; the Queen is lounging "supine on a couch"; a Maid of Honour, looking out from a window with a fringe of green-veined bougainvilleas, at the clouds, like great knots of pink roses, that speed slowly above the town, dreams of marrying the languid Prince Yousef; all about one feels the rustle of the court, the glitter of state dinners, where the very hangings seem to be vibrant with an insatiable sensuality that provides, only a little disguised by the ceremony of office and fashion—though itself phantasmal and fragile—one of the only real incitements to activity. I have heard Ronald Firbank called trivial, and in one of his phases he is; but he is certainly more serious as an artist than he is commonly credited with being. He can create a very sharp impression—about trivial matters, if you like—with extraordinarily few words. It is not merely—though for this he is perhaps most famous—a question of suggesting the improper so inobviously and so lightly that it is difficult to put your finger on the phrase that has prompted the indecent idea; he is also able to make details, exquisitely selected and placed, tell strongly in securing effects of a certain aesthetic intensity—as when Laura looks out later at the royal wedding of the prince she had hoped to marry, from the spike-fringed walls of a convent.

What one finds in both these books is a last survival of the fin de siècle: despite their occasional dallyings with the movies and other features of the twentieth century, they belong essentially to the *Yellow Book* era. But it is curious to contemplate the change that has come over the decadence of the nineties since the heyday of Beardsley and Wilde. The school which began with Baudelaire and is now dissolving with Arthur Symons derived its principal force from its constant conviction of sin. The decadents talked much about "paganism," but their point of view was not pagan: it was a reaction against Victorian Christianity by people who were still Christians and Victorians. The fascination with which they succeeded in investing certain ideas and situations was dependent on the extent to which they could make you believe that these were sinister. They wanted you to be afraid of sin, as sin—that is, as something to be detested—yet at the same time to celebrate it as something to be desired: an impossible moral position, sure to involve insincerity on one side or the other. How can you believe that sin is "the good" and at the same time believe it to be sin? From the point of view of the person who is really convinced of the sinfulness both of the pleasures of the flesh and of the play of the intelligence, they are things to be sedulously shunned; from a point of view really pagan, they do not become an issue at all. But Baudelaire had to pretend to take the Devil seriously while he was spending his artistic life endeavoring to make him attractive; and his successors followed his example.

This is perhaps why the writers of the end of the century seem today diminished in stature. Who can read *Les Fleurs du Mal*, *À Rebours*, *The Picture of Dorian Gray* or Swinburne's *Poems and Ballads* with the enthusiasm of their contemporaries? The effectiveness of the subjects dealt with depends upon one's being shocked by them, and when the prejudices to be baited have been removed, the works of art are no longer exciting. I can think of only two writers of that period and school who escaped the moral confusion of the reaction against respectability: Aubrey Beardsley and Paul Verlaine. It is, of course, true that Beardsley very often exploited in his drawings the fascination of Evil as evil; but he also wrote the opening chapters of rather a remarkable erotic romance called *Venus and Tannhäuser*, in which he does succeed in investing a sort of pagan world with the artificial graces of the nineties without allowing it to become darkened and tragic with the fumes of a burning orthodoxy; his Venus, unlike the Venus of Swinburne or the Harlot of Oscar Wilde, is not destructive and terrible, but girlish and agreeable. The grotesqueries and orgies of her court are to her all quite natural and harmless; she really approaches much nearer to the naïve naughtiness of the eighteenth century than anything to be found in Wilde. As for Verlaine, he unquestionably vacillated between "paganism" and piety; but, unlike Baudelaire, he did not try to be pagan and pious at the same time. When Verlaine was a faun, he was wholly a faun, untroubled by moral compunction. And in these moods he created, too, a neo-eighteenth-century world, erotic, lighthearted and skeptical, not unlike the world of *Venus and Tannhäuser*.

Now, Mr. Van Vechten and Mr. Firbank are also able to take their heresies and pleasures lightly. It may be that Mr. Firbank has gone to school to Beardsley. But it is probably no longer possible for practitioners of this species of fantasy to become either worried or fervent. The generation of Beardsley and Wilde had been brought up on Ruskin and Tennyson; but the generation of Firbank and Van Vechten has been brought up on Beardsley and Wilde, and their prejudices were undermined early. The conviction of sin has been removed, and it is possible for the "sinner" to be amiable again. This fin de siècle genre may be destined to grow dimmer and dimmer, but at least it fades away with a smile.

October, 1923

Greenwich Village in the Early Twenties*

I. The Road to Greenwich Village

I NEVER went to school very much. When I was a girl, they figured out that it would be a good thing for me to do the work and to get an education—and I did the work so well they forgot about the education. My father left me at a girl's school in Greeley Valley, Colorado, but I was only there a little while. They were awfully narrow-minded there. I told the girls some things that they weren't supposed to know—my father was a doctor, and I used to read his medical books, see. I told them that a baby before it's born looks like a kind of a tadpole. Some of the girls told the teachers, and the teachers bawled me out. They told me that if I ever said anything like that again I'd have to leave. The whole school was stirred up about it—and the girls I'd told that I'd been friends with, finally got to be the worst of all—they wouldn't speak to me any more. So I couldn't stand that—I left, myself. I saw one of them afterwards and she told me that she was sorry, because, after I had gone, some of them looked it up and they found out I was right.

I was married when I was fourteen and went up to Washington. On the train when I was on my way up there, a man got in from Idaho, and when he heard I was going to Washington, he said, "You're going to Washington, are you? Well, when you've been there a little while, you'll be all covered with moss—you'll have moss growing on your eyebrows and hanging out of your ears, and your hair will be full of moss!" I didn't think that sounded very cheerful, but I went up there, and I was in the woods almost fifteen years. The camp was 'way up the mountain—from where we were, Mt. Rainier looked like you could just lean right over and touch it. When we first got there, we started out for the mountain in a buckboard: the driver was a man who had been hit by a limb, and his nose was squashed all over his face. Pretty soon, he pointed out ahead and said, "You see that loblolly over there?" I looked out and

*The first of these sketches is from life; the second, imaginary.

saw a great big sheet of mud. "Well," he said, "we're goin' right through it!" And he lashed up the horses and plunged right in. When we got out, I looked back and saw the poor dog that had been tied to the back of the buckboard—he was all fulla mud and almost dead. So were we. Then to go up the mountain, we had to ride. I never had ridden very much, and I made some big mistakes. I couldn't understand why the horse always had to go zigzag along the path and I decided I'd make him go straight—and the first thing I knew I was off on the ground rolling down the slope. The horse had stumbled on a cedar-snag—those cedar-snags are as slick as glass, you know. If I had left him alone, he would have avoided them. He was what they call woodsbroke, and I wasn't yet.

Well, as I say, I was up there almost fifteen years and I certainly got awfully lonesome. I used to feel like I was sunk in a deep well: it's so close with the trees up all around you that you feel like you can hardly breathe. It's so hot in the daytime you can hardly stand it and so cold at night you can hardly stand it. I almost put my eyes out reading by a lantern in the evenings. I used to sit there and hear the mice running round and round like a racetrack. The woods are fulla mice—the mice get into the walls, and the skunks go in after the mice and they get fastened there. I couldn't get very many books—all they had up there was the seed catalogue and the almanac—and I had to get them brought up from the circulating library in Seattle. I read E. P. Roe's *The Opening of a Chestnut Burr* and *He Fell in Love With His Wife*—old stories about New York, you know—but I thought they were great. I used to read them and just think it must be wonderful to live in New York. Once I cooked for a camp of sixty men where the cook had gone away. It's quite a stunt in itself to learn to cook up there. What they eat up there is sourdough—that's a kind of pancake dough that isn't affected by the cold. It's so cold up there that you can't do much with food—our Indian, Jake, used to take his bread and his bottle of potato-water to bed with him at night to keep them from freezing.

I'll never forget the first time I made bread. In the first place, they don't have any regular kind of yeast—like Fleischmann's —they only have one kind—a brand called Owl—and you have to put in about twelve cakes of that to get any results at all. I tried to knead it on a table, but I couldn't do anything with it—the bottom of the pan would just clink back and forth—it was so big and weak. Finally, the old man that was there took it and put it down on the floor and went to it with his whole strength—that was the only way you could make any impression on it. What I missed most—I never thought I would—but what I missed most was a woman. I didn't see a woman for years, and then when I did, she was more like a man than a woman. She was a woman who had come up there with her husband, who was a Civil War veteran and had a homestead. She helped him cut the trees and everything—sure, she used to work on the business end of a cross-saw! Then he drank so that she left him and went down to Tacoma and went into business—and she bought up the tideland flats for twenty-five dollars an acre. They were just an expanse of mud then, and everybody gave her the big ha-ha, but it turned out that they were valuable for machine shops—she evidently knew that—and she sold them for a lot of money. Her name was Larry Larson.

Well, when she was selling out her ranch she came over to see my husband. I couldn't take my eyes off her, I hadn't seen a woman in so long. But she didn't notice me—didn't know I was there, see. I was standing cooking potato cakes over the fire—we didn't have any stove, we just had to cook over the blaze—and I was changing my frying pan from hand to hand and trying to hold my face away from the fire. Pretty soon, she came over, still talking to my husband, and put on a man's old slouch hat down over her eyes, and took the frying pan away from me and held it right out over the blaze and kept it there without ever changing hands and you ought to have seen her flip the potato cakes over, holding it out like that—still talking business all the time. Made me feel so cheap! Finally, we had a kind of a bust-up. I got tired of living up there, and my husband thought I was interested in another man—but you had to be interested in something up there—and I took my boy—he was born up there—and went south again. I really guess it's only a woman like Larry Larson that can succeed up there.

When I first went up to Washington, I'd see all those wives of homesteaders with picket fences around them—Mrs. Shafer and Mrs. Huckaby and Mrs. Smith—and I resented that the wives always died but never the men—all except Huckaby, and he had to be shot! One woman got so desperate one winter, when her husband was off on a spree, that she killed her four children with a butcher knife and tried to get away with herself. It seemed as if it was hearing the cougar scream that she got so she couldn't stand. They give the most awful scream that just sends the shivers right through you—just like a woman, you know. She tried to drown herself, but when she struck the cold water, it sort of knocked her sane or something. The man who told me about it thought that was funny! Only the baby survived.

My husband was mean and cruel—he said he had Indian blood. He always did have a grudge, but it was him that always brought it up himself—I don't think he had any Indian blood. His father was mean—that's why his wife left him, he was so mean—but my husband improved on his meanness. He was a teaser, and when they grow up and don't get over it, it is pretty bad. The old man got kind of crazy one winter and tried to poison me. He'd sit around in the evening and say, "John L. Sullivan's dead," when he wasn't dead at all—and then he thought that I was a spy on-um that his wife had sent. I guess he'd been up there so long alone brooding in his homestead that he finally went off-uz head. Well, anyway, one night he tried to poison me. Strychnine—they use it for traps, you know. That night was a different night from the other nights—all the days were just the same, but this day was a different day. He got up and went out for a walk after dinner, instead of going right in for a nap, like he usually did. Well, anyway, at dinner be offered me this piece of meat—deer-meat—and I didn't want it, but I wanted to be polite to the old man, so I waited till he'd went out and then put it back on the plate, and in the evening he ate it himself and was so sick! But he knew what to do. I wouldn't have and might have died—but he ate a lot of lard. Now he's my best friend: we write to each other all the time. He told me afterwards he guessed he was queer that winter. They called him Abe Lincoln up there.

I had two children up there, and the third one died before it was born—a month before it was born—and poisoned me. And I wanted to die: I was so sick, and my husband was such a mean monster. I couldn't remember anything—that was really terrible, that muddled mind I had—and whenever anybody would ask me a question, it would be just like a big blank wall up in front of me. I couldn't even remember the things I had to buy when I went to the store—I used to have to memorize them on my fingers. The doctor—Dr. Smiley, who was new up there then—came in, and he felt right away what was the matter, and he said, "You don't want to get well!," and I said, "Oh, yes, I do," and he said, "No—you don't,"—so then, of course, finally, I had to admit that I didn't. And he pled with me to try to get well, because he said he was new there, and if one of his patients died, they'd figure he wasn't any good. So finally I got well. But when I went to court for the divorce, I couldn't answer any of the questions they asked me: I'd just stand there like a dumb ox.

I went down to Oklahoma where my father was—my father had set up as a doctor—I don't know if he ever knew how to give anything but calomel, but he certainly gave plenty of that —and the whole community down there got to be practically dependent on him—he learned by experimenting on them, too. That was in Eagletown, which is halfway between Broken Bow, Oklahoma, and De Queen, Arkansas—that's a district they call the Sticks because there's so much timber there. The country is really beautiful: they have all these yellow pines and what they call ironwood that turns first brown and then yellow, and sort of a henna-colored soil—but the people don't do anything with it. Where we were, the Choctaw Lumber Company had come in and put them to work—somebody has to do something with them—they'd just sit and rock, otherwise. Each family owns a cow, and if they're ambitious they have a "hawg" and they'd let it go at that. I tell you, you have to go down and live among them to believe that there are such people! They won't talk—all you can get out of them is "yes" and "no" and "Ah reckon." But they watch everything you do —the first morning I was there, all the women hung around and watched me get washed. You ought to have seen their faces when they saw some of the things I did—they thought I was outlandish—they didn't have to do that, see! And when I brushed my teeth! They couldn't make out what it was. They don't have any toothbrushes down there—they use snuff-sticks instead. And the women would watch me from the house

across the street when I got undressed at night. The only way
they know how to amuse themselves is to play craps—that's
their diversion. My father had a mechanical piano brought
down to try to entertain them, and you ought to have seen the
crowd around the house every night—they just stood there
and stared with their mouths open. They'd never heard any
music before—only just these old fiddles they have.

They played that mechanical piano every night for a month,
and I couldn't stand it any longer finally. I walked out one
night and said, "Golly! I can't stand this tinned music any
more!" They looked at me real sore and said, "Didja ever hear
any better?" Later on, they had pictures there—in the same
room that was the school and the church; but most of the
older people didn't go—that was kind of new, see. I used to go
and see films of New York, and it would make me just wild to
go there. I got in wrong with them all around.—In the first
place, I didn't make my boy go to church, and they're all very
moral—or claim to be. And they couldn't understand why I
read books—if they saw me reading a book, they'd put me
through a regular cross-examination—they'd want to know
what it was and why I wanted to read it. They didn't even read
the Bible—they figured they wouldn't know about it. I read
Darwin and some of Haeckel down there that my father
had and *The Wandering Jew* by Eugene Sue. Now I like to read
D. H. Lawrence and Michael Arlen. And then another thing I
did they didn't like was to speak to niggers I knew in the
street—you're not supposed to do that—it's as much as your
life is worth to speak to a nigger. I used to go out for long
walks with a book and that made them very suspicious—they
wanted to know why I wanted to go out for a walk alone.

Finally, they decided that I was some kind of a fancy woman,
who was meeting men in the woods—they began to talk about
me like I was a menace to the town. At the same time, when I
went out, the men would always follow me. There was a man
with a wooden leg who used to get on my nerves—he was the
most persistent of all. I used to hear his wooden leg stomping
behind me wherever I went, and I used to have to dodge him
among the trees. Some of the men had been in the war, and
they'd been away and weren't quite so narrow-minded as the
other people—one of them told me about how he was in an

attack and he saw a German coming toward him with his thumb, which had been cut off, just hanging loose by the skin. "Ah couldn't kill him," he said, "so Ah just took him to the hospital." I asked him why he had gone into the war—"Why," he said, "Ah figgered that if we didn't go over there and git them, they'd come over here and git us. That's what the newspapers said. Why? wasn't it true?" He was nice—but most of the men were the kind that tar and feather people. In fact, finally, one day I was out for a walk with an engineer, who was the only man in the community I could talk to—and we were sitting on the railroad track, and all of a sudden a man jumped out of the bushes and pointed a shotgun at us and said, "What are you doing on that railroad track?" I was mad, I can tell you! I stood up and I said, "You must think we want to go some place to make love—to go out on the railroad track! But go ahead and shoot me! Here I am! You'll never have a better target!"

That was too much for me—I decided to leave and take a chance on New York. First I lived in the Bronx, and that was terrible. But I'd heard about the Village. There was a Greenwich Village girl in Seattle—a little Roumanian Jewess. I got to know her when I left the woods and lived with her while I was sick. She had painted fans and things—I'd never seen anything like that. So finally I came to the Village. I did sewing. Now I run this little store, and I like it, because I always had a sort of an original taste in decorations and things. I make these blouses myself—they're not afraid of having them too bright down here. Another thing is that nobody cares what you do down here—nobody expects you to cook or to go to church —and you can always talk to interesting people. I tell you, the West is all right, but it's a great relief to get some place where you can feel a little bit free. I know all about those great open spaces.

April 15, 1925

II. *Fire-Alarm*

The first expressionist play we ever did at the Hole-and-Corner Playhouse was a piece called *Fire-Alarm* by a man named DeGross Wilbur. We put it on because the author had offered to finance it himself. The play was in eighteen scenes and dealt with the nervous breakdown of a worker in a paper-box factory. In the first scene, you saw him making boxes: he and the other workers wore pasteboard masks of the same material as the boxes and performed monotonous movements in unison. Finally, a gong is sounded for quitting time, and all the workers leave except the hero (who, in the program, was called simply The Man): he gets up and looks about him; the lights have been turned on the scenery (which has been hitherto left in darkness), and he realizes that he is imprisoned in a great paper box. Then the sides of the box become transparent, and he sees the families of the officials and the shareholders of the paper-box business parading pompously about him. A pretty girl seems to smile at him, and he tries to go to meet her, but finds that he is balked by the sides of the box. A policeman threatens him, and he falls to the ground in despair. The next scene is a long soliloquy: the stars have come out in the sky, and the Man can see them through the paper box. They are red, yellow and green and are continually going on and off (DeGross declared it was silly to have stars of the conventional kind, when no one saw them that way any longer: these were modern American stars and ten times the ordinary size). The Man apostrophizes the stars: "Oh, little jazz-babies," he says, "oh, little jazz-babies, twinkling so bright as you dance the shimmy of the spheres! Oh, little jazz-babies, winking, with the mascara of night on your eyelashes!—look down on the great smoky city and tell me where my sweetie is!" This goes on for some time. The next scene is still in the box. The owner of the factory appears and tries to induce the Man to go back to work; then a member of the union comes in and tries to induce him to strike. Both were played by the same actor, with the same make-up but different clothes. The Man sends them both away, telling them that their aims are identical and that he has no use for either. Then the man has another long soliloquy; then a Physicist appears. The Physicist explains to the

Man that he has discovered a new system of morality based on the quantum theory. He has learned to disintegrate matter, and, by the application of powerful rays, he makes the paper-box prison disappear. Thereafter, the play presents the adventures of the Man and the Professor of Physics in their pursuit of the new code of morality. This code is based on discontinuity: you suddenly do the opposite of whatever you have previously done. This enables you to rob trusting friends, to trip up people walking in the street and to put knock-out drops in the cocktails of people you have invited to dinner. The Man and the Professor of Physics experiment with all these things, but they are all very disappointing. The jewelry stolen from the trusting friends turns out to be bogus, and the drugged guests have nothing in their pockets but ragged pocket-handkerchiefs and are wearing false dress-shirt fronts and made-up hook-on ties. The people tripped up in the street turn upon the practical jokers, and one of them hurls the Man through the plate-glass window of a fashionable modiste. There he encounters the girl who smiled at him and whom he has ever since been seeking, but she turns out to be a wooden mannequin. In his chagrin at this disillusion, be promptly puts into practice the morality of the Professor by assassinating him on the spot and throwing him down a drain. But, in a moment, the Physicist reappears, made unearthly by a colder kind of light. We realize now for the first time that the Physicist represents Truth, which is unchangeable and indomitable. This is conveyed to us in a soliloquy by the Man. Toward the end of this soliloquy, a large rhomboid in the backdrop begins to glow. "Come with me," says the Physicist, "into the Light!" And both advance into the mercury-tube dawn.

When I first read the script of this play, I felt a good deal of interest in a young paper-box worker—I had been given to understand that the author was himself a worker—who had developed such a singular vein of fancy. But when I met De-Gross Wilbur, I discovered that he was a pale vain young man, who not only had never seen a paper-box factory in his life, but had never even been near the textile mills where his father made bathing-suits. It was the money from the bathing-suits, however, which financed DeGross's play. I asked him how he had come to write the play, if he had had so little real feeling for the workers; and he answered that he simply believed that the time had now arrived for plays of that sort to be written. I asked him why he called his play *Fire-Alarm*, and he said that, as he had originally written it, it had ended with the Professor and the Man heading a peace delegation to the President and then setting the White House on fire; and that, even though this scene had been taken out, the title was still true to the spirit of the play, which was frankly one of revolution. Later on, however, I heard him telling someone that *Fire-Alarm* was intended to have no political significance but to be taken as a "farce for live puppets, of which the moral was a Buddhistic resignationism." "You must always play for laughs," he told us. "In the dinner scene, where the Physicist and the Man pick the pockets of the guests they have drugged, you must have the guests come to life and turn seltzer bottles on them. It is years and years since a seltzer bottle has been seen on the American stage. They have been banned by the dollar-chasing 'refinement' of the uptown commercial theater. But we shall never have a real native American Drama till the seltzer bottle squirts again!" Three days before the opening, he told us that it had always been his idea to have a fire bell and a siren continuously sounding between each two scenes; otherwise, he said, the title would be meaningless. And this we tried for awhile.

I cannot say that the play was well directed: it was scarcely directed at all. The titular director was a fellow named Bob Mott, who had done a little of everything in the Village. In those days, in Greenwich Village, wherever you went to a party, there was always an impressive person who seemed so free from affectation that you took him for one of the distinguished artists who sometimes lived down there. He would sit in a corner and smoke with a homely or rugged assurance that seemed to mask treasures of subtlety and wit, and people would gather about him to hear his judgments on all sorts of subjects. Bob Mott was one of these persons. He went striding around the Village with a thick and knobby cane, a rough-and-ready old soft hat and a large pipe, which he usually kept in his teeth all the time he was talking; but, when you really got to know him, you found out that the basis of his character was a smug invincible limpness. He was, therefore, not a very good director. It cannot be said that Bob did not appreciate the play: on the contrary, during the rehearsals, he spent so much time laughing at the jokes that he never got around to finding means for making them effective with the audience; and, at the end of a scene which moved him strongly, as certain scenes invariably did when the actors remembered all the lines and went through them without halting, he would turn to the nearest bystander and, with his pipe clenched between his teeth, whisper loudly, "God! what a punch!" He used to watch the rehearsals very knowingly, always pulling his pipe; but he never gave the actors any useful instructions, except occasionally to take them aside and hold whispered conversations with them —conversations that were mostly intended to promote Bob's relations with the actresses rather than the progress of the play. He was usually more or less drunk. He and DeGross Wilbur used to have terrific quarrels.

Jane Gooch, who also designed the costumes and managed the publicity end, did most of the real work of direction. She made a point of looking in on the rehearsals every other day or so to see that the actors were managing to get on and off the stage and taking each other up on their cues. But she was never able to stay very long and so could not enforce the discipline and keep the actors up to the efforts which are required for a successful production. All sorts of other people used to drift in and out while the rehearsals were going on. They would make all sorts of suggestions to Bob Mott and to the actors. There was one man who ran a book shop who was jealous of one of the actresses, a girl with whom he had been living and whom he had begun to suspect of an interest in one of the members of the cast. He would come and sit there every day, and sometimes conceal himself behind the scenes, where the actors would fall over him as they were making their exits. Bob Mott had a police-dog named Hindenburg, which he always brought to the theater with him and which barked at the fire-alarm and the scenes in which people were knocked around. There was also a Polish girl, who drank and was in love with Bob Mott. We used to hear her sobbing in the pauses. The day of the dress rehearsal, Jane Gooch, who had been overworking, arrived in

the afternoon, and, after witnessing a scene or two, broke
down and had hysterics. She recovered, however, and did what
she could.

Fire-Alarm did not run very long, but the run was extremely varied. On some occasions, the audience would hiss;
and, on others, they would sit in utter silence. At one performance, a single spectator laughed harshly at one of the
satiric lines and the rest of the audience hushed him. Sometimes we could hear people weeping; and sometimes they
laughed so wildly that they broke the actors up. ("I am perfectly satisfied," DeGross would say. "The play has a thousand
facets.") Sometimes they had nearly all left before it was half
through. Nor did this altogether depend on the accidental
mood of the audience: the performances differed remarkably.
The prompter, whose English was poor, had difficulty in following the lines, so that parts of the play were dropped out
when the actors forgot their speeches. The soliloquies were
particularly treacherous and were often abruptly telescoped by
the omission of long passages, before the actors who were supposed to play the following scenes had had time to arrive in
the wings and pick up their cues. Sometimes the stage manager, who was also the electrician and who was having a crisis
with his wife, would forget to lower the curtain, so that the actors, at the end of an act, had to hold their positions like living
statues. One night, during the final scene, when the Professor
took the hero by the arm and led him toward the dawn of
Truth, the electric rhomboid, at the back of the stage, instead
of bursting into brightness, merely gave a momentary glow
and then began to grow fainter and fainter. When the Professor delivered his exhortation, "Come with me into the
Light!", the stage was entirely dark. There was a good deal of
laughter at this, and DeGross asked us to do it this way every
night, because it made the ending more ironic. He said that, in
allowing the play to end on a note of hope, he had been sub-
consciously affected by the pressure of the popular taste in favor of a happy ending, and that this accident had made him
realize how much finer it was to end in darkness. We dissuaded
him from this, however.

According to a tradition of the theater, the last night of a
run is a special occasion: the actors play practical jokes, which

are usually unnoticed by the audience, and try to break one another up. Now, the actors in *Fire-Alarm* had been through a good deal for the play, and they felt that they had the right to express their relief at its closing by hoaxes of an exceptionally elaborate kind. The stage manager, who was feeling more cheerful because his wife had come back, also entered into the spirit of the occasion and spent hours, unknown to the actors, arranging surprises and pitfalls. Thus, for the first scene, in which the hero tries to break through the sides of the box, he made invisible slits in the gauze so that the actor put his leg and arm through and had to pull them back again. And when the Employer in a later scene picked up his silk hat from the table, a shower of pretzels fell out. The guests in the dinner scene took the wind out of the hero's indignation by wearing real dress shirts instead of false ones and having large rolls of bills in their pockets. (During this scene, Bob Mott's police-dog also wandered in from the wings and licked one of the corpses on the nose.) The stage manager's most ingenious effect occurred in one of the interior sets: the Professor was supposed to open a door and enter from the outside; but the door had been fixed so that its hinges were at the bottom instead of at the side, and it came down on the stage like a portcullis; the actor had to walk in over it. When he later tried to make his exit through the door on the other side and pushed at the knob to open it, it turned out to have been taken off its hinges altogether and, evading the Professor's grasp, was wafted away into space by someone on the other side. In the midst of the final soliloquy, which the hero delivered from a high set of steps, these steps were rolled slowly behind the scenes, carrying the soliloquy with them; and when the Professor began talking about the Light, a flashlight was set off right in front of him, which upset the actor so much that he began again several speeches back and started to play the scene over.

Most of the audience laughed: there were not very many there. But after the performance, a strange rigid woman—a spinster of about forty-five, who wore spectacles and was dressed in hideous clothes of some remote age and place—appeared at the stage door and desired to meet the author. She talked nervously, as if under intense pressure, and I thought she was a little mad. When DeGross Wilbur appeared, she complimented him on his play with a curious acid eagerness that sounded as if she were so unaccustomed to expressing herself with enthusiasm that she lacked the appropriate accents. "Tell me, please, Mr. Wilbur," she demanded, "have you ever been in Gibson, Colorado? I am sure you must have been in Gibson!" DeGross said that he had never been there. "What you have given us," she went on, "so insolently—I might almost say, so atrociously—with a defiance so categoric—is a compendium of all its laxities, its brazennesses, its eclipses, as well as of its few limpid lovelinesses. I should have said that no one could have written that play who had never been a schoolteacher in Gibson! The Employer's coarse market-mindedness, so sickeningly submerged in the foodstuffs by which alone man cannot live! All his purposes are directed toward it! Above it his thoughts cannot leap!" (She was speaking of the shower of pretzels.) "I have seen it a thousand times! And the stars that do but caricature our passions when we cry to them in their coolness and clearness—and the dreadful doors of our rooms that seem to topple inward upon us or to waver away at our touch, as we pass from cell to cell of torment!"

As I say, I thought she was mad. That was my first meeting with Isabelle Griffin. I did not know that she was eventually to become the first woman dramatist of importance in the history of the theater. And I was even further from guessing that this immature and incoherent play of Wilbur's was actually to show her the way to her own creative development. She had come on to New York for the first time and for only a very brief visit, and if she had not seen *Fire-Alarm* at the suggestion of another schoolteacher with whom she was staying in St. Luke's Place, it is unlikely—since she read almost nothing but seventeenth-century poetry—that she would ever have come into contact with the methods of German expressionism, which, imperfectly assimilated and exemplified as they were in *Fire-Alarm*, were in her case to prove so fruitful. Today, one speaks of Isabelle Griffin and Strindberg. Nor was it merely the calculated effects of the play that influenced her own technique: she was also, to some extent, happily inspired by the accidents and jokes of the final performance. The Physicist's sudden setback when the flashlight was set off at the end provided Miss Griffin, for example, with scenes of a curious effectiveness, in which whole passages of dialogue were repeated.

DeGross Wilbur himself soon sloughed off the modernist tricks which he had been at such pains to acquire and took to writing those amusing comedies which began with satiric pictures of the country-club life of industrial towns and ended on the Riviera with the international cocktail set.

April 20, 1927

Sherwood Anderson's 'Many Marriages'

I CANNOT regard *Many Marriages*, the new novel by Sherwood Anderson, as a quite worthy successor to *The Triumph of the Egg*. It takes the subjective method of the last story of that book, *Out of Nowhere Into Nothing*—which was already rather too long—and applies it on an even more elaborate scale. It may be that I am not in a position to judge *Many Marriages* quite fairly, because the author, at the time he was writing it, once told me the story at length. It then seemed to me fresh and surprising, like a dream that was remembered with vividness and that kept for the dreamer some strange special significance. In the telling, it had all of the quality that has often brought Anderson, at his best, closer to the art of the poet than to that of the writer of fiction. But when I came to read the story in its extended form, I found it tedious and sometimes flat. It is as if Mr. Anderson had diluted his ideas until they had lost a good deal of their force. The incident, for example, of the meeting between the girl and the boy, when both find themselves for the moment delivered from the sense of shame, and she swims to him out of sleep like a diver from profound waters, is certainly very fine; but one has to hear too much about it—or rather, what one keeps on hearing adds too little to what one has already heard. Mr. Anderson's repetitions, which are intended to, and which do at their best, give the effect of the rhythms of living, become here indefensibly boring. We have, for example, to listen twice to a complete and detailed description of the finding of the little green stone which is to stand as a symbol of life, and whenever it is mentioned later, this description is partly repeated. It is a little like *The House That Jack Built*.

It is a habit of Mr. Anderson's to divest his characters of their incidentals, their furniture, their houses, their clothes, their ordinary social relations; and he produces in the best of his stories an impression of classic simplicity. But this feature of his writing, also, comes off badly in *Many Marriages*. The characters seem strangely pale, as if they had been stripped of their personalities, too. The wife assigned to the hero is quite inconceivable as a human being. She presents the blank face of a phantom. When her husband announces that he is leaving her, she accommodatingly poisons herself without uttering a word of remonstrance. Such a woman, however sexless, might be expected at least to have some existence in connection with her family and her household; but Mrs. Webster gives up her daughter without making the faintest struggle. It is like something in a children's charade or one of those comic-strips, in which people fall dead, amid a galaxy of stars, at some catastrophic "wisecrack." We seem to see Mrs. Webster clasping her hand to her forehead and shooting up several feet into the air. It is true, of course, that poor Mrs. Webster is intended as an example of death-in-life; but even a corpse should be human. And in the case of Nathalie Schwartz, the mistress, who is played off against the wife, this explanation cannot apply. We are repeatedly told how strong she is, yet Nathalie, too, is a specter whose voice we are never allowed to hear. We end with an irritated feeling that the hero has simply dropped one lay-figure in order to pick up another.

Yet, in spite of the feebleness, even flabbiness, of the texture of *Many Marriages*, the book is not wholly devoid of the queer and disquieting impressiveness which one feels in all Anderson's work. Here as elsewhere, we are soothed as well as disturbed by the feeling of hands thrust down among the inner organs of life—hands that are delicate and clean but still pitiless in their explorations. My only quarrel here with Mr. Anderson is that he has not thrust down so far as usual. He takes up the familiar theme of the husband who tires of his wife and goes off with someone else, and he leaves it much more nearly as he found it than it has been his wont to do with the cases with which he deals. Awakening husband and frozen wife are not quite different enough from the people in Miss Cather's *One of Ours* or Mr. Hergesheimer's *Cytherea*. Yet even when Sherwood Anderson cannot save a banal theme from banality, his banality is something distinct from the banality of other people. He has arrived at it all by himself. At his best, Sherwood Anderson functions with a natural ease and beauty on a plane in the depths of life—as if under a diving-bell submerged in the human soul—which makes the world of the ordinary novelist seem stagy and superficial. At his worst, as in *Many Marriages*, one feels, as one cannot feel in the cases of so many of his contemporaries, that he is at least, in the pursuit of his own ideal, making his own mistakes.

April, 1923

Ring Lardner's American Characters

MR. RING LARDNER is a popular journalist who writes for the New York *American* and who also provides the text for a syndicated comic strip. It has therefore been thought appropriate to present his new collection of short stories as if it were a volume of popular humor. There are a preface in the vein of Bill Nye and a jocose introduction to every story, and the title page is brightened by a humorous cut that is evidently by John Held. The book itself, from its burlesque preface, is called *How to Write Short Stories*, instead of, as it ought to be, *Champion and Other Stories*.

Is all this an idea of the publishers, who do not want to forfeit the prestige of Mr. Lardner's reputation as a humorist, or is it due to Mr. Lardner, who is timid about coming forward in the role of serious writer? The fact is that this new book of his, instead of belonging to the gruesome department of, say, Irvin Cobb's *Speaking of Operations*, contains some of the most interesting work that Ring Lardner has yet produced. These stories, he observes in his preface, "will illustrate in a half-hearted way what I am trying to get at." But the stories are not half-hearted: it is the jokes that he intrudes among them. The nonsense of his introductions is so far below his usual level that one suspects him of a guilty conscience at attempting to disguise his talent for social observation and satire. For, aside from a very few things, such as *The Facts*, that seem a little magazine-made, what one finds in *How to Write Short Stories* is a series of studies of American types almost equal in importance to those of Sherwood Anderson and Sinclair Lewis.

It may, indeed, be said of Ring Lardner that, if we compare him with these other two writers, he shows a certain specific advantage over each of them. In those of Mr. Lardner's stories in which he attempts something rather similar to Sherwood Anderson's *The Egg* or *I'm a Fool*, he shows a firmer grasp both of the Western vernacular and of the external realities with which he is dealing. In a sense, he is closer to life. It is curious to speculate what would have happened to some of the stories in this collection if they had been written by Sherwood

Anderson. Two of Lardner's baseball players—Alibi Ike and a scout who is willing to risk ruining his team for the sake of a perfect quartet—may almost be called neurotics; and a third—the demon batter in *My Roomy*—is evidently quite insane. What startling preoccupations might not have been revealed to the reader if Anderson had X-rayed their deepest insides! Is not the mysterious Elliot, who insists upon shaving in the middle of the night and cannot sleep unless the water in the bathtub is running, a brother to John Webster of *Many Marriages*, who appeared before his daughter naked, and to the girl in *Out of Nowhere Into Nothing*, who used to listen to the waterpail slopping over? With Anderson, you are sometimes so far submerged in the spiritual sensations of these characters that you lose sight of them as actual people in an actual Western community; with Lardner's queer cases, however, you are never taken inside them; you see them only in their relations with other people. And when Lardner comes closest to Lewis, as in the story called *The Golden Honeymoon*, he is less likely than Lewis to caricature, and hence to falsify, because he is primarily interested in studying a kind of person rather than in drawing up an indictment.

But Mr. Lardner has, of course, not as yet attained the stature of either of these men. Anderson has a poet's sensibility; Lewis, a satirist's fury. But what Lardner may have to match these he has never yet fully revealed. For all his saturnine tone, his apparent scorn of vulgar values, he seems committed to popular journalism. He does not even care to admit that he has tried to do work on a higher level—hence the clownish presentation of these stories. Yet he would seem to come closer than anyone else among living American writers to possessing the combination of qualities that made *Huckleberry Finn* a masterpiece. For one thing, he has ready invention —which most American realists have not; and for another— what is even rarer—an unmistakable personal accent which represents a special way of looking at things. Even such important examples of recent American realism as Sinclair Lewis's *Main Street* and *Babbitt* have been put together largely out of literary materials that the author found ready to hand—the pre-war English novel of Bennett and Wells. But Ring Lardner seems to have imitated nobody, and nobody else could repro-

duce his essence. You have to read the whole of a novel of
Lewis to find out that there is anything remarkable about it;
but there is scarcely a paragraph of Lardner's which, in its irony
both fresh and morose, does not convey somehow the sense of
a distinguished aloof intelligence. And he has shown an unexcelled, a perhaps unrivalled, mastery of what since the publication of Mencken's book, has come to be known as the
American language. Mark Twain, in his foreword to *Huckleberry Finn*, explained that he had taken great care to differen-
tiate between "the Missouri Negro dialect; the extremest form
of the backwoods Southwestern dialect; the ordinary 'Pike
County' dialect; and four modified varieties of this last." So
Lardner has marked the distinction between the baseball
player's and the prize-fighter's slang, can speak the language of
the Chicago song-writer of *Some Like Them Cold*, who has
come to New York to make his fortune, and has equally at
his command the whole vocabulary of adolescent clichés of the
young girl who writes to the songwriter, and of the quite different set of clichés of the middle-aged man from New Jersey
who goes to Florida for his golden honeymoon. And he understands the difference between the spoken language of these
semi-literate types and the language they will use when they
write. Finally, what is most important, he writes the vernacular
like an artist and not merely like a clever journalist—as George
Ade or O. Henry did. There is nothing artificial or forced
about the use of slang in these stories; it is as natural as it is apt.
Lardner's language is the product of a philologist's ear and a
born writer's relish for words.

    Will Ring Lardner, then, go on to his *Huckleberry Finn* or
has he already told all he knows? It may be that the mechanical
repetition of a trick that one finds in such a story as *Horseshoes*
and the melodramatic exaggeration of *Champion* indicate limitations. But you never know: here is a man who has had the
freedom of the modern West no less than Mark Twain did of
the old one, who approaches it, as Mark Twain did, with a perceptive interest in human beings instead of with the naturalist's formula—a man who lives at a time when, if one be not
sold irredeemably into bondage to the *Saturday Evening Post*,
it is far easier for a serious writer to get published and find a
hearing than it was in Mark Twain's day. If Ring Lardner has

anything more to give us, the time has now come to deliver it. He has not even popular glory to gain by pursuing any other course. His popular vein is about worked out; and he has always been too much of an artist to make the biggest kind of success as a clown; his books have never sold so well as Stephen Leacock's or Irvin Cobb's. When Lewis himself, in his earlier phase a humorist for the *Saturday Evening Post*, took a chance and composed in *Main Street* his satire upon its readers, he received unexpected support. It turned out that there were thousands of people who were ready to hear what he wanted to say. What bell might not Lardner ring if he set out to give us the works?

July, 1924

Eugene O'Neill and the Naturalists

I. Eugene O'Neill as Prose-Writer

THE new volume of Eugene O'Neill's plays contains *The Hairy Ape, Anna Christie* and *The First Man*. The first of these seems to me almost the only thing that Mr. O'Neill has yet written that has very much value as literature apart from its effectiveness as drama. As a rule, the plays of O'Neill are singularly uninviting on the printed page. The dialogue is raw and prosaic, in texture quite undistinguished, and the author has made no attempt to appeal to the imagination by way of the stage directions, which are not lifted above the baldness of the prompt-book. These plays appear too often, in short, as rather second-rate naturalistic pieces that owe their eminence, not to their intrinsic greatness, but, as Marx said of John Stuart Mill, "to the flatness of the surrounding country." The dialogue of *The First Man*, which I have not seen on the stage, proves in the reading so tasteless and dreary that one does not see how one could sit through it.

But Eugene O'Neill has another vein in which he is a literary artist of genius. When he is writing the more or less grammatical dialogue of the middle-class characters of his plays, his prose is heavy and indigestible even beyond the needs of naturalism. People say the same things to one another over and over again and never succeed in saying them any more effectively than the first time; long speeches shuffle dragging feet, marking time without progressing, for pages. But as soon as Mr. O'Neill gets a character who can only talk some kind of vernacular, he begins to write like a poet. We had already had evidence of this in the Negro hero of *The Emperor Jones* and in the first act of *Anna Christie*, but when one saw *The Hairy Ape* produced by the Provincetown Players, one had the feeling that Mr. O'Neill had for the first time become fully articulate. As Walter Pritchard Eton said, he wrote slang like "a sort of wild organ music." The scenes in which the non-illiterate characters talk are as clumsy and dead as ever, but the greater part of the play, in which Yank, the stoker, discourses, has a mouth-filling rhythmical eloquence very rare in naturalistic drama.

When the speeches came to life in this way, the drama was always more moving. One felt that Mr. O'Neill, in his gift for drawing music from humble people, had a kinship with Sherwood Anderson. For *The Hairy Ape* is the tragedy not, as in the common formula, of the American pitted against his environment nor even of the proletarian pitted against capitalism, but of the universal human being pitted against himself. It is, as Mr. O'Neill has labelled it, a play "of ancient and modern life." I have heard this disputed by people who had got the impression from seeing the play that the hero of *The Hairy Ape* is thwarted by the forces of society instead of by his own limitations. But I believe that if anyone will read the last scenes in the printed text, he will see that though it is a consciousness of social inferiority that gives the first impetus to Yank's débâcle and though he himself at first supposes that it is society he has to fight, the Hairy Ape's ultimate struggle for freedom takes place within the man himself. I am not sure that Mr. O'Neill always gives enough dramatic emphasis to his most important ideas. The significance of these last scenes of *The Hairy Ape* was not thrown into relief on the stage. People seemed to understand the play better when they saw it a second time. This is a reason—aside from the fact that the *Ape* is good literature—that it is useful to have it in a book.

November, 1922

II. All God's Chillun and Others

Catskill Dutch by Roscoe Brink was a long, conscientious, rather boring play about rural life on the Hudson after the Civil War. There is a good deal of this sort of naturalism now being turned out in America. No longer than a decade ago, our critics were still complaining of the scarcity of sober realism in American fiction and drama; that was the period of the great ascendancy of the school of Arnold Bennett and Stanley Houghton, and almost nobody but Dreiser, in the United

States, was doing anything of the sort for us. Now the formula has been discovered, and dozens of people are applying it. The writer had occasion recently to go through the manuscripts submitted in a magazine short-story contest and, even knowing the popularity of novels like Lewis's and Willa Cather's, was astonished by the unanimity with which this formula had been adopted: of the three ablest writers who emerged, one dealt with the Jews on the New York East Side, another with the Southern Negroes, and a third with the suburbs of San Francisco. All three, like Mr. Brink, wrote competently and sincerely; but none of them had anything much that was personal or vivid to communicate. They tended, like Mr. Brink, to be duller than the life they described.

Thus we are getting the backwash of the naturalistic movement—as we have of so many other movements—when Europe is just leaving it behind. What in the theater is called expressionism represents an attempt to escape from the literal methods of realism—as the cubism of Braque and Picasso represents an attempt to escape from the photographic ideals of nineteenth-century painting. The expressionistic method, as Mr. Stark Young has said, is "merely the poetic method"; but it has produced a genre that differs from any previous dramatic poetry, because it is practised by people who have had to break away from naturalism. It was not a problem for Shakespeare to disregard literal realism and to have any sort of character give vent to his inmost thoughts in the non-colloquial language of the imagination, because Shakespeare did not have to make the effort of unlearning Ibsen and Shaw. But the dramatic poet today has to take a naturalistic subject and try to knock poetry into it—just as the modern painter has to take a conventional still-life and by main force hack it to pieces and shuffle up the fragments in a novel pattern. Hence the discordant conceits, the limping allegories, of such a play as *The Man Who Ate the Popomack*—a pioneer English expressionistic comedy by W. J. Turner. *The Man Who Ate the Popomack*, though it has a dash of wit and some charming speeches (particularly in the Chinese scene), is, on the whole, rather an unsatisfactory medley of a little Shaw, a little Galsworthy, a little expressionism and a residuum of jokes from *Punch* (the man who comes to dinner in a diving suit). The difficulties of presenting a fairy-tale mixed

up with a drawing-room comedy seem acutely to have been
felt by the producers, who have radically altered Mr. Turner's
text and presented as a conventional dream what the author, as
appears from the printed play, meant to be shown as actually
happening. I don't think they have improved matters by doing
this; I prefer Mr. Turner's version. But then it is true that the
author has not solved the problem himself.

A much better play than either of these, *All God's Chillun
Got Wings* by Eugene O'Neill, also shows signs of an effort to
impose subjective fancies upon an idea objectively conceived.
The Provincetown Players, in producing the play, have not
tried to carry out the idea that appears in the author's text, of
having the walls and ceiling of the interior set contract as the
situation becomes more oppressive, but they have made him a
present of a curious church with a waist like a human being's
and flying buttresses of brick that seem to be streaming away
in the wind. These devices, both author's and producer's,
strike one as a little mechanical, as not quite belonging with
the rest of the play; but, in any case, they are unimportant and
not typical of the treatment of the whole. Mr. O'Neill has
made a much more effective departure from the cumbersome
naturalism of the "transcript from life" of the type of *Catskill
Dutch*, by simply throwing overboard most of its detail. He
has sheared away, in *All God's Chillun*, almost everything except the relation between his two central characters, and, in
doing so, has gained intensity, one of the qualities our realism
most needs.

For the rest, *All God's Chillun Got Wings* is one of the best
things yet written about the race problem of Negro and white
and one of the best of O'Neill's plays. Two of Mr. O'Neill's
chief assets are, first, a nervous driving force that carries the
audience inescapably along; and, second, a gift for the eloquent use of the various forms of the American vernacular.
Both of these *All God's Chillun* has. It is not quite so consistently compelling or well-written as *The Emperor Jones* or *The
Hairy Ape*; it has its harsh notes and its raw expanses. But
then, it has a certain advantage over either of these other plays
in presenting two characters equally strong, in collision with

one another, instead of one central character who only contends with himself.

Mr. O'Neill has another qualification which sets him completely apart from the other American dramatists, who have so far done very little more than modify the conventional American comedy in the direction of Shaw or Sinclair Lewis: he nearly always, with whatever crudeness, is expressing some real experience, some impact directly from life. The characters and the scene in O'Neill are sometimes forbiddingly bleak—as in the latter part of *All God's Chillun*—but they are likely at any moment, by taking on the power and the awfulness of naked natural forces, to establish a violent contact between themselves and us. This was true of even *Welded* (on the stage), a monotonous drama of marriage—which failed principally, it seems to me, through not having been well enough written. Mr. O'Neill, with this sort of subject from ordinary middle-class life, does not pay enough attention to style. A play, like anything else that is built of words, is primarily a work of literature, and even the most vigorous dramatic idea cannot be trusted to make its effect without the right words to convey it. All but the greatest of actors are liable to betray a careless text, but an accurate and brilliant text will manage to speak for itself in spite of the very worst. The expressiveness of Mr. O'Neill seems to diminish in direct proportion to his distance from the language of the people. At one pole, you have *The Hairy Ape*, certainly his best-written play; at the other *Welded*, perhaps his worst. In *All God's Chillun Got Wings*, you see his quality rising and falling—between the stale language of stock-company melodrama and the vivid, the racy, the real.

May 28, 1924

The New American Comedy

TEN years ago people flocked to comedies like *It Pays to Advertise*, in which the heroes were breezy business men who made a great deal of money in the last act, or to sentimental dramas like *Turn to the Right*, in which the simple American home was glorified. Today, they go to the theater to see satires like *Beggar on Horseback* by Marc Connelly and George S. Kaufman, in which business is made ridiculous; or comedies like George Kelly's *The Show-Off* and J. P. McEvoy's *The Potters*, in which business is made obnoxious and the American home hideous. It is not merely that these plays find producers but that they actually become very popular. *The Potters* is now in its seventh month, and *The Show-Off* has celebrated its hundredth performance. The work of a younger generation who have served their apprenticeships to the bond-selling business and the advertising agencies, to the ideals of Main Street generally, and who, encouraged no doubt by Lewis's example, have decided to trust their instincts in caricaturing these things, these plays find, as Lewis's novels did, audiences with similar instincts, who want nothing better than a chance to guffaw at their own preposterous dullness. Such comedies and their public are a sign—if not quite indubitably that America is becoming more intelligent—at least that a good many Americans have reached a point of supersaturation with our current commercial ideals. We have at last become aware that our commercialism has certain unattractive aspects and have begun to satirize ourselves. The crass business man, indeed, as well as the romantic advertiser, are already showing signs—in the pages of *Life*, for example—of passing into the popular mind as stereotyped comic characters, like the dude or the hayseed of yesterday.

Our satirists, nevertheless, have retained a good deal of the machinery, and hence of the point of view, of the business man's comedy upon which they have improved. The homely little old mother of *Turn to the Right* still survives—though in a modified form—as a fundamental element in *The Show-Off* and even in *Expressing Willie*; and the principal male charac-

ters, however absurd or hollow, do not fail to make a great deal
of money at the end of the last act, like the hero of *It Pays to
Advertise*. Aubrey Piper in *The Show-Off* saves his brother-in-
law from being swindled out of the profits of his invention,
and Mr. Potter turns out, after all, not to have sold the valuable oil lease. Once our writers of comedy depart from the
more obvious kind of satire that depends on intensifying ugliness, they gravitate toward the commonplace—nor does it
seem to me that the pessimistic heresies of the last scenes of
Elmer Rice's *The Adding Machine*, for example, are very much
less commonplace than the reassuring conventions I have
mentioned. There can, however, be no doubt whatever that in
effects of ferocious ugliness our dramatists have recently distinguished themselves. The almost half-witted joviality of *The
Show-Off*; the cooped-up poisoned interiors of *The Adding
Machine*; and the series of messy collisions between people
living too hurriedly or too close together that makes *The
Potters* like a long headache: conversations shattered by the
subway, meals bolted while transacting business, the love affair
on the piazza that is suddenly arrested by the headlights of another pair of lovers who are parking their car in the street, the
exasperated members of a family, all with mutually conflicting
aims, continually coming and going to the din of the door
bell, the telephone, the phonograph and the radio—it is in
such heightenings of the surface horrors of modern American
life that our theater at present excels.

What one misses, however, in these plays, even at their
strongest as satire, is a feeling for literary style. Our American
dramatists do not write very well. Marc Connelly and George
S. Kaufman deal more fancifully and more gaily than these
others with the office building and the suburban sitting-room,
but they do not write any better. Zona Gale, who writes well
in her novels, loses most of her distinction when she works for
the stage. Rachel Crothers, who, in *Expressing Willie*, presents
the successful business man going in for culture, has invented
some amusing patter for the conversational artist and the psychoanalytic siren into whose hands her hero has fallen, and
shows in general a gift for dialogue. Scott Fitzgerald, in his
play *The Vegetable*, which has been published and tried out on
the stage but never yet brought to New York, has applied to

this comedy of commercial mediocrity an imagination further from the commonplace than that of anyone else who has tried it, but his uncertain grasp of his subjects, more dangerous in a play than a novel, seems unpropitious to its success on the stage.

What might we not get, one asks oneself, if Ring Lardner were to write a play? He has already done several amusing sketches, and there is a rumor that he is now composing, in collaboration with George Gershwin, a version of *Carmen* in "the American language." His new book of short stories seems to me to establish him as something much nearer an artist than either Mr. Kelly or Mr. McEvoy—I might almost say than Mr. Rice. He has a charming imagination and he writes Americanese with a real sense of style. If anyone is capable of doing a one-hundred-percent American comedy that would also be dramatic literature, it is probably Mr. Lardner. But in the meantime, he is busy supplying the text for a syndicated daily comic strip—just as Mr. McEvoy has recently taken the Potters into the comic section with a daily strip of his own. That is the trouble with American comedy. If, on the one hand, it still stays too close to the comedy of yesterday, it is drawn, when it pulls away, toward the slapstick of the funny papers. The dramatists I have mentioned above put before us the materials for a national comedy but they apply to them the methods of the comic strip. What is needed is someone to color them with the temperament of the artist.

June 18, 1924

A Vortex in the Nineties: Stephen Crane

M R. THOMAS BEER'S *Stephen Crane: A Study in American Letters* is the latest and not one of the least satisfactory additions to the twentieth-century portrait gallery of nineteenth-century celebrities inaugurated five years ago by Mr. Lytton Strachey. Since *Eminent Victorians*, biography in English has become what it has long been in France: a form of literary art. "Those two fat volumes," at seven-fifty a set, which Mr. Strachey deplored in 1918, have already begun to disappear, and instead we have, if not always masterpieces of Stracheyan compression and point, at least narratives that are critical and selective and of dimensions appropriate to their subjects.

Mr. Beer, however, differs from most of his fellows in not imitating Strachey's style as well as his economy and form. Mr. Beer has gone for his style to a writer who had already before Strachey brought something of Strachey's accent to the chronicle of the nineteenth century: he has gone to our own Henry Adams. He patronizes American politics in very much Adams's manner and even imitates those curious transitions—the result, perhaps, in Adams's case, of the effort to impose a unity on a set of historical phenomena that appalled him by their apparent inconsequence—which in his *History of the United States* and *The Education of Henry Adams* suggest sometimes that the smooth-flowing garment of style has been arranged with a view to draping rather vague intellectual contours. We find Mr. Beer writing: "This jape [a bon mot of Mark Twain's at the expense of Henry James] was in London six months later, but Crane, a few blocks to the north of its making, was far from well," or, "He had read with appreciation Knut Hamsun's *Hunger* when Karl Harriman brought the book to Brede in summer, but appetite ceased and Mrs. Crane had agitated conferences with friends as to Switzerland and the Black Forest." Was there really any point to be made by combining in the same sentence Hamsun's *Hunger* and Crane's illness?

But Mr. Beer, in spite of this and some other defects of style, has written an incredibly entertaining book about one of the most unpromising of periods. The eighties and nineties in America appear—at least to one who was born on the hither edge of them—perhaps the most provincial and uninspired moment in the history of American society. It sometimes seems to me that it is even possible to detect a distinct intellectual decline between Americans educated in the seventies and Americans educated in the eighties. In the seventies, men were still living on the culture and believing in the social ideal which had survived from the founding of the Republic. The doctors, the professors, the lawyers and the churchmen who were graduated from college in the seventies had at once a certain allaround humanism and a serious and dignified attitude toward life; they were carrying on an integrity of moral ideal. But by the eighties Business was flooding in and ideals were in confusion: the old-fashioned lawyer was on his way to becoming a corporation lawyer whose principal function was to keep Business from going to jail; the doctor was on his way to becoming a modern "specialist" and sending Business to a sanitarium; and the church and the university were beginning to be abandoned by first-rate men altogether. In the meantime, the men of the eighties, with whatever sound culture and honest aims, were finding themselves launched in a world where there was a great deal of money to be made and most people were trying to make money. Humanism went by the board; moral scruples were put to rout; and seriousness about man and his problems was abrogated entirely in favor of the seriousness of Business about things that were not serious. The State became identified with Business; ideas were shot on sight. The people who acquired money had a pretty good time, one supposes; at least they spent a great deal of money. But life, in the long run, by the turn of the century, seemed to many unsatisfactory. What was a man to do who had been educated for the old America and who once might have served the Republic or followed an interesting profession in a society which offered stability and leisure? Become the slave of Business at one extreme or drink himself to death at the other, but in any case absorb, perhaps unconsciously, enough of the commercial ideal to neutralize any others with which he might have started out. For one of the most depressing features of the American world of this period was that it hardly knew what was the matter with it. It was only at a later date that people like Edith Wharton and Van Wyck Brooks began to diagnose and describe.

Now, Mr. Thomas Beer's success with this unselfconscious epoch has been attained in this book not merely through his minute knowledge of it and his exquisite appreciation of its humors, but from the fact that he has found in the sprawling and unorganized, the prosaic and Philistine America of the end of the nineteenth century a point of intellectual dignity from which it is possible to focus it. Stephen Crane was a vortex of intensity in a generally stagnant sea. He was an artist not as the age understood that word but as the world at large understands it. I do not say that he was a great artist or that he was even of the first rank, but what he had was the real thing and he adulterated it with nothing else.* Stephen Crane had arrived in prose, apparently without having read Maupassant or knowing anything of the school of Flaubert, at precisely their objective method and their ironic point of view, and in poetry, at a terse vers libre which at its best has scarcely been surpassed by any of the more profuse vers librists who have since received more liberal publicity; and he managed to practice his art without any journalistic infection. Mr. Beer says, in fact, that Crane, after years of newspaper training, was never able to write copy successfully: he could no more suspend his artistic sincerity to turn out a half-column on a fire than he was able, in *Active Service*, to concoct a popular novel. And, as a result of this undeviating devotion to a purpose which was, in that period, as little comprehensible to Richard Watson Gilder as it would have been to Mrs. Astor, he seems to have been regarded with almost universal suspicion. Joseph Conrad, who knew him well and who contributes an introduction to Mr. Beer's study, and Mr. Beer, who has been at pains to investigate, both bear witness that Crane could never really have been described as dissipated; and his writing is certainly the

---

*I should certainly say today that Stephen Crane was an artist of the first rank, but I have left this opinion of the twenties as typical of our contemptuous attitude toward the nineties and our diffidence in making claims for the American writers of the past. It will be noted that, when I mention Crane later in *The All-Star Literary Vaudeville*, my opinion of him has already gone up; and still later, in *The Critic Who Does Not Exist*, I give him a place among American classics.

product of a mind of unblunted edge. Yet Stephen Crane, in the United States, at the time of his great reputation, was accused of every vice and crime from drug-taking and dying in delirium tremens to seducing country girls and attempting to burn James Gordon Bennett's yacht. As he remarked, in 1896: "When people see a banker taking a glass of beer in a café, they say, 'There is Smith.' When they behold a writer taking a glass of beer, they say, 'Send for the police!'"

The effect of Mr. Beer's study is, however, as I have suggested, to bring out in these barren decades in which Stephen Crane lived a certain importance and interest which they owe to Stephen Crane's having lived in them. The happenings and habits of the era—the Bowery, the Cuban War, Clyde Fitch and Lillian Russell, the debaucheries of the Haymarket and the racing days on the Jersey coast—though they may have for us a charm of memory, do not usually wear for us the aspect of having been in themselves enchanting; but they take on a certain literary glamor when we watch them through Stephen Crane's eyes. What is exciting is to see this life experienced and criticized by a man of first-rate intelligence who was also living in the thick of it—to see its literature tried by the touchstone of a practicing artist who could feel the hollowness of Stevenson and the value of Henry James, who realized that *Huckleberry Finn* was spoiled as a perfect novel by its final pages of farce and—as I learn from another source than the biography of Mr. Beer—sometimes amused himself by trying to cut down specimens of contemporary American poetry to the minimum of idea or emotion that, on scrutiny, he found them to contain. What is touching, and perhaps most startling of all, to an American young enough to remember the banter and slang of the nineties as the language of a lost world, of an innocently rakish youth that had nothing to do with art or ideas, is to hear that language mordantly talked by an intensely serious man: "I will bet my marbles and my best top that Walter Besant is forgotten in twenty years"; "Mr. Yeats is the only man I have met who talks of Wilde with any sense. The others talk like a lot of little girls at a Sunday School party when a kid says a wicked word in a corner." Other personal qualities come through in a letter to a runaway boy whom he had found without money in San Antonio: "Dear Deadeye Dick: Thanks for sending back my money so fast. The hotel trun me out, as my friends of the Bowery say. . . . Now, old man, take some advice from a tough jay from back East. You say your family is all right and nobody bothers you. Well, it struck me that you were too young a kid and too handsome to be free and easy around where a lot of bad boys and girls will take your pennies. So better stay home and grow a mustache before you rush out into the red universe any more."

In any case, Mr. Beer has put Stephen Crane squarely back in his place on the literary map. He was partially excluded by his own time and has remained something of an outlaw even in ours. His biographer has shown him here as one of the most intellectually respectable Americans of the latter part of the century; and his works, if they are republished now, as there is a rumor they are to be, will have a lesson of artistic discipline to teach an age of easy writing.

January 2, 1924

Emergence of Ernest Hemingway

O N October 21, 1923, the following note appeared in Burton Rascoe's *A Bookman's Daybook*, a feature of the Sunday edition of the New York *Tribune*, of which Rascoe was at that time literary editor:

> Called upon Mary and Edmund Wilson late in the afternoon, and Wilson called my attention to some amusing stuff by Ernest Hemingway in the new issue of the *Little Review*.* [Lewis] Galantière sent me a copy of Hemingway's *Three Stories and Ten Poems*, which was published in Paris, and said that I would find it interesting, but I have not yet got around to reading it. Wilson was ill with a cold and complained that the difficulty with New York is that it is hard to keep feeling well here, that it ties one up nervously and residents of Manhattan are always having colds.

I presently had the following letter from Hemingway, who was then working on a newspaper in Canada:

November 11, 1923

Dear Mr. Wilson:

In Burton Rascoe's Social and Literary Notes I saw you had drawn his attention to some writing of mine in the *Little Review*.

I am sending you *Three Stories and Ten Poems*. As far as I know it has not yet been reviewed in the States. Gertrude Stein writes me she has done a review but I don't know whether she has gotten it published yet.

You don't know anything in Canada.

I would like to send out some for review but do not know whether to put a dedication, as compulsory in France, or what. Being an unknown name and the books unimposing they would probably be received as by Mr. Rascoe who has not yet had time, after three months, to read the copy Galantière sent him. (He could read it all in an hour and a half.)

The Contact Publishing Co. is McAlmon. It has published Wm. Carlos Williams, Mina Loy, Marsden Hartley and McAlmon.

I hope you like the book. If you are interested could you send me

---

*These contributions were *In Our Time*, comprising six of the little vignettes that afterward appeared in the two books of that title, and a satirical prose poem called *They Made Peace—What Is Peace?*

the names of four or five people to send it to to get it reviewed? It would be terribly good of you. This address will be good until January when we go back to Paris.

Thanking you very much whether you have the time to do it or not.

Yours sincerely,
Ernest Hemingway

1599 Bathurst Street
Toronto, Canada

I acknowledged the book when I got it, mentioning that I might do a note on it in the *Dial*, and had from him the following reply:

November 25
1599 Bathurst Street
Toronto

Dear Mr. Wilson:

Thank you ever so much for the letter. It was awfully good of you.

The book is a silly size. McAlmon wanted to get out a series of small books with Mina Loy, W. C. Williams, etc. and wanted me in it. I gave him the stories and poems. I am glad to have it out and once it is published it is back of you.

I am very glad you liked some of it. As far as I can think at the minute yours is the only critical opinion in the States I have any respect for. Mary Colum is sometimes sound. Rascoe was intelligent about Eliot. There are probably good ones that I don't know.

No I don't think *My Old Man* derives from Anderson. It is about a boy and his father and race-horses. Sherwood has written about boys and horses. But very differently. It derives from boys and horses. Anderson derives from boys and horses. I don't think they're anything alike. I know I wasn't inspired by him.

I know him pretty well but have not seen him for several years. His work seems to have gone to hell, perhaps from people in New York telling him too much how good he was. Functions of criticism. I am very fond of him. He has written good stories.

Would it perhaps be better to postpone the "Briefer Mentions" in the *Dial* until *In Our Time* comes out sometime next month and I will send it to you. You can get from it what I am trying to get at and the two of them together could make one review.

I am awfully glad you liked the *In Our Time* stuff in the *Little Review* and it is where I think I have gotten hold of it.

There is no use trying to explain it without the book.

It is very sporting of you to offer to help me get a book before the publishers. I don't know any of them.

Edward O'Brien wrote me the other day asking formal permission to reprint *My Old Man* in his *Best Short Stories of 1923* and asking if he could dedicate the book me. As the book isn't out that is confidential. He prints bum ones and good ones. He asked me if I had enough stories for a Boni and Liveright book. I don't know whether that means he could get them to publish it. I will write and ask you about it when the time comes if you don't mind.

E. E. Cummings' *Enormous Room* was the best book published last year that I read. Somebody told me it was a flop. Then look at *One of Ours*. Prize, big sale, people taking it seriously. You were in the war weren't you? Wasn't that last scene in the lines wonderful? Do you know where it came from? The battle scene in *Birth of a Nation*. I identified episode after episode, Catherized. Poor woman she had to get her war experience somewhere.

The thing in the *L.R.* was a joke.* I wrote it in the wagon-restaurant going back to Lausanne, had been at a very fine lunch at Gertrude Stein's and talked there all afternoon and read a lot of her new stuff and then drank a big bottle of Beaune myself in the dining car. Facing opening the wire again in the morning I tried to analyse the conference.

Her method is invaluable for analysing anything or making notes on a person or a place. She has a wonderful head. I would like to write a review of an old book of hers sometime. She is where Mencken and Mary Colum fall down and skin their noses.

Please excuse this very long letter and thanks again ever so much for your letter and the good advice. I would like to see you very much when we go through N.Y.

> Very sincerely,
> Ernest Hemingway.

He looked me up on his next visit to New York and sent me the first *In Our Time* (lower-cased *in our time*), which was published in the spring of 1924 in an edition of a hundred and seventy copies by the Three Mountains Press in Paris. This contained only eleven of the fifteen stories that appeared in the Boni and Liveright edition of 1925.

I wrote a review of *in our time* and *Three Stories and Ten Poems*, which appeared in the *Dial* of October, 1924. Though it is not of much interest in itself, I am proud of it because it is,

---

* *They Made Peace—What Is Peace?*

so far as I know, the first criticism of Hemingway that appeared in print. (It is not, however, listed by Louis Henry Cohn in his *Bibliography of the Works of Ernest Hemingway*. The first article noted by him is of November, 1925: a review by Burton Rascoe of the expanded *In Our Time*.)

Mr. Hemingway's Dry-Points

Three Stories and Ten Poems. By Ernest Hemingway. 12mo. 58 pages. Contact Publishing Company. Paris. $1.50.

In Our Time. By Ernest Hemingway. 12mo. 30 pages. The Three Mountains Press. Paris. $2.

Mr. Hemingway's poems are not particularly important, but his prose is of the first distinction. He must be counted as the only American writer but one—Mr. Sherwood Anderson— who has felt the genius of Gertrude Stein's *Three Lives* and has evidently been influenced by it. Indeed, Miss Stein, Mr. Anderson and Mr. Hemingway may now be said to form a school by themselves. The characteristic of this school is a naïveté of language, often passing into the colloquialism of the character dealt with, which serves actually to convey profound emotions and complex states of mind. It is a distinctively American development in prose—as opposed to more or less successful American achievements in the traditional style of English prose —which has artistically justified itself at its best as a limpid shaft into deep waters.

Not, however, that Mr. Hemingway is imitative. On the contrary, he is rather strikingly original, and in the dry compressed little vignettes of *In Our Time*, has almost invented a form of his own:

"They shot the six cabinet ministers at half-past six in the morning against the wall of a hospital. There were pools of water in the courtyard. There were dead leaves on the paving of the courtyard. It rained hard. All the shutters of the hospital were nailed shut. One of the ministers was sick with typhoid. Two soldiers carried him downstairs and out into the rain. They tried to hold him up against the wall but he sat down in a puddle of water. The other five stood very quietly against the wall. Finally the officer told the soldiers it was no good trying to make him stand up. When they fired the first volley he was sitting down in the water with his head on his knees."

Mr. Hemingway is remarkably successful in suggesting

moral values by a series of simple statements of this sort. His more important book is called *In Our Time*, and, behind its cool objective manner, it constitutes a harrowing record of the barbarities of the period in which we live: you have not only political executions, but hangings of criminals, bull-fights, assassinations by the police and the cruelties and horrors of the war. Mr. Hemingway is unperturbed as he tells us about these things: he is not a propagandist even for humanity. His bull-fight sketches have the dry sharpness and elegance of the bull-fight lithographs of Goya. And, like Goya, he is concerned first of all with making a fine picture. Too proud an artist to simplify in the interests of conventional pretenses, he is showing you what life is like. And I am inclined to think that his little book has more artistic dignity than anything else about the period of the war that has as yet been written by an American.

Not perhaps the most vivid book, but the soundest. Mr. Hemingway, who can make you feel the poignancy of the Italian soldier deciding in his death agony that he will "make a separate peace," has no anti-militarist parti pris which will lead him to suppress from his record the exhilaration of the men who had "jammed an absolutely perfect barricade across the bridge" and who were "frightfully put out when we heard the flank had gone, and we had to fall back." It is only in the paleness, the thinness of some of his effects that Mr. Hemingway sometimes fails. I am thinking especially of the story called *Up in Michigan*, which should have been a masterpiece, but has the curious defect of dealing with rude and primitive people yet leaving them rather shadowy.

In Our Time has a pretty and very amusing cover designed from scrambled newspaper clippings. The only objection I have to its appearance is that the titles are printed throughout without capitals—thus: "in our time by ernest hemingway—paris." This device, which had a certain effectiveness when the modernists used it first to call attention to the newness of what they were offering, is now becoming a bore. The American advertisers have taken it over as one of their stock tricks. And it is so unsightly in itself that one does not like to see it become—as in the case of Mr. Hemingway's book and Mr. Hueffer's*

---

*Ford Madox Ford, who changed his family name from Hueffer.

trans-atlantic review—a kind of badge for all that is freshest and most interesting in contemporary writing.

October, 1924

In connection with this review, Hemingway wrote me the following letter:

113 Rue Notre Dame des Champs
Paris VII
October 18, 1924

Dear Wilson:

Thank you so much for writing the review in the October *Dial*. I liked it very much. You are very right about the lack of capital letters —which seemed very silly and affected to me—but Bird had put them in and as he was printing the *In Our Time* himself and that was all the fun he was getting out of it I thought he could go ahead and be a damn fool in his own way if it pleased him. So long as he did not fool with the text.

I'm awfully glad you liked it.

How are you anyway? and did you ever get Chaplin for your ballet?

We have lived very quietly, working hard, except for a trip to Spain, Pamplona, where we had a fine time and I learned a lot about bull fighting, the inside the ring scene. We had a lot of minor adventures.

I've worked like hell most of the time and think the stuff gets better. Finished the book of 14 stories with a chapter on *In Our Time* between each story—that is the way they were meant to go—to give the picture of the whole between examining it in detail. Like looking with your eyes at something, say a passing coast line, and then looking at it with 15X binoculars. Or rather, maybe, looking at it and then going in and living in it—and then coming out and looking at it again.

I sent the book to Don Stewart* at the Yale Club about three weeks ago. When he was here he offered to try and sell it for me. I think you would like it, it has a pretty good unity. In some of the stories since the *In Our Time* I've gotten across both the people and the scene. It makes you feel good when you can do it. It feels now as though I had gotten on top of it.

Will you get over here this winter do you think? We will probably be in Paris all winter. Not enough money to get out. The baby is very well and husky. Hadley is working on the piano.

*Donald Ogden Stewart.

She sends her best regards to you and Mrs. Wilson.

Hope everything is going well with you and that you have a good winter. I would like to hear from you and I did appreciate the review. It was cool and clear minded and decent and impersonal and sympathetic. Christ how I hate this terrible personal stuff. Do you remember my writing from Toronto wanting some reviews and publicity? and then got some and it turned me sick.

I think there's nothing more discouraging than unintelligent appreciation. Not really discouraging; but just driving something back inside of you. Some bright guy said *In Our Time* was a series of thumbnail sketches showing a great deal of talent but obviously under the influence of Ring Lardner. Yeah! That kind of stuff is fine. It doesn't bother. But these wordy, sentimental bastards. You are the only man writing criticism who or whom I can read when the book being criticized is one I've read or know something about. I can read almost anybody when they write on things I don't know about. Intelligence is so damn rare and the people who have it often have such a bad time with it that they get bitter or propagandistic and then it's not much use.

With best wishes to you and to your wife,

> Very sincerely,
> Ernest Hemingway

Is this *What Price Glory?* really a good play. I don't mean a good *play*—it sounds fine over here.

I have learned, since the above was written, that my review of *In Our Time* was not the first. An earlier one, signed M. R., had appeared in Paris in the April, 1924, issue of *the transatlantic review*. 1953.

Imaginary Dialogues

I. The Poet's Return

Mr. Paul Rosenfeld and Mr. Matthew Josephson

MR. ROSENFELD. I was very much interested, Mr. Joseph-son, to read in a recent number of *Broom* your review of Elinor Wylie's poetry. I had never precisely understood your position before, but you have now made it quite clear.

MR. JOSEPHSON. It is a point of view of which a plain state-ment has, I think, been long overdue in America; it is the only point of view, I am sure, which will make it possible for Amer-icans to realize themselves creatively. I was really very much surprised on my return from a prolonged absence abroad to find that none of the professional literary people had had the boldness or the intelligence to formulate it—though the ne-cessity for it is perfectly obvious. Gilbert Seldes, in his articles on the movies, the jazz-band and the comic strip, has come nearer to it than anyone else; but even he is still somewhat intimidated by the pretentions of the officially "artistic": he in-sists upon trying to believe in Bugs Baer and Sherwood Ander-son both at the same time; he will not admit that Irving Berlin has rendered Schoenberg uninteresting and unnecessary.

MR. ROSENFELD. I see; but it seems to me that Seldes's po-sition is easier to defend than yours. For whereas Seldes merely wants to call attention to the neglected virtues of the vulgar, you are attempting also to discredit things that are fine. You say, for example, in your review of Mrs. Wylie, "The large imaginative, daring, formidable people in America are mostly to be found on the vaudeville stage, in the movies, the adver-tising business, prize-fighting, railroads, Wall Street. One is led to this conclusion by observing to what an alarming extent those who produce poetry lack such virtues. Art is purveyed for small persecuted colonies, dispersed throughout this conti-nent, and hidden away among its stone walls and steel founda-tions. They simply do not join in the great funny time that is being had by all. . . . Thus, while the age itself is given to

upheaval, our poets, insensibly enough, strike perfectly traditional poses and have nothing to say which would place them
in this time rather than in Heine's or Landor's time." Now, in
the first place, I should deny that Mrs. Wylie fails to express
any contemporary reality. She may not, to be sure, give voice
to the emotions of a vaudeville actor, a pugilist or an advertising man; but she does convey something that lies concealed
below the lives of many educated Americans—and that is not
merely an imitation of the emotions of Heine or Landor, but a
feeling which, when it finds vent at all, acquires a peculiar intensity and brilliance from the hardness of the unsympathetic
surface that society opposes to it and the severity of the Puritan tradition that has hitherto held it in check. Elinor Wylie is
the Edith Wharton of our poets. Her pride, her submerged
passion and her museum show-case culture are all characteristically American; her images of glass and bronze and gold and
graved flint and crystal lenses have the hardness and exactitude
and glitter of the world in which she has lived; they could have
been cast in no other society than that of the American East.
When I read Mrs. Wylie, I think of high rooms in dustless
expensive houses, of old mirrors and silverware kept up to
looking gleamingly new, of gilt backs of Congreve and Keats
behind the panes of mahogany book-cases. Or rather she is the
symbol of the soul which has learned to subject itself to the
discipline of these things and which finds itself at last in revolt
against them, which feels that stirring within her that would
sever its bonds and be off, that would make her to arise and
follow after the milk-white hounds of the moon. She is the
pang of the heart that is transfixed by the splinter-sharp ice of
lack, the woman-cry in its sheerest bell-timbres—snow-silvers,
white-golds, copper-blues—

MR. JOSEPHSON. Go on; that is very amusing; but I hope
you don't consider it criticism.

MR. ROSENFELD. What do you mean? I thought that Elinor
Wylie did express something real and I was trying to explain
what it was.

MR. JOSEPHSON. That is precisely the kind of thing that has
compelled my colleagues and me to write about you so much
and so bitterly. The day for irresponsible rhapsody as a substitute for exact analysis has now long passed. What you publish

as critical essays are, of course, merely opium visions: they have no real relation to their subjects. They are simply romantic fantasies exfloreating a century too late. Like all romantics, you are under the delusion that in order to produce literature, the only thing necessary is to let one's feelings go. Now, if you measured your feelings against the fact, you would realize that your outburst just now has nothing to do with Elinor Wylie; it probably expresses some emotion of your own. And if you measured Elinor Wylie against the fact, you would see that she is not important. Neither you nor Elinor Wylie exists in the face of the great American Fact!

MR. ROSENFELD. Well, I may be more or less of a romanticist but I understand the value of tradition; and, to return to your review of *Black Armour*, I do not see why Elinor Wylie should not build on Landor and Heine. Every artist invents his own language, and the language of art changes with the changes of civilization. First Beethoven is unintelligible; then Wagner; then Stravinsky; but in the end the world has always to recognize that the language of art is its own. And in the meantime each one of these men has built on his predecessors and without him could not have existed. Did not Virgil derive from Homer, and Dante derive from Virgil? Yet all three are completely different: they have written the poems of three different worlds. It is not merely a question of taking over a technique or of reflecting a point of view but of living up to a standard of excellence. Let me remind you how much Joyce's *Ulysses* is obviously indebted to Homer, and how devotedly T. S. Eliot has gone to school to the Elizabethans.

MR. JOSEPHSON. Precisely: and on that account neither one of them is of very much interest to us. You are like all Americans who think themselves modern; you feel the thrill of doing something sensational when you come out for *The Waste Land* or *Ulysses*. But the one is only the last excretion of naturalism as the other is the last gasp of romantic poetry. Joyce tries to brace himself to his dreary task of reporting bar-room conversations by playing a game with the structure of Homer, just as Eliot, shrinking from a world which he cannot embrace and enjoy, flees for refuge to Tourneur and Webster; there is scarcely an original word in *The Waste Land*—there is scarcely a line which is not either a quotation or an echo of someone else.

And yet you American critics have been making an extravagant fuss about it and calling it an authentic interpretation of the world in which you live, and you have thus joined the party of defeat. It is the same with Arnold Schoenberg, whom you praise and a passage from whose *Pierrot Lunaire* you have compared to *Tristan und Isolde*: you are right about that, of course; but Schoenberg is the death of Wagner, the dissolution of a romantic corpse; he is the creaking of the rusty hinges in the ruined palace of Klingsor. Like Eliot, he has nothing to offer but the whine of a dry complaint. We who have been lately in Germany and France and who have had the advantage of acquaintance with some of the more tonic figures of the younger generation, such as Tzara and the other dadaists, can see clearly that Eliot and Schoenberg and Joyce are as dead for the purposes of the present as Shakespeare, Flaubert and Wagner. The man who would master the gigantic, the gorgeous, the fantastic world of the twentieth century must be able to identify himself with it, not cry out against it as they do, not for ever be wailing over something that is gone and that nothing now can ever bring back. That is why I have said in the review to which you take such exception that the time "demands hardier poets, such as can straddle the language of our people, or know the genius of this people as well as a vaudeville comedian or an advertising copy-writer." You do not understand my position at all if you suppose that you can prove your case by the example of Eliot or Joyce. You have, besides, with your romantic inexactitude, misstated my position completely: you assume that Elinor Wylie, in imitating her predecessors, has created a language of her own, but I do not admit your contention that she has anything new to express. What I wrote was that "our poets have nothing to say which would place them in this time rather than in Heine's or Landor's." Elinor Wylie translates Greek epigrams just exactly as Landor did; she writes a lyric on a Nocturne of Chopin. Of what use is that to anybody? The Greeks and Landor and Chopin were all very well in their time, but they do not represent *our* reality.

MR. ROSENFELD. The life of feeling is always real. I grant you that its language changes—but man himself does not change so quickly in a mere two thousand years. He suffers the same chagrins; he is roused by the same passions. So long as he is capable of love and pain, he will continue to read Sappho and Catullus, Heine, Musset and Keats; his emotions will find lyric expression very much as theirs have done. The language of the heart which has already survived from the Greek and Roman worlds to Heine's has not become obsolete in the space of a hundred years!

MR. JOSEPHSON. Your case is even worse than I thought: you have not only failed to adjust yourself to the great revolution that has taken place; you apparently do not even realize that there is any adjustment to be made. You still entertain the delusion that you are living in the early nineteenth century. I am sure that you read Goethe in the subway and sing Schumann and Schubert in the shower. Yet the subway and the shower themselves are more magnificent poems than anything by Schubert or Goethe. Isn't it marvellous, an obus of steel, loaded with human beings and thundering under the earth through a tunnel a hundred miles long! A marble cell with a gleaming canopy that releases at a touch of the hand a cascade of crystal needles! What does the shower or the subway train have to do with the language of the heart? What did the people who created them care about it? What have Sappho and Catullus and Heine and Schubert and Elinor Wylie to say to the people whose privilege it is to revel in this monstrous poetry, whose lives are all compounded of it, who are themselves the improvisatori of a prodigious mechanical fantasy? Our American engineers, our industrialism, our business and finance themselves, have created this astounding world. To interpret it, you must take it on its own terms. The great processes of manufacture and distribution and organization go on with stupendous and resistless gestures; they are for America today what the conquests and the explorations were for the Renaissance. And today it is the vaudeville comedian or the artist of the comic-strip who truly conveys the excitement of America's hilarious brutality, the gusto of its gargantuan appetite. It is the writer of advertising copy who forges its literature. "Meaty Marrowy Oxtail Joints": there is the beauty of our real world, the satisfaction of producing a savory soup and the uninhibited joy of consuming it! "The velvety clutch responds to the merest pressure . . . the pliant but positive

gears engage silently at a touch of the convenient control":
there is a cadence from motoring, from the delicacy of a sensuous machinery. People who are employed in washing themselves in silver-fitted snow-dazzling bathrooms, with fragrant
non-sinkable soap, in eating such an abundance of different
kinds of food as no nation in the world has ever known, in
transporting themselves through the air, under the earth or
across its surface at a speed hitherto unimagined, and in selling
all these marvels to other people who are eager and delighted
to buy, such a race has ceased to feel the need for what you call
the "language of the heart." They have learned to do without
"the heart"; their life is all in appetite and action. You will
never be able to interest them in the old kind of literature
again. Or music. Or plastic art. What does "literature" amount
to now? The last complaints of the dying poets! What is music?
You admire Varèse; but what is Varèse at his boldest but the
echo of the music of the streets?—and the streets do it better
than he. The hawking taxis, the screaming sirens, the joyous
yell of the mechanical life, all this we hear every day; it is the
rhythm to which we dance, to which the power-drunken city
exults. It is an impertinence for a modern composer to think
himself a clever fellow for capturing a few of these noises, so
glorious and wild in their native state, and clipping them and
toning them down to be handled by the instruments of an orchestra and performed at a single little concert to which a few
hundred people will listen. And what is painting? What is
sculpture? A bad monument to celebrate a battle, a landscape
not much larger than a playing-card in a gallery like a mau-
soleum, which only a handful of people in New York will ever
come in to see and which the millions in the rest of the country will not even hear about! How can you set up these trivialities as rivals to the electric sign, which thousands of people see
every day—a triumph of ingenuity, of color, of imagination!—
which slings its great gold-green-red symbol across the face of
the heavens themselves and tells the world that it has made a
new Chewing Gum or a Pickle or a Cigarette that will give you
a new sensation! I tell you that culture as you understand it is
no longer of any value; the human race no longer believes in it.
That is why I am giving my support to the campaign for
Henry Ford for President! Henry Ford never listens to music

nor looks at pictures nor reads poetry; it is, in fact, even a matter of doubt whether he is able to read at all. He has said openly that he would not give ten cents for all the art in the world. But he Gets Things Done; he Gives Us a Laugh; he takes the Whole World for a Ride! He sends tractors to the lumber camps and cuts in half their titanic labor; he charters a ship and sets out for Europe to put an end to the war; he succeeds in making Congress turn over to him the federal water plant at Muscle Shoals on a lease of a hundred years. And these things Henry Ford can do just because he ignores the past, just because the restraints and the pieties that your schooling imposes on you do not exist for him. It is only such a figure as Ford that America really respects and who will eventually be able to rule it. As I have written, "There shall be one great Powerhouse for the entire land, and ultimately a greater one for the whole world. . . . Let Ford be President. Let him assemble us all into his machine. Let us be *properly* assembled. Let us all function unanimously. Let the wheels turn more swiftly."

MR. ROSENFELD. I am afraid that you have come back to America—after living so long abroad—with rather a mistaken idea of what the life here is like. You have been influenced by the notions of America of such people as Léger and Cocteau—

MR. JOSEPHSON. You must not imagine that my point of view has anything in common with Jean Cocteau's! Cocteau is as old-fashioned now as Anatole France or Verlaine. He is merely a belated aesthetic who tries to be up-to-date—he would have been more at home in the eighties. Between Cocteau and myself there is scarcely communication. My affiliations have been with the dadaists, with Tzara, Breton, Soupault—

MR. ROSENFELD. —You have been influenced by the dadaists, then. In any case, my point is this. Your dadaists, like Cocteau, have made a sort of cult of America. The United States looks so exotic to people who have never been here. I have had the same illusion myself when I have been living a long time abroad. The truth is that the French have seen pictures of our skyscrapers and enormous bridges, they have been thrilled by the pace of our movies and excited by our Negro jazz, and, being nowadays the most cautious and balanced, the least precipitate people in the world, they are fascinated by the

idea of a country where such excesses are of common occurrence. They have been using America as a war-cry with which
to rally against the staleness and banality into which their classical tradition has fallen, never dreaming how much more banal five-eighths of America is than the dirtiest and poorest
French town. A European whom I know and who had been
much in Paris with the modern composers and writers, came
recently for the first time to America and was very much disappointed. "Is this New York?" he exclaimed when he landed.
"Why, it is just exactly like Europe!" He had expected to see
people riding automobiles up the sides of enormous buildings,
as they do in the comic films; impossible elevated railroads
running on top of one another in tiers; skyscrapers as high as
the Matterhorn, and Heaven knows what else. Now I cannot
help feeling a little that you have caught this point of view.
When you are back in American life again, I do not know if
you will be able to preserve it—I do not know if you will enjoy
"the great funny time that is being had by all." You seem to
think that the people who compose the ads necessarily believe
in the things they write, that their enthusiasm for their products is genuine. But actually, the chances are that the man who
writes the paeans to oxtail joints has never seen one in his life
and would not care to eat it if he did. The chances are that he
is sickened by advertising and everything that reminds him of
it. Sherwood Anderson until very lately was a writer of advertising copy; but do you think he found that inspiring? Do you
imagine he shared your view that selling manufactured goods
was the highest form of creative activity? On the contrary, he
devoted all his leisure to working at that kind of literature that
you say you regard as futile—to fixing, in his stories, those visions that reveal with a poet's art the limited, the stunted lives
of the people of the factories and the farms, the gentleness and
the fineness that lie quivering underneath the burden of the
cities and the barrenness of the fields, the soul of man so long
exiled from its heritage that it scarcely dares recognize itself
nor remember to what visitations it once had been opened
wide. No: surely, only one point of view is possible at the present time for the writer of good faith in America—or for the
artist of any kind—and that is *against* all the forces which you
are making an effort to flatter—against the America which

would starve us all and exhaust us and grind us under, so that the machine might "function unanimously" and "the wheels turn more swiftly." These artists like Sherwood Anderson, whom you describe as "small persecuted colonies," as if they were cowards or defective people unable to ride the whirlwind and direct the storm, are perhaps now our only real heroes because they have dared to oppose themselves to it and to blurt out one desperate word, in the teeth of routine and vulgarity, for the honor of the human spirit!

MR. JOSEPHSON. The Honor of the Human Spirit . . . the Principles of Justice and Humanity . . . Liberty, Fraternity, Equality . . . the Dawn of a New Day . . . Workers of the world, unite! you have nothing to lose but your chains! . . . E. E. Cummings could make an amusing poem by mixing them all up together and sticking in the Paris urinal and the venereal affiches. My dear fellow, you take it all too seriously. In Europe no one takes those things seriously. Those clichés, from the eighteenth century, old campaign cries and catchwords and shibboleths, are as stale and as lifeless now as old newspapers of the war. The world was hysterical then and still babbled a romantic liberalism; but, now that its fever has subsided, it has settled down to give itself up to the working out of economic forces, and it finds that that will do very well. They may prove to have a wisdom of their own. It can even enjoy its own absurdity and make a lark of its fantastic confusion. And that is where dada comes in. It was dada that awakened laughter when humanity had been worrying too long about the honor of the human spirit and all those other insipid abstractions. The younger and more alert minds of the countries involved in the war now feel free to be gay without shame. The time has now come to amuse ourselves. We have worked and suffered enough—and for what? For the most colossal farce of all time! For Mussolini, for the starvation of Russia, for a war between England and France. Not that I object to wars, which are among the livelier numbers in the universal vaudeville; nor that I disapprove of Mussolini, whom I admire for his buffoonery and his vigor. But they are certainly not what anybody wanted nor what anybody thought he was fighting for. The results of the war are nonsense, superb nonsense! from any point of view. Think of Wilson taking on the combined prestige of

Lincoln, Cromwell and Christ, assembling thousands of words on World Peace, day after day, night after night, marshalling them together, sending them forth, army upon army of words, besieging an imaginary citadel with celestial storm-clouds of words—then finally choking, collapsing deflated in the great content uncomprehending West and having the gross of green spectacles that he had brought back with care from Versailles thrown casually out behind the house by people who had not paid the slightest attention to a syllable he had been saying! What is the next turn? Landru? D'Annunzio? The Harding administration? Léon Daudet turning the suicide of his son into a gigantic piece of publicity? Morris Gest turning Reinhardt's *Miracle* into a Barnum and Bailey circus? The Oil Scandal? The *Dial* Award? Dada makes the most of them all and turns them all upside down. For dada is the spirit of play, of the fascinating idiocy of things. It shows the lack of connection between everything with a dazzling quickness of mind. And so it is the nonsense comedian like Ed Wynn or Joe Cook, the humorist like Lardner or Benchley, who comes nearest among Americans to the disintegrating laughter of dada and is truest to the spirit of the time. A lady in décolleté steps forward to sing an aria from some popular and saccharine opera, but before she has got further than the opening bars a screen is dropped down in front of her, and Joe Cook appears before it in a burlesque juggling act; then the screen is lifted again and the soprano, who has never stopped singing, complacently completes her aria. Or, in a farce of Ring Lardner's, three men are discovered fishing in boats; from time to time one of them rings a bell and a maid brings them trays of drinks, walking across the water. "Can you imitate birds?" asks one of them, at the end of a long silence. "No," the other replies, "but I can construct a shack suitable for occupancy by six persons." For after all, what is life as we know it but a series of delicious inconsequences? So why not come out frankly for the leaders with the greatest capacity for absurdity? They will provide the greatest amount of fun. That is why we say, "Vote for Henry Ford! the Master Dadaist of the twentieth century!"

MR. ROSENFELD. Yes, I see: that, I suppose, is the real difference between us. For me, it is a serious matter, but for you, it is only a game. I read your manifestos printed upside down, your assertions that "*Oui = Non*" and your plays in which the different acts have nothing to do with each other, and I see the point of their pointlessness; but I cannot quite laugh at the joke. You keep saying that this or that lacks reality or does not represent anything real, but for me the artistic life of Europe, the life of feeling which it makes articulate, is the only authentic reality. When I hear of young musicians killed in the war or starving to death in Russia, of distinguished conductors insulted and great operas banned from the stage, when I see the desolation of a people who, through devotion to such ideals as Henry Ford's, have at last been reduced to a condition in which they live without even such music as the old New England singing societies provided, relegating it to dreary old concert-halls in a few of the largest cities and to the luxury and the banality of the insufferable Metropolitan—I cannot help being saddened. Perhaps I do err through overseriousness; I dare say you are right about that. It may be true that I have been extravagant in expressing my indignation over the later works of Richard Strauss, because I felt that by the surrender to a cheap success he had betrayed the great tradition of German music; and that I ought not to have worried so much about the artistic failure of Mahler. And there are times when my conscience reproaches me for my treatment of poor old Saint-Saëns, whom I accused of selling his soul, when perhaps he had none to sell. One of you younger men could no doubt have done all this much better; you would have been able to snuff out Strauss or Saint-Saëns with a single bizarre sneer. But I shall always be convinced that the thing with which all these men were trying, with however imperfect success, to identify themselves is the only thing in the world from which one can derive any faith to lift one above the nonsense of events. I would save, not the warring states, not the bankers and the politicians, not even the peoples, with their wretched lives, if they had never made anything beautiful, but the fatherland of Goethe and Bach, of Shakespeare and Wagner and Musorgsky, of the imagination of Europe. It is to citizenship there that I have been bred, and I can understand no other allegiance.

MR. JOSEPHSON. That fatherland has been defeated: America is its defeat.

MR. ROSENFELD. It is a defeat I am ready to share.

MR. JOSEPHSON. What bravado of the romantic spirit that goes on striking noble poses even after it has been abolished! Gestures of that sort, however—though spirited and touching in themselves—can never nowadays seem anything but ridiculous. It is all very well to say that I have lived too long abroad and that I don't understand America; but there is one thing I can tell you with assurance I appreciate as the Americans appreciate it that you seem to have lived here all your life without ever being aware of at all. You think you are up to the minute in following American music, that you are generously promoting its advance, when you contribute an article to the *Dial* on Leo Ornstein or Roger Sessions. But where are your fanfares for Lopez and Whiteman? for the rich rhythms of the Negro revues? You say that we exist without music at precisely the time when our jazz—a gorgeous and disturbing carnival, one of the most vital expressions of our time—has been making the whole world delirious! And you have not yet, so far as I know, written a word about it. You have no ear for the popular voices. You always refer to vulgarity with loathing. Life for you must be thinned and refined and laid away in an elegant score before you can consent to touch it. You talk about the desolation of a people who have no use for music. But I, all new to the States as I am, see people dancing everywhere to their music, and I throb to the prodigious orgy. There is no desolation in that music—only the drunkenness, the dizziness of life —vulgar life, unrestrained, taut-nerved, hurtling out with its howling trombones in its great gaudy circus parade toward the unknown mechanical future. I have heard that music in the streets, intrepid, cacophonic, triumphant, and I have thrown up my hat for joy! But you have preferred to remain indoors while the parade went by outside. You stagnate in the quietude of the library where Schoenberg and Bach are alike entombed.

MR. ROSENFELD. On the contrary, I have listened to that music, too; and I confess that it has given me pain. I have even had moments of depression when I have fancied that what you say might be true. But make no mistake, my friend: if art is to be defeated, you will be among the victims. You are a poet, like Elinor Wylie; you are a critic, like myself. You can never march with that procession; they have no place for critics or poets. You can only get yourself cut to pieces by prostrating yourself before Juggernaut, in amazement and awe at his might. If you choose to pretend to enjoy it, that is your own affair.

April 9, 1924

II. The Delegate from Great Neck

Mr. F. Scott Fitzgerald and Mr. Van Wyck Brooks

MR. FITZGERALD. How do you do, Mr. Brooks. I'm afraid it's an awful nuisance for you to see me.

MR. BROOKS. Not at all. I'm very glad to. I'm only sorry to have had to put it off. But I've been so frightfully busy with my book that I haven't been able to do anything else.

MR. FITZGERALD. What's that—the James? I suppose you're hurrying to have it out in time to get the benefit of the publicity of the *Dial* award.

MR. BROOKS. Oh, no: it may take me a long time yet. But it's really rather a complicated job, and I don't like to drop a chapter in the middle or I lose all the threads. I've just come to a breathing-space.

MR. FITZGERALD. I should think you'd want to rush it right through and get it out now: it might double your sales.

MR. BROOKS. Oh, I couldn't possibly: I still have a good deal of work to do on it.

MR. FITZGERALD. I suppose you must read hundreds of books, don't you? How many books do you suppose you've read for the James? Two hundred? Five hundred?

MR. BROOKS. Oh, I don't know, I'm sure—everything I could get hold of that threw any light on him.

MR. FITZGERALD. I suppose you must quote on an average of four or five books on every page of your biographies, don't you?—and you probably refer to four or five others—and you've probably read half a dozen others that you didn't get anything out of. That makes fifteen or sixteen books to a page. Think of it! Reading fifteen or sixteen books just to write a single page! For a book of two hundred and fifty pages that would be—

MR. BROOKS. They're not all different books, you know. One uses the same books again and again.

MR. FITZGERALD. I know: but even so—it's perfectly amazing! I suppose you must know more about American literature than anybody else in the world, don't you?

MR. BROOKS. Oh, no! not by any means.

MR. FITZGERALD. Well, you're the greatest writer on the subject, anyway. That's the reason we've sent you this letter. As I told you, I've been delegated by the Younger Generation of American writers to congratulate you on getting the prize. They chose me as really the original member of the Younger Generation. Of course, there were a lot of people writing before *This Side of Paradise*—but the Younger Generation never really became self-conscious till then nor did the public at large become conscious of it. My slogan is that I am the man who made America Younger-Generation-conscious.

MR. BROOKS. I am certainly very much flattered—

MR. FITZGERALD. Besides, I'm about the only one who still looks really young. Most of the others are getting old and bald and discouraged. So they picked me out to represent them. They thought they ought to send somebody under thirty. —Well, could you stand to have me read you the letter they've written you or would you rather read it yourself?

MR. BROOKS. No: Certainly—read it. Do!

MR. FITZGERALD (*reading*). "Dear Van Wyck Brooks: We, the undersigned American writers, desire to offer you our heartiest congratulations on the occasion of your receiving the *Dial* award. If it is a question of critical service to American letters, we believe that there is no one living to whom it might more fitly be given. We soon found, when we first began writing, that your books were among the few that could help us to orient ourselves."—This first part's pretty heavy—but it gets a little more interesting later on.—I didn't draft the letter myself.

"You yourself had called a caustic roll of the critics whom we found in authority: Professor Irving Babbitt, who, refusing to see in romanticism one of the great creative movements of our time, could do nothing but scold at young writers who derived inspiration from it; Mr. Paul Elmer More, who, for all his sound standards of learning and literary competence—an anti-romantic like Professor Babbitt—had denounced as a form of debauchery what is actually a necessary condition of any artistic activity: the response to irrational impulse, and who thus, if he could have enforced his injunction, would have shut off the arts at their source; and Professor Stuart P. Sherman, who, borrowing the severity of Mr. More's manner without sharing his moral convictions, soon gave out such discordant sounds that he has now been forced to change his tune in the interests of a liberal sweetness. These critics had been preaching restraint to a people bound hand and foot. The country at large may have been suffering, as they thought, from a phase of anarchic expansion; but the failing of our literature was the timidity of the 'genteel tradition.' You were among the first to stand up for the romantic doctrine of 'experience for its own sake' and to insist on the importance of literature as a political and social influence. These ideas are perhaps open to criticism as a definitive aesthetic program; but they have served at least to awaken us to a sense of the drama in which we were playing. Our fathers had been further than our grandfathers from the civilization of Europe, and you goaded us back to our place in the world. You roused us with the cry that the hour had come 'to put away childish things and to walk the stage as poets do.'

"For all this we are forever in your debt, and we have wished to express our gratitude. Do not think us ungracious, we beg, if we accompany it with a plea. You were almost alone, when you first began to write, in taking American literature seriously —in appraising it as rigorously as possible, in comparison with other literatures, and in exhorting us to better our achievements. Yet, in your zeal to confess our deficiencies, you seem sometimes to create the impression that we have so far accomplished nothing. The older generation of critics had fallen down, primarily, as humanists—that is, they had been weak, not in intellect, but in aesthetic sensibility. They had not been able to feel the value of the widely varying forms of beauty which the men of other races and ages had distilled from their varied experience. Can it be that, with more generous intentions than theirs, you, too, with different preconceptions, are tending to fail in appreciation? After all, a good many of the Americans whose inadequacies you have analyzed so damagingly have had each his peculiar sense of life, his particular aspect of America, that he succeeded in getting on paper in some more or less vivid form. Emerson pursuing happy guides through the winey yet fumeless air in his commerce, so blithe and so homely, with the high places of light; Thoreau with his compact prose and his strong and dense colors, like the white of opaque clouds against blue Massachusetts sky, like the clustered green masses of trees around foursquare New England houses—both these men have conveyed to us the beauty of a particular kind of life. We feel in them a freshness and a freedom as of lawns that slope away to fenceless meadows, and we taste a frosty sea-captain sarcasm that seasons ideal and discipline. So Mark Twain has most poignant pages which give us something that we scarcely find in your *Ordeal of Mark Twain*; it is not only the sadness of the Mississippi in the days when life there was poor, but the romance and the humor of the pioneers straying wide across the empty continent; and we recognize in that sadness, that rough romance and that humor, at once genial and cruel, something more than the outlandish product of a particular time and place: we are moved by the troubling compound of life at all times in all places."—

MR. BROOKS. Will you forgive me if I interrupt you a moment? I don't want to find fault so much with your description of the New England writers—though I'm not sure that even there you haven't allowed distance to gild with an imaginary glamor a society that turns out, when we examine it, rather disappointingly barren—but in regard to the West, one is driven, when one comes to look into the subject, to the conclusion that its reputed romance and humor are almost entirely fictitious. The life along the Mississippi that Mark Twain knew in his boyhood was depressing in the extreme—a mere matter of lonely villages scattered along a muddy shore; and such excitement as he afterwards found in Nevada and California was mainly limited to drinking and gambling, with outbursts of violet profanity and occasional outbreaks of murder. The lies and the practical jokes that constituted frontier humor were merely, like those other manifestations, in the nature of hysterical relief from intolerable privations and repressions.

MR. FITZGERALD. Well, I come from the West—the *Middle* West—myself, and of course it's pretty bad in some ways. But don't you think there must have been still a certain romance about it at the time that Mark Twain went there? Don't you imagine even a pilot on the Mississippi, like Mark Twain was in his youth, must have felt a real thrill at knowing that he was personally playing a part in dominating the American continent? And there must have been a marvellous kind of comradeship in the ranches and the mining-camps—when they called each other Captain and Colonel. I always have a feeling of something heroic in the old songs and stories of the West. Think of the men from New York and New England who first dared to build their settlements in the gigantic amphitheaters of Utah, where the great black rock-ranges wall you round like the ramparts of the world! And the red sandstone hills of Nevada! Can you imagine what it must have been like to try to live the white man's life among those fantastic shapes, in the presence of those faceless prehistoric gods? And the first men who went to California, the prospectors of Mark Twain's sixties —they must have been drunk with the sunshine even more than the San Franciscans today—as well as with liquor, of course. I imagine them shaking off their hardships in a tremendous exhilaration when they first found themselves on that golden coast, where no worry from the old world ever comes, where Time itself seems to have been left behind like some tyrannous medieval institution, where man's life seems restored at last to the primeval leisure of Eden, where it is always summertime and always afternoon! Have you ever seen the mountains turning purple at sunset and the purple-fringed sea? Think of the men from the shacks and the diggings looking out on that new horizon, that new ocean that opened to the Orient, and hearing the drums of the surf that beat out the somnolent rhythms of the reefs and white sands of the South Seas! No older generation and no taboos! Big fortunes easy to make! Don't you think that, if ever Americans have really felt free in America, those early Californians must have?

MR. BROOKS. The condition of survival for the pioneer, even in California, was the suppression of all those instincts which might tend to conflict with his adjustment to his rude environment. You assume that a man of Mark Twain's generation would have been capable of the enjoyment of landscape. But we find no evidence that this was the case. The enjoyment of landscape results in an enrichment of the spiritual soil which bears its fruits in artistic creation, and the generation of Mark Twain—who can doubt it?—throttled its impulse to delight in natural beauty as an interference with its concentration upon its immediate material task. The psychology of the Puritan and the pioneer has always, it seems to me, made Americans rather blind to natural beauty. It may, in fact, be seriously questioned whether America has ever had a writer who can be said to have appreciated it properly. Think of the vital relation to natural objects that one finds in a Ruskin or a Jeffries, and then summon the most distinguished examples that our literature is able to show. How meager, how relatively pale, how lacking in genuine significance, the latter must inevitably appear!

MR. FITZGERALD. Well, I really oughtn't to try to talk about it because I don't know the subject the way you do.—I dare say that that part of the letter does lay it on pretty thick, but they wanted a purple passage to show you what they meant about enthusiasm.—Shall I go on reading?

MR. BROOKS. Do.

MR. FITZGERALD. "In the case of Henry James, again, we have been a little disappointed as we have read the published chapters of your forthcoming book about him. What we had hoped for was a definitive study of a novelist of genius who, fortunately for us, happened to be an American; but what we seem to be getting is the tragedy of an American who was rash enough to try to become a novelist. Yet, for all James's partial failures at filling in the outlines of his canvases, he was surely a first-rate artist, one of the few real masters of literature that the United States has produced; and his position as an American expatriate must have given him a peculiar advantage as an international critic of society that made up for whatever he had missed in intimate experience of American life. Must we believe that his social maladjustment as an American of his period had really for his work the disastrous results on which you insist in these chapters? Your first instalment is based on James's own autobiographical volumes; yet what interests us when we read these books is less the record of the provincial background and the writer's relation to it than the wonder and excitement of the artist enchanted by the spectacle of life—life even in the nineteenth century, even in the United States. Do not, we beg you—it is the burden of our plea—lose too much the sense of that wonder!"—

MR. BROOKS. I beg your pardon: but I really do think you

overestimate those autobiographical volumes! To me, there has always seemed to be something rather flaccid and empty about them. Think how much more colorful and spirited is Cellini's autobiography! How much more candid Rousseau's! How infinitely much more alive to the intellectual currents of their time the autobiographies of Renan and Mill! How much richer in psychological interest the memoirs of Marie Bashkirtseff! James wrote in his later years, you know, of "the starved romance of my life." And what I feel in his autobiography is the starvation rather than the romance. What American can fail to recognize the inexorable spiritual blight of which James himself spoke so often? Have we not all run up against it—an impotence and a blindness of the soul—like one of those great blank implacable walls that balk the view in American cities?

MR. FITZGERALD. The Puritan thing, you mean. I suppose you're probably right. I don't know anything about James myself. I've never read a word of him.—Just let me finish this letter; there's not very much more.

"We thus deprecate your gloomy verdicts on the value of the American classics; yet, feeling as we do the force of your criticism of our general culture, we should never have thought of complaining, if we had not lately come to fear that, intent upon the diagnosis of the diseases from which we have suffered, you have ended by becoming inhibited by an a priori theory which prevents you from hoping for improvement. You have discovered so many reasons why artistic achievement should be difficult that you seem to have become convinced that it must always remain impossible. When you write of contemporary literature, it is politely but without conviction: the modern writers who have been most successful in realizing the ideal you proposed have not received your accolade. And the effect, in the long run, has been more than a little discouraging. The other day, one of the youngest of our number, reading your essay *The Literary Life*, broke down into a wild fit of weeping and cursed God for having made him an American."—

MR. BROOKS. Dear me! How distressing! Really—

MR. FITZGERALD. Oh, that's just a silly joke! It didn't really happen, of course. I made it up myself and had them put it in. It's the only part I wrote.—I'm sorry: I suppose it was bad taste!

MR. BROOKS. No—no: not at all! I see! I beg your pardon.
Go ahead.

MR. FITZGERALD. "It is true that our newer critics tend to
err through too easy enthusiasm: it is usually enough for a
book to make pretensions to artistic seriousness for them to
hail it as a masterpiece. But their indiscriminate excitement
hardly compensates us for your indifference. It is certainly a
mistake to behave as if all our contemporary writers were
equally successful as artists, but we have the uncomfortable
feeling that you may think them all equally deplorable—merely
the most recent examples of the various depressing ways in
which writers may fail in America—not the beginnings of a literary renascence but fresh waxworks for a Chamber of Horrors;
and we wonder whether your disinclination to write anything
about your contemporaries may not be due merely to a delicacy that prevents you from cutting up people before they are
quite dead.

"Yet the younger generation of writers have been trying to
put your precepts into practice. They have not blenched before
the boldness of the European masters, as you accuse their
fathers of doing: they have tried to follow great examples.
They are interested, as you urged them to be, in the life of
their own country; and they have opened their souls to experience. For all their pessimistic pronouncements, they are confident, hopeful and gay. But when they have looked for your
snow-white banner flying beside their more motley ones, they
have found you still brooding the wrongs of an earlier generation, the defeats of an older army. They find you shivering
among the archives, and they shiver at the sight of your chill.
Meantime, there is life in America—artistic life even—to warm
us all. If we reproach you for failing to enjoy it, we are only
giving back to you a gospel we have learned from your own
books."

And then the names—I won't read the list—but practically
everybody, you see.

MR. BROOKS. It was really awfully kind of you to take the
trouble to write me like this. I'm very much interested in what
you say.—But I can't reconcile the picture that you draw of
yourselves at the end of your letter with the account that you
gave me yourself when you were talking about your friends

just now. You said, I think, that the younger generation was "getting old and bald and discouraged," and that is not a very cheerful picture. I appreciate your gallant effort to make the best of your situation; but I am afraid that your admirable spirit has already been partly broken by the indifference of a commercial society, that your gestures are lost in the void.

MR. FITZGERALD. Oh, I was just kidding about that. They're not really old and discouraged. I'm the only one that's discouraged, because I find that I can't live at Great Neck on anything under thirty-six thousand a year, and I have to write a lot of rotten stuff that bores me and makes me depressed.

MR. BROOKS. Couldn't you live more cheaply somewhere else?

MR. FITZGERALD. Nowhere that's any fun.

MR. BROOKS. I can't help thinking it a pity that a writer as gifted as you should be let in for such heavy expenses. As you say, it lays you open to exploitation by the popular magazines; and, though you charge me with indifference, I can tell you that that is something I regret very much. I should hate to see your whole generation fall a victim to that sort of thing. You are "the man," you told me, you know, at the beginning of our conversation, "who has made America Younger-Generation-conscious." Did you realize, when you used that expression, that you had dropped into the language of advertising? In describing your literary activities, you could not avoid the jargon of business; and it strikes me that the production of books by the younger generation has now become an industry much like another. The first crop of younger writers had scarcely scored their first successes when a new race of editors and publishers met them with open arms, eager to commercialize them—not by turning them into hacks of the old sort who would have had to do work of a kind altogether against their conscience but by stimulating them to write much and often rather than responsibly and well, by putting a premium on their second-best; so that, instead of improving on their first attempts, they have often, it seems to me, sunk below them. A half-educated public has created a demand for half-baked work. And I'm not at all sure that you younger writers are very much better off than your predecessors were: in the eighties and nineties, at least, there was a small cultivated public and not much question of pleasing the rest. I will say of the distinguished writers of the day before yesterday, whom you accuse me of undervaluing, that they usually followed their art with a very high sense of its dignity, so that even their journalism sounds like the work of serious men of letters—and this is true of Stephen Crane as much as of Henry James; whereas, in the case of you younger men, one sometimes cannot help feeling that your most ambitious productions are a species of journalism. Is it possible to resist the conclusion that you are succumbing to our capitalist civilization in a way you could never have foreseen?

MR. FITZGERALD. I knew that what I said about making America Younger-Generation-conscious sounded like advertising. I was just making fun of the way that the advertising people talk.

MR. BROOKS. Let me remind you that Freud has shown us that the things we say in jest are as significant as the things we say in earnest—they may, in fact, be more significant, because they reveal the thoughts that are really at the back of our minds and that we do not care to avow to the world. I was struck, also, by that other joke, which you contributed to the letter— I mean about the man who cursed God for having made him an American. Who can fail to detect in this desperate image an involuntary tragic cry which contradicts everything else you have been straining so hard to affirm?—Another detail that betrays: I notice that when you mention the signatories, who explicitly include yourself, you always speak of them as "they" instead of "we." In doing so, I can't help feeling, you furnish irresistible evidence that the unity you assume in collaborating is more or less artificial, that you are actually, in spirit and point of view, as isolated from one another as it has always seemed that literary men are bound to be in America. In allowing your art to become a business, you have rendered true unity impossible and have given yourselves up to the competitive anarchy of American commercial enterprise. You can at best, I fear, gain nothing but money and big hollow reputations—each man out for himself—and these things for fifty years in America have brought nothing but disillusion.

MR. FITZGERALD. Don't you suppose, though, that the American millionaires must have had a certain amount of fun making and spending their money? Can't you imagine a man like Harriman or Hill feeling a certain creative ecstasy as he piled up all that power? Just think of being able to buy absolutely anything you wanted—houses, railroads, enormous industries!—dinners, automobiles, stunning clothes for your wife, clothes like nobody else in the world could wear!—all the finest paintings in Europe, all the books that had ever been written! Think of what it would be like to give parties that went on for days and days, with everything that anybody could want to drink and a medical staff in attendance and the biggest jazz orchestras in the city alternating night and day! I confess that I get a big kick out of all the glittering expensive things. Why, once, when I'd just arrived in New York with a lot of money to spend, after being away in the West, and I came back to the Plaza the first night and looked up and saw that great creamy palace all blazing with green and gold lights, and the taxis and the limousines streaming up and down the Avenue— why, I jumped into the Pulitzer fountain just out of sheer joy! And I wasn't boiled either.

MR. BROOKS. Are you sure you weren't a little hysterical?

MR. FITZGERALD. No: I've been hysterical, too. This was exhilaration.—Look: I don't suppose you could possibly be persuaded to come down to Great Neck this weekend. We're having a little party ourselves. Maybe it would bore you to death—but we're asking some people down who ought to be pretty amusing. Gloria Swanson's coming. And Dos Passos and Sherwood Anderson. And Marc Connelly and Dorothy Parker. And Rube Goldberg. And Ring Lardner will be there. You probably think some of those people are lowbrow, but Ring Lardner, for instance, is really a very interesting fellow— he's really not just a popular writer: he's pretty morose about things. I'd like to have you meet him. There'll be some dumbbell friends of mine from the West, but I don't believe you'd mind them. And then there's going to be a man who sings a song called, *Who'll Bite your Neck When my Teeth are Gone?* Neither my wife nor I knows his name—but this song is one of the funniest things we've ever heard!

MR. BROOKS. Why, thank you ever so much. I'd like ever so much to go—and I'd like to meet all those people. But I'm really afraid that I can't. I'm not nearly done with the James, and I have to devote all my free time to it. And, since you feel that I'm being unfair to him, I must go over my material again and think about it from that point of view.—You know, I appreciate very much your taking the trouble to write me. I'm sorry you find me discouraging: of course, I don't mean to be. On the contrary, I think that your generation is showing a great deal of promise.

MR. FITZGERALD. Well, I'm sorry if I've been a nuisance. It was good of you to listen to the letter.

MR. BROOKS. It was very good of you to write it.

MR. FITZGERALD. Well, I won't bother you any longer.— I'm sorry you can't come down Saturday.

MR. BROOKS. Thank you ever so much. I wish I could!

April 30, 1924

Gilbert Seldes and the Popular Arts

I. *The Seven Lively Arts* (1924)

M R. SELDES has written a valuable and enormously entertaining book on the vulgar arts of vaudeville, jazz music,
newspaper satire, the movies, the revue, the circus, and the
comic strip. He has tried to do for the field of popular entertainment very much what Mr. Mencken has done for philology
in his treatise on the American language; and everybody interested in American culture should pay attention to the results of
his researches.

Unfortunately, Mr. Seldes has not to the same degree as
Mencken the gift of lucid presentation. He does not seem
to realize that the function of his book is primarily one of
exposition—the conveying of information, the unfolding of
novel ideas—and that in order to do this successfully, you must
cultivate patience and order. Mr. Seldes proceeds obliquely by
means of metaphysical discussions of theory and elliptical literary allusions, jokes, curses, cries of ecstasy and hysterical
revelations—the whole rather bewilderingly distributed among
chapters of the normal kind, open letters and imaginary dialogues, which are supplemented by footnotes, appendices and
parenthetical interpolations. You have a feeling that the quick-
silver ideas are escaping through the interstices of the ill-
woven sentences. There are passages in *The Seven Lively Arts*
that I cannot understand at all, and others that I should not
understand unless I happened, in the particular case, to possess
some independent knowledge of what the author is trying to
tell me about. I cite, for example, the footnote on page 336: "I
haven't seen The Covered Wagon. Its theme returns to the
legendary history of America. There is no reason why it should
not have been highly imaginative. But I wonder whether the
thousands of prairie schooners one hears about are the film or
the image. In the latter case there is no objection." Now what
does he mean by this? On the opposite page I find: "By corrupting the action [of novels and plays which were being turned
into movies] the producers changed the idea; bad enough in

itself, they failed to understand what they were doing and supplied nothing to take the place of what they had destroyed." I
can see that a possible sense might be given to this passage by
interchanging the semicolon and the comma, but there are so
many other passages like it that it is impossible to tell whether
this particular one has been misprinted or not. Again: "You
[the 'movie magnates'] gave us Marguerite Clark in films no
better than the 'whimsy-me' school of stage plays." Now I
know what Mr. Seldes means when he refers to the "whimsy-
me" school of drama, because I happened to be present on the
single night when the Algonquin group of humorists put on
the entertainment called *The No-Siree*, and saw their burlesque
of A. A. Milne in which an old gentleman said, "Ah, whimsy
me!"; but if I had not, I should barely have been able to guess
what Mr. Seldes meant by this passage.

Mr. Seldes does succeed, none the less, for all his tendency
toward woolly writing, in disengaging some judicious observations. The chapter from which I have just quoted, for example,
contains admirable criticism of the movies; and the discussion
of the technique of vaudeville is, it seems to me, equally
sound. And, though his bons mots do not always come off, he
strikes at times—as in his passage on Christopher Morley—a
debonair vein of wit that has the air of unexpectedly igniting
when he is not trying for it especially. But where he seems to
me most successful is in simply reporting the things that he has
seen. It is then that he writes his best prose and produces his
most persuasive effects. The descriptions of the Chaplin films,
the Krazy Kat comic strip and the antics of the Fratellini clowns
really bring them most vividly before us: we laugh with delight
as we read. Mr. Seldes, I suppose, is surest here because he is
closest to his object. As soon as he stops looking at his object,
he has a way of becoming bedazzled by strange intellectual
fancies, and is almost as likely to come out with something
wildly inappropriate as with something penetrating and true.
How, for example, did he arrive at the following: "It was odd
that in *Vanity Fair*'s notorious 'rankings,' Krazy tied with
Doctor Johnson, to whom he owes much of his vocabulary."
In what way does Krazy Kat's vocabulary resemble Doctor
Johnson's? The romantic passages quoted certainly fail to convince one of this. Mr. Seldes describes Krazy Kat, also, as "a

creature more like Pan than any other creation of our time"—
though it is difficult to see how Krazy Kat is much more like
Pan than he is like Doctor Johnson. And on what evidence
does he prophesy that Ring Lardner is capable of becoming a
second Mr. Dooley? Ring Lardner, so far as I know, has never
shown a taste for political satire; his recent tendencies have
been, on the one hand, toward sheer nonsense and, on the
other, in such short stories as *The Golden Honeymoon*, toward a
sort of realistic fiction. Nor is it possible to understand what
the passage about the kittens that Mr. Seldes quotes from
Lardner has to do with the "Black Beauty-Beautiful Joe style
of writing," of which Mr. Seldes says it is a parody. "It may
shock Mr. Lardner," says Mr. Seldes, "to know that he has
here done in little what Mr. Joyce has done on the grand scale
in *Ulysses*." It is not only Mr. Lardner who is likely to be surprised by this statement; and he will not be more surprised
than the composers of *I Wonder Who's Kissing Her Now* when
they learn from Mr. Seldes's book that they have "skillfully
built up a sentimental situation in order to tear it down with
two words." These shots go too far or miss, but Mr. Seldes
often does hit the mark—as when he says that Mr. Dooley, in
respect to the Dreyfus case, was performing the same service
for Americans that Anatole France performed for the French.
The difference was, as he notes, that a different sort of audience required a different vehicle of satire. What Mr. Dooley
had to say was essentially no more genial than what Anatole
France had to say, but it was only his good humor and his dialect that made it possible for him to say it at all. So, in our
generation, when manners have passed from back-slapping
to brutality, we have Mencken using a bludgeon on a society
that understands nothing but bludgeons. We have never yet
reached the stage when an Anatole France could be influential.

Much of the clouding of Mr. Seldes's judgment in individual cases arises, I fancy, from his feverish approach to his subject as a whole. In his most ecstatic moments, he is given to
making extravagant claims—as when he asserts that Charlie
Chaplin and George Herriman, the inventor of Krazy Kat, are
the only two "great artists" in America, and that Krazy Kat is
our "most satisfactory work of art"; then, apparently in reaction from such excesses, he will protest for whole chapters at a

time that he is not really trying to compare Herriman with Picasso and Irving Berlin with Stravinsky, but merely backing them against the "faux bon," the "bogus" imitations of the fine arts—thus creating, with an immense amount of pother, what is, so far as I can see, very largely an artificial issue, and one that lands Mr. Seldes in a foolish and inaccurate disparagement of opera and the drama. Why shouldn't it be possible for him simply to go ahead and write a book about the popular arts, without all these protestations? They have been written about before—by Anatole France, for example, who did not think it necessary to denigrate the theater in order to justify the café chantant. Well, there is a real reason, no doubt, why the popular arts should present a slightly more difficult problem in America than they do in a country like France. The French have a culture which diffuses itself more or less through all their social classes and their various fields of activity. The same thing which you find at its highest pitch of purity and intensity in a comedy of Molière appears also in a farce by Guitry, a topical revue by Rip, an illustrated joke in *Le Rire* or even in a conversation between strangers in a railway coach. But in America we have no such homogeneous culture penetrating our whole society. Today a whole race of Americans goes to school and arrives at maturity without more than the sketchiest acquaintance with the classic Anglo-American culture that has been so far our only heritage; and it is inevitable that, among this race, individuals should sometimes appear who, working in some department of popular slapstick humor and with no other language than the common slang, should achieve distinction or brilliance. Such a popular humorist as this may not only go unrecognized as an artist; he may not know that he is one himself. Herriman, I suppose, is such a man; so, perhaps, is Ring Lardner. And Mr. Seldes, in *The Seven Lively Arts*, has performed a feat of some daring in bringing them within the field of criticism. He has overdone it a little, and his case may suffer in consequence; but if he had not been capable of overdoing it, he might never have done it at all.

One thing which, I suspect, has had much to do with making Mr. Seldes self-conscious in his relation to the popular arts is the fact that, unlike most Americans, he has not been brought up on them from boyhood, that he has not learned to take them for granted. He tells us that he had scarcely in his youth ever been either to a circus or to a vaudeville show; and his failure to discuss either the early work of Opper (save for a bare mention of Happy Hooligan) or the burlesque of Weber and Fields, suggests that he may never have known them. This lack of familiarity has the advantage of putting Mr. Seldes in a position to see in the vulgar arts certain qualities of style and imagination which are likely to be missed by people who do not expect anything of them, because they have left them behind with childhood, but it also has the disadvantage of allowing Mr. Seldes to approach them with a sensibility so sophisticated, that, not, for example, having been entertained by a given vaudeville act at the mental age for which it was intended— that is, at the age that Mr. Seldes was about twenty years ago and that the average vaudeville audience is forever—he tends either to reject it angrily as an unsuccessful attempt to do something artistically dignified or to read into it all sorts of profundities that do not have any actual existence.

As a result of this deficient background, we find Mr. Seldes neglecting an interesting aspect of his subject which I should very much like to see discussed: I mean, the revolution in humor that seems to be taking place in New York. In the old days of Weber and Fields, the latter would look down from his bullying height at the former's flowered vest and say, "Aha, now I know vere de lounge vent!" Nowadays, Joe Cook asks "the Senator," his stooge, "How's your uncle?"—and the Senator answers, "I haven't got an uncle." "Fine," says Cook. "How is he?" The difference is that the Weber and Fields joke is a "gag": it is fantastic but it makes sense; whereas Cook's is simply idiotic: you laugh at it, if you do, because it is perfectly pointless.

I should like to bring to the notice of Mr. Seldes two of the older vaudeville comedians who seem to have been transition figures in this change from the smart to the silly: Charlie Case and James J. Morton. Charlie Case was a black-face monologist with a Chaplinesque overtone of pathos who used to sing curious unrhymed songs to a monotonous dirge-like accompaniment. He had developed a vein of his own which was refreshingly unconventional, since it did not depend on gagging,

and his death is said to have been hastened by disappointment
at his failure to establish himself with anything like the public
he deserved. If he had been launched only eight or ten years
ago, he would probably now have a show of his own—like
Frank Tinney who is, to my mind, a much less gifted performer than Case. As it was, Charlie Case was the object of a
cult on the part of a few fans like F. P. A., who printed Case's
songs in his column at the time of the latter's death. James J.
Morton, the other of these comics, was a large solemn middle-
aged man in an ill-fitting frock-coat, who gave a schoolboy
recitation that began, "Hark, mother! I hear the sound of
footsteps in the village street," to the accompaniment of deaf-
ening off-stage noises, and told interminable pointless stories
rather in the manner of Ed Wynn. Neither Case nor Morton
had much in common with the typical comedians of that era:
the Jimmy Powerses, the Nat M. Willises, the McIntyres and
Heaths. They were more subtle, more intellectual, more like
the comedians in vogue today. One can see in them the first
faint foreshadowings of the Algonquin school of humor—the
cult of the flat joke, the irrelevant remark, the sophisticated
naïveté.

That this cult has some meaning as a sign of the times and is
not merely a local fashion would seem to be indicated by its
kinship with the European movement called dadaism. It has
always been natural for the people of the English-speaking
countries to amuse themselves with what they call nonsense,
and, though the nonsense of Joe Cook and Robert Benchley is
distinct from that of Carroll and Lear, it is not in itself a phenomenon that has anything abnormal or surprising about it.
But that our cultivation of nonsense of this special kind should
have been paralleled in France by the development of a similar
school of nonsense suggests a common cause. For the French
have never been given to nonsense; they have scarcely even
understood it. French jokes, unlike English jokes, are usually
funny, not because they are silly, but because they reveal some
truth. The French, since the war, however, have suddenly discovered nonsense. Jean Cocteau's *Le Potomok* and *Les Mariés
de la Tour Eiffel* came close to Carroll and Lear, and the dadaists
have gone all the way in the direction of a deliberate lunacy.
Though the French have made an issue of their nonsense, an

occasion for polemics and riots, as Benchley or Lardner would never do, the non sequiturs and the practical jokes of the French and the American humorists (though the dadaists pretend to grim seriousness) seem the product of similar situations: in France, the collapse of Europe and the intellectual chaos that accompanied it; in America—what is perhaps another aspect of a general crisis: the bewildering confusion of the modern city and the enfeeblement of the faculty of attention. It relieves some anxiety for people to watch acts or listen to stories that are completely inconsecutive and pointless, because that is the way the world is beginning to seem, the way their own minds are beginning to work. They have to think about too many things and the relation between all these things is not in the least clear. It is comforting to hear Joe Cook when he is genially incoherent: our laughter both confesses and dismisses our fears.

In any case, *The Seven Lively Arts* is a genuine contribution to America's new orientation in respect to her artistic life which was inaugurated in 1915 by Brooks's *America's Coming of Age* and two years later more violently promoted by Mencken's *A Book of Prefaces*. Mr. Seldes's view of the arts has perhaps been a little confused by his evidently quite recent discovery that it is possible to appreciate, not only Krazy Kat at the same time as James Joyce, but both Krazy Kat and Joyce at the same time as "the *Medea* of Euripides"; but his book contains a brilliant chronicle of the high spots in our popular entertainment. If not all these forms of entertainment have really quite reached the dignity of arts, Mr. Seldes has succeeded in inventing them as such: it is he who is the artist here. He has precipitated pure crystals of irony from the cheap adulterated compounds in which it is usually sold; he has caught the enchanting echoes of our popular gaiety and melody as they drift in the city air. To read his book is to live again the last ten years of vaudeville and revue, newspapers and moving pictures, but in a purified and concentrated form—tasting nothing but the magic tune, the racy flash of characterization, the moment of mad laughter. As for the trained dogs, the melodramatic playlet and the sentimental soloist, they, too, become entertaining through the wit of our guide's comments.

If he were only a little less fanatical about magnifying the importance of the whole affair, he would make the perfect companion.

September, 1924

II. *The Great Audience* (1950)

In 1924, Mr. Gilbert Seldes published a book called *The Seven Lively Arts*, the object of which was to show that the popular arts in America were remarkable for vitality and imagination and that the best they had produced was to be preferred to the "faux bon" of our respectable arts. There were chapters on vaudeville, movies, revues, newspaper humor, the comic strip, ragtime and jazz music, and Mr. Seldes's heroes were Joe Cook, Charlie Chaplin, Florenz Ziegfeld, Ring Lardner, Krazy Kat, Al Jolson and Irving Berlin. That was the epoch, in the United States, of the liquidation of genteel culture, and Mr. Seldes's audacious book marked one of the steps in this process. He had at that time just resigned from the managing editorship of the *Dial*, a literary and artistic monthly that maintained very close relations with everything that was newest in Europe, and *The Seven Lively Arts* had its connections with the more general movement of which the jazz rhythms of Stravinsky and Edith Sitwell, the ballets of Jean Cocteau and the premeditated delirium of the dadaists were among the manifestations. Gilbert Seldes had at that time, in common with these, a touch of that upside-down snobbery of the café chantant and the music hall that probably stemmed from Toulouse-Lautrec. The Fratellini clowns of the Cirque Médrano figured among his favorites, along with Ed Wynn and Joe Jackson.

During the twenty-six years that have elapsed since the appearance of this early book, Mr. Seldes has been up to his neck in the seven lively arts, as well as in a couple of new ones that had not yet arrived at that time. He has not only continued, as a critic, to follow and comment on the various phases of popular entertainment; he has served on the production end of several of them and got to know them from the inside. Between 1937 and 1945, he was head of the Television Program Department of C.B.S., functioning also as producer, director, writer and M.C., and he has also been associated with the radio side of C.B.S. and has intermittently written radio scripts and delivered series of broadcasts. He has collaborated on movie documentaries and he has sweated out his term in Hollywood on the writing staff of Paramount. Through all this, he has steadily worked—as a check on his activities shows—to realize the best possibilities, aesthetic and educational, of these new techniques of mass amusement; and he has now written a large-scale study of television, radio and movies, with a section on comic books, summing up his conclusions about them.

Seldes's new book, *The Great Audience*, is quite different from *The Seven Lively Arts*, but it is a logical sequel to it, which makes, also, a dramatic contrast. The early book was a series of essays celebrating distinguished artists. The new one has little to say about individual writers and performers; it uses them only as illustrations. It is a solid and sober report, authoritatively documented, of the industries with which it deals: a history of their development, an analysis of their economic and technical problems, a survey of their present condition and an estimate of their probable future. It is also a critical essay, the most comprehensive and searching I know, on mass entertainment in the United States—an essay which draws conclusions that could never have been foreseen by the early Seldes or by anybody else at that stage. These analyses, predictions and conclusions will undoubtedly provoke objection, but they cannot fail to carry weight. This is the first time, so far as I know, that a man of intelligence and taste, with a sound enough education to give him cultural and historical perspective, who has at the same time a practical grasp of the technical and financial aspects of the entertainment business, has set out to attack the whole subject: to describe it, to explain it, to assess it, to assign it to its place in society; and before one goes on to discuss the special questions that Mr. Seldes raises, it should be said that *The Great Audience* seems one of those "definitive" works that, taking advantage of a crucial moment, sum up and deliver

judgment on some phase of human activity; that make us
understand what has happened, that establish enduring assumptions and that remain indispensable landmarks.

It is not possible to summarize briefly the contents of Mr.
Seldes's book, but its main conclusions are these:

The movies, he says, have been losing their public. Between
1947 and 1950, a thirty-percent drop has taken place, and the
movie-theater audience is mainly made up of teen-agers; after
twenty, people go less often, and after thirty, almost not at all.
The films are mostly aimed at the young and, in consequence,
have become, at the present time, repetitions of stereotyped
myths that have no roots whatever in reality. Mr. Seldes is at
his most brilliant in his descriptions of the imaginary worlds
presented by the mass entertainments. He shows that the contemporary world of the films is one in which men and women
are never allowed to have sexual relations. Extramarital liaisons
are barred, and even when people get married, the consummation is infinitely delayed by a series of unfortunate accidents.
Later on, when the wives have acquired children by some par-
thenogenic process, the marriage may be threatened by a bad
woman whose badness consists of an interest in sex; but Providence will always arrange that the couple shall be brought together by the injury or illness of a child. In the meantime, the
hiatus left by the exclusion of sensual passion that is imposed
by the censorship is filled by a strangely uncensored sadistic indulgence in violence. A woman may not be desired but she
may be indecently spanked or given a sock in the jaw. And the
hero and heroine never work; it is enough for the young man
that he should marry the boss's daughter, or, in the case of a
composer, that he should write "a great song or symphony in
a single blinding flash of inspiration." Only the milkman and
such people work, and these workers are invariably good-
natured and respectful toward the more fortunate class they
serve. The married couples remain immature till the children
begin to grow up, whereupon they revert to the springtime of
youth and are saved from amorous follies only through the intervention of their bright adolescent children. No one, says
Mr. Seldes, ever really grows up in the movies, and that is the
reason they do not interest adults.

While the movies, in the thirties and forties, were petrifying into these formulas, the radio had been developing two new kinds of formularized commodity: the news broadcast and the daytime serial. The problems of free speech and good taste that arise in connection with news commentators and the commercial announcements of sponsors have been decided in different instances, the most important of which are recorded by Mr. Seldes, in a variety of different ways; but, with the recent decline in radio, in proportion as television has been taking its place, the barriers against propaganda and the plugging of obnoxious products have been largely broken down. You can now buy time for almost anything: a laxative that is advertised at mealtime or a bigoted religious program. As for the daytime serial, it is a dreary and insipid story that is made to creep on from day to day in such a way that as little as possible will happen in any given instalment and that that little will take as long as possible. The typical situation here is one in which a decisive and self-dependent woman intervenes in the lives of others. She must never meet another character who is vigorous and determined also, because that would precipitate action. Her husband is invariably unready and hesitant; he probably suffers from impotence. She herself is probably frigid. A check on radio audiences has shown that the listeners to these serials are housewives with impoverished lives, themselves lacking competence and resolution. The continual small anxieties created by the situations in the serials correspond to their own anxieties and afford the humble satisfaction of hearing them vicariously resolved. But it is probable, Mr. Seldes believes, that this interminable purveying of anxieties has the effect of keeping up artificially the state of mind it appears to soothe, just as the playing down to immaturity, in the case of the young movie audience, has become perhaps the principal influence that induces it to remain immature.

What, then, about television, with which Mr. Seldes has been involved almost since its commercial inception and to which, though he does not say so, he has contributed his own best efforts with a view to directing its development toward a respectable art of its own? He admits that, at its present stage, TV has produced nothing really new, but he believes that since it has the advantage of letting you both see and hear its

performers while their performance is going on, it should encourage a more natural relation between the performer and his
audience than either radio or movie does, and he hopes that,
in its handling of drama, it will approximate to the regular
stage in allowing us to see characters in the round. Unfortunately, the only examples that Mr. Seldes is able at this time to
invoke in order to persuade us of these possibilities are such
features as Milton Berle and the puppets Kukla, Fran and
Ollie, about whose quality he makes it plain that he is not
enthusiastic, and he has already chilled the reader's blood by
introducing his section on this subject with the heading *Pan-
dora's Box.*

Mr. Seldes has tried to be as hopeful as the conditions will
possibly permit; he does not want to accept dead ends. Television, if it only will, can, he says, give us real theater in the living room. The movies can retrieve their slipping public by
appealing to an untouched audience—that of mature men and
women. He preaches to the public as a whole the need for
non-official protests on the part of groups of citizens—though
he has noted the discouraging apathy of the people who pa-
tronize these mass media. To those who don't listen to radio,
who don't look at television, and who rarely go to the movies,
he insists that this will not save them. They must live in a common society conditioned by the effect of these things. Might
not a man who had never turned on the radio find himself
being trampled to death by a panic-stricken mob driven frantic
by some such broadcast as Orson Welles's *War of the Worlds?*
On the other hand, the remedy proposed for minimizing this
kind of hazard seems a heavy price to pay for escape from even
such a fate as this. In order to keep informed as to what is
going on in these departments, the non-lover of television and
radio will be obliged, Mr. Seldes suggests, to "suspend whatever he is doing and look for an hour or two at the best that is
now offered." But "if a nation cannot survive half slave and
half free, a democracy cannot endure if the forces making for
free minds are apathetic and the forces of invincible ignorance
are aggressive and brilliantly managed and irresponsible. If it is
already inconvenient to attack them, it will be dangerous in
five years, and it will be impossible in ten." If no pressure is
brought by the public to have the level of these media raised,

the result may be simply that the movies will be superseded by
television, and that radio will go bankrupt in the attempt to finance its successor before television has had the chance to outgrow its rudimentary stages. This would greatly facilitate the
step that is Mr. Seldes's principal bug-bear, as it may well be
anyone's: the taking over of the mass media by the government and the use of them, not for more or less legitimate
informative and cultural purposes, as the B.B.C. has used them,
but for unscrupulous total control of a spineless depersonalized public. The exploiters of mass entertainment, in aiming,
for steady and sure returns, at the lowest common denominator, have in some departments been losing their audience, but
they have also been stultifying those who share in this lowest
common denominator and artificially extending its realm.

We are almost as far here from the Seldes who delighted in
the *Ziegfeld Follies* and the vaudeville turns at the Palace as we
are from the Toulouse-Lautrec who frequented the Nouveau
Cirque or, for that matter, from Toulouse-Lautrec's predecessor, the seventeenth-century Jacques Callot, who amused himself in Italy at the *commedia dell'arte*. This book is about the
audience, not about the artists. Mr. Seldes says he cannot take
time to pay his compliments to the shows and the actors that
have given him particular pleasure, but, after all, the films as
we have them could hardly produce a new Chaplin. Mr. Seldes
has told briefly here the story of Walt Disney's capitulation, in
competition with the comic books and under pressure to pay
off his financing, by turning out long features in quantity. He
might have added that of Jimmy Durante, surely the greatest
comic that has appeared since Mr. Seldes's first book, who has
been compelled to descend from the wild poetry of the Parody
Club to the routine personality gags of his work on the screen
and air. Mr. Seldes mentions in passing that Li'l Abner may
perhaps "to a degree" take the place of Krazy Kat; but he is occupied chiefly with the problem of curing the degenerate tendencies of the seven hundred million comic books that are
now printed every year.

Mr. Seldes, since he left the *Dial*, has been cultivating certain conceptions that sometimes land him in a false position.
He asserts that the more serious American writers have always

been contemptuous of "the average man," that they have vili-
fied American life and made no effort to understand America.
He even goes to the length of implying that Walt Whitman
was deficient in sympathy for ordinary American humanity and
indifferent to the Civil War. It is a pity that Mr. Seldes should
so long ago have taken up a position that has prevented him
from becoming as well-acquainted with the history of American thought as he is with that of our popular arts. Since this
question, in his latest book, is raised only incidentally, one
need not go into it here any further than to make the point
that the better American writers have given expression to a variety of points of view and that these points of view themselves
have varied in response to varying epochs. Mr. Seldes's own
point of view seems rather to belong to the category of what
Frank Moore Colby meant when he called one of his books
Constrained Attitudes. This attitude is contradicted on almost
every page of Mr. Seldes's book by what he thinks and says and
is. Such occasional pokes as he takes at his antagonist, the
straw-man "intellectual," who is supposed to disdain the popular arts, are quite inconsistent with the bitter complaints of
"anti-intellectualism" that he brings against the radio and
movies for their habit of representing schoolteachers as invariably either "angular spinsters" or "absent-minded professors,"
who are treated "the former without sympathy, the latter without respect," and their convention that all studious young
people are absurd little prigs and bores.

The truth is, of course, that Mr. Seldes is nothing if not an
intellectual himself, and, as *The Great Audience* proves, an exceptionally able one. He has come out of his twenty years of
wrestling professionally with the lively arts even less well-
disposed toward mediocrity, toward the facile, the false and the
trashy, than he was at the time when he was editing the *Dial*
and when the floods of that rubbish were not threatening to
swamp us. Mr. Seldes's whole appeal to the public is based on
the hope—I believe quite justified—that there are still a great
many Americans who are also intellectuals, to the degree, at
least, of not being satisfied with the goods that the mass media
are putting out. His "intellectual" and his "average man" are
in reality demagogic devices, taken over from the very agencies
against which he now protests; they have never been anything

other than masks to mislead the simple. Mr. Seldes shows them up at once when he comes to grips with his subject, as in his section called *Nine P. M. Tuesday*, in which he tells us that "the average man lives at many emotional and intellectual levels," and when he declares, in *The Menace of the Years*, that "the people desperately need arts that are serious." Intellectual that he is, he cannot help expressing a doubt whether, at this point, the people are "capable of accepting" them; and no critic of our post-Civil War period or of the Mencken and Lewis era has ever taken a gloomier view of the results of American commercialism or issued a grimmer warning. The radio and movies, Mr. Seldes says, "are the great engines of democratic entertainment and culture," yet, through their imposition of uniformity, "they are committed to the destruction of democracy."

October 28, 1950

Houdini

HOUDINI is a short strong stocky man with small feet and a very large head. Seen from the stage, his figure, with its short legs and its pugilist's proportions, is less impressive than at close range, where the real dignity and force of the enormous head appear. Wide-browed and aquiline-nosed, with a cleanness and fitness almost military, he suggests one of those enlarged and idealized busts of Roman consuls or generals. So it is rather the man himself than the stage personality who is interesting. Houdini is remarkable among magicians in having so little of the smart-aleck about him: he is, of course, a tremendous egoist, like many other very able persons, but he is not a cabotin. When Houdini performs tricks, he does it with the directness and simplicity of an expert giving a demonstration and he talks to his audience in a quite different way from that of the ordinary conjuror: straightforwardly, with no patter. The formulas—such as the "Will wonders never cease?" with which he signalizes the end of a trick—have a quaint conventional sound, as if they were perfunctory concessions to the theater. For preëminently Houdini is the honest craftsman which his plain speech and German accent suggest—thoroughgoing, earnest, enthusiastic.

Houdini is in fact a German Jew (Houdini is not his real name)—born in the state of Wisconsin. In his youth, he served an apprenticeship to circuses and dime-museums. He mastered the whole repertoire of magic and took his place, with a show of his own, as a magician of the first rank. Houdini has until recently been most celebrated for the specialty known as the "escape." He has succeeded in extricating himself from every conceivable kind of strongbox, straitjacket, handcuffs and chains under every conceivable kind of circumstances; and, though this is a department of trickery which has always seemed to the present writer less artistically interesting than others, it is characteristic of Houdini that, not content with the ingenuities of illusion and the perfection of sleight-of-hand, he should have chosen to excel in that branch of magic which offered the most dangerous challenge and the best chance of performing feats unlikely to be duplicated, and which also took him farthest from the masks of the theater. Lately, however, Houdini has achieved a new kind of celebrity in connection with the investigation of spiritualism. It was formerly the custom to have spiritualistic phenomena authenticated by scientists of various sorts, and, as a result of this method of research, many surprising discoveries were reported —culminating, at the end of the war, in the ectoplasm revelations. When the French magicians, however, of whose committee Houdini had been made a member, challenged the ectoplasm mediums to admit magicians to their séances, they refused to perform under those conditions; and when Houdini was later included in the *Scientific American*'s committee to investigate Mrs. Crandon, the Boston medium, who nearly succeeded in winning the prize offered by that publication for the production of genuine phenomena, he detected her tricks at once and proceeded to construct a cabinet which would make it impossible for her to repeat them. The truth is, of course, that in a committee of scientists on which Houdini sits, it is Houdini who is the scientist. Doctors, psychologists and physicists are no better qualified to check up on spiritualistic phenomena than lawyers, preachers or poets. They are deceived just as readily by magicians on the stage as anybody else in the audience, and it is equally easy for them to be deceived by magicians as mediums. The problem is whether the "medium" is a real medium or merely a conjuror, and this is something that only a conjuror is really equipped to find out.

Houdini is thus perhaps the first investigator of spirtualism who is competent for the task. He is one of the most accomplished magicians in the world, and—what is rare—he has brought to the study of trickery a true scientific curiosity: he seems now to have become more interested in understanding how effects are produced than in astonishing people with them, and to derive more satisfaction from lecturing on the methods of the mediums than from contriving illusions of his own. He has collected a library of books on trickery, occultism and kindred subjects which is said to be the largest in the world; and he has himself published a book on spiritualism called *A Magician Among the Spirits* and a pamphlet setting forth his observations in connection with Mrs. Crandon and

with Argamasilla, a Spanish clairvoyant who claimed to be able
to read through metal. He has even taken the trouble to attempt a retrospective exposé of Daniel Home's famous levita-
tion of fifty years ago, visiting the London hotel at which
Home is supposed to have floated out of the window of a
room and in at the window of the room next door and discovering that the passage from one ledge to the other could
easily have been made with a rope. As a result of his study of
the supernatural, Houdini has come to the following conclusions. He believes that, so far as the evidence goes, the phenomena of spiritualism are fraudulent, because, in all the cases
on record in which experts on magic have been called, their
testimony has gone against the mediums; he asserts that
telepathy does not exist and that he himself can reproduce by
trickery any telepathic phenomena of which he has ever heard;
that the miracles of which the legends are always reaching us
from the East—the Indian Rope Trick, the stopping of the
pulse and the Yogis who survive being buried alive—are either
tricks long understood by magicians or travellers' tales which
have never been authenticated; and that all other supposed
supernatural occurrences are to be put down either to coinci-
dence or to momentary hallucination.

Houdini declares that he has never been duped, that he has
never failed to see through a trick, but that he lives in continual terror of someday being outwitted by a telepathist or a
medium—in which case his dogmatic denials would be made
to look ridiculous. And this has given him a certain edge, a certain nervous excitement, as of a man engaged in a critical fight.
Where he once challenged the world to tie him up, he now
challenges it to convince him of the supernatural; and, in spite
of his apparent self-confidence—sometimes thought excessive
—he is very keenly aware of the perils of his position. It may
be indeed that Houdini has appeared at a crucial moment in
the history of spiritualism and that he is destined to play an
important role. For a spectator at one of his Hippodrome performances, it is difficult to understand how a credulous disposition toward mediums can long survive such public
exposures. Here one can see Houdini reproduce the classical
phenomena of the megaphone that floats, the bells that ring
and the ghostly hands that brush one's face, in full sight of the

audience, who see how the tricks are done, but to the bewilderment of a blindfolded man who sits with him on an isolated platform. When one has watched Houdini, with his hands and feet both held by his vis-à-vis, get hold of a megaphone by his teeth, one does not find it surprising that the editors of the *Scientific American* should have been fooled by the same trick performed by Mrs. Crandon in a dark room. And when we have heard him, by means of devices that he afterwards gives away, tell members of the audience whom he has never seen before, their names and their addresses and facts about their private affairs, we are prepared to accept any marvels of this kind that the mediums, with their elaborate intelligence service, are reported to be able to accomplish.

The real situation, however, is of course that with the people who frequent séances, the difficulty is not for the mediums to convince them that the phenomena are genuine but for the tricksters to handle things so badly as to make their clients suspicious. A friend of mine was once told by a professional medium of a séance that had gone wrong when he had found that he could not get his hand free; he had tried to represent the spirit by touching the client with his cheek and then in a panic remembered that he had not yet shaved that day; but the lady allayed this fear, as soon as the séance was over, by telling him that the manifestations that day had been certainly their most successful, since the supernatural essence of the spirit had startlingly communicated itself by a sharp electrical pricking. One thinks also of the French savant who, as a result of methodical research, undertaken at the behest of the government, reported his success in establishing that spirits had hair on their heads, that they were warm, that they had beating hearts, that their pulse could be felt in their wrists, and that their breath contained carbon dioxide.

June 24, 1925

Poe at Home and Abroad

THE RECENT revival of interest in Poe has brought to light a good deal of new information and supplied us for the first time with a serious interpretation of his personal career, but it has so far entirely neglected to explain why we should still want to read him. In respect to such figures as Poe, we Americans are still perhaps almost as provincial as those of their contemporaries who now seem to us ridiculous for having failed to recognize their genius. Today, we take their eminence for granted, but we still cannot help regarding them, not from the point of view of their real contributions to western culture, but primarily as fellow-Americans, whose activities we feel the necessity of explaining in terms of America and the circumstances of whose personal lives we are, as neighbors, in a position to investigate. Thus, at a date when "Edgar Poe" has figured in Europe for the last three-quarters of a century as a writer of the first importance, we in America are still preoccupied—though no longer in moral indignation—with his bad reputation as a citizen. Thus, Dr. J. W. Robertson, who perhaps started off the recent researches, five years ago published a book to show that Poe was a typical alcoholic. Thus, last year we saw the publication of Poe's correspondence with his foster-father. Thus, we are promised the early revelation of Poe's plagiarism of his plots from a hitherto unknown German source (as James Huneker has pointed out that Poe's later and most celebrated poems must certainly have owed a good deal to an obscure American poet named Thomas Holley Chivers). Thus, a Miss Mary E. Phillips has just published an enormous biography running to sixteen hundred and eighty-five pages—*Edgar Allan Poe, the Man*—a monument of uncritical devotion which it must have taken a lifetime to compile, stuffed with illustrations that include not only photographs of the little Scotch town from which Poe's foster-father came, of the librarian of the University of Virginia at the time when Poe was a student there and of the clock on the mantle-piece of Poe's cottage at Fordham, but also maps of New York, Richmond and Baltimore at the time when Poe lived in those cities; and containing embedded in its pudding-stone prose perhaps more miscellaneous facts about him than have ever before been assembled.

The ablest and the most important of recent American books on Poe, is, however, without any doubt, Mr. Joseph Wood Krutch's *Edgar Allan Poe: A Study in Genius*. Mr. Krutch has made an attempt to go beyond Doctor Robertson in diagnosing Poe's nervous malady, and his conclusions are by this time well known: he believes that Poe was driven in the first instance into seeking a position of literary eminence by a desire to compensate himself for the loss of social position of which his foster-father had deprived him; that, in consequence, perhaps of a "fixation" on his mother, he became sexually impotent and was forced, as a result of his inability to play a part in the normal world, to invent an abnormal world full of horror, repining and doom (the universally recognized concomitants, according to Mr. Krutch, of sexual repression of this sort) in which he could take refuge; that his very intellectual activity, his love of working out cryptograms and crimes, had been primarily stimulated by the desire to prove himself logical when he felt he was going insane; and, finally, that his critical theory was merely a justification of his peculiar artistic practice, which was itself thus, in turn, a symptom of his disease. It must be said, in fairness to Mr. Krutch, that he does not fail to draw, at the end of his book, the conclusions about artists in general which follow from his particular conclusions. Mr. Krutch fully admits that, if what he says about Poe is true, it must also be true of "all imaginative works," which, in that case, should be regarded as the products of "unfulfilled desires" springing from "either idiosyncratic or universally human maladjustments to life." This does not, however, prevent Mr. Krutch from misunderstanding Poe's writings and seriously undervaluing them, nor even from complacently caricaturing them —as the modern school of social-psychological biography, of which Mr. Krutch is a typical representative, seems inevitably to tend to caricature the personalities of its subjects. We are nowadays being edified by the spectacle of some of the principal ornaments of the human race exhibited exclusively in terms of their most ridiculous manias, their most disquieting neuroses and their most humiliating failures. Mr. Krutch has chosen for the frontispiece of what he calls a "study in genius" a daguerreotype of Poe taken in 1849, shortly before his death: it shows a pasty and dilapidated personage with untrimmed untidy hair, an uneven toothbrush mustache and large pouches under the eyes; the eyes themselves have a sad unfocussed stare; one eyelid is drooping; one hand is thrust into the coat-front with an air of feeble pretentiousness. The dignified solemnity of the figure is as ludicrous as a bad old-fashioned actor attempting to play *Hamlet*, and its visible disintegration unpleasantly suggests an alcoholic patient recently admitted to a cure. And something like this is the final impression left by Mr. Krutch's book. Mr. Krutch quotes with disapproval the statement of President Hadley of Yale, in explaining the refusal of the Hall of Fame to accept Poe among its immortals: "Poe wrote like a drunkard and a man who is not accustomed to pay his debts"; and yet Mr. Krutch himself, so interesting as a psychologist, is almost as unperceptive when he tells us, in effect, that Poe wrote like a dispossessed Southern gentleman and a man with a fixation on his mother.

For the rest, Mr. H. L. Mencken has written with admiration of Poe's destructive reviewing—that is, he has paid a tribute to an earlier practitioner of an art of his own; Mr. Van Wyck Brooks has examined Poe's work for evidences of the harshness and the sterility of a Puritan-pioneer society, and found it unsatisfactory as literature; and Mr. Lewis Mumford, in *The Golden Day*, seems to have taken his cue from Mr. Brooks when he finds in the hardness of Poe's effects the steel of the industrial age. It may, I believe, be said that no recent American critic, with the exception of Mr. Waldo Frank in his article on the Poe-Allan letters, has written with any real appreciation of Poe's absolute artistic importance.

II

One of the most striking features of all this American criticism of Poe is its tendency to regard him as a freak, having his existence somehow apart not merely from contemporary life but even from contemporary literature. "That his life happened to fall," writes Mr. Krutch, "between the years 1809 and 1849 is merely an accident, and he has no more in common with Whittier, Lowell, Longfellow or Emerson than he has

with either the eighteenth or nineteenth centuries in England.
. . . His works bear no conceivable relation, either external or
internal, to the life of any people, and it is impossible to account for them on the basis of any social or intellectual tendencies or as the expression of the spirit of any age." Worse
than this, we are always being told that Poe has no connection
with "reality," that he writes exclusively of a "dream world"
which has no point of contact with our own. The error of this
second assertion immediately becomes apparent when we consider the falsity of the first. So far from having nothing in common with the spirit of the first half of the nineteenth century,
Poe is certainly one of its most typical figures; that is to say, he
is a thorough romantic, closely akin to his European contemporaries. Thus, his nightmarish vein of fantasy is very much
like that of Coleridge; his poetry in its earlier phase derives from
Shelley and Keats; his "dream fugues" resemble De Quincey's
and his "prose poems," Maurice de Guérin's. His themes—
which, as Baudelaire says, are concerned with "the exception
in the moral order"—are in the tradition of Chateaubriand and
Byron, and of the romantic movement generally. It is, then, in
terms of romanticism that we must look for reality in Poe. It
shows a lack of historical sense to expect of him the same sort
of treatment of life that we find in Dreiser or Sinclair Lewis
and the recent preoccupation with which seems so to have
misled our critics. From this modern sociological point of
view, the European writers whom I have named above had no
more connection with their respective countries than had Poe
with the United States. Their settings and their dramatis per-
sonae, the images by which they rendered their ideas, were as
different as those of Poe from the images of modern naturalism, and they used them for a different kind of story-telling
which conveyed a different kind of moral.

What, then, are the morals of Poe, the realities he tried to
express? The key is to be found in Baudelaire's phrase about
"the exception in the moral order." The exception in the moral
order was the predominant theme of the romantic movement.
It is absurd to complain, as our critics do, of Poe's indifference
to the claims of society, as if this indifference were something
abnormal: one of the principal features of romanticism was,
not merely an indifference to the claims of society, but an

exalted revolt against them. The favorite figure of the romantic writers was the sympathetic individual considered from the
point of view of his non-amenability to law or convention.
And in this, Poe runs absolutely true to type: his heroes are the
brothers of Rolla and René; of Childe Harold, Manfred and
Cain. Like these latter, they are superior individuals who pursue extravagant fancies, plumb abysses of dissipation or yield
to forbidden passions (Poe made one or two experiments with
the common romantic theme of incest; but his specialties were
a frigid sadism and a curious form of adultery which never
took place till the woman whom the hero betrayed was dead).
And, as in the case of the other romantic heroes, their drama is
the conflict of their impulses with human or divine law. This
impulse of the individual does not, however, in Poe, take
often, as it does with the other romantics, the form of a too
generous passion overflowing the canals of the world; but assumes rather the sinister character of what Poe called the "Imp
of the Perverse." Yet this very perversity of Poe, the kind of
dizzy terror it engenders, due to whatever nervous instability
and whatever unlucky circumstances, have their poetry and
their deep pathos—from those lines in one of the finest of his
poems in which he tells how the doom of his later life appeared
to him even in childhood as he gazed on "the cloud that took
the form (When the rest of Heaven was blue) Of a demon in
my view," to that terrible picture of the condemned man,
"sick—sick unto death with that long agony," when "first [the
candles] wore the aspect of charity, and seemed white slender
angels who would save me; but then, all at once, there came a
most deadly nausea over my spirit, and I felt every fibre in my
frame thrill as if I had touched the wire of a galvanic battery,
while the angel forms became meaningless specters, with heads
of flame, and I saw that from them there would be no help.
And then there stole into my fancy, like a rich musical note,
the thought of what sweet rest there must be in the grave."
And it is the lifelong "agony" of his moral experience that
gives to Poe's *William Wilson* its superior sincerity and intensity over Stevenson's *Doctor Jekyll and Mr. Hyde*. In Stevenson,
it is the virtuous half of the dual personality that destroys the
divided man by exorcising the evil; but, in Poe, it is the evil
half that does away with the good and that is even made to tell

the whole story from its own point of view. Yet does not *William Wilson* bring home to us the horror of the moral transmutation more convincingly than the melodramatic fable of Doctor Jekyll and Mr. Hyde?

There is one special tragic theme of Poe's which deserves to be noted in this connection. Mr. Krutch says that Poe was impotent, and that, for this reason, though perhaps unconsciously, he chose to marry a girl of thirteen with whom it would be impossible for him to have regular conjugal relations. Mr. Krutch does not offer any proof of this, but we do not have to assume it to be true in order to agree with Mr. Krutch that Poe's marriage with Virginia Clemm was somehow unsatisfactory, and that it plays a strange role in his work. Virginia was Poe's first cousin, and it may be that, on this account, he had scruples about consummating the marriage. In any case, she became tubercular, and, twelve years after their marriage, died; while Poe himself grew neurotic, irritable and at last unbalanced. He was obsessed by desperate fantasies and seems, after her death, to have been almost insane. It is possible to follow Mr. Krutch in admitting that the atrocious sadism of many of Poe's later tales must have been due to some emotional repression. Though he undoubtedly adored Virginia, he seems at the same time to have wished her dead. He is always imagining, in his tales, long before her actual death, that a woman like Virginia has died and that her lover is free to love other women. But even here, the dead woman intervenes: in *Ligeia*, she reincarnates herself in the corpse of her successor, who has also died; in *Morella*, in her own daughter. And it is evidently this conflict of Poe's emotions which inspires, not merely these bizarre fancies, but also the unexplained feelings of remorse that so often haunt his heroes. After Virginia has actually died, the situation he has foreseen in the stories seems to be realized. He conducts flirtations with other women; but they are accompanied by "a wild inexplicable sentiment that resembles nothing so nearly as a consciousness of guilt." "I was never really insane," he writes to Mrs. Clemm just before his miserable death, "except on occasions when my heart was touched. I have been taken to prison once since I came here for getting drunk; but then I was not. It was about Virginia." The story of Poe and Virginia is a painful and rather unpleasant one; but it is perhaps worth discussing to this extent, for we recognize in it the actual relation which, viewed in the light of a romantic problem and transposed into romantic terms, fills Poe's writings with the ominous sense of a deadlock between the rebellious spirit, the individual will, on the one hand, and both its very romantic idealisms and its human bonds, on the other. "The whole realm of moral ideals," says Mr. Krutch, "is excluded [from Poe's work], not merely as morality *per se*, but also as artistic material used for the creation of conflicts and situations." What, then, does he suppose such stories as *Eleonora* and *Ligeia* are about? He goes on to say that horror is the only emotion which is "genuinely Poe's own" and that this "deliberately invents causes for itself," that "it is always a pure emotion without any rational foundation." How, he would no doubt ask, can anything describable as moral interest be found in the *Descent into the Maelström* or the *Case of M. Valdemar*? This question I propose to discuss in a moment.

III

Poe was, then, a typical romantic. But he was also something more. He contained the germs of a further development. By 1847, Baudelaire had begun to read Poe and had "experienced a strange commotion": when he had looked up the rest of Poe's writings in the files of American magazines, he found among them stories and poems which he had "thought vaguely and confusedly" of writing himself, and Poe became an obsession with him. He published in 1856 a volume of translations of Poe's tales; and from then on, the influence of Poe became one of the most important in French literature. M. Louis Seylaz has recently traced this influence in a book called *Edgar Poe et les Premiers Symbolistes Français*, in which he discusses the indebtedness to Poe of the French symbolist movement, from Baudelaire, through Verlaine, Rimbaud, Mallarmé (who translated Poe's poems), Villiers de L'Isle-Adam and Huysmans, to Paul Valéry in our own day (who has just written some interesting pages on Poe in a preface to a new edition of Baudelaire's *Les Fleurs du Mal*).

Let us inquire as to precisely in what this influence of Poe consisted that was felt so profoundly by the French through a

whole half-century of their literature, yet which has so completely failed to impress itself upon the literature of Poe's own
country that it is still possible for Americans to talk about him
as if his principal claim to distinction were his title to be described as the "father of the short story." In the first place, says
M. Valéry, Poe brought to the romanticism of the later nineteenth century a new aesthetic discipline. Perhaps more than
any other writer, French or English, of the first half of the century, he had thought seriously and written clearly about the
methods and aims of literature. He had formulated a critical
theory, and he had supplied brilliant specimens of its practice.
Even in poetry, by the time that Poe's influence had begun to
be felt in France, it had been the ideals of naturalism that the
post-romantic generation had tried to bring into play against
the extravagance and the looseness of romanticism running to
seed. But the American was now to provide them with a new
and logical program that would aim to lop the overgrowths of
romanticism and yet to achieve effects that can only be called
romantic. What *were* these ultra-romantic effects which had
first been described by Poe, and by what means did he propose
to attain them?

"I *know*," writes Poe, "that indefiniteness is an element of
the true music [of poetry]—I mean of the true musical expression . . . a suggestive indefiniteness of meaning with a view
of bringing about a definiteness of vague and therefore of spiritual *effect*." This is already the doctrine of symbolism. Poe had
exemplified it in his own poems. Poe's poetry is rarely quite
successful; but it is, none the less, of first-rate importance. He
tells us rather pathetically, in his preface to his poems, apolo-
gizing for their imperfections, that "events not to be controlled" have prevented him "from making, at any time, any
serious effort in what, under happier circumstances, would
have been the field of my choice." The immaturity of his early
verse, where he is imitating Shelley and Coleridge, is certainly
not redeemed by the deliberate tricks of his later, which he
seems to have borrowed from Chivers and which are always a
little trashy. Yet all of Poe's poetry is interesting, because more
than that of any other romantic (except perhaps Coleridge in
Kubla Khan), it does approach the indefiniteness of music—
that supreme goal of the symbolists. That is to say that, from

the ordinary point of view, Poe's poetry is more nonsensical than that of any of the other romantics—and nonsensical in much the same way as, to the ordinary point of view, much of our best modern poetry appears. To note but a single instance: one of the characteristic traits of modern symbolism is a sort of psychological confusion between the impressions of the different senses. This confusion distinctly appears in Poe: thus we find him, in one of his poems, *hearing* the approach of the darkness; and, in the marvellous description in one of his tales of the fusing sensations that follow death, we read that "night arrived; and with its shadows a heavy discomfort. It oppressed my limbs with the oppression of some dull weight, and was palpable. There was also a moaning sound, not unlike the distant reverberation of surf, but more continuous, which, beginning with the first twilight, had grown in strength with the darkness. Suddenly lights were brought into the room . . . and issuing from the flame of each lamp, there flowed unbrokenly into my ears a strain of melodious monotone."

Poe's theory of short-story writing was similar to his theory of verse. "A skilful artist," he writes, "has constructed a tale. If wise, he has not fashioned his thought to accommodate his incidents; but having conceived, with deliberate care, a certain unique or single *effect* to be wrought out, he then invents such incidents—he then combines such events as may best aid him in establishing this preconceived effect." So the real significance of Poe's short stories does not lie in what they purport to relate. Many are confessedly dreams; and, as with dreams, though they seem absurd, their effect on our emotions is serious. And even those that pretend to the logic and the exactitude of actual narratives are, nevertheless, also dreams. The happenings in them differ from the mere macabre surprises and the astonishing adventures and voyages of such imitators of Poe as Conan Doyle. The descent into the maelström is a metaphor for the horror of the moral whirlpool into which, with some justification, Poe had, as we know from more explicit stories, a giddy apprehension of going down; the precariously delayed dissolution of M. Valdemar stands for that horror of living death that figures also in *Premature Burial*, which, arising from whatever blight, haunted Poe through all his later life. No one understood better than Poe that, in fiction and in poetry both, it is not what you say that counts, but what you make the reader feel (he always italicizes the word "effect"); no one understood better than Poe that the deepest psychological truth may be rendered through phantasmagoria. Even the realistic stories of Poe are, in fact, only phantasmagoria of a more circumstantial kind. Any realism of any age which does not convey some such truth is, of course, bound to be unsatisfactory. And today when a revolt is in progress against the literalness and the superficiality of the naturalistic movement that has come between Poe's time and ours, he ought to be of special interest.

"Poe's mentality was a rare synthesis," writes Mr. Padraic Colum. "He had elements in him that corresponded with the indefiniteness of music and the exactitude of mathematics." Is not this what modern literature is tending toward? It was Poe who sent out the bridge from the romanticism of the early nineteenth century to the symbolism of the later; and symbolism, as M. Seylaz points out, though scarcely any of its original exponents survive, now permeates literature. We must not, however, expect that Poe should be admired or understood in his capacity of suspension across this chasm by critics who are hardly aware that either of its banks exists.

December 8, 1926

The Tennessee Poets

I. A Water-Colorist

Mr. John Crowe Ransom is a poet of much charm and a certain amount of originality. The narrative in sonnet sequence which gives its title to his new book—*Two Gentlemen in Bonds*—does not represent him at his best: it is prettily enough done, but all in a vein of rather too mild, too quaint, too sweetly wise irony—an irony somewhat suggestive of Mr. E. A. Robinson, but without the fine and delicately cutting edge which that poet occasionally unsheathes. In general, a cutting edge of some sort is what we chiefly miss in Mr. Ransom. Skillful, agreeable and personal as are the casually broken rhythms of his inveterate iambic pentameter, we come to wish at last that the good-natured iambs, which so easily allow themselves to forfeit the beat of their meter in the interests of a tone of conversation, would decide to set straight their slipped stresses, to vindicate their true accent, and to march, to sound their trumpets or to strike. We have, however, to have had a good deal of Mr. Ransom before we arrive at this state of mind. In the meantime, we can read him with the same sort of pleasure that we get from Edith Sitwell or Wallace Stevens, to whom he is closely akin. Mr. Ransom is not a great poet, but he is a delightful and distinguished one, one of the very few American poets of whom we may be sure that he will never bore us or let us down into banality. His humor and his grace never fail him; and we find in the best of his poetry the light and translucent loveliness—deliciously satisfying and more precious than so much more pretentious work—of a master of water-color:

Go and ask Robin to bring the girls over
To Sweetwater, said my Aunt; and that was why
It was like a dream of ladies sweeping by
The willows, clouds, deep meadowgrass and the river. . . .

Let them alone, dear Aunt, just for one minute
Till I go fishing in the dark of my mind:
Where have I seen before, against the wind,
These bright virgins, robed and bare of bonnet,

Flowing with music of their strange quick tongue
And adventuring with delicate paces by the stream—
Myself a child, old suddenly at the scream
From one of the white throats which it hid among!

February 2, 1927

II. *Fugitives*

This anthology contains a selection from the work of eleven
poets who published for four years in Nashville, Tennessee, a
magazine called *The Fugitive*. Three of them—John Crowe
Ransom, Laura Riding and Donald Davidson—have since
brought out books of their own; and others have become
better known through the appearance of their poems in New
York magazines. But these poets, aside from their individual
merits, have a special importance as a group; and this anthology makes it possible to see how much alike they are, how far
their ideas and their style have been affected by their close association. It may, I suppose, be said that Mr. Ransom was the
leader of the Fugitives; and there is perhaps not one of these
poets who does not seem in some way to derive from him.
What they all have in common with Mr. Ransom are an into-
nation of irony, a "metaphysical" turn and a rich English vocabulary. It is true that these are characteristics which they
share with many other modern poets; but the strength of their
position as a group has enabled them to develop an original
vein of imagery and even a rhythm of their own. They have
constituted an organism vigorous enough to throw off the influence of T. S. Eliot, to which so many other poets have succumbed but of which relatively few traces are to be found in
the work of the Fugitives.

In another respect, also, the Fugitives are interesting in their
group aspect. They are one of the many recent manifestations
of the creative awakening of the South. We had become accustomed in this quarter to old-fashioned florid oratory and early
nineteenth-century romanticism. Not even George W. Cable,
a man of first-rate intelligence and considerable literary ability,
was altogether unaffected by the decomposition of the Southern style; and James Branch Cabell, in transposing it to the

Middle Ages, did not escape its vices. But now, from New
Orleans, from Richmond, from Nashville, from South Carolina
itself, we are beginning to get a new literature that is as free
from the flowers of rhetoric as it is from the formulas of gallantry. It is capable, in fact, as the Fugitives are, of showing itself cruel and astringent. But, although it has sloughed off
these demoded trappings, it has kept much of the grace and
distinction with which they were formerly worn. By reason of
the very slow tempo of the South, its leisured detachment from
the industrial world and the persistence of its local tradition, the
Southern writer at the present time enjoys certain peculiar advantages; and it is possible that the literary South may eventually come to play, in relation to the great centers of the North
and the West, a role in some respects similar to that which
eighteenth-century Ireland has played in relation to London.

The standard of the Fugitives is high. Of the poets who have
not published books, I have found Mr. Allen Tate and Mr.
Robert Penn Warren the most interesting. Mr. Warren, in fact,
gives the impression of being one of the most promising
young poets who have recently appeared on the scene. His
characteristic style is nodulous, tough and tight:

> Of old I know that shore, that dim terrain,
> And know how black and turbulent the blood
> Will beat through iron chambers of the brain.

He is, in fact, we feel, a little *too* tight: we are conscious of the
iron chambers rather than of the blood beating through them.
We suspect that Mr. Warren suffers from a trouble one often
finds in young poets: his mastery of language and his subtlety
of mind seem at the moment developed disproportionately to
his emotions and his ideas, which are still rather vague and immature. This accounts, I believe, for his frequent obscurity.
Some of the poems of Mr. Warren which I most admire—for
example, *Croesus in Autumn*—I have read carefully several
times, yet I cannot really understand them. Lines and images
burn with a life of their own more intense than any life I can
feel informing the poem as a whole—"Now green is blown
and every gold gone sallow"—and I suspect that Mr. Warren's
real poems still remain to be written.

Mr. Allen Tate, however, is older than Mr. Warren, and his

work is quite mature. There is something too much of Eliot in *Causerie II* and an image from Valéry at the end of the *Ode to the Confederate Dead*; but even where Mr. Tate is imitative he possesses a strange originality, a special vein of macabre imagination, a deeply stained color, of his own. What commands our admiration in these two longest of Mr. Tate's poems is his capacity for sustained phrasing—there are no lapses and no blanks, no stop-gaps. But though, line for line, these poems are amazing, they seem, in some way, as wholes, to lack emphasis, to fail of cumulative effect (the *Causerie* especially; the *Ode* somewhat less). In the case of Mr. Tate's shorter poems, however, these objections do not hold. *Mr. Pope, Death of Little Boys* and *Idiot* are like elaborate oriental ornaments which have been produced at an immense expense of materials, patience and cunning skill. We can have them around us and pick them up to examine them again and again, and we find that we do not get tired of them: they are as intricately patterned as cloisonné vases, as heavy as little bronzes (they differ in this from the inveterate lightness, sometimes flimsiness, of John Crowe Ransom). We admire the silver wire embedded in the blue and green enamel and the beautiful polish and glaze; we consider the precious alloy that has gone to make the grotesque image. One could give no idea of these extraordinary poems save by quoting them in their entirety. It is only possible here to include a few striking lines that make their effect by themselves.

Of the urn containing Pope's ashes:

> The urn gets hollow, cobwebs brittle as stones
> Weave to the funeral shell a frivolous rust.

A railroad train:

> Far off, a precise whistle is escheat
> To the dark . . .

A sick child:

> the windowpane extends a fear to you
> From one peeled aster drenched with the wind all day.

March 7, 1928

The Muses Out of Work

WHEN one looks back on the American poetry of the season, one is aware of only two events which emerge as of the first interest: *The King's Henchman* by Miss Edna St. Vincent Millay and *White Buildings* by Mr. Hart Crane. Mr. E. A. Robinson's *Tristram* has been extravagantly admired in some quarters; but, though it is undoubtedly more easily readable than his other Arthurian poems, though it contains a better story more energetically told and though it is by no means poor in those flashes of moral vision that make the weaker poems of Robinson more interesting than the strongest of a good many of his contemporaries, it seems to me that these luminosities are too low-burning and evanescent to justify the whole of a long narrative that reads at its worst like a movie scenario and at its best like a novel of adultery of the nineties, full of long well-bred conversations of which the metaphysical archness sounds peculiarly incongruous in the mouths of the heroes of medieval legend. What is admirable about *Tristram* is that now, after so many years during which Mr. Robinson's work has been growing more and more spectral, he should suddenly come to life to write a poem with so much vividness and animation, if not precisely with much poetic reality or much poetic art. But, with all respect for a fine poet and for one of the most honorably won of our contemporary reputations, I would still exchange the whole of Mr. Robinson's Arthurian cycle, with its conventional romantic stage properties of castles and seas and wars and its false starts at passionate expression always foundering in "before we knew what we were yet to see" or "until we saw as far as we should know," for one of his New England elegies. Miss Millay's poetic drama (which in its published form is considerably longer than the libretto used for the opera) has a theme very much like Mr. Robinson's and, though she treats it but little less conventionally, gets out of it better poetry. Miss Millay has an instinct for drama, but not much imagination for character; and, in writing *The King's Henchman*, she seems to have been somewhat hampered by the traditions and the requirements of the opera libretto. Nor do I think her last act so effective as her situation warrants. But the *Henchman*, in point of style, is remarkably well-sustained and quite out of the class of her other plays: the language remains simple without ever ceasing to be personal, terse and, as it were, well-seasoned. And at its high point, in the love scene of the second act, Miss Millay, instead of merely allowing her lovers, as Mr. Robinson does, to debate about their love at length, is able to find for their emotions an equivalent in poetic music.

It is precisely to this mastery of Miss Millay's of the music of English verse that she owes her present preëminence (not that Mr. Robinson is not himself sometimes a master of this, but his music is mostly confined to the pathetic or ironic "dying fall"). The imagist movement, it seems to me, has caused to be accepted in America an entirely inadequate ideal of what poetry ought to be: the imagist poets have popularized a sort of surface-poetry, poetry of description, poetry for the eye—the poetry of Amy Lowell, Mr. Sandburg and Mr. Fletcher—a poetry that is based on the cadences of prose and that is full of flat prose vowels. A few years ago, the writer was discussing English poetry with a number of young men, all of them persons of reading and taste and one of them a distinguished follower of the imagist tradition: it appeared, in the course of the conversation, that none of them had any use for Milton. When one confronted them with particular passages, the reason became quite plain: they were tone-deaf to Milton's effects. Compelled to apprehend *Paradise Lost* through the eye and the intellect alone, they could see nothing in the most splendid passages but the bad taste of mixed mythology, the dreariness of obsolete theology, the clumsiness of an inexact imagination and the affectation of a tortured tongue. Wordsworth fared even worse: they thought Wordsworth about the same thing as Longfellow. They could not *hear* the difference between Wordsworth and Longfellow any more than they could hear the kinship between Wordsworth and Milton. The influence of the imagist school has done much to deprive American poetry, as it were, of the dimension of sound. And the dangerous example of Walt Whitman (himself a very great poet) has, paradoxically, rendered it more prosaic: in borrowing from Whitman, his followers seem never to appropriate anything but the formulas of Whitmanesque rhapsody and, for the most part, to have remained insensible to the extraordinary musical gift which makes the best of his long poems symphonic and which enables him, in rendering bird-song, to hit, not merely upon lyrical rhythms but even upon sound-combinations surprisingly similar to those that Aristophanes had found in *The Birds* to mimic the nightingale.* To look only at the poetry of the present season, the work of Miss Lola Ridge, Mr. James Rorty, Mr. Virgil Geddes and Mr. Eugene Jolas all, in one way or another, show evidence of this untuning of verse. Now, Miss Millay, who is perhaps a little deficient in visual imagination, writes verse as a pupil of Shakespeare and Bach; and, in the second act of *The King's Henchman*, as a pupil not unworthy of her masters. In the exquisite music of the love scene, at once so irregular and so smoothly running, at once so exact and so free, she has reached one of the high points of her poetry. It is the magic strain that strikes our ear, seeming wordlessly—by the very clear outline of its phrases, the definiteness of its images—to convey the exaltation of young first love, all its awkwardness turned to beauty.

As for Mr. Hart Crane, he is a singular case; he, too, commands a diapason. But it is a diapason of which the phrases are anything but clearly outlined, the images anything but definite. Mr. Crane has a most remarkable style, a style that is strikingly original—almost something like a great style, if there could be such a thing as a great style which was, not merely not applied to a great subject, but not, so far as one can see, applied to any subject at all. Mr. Crane's "corymbulous formations of mechanics—Who hurried the hill breezes, spouting malice Plangent over meadows" and his "great wink of eternity, Of rimless floods, unfettered leewardings, Samite sheeted and processioned" remind us a little of the poet Chivers, from whom Poe borrowed his later style and who wrote of "cataracts of adamant uplifted into mountains" and of "the rising golden glory of the sun in ministrations, Making oceans metropolitan of splendor for the dawn." One does not demand nowadays of poetry that it provide us with logical metaphors or with an intelligible sequence of ideas: Rimbaud is inconsecutive, his im-

---

*Compare the passages of bird-song in *Out of the Cradle Endlessly Rocking* with *The Birds*, 676-684.

agery is sometimes confused. Yet, with Rimbaud, whom Mr. Crane a little resembles, we experience intense emotional excitement and artistic satisfaction; we are dazzled by the eruption of his images, but we divine what it is he is saying. With Mr. Crane, though he can sometimes move us, the emotion is oddly vague:

> Still fervid covenant, Belle Isle,
> —Unfolding floating daïs before
> Which rainbows twine continual hair—
> Belle Isle, white echo of the oar!
>
> The imaged Word, it is, that holds
> Hushed willows anchored in its glow.
> It is the unbetrayable reply
> Whose accent no farewell can know.

Lines even so explicit as these are rare with Mr. Crane. His poetry is a *disponible*, as they say about French troops. We are eagerly waiting to see to which part of the front he will move it: just at present, it is killing time in the cafés behind the lines.

This development of language beyond its theme is characteristic of a whole group of contemporary American poets. Among writers who have published volumes in the course of the present season, one may cite Mr. John Crowe Ransom, Mr. Foster Damon, Mr. Maxwell Bodenheim and Mr. Archibald MacLeish. Each of these, in greater or less degree, is an example of distinguished style or inventive language in the service of a soul which, at least at the moment, does not strike us as sufficiently interesting. Mr. Ransom is much the best of these —I have paid my respects to him elsewhere—but for so subtle and brilliant a writer, the impression he makes upon us is singularly mild. Mr. Bodenheim's new volume, *Returning to Emotion*, seems to me to have many ingenious figures, but little more emotion than his previous ones (yet Mr. Bodenheim is a poet, and, though his books are rather disappointing when we set out to read them through, he appears to excellent advantage in the selection made by Conrad Aiken for the anthology called *Modern American Poetry* in the Modern Library Series). And Mr. MacLeish, though he is polished and lettered where Mr. Crane is careless and wilful, presents also a case of a fine style which has not yet been called to the front. Mr. MacLeish simply now writes well as a poet of the age of Eliot where he formerly, when he was first out of Yale, wrote well, if I am not mistaken, as a poet of the age of Masefield. He fails completely, in his present phase, to convince one of the moral necessity of his desperate invocation of the void (he is perhaps at his best in his satires and trifles): it is the literary fashion which has changed and not Mr. MacLeish who has grown, who has found his poetic identity. He writes admirable English verse: his instrument is of the very best make; but, emotionally and intellectually, I fear that a good deal of the time he is talking through his new hat. The influence of T. S. Eliot seems to have its unfortunate side: it is making the young men prematurely senile. It was bad enough for Mr. Eliot to imagine himself Gerontion at thirty, but with him the state of mind was real and the poetry had its poignancy; with his followers, it is largely a pose.

In connection with a good deal of the American poetry of the kind I have discussed above, one gets the impression that, if it is true that the manner of it is often more interesting than the matter, this is perhaps because the poets themselves do not lead very interesting lives. Does it really constitute a career for a man to do nothing but write lyric poetry? Can such a man expect the world to be concerned with what he has to say? In certain cases, such a career may justify itself. But more often, I believe, it fails to. Think of the poets of Johnson's *Lives*— almost all of them clergymen, physicians, ambassadors, statesmen or courtiers. Waller sat in Parliament and engineered a Royalist plot; Milton was Cromwell's Latin secretary and narrowly escaped the scaffold at the time of the Restoration; Prior was ambassador to France and took part in negotiating the Treaty of Utrecht. These three poets, in everything else so different from one another, have it in common that their work is distinguished by an interest in public affairs and a large experience of the world. Even in the case of those poets who, in the Rome of Virgil and Horace as well in the England and France of the seventeenth century, played no active part in the life of their time, they benefited much by their contact with the Court, where the civilization of the age had in some respects been brought to its highest point and where the problems of the day were in the air. It is no doubt partly the fault of the American world that the poet has no share in its affairs: politics is unattractive to people of the quality of intelligence that is needed for the writing of poetry; the specialization and high pressure of the professions make the cultivation of literature difficult; and a central social point of vantage from which all the activities of the time may be more or less surveyed-—as from Paris, London or Rome—is for the United States apparently impossible. But the writer, from his experience of poetry and poets, has finally been brought to the conclusion that a young poet in America should not be advised at the outset to give up all for the Muse—to seclude himself in the country, to live from hand to mouth in Greenwich Village or to escape to the Riviera. I should not advise him even to become a magazine editor or to work in a publisher's office. The poet would do better to study a profession, to become a banker or a public official or even to go in for the movies. What is wrong with the younger American poets is that they have no real stake in society. One does not want them to succumb to society; but one *would* like to see them, at least, have some sort of relation to it. If the relation is an uncomfortable or a quarrelsome one, so much, perhaps, the better. As it is, the conflicts of feeling and the criticism of society are left largely to the novelists and the dramatists; and the poets content themselves with expressing the chagrin of sterility. Those who admire Yeats and who have put themselves to school to him would do well to consider how much of his strength is derived from his identification of his own aims with those of his people and party. It is perhaps only the political partisan, like Yeats—or like Dante—who has the right to be disillusioned with politics; as it is perhaps only the man of the world, like Catullus or like Byron, who has the right to be insolent to the great.

One of the ways in which American poets—the poets of the opposite camp from those I have just been discussing—do try to establish themselves in some sort of solidarity with society is by trying to immerse themselves, usually by way of Carl Sandburg and Walt Whitman, in the common life of their time. Mr. James Rorty has tried to do this and, to the writer's mind, has failed: his Canadian and Californian "landscapes" are charming, a really fresh and agreeable poetry of the West; but as a prophet of the *New Masses*, Mr. Rorty will convince nobody. Mr. Rorty is at home, and a poet, in the solitudes of the mountains and the prairies, but not yet among the crowds. Mr. Eugene Jolas, in *Cinema*, approaches the vulgar life of America, not through Sandburg and Whitman, but by way of Guillaume Apollinaire and the other up-to-date French fanciers of American skyscrapers and movies; but, on the whole, for all his bold and pyrotechnic images, he seems to write of American life from the outside, better informed than his European masters, but still preoccupied with the phenomena of the surface. (Mr. Jolas is, however, quite successful in writing about railroad journeys.) I do not, of course, disapprove of the policy these poets have followed. I am merely discussing the degrees of success attained by particular poets. And before passing on from this school, I should like to call attention to the very individual work of Mr. Kenneth Fearing which has been appearing in the *New Masses*. Mr. Fearing seems the most promising hard-boiled poet of the younger generation. He has an original flavor and accent and what seems a true intensity. One hopes that he will soon publish a book.

Two poets of this recent lot deserve a separate mention: Mr. Scudder Middleton, author of *Upper Night*, and Mr. Mark Van Doren, author of *7 P.M.* Though neither has a very wide range, both possess musical instruments: they practise English poetry successfully. Neither one is either an eccentric or a follower of the literary fashion; and both seem to write their poetry "on the side," as a natural function of lives that are well occupied with other matters. These other matters do not in themselves appear to be particularly stimulating: Mr. Van Doren conveys an impression of amiable reflective well-being and Mr. Middleton presents an attitude of slightly frustrated equanimity which are perhaps characteristic, in America, of the milieux in which one finds people at once comfortable and sensitive and cultivated. But this poetry in its kind is authentic. Mr. Middleton's *Children of Blossom* and *Burial* and Mr. Van Doren's *7 P.M.*, *Apple-Hell* and *The Crime* are among the best things of the season.

*

If it is true, as I have suggested, that some of the most gifted of American poets might become even better worth reading if they did not make the writing of poetry their only serious occupation, it is possible that we have here an explanation of the fact that in the United States the women who are writing poetry seem, in certain ways, more interesting than the men. Merely to be a woman is, as a rule, a career in itself, of which her poetry is bound to be a by-product, but a by-product that may reflect fundamentals. I have spoken above of Miss Edna Millay; Miss Léonie Adams, in the past year, has published in magazines a considerable amount of work brilliantly up to her best; and Miss Louise Bogan, a set of poems which surpass her best previous work. Miss Laura Gottschalk of the Fugitives group has brought out a first volume of verse, metaphysical rather than passionate, but distinguished by a fancy and an irony of a highly personal kind.

The writer has been sometimes accused of overrating the more popular irony of Mrs. Dorothy Parker. It is true that Mrs. Parker's epigrams have the accent of the Hotel Algonquin rather than that of the coffee houses of the eighteenth century. But I believe that, if we admire, as it is fashionable to do, the light verse of Prior and Gay, we should admire Mrs. Parker also. She writes well: her wit is the wit of her particular time and place, but it is often as cleanly economic at the same time that it is as flatly brutal as the wit of the age of Pope; and, within its small scope, it is a criticism of life. It has its roots in contemporary reality, and that is what I am pleading for in poetry.

May 11, 1927

This article, which appeared in the *New Republic*, was not very well received by some of the poets discussed. Hart Crane, when he read it—as later appeared in Philip Horton's biography of him—wrote to Yvor Winters as follows:

"You need a good drubbing for all your recent easy talk about the 'complete man,' the poet and his ethical place in society, etc. . . . Wilson's article was just half-baked enough to make one warm around the collar. It is so damned easy for such as he, born into easy means, graduated from a fashionable university into a critical chair overlooking Washington Square, etc., to sit tight and hatch little squibs of advice to poets not to be so 'professional' as he claims they are, as though all the names he had just mentioned had been as suavely nourished as he—as though four out of five of them hadn't been damned well forced the major part of their lives to grub at *any* kind of work they could manage by hook or crook and the fear of hell to secure! Yes, why not step into the State Department and join the diplomatic corps for a change! Indeed, or some other courtly occupation which would bring you into wide and active contact with world affairs! As a matter of fact, I'm all too ready to concede that there are several other careers more engaging to follow than that of poetry. But the circumstances of one's birth, the conduct of one's parents, the current economic structure of society and a thousand other local factors have as much or more to say about successions to such occupations, the naïve volitions of the poet to the contrary. I agree with you, of course, that the poet should in as large a measure as possible adjust himself to society. But the question always will remain as to how far the conscience is justified in compromising with the age's demands."

Mr. John Crowe Ransom addressed a letter to the *New Republic*, which was published in part, with a reply by me, in the issue of July 22, 1927:

Sir: I address myself not to the editorial godhead in its indivisible oneness, but to the portion incarnated recently by Mr. Edmund Wilson, whose *The Muses Out of Work* appeared in the issue of May 11.

Your taste in poetry seems to me admirable; which means, of course, that your likes and dislikes among the poets of the season are much the same as mine. In fact, I admire your natural taste all the more, since your reasoning, by which you go through the motions of fortifying your judgment, seems to me brutal and absurd. May I review your achievement? It is my thesis that you judge well of poetry without knowing why you judge, and that you invite the world to judge of poetry on grounds which are thoroughly insufficient.

You undertake to review the season's poetry according to a single consideration, which you phrase in several ways: Poetry must "have its roots in contemporary reality"; its theme must be important and contemporary; its tone must indicate that the poet "has a stake in society," leads "an interesting life," and has a successful "career," of which the poetry is strictly the by-product.

Permit me to observe that in hardly a single instance has this principle permitted you to make an aesthetic judgment.

Certainly you do not apply it to Miss Millay's poetry. You prefer to ascribe her preëminence to a very different principle (which seems also to be highly dubious): "precisely to her mastery of the music of English verse." Your liking for her verse was in defiance of your doctrine, which she violated. Personally, I was astonished when I heard that the great American opera had at last come to pass with a libretto that harked clear back to the Anglo-Saxon; you must have been appalled, with your bias in favor of the Hotel Algonquin; but, not sharing your bias, I did not have to share your embarrassment, and could honor *The King's Henchman* without damaging a pet theory. That you, too, honored it, under the circumstances, shows a magnanimity.

You do not seriously apply it to Mr. Robinson's *Tristram*, which just as plainly is a poet's abnegation of the contemporary reality.

You are on the point of applying it to Mr. Hart Crane's *White Buildings*, but again you save yourself; what you admire there you do not succeed in saying, but it is despite the fact that you remark the poet's lack of a satisfactory contemporary theme.

You seem to apply it with favorable results to Mr. Van Doren's *7 P.M.*, forgetting that you have just now disqualified him with the stipulation that the "career" you have in mind for the poet must not include the career of an editor.

You do not apply it anywhere very thoroughly, and the fact is to your credit. It is a village schoolmaster's principle, and requires you to be presumptuous every time you apply it in an unfavorable sense, and you very decently prefer to be evasive for the most part, and let the principle go.

In opposition to your principle, I venture to submit a counter set of related propositions. Poetry is automatically and inevitably contemporary, and in reflecting the most actual and important experiences of the poet reflects indubitable contemporary data. Sometimes its comments upon these data are direct, and sometimes they are by way of indirection; and the latter case is not the less significant, though it is the more difficult for the critical analysis. The prime virtue of poetry as a contemporary document is not its directness, in which it is greatly exceeded by prose, but its sincerity, in which it is reputed to have no equals. There is as much of the poet in a *King's Henchman* as in a *Figs from Thistles*, and vice versa. It is impossible to find in the surface "theme" of a poem any index to the degree of the poet's emotional excitement, since any theme pursued far enough involves the poet's whole mind and all his experience. The "interest" which attaches to a poet's theme is fundamentally the poet's interest, and the single isolated critic is in no better position than the poet to determine whether this is a universal interest; that question must hang in the balance for the process of time to bring to an answer.

These propositions I cannot here contend for; they seem to me to be very nearly axiomatic for critical theory. The general doctrine might be called a Critical Positivism: it is deeply informed with the conviction that critics must renounce their a priori formulas and their ex-cathedra manners. They must prepare themselves to admit that their formulas will never fully explain the poem, and will probably not even fully explain their judgment of the poem. . . .

John Crowe Ransom

Nashville, Tennessee

Mr. Ransom has misunderstood me—perhaps I should have stated my position more explicitly. In the first place, I did not "undertake to review the season's poetry according to a single consideration"—that the poet should "have a stake in society," etc. This—like my remarks on "the music of English verse"—were not definitive critical principles, but merely reflections by the way. I am well aware that no set of critical formulas can ever succeed in explaining a poem, and I do not pretend that my own primary judgments as to what is good poetry or what is not are anything other, in the last analysis, than mysterious emotional responses. In any field of literature, however, it is possible, and perhaps profitable, to speculate as to what makes certain productions more satisfactory than others. As for the question of "a stake in society," I never either made such a statement or went upon such an assumption as Mr. Ransom takes for granted on my part: I quite agree with him that the reality and the intensity of the experience which has gone to make a poem, and the excellence of the poem, are not at all to be measured by the contemporaneity of the subject or the form. I have no a priori objections to any sort of subject or form whatever—not even to the Arthurian legends. My contention was simply that the work of certain poets—among whom I did not include Mr. Robinson or Miss Millay—granting them whatever settings and puppets or whatever veins of imagery were congenial to their various temperaments, did not seem to be drawn from a particularly deep or a particularly interesting experience. If I had meant what Mr. Ransom thinks I meant, I should scarcely have spoken with admiration of Milton: Milton's personal emotional experience and his experience of the contemporary world both play prominent parts in his poetry, but the "surface theme" of *Paradise Lost*, for example, relating as it does to the Garden of Eden, is anything but contemporaneous.   E.W.

Upton Sinclair's 'Mammonart'

M R. UPTON SINCLAIR, having supplied successively economic interpretations of American journalism, American religion and American education, has undertaken, in his new book *Mammonart: An Essay in Economic Interpretation*, to perform the same service for literature and art. "It is my intention," he writes, "to study these artists from a point of view so far as I know entirely new. . . . The book will present an interpretation of the arts from the point of view of the class struggle." One does not see how Mr. Sinclair, who has been intimately associated for so many years with radical ideas and literature, can imagine that this point of view is new. On the contrary, it has become so familiar that, as soon as we have learned what his book is about, we can predict almost exactly what we shall find in it—even though we may be unprepared for the extreme results in certain cases of the author's application of his point of view. Here, for example, is Mr. Sinclair's economic interpretation of *Kubla Khan*: "Note that every one of these images appeals to reactionary emotions, fear or sensuality. By sensuality the reason is dragged from its throne; while fear destroys all activity of the mind, causing abasement and submission. Moreover—and here is the point essential to our argument—almost every image in this poem turns out on examination to be a lie. There is no such place as Xanadu; and Kubla Khan has nothing to teach us but avoidance. His pleasures were bloody and infamous, and there was nothing 'stately' about his 'pleasure-dome.' There never was a river Alph, and the sacredness of any river is a fiction of a priestly caste, preying on the people. There are no 'caverns measureless to man'; while as for a 'sunless sea,' a few arc-lights would solve the problem. The 'woman wailing for her demon lover' is a savage's nightmare; while as for the 'Abyssinian maid,' she would have her teeth blackened and would stink of rancid palm oil. From the beginning to the end, the poem deals with things which are sensual, cruel and fatal to hope."

It would, however, be unjust to Mr. Sinclair to suggest that he does not appreciate *Kubla Khan*. It is true that he announces his intention of proving that "present-day technique is far and away superior to the technique of any art period preceding" and that he attempts to do so by comparing a sonnet of Milton's to one by Mr. Clement Wood to the disadvantage of the former. But, whatever Mr. Sinclair may say for the good of the socialist cause, he has a real appreciation of literature and this somewhat interferes with his indictment. In *The Brass Check*, his book on journalism, he set out to expose a field of which he had had little inside experience and for which he felt, in consequence, no sympathy; but he is dealing in *Mammonart* with the products of his own craft, and the result, from the doctrinaire point of view, is one of the least effective of his books.

Bernard Shaw, with his more rigorous mind, has made a similar revaluation of literature, but he carried it through more logically. He began by assigning all literary works to either one of two departments, according to whether these works were or were not designed to ameliorate social conditions; and he laid down the uncompromising principle that, artistic merits being equal, the second was inferior to the first. But Upton Sinclair has not based his discussion upon any such clear proposition—which at least keeps the artistic question distinct from the moral one. He has tried to write a treatise on art which should function as a socialist tract by asserting that "all art is propaganda" and then justifying this assertion by assuming that any work of art which implies a philosophy, a point of view or even a sensation or an impulse is a piece of propaganda in favor of it. Since no human work can exist that does not rest on some sort of assumptions on the part of the person who produced it, Mr. Sinclair can make out a case; but his book, as a socialist exposé, is by no means the bombshell he has promised. What he has written is an outline of literature (since he has little to say about the other arts) by an able pamphleteer with a real taste for books but some moral and political prejudices which do not seem to prevent his enjoying certain works that run counter to these prejudices but which at least make him protest that he shouldn't. As such an outline, *Mammonart*—at any rate, the latter part—is not at all bad. Mr. Sinclair's memory occasionally lets him down, as when, evidently confusing Paul of Tarsus with the fourth-century Saint Paulinus, he tells us that Saint

Paul was "a renegade Roman gentleman and former official of the empire" and writes scathingly of Thackeray's sentimentalizing over the death of Major Pendennis under the impression that Major Pendennis died the death of Colonel Newcome. But, on the whole, he is quite well-informed as to history and literature and knows how to place the writers with whom he deals in relation to the life of their times. He is particularly interesting in his treatment of the American writers of the last generation. Mr. Sinclair is himself a survivor of the era of Frank Norris and Richard Harding Davis, and his account of this is probably unique in its combination of inside knowledge with unorthodox point of view. On Jack London, whom he knew well, he is especially illuminating. One has seen, in fact, a good many less readable and less intelligent literary histories than this of Upton Sinclair. Intending, in his role of political oracle, a devastating social criticism, what he has given us, in his character of literary man, is a book that stimulates one's interest in the arts of God and Mammon both.

What is vulnerable in *Mammonart* is the thinking of Upton Sinclair rather than his literary taste. If, for example, he had begun by reflecting what *Art for Art's sake* really means, he would not have felt obliged to denounce it from beginning to end of his book. *Art for Art's sake*—an excellent slogan—means simply that the artist has the right to practice his art with a view to the perfection of his own kind of product—that he should not be expected to meet the requirements of specialists of other kinds. If somebody, that is to say, is constructing from the phenomena of experience a satisfactory artistic system, it should not be demanded of him that he construct either a political or a moral system, and the critic should not take him to task if his pattern fails to match the patterns of other people's political and moral systems. The artist has his own technique for formulating his vision of truth, and he cannot be expected to worry about the constructions of other people who are working in different materials. Mr. Sinclair comes quite close to this point of view when he writes in connection with Strindberg: "Let the artist give us truth, and we can always find use for it." And I suppose he would not oppose a program of *Mathematics for Mathematics' sake*. He speaks somewhere with admiration of the achievements of modern physics. Yet if mathematicians had not been permitted to indulge in *Mathematics for Mathematics' sake*, these discoveries would have been impossible. When Karl Friedrich Gauss worked out his fourth-dimensional coördinates, he was engaged in a speculation which not only was quite devoid of political or moral significance but did not even appear at the time to be susceptible of practical application. Yet it was precisely by the aid of these exercises in pure mathematics and of others in the same direction that Einstein arrived at his new discoveries; and it is in the light of Einstein's discoveries that Mr. Sinclair's physicists in California are conducting their researches into the structure of the atom. A work of pure literature of which Mr. Sinclair disapproves is Gautier's *Émaux et Camées*. I take it that he would like to discourage the writing of any more such books. But how can he be sure that putting an end to writers of the type of Gautier might not mean inflicting on literary culture the same sort of injury that would have been inflicted on mathematical and physical culture if Gauss's experiments had been prevented? One of the first rules of civilization should be freedom for the artist and the scientist, and for every other kind of intellectual creator, to pursue his own researches and produce his own kind of work. If the Socialist Coöperative Commonwealth to which Mr. Sinclair looks forward is going to interfere with this, it is difficult to see how its culture will deserve to be considered superior to our own individualist one.

April 22, 1925

'The Pilgrimage of Henry James'

I T IS becoming a commonplace to say of Mr. Van Wyck
Brooks that he is really a social historian rather than a literary critic, but one cannot avoid raising the question in connection with his new book. *The Pilgrimage of Henry James*, like
The Ordeal of Mark Twain, is a page of American social history:
in it, Henry James figures as the type of sensitive and imaginative American who, in the later nineteenth century, found the
United States too barren and too crude for him and sought a
more congenial environment in Europe. Mr. Brooks points
out James's original isolation as the son of the elder Henry
James, that well-to-do wandering philosopher who travelled
back and forth between Boston and New York, between the
United States and Europe, without finding himself quite at
home anywhere; and he traces James's first saturation with European impressions during the formative years of his teens; his
attempt at the beginning of his career to establish himself in
America as an American novelist working with native material;
his discouragement, his longing for Europe, his experiments
with France and Italy and his dissatisfaction with his life there;
his decision to live permanently in England and to find a field
for his art in the depiction of English society; his failure, after
years of living among them, to establish intimate relations with
the English and his disillusioned reaction against them; the
bankruptcy of his imagination, his homesickness and his visit
to the United States; his consternation and despair at the spectacle of modern America, and his final return to England. In
short, Henry James's tragedy, according to Mr. Brooks, was
that of the literary artist who has lost contact with his own society without having been able to strike roots in any other.
And of all this aspect of James's career he has given the most
intelligent and the most exhaustive account that we have yet
had; in fact, it may be said that James's social significance and
the part that his social situation plays in his work have here
been properly appreciated for the first time. Mr. Brooks has
made a contribution of permanent value toward the criticism
of Henry James. He has interpreted the complex subject with

all his incomparable instinct for divining the feelings and motives of Americans, for getting under their skins; and he has presented his logical theory with the consummate orderliness, neatness and point that he always brings to making out a case. When, for example, he disentangles James's reasons for turning playwright at one period of his career, he generates a kind of excitement in the process of demonstration that seems almost to be independent of the interest of what is being demonstrated. And he has reduced the whole to an entertaining narrative colored by imagination and written with grace. From the point of view of literary form, Mr. Brooks's *Henry James* is, in fact, probably the best of his books.

Where the book is unsatisfactory is in its failure to recognize the real nature and development of James's art. Mr. Brooks has completely subordinated Henry James the artist to Henry James the social symbol, with the result that James's literary work, instead of being considered in its integrity on its own merits, has undergone a process of lopping and distortion to make it fit the Procrustes bed of a thesis. According to Mr. Brooks's simplification, Henry James was at first a very good novelist and then, later on, a very bad one. Mr. Brooks admires James's earlier fiction as a Turgenev-like social document and writes a warm appreciation of it—that is, he admires James in direct proportion as James performs the same sort of function as Mr. Brooks himself. But what he says, in effect, is that, after the publication of *The Bostonians* in 1886, James's artistic record is an almost total blank: when James had settled in England and had used up his American impressions, his failure to make anything of his English material was virtually complete. Mr. Brooks here lumps together the work of thirty years and, in the interest of an a priori theory, refuses to admit distinctions among some thirty volumes of fiction of widely differing character and merit. The truth is that the work of James's English residence falls into three distinct periods. During the second of these—after *The Bostonians* and while he is already dealing chiefly with English material—he reaches what seems to me indisputably his completest artistic maturity: he has got over a certain stiffness, a certain naïveté, which characterized his earlier work and he has acquired a new flexibility and a personal idiom. He has come for the first time into the full possession of his language and form, and he has not yet lost any of the vividness of his youthful imagination. He has ten years ahead of him still before that imagination will begin to show signs of flagging in such books as *The Awkward Age*, and longer still before that style runs to seed in the thickets of the later novels. In the meantime, in the fiction of this period—particularly, perhaps, in the shorter novels which were characteristic of it: *What Maisie Knew*, *The Aspern Papers*, etc.—he is to produce what seems to the present writer his most satisfactory and distinguished work. As for the deterioration which afterwards sets in, it is to be ascribed chiefly to advancing age. An important thing to remember in connection with James's latest novels—which Mr. Brooks treats with such severity—is that *The Ambassadors*, *The Wings of the Dove* and *The Golden Bowl* were all written when James was in his late fifties. Their abstraction, their comparative dimness and their exaggerated mannerisms are such as not infrequently appear in the work of an artist's later years. George Meredith and Robert Browning, who did not labor under the handicap of being expatriated Americans, developed somewhat similar traits. These later novels of James are, in any case, not as Mr. Brooks asserts, fundamentally unreal and weak. Intellectually, they are perhaps the most vigorous, the most heroically conceived, of his fictions; but they are like tapestries from which, though the design and the figures still remain masterfully outlined, the colors are fading out.

When all this has been said, however, there still confronts us, in connection with James, the question of a lack in his work of direct emotional experience—a lack which is naturally felt more disconcertingly in his later than in his earlier books, since it is less easily comprehensible in a mature than in a callow man. One can agree here with Mr. Brooks that this insufficient experience of personal relations may be partly accounted for by James's isolation among the English. Yet to throw all the emphasis thus on James's social situation, as Mr. Brooks seems to do, is surely to proceed from the wrong direction. James's solitude, his emotional starvation, his inhibitions against entering into life, were evidently the result of his fundamental moral character, not merely an accident of his social maladjustment; and with the problem of that fundamental character Mr.

Brooks never adequately deals. "An immortal symbol," he sums James up, "the embodiment of that impossible yearning of which Hawthorne somewhere speaks—the yearning of the American in the Old World" for the past from which he has been separated. But this theory that a man's whole career may hinge on his yearning for the European past is humanly unconvincing.

It is precisely because Mr. Brooks's interest is all social and never moral that he has missed the point of James's art. It is possible for him to find James's work so empty and disappointing only because he insists on comparing it with that of writers with whom James has little in common: Hardy, Dickens, Tolstoy and Balzac. One would be in a position to appreciate James better if one compared him with the dramatists of the seventeenth century—Racine and Molière, whom he resembles in form as well as in point of view, and even Shakespeare, when allowance has been made for the most extreme differences in subject and form. These poets are not, like Dickens and Hardy, writers of melodrama—either humorous or pessimistic, nor secretaries of society like Balzac, nor prophets like Tolstoy: they are occupied simply with the presentation of conflicts of moral character, which they do not concern themselves about softening or averting. They do not indict society for these situations: they regard them as universal and inevitable. They do not even blame God for allowing them: they accept them as the conditions of life. Titus and Bérénice, Alceste and Célimène, Antony and Octavius—these are forces which, once set in motion, are doomed to irreconcilable opposition. The dramatist makes no attempt to decide between competing interests: he is content to understand his characters and to put their behavior before us.

Now, it was James's immense distinction to have brought to contemporary life something of this "classical" point of view. The conflicts in his early novels are likely to be presented in terms of European manners and morals at odds with American ones—with a predisposition in favor of the latter. But later on, James's contrasts tend to take on a different aspect: they represent, not merely national divergences, but antagonisms of ideals and temperaments of a kind that may occur anywhere. I cannot agree with Mr. Brooks when he says that in James's

later novels "the 'low sneaks' have it all their own way . . .
the subtle are always the prey of the gross . . . the pure in
heart are always at the mercy of those that work iniquity." On
the contrary, the leaning toward melodrama that allowed James
in his earlier novels to play virtuous Americans off against
scoundrelly Europeans has almost entirely disappeared. *The
Ambassadors* is obviously a sort of attempt to re-do the theme
of *The American*, as *The Wings of the Dove* is to re-do that of
The Portrait of a Lady, but one has only to compare the two
pairs of books to realize that James no longer sees life in terms
of the innocent and the guilty. The Bellegarde family in the
earlier novel are cold-blooded and impenitent villains, whereas
Mme. de Vionnet, who plays a somewhat similar role in *The
Ambassadors*, is shown in as attractive a light as the American
to whom she is morally opposed; in the same way Gilbert Os-
mond and his mistress, who make Isabel Archer miserable, are
a good deal more theatrical than Kate Croy and her lover, who
try to exploit Milly Theale. Mr. Brooks's account of *The Wings
of the Dove* seems almost perversely unintelligent. He melodra-
matically describes Milly Theale as the "victim of the basest
plot that ever a mind conceived"; yet one of the most remarkable things about *The Wings of the Dove* is the way in which,
from the very first pages, Henry James succeeds in making us
sympathize with the author of this unquestionably ignoble
plot, in making us feel that what she does is inevitable. Kate
Croy, though hard and crass, is striving for the highest aspirations she is capable of understanding, just as the more fastidious Milly is.

It is thus, in James's later novels, not a case of the pure in
heart invariably falling a prey to the guilty, of the low sneaks
having it their own way. It is simply a struggle between different kinds of people with different kinds of needs. I do not
know what Mr. Brooks means when he writes of "the constant
abrogation of James's moral judgment, in these years of an enchanted exile in a museum-world" nor when he says that
James "had seen life, in his own way, as all the great novelists
have seen it, *sub specie aeternitatis*; he was to see it henceforth,
increasingly, *sub specie mundi*." On the contrary, James, in his
later works, is just as much concerned with moral problems,
and he is able to see all around them as he has not been able to

do before. He has come to be occupied here even more than in his earlier work with what seem to him the irremediable antagonisms of interest between people who enjoy themselves without inhibitions, who take all they can get from life, and people who are curbed by scruples of aesthetic taste as well as of morality from following all their impulses and satisfying all their appetites—between the worldly, the selfish, the "splendid," and the dutiful, the sensitive, the humble. This humility, this moral rectitude takes on in Henry James the aspect of a moral beauty which he opposes, as it were, to the worldly kind; both kinds of beauty attract him, he understands the points of view of the devotees of both, but it is one of his deepest convictions that you cannot have both at the same time. The point of *What Maisie Knew*, for example, lies in the contrast between Maisie's other guardians—the vivid, the charming or the bold —who live only for their own pleasure and advantage and refuse to be bothered with her, and Mrs. Wix, the ridiculous old governess, who, by reason of her possession of a "moral sense," is left with the responsibility of Maisie, "to work her fingers to the bone." So, in *The Golden Bowl*, the brilliant figures of Charlotte and the Prince are contrasted with the unselfishness and the comparative dreariness of Maggie Verver and her father. Almost all Henry James's later novels, in one way or another, illustrate this theme. Surely this, and not, as Mr. Brooks suggests, any mere technical pattern, is that "figure in the carpet" that is hinted at in the famous short story; and in this tendency to oppose the idea of a good conscience to the idea of doing what one likes—wearing, as it does so often in James, the aspect of American versus European— there is evidently a Puritan survival that Mr. Brooks, in his capacity as specialist in American habits of thought, might have been expected to treat more prominently. As it is, he only touches upon it by way of a different route.

Of Mr. Brooks's queer use of his documents for the purpose of proving the artistic nullity of the latter half of James's career, many instances might be given. We sometimes get a little the impression that, instead of reading James's novels with a sense of them as artistic wholes, he has been combing them intently for passages that would seem to bear out his thesis even in cases where, taken in context, they clearly have a different meaning. The extreme abuse of this method is to be found in the chapter in which Mr. Brooks attempts to prove the inadmissible assertion that none of James's later novels is "the fruit of an artistic impulse that is at once spontaneous and sustained," that they "are all—given in each case the tenuity of the idea—stories of the 'eight to ten thousand words' blown out to the dimensions of novels." One would ask oneself at once: In what way can the "ideas" of *The Ambassadors* and *The Wings of the Dove* be described as being any more "tenuous" than those of their predecessors? How could either of them conceivably be a short story? They cover as long a period as the early novels, they contain just as many important characters, they deal with themes of just the same nature and they are worked out on just as elaborate a scale. But Mr. Brooks does not even pretend to go to the novels themselves in order to justify his critical conclusions about them: he bases his whole case on three passages which he has found in James's correspondence. When we come to examine these, we discover that two of them are references, respectively, to the "long-windedness" of *The Wings of the Dove* and the "vague verbosity" of *The Golden Bowl*—which certainly does not prove in the least that the author thought their *ideas* tenuous. It is in the third of these references that the phrase about "the tenuity of the idea" occurs, in an entirely different connection. James writes apologetically to Howells in regard to *The Sacred Fount* that it had been "planned, like *The Spoils of Poynton*, *What Maisie Knew*, *The Turn of the Screw* and various others, as a story of the 'eight to ten thousand words'" and had then spun itself out much longer. He goes on to explain that he might, perhaps, have "chucked" *The Sacred Fount* in the middle if he had not had a superstition about not finishing things. He does not, however, say that he considers these other novels as unsatisfactory as *The Sacred Fount* nor that he had any impulse to chuck them. In the only part of this passage, moreover, that Mr. Brooks omits to quote, he gives a quite different explanation from Mr. Brooks's one for his practice, at this particular time, of projecting short stories instead of novels: "*The Sacred Fount*," writes James, "is one of several things of mine, in these last years, that have paid the penalty of having been conceived only as the 'short story' that (alone apparently) I could hope to work off somewhere (which I mainly failed of)." That is, he planned short stories rather than novels, because he thought that short stories were more salable. That, against this intention, he should have found the short stories growing uncontrollably into novels would seem to prove, not, as Mr. Brooks says, that James's "artistic impulse" was not "spontaneous and sustained," but, on the contrary, precisely that it was.

Mr. Brooks's misrepresentation of the obvious sense of this passage, his readiness to found upon such meager evidence so sweeping and damning a case, throws rather an unreassuring light on the spirit of his recent criticism. That spirit is one of intense zeal at the service of intense resentment. What Mr. Brooks resents and desires to protest against is the spiritual poverty of America and our discouragement of the creative artist. But, in preaching this doctrine, Mr. Brooks has finally allowed his bitterness to far overshoot its mark and to castigate the victims of American conditions along with the conditions themselves. In the latter part of *The Pilgrimage of Henry James*, we have the feeling that he has set out to show James up, just as, in his earlier one, he set out to show up Mark Twain. The story of Henry James, like that of Mark Twain, might have excited both our pity and our admiration; but in Mr. Brooks's hands, it gives rise to little but irony. Like Mr. Sinclair Lewis, that other exposer of the spiritual poverty of America, Mr. Brooks has little charity for the poor, and his enthusiasm for creative genius is not today sufficiently generous to prevent him, one is coming to feel, from deriving a certain satisfaction from describing its despair and decay.

There are, however, in any case, two reasons why Henry James is not a very happy subject for Mr. Van Wyck Brooks. In the first place, for all the sobriety of Mr. Brooks's tone, he is in reality a romantic and a preacher, who has little actual sympathy or comprehension for the impersonal and equanimous writer like James. One remembers in this connection a curious passage about Shakespeare in *America's Coming-of-Age*: "Why is it," asked Mr. Brooks, "that Shakespeare is never the master of originating minds? Plato may be, or Dante, or Tolstoy . . . but not Shakespeare . . . certainly anyone who requires a lesson of Shakespeare comes away with nothing but grace and good humor." The truth is that Mr. Brooks cannot help expecting a really great writer to be a stimulating social prophet. He can understand the lessons conveyed by a Plato or a Tolstoy, but he seems not much more responsive to Shakespeare than he is to Henry James. From Shakespeare he comes away with "nothing but grace and good humor," and from James with almost nothing at all. In the second place, Henry James lends himself to Mr. Brooks's treatment a good deal less satisfactorily than, say, Mark Twain, because the latter was admittedly a remarkable figure who wrote a few very fine things but the bulk of whose books, partly hack-work, have very little literary interest. In this case, it may be said that the man is more impressive than his work, and Mr. Brooks is in a position to tell us something important about him which is not to be found in his writings. But, in the case of Henry James, the work he accomplished in his lifetime is infinitely more interesting than the man. Henry James was not an intimidated and sidetracked artist, but a writer who understood both himself and the society in which he was living and who was able to say just what he meant about nations and human beings. It is difficult for Mr. Brooks to tell us anything about Henry James that James has not told us himself. *The Pilgrimage of Henry James*, which is shorter than its predecessor, falls short of it, also, in life and force. The *Mark Twain* was driven along by the author's passion of discovery and his fury of indignation to a conclusion which is, I suppose, so far Mr. Brooks's highest point of eloquence; but it is perhaps, in the later book, a sign of the critic's failure to be fully possessed by his subject, of his comparatively feeble reaction to it, that the last page, instead of leaving us, as its predecessor did, with a dramatic and significant image, should be evidently an unconscious imitation of the last page of Lytton Strachey's *Queen Victoria*.

May 6, 1925

The All-Star Literary Vaudeville

T HE WRITER of this article is a journalist whose professional activities have been chiefly concerned with the
American literary movement of the last fifteen years.* He has
written reviews of the productions of that movement and
worked on magazines which were identified with it; he has
lived constantly in its atmosphere. And he feels a certain human sympathy with all of its manifestations, even with those of
which, artistically, he disapproves. It is to him a source of deep
gratification that literature has been "sold" to the American
public, and, on principle, in the face of alien attack, he will
stand by even the least intelligent, the least disinterested, of its
salesmen: he has served in that army himself. But it has recently occurred to him that, when he comes to take stock and
is perfectly honest with himself, he must admit to feeling only
the mildest interest in most of the contemporary literary goods
which now find so wide a market, and that he is disaffected to
the point of disgust with the publicity service which has grown
up in connection with them. He has to take account of the fact
that it is scarcely possible nowadays to tell the reviews from the
advertising: both tend to convey the impression that masterpieces are being manufactured as regularly as new models of
motor-cars. In the early days of the present era, the reviews of
H. L. Mencken, Francis Hackett, Floyd Dell and Louis Untermeyer set an example of honesty and boldness. Today these
journalist critics, having got the kind of literature they want,
are apparently quite content; and most of the reviews are now
written by people who do not try to go beyond them. The
present writers on American literature all have interests in one
phase or another of it: either the authors know one another
personally or they owe one another debts of gratitude or they
are bound together by their loyalty to some stimulating common cause. And almost all forget critical standards in their devotion to the great common causes: the cause of an American
national literature in independence of English literature, and

*This essay first appeared anonymously.

the cause of contemporary American ideas as against the ideas of the last generation. Even Stuart P. Sherman, once so savage in the opposite camp, has become as benevolent as Carl Van Doren and now occupies what has perhaps become, from the popular point of view, the central desk of authority, to which each of the performers in the all-star circus, from Ben Hecht to Ring Lardner, steps up to receive his endorsement. The present writer has, therefore, for his own satisfaction, for the appeasement of his own conscience, made an attempt to draw up a balance-sheet of his opinions in regard to his contemporaries, not merely in disparagement of those whom he considers rather overrated but in justice to those he admires. If he succeeds in disturbing one editor or reviewer, in an atmosphere where now for some time politeness and complacency have reigned, he will feel that he has not written in vain.

To begin with the contemporary American novel—which is commonly assumed to be our principal glory—I must confess that I have difficulty in reading our novelists. We compare our fiction with English fiction and conclude that we have been brilliantly successful in this field; but the truth is merely that the English novel is just now at a particularly low ebb. We have no novelist of the first importance, of the importance of James, Joyce or Proust; or of that of Balzac or Dostoevsky. Dreiser commands our respect; but the truth is he writes so badly that it is almost impossible to read him, and, for this reason, I find it hard to believe in his literary permanence. To follow the moral disintegration of Hurstwood in *Sister Carrie* is to suffer all the agonies of being out of work without being rewarded by the aesthetic pleasure which art is supposed to supply. Sinclair Lewis, with a vigorous satiric humor, has brought against certain aspects of American civilization an indictment that has its local importance, but, when one has been through *Main Street* and *Babbitt*, amusing though they certainly are, one is not left with any appetite to read further novels by Lewis: they have beauty neither of style nor of form and they tell us nothing new about life. Joseph Hergesheimer, though he knows how to tell a story, writes nearly as badly in a fancy way as Dreiser does in a crude one: the judgment of him that I most agree with is the remark attributed to Max Beerbohm:

"Poor Mr. Hergesheimer, he wants so much to be an artist."
Cabell, though a man of real parts, is, at his worst, a case of the
same kind: *Beyond Life* I regard as one of the most obnox-
iously written books I have ever read. *Jurgen* certainly had its
merits: it was well-planned and curiously successful in the artificial evocation of the atmosphere of primitive folklore. But,
except at Cabell's moments of highest imaginative intensity,
which are neither very frequent nor very intense, he is likely to
be simply insipid. His genealogies and maps of Poictesme bore
me beyond description, and the whole Poictesme business
strikes me as the sort of thing with which ingenious literary
schoolboys sometimes amuse themselves. I dislike also Cabell's
Southern sentimentality, which leaves him soft when he thinks
he is most cynical. One cannot help feeling that, in the impression he gives of living and working in a vacuum, he furnishes a
depressing illustration of the decay of the South since the Civil
War. Willa Cather is a good craftsman, but she is usually rather
dull. In spite of a few distinguished stories, she suffers from an
anemia of the imagination and, like that other rather distinguished novelist, Zona Gale, is given to terrible lapses into
feminine melodrama. As for Waldo Frank, he writes in a style
—to me, never quite satisfactory—that combines James Joyce
with the Hebrew prophets. At his best, he touches tragedy
and, at his worst, embraces melodrama. He possesses a real
poetic sensibility and is refreshing in so far as his vision is different from that of any one else; but, in his novels, where we
hope to see him stage a drama, he is usually content to invoke
an apocalypse. I consider Jean Toomer's *Cane* rather better in
literary quality than Frank's somewhat similar *Holiday*. I feel
more interest in John Dos Passos and F. Scott Fitzgerald than
in any of the writers mentioned above: they are younger than
the others, and one does not feel as yet that one knows exactly
what to expect of them. Dos Passos is ridden by adolescent
resentments and seems given to documenting life from the
outside rather than knowing it by intimate experience; but,
though, like Lewis, that other documentator, he is far too
much addicted to making out cases against society, he is a
better artist than Lewis and has steadily progressed in his art.
Scott Fitzgerald, possessing from the first, not merely cleverness, but something of inspired imagination and poetic literary

brilliance, has not until recently given the impression of precisely knowing what he was about; but with *The Great Gatsby* and some of his recent short stories, he seems to be entering upon a development in the course of which he may come to equal in mastery of his material those novelists whom he began by surpassing by vividness in investing it with glamor. Besides these, there are the other fabricators of fantasy and the realists, satiric and plain; but the former, so far as I have read them, are either tawdry, like Ben Hecht, or awfully mild, like Carl Van Vechten; and the latter, though both in novel and drama they have learned to apply the formulas of naturalism to almost every phase of American life and have, therefore, a certain interest in the history of American culture, are otherwise especially uninteresting at a time when naturalism has run its course and everywhere except in America is either being transformed or discarded. And we have also had the Wellsian social novel, at various levels of mediocrity.

Sherwood Anderson is a different matter. In his novels, despite excellent pages, I invariably become exasperated, before I have got to the end of them, by the vagueness of the characters and the constant repetitiousness of the form. But his short stories and his symbolist prose-poems have a kind of artistic authenticity that neither Lewis's richer resources nor Miss Cather's technical efforts have been able to win for those writers. Without ever having learned the tricks of his trade, Sherwood Anderson, in the best of his stories, has shown an almost perfect instinct that fashions, from what seems a more intimate stratum of feeling and imagination than our novelists usually explore, visions at once fresh and naïve and of a slightly discomfiting strangeness. He could stand to learn something, however, from the methods both of Miss Cather and of Lewis: too much of his material has evaporated in his hands from his not knowing how to deal with it. It can probably be said that, in general, the newer American writers have so far been distinguishing themselves in the short story rather than the novel. The short stories of Sherwood Anderson, Ernest Hemingway's *In Our Time* and Gertrude Stein's early *Three Lives*, to which should be added the best of Ring Lardner, constitute an impressive group and one quite free from the outworn conventions and the suggestion of second-rate imitation that make many of the novels unsatisfactory. It is interesting to note that all four of these writers have certain characteristics in common, that they may almost be said to form a school, and that, remote though they may seem from one another, there is a fairly close relationship between them. Thus, Anderson has read Gertrude Stein and seems to have been influenced by *Three Lives*; and Hemingway has evidently read and been influenced by all three of the others. Each of these four writers has developed what seems only a special branch of the same simple colloquial language, based directly on the vocabulary and rhythm of ordinary American speech; and, if there can be said to be an American school of writing, aside from American journalese or from the use of American slang in otherwise conventional English prose, these writers would seem to represent it. It is a genre that has already produced one masterpiece in Mark Twain's *Huckleberry Finn*, a work to which Anderson, Hemingway and Lardner are probably all indebted.

As for the dramatists, there is still only O'Neill, who, for all his efforts to break away from naturalism, remains a typical naturalistic dramatist of something under the very first rank. He is a writer of the same school as Hauptmann, with much the same kind of merits; but, where Hauptmann is as steady as Shakespeare, O'Neill is hysterically embittered. He forces his tragic catastrophes and, at the same time, fails to prepare them; and, despite the magnificent eloquence of which he is sometimes capable, especially when handling some form of the vernacular, he has grave deficiencies of literary taste which allow him to leave great areas of his dialogue either banal or bald. John H. Lawson has a wit and a fancy which have found their proper vehicle in the theater; but, even more than his ally, Dos Passos, he is given to adolescent grievances and adolescent enthusiasms.

We come now to literary criticism. In my opinion, H. L. Mencken (who is perhaps a prophet rather than a critic) is ordinarily underrated as a writer of English prose. Belonging himself to the line of Butler and Swift rather than to that of Pater and De Quincey, he cherishes a rustic reverence for the more "aesthetic" branch and is never tired of celebrating the elegances of such provincial fops as Lord Dunsany,

Hergesheimer and Cabell, who have announced—it is, I think, Mr. Cabell's phrase—that they aim to "write beautifully about beautiful things." But although it is true that Mencken's style lends itself to excesses and vulgarities, especially in the hands of his imitators, who have taken over the Master's jargon without possessing his admirable literary sense, I believe that his prose is more successful in its way than that of these devotees of beauty usually is in theirs. The ideas themselves behind Mencken's writing are neither many nor subtle and, even in his most serious productions, even in *The American Language*, he overindulges an appetite for paradox. But some strain of the musician and poet has made it possible for Mencken to turn these ideas into literature: it is precisely through the color and rhythm of a highly personal prose that Mencken's opinions have become so infectious. He has now been repeating these opinions with the same pugnacious emphasis for fifteen or twenty years, and one has become rather tired of hearing them; yet he sustains a certain distinction and affords a certain satisfaction. Consider, for example, the leaflet he recently circulated on the adventures of the *American Mercury* with the Boston Watch and Ward Society: this statement, of no literary pretensions, in which he appears without war-paint or feathers, displays most attractive eighteenth-century qualities of lucidity, order and force, for lack of which the youngest of the younger literary generation, who have thrown Mencken overboard, have proved so far rather ineffective.

Paul Rosenfeld is another critic very unpopular with this youngest generation who seems to me an excellent writer. Though he, too, has his faults of style, which include a confusing weakness for writing French and German locutions in English, his command of a rich English vocabulary is one of the things that make him exceptional among recent American writers—who are not infrequently handicapped by not having at their disposal a large enough variety of English words, or, if they have them, by not knowing what they mean. Mr. Rosenfeld, at his worst, is given to overwriting: receiving in his soul the seed of a work by some such writer as Sherwood Anderson, himself one of the tenderer plants, he will cause it to shoot up and exfloreate into an enormous and rather rank "Mystic Cabbage-Rose." On these occasions, his prose seems sometimes rather coarse in quality and his colors a little muddy; but, at his best, Mr. Rosenfeld's writing is certainly among our soundest and his colors are both brilliant and true. He is sensitive, intelligent, well-educated and incorruptibly serious; and he is perhaps the only American critic of the generation since that of James Huneker who has written anything of any real value on the current artistic life of Europe. Van Wyck Brooks, who also writes excellent prose, though of quite a different sort, I propose to discuss in another connection.

George Jean Nathan is a wonderful humorous writer and a better critic of the theater than A. B. Walkley, in a recent article, gave him credit for being; but his writing, which superficially resembles Mencken's, is usually lacking in the qualities that give Mencken's its durable texture. Willard Huntington Wright, some years ago, gave the impression of being some one important; and Lewis Mumford now gives the impression of some one perhaps about to be. Gilbert Seldes, through his activities as an editor of the *Dial* and his cultivation of the popular arts, has filled a role of considerable importance; but his principal literary quality is a kind of undisciplined wit which figures too often in his writings at the expense of lucidity and taste. He has lately become addicted to aesthetic editorial writing, a department for which his alert and vivid but glancing and volatile mind, is perhaps not very well adapted. In my opinion, he is seen at his best in passages of straight description of some movie or vaudeville act which has aroused his imagination. Burton Rascoe has performed the astonishing and probably unprecedented feat of making literature into news. A master of all the tricks of newspaper journalism, which he has introduced into the Sacred Grove to the horror of some of its high priests, his career has yet been singularly honorable in its disregard of popular values; and the cause of letters has profited more from his activities than the proprietors of popular newspapers who have inevitably discovered in the long run that they would feel more comfortable with a literary editor who did not find books so exciting. Mr. Rascoe has always written respectably and, at his best, with much ease and point. Most of the younger generation of critics either are badly educated or have never learned to write, and many suffer from both disabilities. At best, we have produced no literary critic of the full European stature. The much-abused Paul Elmer More still figures as our only professional critic whose learning is really considerable and whose efforts are ambitious and serious. His prose is quite graceless and charmless, but always precise and clear; his point of view, though the Puritan rationalism of which it is a late product has imposed on it some rigid limitations, has the force of a deep conviction and the advantage of a definite formulation. Mr. More, although hopelessly inhibited in the exercise of his aesthetic sensibility, has become, insofar as is possible without the free range of this, a real master of ideas.

The new post-war method of biography, based on Strachey and psychoanalysis, has had many practitioners in America: Katherine Anthony, Van Wyck Brooks, Thomas Beer, M. R. Werner and others; but, though it has turned out a number of agreeable books, I have not seen any except Brooks's *Mark Twain* that seemed of first-rate importance. In the special departments of scholarly and expository writing, the general inferiority of the level of our culture to that of Great Britain or France becomes inescapably plain. There are not many of our college professors who can command the attention of the reading public. Professor John Dewey writes much and his influence has been considerable, but he has not inherited with pragmatism William James's literary gift. Professor Morris Cohen, who does possess a literary gift, has so far published nothing but reviews, and not very many of them. In the classics, Professor Tenney Frank seems the only representative of a new generation; but Professor Frank, although competent in a literary way and bold in interpretation, appears to be rather indifferent to the literary interest of the classics. Professor Paul Shorey of Chicago is perhaps the only other scholar who writes readable books in this field. We have, in short, no university professor with a literary reputation equal to that of Garrod, of Gilbert Murray, of Mackail, of A. E. Housman, or of Whitehead or Bertrand Russell or Lowes Dickinson. I can remember no recent book by an American professor which has been widely read on its literary merits, except Professor Warner Fite's *Moral Philosophy* and Professor Samuel Morison's *Maritime History of Massachusetts*. In science, we have some readable popularizers in the rousing modern manner, but they are mostly undistinguished writers: Doctor Fishbein, Doctor

De Kruif and Doctor Dorsey. Edwin Slosson is rapidly becoming a sort of William Lyon Phelps of scientific culture. The zoölogist William Beebe writes a prose that is shamelessly journalistic; but he is a man of some literary ability, who deserves to be read by writers. One of his assets is an extraordinary vocabulary, which blends scientific with literary language in such a way that his scientific words are imbued with a new life and color. I doubt, however, whether the cable to the *New York Times* is a very good school of writing. I am sorry not to be able to do justice to our recent political writers. I believe that in this department we are somewhat better off than elsewhere; but it is the one in which I have lately read least.

As for poetry, the new movement of twelve years ago seemed at the time to assume impressive proportions. But who can believe in its heroes now? Edgar Lee Masters did one creditable thing: *The Spoon River Anthology*; but, except for a single fine poem called *Silence*, I have seen nothing by him since that I could read. Vachel Lindsay's best poems, such as his *Bryan*, are spoiled by the incurable cheapness and looseness which are rampant in the rest of his work. Carl Sandburg, unlike Masters and Lindsay, has a genuine talent for language; with a hardboiled vocabulary and reputation, he offers what is perhaps the most attractive surface of any of the men of the group. But, when we come to read him in quantity, we are disappointed to find him less interesting than we had hoped; his ideas seem rather obvious, his emotions rather meager. The work of Amy Lowell is like a great empty cloisonné jar; that of John Gould Fletcher a great wall of hard descriptive prose mistakenly presented as poetry. Conrad Aiken, except in a few of his lyrics, is one of those curious people, like William Vaughn Moody, who can turn out a rich-looking texture of words and who can make at first glance the impression of being true and highly gifted inheritors of the English tradition of the nineteenth century, but who leave us, on closer reading, with a feeling that they have not quite got the "afflatus" that their themes and their style imply. Robert Frost has a thin but authentic vein of poetic sensibility; but I find him excessively dull, and he certainly writes very poor verse. He is, in my opinion, the most generally overrated of all this group of poets. Ezra Pound, who

deserves all honor as a champion and pioneer, has worked conscientiously and stubbornly as one who understands very well,
and as few of his contemporaries do, in what the highest
poetry consists, but who has rarely been able to affect us as the
highest poets do. His cantos of a "poem of considerable
length," so ambitious and so full of fine passages, passages that,
standing by themselves, might lead us to believe them mere
ornaments from a masterpiece on the great scale, seem entirely
composed of such fragments; a mosaic which fails to reveal a
pattern, a monument, in its lack of cohesion, its lack of driving
force or a center, to a kind of poetic bankruptcy. The other
poets of the literary Left, though, like Pound, they can often
write, seem to suffer from a similar sterility. Marianne Moore,
for example, is sometimes very fine; but, as she herself has
shrewdly noted in choosing a title for her collected verse, the
bulk of her work answers better to the description of "Observations," than to that of poetry. From a slag of intellectual processes that has only a viscous flow, there emerge intense and vivid
images that seem to have been invested with a sharp emotional
meaning but that are rarely precipitated out in such a way as to
make the piece a poem. H. D., like Carl Sandburg, writes well;
but, like Sandburg, there is not much in her. Wallace Stevens
has a fascinating gift of words that is not far from a gift of nonsense, rather like that of Edith Sitwell, and he is a charming
decorative artist. Alfred Kreymborg has his dry distinction, but
he tends fatally toward insipidity. I think I prefer the oddity of
his early work, frankly prosaic and dry, to his later more pretentious sonnets. E. E. Cummings possesses, in some respects,
a more remarkable lyric gift than any of the poets reviewed
above; his feeling is always spontaneous, and his words run
naturally into music. But, as in his rather limp line-drawings,
the hand does not seem very firm: all sorts of ideas and images
have come streaming into his head, and he doesn't know how
to manipulate them to make them artistically effective. W. C.
Williams and Maxwell Bodenheim I have tried my best to admire, but I have never been able to believe in them.*

*It was at about this time that Maxwell Bodenheim described me in some
such phrase as "a fatuous policeman, menacingly swinging his club." In
rereading this essay—in which I have qualified or softened some of the original judgments—I have sometimes been reminded of this.

Since these poets made their first reputations, the general appetite for poetry seems to have somewhat abated. Among the younger poets, for example, even those of most brilliant promise are having difficulty in getting their poems printed, not by the publishers only, who have evidently come to the conclusion that poetry is bound to be unprofitable, but even by the magazines. The editors of the magazines, who have brought out, since the poetic revival, two or three crops of poets, seem content now to close the canon, and have no place for the poetry of unknown men—even if so obviously gifted as Phelps Putnam or Allen Tate—who cannot be found in Mr. Untermeyer's anthologies or among the original contributors to the *Dial*.

I have left aside the women lyric poets in order to discuss them as a group by themselves. On the average, though less pretentious, I think I find them more rewarding than the men: their emotion is likely to be more genuine and their literary instinct surer. Miss Lizette Woodworth Reese, the dean of the guild, astonishes one by continuing to write, not only with the same fine quality, but almost with the same freshness, as forty years ago. Sara Teasdale, the monotony of whose sobbing note caused her to become rather unfashionable when a more arrogant race of young women appeared, has made definite progress in her art since her earlier books of poems and has recently written some of her most charming lyrics. Miss Edna St. Vincent Millay has now, in turn, grown so popular that she, too, is in danger of becoming unfashionable; but she remains the most important of the group and perhaps one of the most important of our poets. Like Mencken, the prophet of a point of view, she has, like him, become a national figure; nor, as in the case of some other prophets, is her literary reputation undeserved. With little color, meager ornament and images often commonplace, she is yet mistress of deeply moving rhythms, of a music which makes up for the ear what her page seems to lack for the eye; and, above all, she has that singular boldness, which she shares with the greatest poets and which consists in taking just that one step beyond where one's fellows stop that, by making a new contact with moral reality, has the effect of causing other productions to take on an aspect of literary convention. Elinor Wylie, in the best of her verse and in her novel

Jennifer Lorn, gives expression to a set of emotions quite different from those of Miss Millay, but one which has also its
typical interest and its own kind of intensity. Her literary profi-
ciency is immense: she is never at a loss for a clever rhyme, a
witty reference or a brilliant image; she can command all the
finest fabrics, the choicest works of art, the most luxurious sensations, the most amusing historical allusions and the most delicious things to eat. And, as a consequence, her inferior work
is almost as well-written as her best; and her best work has
both a style and a splendor of a kind very rare in America—
where, even when these qualities do appear together, as they
did to some extent in Amy Lowell, they too often remain hollow and metallic from the lack of a heart at the core. Edna Millay's inferior work has no such embroidery to deck it; and, save
in her vein of classical austerity, she has for her best but the imagery of the sorrel or mullein stalk of the barren and rocky pastures, the purple wild sweet-pea dragging driftwood across the
sand, the dead leaves in the city gutters, the gray snow in the
city street, the kettle, the broom, the uncarpeted stairs and
the dead father's old clothes—grown strange and disturbing
now, to this reader's sense, at least, as the prison cell of Verlaine
or Catullus's common crossroads. Louise Bogan plucked one
low resounding theme on tensely strung steel strings, but it is
now the vibrations of this rather than a further development
that are ringing still in the air. Léonie Adams's *Those Not Elect*
is a very remarkable book, of which the language, which seems
to branch straight from the richest seventeenth-century tradition, strikes music from the calm summer starbreak, the bright-
washed night after rain or the blue translucence of evening,
where a gull or a pigeon that flies alone, seeking freedom in
that space and clarity, is lost in a confusion of cloud and light.
An anthology of these women poets should include, besides
those named above, the *Cinquains* of the late Adelaide Crapsey
and the best of Miss Genevieve Taggard, Miss Babette Deutsch
and several others, of whom the younger Laura Gottschalk
may turn out to be one of the most interesting and in whose
company Dorothy Parker, long known as a humorous writer,
has recently, it seems to me, fully proved her right to belong.

I have left to the last the two poets whom, among the men,
I admire most: T. S. Eliot and E. A. Robinson. T. S. Eliot,

though heavily infected with the Alexandrianism of the Left, has been able to imbue with a personal emotion, not only his inveterate literary allusions and his echoes of other poets, but even the lines that he has borrowed from them. He deserves, both as critic and as poet, his present position of influence. I deplore the fatigued and despondent mood that seems lately to have been drying up both his criticism and his poetry; but I cannot believe that a passion for poetry so serious and so intense can be permanently stifled or numbed. E. A. Robinson is the last and, artistically (leaving the happiest flashes of Emerson aside), the most important of the New England poets. Though he has recently run much into the sands of long and arid blank-verse narratives, I believe that he is one of the poets of our time most likely to survive as an American classic. He and Eliot both, though there are times when they disappoint us by the tendency of their motors to stall and times when they get on our nerves by a kind of hypochondria of the soul, have possessed the poetic gift and the artist's mastery of it.

The subject of Mr. Robinson may lead us to some more general observations. I have said that E. A. Robinson is the last of the New England poets, and it is true that he really belongs to an earlier period than the present and has little in common with the writers in whose company the anthologists now place him. (He is closer to Hawthorne and Henry James.) When we look back on the literary era which preceded the recent renascence, we are surprised, after all that has been written about its paleness, its tameness and its sterility, to take account of the high standard of excellence to which its best writers attained. When we consider Henry James, Stephen Crane and even such novelists of the second rank as George W. Cable and William Dean Howells, with such critics as Irving Babbitt, W. C. Brownell and Paul Elmer More, who belong essentially to the same era, we are struck with certain superiorities over our race of writers today. It may be said of these men, in general, that, though their ideas were less "emancipated," they possessed a sounder culture than we; and that, though less lively, they were better craftsmen. They were professional men of letters, and they had thoroughly learned their trade. Note the intense concentration, the incapacity for careless writing, of even

Stephen Crane, who passed for a clever newspaper man and an outlaw to respectable literature, but whose work astonishes us now by an excellence of quality by no means incomparable—as how much of our present fiction is?—to the best European work in the same kind.

Another writer who, like Mr. Robinson, is bound closely, through her craftsmanship and her culture, to this earlier American tradition, but who, by reason of her critical point of view, makes a connecting link with our own, is Edith Wharton. Often described as an imitator of Henry James, she was really, in her important novels, a writer of a different kind. Henry James, except at very rare moments, was never a preacher or a bitter social satirist; but Mrs. Wharton was perhaps the first American to write with indignant passion *against* American values as they had come to present themselves by the end of the last century. Her recent books, since *The Age of Innocence*, have been of rather inferior interest; but, in her prime, she produced what I strongly believe are the best examples of this kind of fiction that we have had in the United States. She was soon followed by Van Wyck Brooks, who represented a similar reaction against a world either brutal and commercial or moribund and genteel. One of the prophets of the present generation, he belongs to the older and more sober tradition and has never, for better or for worse, learned any of the methods of the new.

Join these writers with the others I have mentioned and it will be seen that they make a remarkable group. They have provided both a picture and a criticism of one period of American life. The writing of our own age will hardly, I fear, present so dignified or so firm a front. We have the illusion of a stronger vitality and of a greater intellectual freedom, but we are polyglot, parvenu, hysterical and often only semi-literate. When time shall have weeded out our less important writers, it is probable that those who remain will give the impression of a literary vaudeville: H. L. Mencken hoarse with preaching in his act making fun of preachers; Edna St. Vincent Millay, the soloist, a contralto with deep notes of pathos; Sherwood Anderson holding his audience with naïve but disquieting bedtime stories; Theodore Dreiser with his newspaper narrative of commonplace scandals and crimes and obituaries of millionaires, in which the reporter astonishes the readers by being rash enough to try to tell the truth; T. S. Eliot patching from many cultures a dazzling and variegated disguise for the shrinking and scrupulous soul of a hero out of Henry James. Let us remember, however, that vaudeville has always been an American specialty; and that the writers we value most highly in the pre-Civil War period have not in general been such as I have mentioned above as typical of the generation just before our own. Emerson, Whitman, Poe; *Walden* and *Moby Dick*: they are all independent one-man turns, and can say that we may not find their peers among our present bill of comic monologuists, sentimental songsters and performers of one-act melodramas?

June 30, 1926

The Critics: A Conversation

MR. HUDNUT. Who has read Hornblende's latest?

MR. BIRD. Not I! I looked into it, and the first thing my eye lit upon was a letter purporting to be written by a Frenchman in which the date was given 1 Janvier with a capital J. After that, I really couldn't go on with it!

MR. HUDNUT. Of course, I think Hornblende's cosmopolitan pretensions are among the most amusing things in contemporary literature. He has never been abroad in his life, you know, but he gets someone over there to supply him with a lot of continental theater programs and menus, which he memorizes for purposes of conversation.

MR. BIRD. Really! Ha-ha-ha! Marvellous! Marvellous!

A LADY. Well, this last book of his almost makes one wonder what one could have seen in the others. It's so *dull*, and so *sentimental*!

MR. HUDNUT. Oh, Bert has always been sentimental—the most sentimental man in the world! All this great show of brutality and ruthlessness with which he tries to impress his readers is merely a screen to defend himself against his own emotions. You know, he always sends a valentine every year to the first girl he was ever in love with—out in South Dakota somewhere.

THE LADY. Well, I'm very much interested to hear that, because that's what I have always felt about him—that he was essentially a weak man trying to disguise his weakness by bluster. It's as if he were continually calling a spade a spade just to show he's not afraid to.

MR. LATROBE. And, after all, everything that Hornblende tries to do has already been done so much better by Charles Lavender.

THE LADY. Oh, yes: Charles Lavender!

MR. HUDNUT. Who is Lavender, Latrobe? I've never heard of him.

MR. LATROBE. Charles Lavender was an exquisite artist, though he's hardly known today.

MR. HUDNUT. When did he live?

MR. LATROBE. All his best work came out in the nineties.

He treated the sort of subject that Hornblende tries to deal with—and I think it's quite obvious what Hornblende's subjects really are—but gracefully, poignantly, charmingly!

MR. HUDNUT. How can you get hold of Lavender's books?

MR. LATROBE. They're almost impossible to find nowadays. I suppose that I am probably the only person in America who has a complete collection.

MR. HUDNUT. I'd like to borrow them some time.

MR. LATROBE. I'm sorry, but I never lend my books— especially my Lavender firsts.

MR. BIRD. I couldn't resist calling Hornblende's blunder to the attention of Jacques Champfleury!

MR. HUDNUT. Yes—tell us about your controversy with Champfleury. I missed the last *Revue Libre*.

MR. BIRD. Well: to begin at the beginning, in 1895, when the old *Revue de Lutèce* was started, an announcement appeared in the first number to the effect that one of the features of the magazine was to be the cultivation of English literature —with all the usual rot about promoting the interchange of ideas between the two countries—and in the very next number there appeared an article on the English novel spelling Dickens D-i-k-e-n-s. D-i-k-e-n-s! I ventured at the time to point out this little error to the editors and received a polite but insincere reply from Camille Vide, who had written the article— professing his profoundest regret and explaining that a correction would be published—which in due course appeared, also polite but insincere. Five months later, in another article, this time on a French subject, Monsieur Vide informed the world that *Le Kiosque Parfumé* of Tristan Kraus had appeared in 1879. Well: there I had him on his own ground! The first edition of *Le Kiosque Parfumé*, limited to twenty-five copies, was privately printed in 1877—two years earlier than that! I wrote an article in excellent French which I called *Les Erreurs de M. Vide* and sent it to the rival magazine, *La Revue des Deux Rives*. Well: to make a long story short, the *Lutèce* crowd have never forgiven me. They reviewed my bibliography of the Mexican drama in the most perfunctory fashion, garbling the passages they translated—

THE LADY (*talking to Hudnut, while Latrobe listens to Bird*). I'm so relieved to hear you say that you don't think

Bertram Hornblende is really such a tremendous figure. That's what I've always felt, but up to this latest book I've never dared to admit it.

MR. HUDNUT. Oh, Hornblende is really afraid of life. He tries to get out of himself but he's hopelessly introverted. That's the real reason he's taken to living in Honduras. The grandeur of the tropical coasts that he goes on about so much has nothing whatever to do with it: what he's looking for is a never-never land, where he can completely get away from reality. His wife keeps house for him and does everything for him, and he lives in a continual daydream.

THE LADY. She's pretty awful, isn't she?

MR. HUDNUT. Oh, I like Edith: Edith's a good sort. Of course, she's not terribly stimulating, but then, for the kind of thing Bert wants, I suppose she's absolutely perfect.—Bert has a physical deformity, you know—one of his legs is shorter than the other—and it has affected his whole point of view. He's morbidly sensitive about it—he always sits with his legs crossed, so that it won't be noticed. And when he's photographed, he always makes a point of having the foot of the longer leg on a step or a stump or something—or he's standing on the side of a mountain. That's the reason he's gone in for mountain-climbing. If Bert can be photographed on the side of a mountain, with an alpenstock and a pretty woman, he's perfectly happy—just like a child!

THE LADY. His wife doesn't make it particularly easy for him to see other women, I understand.

MR. HUDNUT. Yes: but her jealousy of poor old Bert is entirely unnecessary. He couldn't—or wouldn't—do anything even if she gave him a chance.

MR. BIRD (*continuing his story*). Well, Vide went over to the *Revue Libre* which his brother-in-law Champfleury was founding, and the *Revue* began to boom Hornblende as the foremost American novelist, because Mme. Champfleury had translated his first novel. He has even been taken up by that unutterable sheet *Hurrah-Moche*, which is published by Lavarnier, who also publishes the *Revue Libre*. The young pro-American French aesthetes hailed Hornblende as one of the prophets of the literature of big machinery. That was before he had gone to Central America—a good joke on them! I wrote them a letter in French, with a translation of the back-to-the-wilderness outburst that he published just before he left. But they never either printed or replied to it. Perhaps they cannot read correct French. The very title of their magazine is gibberish! They have taken the English word "hurrah," which they have picked up and think very smart, and have affixed to it a French slang adjective. Together the two words mean nothing. It is nonsense! It is neither good French nor good English! An insult to the intelligence!

MR. HOSKINS (*speaking for the first time*). It seems to me that, in all this discussion of Hornblende, we have really failed so far to face the aesthetic problem he raises. I must say I disapprove of this habit, which seems to be becoming so prevalent, of making personal gossip do duty for an intellectual approach to literature. Hornblende's real weakness, it seems to me, becomes plain when we subject him to an aesthetic analysis. I begin by dividing works of literature into three clearly distinguishable classes, whose nature I can indicate best by an analogy from mathematics. I identify these three classes, also, with the three states of higher consciousness defined by Gundeljeff in his Eurasian yogi system. The first of these classes includes literary artists who represent some simple aesthetic entity multiplied by itself to a higher power—they correspond to the cubes, the squares and the other powers of algebra. Such writers are Victor Hugo, Horace, Metastasio, Milton and Trollope. This is Gundeljeff's ectogenetic state of consciousness: the works of art are given off by the artist from *the outside*. The third class is that which includes almost all the greatest figures in literature: it has its mathematical equivalent in the irrational numbers we call surds—that is, numbers that are not susceptible of having rational roots extracted—and its philosophical equivalent is the engenetic state of Gundeljeff: the work of art is gestated *within* the artist and never wholly emerges. Into this class fall Mallarmé, John Donne, Herman Melville, the author of the *Kalevala*, Oscar Pilseck and the best parts of Pindar. It was because we wished to insist upon this fundamental aspect of literature that Pilseck and myself have called our magazine $\sqrt{2}$, and, by resorting to a different technique of analysis from any that has yet been applied, we have been able to extract, to an approximation equivalent to ten places of decimals, the root of the aesthetic blend of elements—susceptible, of course, of a qualitative as well as a quantitative analysis—that, raised to the x power, have resulted in the work of art. Performing the inverse operation, we shall also be able to approximate the production of works of art of the irrational engenetic kind, and our essay in the first issue in reality provides prolegomena to the method of a new body of literature, in which what has hitherto been produced by the freaks and the flukes of individual genius will be forged by the application of a rigorous intellectual discipline. There is, however, a second intermediate class, to which Bertram Horn-blende belongs—

The conversation is suddenly terminated by the downfall of Western civilization.

August 5, 1925

Pope and Tennyson

M R. LYTTON STRACHEY, by a recently published paper—
Pope: The Leslie Stephen Lecture for 1925—seems to have
revived a flicker of the old nineteenth-century controversy
about the poetic merits of Pope. His defense has already provoked a demurrer from Mr. Conrad Aiken. Mr. Strachey's defense rests, however, on entirely different grounds from the
championship of Pope by Byron against the attacks of the romantics. The special issue of that time now means little to us:
we pride ourselves indeed today on disregarding all the special
issues of literature, of taking up no position that can limit our
play of intelligence. We have the illusion of appreciating without prejudice the good writing of the most various schools,
applauding in each its peculiar success in what it has attempted
to do. And yet, like the romantics and the eighteenth century,
we must tend to admire in the past only the qualities we cultivate ourselves. We pick out in the poets we seek to revive precisely those lines that, removed from their context, will make
them appear more modern. Certain critics by this method
have recently performed some veritable conjuring tricks with
Dryden; and Mr. Strachey now perhaps does a little for Pope
what he makes fun of Pope for doing for Homer: he makes
him look like a poet of our own time.

Assuming, however, the standards by which we judge poetry
today, one is persuaded that Mr. Strachey has made out the
strongest possible case for Pope and has appreciated certain aspects of his genius as they have never yet perhaps been appreciated. That there were aspects of Pope which were not much
appreciated even in his own century seems to be strikingly
proved by Dr. Johnson's comment on a couplet that Mr. Strachey quotes with special enthusiasm:

> Lo! where Maeotis sleeps, and hardly flows
> The freezing Tanaïs thro' a waste of snows.

Pope is supposed to have considered these lines the most successful he ever wrote; and Johnson could not understand this.
But if the story is true, it is evident that Pope must have aimed,

in his verse, at something a good deal more artistically interesting than the "rocking-horse" aphorisms for which he was
denounced by Wordsworth and for which he is still commonly
condemned. These lines, with their self-contained pattern,
their frozen coldness and retarded flow, have a perfection of
linguistic harmonics and an accurate descriptive brilliance that
are typical of Pope at his best, but in which the romantics, except for Keats, did not as a rule excel. Mr. Strachey is also particularly happy in citing to support his case two passages in
which his poet pulls out a fuller stop than is usual with him:
the "fate of old women in society" and the death of Bucking-
ham. These passages are malicious, to be sure, like almost all
the effective things in Pope, but they are also undeniably tragic.

                                    II

It is curious to compare Pope with Tennyson, a poet whom,
on one of his sides he resembles.

> The silver eel, in shining volumes roll'd,
> The yellow carp, in scales bedropp'd with gold.

If it weren't for their metallic weight and ring, which are characteristic of Pope and which perhaps make the gold and silver
a little more real than the fish, these lines might have been
written by Tennyson; yet they come from *Windsor Forest.* So
much of the description of Tennyon also represents a triumph
of artifice, and it does not always carry him much further than
Windsor Forest carries Pope! Consider even the lyrics in *The
Princess,* always played by admirers of Tennyson as among
their strongest cards. *Blow, Bugle, Blow!* is unquestionably a
very fine poem so long as it sticks to rendering the bugle, but
the poet in the last stanza tries to deepen its music by a moral
note:

> O love, they [the echoes of the bugle] die in yon rich sky;
>   They faint on hill or field or river:
> Our echoes roll from soul to soul,
>   And grow forever and forever.
> Blow, bugle, blow! etc.

Is this kind of deliberate morality, of which Tennyson and so

many of his contemporaries—especially in America—were full,
any less artificial than that of Pope? If Tennyson were able to
convince us that he had felt the reverberations of human relationships in connection with the sound of the bugle (as Wordsworth felt the fading of the wonder of life in connection with
the countryside of his childhood), we should accept this as
an integral part of the poem; but we feel that these lines are
synthetic. As for *Come down, O maid, from yonder mountain
height*, it is as sheer a piece of virtuosity as anything in Pope.
Compare the freezing Tanaïs of *The Dunciad* with "the firths
of ice That huddling slant in furrow-cloven falls." Though this
poem fixes so many vivid images, it conveys little lyric emotion. With Pope, who seems to make no pretence to be anything but superlatively witty, we are delighted when we find him
rising to something like the passion of great poetry; with Tennyson, who pretends to the highest prestige of emotional and
moral profundity, we are sometimes disappointed to get only
wit. Did not Pope, in his most characteristic vein of eighteenth-
century irony, hit off at least one charming lyric?

All hail, once pleasing, once inspiring shade!
    Scene of my youthful loves and happier hours!
Where the kind Muses met me as I stray'd,
    And gently press'd my hand, and said, "Be ours!"—
Take all thou e'er shalt have, a constant Muse:
    At Court thou may'st be liked, but nothing gain:
Stock thou may'st buy and sell, but always lose,
    And love the brightest eyes, but love in vain.

Do we not accept the music and the feeling of this precisely
because the poet has not tried to write in the least in the manner of Milton on his blindness? Do we not reject much of
Tennyson—and of many of his contemporaries—because we
suspect them of exaggerating the dignity of their emotions?

III

It would, of course, be unfair to leave Tennyson at this. I have
said that *Come down, O maid, from yonder mountain height*
conveys little lyric emotion. What it does convey very successfully is the satisfaction in smooth English lawns and rich

"immemorial" trees which, as Mr. Harold Nicolson has pointed out in his admirable biography of Tennyson, became the grave of the real poet. When Tennyson is deeply troubled, as he was by the death of his friend, he writes in a different strain. It is interesting to see what he does with a subject that really moves him in that other famous lyric from *The Princess: Tears, Idle Tears*. Here he is dealing with an emotion as fleeting, as elusive and as complex as anything in French symbolist poetry—the strange poignancy, at once fresh and desperate, of some unexpected echo from the past. One knows from such a poem as,

> Les faux beaux jours ont lui tout le jour, ma pauvre âme,
> Et les voici vibrer aux cuivres du couchant.

how Verlaine would have treated this theme. But, instead of resorting to the telescoped metaphors and the medley of images of symbolism, Tennyson reduces his difficult subject to a series of lucid statements almost as precise, antithetical and realistically accurate as Pope's:

> Fresh as the first beam glittering on a sail,
> That brings our friends up from the underworld,
> Sad as the last which reddens over one
> That sinks with all we love below the verge.

He summons an elaborate simile, based like Pope's upon observation, which renders exactly what he wants to say:

> Ah, sad and strange as in dark summer dawns
> The earliest pipe of half-awaken'd birds
> To dying ears, when unto dying eyes
> The casement slowly grows a glimmering square.

In *Tears, Idle Tears*, Tennyson wrote what is not perhaps merely, as Mr. Nicolson suggests, one of the most successful of his own poems, but one of the best poems of his time. In this vein, the Victorian poet was nearer to the school of Verlaine than it is likely to occur to us to notice. Tennyson's peculiar achievement was to have caught in a classic regularity the exquisite moments of a temperament as sensitive as Verlaine's.

September 16, 1925

A Letter to Elinor Wylie

D EAR MADAM,
It is now two years since you were so kind as to send me the first of your novels, which the vexation of other business and the exigencies of other studies then prevented me from reading. It has, in the meantime, been your reproach, that, whereas you, a year ago this autumn, were prompt to be present at and eager to applaud my tragedy (a kindness, I must confess, uncommon), I have allowed another year to pass without troubling to open your book; and that, although, on the first publication of your poems, I was among the foremost to commend them, my enthusiasm for your genius has so far abated that I have been willing to neglect in private what I have forborne to notice in publick. Let these complaints now cease: as I have offered in excuse of my protracted delay the constant press and perplexity of my affairs, so now, receiving your second novel in a moment of tranquillity and leisure, I have taken the opportunity to prove my candour by a careful perusal of both.

Of the first, it may now seem too late to say much, since it has already been abundantly praised. It was your habit, at the time when I had not yet read it, to call to my attention the extravagant eulogies which had been lavished upon it by Mr. Van Vechten and Mr. Van Doren; but of these two criticks, the first is of so particular a taste as to render him insensible to the beauties of many works, and those among the greatest; so that whatever falls in with his humour obtains the suffrage of his judgment; and the second, like the sun of tropical latitudes, which sheds its warmth all the year around, diffuses his mild benignance upon the excellent and the unworthy alike, until, by its uniformity, it causes us to long for the asperities of more inclement climates. Posterity must, therefore, be as little persuaded by the eloquent caprice of the one as convinced by the universal patronage of the other; and it should be enlightening to the publick, as it must be gratifying to you, for me to add my commendation to theirs. The merits of *Jennifer Lorn* must command a respect far beyond what we are accustomed to

accord to light tales of this species, which, as they are written
merely to amuse, do not often move us to admire. We are as
much instructed by your knowledge of mankind as delighted
by your felicity of invention; and amazed no less by the brilliance exhibited in the splendours of the style than by the
vigour displayed in sustaining them. Of the character of Gerald, it may be said that our literature affords no more ingenious, and, at the same time, no more dreadful, illustration of
the truth, that the most polished taste and the highest accomplishment may coexist with selfishness and cruelty; and the exercise of great abilities have for accompaniment the contempt
of religion. Nor, though you stimulate us at first to admire, do
you fail at last to provoke us to despise, when one who has
commenced as an Atheist, is finally shewn as a thief.

Your second novel, *The Venetian Glass Nephew*, now remains
to be examined; and it will not be surprising if you have not
found it possible to repeat so remarkable a success in so short
a time. I must say first that your choice of a subject seems less
happy than in the case of its predecessor: your ignorance of the
Italian language and your lack of acquaintance with the country to which it is native have rendered your scenes, on the
whole, less natural and easy than in *Jennifer Lorn*. If you reply
that a full third of the earlier tale is supposed to take place in
Persia, a country of which you know even less than you do of
Italy; I must answer that, as Persia, like Arcadia, is a country
of which no one knows anything, we may be free, without fear
of reprehension, to write anything of it we please; but that, in
the case of Venice, we are certain to have among our readers
many persons who have been there, and whom it will displease
to find the scenes inappropriate or the manners reported inex-
actly. I must object further that you have mingled the fictitious
with the real in a manner hardly allowable; in as much as,
though introducing such actual and known personages as
Count Gozzi and Cardinal de Bernis, you have juxtaposed to
them an imaginary character whose name is a paraphrase of
Casanova's and who, though in some cases spoken of in connexion with names that paraphrase those of the impostor's associates, in others is represented as the hero of Casanova's own
exploits, such as the escape from the Leads. If you should
plead that, since Casanova has left a history of his own life in

which its events are recorded with some fulness, and that it would be incredible to ascribe to him an adventure which is not included in that account; I must reply that the same is true of Gozzi, who nowhere mentions in his memoirs the circumstances you relate.

As for the style, though distinguished by elegance and enlivened by wit, which no production of yours can fail of, I fear that the imagery has here become so copious as somewhat to impede the progress of the action. Where we are bewildered by the profusion of the trees, we become incapable of perceiving the forest. Your story is obscured by a luxuriance of phrases, which seems less suited to a novel than a poem, where exfoliation of this kind is more easily accepted; and we are forced to conclude, when we have reached the end, that the plot has not been very carefully contrived. Our attention is directed first to the Cardinal, but we presently discover that he is not among the chief actors; then we are entertained by a long conversation between the Cardinal, the Chevalier and the Count, which occupies a good third of the book, yet appears to lead nowhither, and to accomplish no purpose which might not have been accomplished better in briefer space. If the style would be more suited to a poem, the same may be asserted of the matter, which, involving so much that is supernatural and whimsical, would not invite in verse the same scrutiny to which it must be subjected in a novel, where we are less content to admit the vagueness of fancy or the abstraction of allegory.

> Indignatur item privatis ac prope socco
> Dignis carminibus narrari cena Thyestae.
> Singula quæque locum teneant sortita decentum.

What is here said of the styles of tragick and comick poetry, must with even greater reason be applied to the more dissimilar styles of poetry and prose.

Of the fable itself, it can only be said that, if it is to be taken literally, it is absurd; and if allegorically, licentious. That a young woman should be converted into porcelain by a ceramical calorification, even with the assistance of the Devil—this is a conception as repugnant to reason as it is monstrous to imagination. But we should prefer the extravagances of childhood to the wantonness of maturity. Remember, Madam, that the progress of age, in which I am so much further advanced than you, should bring, not, as we grow accustomed to the spectacle of vice, a cynical indifference to virtue; but a more scrupulous attention to morality and a constant determination to leave no line which could offend it, as we approach more closely to the awful Judgement Seat before which we must all one day stand. I am, dear Madam,

                    Your most affectionate humble servant,
                              Sam. Johnson

                                        October 7, 1925

Firbank and Beckford

R ONALD FIRBANK, the English novelist, died at Rome on
June 7. His last novel, *Concerning the Eccentricities of
Cardinal Pirelli*, has been published in England, but not yet in
the United States. This is in some ways, I believe, the best book
of Ronald Firbank's I have read—certainly one of the very best
written and one of the freest from the curious "gagging" with
which Firbank has had a way of shutting off the vividness and
charm of his characters by reducing them to the mere comic
names of a sophisticated funny-paper. Ronald Firbank has usually been treated as a less important representative of the fashionable school of ironic romance (Van Vechten, Aldous Huxley,
etc.); but, though at first glance he looks the most trivial, he
seems to me to have felt the artist's vocation more authentically than many of the others. These others, in general, are
graceful writers; but Firbank is not really a graceful writer: he
works always in brief discontinuous strokes which appear to
have cost him some pains. Whatever else he may not take seriously, he is serious about literature. The "painted, love-tired
hands" of the toreador's mistress opening and closing her fan;
the "still deep pools" of the Moorish water-garden, in which
the Cardinal sought "like some Adept to interpret the mirrored
music of the sky"; the Pope with "the head of an elderly lady's-
maid," in his twentieth-century Vatican, remarking, "It's a
bore there being no lift!" as he dismisses the Cardinal with a
benediction: these do afford something of the pleasure and
surprise that we get from the vision of the original artist.

But Firbank, in some ways so highly developed, is fatally deficient in others. As an artist, he presents the disconcerting
spectacle of one of those sea-crabs one sometimes finds on
which a claw that has been broken off has not yet had time to
grow again, and we are shocked by the disproportion between
the formidable normal claw and the helpless rudimentary one.
In their subjects themselves, Firbank's novels seem to reflect
some fundamental malformation; it is not merely the reader
who finds them unsatisfactory, but the author who expresses
dissatisfaction. All the heroes and heroines of Firbank—in

those books that I have read, at least—have the most unfortunate fates; possessed by a bizarre variety of passions, they are almost invariably frustrated in their efforts to satisfy them. This final novel, indeed, seems a fable for the author's own case: can we fail to recognize in the Cardinal, with his "very great distinction and sweetness," whose ecclesiastical career is blighted by his worldliness and frivolity, by his inveterate excessive indulgence toward the weaknesses and vagaries of his flock, a symbol of the fate of that English novelist, distinguished by some very rare qualities, who never came to anything in the world of letters represented, in another of his books, by a delegation consisting of E. V. Lucas, Robert Hichens and Clutton-Brock?

It is interesting to compare Ronald Firbank with another highly special literary case—William Beckford, the author of *Vathek*. Beckford, like Firbank, was a very rich man of unusual literary ability, who never, however, accomplished as much as his brilliance seemed to warrant—an Englishman who lived much out of England and had a taste for the Mohammedan world (both Firbank and Beckford liked to dwell on the excesses of the pre-Adamite Sultans). They both had luxurious tastes and eccentric curiosities. They both derived from French sources; but Beckford is as different from his master Voltaire, and in very much the same way, as Firbank from his master Anatole France. For the cynicism and irony of Beckford do not imply a criticism of society; they seem merely to satisfy a perverse impulse. And Beckford's fancy has the slightly mad silliness that we also find in Firbank. "In vain did she renew her fumigations," writes Beckford of the Princess Carathis, as she is making her supreme effort to put herself in harmony with the powers of darkness, "and extend herself upon the roof to obtain mystic visions. Nothing more could she see in her dreams than pieces of brocade, nosegays of flowers, and other unmeaning gewgaws." One cannot think of any other English writer up to our own time who would be likely to have written this; but it is the sort of thing one does find in Firbank. The unexpected and tragic force of the burning hearts of the Hall of Eblis is also akin to the incongruous bitterness which sometimes makes itself felt in Firbank. Beckford and Firbank both

have a cool and trivial cruelty that we might call cattily feminine if it were not so plainly something else. And in their sensitiveness, their subtle intelligence, their taste for fine and
gorgeous things, as well as in their malice, their manias and
their incurable tic of silliness, they have both much in common
with the uncomfortable character of Proust's M. de Charlus.

September 8, 1926

A Preface to Persius

Maudlin Meditations in a Speakeasy

T HE OTHER EVENING I had to dine out alone, and, stopping
in on my way at a book store, bought a little eighteenth-
century edition of Persius, with notes and a translation. The
editor and translator was a man named William Drummond,
who had also been a member of Parliament. The attractive
duodecimo was bound in green morocco and stamped in gold,
and, inside the cover, had gray marbled paper with green and
yellow runnings. There was a medallion of Aulus Persius Flac-
cus, with crisp metallic curls on the title-page, and the whole
volume, with the edges of its pages gilded on all three sides
and its well-spaced and small clear type, had the aspect of a
little casket in which something precious was kept. I went to
an Italian restaurant and, while I was waiting for the antipasto,
I began to read the preface. "In offering to the public," it ran,
"a new English version of Persius, my object has rather been to
express his meaning clearly, than either to translate his words
literally, or to copy his manner servilely. The sentiments of this
satirist are indeed admirable, and deserve to be better known
than they are; but his poetry cannot be praised for its elegance,
nor his language for its urbanity."

The plate arrived, with a glistening sardine, little purple
olives, two pearly leeks, bronze anchovies and bright red
pimiento slices that looked like little tongues, all against a lin-
ing of pale lettuce. There were also a bottle of yellow wine and
a goblet of pale green glass. I wondered what had become of
the sort of thing that this editor of Persius represented. In the
middle of the room where I sat was a party of men and women,
all pink and of huge size, who were uncorking loud sour laughter; across the room was a quite pretty young girl, of an obviously simple nature, who had some sort of keen professional
interest in pleasing a rather defective-looking half-aquiline
man, whose eyes one couldn't see through his eyeglasses.
Craning around behind me, however, I caught sight of E. E.
Cummings. Cummings, I reflected, was a cultivated fellow and

a good writer and came from Boston, but was not a bit like William Drummond. For a point of view like that of Drummond, who would have reproached the inelegance of Persius's poetry yet applauded his admirable sentiments, one would have to go to our own eighteenth-century literature—to Joel Barlow or Philip Freneau. But Drummond was a fancier of letters and a political figure at the same time—Jefferson might have thought and written so. Some of the logic, some of the elegance, some of the moderate and equable opinion which seemed to be the qualities—here found, as it were, in their pure state—of this preface to an ancient classic had gone to the announcement of our national policies and the construction of our constitution. But new interests had taken over the government; and I had been reading in the paper that day of a typical example of their methods—an assault by the state constabulary on a meeting of Italian miners; men clubbed insensible, children gassed, old people badly beaten, a nursing woman knocked down. With the exception, I reflected, of Cummings, and possibly the Italian waiters, there was probably not a person in that room who would not either approve this action or refuse to believe that it had happened; and Cummings was as powerless to prevent its recurrence as the illiterate waiters would be. Perhaps the only element in sight which had anything in common with Drummond on Persius was the Italian dinner itself, of which a bowl of minestrone, with its cabbage, big brown beans and round noodles, had just reached me as the second course, and in the richness and balance of whose composition I could still see the standards of a civilization based on something more comfortably human than commercial and industrial interests. Yet how few generations of Italians speaking English and competing with the natives would it take for them to forget their cooking and their ideal of a good dinner and to go in, as one already saw them beginning to do, for expensive à la carte restaurants with heterogeneous and uninteresting menus?

"The defects of Persius, considered with respect to composition, cannot perhaps be easily defended. Even Casaubon, his fondest admirer, and most successful interpreter, admits that his style is obscure. If, however, any apology can be made for this first sin against good writing, it is in the case of a satirist,

and above all, of a satirist who dared to reprobate the crimes, and to ridicule the follies of a tyrant. If Persius be obscure, let it be remembered, he lived in the time of Nero. But it has been remarked, that this author is not obscure, only when he lashes and exposes the Roman emperor. It was very well, it has been said, to employ hints, and to speak in half sentences, while he censured the vices of a cruel and luxurious despot; but there could be no occasion for enveloping himself in obscurity, while he expounded the doctrines of the Stoics to his friend Cornutus, or expatiated to the poet Bassus on the true use of riches."
—I looked up, as the chicken and greens were being set down before me, and saw Cummings, who had finished and was leaving. If they had felt that way about Persius, what would they have thought of Cummings? And what was the use, in the eighteenth century, of the critics' having cultivated those standards, if Cummings was what the future had in store? He stopped at my table, and I asked him where be had spent the summer. "I thought of going to Boston," he ejaculated, "to see the machine-guns!*—but we've all seen plenty of machine-guns!—commonest thing in the world!—so I walked around New York, expecting to be blown up any moment—be a fine thing to blow the subways up!—of course, my attitude toward this whole thing—I mean, it's just unfortunate—it's a bore, like somebody losing his pants—it's embarrassing, but it oughtn't to be a surprise to anybody—what surprises me is that they managed to stay alive for seven years!—why, I've seen them shoot people first and search them afterwards—and if they've got any bullets in them, they arrest them for carrying concealed weapons!" He slipped away with his spirited crest of hair and his narrow self-regarding eyes. I addressed myself to the salad. So Persius, in another age that combined moral anarchy with harsh repression, had, it seemed, expressed himself confusedly, inelegantly, and obscenely. And it is Persius who is the writer and not the complacent Drummond, as it is Cummings and not the persons who publish books on American poetry. Where life is disorderly, the poets will express themselves in nonsense. I had looked at the beginning of Persius—

*Sacco and Vanzetti had been executed in Boston on August 23, 1927, and the demonstrations in protest against this had alarmed the city authorities to the point of having the State House guarded with tommy-guns.

"*O curas hominum! O quantum est in rebus inane!*"—it seemed to me entirely in the modern spirit.

I went on reading the preface: "While, therefore, I fully admit the charge against Persius, I cannot allow to it that weight, which it would have in most other cases. Indeed, we may as well complain of the rust on an ancient coin, as of the obscurity of an ancient satire. Nature, it is true, always holds up the same mirror, but prejudice, habit, and education, are continually changing the appearance of the objects seen in it. The objections which have been made to my author in some other respects, are more difficult to answer. His unpolished verses, his coarse comparisons, and his ungraceful transitions from one subject to another, manifest, it is said, either his contempt or his ignorance of elegant composition. It cannot, indeed, be contended, that Persius displays the politeness of Horace, or that he shows himself an adept in the *callida junctura*. His poetry is a strong and rapid torrent, which pours in its infracted course over the rocks and precipices, and which occasionally, like the waters of the Rhone, disappears from view, and loses itself underground." Yes: like Cummings's poetry and conversation. Yet Drummond had his poetry, too: "the rust on an ancient coin," "a strong and rapid torrent, which pours in its infracted course"—and it appeared that he was, after all, sympathetic with the unpolished Persius and had earnestly undertaken to defend him against the taste of the time. That was the paradox of literature: provoked only by the anomalies of reality, by its discord, its chaos, its pain, it attempted, from poetry to metaphysics, to impose on that chaos some order, to find some resolution for that discord, to render that pain acceptable—to strike some permanent mark of the mind on the mysterious flux of experience which escapes beneath our hand. So with Persius, poised, as it were, on the edge of the collapse of the Empire, for whom the criticism of the satirist, the philosophy of the Stoic—at the least, the hexameter itself—were all ways, for even so "inelegant" a poet, of introducing some logic and some meaning into the ceaseless struggles of men to make themselves at home in the universe. Then, as it were, relieving the poet, the critic who studies him, in turn, must stand firm against these miseries and horrors, these disquieting shocks of reality—he must pick up the poet's

verses, all twisted where disaster has struck them, and he must
carry them further, like Drummond, to where there is tranquillity and leisure enough for him to point out what form and
what sense the poet had tried to give them, to supply by his
own judicial comments the straightness and the soundness
they lack. Yet, even beneath the shelter of that firmament
of eighteenth-century order, he, too, has felt the shock of
reality—the dullness of a rusted coin, the turbulence of a river.
For without the impulse from reality, neither criticism nor
poetry nor any other human work can be valid.

I had finished the apple, the Brie cheese and the little black
demi-tasse, and I turned to the book again: "I cannot conclude this Preface, without lamenting that an early and untimely death should have prevented the Poet, whom I have
translated, from giving a more finished appearance to his
works." How extraordinary that William Drummond, almost
two thousand years after Christ, should have felt this solidarity
with Persius, that, bridging the ruin of Rome, bridging the
confusion of the Middle Ages, we should find him lamenting
this early death as if it were that of some able young man
whom he had known in his time in London, some young man
who had been educated at the same institutions and shared
with him the same values. The discord and chaos of reality!
From the point of view of civilization, the whole of the West
had caved in. The geographical void of Europe had been too
big for Rome to fill; and then later—to change the metaphor,
as my wine made it easy to do—when plantations that had
been ploughed under had scattered their seed abroad, and at
last there had been bred all through Europe such a race as had
formerly flourished only on the Mediterranean, a new race to
whom Persius could speak as men of his own education—
when this had been achieved, there opened, as it were in another dimension, a new void, the social void, below the class of
educated people to which Persius and Drummond belonged,
and into that yawning gulf of illiteracy and mean ambitions,
even while Drummond wrote—the book was dated 1797—
Europe heavily and dully sank, not without some loud
crackings of her structure. America, in a sense, was that gulf.

I had finished the bottle of wine, which was certainly better
than they had had last year—they were really making an effort,

I thought, to improve the quality of their wine. How much, I wondered, was it due to the wine that I now myself felt so warmed by this sense of continuity with the past, with Persius and William Drummond, by this spirit of stubborn endurance? Suppose that the federal agents should succeed in suppressing these restaurants where pretty good wine was still served. These restaurants were run by Italians, and it had lately been against Italians that the machine-guns of the State had been trained and the police incited to butchery. In the meantime, there was nothing to do save to work with the dead for allies, and at odds with the ignorance of most of the living, that that edifice, so many times begun, so discouragingly reduced to ruins, might yet stand as the headquarters of humanity!

I left the restaurant in meditation, and, on my way out, had a collision that jarred me with a couple of those bulky pink people who had stopped laughing and were dancing to the radio.

October 19, 1927

Burlesque Shows

I. The National Winter Garden

T HERE IS a rumor that the National Winter Garden Burlesque has fallen a victim to the current purity wave and been obliged to abate the Aristophanic license for which it was formerly celebrated. The management of the National Winter Garden (not the Broadway Winter Garden, of course, but the one at Second Avenue and Houston Street) has been kind enough to supply the *New Republic* with a season pass, and, as the result of a recent visit, the writer of these notes is happy to announce that this report is entirely without foundation and to recommend the Minsky Brothers' Follies as still among the most satisfactory shows in town. The great thing about the National Winter Garden is that, though admittedly as vulgar as possible, it has nothing of the peculiar smartness and hardness one is accustomed to elsewhere in New York. It is refreshing because it lies quite outside the mechanical routine of Broadway. Though more ribald, it is more honest and less self-conscious than the ordinary risqué farce and, though crude, on the whole more attractive than most of the hideous comic-supplement humors of uptown revue and vaudeville. Nor is it to be confounded with the uptown burlesque show of the type of the Columbia, which is now as wholesome and as boring as any expensive musical comedy. The National Winter Garden has a tradition and a vein of its own.

For one thing, the Minsky Brothers go in for a kind of beauty which has long passed out of fashion elsewhere. The National Winter Garden has no use for the slim legs and shallow breasts the modern American taste for which has been so successfully exploited by Ziegfeld and the other uptown producers. Save for their bobbed hair and modern shoes, the chorus at the National Winter Garden might have come out of the pictures of Casino girls in old *Munsey's Magazines* of the nineties. And the humor of the National Winter Garden differs, also, from the humor of other shows. It mainly consists of gags, to be sure, but they are not the gags you are used to. For all their violence, the comic interludes have a certain freshness and wit. In the current version of *Anthony and Cleopatra*, a perennial Minsky classic, Julius Caesar, in a tin helmet and smoking a big cigar, catches Anthony (the Jewish comic) on a divan with Cleopatra (the principal strip-tease girl) and wallops him over the bottom with the flat of an enormous sword. "I'm dying! I'm dying!," groans Anthony, as he staggers around in a circle; and Caesar and Cleopatra, the Roman soldiers and the Egyptian slave-girls break into a rousing shimmy to the refrain of "He's dying! He's dying!" "I hear de voices of de angels!" says Anthony. "What do they say?" asks Caesar. "I don't know: I don't speak Polish." He is groggy; he totters; he faints. "I hear de cockroaches calling me!" he cries; and from the orchestra sounds, acrid and sinister, the cry of the expectant roaches. "Bring me the wassup," says Cleopatra, and her slave-girl, kneeling, presents a box, from which Cleopatra takes a huge property phallus. (At some point in the development of the ancient act, the word *asp* was evidently confused with *wasp*.) It is impossible to report in these pages all the incidents of the scenes that follow. Cleopatra falls prone on her lover's body, and Caesar, with pathetic reverence, places on her posterior a wreath, which he waters with a watering-pot. Charmian and Britannicus, after some play of their own with the wassup, finally fall lifeless, too, the girl as she flops on the soldier exploding a toy balloon which he has been wearing as a false chest. This curious piece of East Side folk-drama has been popular at Minsky's for years, and it is always a little different. Sometimes Caesar makes his entrance on a bicycle, blowing his own bugle; sometimes his entrance is heralded by a flourish of trumpets from the orchestra, as the company lines up and looks out the wings: Caesar enters from the other direction and gooses the last man, so that the whole row fall down like dominoes. There is also a remarkable gallows skit, which begins as an affecting piece of realism and ends as a low joke.

The orchestra at the National Winter Garden is energetic even in summer. The girls are not only robust but take a certain jolly interest in the show and sometimes betray their roles by laughing inappropriately at the jokes. The audience are keenly appreciative, and the house peals with easy thunder more infectious than the punctual crashes uptown. The theater, at

the top of an office building, is very well ventilated; and just
now you can see through an open exit the foothills of the
downtown buildings against a pale lilac-gray sky. After the
show, you can walk down the fire-escape.

The most celebrated performer of the National Winter Garden was a Yiddish comedian named Jack Shargel, who has now
retired from the stage. To these raw buffooneries he is said to
have brought a touch of the wistfulness of a Lew Fields or a
Charlie Chaplin. A connoisseur of the theater in its best days*
has described to me a scene in which Jack Shargel received a
rose from a beautiful lady just going off the stage. He kissed it,
he smelt it in ecstasy, then, with a graceful and infinitely tender
gesture, he stretched out his hand and tossed it away: it fell
with a crash of glass.

                                                    July 8, 1925

II. *Peaches—A Humdinger*

The National Winter Garden Burlesque has been subjected
to a renovation since I wrote about it last summer. The poets,
the artists, and the smart magazines have been making it fashionable; and Mr. Minsky, the manager, feeling perhaps that the
shabbiness of the old productions was unworthy of his new
clientèle, has provided brighter and more elegant settings and
a slenderer bevy of girls, with a fresh repertoire of costumes.
At a recent performance I witnessed, one of the actors made a
speech in the intermission, in which he said that a critic had
written, apropos of some risqué Broadway musical comedy,
that if he wanted to hear "dubble entenders," he would rather
go to the National Winter Garden, "because here's where you
get burlesque as you like it, without any camouflage—sincere
dubble entenders." Nevertheless, a restraining taste has been
exercised, since I last was there, on the traditional Minsky humor. There is even a rumor that a gifted representative of the
non-commercial artistic theater is to write and design a sketch

---

*This was E. E. Cummings, who loved burlesque and was able to make
some use of its methods. See the piece that follows on his play *Him*. He made
a drawing of Jack Shargel, which appeared in the *Dial*.

for the National Winter Garden. At this rate, it will presently be hardly distinguishable from the Music Box Revue.

To find burlesque in its primitive form, you must go to the Olympic on Fourteenth Street. The Olympic, with more limited resources than the National Winter Garden, makes no attempt to give its patrons anything beyond the fundamentals —that is, instalments of sidewalk conversation alternating with instalments of girls. As for the former, it is mainly manufactured by three unvarying comedians, who reappear time after time in front of the same prosaic backdrop advertising the Monte Carlo Spaghetti House, the Cabin Dancing Academy, the White Rats Tonsorial Parlors and the D. and S. Pants Shop. (An act like the Anthony and Cleopatra of the National Winter Garden would be quite out of the range of the Olympic.) Of these merry-andrews and kings of fun, the leader is, of course, a spruce young man with a clean-shaven face and a straw hat. But, whereas, at Minsky's in its present phase, this conventional role has been given to a comparatively prepossessing fellow not unlike a musical-comedy hero, the "straight man," as he is called, at the Olympic follows the true burlesque tradition by making us feel that, though his neatly pressed clothes contrast with those of his disreputable companions, he is the greatest rogue of the three. The other two, the low comedians, have the appearance of unhappy monstrosities. One is dwarfish, with a very big head and the toil-toughened, staring and honest face of a German nibelung, and he embarks on his comic adventures invariably with the utmost solemnity; when these end in cruel disaster at the hands of his straw-hatted tormentor or of one of the disdainful cuties with bare legs and a brassière, he apostrophizes the audience in Yiddish on a note of bewildered complaint or rage. The other, more nondescript and stunted still, is dressed in clothes which produce a disconcerting effect, like those of a trained chimpanzee, from his inability to wear them in a human fashion, and his face presents no human expression but a heavy and cretinous mask, of which the closed-up slits of the eyes give the impression of some helpless abortion in which the faculty of sight has been scarcely developed. The dialogue of these three artists suffers sadly from a poverty of invention. Here are a couple of examples. One of the Girls: "I'm in love! I'm in love! I'm gonta jump off the Brooklyn Bridge!" The Man with the Straw Hat: "Don't do that: you'll get the water dirty!" The Man with the Straw Hat, who is trying to play a cornet, addressing the Nibelung: "Say, don't look at me! Don't look at me! I can't play when you look at me! Say, you've got the kind of face that only a mother could love! If I had a dog with a face like that, I'd shootum!"

The main thing, however, is the girls. The Olympic, like Earl Carroll's Vanities, is equipped with a double runway. This runway, though it is studded on the inside edge with a row of pink electric-light bulbs, has the aspect—to which, besides, the general appearance of the theater and the shirt-sleeved audience of men contribute—of some sort of bowling alley; but it figures, none the less, for the spectators, as the principal source of glamor. The leading women, with their sinewy thighs and their muscular abdomens, have learned the rhythmic contortions of the stomach-dance; and the chorus does its best to live up to them with such shaking of hips and breasts as it can clumsily manage. Some, evidently accepted for their beauty rather than for theatrical gifts, are too stolid or untrained to dance at all and, smiling at the audience below, merely parade back and forth on the runway. Some do not even smile. But all have their powerful effect on the clientèle of the house.

What strikes you at first, however, when you are new to this more primitive form of burlesque, is the outward indifference of the spectators. They sit in silence and quite without smiling and with no overt sign of admiration toward the glittering and thick-lashed seductresses who stand on a level with their shoulders and who address them with so personal a heartiness. The audience do not even applaud when the girls have gone back to the stage; and you think that the act has flopped. But as soon as the girls have disappeared behind the scenes and the comedians come on for the next skit, the men begin to clap, on an accent which represents less a tribute of enthusiasm than a diffident conventional summons for the girls to appear again. This is repeated from four to six times for every number in the show. The audience never betray their satisfaction so long as the girls are there; it is only when the performance is finished that they signify their desire to renew it. They have come to the theater, you realize, in order to have their dreams made objective, and they sit there each alone with his dream. They call the girls back again and again, and the number goes on forever. When the leading performer begins to strip, they watch the process in silence, recalling her with timid applause when she vanishes behind the wings. Finally, she shows them her breasts, but her smile is never returned; nor is there any vibration of excitement when she has finally got down to her G-string— merely the same automatic summons, to which this time she does not respond. In one of the numbers, the girls come out with fishing-rods and dangle pretzels under the noses of the spectators; the leading ladies have lemons. The men do not at first reach for them; they remain completely stolid. Then suddenly, when the lures have been played for some minutes, a few begin to grab at the pretzels, like frogs who have finally decided to strike at a piece of red flannel or like cats who, after simulating apathy while watching a cork on a string, at last find the moment to pounce on it. When they catch the pretzels, however, they do not take them off the strings or playfully refuse to release them; they let them go at the first jerk and relapse into their impassivity.

The truth is, I suppose, that this audience are struck by a kind of awe, as if before priestesses of Venus, in presence of these gorgeous creatures. Their decorum is not undermined by this brazenly sexual exhibition: on the contrary, it makes them solemn. They have come for the gratification that they hope to derive from these dances; but this vision of erotic ecstasy, when they see it unveiled before them—though they watch it with fascination—frightens them and renders them mute.

August 18, 1926

E. E. Cummings's 'Him'

M R. E. E. CUMMINGS, the poet, has published a play called *Him*, of great length and of the utmost impracticability. It is, in fact, rather a dramatic poem in prose, and ought to be judged as such. As a poet, E. E. Cummings occupies a unique and curious place. He is, perhaps, the writer of the younger group who most widely and vividly interests, and who most profoundly influences, other young people writing poetry. And he has certainly deserved this eminence: he has deserved it by his gift for delicious, if frequently incoherent, song, which he seems to shake out so high-spiritedly while most of his fellow-poets are busy stitching images together; by his audacity, and by his original personality, his personal habit of speech, which, until other people began to imitate him, made his poetry quite unlike that of anyone else. Yet Mr. Cummings has always, so far, seemed as an artist rather unsatisfactory. Spontaneity and naïveté are excellent qualities for lyric poetry, but the poet should have at least the patience to calculate his effects and the expertness to carry them out; whereas Cummings seems self-indulgent, as if he never could restrain himself from an extra trick or a silly joke. One suspects in him an incapacity for putting himself in the place of the person who is going to read him. And *Him*, which comes nearer than Mr. Cummings's poetry to letting us see his mind at full length, confirms this impression of self-indulgence. It is characteristic of Cummings that he seems to understand things instantaneously, that he seems to understand everything, but that he rarely seems to try to systematize the flood of impressions that reaches him. This play is the shimmering scaturience of an intelligence and a sensibility of the very first distinction—but a drama deficient in dramatic logic. The main action of *Him* is evidently an ether-dream in the mind of the heroine; and the climax the revelation of the reason for her being under ether. There reënact themselves within her dream the various phases of the love affair that has brought her to her present pass, intermingled with a phantasmagoria of the imaginings of her lover, who, at the time the affair had been going on, had been

engaged in writing a play. But the development of the love affair and the connection with it of the phantasmagoria are obscure even to the reader, and one would think that for a
theater audience they must prove completely baffling. One's
impression is that Mr. Cummings has never really thought out
the problems of his very complicated subject. Though he has
tried for a dramatic structure, he has still left his materials
rather chaotic.

But when all this has been said on the negative side, the remarkable merits of *Him* remain. In the first place, there are
comic ideas which would make Mr. Cummings's fortune, if he
would only take more thought to exploit them. The burlesque-
show Mussolini with his epicene admirers; the morose American traveller bellyaching over the dreariness of a European city
in which the inhabitants are starving; the three Fates who,
throughout the action, sit knitting and rocking and talking
eerie nonsense—all these are capital conceptions that have moments of brilliant vitality, though the author, with a strange
lack of instinct for climax, either lets them go on so long that
they lose their hold on our interest or allows his scene to trail
off in an ineffective ending. Here is a specimen of the happy
vein of the brooding conversation of the Fates:

FIRST. George says he doesn't see why guinea-pigs can't have
children if children can have guinea-pigs.
THIRD. A clean tooth never decays.
SECOND. Do children have guinea-pigs?
FIRST. Oh yes, more's the pity. Mine often have it.
THIRD. Your nails show your refinement.
SECOND. Badly?

Mr. Cummings also reveals an astonishing faculty for mim-
icking and caricaturing the speech of a variety of kinds of
people: his soap-box orator, his sideshow barker and his American ladies in Paris are both made lifelike and thrown into relief
with something of comic genius.

It is, however, in the scenes between the lovers that Mr.
Cummings's genius principally appears. They are, to my mind,
more successful than anything in his poetry. Here the blurri-
ness and lack of direction of the mind which does not construct
is carried off by the extraordinary sensitiveness which is itself a

kind of intelligence. Here Cummings is occupied, as in many of his poems, with the attempt to render shades of feeling so special and so complex that language can scarcely follow them. The effort to seize these feelings and to fix them, not by trying to press them into the mold of an accepted convention, which must falsify unique sensations, but in the flux, in the raw confusion, with which they visit our body and spirit, has always, of course, been a primary cause of the obscurity of Cummings's verse. Now in *Him*, where the poet has imposed upon himself the discipline of dramatic dialogue, he has succeeded, with an original and marvellous eloquence, not merely in letting us hear what the lovers say to one another, but also in making us feel what they feel, experience what they experience. These scenes—and especially the one at the beginning of the third act—seem to me the very best things that Cummings has so far done. They make *Him*, for all its stretches of balderdash and its admixture of puerilities, a book which should be read by all persons who prefer the real thing in literature, no matter how drunk and disorderly, to the well-intentioned imitation, no matter how carefully dressed.

It may be that in the wit, the fantasy and the lyric beauty of *Him* we find the germ of an important dramatic poet. The qualities that have gone to make this play are under notably less efficient control than those that went to make *Peer Gynt*, but the two pieces have something in common. I have said that *Him* is impracticable, and so, in its present form, it is; but why does not someone induce the author to reorganize it and cut it down, and try the experiment of producing it?* Our American expressionist dramas have too often been fatally deficient in precisely those elements of eloquence and genuine imagination in which Cummings's play is so rich: they have commended themselves to our interest on the basis of their artistic merits, and then have turned out to suffer from the primary disadvantage of being written by persons who could not write. E. E. Cummings lacks theatrical craft, but he is equipped with a lively dramatic sense, and—what is rarest of all—with a poet's pen.

November 2, 1927

* *Him* was produced at the Provincetown Theater in Macdougal Street on April 18 of the following year and has twice been revived.

A Great Magician

T HE TRUE STORY of Houdini's death is told for the first time, apparently, in a new biography: *Houdini, His Life Story*, by Harold Kellock, from the recollections and documents of Beatrice Houdini. Houdini had broken his ankle in Albany while performing his Chinese Water Torture trick, in which he was suspended by the feet in a small cabinet full of water. He had lately been over-working, even more than was usual with him, and had not been to bed for three nights; he had also been very much worried about Mrs. Houdini, whom he had had to leave ill in Providence. When he arrived in Montreal, his ankle was still so sore that he was obliged to spend most of the time on a couch. In this condition, in his dressing-room, he received three students from McGill University, where he had just delivered a lecture on spiritualism. One of the students asked whether it were true "that Houdini could withstand heavy blows without inconvenience. The magician replied that he could do so, if he had warning to brace himself. He then picked up some letters. The student said something about testing Houdini's ability then and there. Houdini, absorbed in a letter, was not paying attention and gave an absent-minded reply, which the boy interpreted as consent. The next instant, Houdini was startled by receiving a series of sharp blows in the abdomen. At the fourth blow, he stopped the young man with a gesture, just as the two other students jumped up in protest. Acute peritonitis developed, and, after a Herculean struggle, he died in the hospital."

There is in this sudden ending to a career which had its heroic aspect something ironic and tragic. It shocks us that Houdini, not much over fifty and at the most interesting point of his career, should thus have fallen a victim to one of the most trivial of his own challenges, to a blow by a college student, given under a misapprehension, when he was ill and reading his mail.

Houdini was the son of a rabbi. His parents had come from Budapest, and settled in Appleton, Wisconsin. The father knew no English; they were poor. Houdini (whose real name was

Ehrich Weiss) went off at the age of eleven to earn his own living. He had already learned to do tricks from the conjurors in circus sideshows, and, while working in a locksmith's shop, had mastered the technique of picking locks: he could already, in fact, open handcuffs. He had from the beginning the magician's vocation. He was by turns a messenger-boy, a necktie-cutter and a Wild Man in a tent of freaks; but his concentration on magic was as fervent and unremitting as Lindbergh's concentration on flying.

Houdini had, thus, in his field, the all-absorbing preoccupation of genius, but he was remarkable also for other qualities, the virtues of his sober, pious and self-respecting German-Jewish family, virtues that he managed to preserve through the humiliations and hardships of his early years. Houdini remained all his life, in spite of considerable egotism, the scrupulous, industrious, loyal and generous son of his parents. It was partly this background of family life—his devotion to his wife and his mother is one of his most striking traits—which gave him his solidity and straightness. When, in Yorkshire once, a former hangman who had retired to run a public-house, attempted to bribe the champion, proposing to bet large sums on his ability to tie him up in such a way that he could not escape and then, when Houdini had "thrown" the contest, to divide the winnings with him, Houdini wrote contemptuously in his diary: "Guess he didn't know how I was brought up."

This magician was also romantic, in an essentially Germanic fashion. The story of his marriage is amazing. Mrs. Houdini was eighteen when he met her: she had been taken by her mother to a show that Houdini was giving at the high school, and, in the course of one of his tricks, the magician upset some acid on her dress. He immediately leapt down from the platform and earnestly apologized. The mother remained indignant; but "I managed to whisper to him," Mrs. Houdini remembers, "'Don't mind Mother. I think you're wonderful.' 'Do you?' he exclaimed, straightening up, and for a long moment our eyes held, while Mother and the rest of the audience were completely forgotten." He brought her a new dress at her house, and though the mother refused to admit him, the girl slipped away and met him outside. He persuaded her to go with him to Coney Island, and made her marry him then and there. The quality of Houdini's imagination sometimes verged on the Gothic. Mrs. Houdini tells the following incident: "The last night the brothers worked together at the dance hall in Coney Island, I had a bad scare. Houdini asked his brother and me to take a walk with him after the evening's work was over. He led us into the country on a dark lonely bridge spanning some swiftly running black water. It was a weird-looking night, with a split moon that seemed to be dodging in and out behind heavy clouds. In the middle of the bridge he halted us, and there we waited for a time silently, I at least in growing trepidation. Finally a distant bell tolled solemnly twelve times. As soon as the last beat ceased to reverberate, Houdini clasped his brother's hand and mine together, raised them aloft and cried: 'Beatrice, Dash, raise your hands to heaven and swear you will both be true to me. Never betray me in any way, so help you God!'" And even in Houdini's later years, when he wanted to go incognito to a spiritualistic seance, he liked to disguise himself in a fantastic and elaborate make-up, which involved a long white beard and a hump, and at the end of the proceedings snatch off the beard and dramatically declare to the discomfited medium, "I am Houdini!"

But all this was quite natural for him, not a part that he deliberately played. His own life was his drama, and he had otherwise little of the actor about him—so little, that when one reads this biography, one feels that he had difficulty in adapting himself to his role of public entertainer. He was, at first, it seems, so poor a showman that he could not arouse adequate interest in feats that were actually unprecedented; and when one saw him in his last years, it was curious to note that his magician's patter was confined to a few quaint perfunctory phrases. Houdini, in his queer chosen line, was scrupulous and serious-minded; and he tended to slough off the charlatanry, innocent though that is, which is essential to the magician's profession.

Houdini mastered conjuring in all its branches, but was far too adventurous and energetic to be satisfied to be merely a conjuror. He had always been interested in opening locks, and he began to specialize in escapes. Now, aside from the exceptional qualities which Houdini applied to these problems, there is nothing particularly fascinating about getting out of bags and boxes by means of various fakes. Yet the tale of Houdini's achievements is an exciting and somehow an impressive one. He has acquired a skill with locks that is probably unrivalled in the world, and he has made himself both lithe and strong. He challenges the world to challenge him, and no prison appears too formidable. He seems eaten by a veritable passion to test himself more and more severely: he must prove to himself and the world that he is invincible, irrepressible, uneclipsable. Here, as I say, if we forget Houdini, the object becomes ridiculous, yet the story which culminates in his breaking out of an inhuman steel "carette" devised by the Russian police for the transportation of prisoners to Siberia—an exploit which seems for the moment to have made him a popular hero in Russia—this story of Houdini's self-liberations has its dignity like the story of any brave man who pits himself against obstacles and bests them.

But Houdini was by no means content with even his undisputed title of Handcuff King. He had also, during all this period, been occupied with scholarly researches: he had been collecting and reading books on magic with a characteristically tireless voracity, and had taken a good deal of trouble to interview retired magicians and investigate all kinds of wonder-workers. He began himself to write on the subject. And in his last years, he did few escapes and for the first time appeared to the public in something like his true character and at something like his full stature. He had been making of spiritualism and mediums the same kind of exhaustive study that he had made of prisons and locks. And he now challenged any medium to show him supernatural phenomena which he could not expose and reproduce. To the demonstrations and lectures of this period, he brought a perhaps even more ardent enthusiasm than he had to his earlier escapes: the deflation of this higher fakery had a certain intellectual and moral interest, and Houdini's campaign against the mediums turned into a veritable crusade. It may be that his famous encounter with the medium called Margery in Boston, who, if it had not been for his exposure of her, would no doubt have received the prize offered by the *Scientific American* for genuine spiritualistic phenomena, will make a landmark in psychic investigation.

In the years before his death, Houdini had come to occupy a unique position. He certainly knew more about trickery than

anyone else in the world. The library he had been accumu-
lating had become one of his chief interests and had now
reached such enormous proportions that he was obliged to employ a librarian to catalogue it and keep it in order. One regrets
that his campaign against the spiritualists should so soon have
been cut short by his death. But it is possible that Houdini, by
this time, had already reached the limits of his capacity and exhausted the possibilities of his field. The systematic study of
trickery, with its far-reaching implications for religion and other
departments, must now be pursued by others from a more scientific point of view. But the student will find that Houdini has
supplied him with valuable data and an excellent practical
method. And, in the meantime, the story of Houdini's life
proves more stimulating than we might have expected, and it
makes us think better of humanity than the lives of many other
figures of more conventional reputation in more distinguished
fields. It is exhilarating, even in a juggler, even in a trapeze performer, to see some human skill or faculty carried to its furthest point, to a point where its feats seem incredible. And
Houdini had much more than this to commend him to our
admiration: he was an audacious and independent being,
whose career showed a rare integrity. To follow his early life
among the East Side cabarets and the dime museums is to be
stirred as one can always be stirred by the struggle of a superior man to emerge from the commonplaces, the ignominies
and the pains of the common life, to make for himself a position and a livelihood among his less able fellows at the same
time that he learns to perfect himself in the pursuit of his chosen work.

October 17, 1928

Mencken's Democratic Man

H. L. MENCKEN'S *Notes on Democracy* adds nothing that is new to his political philosophy: its basic ideas are precisely those which he has been preaching for many years and which already appear in his book on Nietzsche, published in 1908. The human race, according to Mencken, is composed of "gentlemen" and "boobs"; the gentlemen, by virtue of their superiority, have made themselves masters of the good things of the world; and the peasants, who, by virtue of their ineptitude, remain fettered to the plough and the bench, are embittered by envy of "their betters." It is this envy which supplies all the issues of politics in a democracy: it is the desire on the part of the peasants to rob the superior classes of rewards unattainable by themselves or to restrain them from the enjoyment of activities that they are unable to understand. The superior classes possess a monopoly not merely of property and pleasure but of the higher virtues as well: they embody all the learning, all the taste, all the fortitude, all the intelligence, all the sense of personal honor and all the sense of social obligation. A government by the people, therefore—that is to say, a government by persons characterized by the opposites of these qualities—is sure to be a scandal and a farce. The United Stares is such a farce and scandal.

Mr. Mencken has here expounded this thesis in greater detail and in more connections than he ever has done before; and he has invoked more authorities to support it. He thus makes the gesture of discussing systematically the machinery of democratic government; he attempts to find corroboration in behavioristic psychology; and he at last receives into his bosom the conclusions of the Binet tests, which he had previously denounced but which he sees now can serve his turn by apparently demonstrating that the majority of the population possess the mentality of schoolboys. Yet, for all this, his book is not really an inquiry: it is Mencken's same old melodrama, with the gentleman, the man of honor, pitted against the peasant and the boob. We are not told what makes people gentlemen or what makes people boobs, or of how it is that both

these species happen to belong to the same human race, or of
how it is that we often find them merging or becoming transformed into one another. With his fierce inflexibility of mind,
Mr. Mencken is capable neither of the sympathy of the historian, of the detachment of the scientist nor of the subtlety of
the philosopher. And his new book is not to be taken as a contribution to political science: it is simply another of his "prejudices," treated on a larger scale than the rest.

Yet although these *Notes on Democracy* are not precisely politics, they are quite remarkable as literature. Poe said of his
treatise *Eureka* that it was to be taken as neither science nor
philosophy, but as what he called a "prose poem," which was,
nevertheless, in its own way, true. The same thing might be
said about Mencken's *Notes*, which is a sort of obverse of *Leaves
of Grass*. Let us, therefore, accept its assumptions and find out
what validity it has. Now, it is plain that a population composed,
as Mr. Mencken says ours is, almost exclusively of beings without courage, ability, honor or aspiration could never have
settled, however crudely, either the West or the East of the
United States or established, let alone maintained, however
unenlightened a federal government—could never, in fact,
have made the efforts or carried out the calculations that are
needed for a single street of shops, could never have preserved
the discipline that is needed to run a first-rate office or a theater or factory or bank, let alone train an army, a navy, a medical profession, a church, a bar or the personnel of any of our
good universities. But let us accept the world that Mencken
imagines as we do the country of the Houyhnhnms or the
country of Erewhon, and we shall find that it has its reality as
these other imaginary places have.

This world which, as I say, has its reality, is simply an abstraction from *our* world of all those features of American life
that fall short of Mr. Mencken's standards. What these standards of Mencken's are I have indicated, and we can accept
them as more or less sound. But the point is that Mencken's
emotions in connection with the things he admires are rarely
of a positive kind: they are negative emotions at missing them,
and they take the form of rage and scorn for the people
who do not represent them. This animus has never been
more effectively—perhaps never so effectively—expressed by

Mencken than it is in this latest book. The *Notes* lack the cumulative power of a pamphlet by Swift or Shaw, because they
do not have the drive of close reasoning to carry us along to
the end; and, as a result, the last of the three sections becomes
rather repetitious and disappointing. But, as a whole, the *Notes
on Democracy* is unquestionably one of the best-written and
most intensely felt of Mr. Mencken's books: with *The American Language* and *A Book of Prefaces,* it constitutes the core
of his work, that part of Mr. Mencken's writing that, whatever
else of his we may skip, certainly ought to be read. He has been
saying the same thing for years, but he has never before succeeded in saying it in so pungent and so terse a language or
with a satiric force so nearly tragic.

These emotions of contempt and anger have projected, as
everyone knows, a ridiculous but terrifying bugaboo: the great
American boob. Some of the items in this latest indictment of
the fabulous Menckenian dunce may sound perhaps a little
fatuous: "What he knows of histology," we learn, "or proto-
zoölogy, or philology or paleontology is precisely nothing.
Such things lie beyond his capacity for learning, and he has no
curiosity about them. . . . Even those applied sciences which
enter intimately into his everyday existence remain outside his
comprehension and interest. Consider, for example, chemistry
and biology. The whole life of the inferior man, including especially his so-called thinking, is purely a biochemical process,
and exactly comparable to what goes on in a barrel of cider, yet
he knows no more about chemistry than a cow and no more
about biology than its calf. . . . He is more ignorant of ele-
mentary anatomy and physiology than the Egyptian quacks of
4000 B.C. . . . He has never so much as heard of ethnology,
pathology or embryology. Greek, to him, is only a jargon spoken by boot-blacks, and Wagner is a retired baseball player. He
has never heard of Euripides, of Hippocrates, of Aristotle or of
Plato. Or of Vesalius, Newton and Roger Bacon. The fine arts
are complete blanks to him. He doesn't know what a Doric
column is, or an etching, or a fugue. He is as ignorant of sonnets and the Gothic style as he is of ecclesiastical politics in
Abyssinia. Homer, Virgil, Cervantes, Bach, Raphael, Rubens,
Beethoven—all such colossal names are empty sounds to him,"
etc., etc. This all sounds a little like M. Jourdain giving Mme.

Jourdain the benefit of his recent instruction in the pronunci-
ation of the vowels (to say nothing of Mr. Mencken's own
notions of the conceptions of modern biology—the barrel of
cider, etc.). Nevertheless, the *Notes on Democracy* contain what
is up to date the author's most effective description of his
"Democratic Man." This character is an ideal monster, exactly
like the Yahoo of Swift, and it has almost the same dreadful reality. This "boob" has impressed himself on the imagination of
our general public in a way that has not been equalled by any
other recent literary creation, with the possible exception of
Scott Fitzgerald's flapper. Sinclair Lewis's *Babbitt* and the inhabitants of his *Main Street* must have been at least partly inspired by Mencken, and they present themselves as merely
species of the genus *American boob*. In the current *New Masses*,
one finds a cartoon with the caption "Immaculate Conception," in which the editor of the *American Mercury* is seen
suckling "the American superman," a rudimentary one-
hundred-percent American, who has been born with a pair of
bone spectacles; and this accurately satirizes the situation. The
conception of the national boob has, one realizes, been firmly
planted, not only in the minds of our writers, but also in the
minds of all those, all the otherwise undistinguished citizens,
who are to be seen in every state of the Union with the *Mercury*
under their arms. We may not always like the heavy-footed superman, who for Mencken is the positive inference to be drawn
from the negative caricature, as we sometimes encounter him
in Mencken's pages, and we may like him even less when we
run into attempts to live up to him on the part of Mencken's
admirers; but we must grant that to have made the Americans
feel the menace of this super-boor and repudiate their fellowship with him is an achievement of some importance.

December 15, 1926

Woodrow Wilson at Princeton

T HE first two volumes of *Woodrow Wilson: Life and Letters*, by Ray Stannard Baker, are now before the public. The first of these deals with Woodrow Wilson's early life up to the time of his going to Princeton as a professor, and the second takes him up to his resignation as president of the University. Mr. Baker has both the vices and the advantages of an official biographer—the vices of a loquacious admiration which cannot refrain from continually exclaiming over the utterances and deeds of his hero instead of allowing them to speak for themselves, and a bias which, from beginning to end, prevents him from permitting his subject to appear for a moment as anything but a perfect gentle knight. The result is that, with the copious documentation of a history, his biography moves in something of the miraculous atmosphere of a saint's legend. You would never find out from this record that Woodrow Wilson was, among other things, a resourceful politician: he is invariably represented as carrying all before him by some divine irresistible authority. But Mr. Baker's advantage lies in the fact that he does have the documents; and it may be said that, allowing for his bias, he seems to use them conscientiously and carefully. His book is not very vivid and not very well-written: it has something of the monotony of vocabulary, the lulling repetitiousness and the dilution of ideas of Woodrow Wilson himself. Thus, after quoting from some one of Wilson's utterances in which the weakness of the latter's thought and style are already sufficiently evident, Mr. Baker will add some such comment as: "The sheer eloquence of the man!" or "The sheer fighting spirit of the man!" or something of the sort, using "sheer" in exactly the way that Wilson was in the habit of doing, with the intention of reënforcing some statement, but with the effect of rendering it feebler. It cannot, therefore, be denied that Mr. Baker has been guilty of some insipidity. On the other hand, the material of his biography has been most scrupulously and clearly arranged: his book is extremely well-ordered. He neglects none of Wilson's activities—political, academic, domestic or recreational—and he tells about everything in its place, proceeding deliberately, step by step, indicating exactly the order of events and patiently going back, when necessary, to fill in some aspect of his subject which, for fear of complicating his main narrative, he has been hitherto obliged to neglect. As a result, we have what is undoubtedly the most valuable work on Wilson which has yet appeared. Mr. Baker has thrust into the shadow some of the angles and colors of his subject, but most of Wilson's character is there: it is quite plain in his acts and in his letters. We do not feel any longer, after reading Mr. Baker's first volume—which deals with that part of his life about which least has been written—that there is anything enigmatical about Wilson.

From the beginning the whole man is before us. We have heard a good deal about Wilson's development and the various phases through which he passed; but we see now that, though he sometimes changed his views, his abilities, his ambitions and his relations with the world remained fundamentally the same. The first fact of importance which emerges in this account of Wilson's early life is the extraordinary homogeneity of his family and his ancestry. All Woodrow Wilson's family, so far back as anything is known about his father's side and for many generations on his mother's, were either Scotch or Scotch-Irish schoolmasters, professors or ministers. Wilson's paternal grandparents were born in the north of Ireland; and his mother was born in Scotland. There were among them a number of men of considerable importance in their home communities. The paternal grandfather appears to have been a highly successful journalist and publisher in the West of the early century: he was a member of the state legislature and was locally known as "Judge." "While Judge Wilson was away in the legislature or in Pittsburgh, where, in 1832, he founded a new tri-weekly paper, the *Pennsylvania Advocate*, the redoubtable Anne Adams [Woodrow Wilson's grandmother] and her sons brought out the Steubenville *Herald*." The maternal grandfather Woodrow, a Scotch Presbyterian minister, after emigrating to America, held pastorates, first at Chillicothe, Ohio, and then at Columbus. One of Woodrow Wilson's uncles studied at Harvard under Agassiz, and at Heidelberg. While a professor at the Theological Seminary of Columbia, South Carolina, he taught his classes evolutionary theories, and, in consequence, was tried for heresy; and, though acquitted, obliged to leave. This did not prevent him, however, from being active in religious work; he published a Presbyterian journal, became a successful business man and the president of a bank, and finally president of South Carolina College. "At one time, after the close of the Civil War, when the state government was at its lowest ebb, he made a bid for the state printing which had been done under the most wasteful of political methods. To the astonishment of everyone at the capital, he secured it. There was great speculation as to whether he would run his presses on Sunday, as all the former printers had been forced to do by the exigencies of publication connected with the legislature. But the people were not long to be in doubt. At twelve o'clock on the first Saturday night, Dr. Woodrow turned out all the lights in his printing office, and the shop remained closed until one o'clock Monday morning." Wilson's father was ordained in Ohio as a Presbyterian minister, taught chemistry and the natural sciences and rhetoric at small colleges in Pennsylvania and Virginia, then became pastor of the First Presbyterian Church at Staunton, Virginia. He later moved to Augusta, Georgia (when Woodrow was a year old), and when the regional schism of the Church occurred as a result of the Civil War, the first Southern Presbyterian Assembly was held in Dr. Wilson's church. The Southern Church was organized there, and Dr. Wilson remained for thirty-seven years its Permanent Clerk. His influence upon his son seems to have been profound—perhaps the most important of Wilson's life. When the boy was only a few months old, "very plump and fat and remarkably quiet," his maternal grandfather Woodrow is reported to have said: "That baby is dignified enough to be Moderator of the General Assembly!"

The whole of Wilson's early life is thus completely enclosed by the horizons of the Presbyterian home. He grows up in the post-war South, and he identifies himself with its fortunes to the extent that, while a student at Princeton, he is capable of turning pale with passion and leaving the room over an argument on the subject of the war; but, except in certain particulars later to be noted, he does not exhibit Southern characteristics. He moves always in the antiseptic atmosphere of Presbyterian public life—that is, lecturing, editorial writing and preaching—and Presbyterian domesticity. But this is enough to provide him with a discipline and a whole set of social ideals which completely command his allegiance. In order to understand Wilson's career, we must consider the virtues and the deficiencies of the Presbyterian society that nourished him, the peculiar advantages of which he probably enjoyed at their best.

One of the features, then, of Wilson's forebears is that they were men and women of principle—that is, though by no means naïve in their relations with the material world, they habitually put moral considerations above material ones. They may turn a hand to real estate or banking; but they are consecrated to higher causes, to education and to the Church. Much of Woodrow Wilson's power was derived from the passionate persistency with which he adhered, in later life, to this ideal of acting on principle. He carried the devotion to principle into fields where people had never thought to see it, and those whom he astonished were invariably at first either demoralized or won. I have complained that Mr. Baker represents Wilson as carrying everything before him as if by irresistible authority; but this, if we do not slight other elements, to a limited degree is true. All that language of oratorical idealism—truth, righteousness, service, faith—which the ordinary public speaker makes use of without believing in it and, as it were, without expecting to be believed—all these phrases were in some sense a gospel with Wilson, and it was the realization of this that arrested the attention of the public. This was the language that Wilson had always spoken: you find it in all the family documents which Mr. Baker has published; you find it in the devoted letters between Woodrow and his father. Wilson continued to speak it all his life: he would, indeed, never learn any other; and, in his lifelong inability to master the language of the world even when dealing with worldlings or himself resorting to methods which were nothing if not of the world, he illustrates one of the weaknesses, as he does also so astonishingly the strength, of his heritage of Presbyterian culture. For it was characteristic of Wilson that he could not express himself on any issue or describe any action of his own except in the terms of the pulpit, the vocabulary of a semi-religious idealism. I do not believe that he was ever a hypocrite: he gives the impression of being always convinced that the values of a given situation are such as he represents them. Woodrow Wilson had never relinquished his original religious faith: he declined to debate religious questions; he would "go crazy," he insisted, in later life, if he did not believe in God. When his fiancée reads philosophy and raises religious doubts, he writes her that, "so far as religion is concerned, discussion is adjourned." And the validity of his own moral principles, the infallibility of his judgment in acting on them, seem to have become for him articles of faith of an almost equal authority. In the whole of Mr. Baker's two volumes, I cannot remember a single passage, not merely among Wilson's public utterances, but in his letters and diaries themselves, where he confesses himself for a moment to be influenced by anything other than the highest and purest motives. He never admits a personal resentment or an impulse of ill-humor or frivolity, a spiritual or physical distemper; he never calculates anything for interest; he can barely allow that he is writing a book or delivering a public lecture because he is in need of money. One can, therefore, find no evidence that Wilson was ever consciously hypocritical. Yet this haughty and persistent refusal to be subject to the accidents of our common humanity is the most unsympathetic feature of his character. Why are we a little unpleasantly affected by Wilson's repudiation, in New Jersey, of the bosses who had supported him in his campaign for governor? Grover Cleveland did much the same thing, but it is always invoked as an example of his honesty instead of his bad faith. The fact is that it is the way in which Wilson expresses himself about this that irritates us—it is his moral indignation: it is his self-righteous inability to accept with realistic frankness the fact that he has himself been a practical politician playing the political game. Why, again, are we inevitably more shocked by certain of Wilson's prevarications, by his categorical denial, for example, in his conference with the Senate committee, that he had ever heard of the Treaty of London—than we are by, say, Bismarck's falsification of the Ems telegram? Simply because Bismarck knows what he is doing and accepts the moral consequences; that is the way in which he chooses to deal with the world; he has never pretended otherwise. But Wilson *has* pretended, and does pretend, otherwise; he appears to pretend even to himself.

The great handicap of this Puritan culture was, of course, its limited scope and its isolation from the world. Wilson knew little of the arts; he was neither widely nor profoundly read; he had little real intellectual curiosity; and he was never, as we shall see, able to appreciate or respect the points of view of worldly people. The characteristic mode of self-expression of the society in which Wilson grew up was the Presbyterian sermon; and Wilson became a master of the sermon: he was essentially, to the end of his life, not a philosopher, but a preacher; and he had only so much learning, and did only so much intellectual work, as is necessary for a preacher. He understood very well, however, in what his genius consisted: he worked within his limitations. It is surprising, in reading this biography, to discover how early and how exclusively he is preoccupied with public speaking. By the time he has graduated from Princeton and from the law school of the University of Virginia, by the time he has tried practising law and given it up after a year, though he goes to study politics at Johns Hopkins, he does not think of himself as a scholar or even as a writer: he knows that he is neither of these things, and he rebels against the kind of apprenticeship to which he finds himself committed. Nor does he want to be a practical politician: the politics of the time appal him; they seem to him to belong to the order of a different planet from that on which he lives. His father has hoped he would enter the Church; and, though he confines himself to public affairs, it is as an inspirational speaker that he sets out to perfect himself. In this purpose he is magnificently successful. Making speeches was the thing he did best, the thing, indeed, that he did supremely well. In reading his published addresses, we are irritated by the vagueness of the language and the unctuousness of the rhetoric. But Woodrow Wilson's delivery was more distinguished than his style. Even when his language was bafflingly evasive or floridly insipid, his voice remained quiet, well-mannered and beautifully distinct, with an edge that made his words seem incisive. He had just enough of a Southern accent and a grace and ease learned in the South to make one forget his square face and rather rigidly looming figure; and, save when the subject of a dreaded opponent pressed the stop of some querulous note of the schoolmaster or the parson, a persuasiveness that was almost hypnotic. He gave the impression of deep conviction and burning zeal, under imperturbable control. Maynard Keynes, in his account of the Peace Conference, has given an excellent description of Wilson's qualities: "He had no plan," he says, "no scheme, no constructive ideas whatever for clothing with the flesh of life the commandments which he had thundered from the White House. He could have preached a sermon on any of them or have addressed a stately prayer to the Almighty for their fulfilment; but he could not frame their concrete application to the actual state of Europe."

One must not, however, make it appear that Wilson—especially in his student days—was nothing better than a facile evangelist. The young man who emerges from the letters and the memoirs of the first volume of this *Life* is an attractive and impressive figure. Stiff, earnest, a little pompous, pursuing his career with a grave concentration that is recognizably Scottish, he is none the less sympathetic by reason of his very seriousness and of the self-dissatisfactions and self-scrutinies of which his letters at this time are full. He already knows his strength, but he is poor and his opportunities seem limited. He had sworn at Princeton with a classmate to a "solemn covenant" that they should "school all our powers and passions for the work of establishing the principles we held in common; that we would acquire knowledge that we might have power; and that we would drill ourselves in all the arts of persuasion, but especially in oratory, that we might have facility in leading others into our ways of feeling and enlisting them in our purposes." "It was not so long ago," he writes to his fiancée from Johns Hopkins, "but that I can still feel the glow and the pulsations of the hopes and the purposes of that moment." He desperately envies a friend who is studying in Germany; he plans, at one time, to go there himself. He is urged by another friend to take steps to have his name put forward for an assistant secretaryship of state: "the office is not much in demand by politicians, and Mr. Bayard, who likes gentlemanly scholarly associates, is finding it hard to fill. . . . Don't you pity me, with my old political longings thus set throbbing again?" But he knows of no one to recommend him, and he is obliged to give up the hope. He produces, at twenty-nine and while still a student at Johns Hopkins, the best of all his books, a book, indeed, quite out of the class of his subsequent ones. The young author of *Congressional Government* is, within the limited scope of his field, a decidedly intelligent man and a lucid and polished writer. Though, characteristically, when he made this study, he had never once been in Washington to watch the houses of Congress in action, he had produced an essay in political history which was realistic as well as original, and the immediacy of his success is dramatic. But even this sudden and brilliant success fails to allay his restlessness. He is excessively shy; he has already a reputation as an accomplished public speaker and as a singer in college glee clubs, but it is difficult for him to meet people, and when he does so, one gets the impression that he does not very closely apprehend them. He is lonely, repressed and uneasy.

During his year of law practice, however, Wilson has fallen in love. He has gone, on business of his mother's, to visit an uncle in Rome, Georgia, and he there meets Ellen Axson, the daughter of the minister of the First Presbyterian Church: "her grandfather, the 'great Axson,' was pastor of the famous Independent Presbyterian Church of Savannah." Wilson's own description of this incident, in a letter to Ellen when she had become his wife, is worth quoting at length: it is typical of the social atmosphere that surrounded him in his youth, that gave its color to his whole career and character. "The first time I saw your face to note it was in church one morning during the first of my last spring's visit to Rome—in April, wasn't it? You wore a heavy crêpe veil, and I remember thinking 'what a bright, pretty face; what splendid, mischievous, laughing eyes! I'll lay a wager that this demure little lady has lots of life and fun in her!' And when, after the service (I think it had been a communion service), you spoke to Mrs. Bones, I took another good look at you, and concluded that it would be a very clever plan to inquire your name and seek an introduction. When I learned that this was Miss 'Ellie Lou' Axson, of whom I had heard so often, quite a flood of light was let in on my understanding, and I was conscious of having formed a small resolution. I took an early opportunity of calling on the Rev. Mr. Axson. That dear gentleman received me with unsuspecting cordiality and sat down to entertain me under the impression that I had come to see only him. I *had* gone to see him, for I love and respect him and would have gone to see him with alacrity if he had never had a daughter; but I had not gone to see him *alone*. I had not forgotten that face, and I wanted very much to see it again; so I asked rather pointedly after his daughter's health, and he, in some apparent surprise, summoned you to the parlor. Do you remember?—and do you remember the topic of conversation? how your father made me 'tackle' that question that was so much too big for me, 'Why have night congregations grown so small?'" They go on long walks and boat-rides and picnics together. She talks to him about George Eliot, about Wordsworth and Browning; she paints, and she tells him about painting. He has never occupied himself with these things, and it is as if she has thrown open a new world to him: he has been refreshed from a richer mind and a more sensitive temperament. Six months afterwards, they are engaged, and he has already become greatly dependent on her sympathy and her responsive imagination, as he is to remain till her death. Their own home is, in most respects, just such a home as that in which he has found her, just such a home as that from which he comes. Ellen Wilson, who, outside her household, commanded so little attention, who found herself overwhelmed by the social responsibilities of her position in Princeton and Washington, devoted herself to her husband's career and to a sort of intensive family culture, with all the energy of her girlhood idealism. She is even said to have played the determining role in some of Wilson's political decisions. The Wilson home was always, in fact, an abode of sweetness and light of an old-fashioned and not undistinguished kind; but it was firmly disciplined and strictly bounded. The books, for example, that the young ladies were allowed to read were censored by vigilant parents; and on one occasion at least in Princeton—as the writer has heard at firsthand—one of the Wilson daughters was embarrassed at not being able to return a volume of the poems of the now faded Aubrey de Vere which her mother had sternly destroyed before she knew it was borrowed. Wilson's marriage had meant for him a fledging of wings, a cultural illumination, one of the major events of his life; yet a fledging and an illumination that had taken place within the confines of the Presbyterian world in which he was born.

II

One of the most striking features of Woodrow Wilson's early life, which Mr. Baker's biography has brought to light, is his passion for drawing up programs and framing constitutions. Already, as a boy in Atlanta, he provided a set of rules for a club that met in a hayloft, and at Davidson, at Princeton, at Virginia, at Johns Hopkins and at Wesleyan colleges, he reorganized the debating societies and turned them, in every case, into something of an almost parliamentary impressiveness. This was always the department of college activity which interested Wilson most. He would arrive; in a very short time, he would gravitate to the head of the society; then, with overwhelming energy and enthusiasm, he would proceed to make it over completely. He would frame a new set of rules and aims that would be laid before the other members with all his compelling eloquence and adopted with the utmost eagerness; the society would appear to be entering upon a new phase of importance and popularity; then Wilson would pass on elsewhere. This becomes the type of his activity everywhere, and even as sponsor of the Fourteen Points. He can draw up a fine lucid program and he can get it accepted by a luminous speech. But much beyond this he cannot go. When Wilson has successfully accomplished this, he will not go on to apply himself to the practical machinery and the boring detail, the adjustments with other personalities, that are necessary to put through his proposals. He can only repeat the performance by starting a new movement somewhere else and drawing up a new set of proposals.

One must not, however, again, imply that this purely forensic activity for which Wilson had so much genius was entirely without use or effect. It did not take them long in New Jersey, after Wilson had ceased to be governor, to pull the teeth of the bills he had passed; but at Princeton his policies were vital, and the edifice founded upon them pretty solidly endures to this day. Wilson, indeed, probably deserves most of the credit for rescuing Princeton, at the end of the nineties, from the extreme disorganization and demoralization of the Patton administration: whatever is sound in the college today was established under the presidency of Wilson. As a professor of jurisprudence and politics, he is said to have been a stimulating lecturer, and his courses were certainly popular; but his students did not do much work. He had himself little or no real passion for learning; and his course was known as a "gut," that is, an easy course. But, once he was elected president, he found himself—and for, perhaps, the first time in his life—with an adequate field for his powers. The faculty was at that time directly appointed by the president. Wilson cleared out the deadwood among the professors with his characteristic combination of radiant enthusiasm and ruthlessness; and even got rid of two trustees who had become involved in an insurance scandal. He then picked out and appointed new professors, with an instinct which today seems brilliant; and got from the trustees an appropriation for fifty younger instructors to be added to the faculty and known as "preceptors," whose function was not to lecture or to hold classes in the ordinary sense, but, by meeting the students semi-formally, to encourage them and supervise their work. He was never, perhaps, more happily inspired than during these early days as president of Princeton. A good many of the professors he brought there are still in the university and among its most distinguished figures. I have been told by men who came as preceptors in the first days of Wilson's administration that they have never at any other time, in the American educational world, seen so much excitement and hope. Wilson was not, however, quite so infallible, quite so triumphantly intelligent, as his biographer represents him. He had his characteristic errors of judgment and mistaken obstinacies. The department of modern languages at Princeton was at that time in a rudimentary state; but Wilson—true, apparently, in this to the Presbyterian tradition—did not much believe in modern languages: he had himself little German and less French, and used to quote with satisfaction a saying of Walter Bagehot to the effect that "a Frenchman can say anything, but has nothing to say."* When the depart-

---

*For this information and much else in this essay, I am indebted to the late Christian Gauss, who came to Princeton as a preceptor under Wilson and built up the Modern Language Department (split later into a Romance and a German Department) virtually from scratch. In the early days of the college, French and German had been barred from the curriculum, "because of the atheistic writings in those languages." Charles Godfrey Leland of the class of 1845 says that, for the same reason, French was not taught in his day. My

ment was being reorganized, the President insisted upon
dictating—and without allowing any discussion on the part of
the instructors themselves—impossible courses of reading. The
students, with their inadequate preparation, were unable to
cope with these assignments, and the department, in the course
of time, was forced quietly to abandon Wilson's program and
substitute one of its own. It was characteristic of Wilson at
Princeton, as it was in 1919 at the Peace Conference, that he
should have shown himself as autocratic in dealing with departments of whose work he knew nothing as with those of which
he had had some experience.

What follows is extremely interesting, and anticipates with a
curious completeness the pattern of Wilson's successes and
failures at Washington. In reading Mr. Baker's biography, we
gradually become aware of a feature of Wilson's character
which already appears in his early letters and which produces at
Princeton its first tragic disaster. Woodrow Wilson is a man of
enormous energy, who is always restless when he is not acting
and who is capable of only one way of acting—the way indicated above. Once he has secured the adoption of a program,
he must immediately pass on to another program. This comes
out strikingly in his writings of this period. Princeton, he complains, is not yet perfect, it is not yet an ideal university. How
could he possibly have expected it to become thus transformed
overnight, with the establishment of the preceptorial system,
or of any other system? It is quite plain that the true reason for
the President's anxiety is to be found in his incapacity to satisfy, to realize himself in any occupation other than his own peculiar kind of statesmanship. Except for politics, he is really not
interested in the subjects that universities teach; and in respect
to politics, he would rather be an actor than a student. He cannot sit patiently for a time and supervise the life of the college.
He looks about him for another constructive proposal, and

---

father, of the class of 1885, was drilled in French with more force than finesse
by an exiled Polish general, who swore at his students as if they were troops.
By the time I came to Princeton, in the class of 1916, the Modern Language
Department was one of the best in the country and had become very much
the fashion with the more intellectual students. This was one of the results of
the Wilson administration, but entirely the creation of Gauss, who had not
always found it easy to get Wilson to accept his proposals.

finds it in the social system. We are here for the first time to encounter a charge that, in the course of his subsequent career, is often to be brought against Wilson—that of reversing a previous position. It is quite true that Wilson reversed his views on many social and political questions, and we may certainly dislike the tone of self-righteous indignation with which he denounces opponents who are merely professing today opinions that he himself professed yesterday. But we should, I believe, be mistaken in supposing that vulgar expediency played anything other than an occasional role among the considerations that moved him. It was rather that Wilson, whose intelligence was not at all far-reaching or subtle, was capable of thinking only about one or two things at a time: when he did think about anything, however, he usually thought in the right direction. He had not so much ideas as divinations, which came forthwith to seem to him self-evident. In this case, it is true that Wilson—Mr. Baker fails to mention this—had contributed a preface to a college handbook in which, with his customary unctuousness, he had written of life in Princeton as incorruptibly democratic. He has, however, come later to see that the undergraduate eating-clubs are a menace: they cultivate social snobbishness, and they break the college up into cliques. He proposes a different system of social units which the university itself should set up and control. This plan was derived from the English colleges and was locally known as the quad system, because the quadrangle around which each of the houses was built would figure as the center of the unit. To each of these houses was to be assigned by the university authorities themselves a group of students and unmarried professors, who would both sleep and eat in the building. Each of these would make a social center, and the clubs were to be abolished.

The writer of the present article is no defender of the Princeton clubs. He believes Wilson's instinct about them to have been fundamentally sound. These eating-clubs are probably the most undesirable of Princeton institutions—not so much because they are snobbish: some sort of snobbishness seems inevitable and perhaps even has its value; but because they are hopelessly dull. Nothing interesting is ever done in them: the students simply eat their meals there and occasionally give house-parties over the weekends. They are not even allowed to live in them, as they are in other colleges in fraternity houses. Movements are put on foot periodically—and on the part of the students themselves—to get rid of them or to do something more sensible with them, for they constitute a force of inertia that has been blocking the development of the university. Yet the buildings are so enormous in bulk and represent such a formidable investment, that it has, so far, been impossible to dissolve the clubs. There is, however, another element to be considered in connection with the problem. In spite of their heaviness and emptiness, the clubs have inevitably become identified with that peculiar idyllic quality which is one of the endearing features of Princeton. It is difficult to describe this quality in any very concrete way, but it has something to do with the view from Prospect Street, from the comfortable back porches of the clubs, over the damp dim New Jersey lowlands, and with the singular feeling of freedom which refreshes the alumnus from an American city when he goes back to Prospect Street and realizes that he can lounge, read or drink as he pleases, go anywhere or dress anyhow without anybody's interfering with him. Now, it was not Wilson's policy about the social system which in itself was ill-advised: it was his methods in carrying it out that were tactless. In the spring of 1907, he put his proposals before the Princeton faculty, introducing them with a speech which those who heard it describe as one of the most eloquent he ever made. The faculty responded almost unanimously and voted some sort of resolution of approval. How far this resolution was supposed to go is a subject of controversy, but it is probable that the professors, for the most part, regarded themselves as voting merely a general endorsement of the principles which the President had suggested. He had brought forward no plausible plan for putting these principles into practice: he had not discussed the problem of expense. Presumably, they were authorizing him merely to prepare a more detailed program. Without waiting further, however, he proceeded to compose and send out a peremptory memorandum to the clubs themselves.

It was commencement, and these institutions were holding their annual banquets. Wilson caused his memorandum to be read at the banquets. Mr. Baker fails to show this incident in its full and true significance. His language about the memorandum

suggests that he must be aware of its having been open to objection, but, quoting from it only a few sentences, he does not
make it possible for his readers to understand its total effect.
The night of these club banquets in June was observed until
recently at Princeton as an occasion of peculiar ceremonies and
supreme conviviality. The freshmen, who had hitherto been excluded from Prospect Street, were for the first time allowed to
invade it. Late in the evening, they would form a parade and,
with red fire and Roman candles, march down between the
rows of clubs. When the older men inside at the banquets
heard the sound of their singing and tramping, they would
come to the doors with glasses of champagne and offer the
freshmen drinks; the more prominent members of the class
were toasted. At the same time, the newly elected sophomores
felt, for the first time, that they were being officially wel-
comed: they had entered the haven of content. And the
alumni had returned with something of that feeling of relief
and exhilaration I have tried to describe above, and no doubt,
also, with that touching need for loyalty—a loyalty far in excess
of the worthiness or interest of its object—which, in a country
with so few institutions that may with dignity command a
man's loyalty, must do its best to satisfy itself with the commercial boosting of cities, with lodges and Rotary Clubs. It
was this moment that Wilson chose for communicating to the
Princeton clubs a note that had the form of an edict—that
seemed brusquely to break the news that they were summarily
to be disbanded, and that even went so far as to recommend
that trustees be appointed at once in whose hands "each club
would vest its property," in order that this property might be
melted up in the unfamiliar quad system. If Wilson had deliberately sought to discover a strategic move which would render a maximum of alumni opinion immediately antagonistic,
he could not have acted otherwise. The proud undergraduates
and the jolly alumni—many of them, no doubt, drunk—must
have felt as if their delightful houses were being snatched from
over their very heads, and that at the moment when they loved
them most dearly; that their joyfully renewed goodfellowship,
their love of Princeton itself, were receiving a cold affront
from the President. In any case, they did not delay to bring
pressure to bear on the faculty, and the faculty, astonished and

frightened, "reconsidered" their resolution. It is quite probable that, if Woodrow Wilson had gone about the matter more
cautiously, and with a sense of the sacred ties of sentiment and
conviviality, he would have secured the adoption of his policy.
At that time, almost everyone was in favor of it—even those,
like Mr. Moses Taylor Pyne, the rich patron of the University,
who afterwards came to oppose it. But Wilson had not been
able to estimate the lengths to which men will go to preserve
for themselves the privilege of an unrestrained freedom and
fun such as he had not hesitated to blight—just as many of the
persons he offended had no doubt never known the ecstasy of
transcendent moral conviction, of the triumph of the personal
will which knows also that it "conquers in this sign," of the
shaping of God's institutions from the baser habitations, however gilded, of the children of this world.

But the forces antagonized by the President were now to
get a spokesman and champion in a figure that Woodrow Wilson would ultimately find it impossible either to persuade or to
subdue—the only man, at that time, in Princeton who possessed enough ambition, self-confidence, persistence and independence to put up a formidable resistance. If it had not been
for Andrew West, then a professor in the Classics Department,
it is probable that Wilson would have won even over the recal-
citrance of the alumni. Now, it is possible to entertain only a
moderate opinion of West either as scholar or as educator, yet
to feel that he, too, derived a certain moral strength from an
ideal of education, and that his collision with Woodrow Wilson
—a collision fatal to Wilson—was partly, at least, the result of
the latter's contemptuous refusal to sympathize with this ideal.
For West, also, had the desire to impose a new pattern on
Princeton. He was obsessed by a beautiful vision which was
based, to some extent at least, on the ideals of classical humanism. He had imagined a super-graduate school, a withdrawn
yet luxurious resort for an aristocratic caste of scholars, all
complete with "dreaming spires" remembering the Middle
Ages as they dominated the Princeton golf-links and with dons
in black gowns having dinner on a daïs, under a sumptuous
stained-glass window and a magnificent organ-loft; of a college
fairly deliquescent with Oxonian Gothic beauty. What was
admirable in this vision Woodrow Wilson did not, perhaps,

understand; its vices were only too plain to him. And, what was probably more important, he came to resent and to fear another powerful egoism which had got into his sphere of influence. In the first stages of his career as president, he treats West with great respect; he writes a preface to a prospectus for the graduate school, smoothly commending the project; and when West is offered the presidency of the Massachusetts Institute of Technology, Wilson requests him to remain at Princeton, assuring him that, if he will stay, he shall presently have his desire. West remains and supports Wilson's policies. When the quad system is proposed, however, West becomes rather uneasy; and when Wilson, in the matter of the edict to the clubs, appears to be acting beyond his authority, he is apprehensive and angry. If the reforms are put into effect, they are certain to be expensive. And if the trustees undertake to supply the money, how can the graduate school be built? There seems no doubt that, in respect to the graduate school, Andrew West had a just grievance: he felt that he had received a pledge from Wilson, that he had stayed on at Princeton on the strength of that pledge, and that the pledge had not been redeemed. The retired Grover Cleveland, who had come to Princeton to live partly on account of his friendship with West and who had been made a member of the board of trustees, sympathized with his friend. He had, moreover, himself, as he thought, some evidence that Wilson was treacherous. Mr. Baker has made no attempt to state or to study the case against Wilson. This question, which is the crux of the controversy, he manages to keep out of his book. He does tell us that Wilson was accused of "bad faith," but he does not say how or why. The truth was, undoubtedly, that Wilson, who had already found himself and West in bitter opposition to one another, had become so exaltedly preoccupied with his new dispensation for Princeton that it was easy for him to brush aside the small-minded and snobbish West and his archaizing graduate school. He could not believe they were really important; and he was able to convince himself that, in matters of no importance, it was not important to keep one's word.

The conflict now reaches a phase extremely unedifying on either side—a phase which presents serious difficulties for Wilson's devoted biographer. A rich lady, a Mrs. Swann, has left

Princeton a bequest for a graduate school, which, according to the terms of her will, is to be built on the campus itself. Mr. Ralph Adams Cram, the supervising architect at Princeton, has designated a site. West, however, has succeeded, to Wilson's alarm, at an early stage of the proceedings, in securing a free hand for the future in everything connected with the graduate school, of which he is himself to be dean. He proposes to make the school completely independent of the University, and even to collect the students' fees through a separate treasurer's office; and he insists now upon having the new college erected at some distance from the campus. It is true that he is balked in this by the terms of Mrs. Swann's will, but he soon obtains another bequest, granted on the opposite condition. Wilson, without warning, is one day handed a letter from Mr. W. C. Procter, a graduate of Princeton and the manufacturer of Ivory Soap: in this letter, Mr. Procter announces to Andrew West that he is prepared to give half a million dollars for the proposed graduate school, if West can raise half a million more; but that he has examined the site on the campus selected by Mr. Cram and that he does not consider it suitable; his offer is only conditional upon some other site's being chosen. Woodrow Wilson, who, though president of the University, has not been notified by Mr. Procter of the latter's visit to Princeton in connection with the graduate school, not unnaturally resents this action. He holds, however, a very strong card in the terms of Mrs. Swann's will, and he attempts to play this card. He calls upon Procter in New York and proposes to him that, since it seems impossible to arrive at an agreement on the matter, two graduate schools be erected—one, with Mrs. Swann's money, on the campus; the other, with Procter's, on the golf-links. This proposal is, of course, preposterous, and Wilson counts on Procter's capitulating to the terms of Mrs. Swann's will. The manufacturer, however, remains obstinate; and Wilson at once sits down in the Jersey City railroad station and writes out to Moses Taylor Pyne a note in which he announces his resignation as president of Princeton. When the board of trustees meet again at the beginning of the next year (1910), the opposition plays a trick on Wilson. Unsuspectingly Wilson attends a meeting of the graduate school committee and is confronted with a letter from Procter in which the latter pretends to

accept Wilson's proposal that two graduate schools be built—
a proposal which had never been intended as anything but a
reductio ad absurdum. Wilson loses his temper, and for the first
time blurts out the truth—that the site of the graduate school
is actually immaterial: "We could make this school a success
anywhere in Mercer County!" The trouble is, it plainly appears, that Princeton is not large enough to hold him and Andrew West both. It is characteristic of him, however, that,
instead of saying merely, "Dean West and I seem to have conflicting ideas that can hardly be reconciled," or something of
that sort, he should declare that "Dean West's ideas and ideals
are not the ideas and ideals of Princeton!" The controversy is
now at its height; the whole community is divided into factions. Dean West, who is a master of money-getting, an irresistible charmer of millionaires, soon secures a third bequest:
another rich alumnus dies, appointing West his executor and
leaving the graduate school a sum then reported as ten million
dollars. The trustees accept it with joy; and Wilson resigns
with relief. He has already had overtures from the New Jersey
Democratic politicians and is preparing to pass on to the
governorship.

In the course of these Princeton controversies, Woodrow
Wilson, from whose point of view, that of a major prophet,
everyone who was not with him was against him, who, as was
said of him by one of his own Princeton supporters, seemed
incapable of understanding that "intellectual error is innocent"
—had behaved toward his opponents with the harshest bitterness. He had been on fairly intimate terms with Mr. John Grier
Hibben, then a professor in the Philosophy Department; but
Hibben had voted against the quad system, and Wilson now
dropped him and cut him—as, to his damage, he was afterwards to do with so many other allies who ventured to dis-
agree with him. When Wilson was President of the United
States and returned to Princeton to vote, Mr. Hibben, then
president of the University, went to the station to receive him;
but Wilson refused to speak to him, turned his back and walked
away. There was in all this a passionate pride: "I am proud and
wilful beyond all measure," he writes to his fiancée, while he is
still a student at Johns Hopkins, and this pride was at the root
of his strength; but Woodrow Wilson presented in an extreme

form one of the paradoxes of the Puritan nature: he was, at the same time, obdurate and ruthless, and excessively thin-skinned. He was sensitive to criticism from friends; he was suspicious and vindictive to his opponents; and he was unable to deal with either except by overwhelming the one and overriding the other. As President of the United States, he repeated after the War his whole tragedy as president of Princeton—with Lodge in the role of West, the League of Nations in the place of the quad system, and the Senate in the place of the Princeton trustees. It is possible to observe in certain lives, where conspicuously superior abilities are united with serious deficiencies, not the progress in a career or vocation that carries the talented man to a solid position or a definite goal, but a curve plotted over and over again and always dropping from some flight of achievement to a steep descent into failure. Casanova's is such a life: his memoirs show again and again the same triumph of impudence and cunning as well as of intelligence and imagination, followed soon by the detection of a fraud that discredits and eclipses the whole man, with the result that he is forced to go elsewhere and begin the whole performance again. Woodrow Wilson's career, in its so different fields and terms, presents similar abrupt fluctuations.

If I have dwelt at length on Wilson's weaknesses, it is not for lack of admiration, but in the attempt to correct Mr. Baker's bias, which has obscured some of the elements in Wilson's story. It may, in general, be said that the public enthusiasm for Wilson, which reached, at the time of the war, both at home and abroad, such almost apocalyptic proportions, has ebbed rapidly—the tragic descent of the curve—since his compromise at Versailles and the defeat of the League of Nations, followed by collapse and death, till there are few to praise him today. The professional intelligentsia, especially, are afraid of taking him seriously. Yet, in the bankruptcy of political idealism which has followed his administration, as in the dreary timidity and stodginess toward which our academic life is always dragged by the force of inertia, we may still find it salutary to look back on Woodrow Wilson's career, and we may read many less profitable books than Mr. Baker's *Life*. In any case, we should certainly do ill to fall in with the cowardice and ignorance of American public opinion which, in spite of his errors and faults, idealized Wilson till he broke, then, in spite of his heroic audacity and his genius for leadership, was willing to deride and forget him.

November 30, 1927

It may be interesting to add here to this sketch of Woodrow Wilson's career at Princeton a story told by Norman Thomas in an interview with Tex McCrary and Jinx Falkenberg, which appeared in the New York *Herald Tribune* of February 13, 1950.

"One thing I have learned," Mr. Thomas says, in speaking of his political fights: "Never give up, but don't nurse a grudge in politics. Woodrow Wilson taught me that lesson.

"In Princeton, I took all the courses available under Woodrow Wilson—no, I never heckled him. That was before I became a Socialist. But in my senior year, we were looking around for some normal healthy mischief to do. There was a big ugly picket fence around the president's house on the campus, and that was our target! We organized a big protest meeting, which turned into a parade—Mr. Wilson was away from Princeton at the time—and we marched over and tore down his fence and took it away and hid it in the woods! As I was to learn later, Wilson never liked opposition of any kind. When he got back and found his fence torn down, he was very angry. But he couldn't very well discipline the whole senior class.

"Years later, when I was editor of the Socialist *World Tomorrow*, and we actively opposed United States intervention in Russia after the first World War, President Wilson's Attorney General thought I belonged in jail even more than Eugene Debs did. Wilson didn't go that far, but he did say to me: 'There is such a thing as indecent exposure of private opinion in public.'

"A few years after Mr. Wilson died, I met his daughter at a reception, and as we were being introduced, she froze—and said, 'I believe I have heard a great deal about Mr. Thomas!' I smiled and asked her which of my political sins she was referring to, and she replied, still angry: 'You were in Princeton, Class of 1905, weren't you? Yes—that was the class that was so cruel to father!' A grudge had been passed on to another generation!"

American Heroes:
Frémont and Frick

JOHN CHARLES FRÉMONT—the subject of a biography by
Allan Nevins: *Frémont: The West's Greatest Adventurer*—was
the illegitimate son of a Virginian lady, who had been married
at seventeen to a sixty-year-old husband. She ran away with a
French émigré, and after some years of wanderings in the
South, in the course of which her lover died, she went to live
in Charleston, South Carolina, where her son came to manhood in the duelling, drinking and racing society of the old
South. He distinguished himself at Charleston College as an
enthusiastic classical scholar: Greek especially, he afterwards
wrote, "had a mysterious charm, as if behind the strange characters belonging to an ancient world I was to find things of
wonderful interest"; but he presently fell in love with a beautiful Creole girl, with large dark eyes and blue-black hair, and
thereafter so neglected his studies that he was finally dismissed
from college. Of his escapades with Cecilia, however, he was
afterwards to write that they were "days of unreflecting life
when I lived in the glow of a passion that now I know extended
its refining influence over my whole life." He was handsome,
and at sixteen already exhibited what were later to prove his
dominant characteristics: "ardor, imagination, ambition, quickness, endurance and reckless impetuosity."

After a brief period in the Navy, the young Frémont was
given an opportunity to participate in a surveying expedition
for the route of a projected railroad between Charleston and
Cincinnati. "The survey," he said, "was a kind of picnic, with
work enough to give it zest, and we were all sorry when it was
over." In the course of it, he fell in love again, and made his
first acquaintance with the Indians: "He sometimes visited Indian feasts which broke up, when the Cherokees became mad
with drink, in furious disorder; he saw them end in bloody
frays, the braves slashing each other with knives." Joel R. Poin-
sett, then Secretary of War, the first describer and the eponym
of the poinsettia, was struck with the young man's abilities and

had him commissioned in the Topographical Corps and included in an expedition, under the Frenchman Joseph Nicolas
Nicollet, to survey the almost unknown region between the
upper Mississippi and the Missouri. Here he encountered voy-
ageurs, scouts, fur traders, frontier soldiers, Indians, buffalo,
prairie fires and, in the lowlands near Lac qui Parle, an astonishing contrast of purple asters with the yellow of goldenrod,
which he was never to forget.

When Frémont returned from this expedition, he went to
live in Washington with Nicollet, upon whom he had made a
great impression, at the house of the superintendent of the
Coast Survey, a distinguished Swiss scientist, who kept a
French chef, did a great deal of entertaining and "used to be
driven through the streets in what he called the 'ark,' a huge
comfortable carriage which he used in visiting his surveying
parties, and which was packed with red and white German
wines, choice foods and soft bedding." Frémont and Nicollet
worked at their maps together and had an astronomical obser-
vatory built on the roof. Frémont fell in love with Senator
Benton's daughter, who was then not yet sixteen. "There came
a glow into my heart," he wrote, "which changed the current
and color of daily life, and gave beauty to common things."
Jessie Benton was high-spirited and strong-willed, as well as
exceptionally well-educated—she had learned French in a convent at St. Louis; between St. Louis, Washington and her
grandfather's estate in Virginia, she had acquired a certain
knowledge of the world. Benton thought her too young to
marry, especially to marry so young and poor a man, and tried
to get Frémont out of the way by having him sent on an expedition along the Des Moines River. When he returned, since the
parents remained obdurate, he and Jessie were married secretly.
When the young couple confronted the Senator, he lived up to
his august role with a scene of repudiation in the old-fashioned
grand manner; Jessie, clutching Frémont's arm, replied with
the words of Ruth, "Whither thou goest," etc. The Senator
did not drive her out; Frémont came to live with them, and
Benton was presently playing the role of his son-in-law's principal supporter in the career of exploration and fighting that so
stimulated the American imagination and made him a national
hero.

Henry Clay Frick (to borrow the formula of the Teasing Tom song in *Patience*)—about whom George Harvey has just written a biography, *Henry Clay Frick: The Man*—was born thirty-seven years later than Frémont (in 1849) in Westmoreland County, Pennsylvania. His parents were German and Swiss; his grandfather, a pious Mennonite, was the original manufacturer of that admirable Old Overholt rye whisky which is still bottled in bond by the government. Frick's father was a small farmer, and, as a boy, the son worked on the farm. His education was very meager: he left school at seventeen, and, in the meantime, he worked in an uncle's store, getting nothing in return but his board and the privilege of sleeping on the counter. He graduated later on to the store of another uncle, where he is said to have been paid three dollars a week. On one occasion, when Henry was at school and the teacher had threatened to whip one of his little cousins, a girl, the boy became furious and averted the punishment by threatening to beat the teacher. It was afterwards recalled of him that he had said, at this time, that his grandfather had made half a million, and that he intended, before he died, "to be worth a million." He also inaugurated the policy which he was to pursue throughout his career of procuring "the best there is": he discarded his ill-fitting farmer's-boy clothes and bought a sixteen-dollar pair of black boots with yellow stitching, which, at the end of six months, he had kept "as bright and spotless as when new." He developed, in this early period, an extraordinary gift for bookkeeping, and later, when he was making first eight, then twelve dollars a week at a larger store, he would go to business school every night, after working from six to eight, to study accounting and banking.

He was later given a place by his grandfather, at a thousand dollars a year, as chief bookkeeper of the Overholt whisky distillery. When, in 1870, old Overholt died, young Henry went into the coke business, with a cousin who had invested in coal lands. They already foresaw the rise of the steel industry in Pittsburgh, and they rightly believed that coke would turn out to be indispensable as fuel for the furnaces. Frick succeeded in borrowing $10,599 and bought with it more lands, and he persuaded his father to endorse countless notes upon which he procured small sums from the farmers of the countryside, "hitching up at dawn and driving all over the country and coming back at night with pockets full of greenbacks." He also preached to the father of Andrew Mellon, who had opened a bank in Pittsburgh, the glorious future of the coking business and borrowed from him $10,000 for the purpose of building fifty ovens: "Judge Mellon was not impulsive; he was notably cautious," but "that he was favorably impressed by the terse representations, direct methods and engaging manners of his confident young customer may well be believed." And even before the first fifty ovens were finished, he was asking for an additional loan in order to build fifty more. Judge Mellon sent a representative to investigate Frick & Co., and was advised not to make the loan, as the director was a mere boy, who had to give part of his time to keeping the books of a large store and whose "half-office and half-living-room in a clapboard shack" was filled with prints and sketches. Later on, however, the Judge again made inquiries and received the following report: "Lands good, ovens well built, manager on job all day, keeps books evenings, may be a little too enthusiastic about pictures, but not enough to hurt; knows his business down to the ground; advise making the loan." The loan was made, and the business prospered.

But in 1873, the panic fell: iron mills were shut down, mines abandoned; Pittsburgh was paralyzed, and the demand for coke began to dwindle. "'It was,' said Mr. Frick nearly half a century later, 'an awful time.'" But Frick & Co. persisted. The young Frick became his own sales agent, and, after rising every morning at six, looking over the ovens and seeing that the work was set going, would take the train to Pittsburgh, where he tramped from factory to factory, soliciting orders for coke. At six he would reach home and "attend to the details of mining till bed-time." At last, however, he became inspired to bring off what his biographer describes as "a truly dashing stroke." There was between Mt. Pleasant and Broadford a small railroad built for transporting coke, which, as a result of the bad conditions, had almost ceased to operate; the stockholders, foreseeing bankruptcy, were eager to sell their shares, and Frick knew that, if the railroad stopped, he would be forced to close his mines. He therefore borrowed a fast horse and drove round to see the shareholders, whom he easily persuaded to sign options on their stock; he then visited the management of the Baltimore & Ohio and preached again the revelation of the future greatness of the coke industry. He pointed out to them the desirability of purchasing now, at the lowest price, a line which must some day become valuable. The B. & O. bought the options at cost and paid Frick himself a commission of fifty thousand dollars, which enabled him to buy, among other things, the fast gray single-footer with which he had rounded up the shares. Judge Mellon was so favorably impressed by the astuteness of this transaction that he granted his young friend a mortgage-loan which now made it possible for him to purchase fifteen thousand dollars' worth of freight cars for the purpose of shipping coke over the road he had just sold and to obtain "a line of discount not exceeding twenty-five thousand dollars."

From this time, the business prospered. By 1897, Henry C. Frick was employing nearly a thousand men and shipping nearly a hundred carloads of coke a day. The price of coke had risen from ninety cents to five dollars a ton. "When springtime came, the various factors of mining, manufacture, transportation and selling had been welded into a smoothly working machine, whose essential attributes required only expansion to assure the ultimate success of the gigantic steel corporation, and the originator of the marvellous system saw his way clear to take his first holiday." This holiday was a trip to Europe with the Judge's young son, Andrew Mellon. Frick proposed two other companions, one a popular young man of their acquaintance, who wrote poems, sang songs and told stories; Henry and Andrew agreed that, being so little lively themselves, it would be a very useful thing for them to have "someone along to do the talking." The other man, however, was notoriously dull, and Mellon demurred a little; Frick explained that there was a "special reason" that he should like to have him of the party. And, in fact, when the excursion was finished and Mellon and Frick had to return home, it was found that the unexplained companion had acquired such an appetite for travel that he was eager to go on around the world and, in order to gratify this desire, consented to sell to Frick, at what was from the latter's point of view a very advantageous price, certain coal lands which he owned in the Connellsville region.

When Henry Frick returned to Pittsburgh, he picked out at once, at a "reception attended by all the élite," a young woman just out of her teens, whom he described as "the hand-somest girl in the room," and, three months after, had married her. As a climax to their honeymoon, the young husband brought his wife to New York and took her to dinner with An-drew Carnegie and his mother at the Windsor Hotel. A sur-prise had been reserved for the end: after dinner, Carnegie announced that he and Frick had gone into partnership. Mrs. Carnegie, who had not been warned of this, remarked drily, in the presence of the guests: "Surely, Andrew, that will be a fine thing for Mr. Frick, but what will be the gain to us?"

Such were the lives of the two remarkable Americans up to the time of their marriages, and up to the thresholds of their greatest successes. The most astonishing adventures and the most important achievements of both men were still, at this point, to come, and no brief condensation would do them jus-tice. If the differences between the explorer of the early half of the century and the capitalist of the latter half seem striking to the point of melodrama, it may partly be due to the unequal value and the differing temperaments of their respective biog-raphers. Professor Nevins has produced an attractive book—well-written, accurate, consecutive, beautifully proportioned and disciplined by a detachment as far from the silly irony that has lately become the fashion as it is from the injudicious im-pulse to magnify or rehabilitate of the fanatical enthusiast; and he, also, persuades us the more easily for the reason that, though he possesses a sense of the dramatic, he refrains from the obvious romantic treatment, the overindulgence in the picturesque, that his subject so temptingly invites, and de-pends for his effectiveness entirely on the quiet arrangement of facts. Colonel Harvey, on the other hand, brings to his task only that shrewdness of the small Vermont shopkeeper which enables him to appreciate, en connoisseur, the shrewdness of the shopkeeper in Frick, in Carnegie and in Rockefeller: he has no literary ability and little imagination, and there is some-thing about his nature profoundly ungracious and sordid, which makes us feel that, though he seems to have tried to present his subject in a favorable light and limited though

Frick himself unquestionably was, the collector of Vermeers and Rembrandts may yet not have lacked distinction to quite the ghastly degree that his biographer's pages do.

Yet a contrast comes out of these books that is real and extremely significant. Frémont had serious weaknesses, and he made a good many mistakes which Mr. Nevins does not try to disguise: he was sometimes incautious, tactless, egoistic, visionary, vain. His conquest of California ended in failure; his career as a general during the Civil War laid him open to damaging criticism; and he was so poor a business man that he allowed his California estate, valued at $10,000,000, to be wrecked by an unscrupulous speculator, and then lost the little that was left in a badly managed railroad enterprise, so that he died, at sixty, an impoverished man, in a New York boarding-house. Frémont's blunders seem mainly to have been due to an incurable lack of prudence: on his return from his first expedition, he insisted upon running, in an elastic boat, the rapids of an impossible canyon on the Platte River, and succeeded in wrecking the whole party; and his almost lunatic passion for crossing the Sierras in mid-winter, though, the first time, it brought him at last to the beauty and abundance of the Sacramento Valley, ended, the second, in horror and disaster. Yet, when we finish the story of Frémont's life, we are ready to say to ourselves: Who would not die in poverty to have won the satisfaction of such a life? and we are willing to agree with the poet that "only the wasteful virtues earn the sun"—as, with Frick, so much of whose strength lay precisely in his impregnable caution, in his incapacity for taking chances with that soundly invested fortune that he had worked so single-mindedly to amass, we wonder at last, as we read of him in his final years, in the solitude of that museum in which he had managed to entomb some of the glories of other ages and places that had known how to live with more joy than the grim Pennsylvania of his boyhood where his love of his few cheap prints had been badly regarded by Judge Mellon's spy—even among his pictures, to which, his biographer tells us, he liked to go late at night, we cannot refrain from asking what is the good of all this prudence and persistency which can only bring a man, late in life and at the expense of millions of dollars, such enjoyment at secondhand of the subtleties of the spirit and the colors of the world as may be bought with the works of art created by other men. The goldenrod and asters of Frémont, the blue-black hair of Cecilia, were an essential part of his life: they were one of the elements that fed it.

It is all too easy, perhaps, to handle this contrast of Frémont with Frick in such a way as to give the former all the aesthetic best of it—to set Frémont's comments on his own adventures, his statement in his memoirs, for example, that he had, on his first expedition, lived "with the fine Greek joy in existence, in the gladness of living," beside the meager memoranda dictated by Frick to his secretary to commemorate incidents of special interest, memoranda in which he himself is referred to in the third person:

"At Sherry's [in 1912] Mr. Grier bet $50,000 to $400 that if Roosevelt gets both Republican and Progressive nominations, he will be elected.

"In Pittsburgh [in 1916] attended Chamber of Commerce dinner, met Senator Warren Harding of Ohio; he looks like fine Presidential timber.

"Movies taken of Mr. F. playing cards. Very life-like.

"Had ten young farmers from Montana on their way to the war at Thanksgiving Dinner. Splendid chaps.

"Hereafter, when I purchase anything from [naming a certain picture dealer] it will be entered in this diary on the day I buy it. If no memo is entered, it is understood that everything is left on approval.

"Dr. Prichett lunched with others and showed up Wilson's character. Mr. F. drew out others but did not express opinion.

"Stopped at Baltimore and saw the Walters Collection.

"Will Hays called. Contribution.

"Mr. F. left Pride's for New York with Mr. Grier. He had refused to take an overcoat, but found one in the car and threw it out of the window to tease his daughter."

It is all too easy to speculate as to whether that fellow-traveller of Frick's and young Andrew Mellon's who exchanged his coal lands, in a bad bargain, for the expenses of a trip around the world did not perhaps, after all, get the better of the deal. Yet Henry Clay Frick makes, in some respects, a by no means contemptible showing beside the explorer and pioneer. For Frick did have his own sort of heroism, his own courage and independence, his own dignity and even honesty. His battle with his employees, for example, over the terrible Homestead strike required boldness as well as obstinacy. We may dislike the narrowness of his mind, the obduracy of his attitude toward organized labor, his stupidity about so many matters in which we should like to see our rich men interested; yet, in his fashion, Frick makes an impressive figure. He is seen perhaps at his best on the occasion, just after the defeat of the strike which had come so near to proving revolutionary, when the anarchist Alexander Berkman attempted to assassinate him in his office. Though Berkman had shot him twice and stabbed him three times, Frick succeeded in pinioning him to the floor. When a deputy sheriff rushed in and was about to shoot the assassin, "Don't shoot!" commanded Frick, "leave him to the law. But raise his head and let me see his face." When this was done, Frick pointed out that Berkman's jaw was moving, and the sheriff extracted from his mouth a capsule of fulminite of mercury sufficient to blow up the whole office. The wounded millionaire was again trying to prevent any violence to Berkman when he grew faint and had to be carried out. While the doctors were treating his wounds, he was arranging that his wife and his mother should be notified in such a way as not to alarm them; and when they came to extract the bullets, he refused to take an anesthetic, suggesting that he might help the doctors in locating them—which he did. He then had himself propped up at his desk and went on with his day's work, "specifying the final terms of a loan which he had been negotiating." Before he left in an ambulance, he dictated the following statement: "This incident will not change the attitude of the Carnegie Steel Company toward the Amalgamated Association. I do not think I shall die, but whether I do or not, the Company will pursue the same policy, and it will win." He would not have a bodyguard after this, but continued to go to and from his office without any kind of protection. He had made himself a rigid agent of that overwhelming power of the steel mills which dominates and drives the lives of employers and workmen alike: he had come to embody in his person its almost extra-human discipline.

While Frick had lain dazed from the assassin's attack, he had imagined that a little daughter who had died the year before at

six and for whom he had grieved ever since, was alive and had
come to see him; and at a time when he was still swathed in
bandages but directing every move in the resistance, not quite
yet at an end, of the now partly scab-manned mills, he was
obliged to look on at the death of a son who had been born
only four weeks before. We may be touched by the curious co-
habitation of the feelings that are tenderest in men with the
will that is implacably callous; but we remember, also, Frémont's return after the first of his great expeditions and his
spreading upon the bed of the daughter who had been born
during his absence the ragged American flag which he had been
the first to raise from the highest peak of the Rockies. And
beside the iron figure of the Bismarck of Homestead, whose
first thought, after the attempt on his life, was to reassure his
wife and mother, there arises the shade of the flighty explorer,
returning from the long Californian trip on which he had lost
touch with his family and was reported to have disappeared,
landing late at night on the levee at St. Louis, throwing pebbles
at the windows of his own house, told by the Negro coachman
that his wife had gone to spend the night at the house of a sick
cousin, and, after first setting out for the cousin's house, sitting
down to wait till morning on a bench in front of a hotel,
because he feared that the shock of his arrival might be harm-
ful to the tubercular relative.

John Frémont found the road to the West and "from the
ashes of his campfires have sprung cities." H. C. Frick produced the coke that made the steel with which were built the
railroads that spanned the continent—those railroads in which
Frémont invested and lost; and Frick's race, too, was one of
giants. They are all here in his biography, these giants—
Carnegie, Gary, Schwab, Morgan, the Rockefellers, and they
inevitably strike us as comic: for all their immense power, they
impress us, in their great transactions, as rather surprisingly
clownish, since—aside from the mere size of their projects—
they are seen to have no dignified aims and, except in a debased
sense, no honor. Trying continually to cheat one another,
whether as rivals or friendly associates, they are the performers
of a colossal rogues' comedy. We have heard, and still hear, a
good deal about the romance of big business, and Americans,
whatever we may say, live much in awe of the rich. Yet the nar-

rative of Colonel Harvey, read immediately after that of Professor Nevins, is almost enough to convince one that Nietzsche was right when he said that there are only three kinds of real creator: the scientist, the artist and the sportsman—because they alone play the game for its own sake, because they alone can be free from the appetite for money or power, or for the vulgar good opinion of their neighbors. Frémont, in his early and most brilliant phase, was a scientist and a sportsman; Nicollet and his associates were scientists; Kit Carson and the other frontiersmen whom Frémont knew in the old wild West were sportsmen. That West which they ranged and studied now no longer exists; we live in the world of Rockefeller, Carnegie, Morgan and Frick; and what leadership or revelation may Americans be sanguine enough still to await either from them or from their agents in the government? The great public have already given evidence of their longing for a different sort of hero in their acclaiming those audacious sportsmen, Charles Lindbergh and Commander Byrd. And what new kind of American in what new field may our country now be ready to breed to provide us with heroes and leaders?

April 4, 1928

The Sportsman's Tragedy

THE REPUTATION of Ernest Hemingway has, in a very short
time, assumed such proportions that it has already become
fashionable to disparage him. Yet it seems to me that he has received in America very little intelligent criticism. One finds
Mr. Lee Wilson Dodd, for example, in the *Saturday Review
of Literature*, with his usual gentle trepidation in the presence
of contemporary vitality, deciding with a sigh of relief that,
after all, Mr. Hemingway (a young man who has published
only three books) is not really Tolstoy or Shakespeare, and describing his subjects as follows: "The people he observes with
fascinated fixation and then makes live before us are . . . all
very much alike: bull-fighters, bruisers, touts, gunmen, professional soldiers, prostitutes, hard drinkers, dope-fiends. . . .
For what they may or may not be intellectually, aesthetically, or
morally worth, he makes his facts ours." In the *Nation*, Mr.
Joseph Wood Krutch, whose review is more sympathetic than
Mr. Dodd's, describes Mr. Hemingway as follows: "Spiritually
the distinguishing mark of Mr. Hemingway's work is a weariness too great to be aware of anything but sensations. . . . Mr.
Hemingway tells us, both by his choice of subject and by the
method which he employs, that life is an affair of mean
tragedies. . . . In his hands the subject-matter of literature
becomes sordid little catastrophes in the lives of very vulgar
people." I do not know whether these critics of *Men without
Women* have never read Mr. Hemingway's other two books or
whether they have simply forgotten them. Do the stories in *In
Our Time* and *The Sun Also Rises* actually answer to these descriptions? Does *Men without Women* answer to them? The
hero of *In Our Time*, who appears once or twice in this new
volume of stories, and the hero of *The Sun Also Rises* are both
highly civilized persons of rather complex temperament and
extreme sensibility. In what way can they be said to be "very
vulgar people"? And can the adventures of even the old bull-
fighter in such a piece as *The Undefeated* correctly be called a
"sordid little catastrophe"?

One of the stories in *Men without Women* also appeared in

the *American Caravan* and was thus twice exposed to the reviewers; yet in all the reviews I have read I cannot remember one which seemed to me to give an accurate account of it. *An Alpine Idyl* has usually been mentioned as a simple tale of horror or a tale of brutality, or something of the sort. Let us examine this story a moment. Two young men have been skiing in the Alps. It is spring and the sun is terrifically strong but in the shade, the sweat freezes in their underclothes. They have begun to find this oppressive and are glad to get down to an inn. On their way, they have passed a funeral, and at the inn they hear the story behind it. The woman who is dead was a peasant's wife who had died during the winter, but the house had been snowbound, and the husband had not been able to bring her out till spring. The man had put the body in the woodshed, laying it on a pile of logs; but when he had had to use the wood, he had stood the corpse up in a corner, and had later got into the habit of hanging the lantern in its mouth. Why, we ask ourselves now for a moment, have we been told about the skiing expedition? Then, immediately, we realize that Hemingway, with his masterly relevance in indirection, has, by telling us of the tourists' oppression, supplied us with the explanation of the brutalization of the peasant. But it is not the mere fact of this brutalization that makes the point of the story. We do not see the point till the end. The peasant comes on to the inn, but he refuses to drink with them there and goes on to another inn. " 'He didn't want to drink with me,' said the sexton. 'He didn't want to drink with me, after he knew about his wife,' said the innkeeper." In a similar way, it is true that *A Pursuit Race* is, as Mr. Dodd would say, a story about a dope-fiend; but what is much more important, it is also a story of a man who has just lost a desperate moral struggle. It is given its point by the final paragraph, in which the manager of the burlesque show, understanding that the struggle has been lost and pitying his recreant advance man, goes away without waking him up. So, in *A Simple Inquiry*—a glimpse of one aspect of army life: that strange demoralization that may bring with it a kind of stoicism—the significance of the incident lies in the fact that the major refrains from dismissing the boy who has just refused his advances.

It would appear, then, that Hemingway's world is not quite

so rudimentary as Mr. Krutch or Mr. Dodd represents it. Even when he is dealing with primitive types—as he by no means always is—his drama almost always turns on some principle of courage, of pity, of honor—in short, of sportsmanship, in its largest human sense—which he is able to bring to light in them. I do not say that the world that Mr. Hemingway depicts is not, on the whole, a bad world; it *is* a bad world, and a world where much is suffered. Mr. Hemingway's feelings about this world, his criticism of what goes on in it, are, for all his misleadingly simple and matter-of-fact style, rather subtle and complicated; but he has, it seems to me, made it plain enough what sort of ideas and emotions he is trying to communicate. His first book was called *In Our Time*, and it was a sequence of short stories about a sensitive and healthy boy in the American Northwest. We were, I take it, to contrast these two series. When Mr. Hemingway gave them this title, he meant to tell us that life was barbarous even in the twentieth century; and that the man who sees the cabinet ministers shot and who finds himself potting the Germans from behind the "absolutely topping" barricade has had to come a long way from the boy who, with the fresh responses of youth, so much enjoyed the three days' fishing trip at Big Two-Hearted River. Yet *has* he really come so far? Is not the principle of life itself essentially ruthless and cruel? What is the difference between the gusto of the soldier shooting down his fellow humans and the gusto of the young fisherman hooking grasshoppers to catch trout? Ernest Hemingway is primarily preoccupied with these problems of natural cruelty and its inevitable obverse of suffering.

The barbarity of the world since the war is also the theme of his next book, *The Sun Also Rises*. By his title and by the quotations which he prefixes to this novel, he makes it plain what moral judgment we are to pass on the events he describes: "You are all a lost generation." What gives the book its profound unity and its disquieting effectiveness is the intimate relation established between the Spanish fiesta, with its revelry, its bull-fighting and its processions, and the atrocious behavior of the group of holiday-making British and Americans who have come down from Paris to enjoy it. In the heartlessness of these people, in their treatment of one another, do we not find the same principle at work as in the pagan orgy of the festival?

Is not the brutal persecution of the Jew as much a natural ca-
sualty as the fate of the man who is gored by the bull on his
way to visit the bull-ring? The whole interest of *The Sun Also
Rises* lies in the attempts of the hero and the heroine to disen-
gage themselves from this world, or rather to arrive at some
method of living in it in such a way as to satisfy some code of
their own. The real story is that of their attempts to do this—
attempts by which, in such a world, they are always bound to
lose out in everything except honor. I do not agree, as has
sometimes been said, that the behavior of the people in *The
Sun Also Rises* is typical of only a small special class of American and British expatriates. I believe that it is more or less typical of certain phases of the whole western world today; and the
title *In Our Time* could have been applied to it with as much
appropriateness as it was to its predecessor.

    Ernest Hemingway's attitude, however, toward the cruelties
and treacheries he describes is quite different from anything
else that one remembers in a similar connection. He has
nothing of the liberating impulse involved in the romantic's
indignation:* he does not, like Byron, identifying himself with
the Prisoner of Chillon, bid the stones of any earthly cell "appeal from tyranny to God"; nor, like Shelley, invite the winds
to "wail for the world's wrong." Nor has he even that grim
and repressed, but still generous, still passionate feeling which
we find in the pessimist-realists—in Thomas Hardy's Tess, in
Maupassant's *Boule de Suif*, even in those infrequent scenes of
Flaubert by which one's resentment is kindled at the spectacle
of an old farm servant or of a young working-class girl at the
mercy of the bourgeoisie. In his treatment of the war, for example, Mr. Hemingway is as far as possible from John Dos
Passos or Henri Barbusse. His point of view, his state of mind,
is a curious one, and one typical, I think, of "our time"; he
seems so broken in to the human agonies, and, though even
against his will, so impassively, so hopelessly, resigned to them,
that the only protest of which he is capable is, as it were, the
grin and the curse of the sportsman who loses the game. Nor
are we always quite sure on which side Mr. Hemingway is

---

*This liberating impulse, however, was later to be brought out in Heming-
way by the Spanish Civil War.

betting. We do sometimes feel a suspicion that the conflict we are witnessing is a set-up, with the manager backing the barbarian. Yet to speak in these terms of Mr. Hemingway is really to misrepresent him. He is not, of course, a moralist staging a melodrama, but an artist exhibiting situations the values of which are not simple. Mr. Hemingway enjoys bull-fighting, as he enjoys skiing, racing and prize-fights; and he is unremittingly conscious of the fact that, from the point of view of life as a sport, all that seems most painful in it is somehow very closely bound up with what he finds to be most enjoyable. The peculiar conflicts of feeling which arise in a temperament of this kind are the subject of Mr. Hemingway's fiction. The most remarkable effects of this fiction, effects unlike those of anyone else, are those, as in the fishing-trip in *The Sun Also Rises*, by which we are made to feel, behind the appetite for the physical world, the tragedy or the falsity of a moral relation. The inescapable consciousness of this does not arouse Hemingway to passionate violence; but it poisons him and makes him sick, and thus invests with a sinister quality—a quality perhaps new in fiction—the sunlight and the green summer landscapes of *The Sun Also Rises*. Thus, if Hemingway is oppressive, as Mr. Dodd complains, it is because he himself is oppressed. And we may find in him—in the clairvoyant's crystal of a polished incomparable art—the image of the common oppression.

December 14, 1927

A Poet of the Pacific*

THE NEW SELECTION, made by herself, of Genevieve Taggard's poems—*Traveling Standing Still*—brings her literary personality before us as none of her previous volumes did. She has here chosen from these three earlier volumes twenty-eight poems; and she has exercised, in dealing with her own work, the same excellent critical judgment which has distinguished her literary reviews. One had always been aware before of this distinction of Genevieve Taggard's and of the integrity of her art; but one had never seen her outline so clearly as that of certain of her sister-poets. One had been aware of her originality but would have found it a little difficult to say precisely in what that originality consisted. She has never stood out so vividly in the literary garden—a plant of unique variety, bringing forth flowers of a certain shape and color—as, say, Elinor Wylie or Louise Bogan or Léonie Adams. But in this book she has so stripped her work down, has so rigorously reduced her writing to a residuum of what is most authentic, that it has, at least for a casual reader, for the first time become possible to recognize her art as something distinct and solid. She seems deliberately to have brought herself to focus.

The impression of Miss Taggard that one gets from this is a little unexpected. If one had tended vaguely to confuse her with a familiar school of women poets—the school which one of their number has recently herself described as the "Oh-God-the-Pain Girls"—Miss Taggard has excluded from this book anything that might encourage it. What we find is a kind of poetry which, however else it may move us, is not in the least "poignant"; and we see that Miss Taggard's point of view, her temperament and her intention must somehow differ from those of the poets with whom, as I say, we tend to class her. She seems, in fact, to differ from her sisters in certain fundamental respects, and I believe that they in some ways are more like one another than Genevieve Taggard is like any of them.

It is probably rather important to remember that Genevieve

*Written in Santa Barbara, California.

Taggard was born in the state of Washington and taken as a
baby to Honolulu, where her parents were American mission-
aries; and that she grew up and spent all her early years (she
was educated at Berkeley) in Hawaii or on the Pacific coast.
Now, we do not, as a rule, in America, get our poets from the
other side of the continent. Most of Miss Taggard's most brilliant sisters were born on the Eastern coast. And when we
come to reflect upon it, we may even be led to ask ourselves
whether the moods and the emotions of lyric poetry are not,
to a considerable degree, the products of varying weather. In
countries where the seasons change, our feelings also run to
extremes: the intensity of our works of art is the result of acute
contrasts of feeling, and these contrasts seem to correspond
with the contrasts of climatic conditions. In our autumns, with
the death of vegetation and the darkening of the skies, we are
reminded of the passing of love, the brevity of human life; in
our winters, we turn in upon and fortify ourselves: as our bodies redouble their calories to cope with the chill of the winds,
so our spirits must generate fire to set off the desolation of the
landscape; and in spring, we feel so much relieved at the revival
of vegetation and the restoration of warmth that our hearts
become hysterically gay. Also, poverty among us is worse; privation deprives us of more. And where life is barren or hard,
we make character to meet our conditions—people who are
rugged without and generous-hearted within, or people who
are cold on the surface and passionate in the spirit. But those
who have lived all their lives on our lower Pacific coast have
hardly been subjected to such heatings and coolings. There
the weather is equable and bright; the sea calm, the scenery
gentle; the flowers bloom all the year round, and there is more
fruit than people can eat. The natives have months of unbroken sun, and they are comfortable, amiable and healthy. In
Southern California, for example, one is surprised even to come
upon a graveyard: one had forgotten that people died; and the
mild and dry earth itself seems to bear its graves lightly.

Now, in the poetry of Genevieve Taggard, we become aware
of this Pacific sun. If most of the lyric poetry we know owes its
vividness, its pathos, its fierceness, to the coldness, the stoni-
ness, the bleakness, the meagerness, the illness, the death, with
which the poets see themselves surrounded—so Genevieve

Taggard's is the wisdom of the Western spaces and suns; and it is something quite other than the wisdom of our keen Eastern winds and constricted streets. The most striking feature of Miss Taggard's temperament, in contrast to the writers of the East, is the fact that her poetry is so rarely the result of a sharp reaction from one extreme to the other: a girl from the Pacific islands does not react against nature, as so many of our New England writers have done, for she has never been led to indulge in those moral and intellectual overdevelopments which make of nature an enemy; and, on the other hand, she does not rebound from the strain of such ascetic states of mind in the direction of nature again, for she has always taken nature for granted and has never divorced herself from it. She is simply and spontaneously physical; she is sensuous as a matter of course. And in the case of many Californians, this means that, since they lack the stimulus of moral dislocation or difficult living to prod them into thought, they do not seem to do any thinking: the problems that perplex, excite and torment the less fortunate parts of the world seem to have no existence for them. One remembers the young Californian girl who, when shown in a Spanish mission a painting of the agony of Santa Clara holding before her her severed breasts on a plate, asked innocently whether they were peaches. Now, Genevieve Taggard is in some respects (and I don't mean to be invidious) rather more like the girl who asked the question than she is like Santa Clara; but she differs from many Californians in the fact that she brings to her sensuous experience a shrewd and a subtle mind—a point of view even rather "metaphysical." And the peculiar interest of her poetry lies in the rare opportunity it gives us for observing such a mind and such a temperament in contact with both West and East.

For Genevieve Taggard, like many gifted Westerners, came early to live in the East. The first effect on her imagination of one of our Eastern winters is to be found in the elaborate *Ice Age*. This remarkable poem is a fantasy by one who has never been frozen-up about people deprived of sunlight. Now, ice has been made terrible in literature as a symbol of the atrophy of human feeling, from the traitors in Dante's Hell, immobilized in the nethermost pit, to the Brand of Ibsen's play, crushed by the avalanche; but Genevieve Taggard's *Ice Age*, vividly imagined though it is, does not bring us to the tragic climax which the poet has led us to expect from her shuddering and effective crescendo. In the end, we are obliged to recognize that the vision has had no moral meaning. Miss Taggard has not written of the cold as a New England writer would. She has merely had a taste of a winter that is colder than the climate she is used to, and it has made her extremely uncomfortable. Just as the dwellers in lands damp and chilly sometimes dream—as the English romantics did—of the languors of tropical climates, so Miss Taggard has been stimulated by New England to imagine a world grown completely cold. With all its sustained brilliance, the poem is a tour de force. Yet Miss Taggard, in coming away from the West, does seem to have quite lost Hawaii: her poems on Hawaiian sun-myths, which are the natural antithesis of the Ice Age, are less, perhaps, rather than more successful. Her memories have only sufficed—in such pieces as *Thirst* and *The Tourist*—for a few little poems of full flavor.

What we finally get is a poet of our common human experience who, despite her fastidious and busy mind, which embroiders it sometimes like lace, stitching it in and out, is singularly close to the ground. Whatever she may say in her bitterer moments—expressing herself in the admirable verses of *The Quiet Woman* and *Dissonance Then Silence*—she accepts what life brings her as natural and right. It is this that has made it possible for her to write, in the piece called *With Child*, the only respectable poem on child-bearing that I remember ever to have seen. The point is that the poet here does not, as is so often the case, repudiate or war with the woman. And even in *B.C.*, where the note is tragic, in warning the mother of Jesus that he will have to face "only agony and another loss of your being" in order to bring forth "an angelic shadow," her tone is not itself agonized, but rather one of sympathetic comprehension and resignation to the common lot. I believe that she is most enjoyable when, as in *Spring Touch* or *Talking Water*, she is most simply sensuous, least anxious.

Yet Miss Taggard has learned the habit of anxiety from her sisters of the East Coast. In a symposium of "statements of belief" that has recently appeared in the *Bookman*, she has told us that, in her early school days, when she had to sing in four-part songs, she always "sat with the altos and sang the dark humming parts." At last, a singing teacher came and identified her as a soprano. The young Genevieve announced her intention of continuing to sing alto. "Very well, and ruin your voice," said the teacher. "You have a real soprano, and you might sing solos." If Miss Taggard does not seem yet, in her poetry, quite to have found her true voice, if she seems sometimes to sing alto with effort, I am inclined to believe that this is not merely due, as she implies, to some anomaly of temperament, but to a certain maladjustment in her relations to West and East. With her eager intellectual appetite, she has devoured our ideas and techniques but she has scarcely been touched by the megrims, the nausea-fits, the moods of sterility that nowadays so often go with them. One looks forward to seeing her take her place as a self-dependent poetic personality, in some ways essentially different from any that we already know.

December 12, 1928

Art Young

ART YOUNG, in *On My Way*, has composed the least pretentious of autobiographies. In fact, the book scarcely pretends to be even an autobiography. He has merely kept a diary for six months, writing down in it every day some reflection, observation or memory. The result is like a series of conversations with a talented but retired and quite unpretentious neighbor, who has seen a good deal of the world and thought a good deal about it and upon whom one might agreeably drop in of an evening in the country.

He talks, as the occasion suggests, of his boyhood long ago in Wisconsin, of the cranks in his home-town who interested him; of his opinion that capitalism is doomed and that socialism will presently supplant it; and he speaks with loyal appreciation of his old master, Bouguereau, and tells how Bouguereau reprimanded him for making a brutal-looking model look too brutal; he says that the trouble with modern New York is that you can see nothing but brick out the windows; he tells about the early days in Greenwich Village: he was present at the celebrated picnic held on top of Washington Arch, when the Village declared itself an independent republic—when people came out the next morning, they all stopped and stared at the balloons flying from the top of the Arch. He used to know Eugene Field, also Jack Reed and Jack London; he tells about his cat, which has had kittens and was disturbed by the men fixing the furnace, so that it carried all the kittens to the attic; he talks about the change in American humor from the days of Bill Nye and Josh Billings; he mimics an old-fashioned Southern Senator whom he used to hear years ago when he was reporting Congress in Washington; he talks about his neighbors in the country; he remarks that if Frank Harris had known all the famous people he said he had, he would have had to be two hundred years old; he explains that Gustave Doré was the great admiration of his youth; he tells you how he used to campaign for municipal ownership, and how he once ran for the legislature on a Socialist ticket, but that he discovered too late that his speeches had all been made outside his own district—perhaps if his constituents had heard him, they would have given him fewer votes; he ruminates on his career as an artist and wonders whether his unpopular political views have really had much to do with the fact that he has never made money.

But as we gradually acquire, with such a neighbor, a tolerably solid idea of his tastes, his disposition, his views, his work and his associations—so with this book of Art Young's, little of it though there is and casual though it sounds, we feel, by the time we have finished it, that, balancing his inconsecutive notes and making them set off one another, he has succeeded in sketching in a rounded picture of his own personality—of the man who has made that long series of drawings that for the last thirty or forty years have been among the least well-advertized but the most distinguished features of American satiric art.

These drawings of Art Young's themselves are not here very well represented. What one would like to have is an album with a selection, well reproduced, of specimens from all the various phases of the artist's long career, but especially from the period of his connection with the old *Masses*, when his talent had its freest scope and he was able to amaze even those who had admired him for years in *Life*, by his wit, his imagination and his sure and incisive line. The drawings in *On My Way* have been usually chosen to supplement the text. There are, for example, many sketches of celebrities which, although they have their own kind of interest—especially those of Mark Twain, in his old age, walking up Fifth Avenue in a silk hat and P. T. Barnum attending divine service—do not represent Art Young at his best. As he tells us himself, he is not a good caricaturist: he is rather a cartoonist than a caricaturist; and he is rather a straight ironic artist of the type of Steinlen and Forain (in whose country he would probably long ago have occupied a position of acknowledged importance) than a cartoonist of the type of Nast. Yet some of his fine things are here. One finds several of the best of his drawings in wash: the Dantesque "world of creepers," anxiously watching their neighbors, stopping their mouths so they may not speak, holding their hats in their hands, all afraid to lift their heads in a wilderness where there is nothing to fear but themselves; and the workman's kitchen, with its heavy human masses and its hands like catchers' mitts, in which the wife is saying to the husband: "There you go! You're tired! Here I be a-standin' over a hot stove all day, an' you workin' in a nice cool sewer!" There is the admirable line-drawing of the self-possessed old farmer that came out first in the *Dial* with the title *American Peasant* (did Art Young supply that title or the *Dial*?). And there are a number of remarkable little drawings which have evidently been made for the book and which recall those plates of Callot in which the human beings are seen on the scale of tiny tin soldiers, set up as a distant set of ten-pins for some general or prince to knock over. As one studies these delicate drawings, one feels that Art Young himself should perhaps have been an engraver. The slender figures of *New York Shadows* have been cut out as clearly in the sunlight (the New York sunlight of yesterday) as their sharp silhouettes on the pavement; and the tree-trunks of *A Speech in the Woods*—through a rift in which a little human figure is seen holding forth to a friend—have been given a palpability of metal. One of the very best things in the book is Art Young's sketch of himself—*Art Young on Trial for His Life*—asleep at the *Masses* trial, when he and the editors, at the time of the war, were being prosecuted for conspiracy against the government: in a few hasty strokes he has caught all that strange non-human moroseness, that engulfing preoccupation, more earnest than any anxiety, that comes over the faces of people who have utterly succumbed to sleep.

The text of *On My Way*, necessarily, lacks the relief of Art Young's drawings; but there is a good deal of insight, and wisdom in the lightly delivered opinions: "I have been reading another book by just another philosopher on the problem of adjusting one's self to this life with a view to harmony. This time it is Keyserling. All of these books, which are becoming more and more frequent, could be summed up as: speculations on how to be happy by ignoring the economic equation in the forming of conduct, health and happiness; or, how to live comfortably in the realm of the spirit while living at the same time in a hard materialistic world. These philosophers are wild-goose-riders. It may not be wilful quackery, but it is quackery of a sort." And though his sketches of celebrities he has known seem sometimes a little perfunctory, they have in other cases a weight of underemphasis. Of Arthur Brisbane, under whom he had worked on the *Journal* and who had said to him, when the *Masses* was started, "You boys are talking to yourselves!," he tells the following anecdote: "Once, after a political campaign meeting, we adjourned to Allaire's, and behind those mugs of ale—such as they served in days gone by—Brisbane talked, mostly about cartoons. When I would express an opinion, he had a beautiful way of saying, 'Do you think so?' Finally he said, 'Young, you ought to be making at least $15,000 a year.'

"Then I said, 'Do you think so?'

"In a few days I went down to Brisbane's office with some cartoons embodying ideas that we had talked over at Allaire's. I felt a little as if I were starting on the high-road to making $15,000 a year, with Brisbane's help. Brisbane looked over the cartoons and said, 'How much do you want for this one?' I named a sum about equal to my unpaid rent and a laundry bill —I think it was seventy-five dollars. Brisbane didn't want to pay that much. He told me the advantages of having my work circulated by the millions in the Hearst papers, and that years hence my cartoons might be worth that, but not now, and besides, he said, 'We can get a boy in the art department to draw the same idea—for thirty dollars a week.' When he got through with me, I felt I was in luck to have my cartoons accepted at all.

"I cite this to show that Brisbane, besides being the highest-salaried editor in the world (even at that time, he told me, he was making as much money as the President of the United States), was also a business man—close on figures. His towering Ritz apartments had not been built then, but he was investing in real estate throughout New York, and had a few seasonal homes. It all added to my wonderment as to how one man could crowd so much responsibility into the span of a lifetime, and why."

Such a story makes Brisbane's career, with all its great profits and its great publicity, seem hollower and more dismal than ever. The personality of such a man, in spite of his air of Olympian power, his ability to operate at a distance, to have himself read in millions of homes, has seemed actually to have been destroyed at some early stage of his life. When you met him, you felt the continual strain, the frustration and even the bewilderment, of one who had irrevocably surrendered to forces outside himself. Such a man does not really control the power he is supposed to represent; he has not made it serve as his weapon: he has himself been absorbed and dissolved. And, beside such a nullity, Art Young is seen to have accomplished a feat which, in modern America, is difficult and rare: at the cost of popular success, and even of regular employment, he has managed to keep the shape of his personality and the quality of his intelligence. A man of Art Young's durability, however little we may publicly acknowledge it, performs an invaluable service in a society such as ours: he provides us with one of the touchstones of which we unconsciously make use in testing the soundness of character.

January 9, 1929

Greenwich Village at the
End of the Twenties*

I. 15 Beech Street

A MONG the empty streets of Greenwich Village, I could catch the rank saline smell of the river. It was as if, now that the people I knew had gone away to Provincetown or Woodstock, now that their world was shut up for the summer, the docks had closed in on our sanctuary. It made me feel rather desolate, and, in the humid dark, through the tangled streets, I drifted to 15 Beech Street. The light in the vestibule there was so dim that I could not see the names on the letter-boxes, so I did not attempt to ring the bell. I opened the heavy double doors and walked into the cavernous hall, with its waste of black-and-white linoleum, its steep and balustraded staircase, its gaunt square-topped radiator and its absolutely grisly hat-rack, of which the varnished ebon antlers and tentacles seemed to have been lopped in such a way as to give it the appearance of the still writhing skeleton of some unidentifiable creature and which was framed in an anomalous niche of imitation and putty-colored marble, the setting, at some prehistoric period, for some unimaginable vase or statue.

I climbed the forbidding stairs and tramped through the vast corridors of several floors—of which even the unexpected sproutings and the mysterious interior windows (closely blinded from the inside with dusty cast-off cloths) seemed inhuman and inexpressive. I had come to see Jane Gooch, but I lingered at other doors. Some had strange cards or no cards, and the names that I knew did not answer. Those high halls, with their dismal lights, with their expanses of stale yellow plaster, with their flat odor of unventilated bathrooms and their monotonous trickle of defective toilets, closed me round with a void of abandonment even more formidable than that of the streets. Well, at least, I thought, here was one house which had not changed since I first came to the Village, which

*The first of these pieces is fiction; the second, fact.

293

had not been demolished overnight to make room for a cliff of apartments, with electric refrigerators, meals "prepared by imported chefs" and, on the street level, smart new drug stores, uptown florists' shops and restaurants with current copies of *The Spur* and *Town and Country* to look at while one waited for a table.

I finally arrived at Jane Gooch's door and made out that her name was still there, and knocked. I waited. She was in: I heard movements at last, sounding ominous and seeming to draw near from a distance. Then she opened the door. She had just been going to bed and received me in a black kimono. The couch had been stripped of its cover and the bed-clothes underneath turned back. It was pleasant and reassuring, after the blank and empty grandeur of the hallways, to find a being so spare and distinguished—as it were, of so clear a significance. Jane Gooch had the straight back, the lankiness, the hatchet profile and the frank direct gaze of the ranches from which she had come: her eyes were very dark, and her smooth black hair, only a little gray, was parted straight in the middle; her gestures with her cigarette had a certain austere elegance.

I asked her if she knew Ralph Davis's address. She had at one time given him asylum in the room adjoining hers, as people often did in the Village and entirely without scandal. "Yes," she said, "he's somewhere out West, you know. I don't hear from him much nowadays, but I have a letter from him somewhere." She got up and began going through the drawers of an old mahogany desk. I looked about the room. Though she did all her cleaning herself, it showed the stamp of her sharp outline and her neatness. On the white walls, above the row of bookshelves, were brass candlesticks with red candles in them, an oval daguerreotype of a rugged Wyoming grandfather, a black bowl of red holly-berries, an Alaskan illustration that Rockwell Kent had given her and two portraits of herself—one a charcoal drawing and the other a painting that presented her with green skin and half-shut eyes and made her look like a corpse. There were also photographs of Joe Livingston, with whom Jane had been in love and who had died of typhoid in Russia; of George Keppel, the Greenwich Village prophet and metaphysical poet, who had developed a Messianic delusion and had finally been put in jail for robbing Seventh Avenue fur stores (he gave all the furs to the poor, and Jane had worked with tireless zeal to get his sentence commuted); and of Linda Fyfe, that fascinating girl painter, who was seen in the misty chiaroscuresque picture with her wild bobbed head thrown back and her long lovely throat revealed: Ralph Davis had once lived with her, and she had gone in for male models—first the pretty young drunken poets, then the waiters from the Italian restaurants—and had almost driven him mad with jealousy.

I asked Jane what she heard from Linda, and she told me that she seemed very happy with the elderly banker she had married. I asked also what had become of the couple who had formerly lived across the hall. I had been rather in love with the girl at one time and had gone there a good deal, lured on by the possibility one always felt in the Village that the ménage might break up overnight: the elements were so unstable, and new combinations formed so quickly. Ross and Peggy had indeed broken up, Jane told me, and both were married now—she to the man who kept the Greenwich Village Rendezvous and made enough money to live uptown by selling bad whiskey and gin to people who came from uptown to drink it, and he to a charming little actress (*he* thought she was charming, Jane said) from a very respectable family in Cleveland, who had made her first appearance on Broadway as the ingénue in some play of Molnar's. Ross had a job now on one of the tabloids, and he had had his old Sullivan Street apartment, formerly one of the "mad-houses" of the Village, made over for his well-brought-up bride. "It's just like what you read about in the old novels," said Jane, "making a 'nest' for the bride! First nest I ever saw down here! All I ever knew them to do at most was have the bed made the night they got married. And they used to be ashamed of getting married!"

I saw that Jane looked tired. "Oh, don't bother any more," I said. She was going through great packets of old letters which she had excavated from the desk. "I'm sorry I've come so late and kept you up." "Oh, I don't mind at all," she said. "I'm glad to see you, in fact. Usually I spend the whole evening alone." "I thought you saw a lot of people," I said, "in connection with *Vortex* and the Hole-and-Corner Players." "I do, but very few of the old crowd." She was ransacking the lower bookshelves now and had struck the files of the *Worker*, which had been dislodged amid a cloud of dust. "How is the *New Worker* doing?" I asked. "Not so well, I guess," she replied. "They haven't got the spirit to make it go. When there were Dick Otis and Fred Bullard and Joe, that was different—because they had a Faith. But now nobody has much faith in the Revolution—I haven't myself. I see that Fritz Binney has grown a great big black beard to make him look like a Bolshevik—but it's more like the Bearded Lady. 'Two owls and a hen, Four larks and a wren, Have all built their nests in my beard!' And so they have—his boy friends that help him with the paper."

I inquired about *Vortex*, the little magazine that she published herself. "Well, we're planning a big hydraulic number," she said (she always said "we," though her original collaborators had long ago ceased to be active), "as soon as we can raise enough money." (It came out at irregular intervals and in widely varying sizes and shapes.) "Hydraulic?" "Yes: pipes and oil pumps and plumbing fixtures—and all those things. We've got some photographs of bathrooms by Leo Kleist that are the most marvellous things you ever saw. There's a series—of washbasins at different angles—that looks just like the tomb of the Medicis. And then there are some paintings by Jacques Ducran of oil stations out on the Coast—bright red and orange and bright blue and gold—they look like something Chinese.—Look at this!" She showed me a still-life in rich brown and yellow, with a background of dazzling white. "Isn't that luscious? That's a rubber bath-sponge and a cake of kitchen soap. Of course, people will laugh at us, but we're used to that—and if anything is going to be done to bring the American public to a real appreciation of art—to a realization of the beauty, of the possibilities for beauty, of these things that they use every day —it will have to be done in the teeth of the hoots and the howls and the jeers of all the kept art critics of the bourgeois magazines. I believe that if we can only raise money enough to have color reproductions made, we'll be able to put over something big. I saw Max Beaumont yesterday, and he promised me half of what it would cost, if I could raise the other half. If I could only get the bills for the last number paid!" (The last *Vortex* had appeared eighteen months before.) "The printers are threatening to sue me. I'll have to give them my salary from the theater this month. And my own bill collectors wake me up at half-past seven every morning!" She laughed. "Oh, here it is!" she said, taking a letter out of its envelope. "Oh, that's fine," I went on to explain: "I'm editing a series of poets, and I wanted to try to get something from Ralph. I always thought he was awfully good and that he ought to have published a book. He had that real disequilibrium of the nerves that seems to make the best poets. The world really looked to Ralph just as wild as the deliriums he describes in his poetry. It made him a little bit difficult personally, because he was always either frightened and suspicious, or full of delusions of grandeur—especially when he was drunk. But life must have been an even worse strain for him than he made it for other people—and when you thought of what wonderful things he wrote, you were willing to put up with anything." "Here's a picture that he sent me," said Jane, taking a photograph out of the letter, "of him and his wife and their cow. Puzzle: find the cow. It was taken to illustrate that article, you know, that he wrote for the *Cosmopolitan: I Have Tried Free Love and Now I Own a Cow*—or something like that, it was called." "Does it tell his address?" I asked. "Yes," she dictated it to me. "Care of the *Weekly Falconer*, Falcon Motors, 1192 Penobscot Boulevard, Detroit."

June 29, 1927

II. Hans Stengel

Hans Stengel, who committed suicide in New York the night of January 28, was a man of considerable gifts who had never found his proper field. His parents were German and at the time that I first met him, he had just come over from Germany, where he had been associated, in Munich, with the group that produced *Simplicissimus*. He had begun by studying painting, but had developed a knack for caricature, which he hoped to turn to account; and, soon after he arrived in New York, he brought his caricatures to the office of *Vanity Fair*, with which I was then connected. They were vigorous and effective drawings of the modern German school, harsh, mordant, sometimes monstrous, sometimes gruesome. But they were, I knew, a kind of thing for which there was little demand. The prevailing taste at that time was for the agreeable triviality and the thin distinction of line of French or English drawing: and Hans Stengel was not merely too harsh, but also, in a sense, too serious. There was then, I believe, in New York, not a single editor of a magazine who would have looked at Stengel's work a second time. The *Liberator*, I think, had already gone out of business; and he could never have made a living by contributing to it. I remember feeling rather ashamed that I could not be more encouraging, that a man of evident talent, who had studied in a sound school, should be met by such a meager prospect of marketing his work in New York. Thereafter, when one encountered his drawings in the magazines and Sunday papers to which, by dint of persistence, he sometimes succeeded in selling them, one saw that he was being cramped by an effort to keep within the limits of what seemed to him the timid and complacent, the unimaginative American taste. He occupied at one time the position of principal caricaturist for the Sunday *Herald Tribune*, and his best work in the United States was probably done for this paper; but, as a German with a strong accent, he had against him both prejudice and fashion; and during the last year before his death he had been reduced to turning out a series for a cheap evening paper, a silly daily "feature" from which he had been obliged to eliminate everything that made his work original and which he refused to sign.

It is always difficult, in a given case, to estimate how far a good artist may have been discouraged from doing his best by a lack of demand for his work. It is possible that a caricaturist of the very first rank might have been able to force New York to accept him. But one cannot doubt, in Stengel's case, that the talent he had was stifled. One felt always that there was a great deal in him that had no field for artistic expression. He was intelligent; he knew a good deal of the world; he talked extremely well. There was more imagination and wit in his ordinary conversation than in anything he drew or wrote (for he sometimes tried his hand at writing). He was the son of a German actor, the director of the municipal theater at Lübeck, and he had cultivated a special instinct, which must have been theatrical in origin, for building up his monologues to cumulative effect and exploiting his personality. He was well-equipped to dominate an audience: he was more than six feet tall; he had served during the war in the German army and he cultivated the shaved head and something of the imperious manner (he had early discarded the monocle) of the traditional Prussian officer. He was therefore to be seen at his best advantage when he was holding the attention of a group of people, at dinner or at one of his Saturday nights; and he had become, with little money to entertain, one of the most popular hosts of Greenwich Village. Mencken, Dreiser and Robert Chanler were among his friends in New York; and at a period when the Village had lost most of its old romance with the most remarkable of its old leaders, he stood out as one of the only personalities capable of attracting about him a regular company of friends and admirers. He displayed, on these occasions, a vein of ironic commentary, fantastic but also acute, which, as I say, surpassed anything in his journalism. He was also, for all his Prussian pose, capable of generosity and a certain sensitive feeling; and he loved to live in the grand style. He was able to succeed, to an extraordinary degree, in interesting people in his personal fate and, in spite of furious quarrellings and fallings-out, in commanding their continued loyalty.

For such a man to wait upon editors and do hackwork for the American newspapers was, of course, peculiarly difficult. He was proud, and when his pride was in question, he would immediately resign his job; and though his incapacity for adjusting himself undoubtedly depressed him more and more, one was always struck, when one saw him after one of these ruptures had occurred, by the unmistakable relief of an independent spirit which would not for a time have to strain any more to conform to the requirements of men less intelligent and bold than he. His career since he had come to New York, in spite of his ups and downs, had always enabled him to live pretty well and would have been thought by many people not unenviable; but for Stengel, it was deeply unsatisfactory. He always seemed to regard caricature itself as rather beneath his dignity; and when, last winter, the proprietor of a night club offered him a large salary to act as master of ceremonies—a position for which his gift of holding the attention of an audience unquestionably fitted him well—he refused to consider it except as a joke. During the last few months of his life, he had set himself to write a novel—a novel in which, apparently, a simple sentimental German boy was to contrast with a cynical and arrogant Junker. Perhaps the most striking feature of Hans Stengel's character was his capacity for passionate feeling: he astounded even the inhabitants of Greenwich Village—by no means free, despite their reputation, from the pervasive indifference and tepidity of contemporary American life—by the violence of his despairs and exhilarations. Just as, in spite of the fact that Stengel spoke excellent English, and the English of a man with a literary ear, he spoke it always with German consonants and with many German locutions, so in New York he remained always a foreigner, who was fascinating to people partly because he represented something exotic, and who was never assimilated. It is natural to put down a failure to survive in one's own community—where we ourselves have no difficulty in prospering—to the deficiencies of the person who fails; but it is sometimes a good idea to inquire into the deficiencies of one's civilization from the point of view of what it destroys. Hans Stengel, in the course of the last year, had talked often of returning to Berlin; but New York had, after all, become his home at the same time that his existence here had come to seem to him hopeless. At one of his evening parties—unknown to the guests, but always with a sense of his audience—he shut himself into the coat-closet, tied a rope to his neck and the doorknob and, pulling against it, strangled himself. He was missed by his guests, and they found him there. His body has been cremated, and his ashes are to be scattered to the waters of that city to which he came so few years ago, a young man with his portfolio of drawings.

February 23, 1928

The Critic Who Does Not Exist

I N PAUL VALÉRY'S address to the Académie Française on the occasion of his succeeding Anatole France, there is a passage in which he describes the literary situation in Paris as he found it in his youth. There were, he says, a number of different parties, each with its own definite set of policies and each with an eminent writer, or group of eminent writers, at its head. There were Zola and the naturalists; Leconte de Lisle and the Parnassians; Renan and Taine and the "*idéologues*"; Mallarmé and the symbolists. These parties stated their programs and defended them against each other: they played roles in a literary politics equally exciting and equally important with politics of the other sort. When five of Zola's followers seceded from his party over the publication of *La Terre*, the event was profoundly significant: it was the first attack in a great campaign. When Valéry, received by the Academy, reasserts the claims of symbolism, at one time a literary minority, in a speech on the career of his predecessor, one of the leaders of a different camp—that is, again, an historic event and marks the success of a revolution. The French writers whom we read most today—France, Gourmont, Proust, Valéry, Gide—all came to intellectual maturity in this atmosphere of debate; and this gives them a kind of interest—the interest of the intelligence fully awakened to the implications of what the artist is doing, that is to say, to his responsibility—very rare in the literature of English-speaking countries, and nowadays perhaps nowhere to be found in any very intense degree save, on a smaller scale, in Dublin. For there is one language which all French writers, no matter how divergent their aims, always possess in common: the language of criticism.

When we come to survey the literary landscape of contemporary America, it seems to us at first that nothing could resemble less the clear political alignments that are nearly always to be found in France. But then, as we examine the prospect more closely, we are surprised to become aware of the presence both of able leaders and of powerful parties, each professing more or less explicitly a point of view and acting more or less consistently on a set of principles. There is, in the first place, H. L. Mencken, with his satellite George Jean Nathan, his disciple Sinclair Lewis, and his literary nursery, the *Mercury*. Then there is T. S. Eliot, who, despite the fact he lives in England and has recently become a British subject, exerts a tremendous influence in America and is always regarded by his American readers as still an American writer. It may be said that Mencken and Eliot between them rule the students of the Eastern universities: when the college magazines do not sound like Mencken's *Mercury*, they sound like Eliot's *Criterion*. Then there is the group of writers—it is a group that does not have any unity and is almost entirely without critical self-consciousness—-of what may be called the neo-romantics, of which Edna Millay and Scott Fitzgerald, with their respective imitators and followers, are the leaders in the present generation, and which had for precursors such writers as Sara Teasdale, Joseph Hergesheimer and perhaps also James Branch Cabell. Then there is the more or less organized and highly self-conscious group of the social revolutionary writers: John Dos Passos, John Howard Lawson, Michael Gold, etc. Their organs are the *New Masses* and the Playwright's Theater. One should mention also—though they constitute a school rather than a group—the psychologico-sociological critics: Van Wyck Brooks, Lewis Mumford (whom I take to be a disciple of Brooks), Joseph Wood Krutch and a number of others.

What we lack, then, in the United States, is not writers or even literary parties, but simply serious literary criticism (the school of critics I have mentioned last, though they set forth their own ideas, do not occupy themselves much with the art or ideas of the writers with whom they deal). Each of these groups does produce, to be sure, a certain amount of criticism to justify or explain what it is doing, but it may, I believe, be said in general that they do not communicate with one another; their opinions do not really circulate. It is astonishing to observe, in America, in spite of our floods of literary journalism, to what extent the literary atmosphere is a non-conductor of criticism. What actually happens, in our literary world, is that each leader or group of leaders is allowed to intimidate his disciples, either ignoring all the other leaders or taking cognizance of their existence only by distant and contemptuous sneers. H. L. Mencken and T. S. Eliot present themselves, as I have said, from the critical point of view, as the most formidable figures on the scene; yet Mencken's discussion of his principal rival has, so far as my memory goes, been confined to an inclusion of the latter's works among the items of one of those lists of idiotic current crazes in which the editor of the *Mercury* usually includes also the recall of judges and paper-bag cookery. And Eliot, established in London, does not, of course, consider himself under the necessity of dealing with Mencken at all. Similarly, George Jean Nathan scoffs at the plays of Lawson and has never been willing to take seriously the movement he represents; and the *New Masses* has never gone further than an occasional gibe at Mencken. Van Wyck Brooks, in spite of considerable baiting, has never been induced to defend his position (though Krutch has recently taken up some challenges). And the romantics have been belabored by the spokesmen of several different camps without making any attempt to strike back. It, furthermore, seems unfortunate that some of our most important writers—Sherwood Anderson and Eugene O'Neill, for example—should work, as they apparently do, in almost complete intellectual isolation, receiving from the outside but little intelligent criticism and developing, in their solitary labors, little capacity for supplying it themselves.

Now, it is no doubt impossible for an English-speaking country to hope for a literary criticism comparable to that of the French: like cookery, it is one of their specialties. But when one considers the number of reviews, the immense amount of literary journalism that is now being published in New York, one asks oneself how it is possible for our reviewing to remain so puerile. Works on history are commonly reviewed by historians, and books on physics by physicists; but when a new book of American poetry or a novel or other work of belles lettres appears, one gets the impression that it is simply given to almost any well-intentioned (and not even necessarily literate) person who happens to present himself; and this person then describes in a review his emotions upon reading the book. How many works of general literature are ever officially discussed in New York by people with any special knowledge of the subjects on which they are invited to write? Since the death of Stuart P. Sherman, who was second-rate at best, there has

not been a single American critic who regularly occupied himself in any authoritative way with contemporary literature. Yet
what might not have been the effect on Sinclair Lewis, for example, and on the great army of Mencken's younger followers,
if Mencken had been systematically and periodically over-
hauled by a critic of equal vigor? What might not have been
the effect on all that new crop of poets who have been made
prematurely senile by imitating Eliot's *Gerontion*, if a critic as
intelligent as the people who ridiculed *The Waste Land* were
stupid had, while doing full justice to Eliot, made fun of this
tendency in time? Do not the champions of proletarian literature deserve the hard-hitting polemics which their appetite for
controversy invites? And might not a critic who enjoyed Lawson's wit and valued his technical inventions have been of some
service in discouraging his bathos and his bad rhetoric? And
those scattered contemporary romantics who, since the war,
have been repeating over here all the poses, the philosophy
and the methods of the Europe of 1830—instead of finding
themselves stalled, bewildered, out of date almost as soon as
they were famous, if their situation had in time been a little
cleared up by a competent criticism, might they not have
already readjusted themselves and applied their brilliant abilities to the production of something more durable? Finally,
with the advent of a new generation, there has emerged from
our literature of the past a number of important names, a
number of writers whom we are all agreed in regarding as of
first-rate quality: Emerson, Hawthorne, Thoreau, Whitman,
Melville, Poe, Stephen Crane, Henry James. Yet so far the
studies by American hands which have dealt with these American classics have been almost exclusively biographical. We have
been eager to expose the weaknesses and curious to probe the
neuroses of these ranking American writers, but have found
little to say that was interesting as to why we should consider
them so. Have we not been unfortunate in the lack of a criticism which should have undertaken, for example, to show how
Hawthorne, Melville and Poe, besides becoming excessively
eccentric persons, anticipated, in the middle of the last century, the temperament of our own day and invented methods
for rendering it?

   I do not of course mean to assert that, except on the lower

levels, any criticism, however able, could make or unmake artists. A work of art is not a set of ideas or an exercise of technique, or even a combination of both. But I am strongly disposed to believe that our contemporary writing would benefit by a genuine literary criticism that should deal expertly with ideas and art, not merely tell us whether the reviewer "let out a whoop" for the book or threw it out the window. In a sense, it can probably be said that no such creature exists as a full-time literary critic—that is, a writer who is at once first-rate and nothing but a literary critic: there are writers of poetry, drama or fiction who also write criticism, like most of the French writers mentioned above and like Coleridge, Dryden, Poe and Henry James; and there are historians like Renan, Taine, Sainte-Beuve, Leslie Stephen and Brandes whose literary criticism is a part of their history. In America, neither kind of criticism has been very highly developed; and I fear that we must take this as a sign of the rudimentary condition of our literature in general. The poets, the dramatists and the novelists too often lack the learning and the cultivated intelligence to give us in works of art the full benefit of the promising material supplied by experience and imagination; and it may in general be said that where our writers of biography and history fail is precisely in their inability to deal adequately with works of literature.

February 1, 1928

A Weekend at Ellerslie

IN FEBRUARY, 1928, I had from Scott Fitzgerald a letter, headed "Ellerslie," Edgemoor, Delaware, which—although it may not at once be clear—was an invitation to visit him:

. . . All is prepared for February 25th. The stomach pumps are polished and set out in rows, stale old enthusiasms are being burnished with that zeal peculiar only to the British Tommy. My God, how we felt when the long slaughter of Paschendale had begun. Why were the generals all so old? Why were the Fabian society discriminated against when positions on the general staff went to dukes and sons of profiteers? Agitators were actually hooted at in Hyde Park and Anglican divines actually didn't become humanitarian internationalists over night. What is Briton coming to—where is Milton, Cromwell, Oates, Monk? Where are Shaftsbury, Athelstane, Thomas à Becket, Margot Asquith, Iris March? Where are Blackstone, Touchstone, Clapham-Hopewellton, Stoke-Poges? Somewhere back at G.H.Q. handsome men with grey whiskers murmured "We will charge them with the cavalry" and meanwhile boys from Bovril and the black country sat shivering in the lagoons at Ypres writing memoirs for liberal novels about the war. What about the tanks? Why did not Douglas Haig or Sir John French (the big smarties) (Look what they did to General Mercer) invent tanks the day the war broke out, like Sir Philip Gibbs the weeping baronet, did or would, had he thought of it?

This is just a *sample* of what you will get on the 25th of Feb. There will be small but select company, coals, blankets, "something for the inner man."

Please don't say you can't come the 25th but would like to come the 29th. We never receive people the 29th. It is the anniversary of the 2nd Council of Nicaea when our Blessed Lord, Our Blessed Lord, our Blessed Lord, our Blessed Lord—

It always gets stuck in that place. Put on *Old Man River* or something of Louis Bromfield's.

Pray gravity to move your bowels. It's little we get done for us in this world. Answer.

Scott

Enjoyed your Wilson article enormously. Not so Thompson affair.

An invidious salutation, which I here omit; the parody in the

306

first paragraph of what Scott evidently imagined to be the attitude of the liberal weekly on which I was then working (I could not make out why the war should be uppermost in his mind); and the reference to my having been obliged to decline an earlier invitation—all combined to produce the effect of a slightly hostile overtone. The Wilson article mentioned in the postscript was the one that appears in this volume under the title *Woodrow Wilson at Princeton*. The "Thompson affair" was an article called *Vanzetti's Last Statement*, an account by Mr. W. G. Thompson, counsel for Sacco and Vanzetti, of his last interview with his clients the day before their execution, which the *New Republic* had reprinted from the *Atlantic Monthly* and a copy of which I had sent to Scott along with the Wilson piece. I gathered that he meant to indicate that he did not necessarily range himself on my side of an issue that had, the summer before, given rise to a split of opinion almost as bitter as that created by the Dreyfus case. I had seen very little of Scott since he had taken his family to Europe in 1924, and I was aware that our personal relations had suffered a certain chill. It was partly that, from college days, when I had been a year ahead of him and the editor of the magazine, he had come to regard himself as somehow accountable to me for his literary career, and that he had been struggling unsatisfactorily with his most ambitious project to date, a novel of matricide, which he had started in 1925. He had learned very fast as a writer; his ideals for his art had gone rapidly up. Each of his three novels, from the point of view of form and conception, had been a startling improvement on the one before. He had now gone on to tackle a subject that might well have taxed Dostoevsky, and he was eventually to find it beyond him. It must have been a psychological "block" as well as the invincible compulsion to live like a millionaire that led him even more than usual to interrupt his serious work and turn out stories for the commercial magazines. At any rate, *Tender Is the Night* did not appear till 1934, when his original subject—the mother theme dropped —was seen to have modulated into something quite different. In the meantime, I had always felt that he was expecting me to point a finger at him and say, "What has become of that novel?" It was his own artistic conscience that accused him, but this was beginning to make our meetings uncomfortable, for any inquiry about his work was likely to bring a sharp retort. But he evidently wanted to see me, so I went.

I had never yet visited the Fitzgeralds in the house just outside Wilmington that they had taken on their return from Europe at the end of 1927, but rumors had reached me of festivities on a more elaborate scale than their old weekends at Westport or Great Neck. Dos Passos had attended a party that Scott had given for his thirtieth birthday, which he described to me as "a regular wake"—Scott had been lamenting the passing of youth ever since his twenty-first birthday, and he had apparently commemorated his twenties with veritable funeral games. I had certainly never seen Scott and Zelda in such a magnificent setting. Ellerslie, Edgemoor, turned out to be a handsome old big square white house, with Greek columns and high-ceilinged rooms. It had been built in the early eighteen-forties and had always up to then been occupied by the managers of the Edgemoor Iron Company. I arrived there with Thornton Wilder, whom I had not known before and whose books I had not read. Scott had had us met at the station, and, in the course of the drive to Ellerslie, we had talked about Marcel Proust. I had just read the final instalment of *A la Recherche du Temps Perdu*, which had reached New York not long before, and was about to describe it to Wilder. There are few things I enjoy so much as talking to people about books which I have read but they haven't, and making them wish they had—preferably a book that is hard to get or in a language that they do not know. But in this case my expectation was disappointed, for it turned out that Wilder had been following Proust just as attentively as I had and had read *Le Temps Retrouvé* as promptly. I had had the impression that his novels were rather on the fragile and precious side, and was surprised to find him a person of such positive and even peppery opinions. He had his doubts about *Le Temps Retrouvé*; he declared that too many of the characters turned out to be homosexual. Charlus was all right, he said; but in the case of Saint-Loup, for example, some further explanation was needed: there was a psychological problem there that Proust had simply shirked. I called his attention to the fact that the novel ended with the phrase "*dans le temps*," as it had begun with the key sentence, "*Longtemps, je me suis couché de bonne heure*," and he said he had noticed this.

Scott met his guests at the door and, the moment their hats and coats were off, took them for a tour of the house, of which he was extremely proud and which he was doing his best to live up to. He would stop in one of the corridors and say mysteriously, "Don't you hear something? Don't you hear something strange?—It's the old Ellerslie ghost." He had posted the butler behind a door to groan and rattle a chain. But at a time when the whole house was buzzing with life and everybody looking forward to cocktails, these sounds did not even attract attention, and the clanking of a chain would, in any case, hardly have meant anything to anyone not fresh from a Gothic novel. We were next taken into a room, where we were given, for our entertainment, a choice of listening to records—which were still a novelty then—of *Le Sacre du Printemps* or of looking at an album of photographs of horribly mutilated soldiers. Scott had discovered the war, and this explained the antiquated allusions of his letter, as well as his just having pointed out to me, hanging on the wall of his study, the trench-helmet which, not having been sent overseas, he had never worn in action. At the time when he had been in the army, he must have been exclusively occupied with the first version of *This Side of Paradise* and his romance with Zelda in Alabama, for it was as if the unpleasant events of 1914–18 were now touching his imagination for the first time. They must have been brought to his notice by his friend Ernest Hemingway, of whom he had seen a good deal in Europe and who was then writing *A Farewell to Arms*. Preliminary drinks were served, but we had not got far with Stravinsky before we were taken outside and involved in a chaotic interlude, of which I can remember—on the darkening lawn—only playing diabolo while carrying on a conversation about Ford Madox Ford.

The crescendo of the evening was well under way when we had our pre-dinner drinks in a large and splendid salon. Gilbert and "Amanda" Seldes were there, and Esther Strachey, the sister of Scott's great friend Gerald Murphy. In a conversation with Seldes and me, Scott somehow got around to inviting us frankly to criticize his character. Gilbert told him that if he had a fault, it was making life seem rather dull; and this quite put

him out of countenance till we both began to laugh. John and
Anna Biggs arrived. John Biggs was an old friend of Scott's
and mine, who had roomed with Scott in college. He practised
law in Wilmington—though he was just about to publish his
second novel—and it was he who had got Scott established at
Ellerslie. I had not seen John since his marriage, and Scott explained Anna to me: "She was one of the famous Rupert
girls—don't you remember the beautiful Rupert sisters that
were such a sensation at the proms?" In the atmosphere of
exhilaration that the Fitzgeralds always generated on these occasions, I was called upon to give them an act that I had sometimes performed years before—after the summer of 1916 at
Plattsburg—at convivial college gatherings. This was an imper-
sonation of a Regular Army officer giving a hoarse-voiced lecture on Scouting and Patrolling. Major Waldron, red-faced and
bespectacled, standing with his heels together and his arms
held stiff at his sides, would bark out, without a gesture or a
flicker of expression, such instructions as: "Places of conceal-
ment: trees and roofs of houses. If you climb on roof of house,
be sure to keep on side that's hidden—side that's away from
enemy. Don't get on side exposed to enemy. Scout that gets
on side exposed to enemy can be seen by enemy and shot.
Scout must keep from getting shot. Scout's no good if he's
dead." I had completely forgotten this, but John Biggs fed it
back to me, and I did my best to oblige, though I was really
not up to it any more. At some point either just before or just
after this, Scott, took me aside in another room and told me
that he had been harboring a grievance against me. It was
something that had happened a long time before—he felt that
I had behaved with him and Zelda in a way that he ought to
resent. I thought it was all nonsense—especially as coming
from him; but since Scott, like Dr. Johnson, considered himself an authority on manners, I tried to explain my offense
away, and something like our old good relations seemed to be
reëstablished.

Then a drove of new people arrived. A play of Zoë Akins'—
The Furies—was being tried out in Wilmington, and the
Fitzgeralds had invited her to dinner, with the designer of the
sets and costumes and three or four other men who were also
involved in the production. At dinner, we were floating di-

vinely on good wine and gay conversation, in which I noted, however, that Wilder, though extremely responsive, remained sharply and firmly non-soluble. He was talking with Esther Strachey about Colette, and saying that there were some of the Claudine books that he thought were pretty good. I sat next to Zelda, who was at her iridescent best. Some of Scott's friends were irritated, others were enchanted, by her. I was one of the ones who were charmed. She had the waywardness of a Southern belle and the lack of inhibitions of a child. She talked with so spontaneous a color and wit—almost exactly in the way she wrote—that I very soon ceased to be troubled by the fact that the conversation was in the nature of a "free association" of ideas and one could never follow up anything. I have rarely known a woman who expressed herself so delightfully and so freshly: she had no readymade phrases on the one hand and made no straining for effect on the other. It evaporated easily, however, and I remember only one thing she said that night: that the writing of Galsworthy was a shade of blue for which she did not care. But as the dinner went on, Miss Akins began to dominate the conversation. She was herself an accomplished performer in a more grandiose tradition than that of the unceremonious twenties, and she was presently holding the table with resounding speeches from Shakespeare. This rather threw out the Fitzgeralds, who were used to the center of the stage and preferred a more playful tone, and when Miss Akins and her companions had left in order to get to the theater, Scott, who had been charming at the beginning of dinner, now grumbled: "All that memorized Shakespeare!" This was followed by a complete anticlimax. Scarcely had we left the table when the Fitzgeralds announced they were going to bed and left the guests to shift for themselves. I soon went to bed myself.

But this, though I saw nothing more, was by no means the end of the evening. The party from Miss Akins' play had been invited to come back when the performance was over, and, with the exception of Miss Akins herself, they did. Zelda, having had her sleep, decided to emerge again, and, coming into one of the spacious rooms, discovered the little designer, alone, leaning moodily on the marble mantel. "Please go away," he said. "I'm thinking, and I don't want to be disturbed."

"Oh, you're not really thinking," said Zelda, for whom, as for all Southern women, any highhanded tone on the part of a man stimulated immediate insolence. "You're just homogeneous!" This could hardly have been due to ignorance: it must have been a species of euphemism intended to soften the remark; but, in any case, its effect was terrible. The young man stalked out of the room and complained to his companions of an insult, and, demanding the Fitzgeralds' car, they all huffily left.

I do not think that Scott, who had slept all night, heard anything about this incident till Zelda got up late the next morning. I remember his sitting around in his bathrobe and reading to Gilbert Seldes and me what must have been one of the early Riviera chapters from his novel then in progress, which was to turn into *Tender Is the Night*. There was especially one dazzling passage with which he had evidently taken much pains and on which he must have counted to stun us. It presented a group of attractive girls—on a beach or in a room, I can't remember—but in any case floating and glowing in richest Fitzgerald glamor. "What do you think of that description?" he asked. We told him we thought it was splendid. "I read this chapter to Dos Passos, when he was here," he said, "and afterwards he said that he liked it 'all except that part,' he said, 'that's so wonderful.' I asked him what he meant, and he said, 'Oh, you know: that part that's so wonderful—that part that's so perfectly marvellous.'" This may have led him to leave it out, or he may have had to scrap it with his original subject, for I cannot now find this passage, in any form I can recognize, in *Tender Is the Night*. Thornton Wilder, who had left early that morning, was, I found, Scott's most recent enthusiasm. He told me that *The Cabala* was the very best thing that had come out, I think, since Hemingway—he did not care so much for *The Bridge of San Luis Rey*. I must absolutely read it—he would send it to me.

But the news of the incident of the night before, when Scott heard of it, profoundly disturbed him. It had been a breach of hospitality, and he must do what he could to repair it. He would look up the offended guests and try to smooth the incident over. He set out in his car after lunch, taking along Esther Strachey and me to talk to him and support his morale. On the way, he questioned the driver—of whom he seemed to have made a trusted familiar—as to what the guests had said while he was taking them home. "Why, the little fellow said, 'Fitzgerald thinks he's got a swell place there, but an uncle of mine's got a house that makes that house look like a dump!'" This visibly depressed Scott, and Esther and I tried to dissuade him from pursuing the matter further; but, "It's only very seldom," he insisted, "that you get a real opportunity to hear what people say about you behind your back.—Didn't anybody," he turned to the driver, "have anything good to say about me?" "There was one that tried to speak up for you," the man replied, "but they had him down on the bottom, with their feet on him." Scott found out in Wilmington that the theater people were not all at the hotel with Miss Akins, and since it looked as if it might take him some time to run them down and to deal with the problem properly, he sent us back to the house. He wanted to make them come back, so that Zelda and he could be nice to them.

The aftermath of a Fitzgerald evening was notoriously a painful experience. I suddenly became terribly irritable and said something sarcastic to Esther about what seemed to me certain chi-chi attitudes that she had recently picked up in Paris. She replied—with great moderation in view of what must have been on my part a very disagreeable tone: "You have an intellectual arrogance that is sometimes very trying." I was somewhat piqued by this—let me say that my friendship of many years with this brilliant and most amiable woman has otherwise been quite unclouded—and I made up my mind that I would leave late in the afternoon. I did not want to see the theater people again; I could not face another evening. It seemed to me the party was slipping, and I knew that when these parties of the Fitzgeralds slipped they were likely to end in disaster. I knew that if I stayed through another night I should be no good Monday. I was getting too old for this kind of thing. I found that I did not, however, have money for the railroad fare, so I asked Scott, when he came back, to cash a check. He had no money either and tried to persuade me to stay. When I insisted, he went away with the check and then came back to let me know that Esther Strachey was the only person in the house who had ten dollars to spare. This was very embarrassing to me, but Esther was neither embarrassed nor embittered, and the whole thing became a joke.

I later heard that Scott had waked up in the night and decided that he had not done justice to the possibilities of the Ellerslie ghost. He put a sheet over his head and invaded the Seldeses' room. Standing beside their bed, he began to groan in a way that he hoped was an improvement on the butler. But Gilbert started up from his sleep and gave a swipe with his arm at the sheet, which caught fire from a cigarette that the ghost was smoking inside his shroud. In the turmoil, something else caught fire, and everybody was rather alarmed.

Scott sent me a copy of *The Cabala*, which I read with much admiration; and that summer I wrote for the *New Republic* the article on Wilder that follows. In rereading it, this Wilmington weekend has come back into my mind so vividly that, in view of the recent interest in the Fitzgeralds and the twenties generally, I have thought it might be worth while to put on record here this specimen of the literary life of a period in which nonsense and inspiration, reckless idealism and childish irresponsibility, were mingled in so queer a way.

1952

Thornton Wilder

NOW THAT Mr. Thornton Wilder has become both a best-seller and a Pulitzer prize-winner, he is in an unfortunate situation. On the one hand, the literary columnists have accepted him as a Reputation and gossip about him with respect but without intelligence; and, on the other, the literary snobs have been driven by his tremendous popularity, by the obsequious gossips themselves, into talking as if they took it for granted that there must be something meretricious about him. Mr. Wilder remains, however, a remarkably interesting writer, with a good deal to be said about him which no one, so far as I know, has said.

One of the things about Mr. Wilder that I do not think has yet been said is that he seems to be the first American novelist who has been influenced deeply by Proust. In devoting some attention to this subject, I do not at all mean to imply a lack of originality on Mr. Wilder's part: on the contrary, it is quite extraordinary that a novelist so young should display, from the first page of his very first book, so accomplished a mastery of a form and a point of view so much his own. The Proust influence seems simply the influence of a first-rate senior writer on a first-rate junior one. And what Mr. Wilder has learned from Proust is not merely Proust's complex impressionism: the side of Proust that Sacheverell Sitwell imitated in *All Summer in a Day* does not figure in Mr. Wilder at all. He has listened to Proust's very heart, and his own has been timed to its beat. It is not so much a formula of style that Thornton Wilder has taken, though there are echoes of Proust's style, too, but a formula of emotion, of the criticism of life. And in order to estimate his work, we should try to discover which part of it represents the poet Wilder himself, from whom quite un-Proustian things may eventually be expected, and which part is mere repetition of cadences caught from the asthmatic master.

One of Proust's favorite formulas, then—which we find in almost every situation of *A la Recherche du Temps Perdu*—is that of an abject and agonizing love on the part of a superior for an inferior person, or at least on the part of a gentle person

for a person who behaves toward him with cruelty. Mr. Wilder
seems infatuated with this, and he leans on it a little too heavily.
It figures less conspicuously in *The Cabala* than in *The Bridge
of San Luis Rey*; but the episode of Alix in the former book,
which seems to me also the episode that carries the least conviction, is simply a reversal of the Proustian relationship in
which we are shown a charming and sensitive man breaking his
heart for an unworthy woman: the part played for Swann by
Odette, for Saint-Loup by Rachel and for Proust's hero by Albertine, is played for Alix by Blair. One finds, also, everywhere
in *The Cabala* unmistakable Proustian turns of phrase; the author has even taken over a favorite expression of Proust's—a
sort of proverbial phrase in French, which I have never seen
before in English: he likes to talk about somebody or other
"making the fair weather" of somebody else, as Swann made
"*la pluie et le beau temps*" of the Duchesse de Guermantes.
And one finds in *The Cabala*, also, one passage where the typical Proustian note of hypochondriacal melancholy is brought
almost to the point of burlesque: a Helen Darrell, a famous
beauty, enters the story suddenly like one of those unan-
nounced characters in Proust's social scenes. We are not told
precisely what is wrong with her, but, like so many of the characters in *A la Recherche*, she is ill and very soon to die; none of
her dearest friends dares to kiss her: they feel that she is blighted
and doomed. "She was like a statue in solitude. She presuf-
fered her death." Yet the unfortunate Alix envies her: "He
would have loved me," she breathes in the hero's ear, "if I had
looked like that. . . . She is beautiful. She is beautiful," he
hears her mutter. "The world is hers. She will never have to
suffer as I must." The dying beauty asks, before she goes, to be
taken to say good-by to a saintly old French poet, who is also
about to die. "One wonders what they said to one another as
she knelt beside his chair: as he said later, they loved one another because they were ill." I have cited this passage at length
because it shows Thornton Wilder when he has slipped into
writing pure Proust and when, as it seems to me, he is least
successful. Proust's characters are always ill, and Proust thinks
that a languishing illness is the most pathetic thing on earth—
but he has in French the special advantage of words made for
him: *malade* and *maladie*, which he is able to introduce with a

mournful and ominous accent that prevents us from becoming impatient with his eternal incurable invalids. Now, the words *ill* and *sick* hardly lend themselves to any such mournful magic: when, in English, you hear that someone is ill, you at once ask what treatment he is taking.

In *The Bridge of San Luis Rey*, the Proustian spirit pervades the book. The Marquesa de Montemayor is made to distil marvellous literature from her love for her selfish daughter, just as Vinteuil in Proust is made to distil marvellous music from his insulted love for his. The Marquesa furthermore, is evidently a transposition from Mme. de Sévigné, who plays herself such an important role in Proust. The bad feature here, however, is that Mr. Wilder has followed Proust in exaggerating the cruelty of the beloved to the lover. This is sometimes hard to swallow in Proust himself, but then there is in Proust a bitterness that seems derived from hard experience; whereas with Mr. Wilder we feel that this violence is merely an effective device. I cannot quite believe, for example, in the harrowing scene in which Esteban is dressing Manuel's wound while Manuel abuses him so harshly, and I cannot believe at all in the scene where La Périchole refuses, after twenty years, to allow Uncle Pio to address her by her first name. Isn't there, also, something rather forced about the pining of Captain Alvarados for his daughter? Isn't it one case of hopeless love too many? At one point, Mr. Wilder allows himself to be carried into rewriting the death of Bergotte (by a natural attraction, certainly: no doubt, like Strachey's death of Victoria, it is destined to be imitated many times): "We come from a world where we have known incredible standards of excellence, and we dimly remember beauties which we have not seized again, and we go back to that world." (*"Toutes ces obligations qui n'ont pas leur sanction dans la vie présente semblent appartenir à un monde différent, fondé sur la bonté, le scruple, le sacrifice, un monde entièrement différent de celui-ci, et dont nous sortons pour naître à cette terre, avant peut-être d'y retourner. . . ."*)

This is not, I must repeat, that Proust has been anything other for Wilder than the inevitable elder master that every young writer must cling to before he can stand on his own feet. Since I have cited so many passages in which Mr. Wilder has filled in with Proust, I must quote at least one in a similar

key which Proust would never have written and which, in Mr.
Wilder's own work, has a quite distinct ring of artistic authenticity: "He regarded love as a sort of cruel malady through
which the elect are required to pass in their late youth and
from which they emerge, pale and wrung, but ready for the
business of living. There were (he believed) a great repertory
of errors mercifully impossible to human beings who had recovered from this illness. Unfortunately there remained to
them a host of failings, but at least (from among many illustrations) they never mistook a protracted amiability for the whole
conduct of life, they never again regarded any human being,
from a prince to a servant, as a mechanical object."

The effect of Thornton Wilder is, in any case, not at all like
the effect of Proust, or like the effect of anyone else one remembers. From what one hears about him, one may get the
impression that he is one of those contemporary writers who
seem still to date from the nineties—that he is simply another
"stylist," another devotee of "beauty"—that one will find him
merely a pretty or a precious writer; but Mr. Wilder, when one
comes to read him, turns out to be something quite different
from this. He possesses that quality of "delightfulness" of
which George Saintsbury has said that Balzac did not possess it
but that Gérard de Nerval did. But he has, also, a hardness, a
sharpness, that sets him quite apart from our Cabells, our
Dunsanys, our Van Vechtens and our George Moores. He has
an edge that is peculiar to himself, an edge that is never incompatible with the attainment of a consummate felicity. This
felicity, which has nothing of the pose, of the self-conscious effort to "write beautifully," of the professional beautiful writer,
is felt through the whole of his work and as much in the conception of the characters and the development of the situations
as in the structure of the sentences themselves. It is the felicity
of a true poet—not merely the contrived "style" of a literary
man with a yearning for old unhappy fancy far-off things—and
it makes possible for Thornton Wilder a good many remarkable feats that we should not have expected to see brought off.
Mr. Wilder, for example, I understand, has never been in Peru,
and ordinarily there are few things more deadly than the
dream-country of the twentieth-century novelist. Yet the au-

thor of *The Bridge of San Luis Rey* has been able to give us a
Peru that is solid, incandescent, distinct. Here is the Marquesa's pilgrimage to Cluxambuqua: "a tranquil town, slow-
moving and slow-smiling; a city of crystal air, cold as the
springs that fed its many fountains; a city of bells, soft and musical and tuned to carry on with one another the happiest
quarrels. If anything turned out for disappointment in the
town of Cluxambuqua the grief was somehow assimilated by
the overwhelming immanence of the Andes and by the
weather of quiet joy that flowed in and about the side-streets.
No sooner did the Marquesa see from a distance the white
walls of this town perched on the knees of the highest peaks
than her fingers ceased turning the beads and the busy prayers
of her fright were cut short on her lips." Then the church, the
hawks, the llama. . . . It is the city of a fairy-tale, of course;
but it is almost of the same quality as *Kubla Khan*. It is not
without its preciosity; but this preciosity of Thornton Wilder's
is at least as sound as that of *Vathek*.

Mr. Wilder has also a form of his own, which is highly individual and which seems to me to promise more than he has
hitherto been able to accomplish. In *The Cabala*, the several
heroes of the several episodes seem first to have nothing in
common save the accident of all being observed by the American who is telling the story; then we learn that they are the
ancient gods fallen on evil times, and we realize that there is
also a significance in their relations with the young American.
In *The Bridge of San Luis Rey*, the different characters appear
to have in common merely the fact that they were killed by the
fall of the bridge; then gradually we are made to understand
that their deaths at that moment had meaning, and that there
is a meaning in the relations of the people who fell to the
people who were left alive. *The Bridge of San Luis Rey* is more
ingenious than *The Cabala*, and more completely worked out;
but I do not find it completely satisfying. God works in too
obvious a way. It is hard to believe that the author believes in
the God of his book. The real higher power at work here is the
author's aesthetic ideal, which is struggling to incarnate itself.

One ought to say something more about *The Cabala*, which
has received less attention than *The Bridge* but which seems to

me, in some ways, more interesting. The circle of clever people
in Rome turn out to be the gods grown old; Christianity and
modern society have finally proved too much for them. The
Puritanism of the young American gives Pan (or Priapus?) such
a feeling of guilt that he is driven to suicide; and Aphrodite
breaks her heart for an American Adonis who pays no attention to her. A brilliant peasant Cardinal, who has spent most of
his life as a missionary to China, robs Artemis—if, as I suppose, Astrée-Luce is Artemis—of her pagan religious faith.
These are the gods of Europe contending with the influences
of alien races. In the end, the young American goes to call on
the Cardinal, whom he finds with *Appearance and Reality*,
Spengler, *The Golden Bough*, *Ulysses*, Proust and Freud on the
table beside him. In the course of the conversation, the Cardinal pushes them all to the floor: "Yes, I could write a book,"
he says, "better than this ordure that your age has offered us.
But a Montaigne, a Machiavelli . . . a . . . a . . . Swift, I
will never be." The moment after, as the visitor is going, the
Cardinal remarks that he would like for his birthday a small
Chinese rug. The young American departs for the States:
"Why was I not more reluctant at leaving Europe? How could
I lie there repeating the *Aeneid* and longing for the shelf of
Manhattan?" The shade of Virgil appears to him. "Know, im-
portunate barbarian," says the poet, "that I spent my whole
lifetime under a great delusion—that Rome and the house of
Augustus were eternal. Nothing is eternal save Heaven. Romes
existed before Rome and when Rome will be a waste there will
be Romes after her. Seek out some city that is young. The secret is to make a city, not to rest in it." . . . "The shimmering
ghost faded before the stars, and the engines beneath me
pounded eagerly towards the new world and the last and
greatest of all cities."

Mr. Wilder himself, however, next turns up in Peru. I have
already praised this fairy-tale country. I am told that it owes
part of its vividness to its grasp of the Spanish character.
Thornton Wilder's feeling for national temperaments—French,
Italian and American—had already appeared in *The Cabala* as
one of his most striking gifts. But I wish, for our sakes, and
perhaps for his own, that he would now follow Virgil's advice

and return for a time to New York. I wish that he would study the diverse elements that go to make the United States, and give us *their* national portraits. Mr. Wilder already knows Europe, and he also knows something of the Orient; and now we need him at home. I believe that this player on plaintive stops has more than one tune in his flute.

August 8, 1928

The Death of Elinor Wylie

ELINOR WYLIE died on the night of December 16, 1928. The account of this given me by her husband, William Rose Benét, was somewhat fuller than that which appears in the memoir of her sister, Miss Nancy Hoyt (*Elinor Wylie: The Portrait of an Unknown Lady*). It had been Sunday, and, after a good deal of going out, they had decided to stay at home for the evening. The day before, Elinor had put in order the man-uscript of her last book of poems, *Angels and Earthly Crea-tures*, which was to go to the publisher on Monday. She had picked up her own novel *Jennifer Lorn* and had read in it for a while; then had closed it in her definite way, saying, "Yes: *Jen-nifer Lorn is* better than *The Venetian Glass Nephew*!" and had gone to the kitchen to get them some supper. In a moment, her husband heard her call, and went in and found her fainting. She asked for a glass of water and when he gave it to her—I learn from Miss Hoyt—said, "Is that all it is?" He carried her to her bedroom, where she died.

The sense of loss expressed in the following article was felt by a good many people. Elinor Wylie had meant to us more than we had always been aware of at the time she was living. With her fine bindings, her formal furniture, her old-fashioned dining-room still-life and her old-fashioned literary culture that made one remember that her godfather had been Horace Howard Furness, the Philadelphia scholar who made the great Variorum Edition of Shakespeare, and her talk that had both style and wit, she occupied a unique position in the region below Fourteenth Street, where, as Frank Crowninshield wrote about her later, she "liked to pretend that she was a Bohemian, but the sham was at all times apparent." Yet it was not this shell that she carried about that gave her her peculiar prestige: it was the fact that, living inside it, she managed to remain a free spirit as few Bohemians are. I was trying to convey this; and the eloquent tone of my article is also explained by the fact that Elinor was the first to die of my close literary friends, the commemoration of whose passing is a recurrent and, I fear, rather depressing feature of this chronicle and its successor.

———

The death of Elinor Wylie hardly yet seems a real event. When people whom we know die, we have usually been prepared for their deaths by some weakening or decay of personality. But in Elinor Wylie's case, a personality still vigorous and vivid suddenly went out of being. A mind alive with thoughts and images, at what seemed its point of fullest activity, was annihilated at a stroke. In a letter she wrote me from England, just before her return in December, she told me that she had never been so happy, had never loved life so much: she had written forty poems, she said—an unusual rate of production for her. I was out on the West Coast at the time of her death, and I found that, even after the news had reached me, I kept unconsciously looking forward to seeing her in New York again. A part of my mind still kept turning toward her—for she had left New York with no farewell, but, on the contrary, with salutations and with the promise that I should see her soon.

It was true that, of recent years, she had been suffering severely from high blood-pressure, and had been warned by the doctors of the danger of a stroke such as that which actually ended her life. She had been told that, if she wished to escape it, she must diet, abstain from coffee and alcohol, be careful not to overtax herself, etc. But she paid little heed to these admonitions, and, as year followed year, used to laugh at her defiance of medical advice and her obstinate survival in spite of it.

In these latest doomed years of her life, her energy seemed actually to increase. When I first knew her, only five years ago, Elinor Wylie was a brilliant amateur, who had produced a few striking poems and started a novel or two, but who had never worked with much application. Yet by the time *Jennifer Lorn* was published, she had become one of the most steadily industrious and most productive writers of my acquaintance. She had always first composed her poems in her head and then simply written them down (in many cases, she never afterwards changed a word); but she now sat at her typewriter day after day, and turned out novel after novel, as well as a good deal of miscellaneous journalism. With a mind that seemed never to flag, she continued up to the last to go out night after night and to meet and talk to all sorts of people. In the meantime, she read insatiably. All her fiction was more or less historical and required special research. For her novel about Shelley, she collected and mastered a whole library. Her labor, in this case, was double, for she had to get up the American West in the pioneering days as well as the English nineteenth-century background. She had authority even for her landscapes, which she would prettily rework in her own colored silks from the narratives of old books of travel. And she seemed to find time, besides, to get through all the poetry and fiction of any distinction or interest that appeared in either England or America.

It was, no doubt, partly her very abnormal condition that so sped up her energy and imagination. Her vitality, during the years after she had come to live in New York, triumphed and flourished at the cost of desperate nervous strain. Though she had sometimes enjoyed fairly long periods of tranquillity, comfort and leisure, her life had been broken up by a series of displacements and emotional dislocations which might have destroyed a weaker nature. In Elinor Wylie's case, it had left her like one of those victims of the war who recover from critical operations and are sent out into life again, but whose condition is a little precarious. Irritation of the old wounds would at once cloud her mind with distress and terror; and one had to remember where they were. Yet in that still scarred and shaken being, who had had to live so long at the mercy of fate and under the domination of others, exasperated inescapably by the recurrent necessity to struggle, there came to birth, in these later years, what seemed to be a new and more powerful personality.

It was like the possession of a poor human life by some strong and non-human spirit, passionate but detached, all-worldly-wise and yet unworldly, generous without devotion, ruthless without spite, laughing with unbiassed intelligence over the disasters of the hurt creature it inhabited, and the mistress of a wonderful language, in which accuracy, vigor and splendor seemed to require no study and no effort and in which it spoke sometimes simply of its own divine estate, sometimes fled to bright and cooling visions for forgetfulness of its human exile, and sometimes tried to entertain by inventing the kind of tales, lending itself to the kind of sentiments, that maudlin human beings enjoy.

Such a spirit, among human beings, can nowhere find itself at home. Received in the conventional world with aversion, suspicion and fear, it creates in that other world where people avowedly live by their wits and their imaginations, an embarrassment almost equally uncomfortable. Yet the inhabitants of both worlds stand in awe of it, for they know that they must look to it for the values which they attach to the things of their worlds, for their very opinions of themselves and for their hopes of life itself. And the presence of such a spirit makes illness and death seem unreal. There are beings—and sometimes among the noblest—who pass their lives in the shadow of death. Putting all faith in the ecstasy of the senses, they cannot but fear the moment when the senses must fade: when the body fails, for them, the world ends. But for a spirit like Elinor Wylie's, death can never quite seem serious. The doctors can never dismay it. And when such a spirit drops its abode, we do not feel in its departure any pathos. Yet in its absence, we find ourselves blank: its vanishing has thrown us out more than we might have expected. It is almost as if the intellect that orders, the imagination that creates—those abstractions which have come to seem to us to have some sort of existence of their own, independent of any individual—had themselves been suddenly cut off. We are here among doubtful human creatures, all quarrelling or herding together, knowing little and thinking less, vague, pig-headed, purblind and violent. We come almost to wonder at last whether that spirit has really been among us—whether it may not have been merely, like the others, a blind, violent and crippled human life. Then we remember that harsh unflurried, that harsh unembittered laughter, and we look up the lovely lines in the book; and we know that in this sea without harbors, our compass must still be set by such magnets as the jest and the verse.

February 6, 1929

Burton Rascoe

A Bookman's Daybook contains a selection of passages from Burton Rascoe's diary, which used to appear with that heading in the Sunday literary section of the New York *Herald Tribune*. On the jacket appears a slender and languid young man, who lies reading in the shade of a tree, surrounded by a flowery mead, while above him the swallows circle. Inside we find something quite different: the literary life of New York in the early years of this decade when there was little fresh air and little leisure. The Bookman who figures in the book is not at all like the young man on the cover; it is the Burton Rascoe we knew in those years—alert, nervous, always in a hurry, always going to so many places and seeing so many people that we can hardly imagine him relaxed or alone. Here is his own description of his impressions on rereading his diary:

"I was struck particularly," he writes, "with the sanguine enthusiasm of this Burton Rascoe of five or six years ago and with his rather breath-taking anxiety to get glimpses of his contemporaries, records of what they were talking about, ideas they were expressing and impressions of his own down on paper, for all the world as though he imagined that a cataclysm might destroy that world he lived in at any moment and that he was making light the labors of some future archeologists and historians. This impression I have of him as taking his mission seriously permits me to understand the fellow's audacity."

Rascoe did take his mission seriously—he did make a desperate effort to get the literary life of New York down on paper, and that he succeeded to a considerable degree is proved by this volume of selections, which in some ways makes a better impression than the original diary did. It has been edited by Mr. Hartley Grattan, who has been able to throw out all the padding, all those long conversations and ruminations that Mr. Rascoe used sometimes to reel out, late at night in the *Herald Tribune* office, when hard-pressed to fill his space and over-keyed-up with coffee. Here we find a great many things which posterity may well be glad to read about: the conversation of Mencken and Nathan and their methods of amusing themselves; the arrival of Joseph Conrad in New York; the controversies over *Ulysses* and *The Waste Land*, which split up dinner tables and divided families; an example of Cummings's top-speed monologues, so difficult to catch and reproduce, but, in their way, as remarkable as his poetry. It is true that we find, also, other matters of a good deal less dignity and interest —glimpses, for example, of the writer of this article, now performing conjuring tricks, now talking about Whitehead through his hat. But all these things serve Rascoe's purpose— all contribute to establishing an atmosphere. I will not say that this atmosphere is a rarefied one. The literary life of New York, as we recognize it in Rascoe's *Daybook*, remains undisguisably a babel of tongues, a round of disorderly parties, an exchange of malicious gossip and a blather of half-baked opinions. But it does have its exhilarating qualities of ready response and variety. It was amusing, if nothing else; and Burton Rascoe was just the man to write about it.

The Rascoe of *A Bookman's Daybook* is a young man just arrived from the West. In Chicago, he has performed the astonishing feat of making good literature exciting to the readers of a great Western paper. True, the spirit of the time has been with him; and he has had, in Chicago, for friends and allies, such writers as Carl Sandburg, Ben Hecht and Sherwood Anderson. But the awakening of a new generation at which he has been assisting has been mostly taking place at a distance; and he has had to develop senses of preternatural keenness. He has had to become almost telepathically aware—at a time when few people were aware at all—of what Mencken was doing in Baltimore. Hergesheimer in Philadelphia, Cabell in Richmond, Conrad Aiken in Boston, of what everybody, in fact, was doing everywhere. Certainly no other American critic at that time, with the exception of Mencken himself, had so prompt and comprehensive an intelligence of what was being written in the United States.

But, scattered though our writers are, the literary center is always New York, and Burton Rascoe decides to shift his base to the East. He arrives full of excitement and high expectations; eagerly he gets to know everybody who is writing, as he already knows everything they have written. He rushes about from one group to another. He attends all the literary teas, the

publishers' luncheons, the theatrical openings, the miscellaneous drinking-parties. And he brings to it all his shrewdness,
his audacity, his humor, his extraordinary memory and his
undiscourageable enthusiasm for literature. He makes us feel,
as we read this record, that there is something really important
in the air, that the work of all these people is interesting, that
their opinions deserve attention.

Nor was this all an invention of Rascoe's. There *was* something going on in those days. One did feel that great books
were being written, that decisive battles were being fought.
The New York journalists who were young at that time are still
bound by a common consciousness of having taken part in
some sort of movement. One has no longer this consciousness
today. Excellent books, to be sure, are being produced; but,
for the most part, the people who write them and the people
who write about them do not see very much of one another.
There are no clear ideas in the air, and no new discoveries
looming. The world of teas, dinners and parties, which appears
when we look back on it now, as we read about it in Burton
Rascoe, to have been a good deal of fun, has come now to be
dominated by Book-of-the-Month Clubs and Literary Guilds,
and organized and exploited by publishers. No sane person of
adult years would go today to a literary luncheon, unless he
had to make a living by reporting such matters; and the first-
rate novelists, dramatists and poets mostly avoid New York like
the plague.

It is partly the character of the city itself that inevitably
makes impossible any close and really profitable exchange
between different kinds of literary people. New York is too expensive for most writers, and even when they do manage to
live here, the distances are usually too great for them to be able
to see much of each other. And the spirit of artistic and intellectual adventure has, as I say, been deadened by the pressure
of the commercial book clubs, which, however discriminating
the tastes of the individual members may be, are bound to illustrate the same principle that is always being brought forward as an apology for the mediocrity of the movies, since their
choices must always represent a compromise between their
personal preferences and the preferences of their vast public in
the provinces. New York, it turned out, had no place for Bur-

ton Rascoe in his original role of popular journalist who persisted in taking literature seriously. The *Herald Tribune* book supplement today is an interesting and attractive survey—it is probably better edited than when Burton Rascoe ran it. But it no longer contains any feature as remarkable as the writing of Rascoe. What one misses is an independent mind surveying the literary world; and one is forced to the conclusion that, in this department, there is really no room on a large New York paper for independent points of view. The result has been that Burton Rascoe has practically given up journalism. He has become, precisely, one of the directors of one of the big book-distributing companies. And aside from this, he plays the stock market, to which he now devotes that special faculty for divining what is likely to become valuable that he formerly displayed in the literary field.

Like most writing people today who still hope to accomplish something, Mr. Rascoe no longer lives in New York. Though he has given up literary journalism, he has not given up literature; he has, he intimates in his foreword, turned to writing novels. And it is reassuring to learn that the irreverent wit, the sure hand at prose and the swift intelligence of the *Bookman's Daybook*, though they have vanished from Manhattan journalism, are still being exercised elsewhere. After all, we reflect, that jacket with the young man reading in the shade of a tree is perhaps more appropriate to Rascoe's book than we had realized when it first met our eye. Burton Rascoe is not only not a product of New York—he is not even a product of Chicago. He was not bred by the city at all. He is a Kentuckian who spent most of his boyhood in the countryside of Oklahoma; and all that he has brought that is soundest to the literary life of the cities has been the fruit of solitude and rural peace—all that is toughest and most vigorous has come out of a provincial country-life perhaps fifty years behind the times, as one thinks of the times in New York. What Rascoe brought with him from the South and the Southwest is invaluable and indestructible. The surest proof of its value—in spite of his inaccuracies, his mistakes of judgment, his occasional faults of taste (some of them perpetuated in this book)—is the difficulty he has encountered in making it survive in New York. He offered us a dramatization of the world of art and ideas; and though

his show, at the time it was running, attracted a certain attention, it has been allowed to go off the boards. I have heard
Burton Rascoe accused of cheapening the material with which
he dealt. But, as I reread the *Bookman's Daybook*, I feel strongly
that it has been we who have let him down, and not he us. At
any rate, he has now been driven to confining his activities in
the city to a lucrative attention to the stock market and re-
treating to the country for serious work—and who will not approve his policy and wish him success at both?

May 29, 1929

Signs of Life: 'Lady Chatterley's Lover'

THIS FINE NOVEL of D. H. Lawrence's has been privately printed in Florence, and it is difficult and expensive to buy. This is a pity, because it may very well be one of the author's best books. About the erotic aspect of *Lady Chatterley's Lover*, which has prevented it from being circulated except in this subterranean fashion, I shall have something to say in a moment. But one ought to begin by explaining that the novel is something more than the story of a love affair: it is a parable of post-war England.

Lady Chatterley is the daughter of a Scotch R. A., a robust and intelligent girl, who has married an English landowner from the Midlands coal-mining country. Sir Clifford is crippled in the war, and returns to his family estate, where he lives amid the unemployment of the decaying industrial towns. He occupies himself at first with writing, sees the literary people in London and publishes some short stories, "clever, rather spiteful, and yet, in some mysterious way, meaningless"; then later he applies himself feverishly to an attempt to retrieve his coal-mines by working them with modern methods: "Once you started a sort of research in the field of coal-mining, a study of methods and means, a study of by-products and the chemical possibilities of coal, it was astounding the ingenuity and the almost uncanny cleverness of the modern technical mind, as if really the devil himself had lent a fiend's wits to the technical scientists of industry. It was far more interesting than art, than literature, poor emotional half-witted stuff, was this technical science of industry."

But Sir Clifford, semi-paralytic, is in the same unhappy situation as the hero of *The Sun Also Rises*, and his attractive wife, in the meantime, has been carrying on an affair with the gamekeeper—himself a child of the collieries, but nevertheless an educated man, who has risen to a lieutenancy during the war, and then, through inertia and disillusion, relapsed into his former status. There has been an understanding between Sir Clifford and his wife Connie, that, since he cannot give her a child himself, he will accept an illegitimate child as his heir. But

Connie has finally reached a point where she feels that she can no longer stand Sir Clifford, with his invalidism, his arid intelligence and his obstinate class-consciousness. She has fallen in love with the gamekeeper; and when she finally discovers that she is going to have a child, she leaves her husband and demands a divorce. We are left with the prospect of the lady and her lover going away to Canada together.

Now, Lawrence's treatment of this subject is not without its aspects of melodrama. It is not entirely free from his ill-mannered habit of nagging and jeering at those of his characters who arouse his contempt or resentment. Poor Sir Clifford, whom his shrill creator cannot refrain from baiting, was, after all, however disagreeable, a man in a pathetic situation for which he was in no way to blame. And, on the other hand, Mellors, the gamekeeper, has his moments of romantic bathos. Yet the characters do, in general, maintain a certain heroic dignity, a certain symbolical importance, which enable them to carry off all this. D. H. Lawrence's theme is a high one: the self-affirmation and the triumph of life in the teeth of all the sterilizing and demoralizing forces—industrialism, physical depletion, dissipation, careerism and cynicism—of modern English society; and the drama he has set in motion against the double contrasting background of the collieries and the English forests has both solid reality and poetic grandeur. It is the most inspiriting book from England that I have seen in a long time; and—in spite of Lawrence's occasional repetitiousness and his sometimes rather overdone slapdash tone—one of the best written. D. H. Lawrence is indestructible: censored, exiled, denounced, snubbed, he still possesses more vitality than almost anyone else. And this one of his books which has been published under the most discouraging conditions and which must have been written in full knowledge of its fate—which can, indeed, hardly yet be said to have seen the light at all—is one of his most vigorous and brilliant.

D. H. Lawrence, in *Lady Chatterley's Lover*, has thrown over the Anglo-Saxon conventions and, in dealing with sexual experience, has decided to call things by their common names. The effect of this, on the whole, is happy. I will not say that the unlimited freedom which Lawrence for the first time enjoys does not occasionally go to his head: the poetic sincerity of the gamekeeper does not quite always save his amorous rhapsodies over certain plain old English terms from being funny at the wrong time; and one finds it a little difficult to share the author's exaltation over a scene in which the lovers are made to decorate one another with forget-me-nots in places where flowers are rarely worn. But, on the other hand, he has greatly benefited from being able, in dealing with these matters, to dispense with circumlocutions and symbols. It gets rid of a good deal of the verbosity, the apocalyptic grandiloquence, into which this subject has so often led him, and it keeps the love scenes human. It may, in fact, probably be said that these scenes in *Lady Chatterley's Lover* contain the best descriptions of sexual experience that have yet been written in English. It is certainly not true, as is sometimes asserted, that erotic sensations either cannot or ought not to be written about. D. H. Lawrence has demonstrated here how interesting and how varied they are, and how important to the comprehension of emotional situations in which they play a part.

The truth is simply, of course, that in English we have had, since the eighteenth century, no technique, no vocabulary even, for presenting such scenes in a novel. The French have been writing directly about sex, in works of the highest dignity, ever since they discarded the proprieties of the age of Louis XIV. For this purpose they have adopted a vocabulary which is conventional and classically abstract; and they have even, for a long time, in their realistic fiction, been printing the vulgar language of the farmyard, the street and the bar. But James Joyce and D. H. Lawrence are the first modern English-speaking writers to put this language into serious books; and the effect, in the case of *Ulysses*, at least, has been shocking to English readers to an extent that must seem very strange to a French literary generation who read Zola, Octave Mirbeau and Huysmans in their youth. But, aside from this question of coarseness in faithfully reporting colloquial speech, we have in English, as I have said, the problem of dealing with sexual matters at all. We have not evolved any equivalent for the literary vocabulary of the French. We have only, on the one hand, colloquial words that will deeply offend some people and no doubt be unintelligible to others, and, on the other hand, the technical words used in works on biology and medicine. Neither kind goes particularly well in a love scene intended to generate an illusion of charm or romance.

This is the problem that Lawrence has tried to solve in *Lady Chatterley's Lover*, and, on the whole, he has been successful. He deserves a special medal from the Republic of Letters for his courage in facing the obloquy to which his experiment was sure to expose him, to say nothing of the other kinds of losses he must take for it—for he cannot have had printed in Italy many copies of the original edition or have made very much money by selling them, and he can claim no rights in the pirated edition that is being printed and sold over here. But there can be no advance in this prohibited direction without somebody's taking losses; and no writer of first-rate merit has done so since Joyce's *Ulysses*, in which it was a question rather of allowing the characters to use certain words than of genuine pioneering in the description of sexual intercourse. All serious writers in the English-speaking countries are much in Lawrence's debt, for even the limited circulation of *Lady Chatterley's Lover* cannot fail to make it easier in future to disregard the ridiculous taboo that the nineteenth century imposed on sex.

July 3, 1929

Dostoevsky Abroad

A TRANSLATION has just appeared—*The Diary of Dostoevsky's Wife*—of the journal of Dostoevsky's second wife during the spring and summer of 1867, when Dostoevsky had been forced to leave Russia to escape from his own and his brother's creditors. From this account, it would appear that the Dostoevskys spent most of their time in Germany quarrelling with waiters over tips, quarrelling and making up with each other, and pawning their belongings to pay the bills when Dostoevsky had lost his money gambling. Anna Grigorevna is simple and touching; Dostoevsky's own complicated character here appears to its worst advantage: he is selfish, disagreeable and silly. It was the range of Dostoevsky's intelligence and the brilliance of his conversation which made people forgive him these qualities. When, for example, we read Baron Wrangel's account of his talks with Dostoevsky in Siberia, or the description of him by Sonia Kovalevsky, the woman mathematician, with whose sister Dostoevsky was in love, we have a vision of a quite different person. Anna Grigorevna, though she frequently speaks of long conversations with her husband, and notes exactly how much everything costs, almost never puts down his opinions. Yet from Dostoevsky's letters of this time, we know that he was already preoccupied with the ideas with which he was afterwards so profoundly to impress himself on Russian thought.

Perhaps the nearest that Mme. Dostoevsky comes to touching on these ideas is in her record of the already famous quarrel between Dostoevsky and Turgenev. Here is her report of the former's account of the visit he paid the latter in Baden-Baden:

"According to him, he is very embittered, even to the point of being venomous and talks the whole time about his new novel, which Fyodr never even so much as mentioned. Turgenev is furious over the notices in the papers, saying he has been most fearfully cut up in *Golos* and *Vaterländischen Nachrichten*, as well as in other publications. He also said that the Russian aristocracy, at the instigation of Philip (?) Tolstoy, had done their best to exclude him from their society, but that none the less nothing had come of it. He added, moreover: 'If you only knew how delighted I should have been!' Fyodr, as usual, treated him none too gently, telling him to procure himself a telescope, for, since he always lived in Paris, he couldn't otherwise expect to know what was happening in Russia, let alone understand it. Turgenev declared he was a realist, and Fyodr said he only thought he was. When Fyodr declared he found the Germans extremely stupid and very apt to be dishonest, Turgenev promptly took offense, assuring Fyodr he had irreparably insulted him, for he himself had now become, not a Russian any more, but a German. Fyodr said that he hadn't known that and greatly deplored the fact. Fyodr said that for the most part he had spoken in a facetious tone of voice, which had obviously annoyed Turgenev considerably, and that he had quite openly told him that his novel had met with no success. But on the whole they parted friends, and Turgenev promised to give him the book. Of all the curious men—how could he possibly be proud of being a German instead of a Russian? I should have thought that no Russian writer on earth would want to repudiate his country and least of all to declare himself a German! What, when all's said and done, has he got to be grateful to Germany for, seeing that he has grown up in Russia, which has supported him and done its very utmost to encourage his talent. And now he breaks right away from it and declares that if Russia were to go under, the world would not be the loser! Of all the appalling things for a Russian to say! Enough of the whole matter—but I know that this conversation with Turgenev has excited Fyodr beyond words, and that he always gets beside himself when people repudiate their fatherland."

It is clear from the first part of this account that Turgenev on this occasion had special reasons for being irritable; and it is equally true that Dostoevsky had special reasons for resenting Turgenev: Dostoevsky had borrowed two years before fifty thalers from the richer man and had never paid them back. Yet there was something more important and interesting than appears from Mme. Dostoevsky's description at the bottom of the quarrel between the two writers, who were contemporaries in age and who had had, as young men in St. Petersburg, their

first successes at the same time. Dostoevsky belonged, like
Turgenev, to the Russian educated class; but his imprisonment
in Siberia had modified his point of view profoundly. The Russian governing classes spoke French, and they looked habitually
toward Western Europe for culture and ideas; they regarded
Russians as barbarians, and could not sometimes, according to
Dostoevsky, even write their own language correctly. Their
liberal aspirations, when they had them, were derived from
Republican France. Dostoevsky had had himself this sort of
education and had at one time shared these ideas. He had belonged to a political and literary club composed of Russian intellectuals of this type, and, as a member of this club, he had
been convicted of conspiracy against the Tsar and sent for four
years to prison. He had found there that, as an educated man,
he was regarded by the ordinary Russians with hatred and suspicion. It had seemed to him then that the gulf between the
educated class and the people was so deep as to make it impossible for even the most sympathetic artists, for even the reformers themselves, to contribute anything really valuable to
the development of the national life. Russian novelists wrote
about Russia, as he himself in his early fiction had done, from
a Western European point of view, from a point of view derived from writers who had been dealing with societies quite
unlike the Russian; and Russian reformers behaved as if a solid
and enlightened bourgeoisie, such as had engineered the
French Revolution, could be counted on to take over in Russia. Neither knew Russian life at firsthand; both, by their very
education, were unfitted to understand it; and both inhabited
worlds of illusion. Contemptuous or despairing of the antiquated social system and the semi-savage population from
which they themselves had sprung, they had removed, either
actually or spiritually, to the other end of Europe; and, even
when intelligent and benevolent, had persistently succeeded
in evading the realities of the national life. The correspondence of Dostoevsky, during these years of his own enforced
exile, is full of hunger for Russia: he devours the Russian newspapers; he complains again and again that a novelist cannot
create in exile. For him, Turgenev was a gifted Russian who
had run away from Russia, who had too easily given up as
hopeless a world that he feared to face, and who patronized

the fellow-countrymen whom he had made his reputation by writing about.

When we read Dostoevsky on this problem, we come to realize that a good deal of what he says applies equally to expatriate Americans in Europe. We feel that the difficult position of the artist or intellectual who turns his back on a provincial country with which he cannot make any wide contact has never—not even by Brooks in *The Pilgrimage of Henry James* —been studied more profoundly than by Dostoevsky. There is, in many respects, a striking analogy between the situation of Russia in respect to Western Europe and the situation of the United States; and it is of special interest to Americans to see how Dostoevsky deals with it.

The course recommended by Dostoevsky was for educated Russians, as far as possible, to clear their minds of preconceived ideas from abroad and, from a firsthand realistic examination of their country and its institutions, to try to understand the Russian character and the Russian point of view. Now, the conditions of Russian life are, and were, very different from our own; but they resemble our own in this: that both are fundamentally different from the conditions of Western Europe. Like the Russians of Dostoevsky's day, we have been used to looking to Europe for ideas; and the ideas with which we have been supplied have, as in Dostoevsky's Russia, been imperfectly suited to our needs. This has always been the problem in America: simultaneously to adapt European culture to the alien conditions of American life and to cultivate from our own peculiar and un-European resources an original culture of our own. But our situation, since the war, has, in some respects, become more serious. Since the war, we have been importing from Europe the emotions and the points of view appropriate to bankruptcy and exhaustion—resignation, futility and despair—into a country full of money and health; while Europe seems herself to be looking to us, as she never has done before: the very books that she sends us denouncing us seem to suggest that she has been disappointed. Yet what America sends Europe, in her famine, are still principally scientific researches uninspired by creative theory and works of art, often illiterate and usually secondhand, imitated from European models. The principal philosophy, so far as one can see, that America has exported abroad during the period since the war, has been Watson's behaviorism—the invention of an experimental psychologist who is certainly not a great thinker and who has since, as a matter of fact, gone into the advertising business.

If, however, we pursue the conclusions to which Dostoevsky's position led him, we come upon a further analogy between the Russian situation and our own. When Dostoevsky had set his face away from Western Europe to direct his attention toward Russian institutions, he found himself confronted by the Tsardom, the feudal system of landowning and the Greek Orthodox Church; and there is something both heroic and embarrassing in the spectacle of one of the most intelligent men of his time making the effort to swallow all these. Thus, in a somewhat similar way, an American who would turn for sustenance to contemporary American institutions will find himself confronted by elements not easy to assimilate. He will find the Chamber of Commerce, the Rotary Club, the American political machine, all apparently the willing instruments of the nationwide commercial solidarity which harasses American communities with company spies and informers and dragoons them on occasion with strong-arm men; which persecutes without justice or mercy Sacco and Vanzetti and how many others!; and the upholders of which it sufficed for an honest municipal servant like Al Smith to speak out with a moderate common sense and a by no means unhampered frankness to strike with panic and fire with resentment.

Yet Dostoevsky's instinct was sound: the fact that the American problem seems a particularly formidable one is no excuse for fleeing or evading it. We must, of course, take European ways of thinking along with our language, our alphabet; but we must try to stick close to the realities of our contemporary American life, so new, and so different perhaps from anything that has ever been known, that, if we cannot find out for ourselves what we want and where we are going, it is improbable, with Europe declining, that anybody else can tell us. Of all this, more presently.

January 30, 1929

Citizen of the Union

THE PUBLICATION of *George W. Cable: His Life and Letters* by his daughter, Lucy Leffingwell Cable Bikle, reminds us how completely this once-popular novelist has now passed into eclipse. Few people read Cable today; and the critics never discuss him. Yet in the eighties and the nineties he was enormously read both at home and abroad; and he deserved the high standing he was given. The decline of Cable's reputation is, I believe, mainly due to the general lack of interest, on the part of the critics of the new generation, in the American literature of the period just behind them. We are rediscovering Irving Babbitt and Paul Elmer More, but we have not yet discovered John Jay Chapman; we leave Stephen Crane in half-shadow, and George Cable in complete eclipse.

The prevalent notion of Cable today seems to be that he was a romantic novelist, of a species now obsolete, who made a good thing of exploiting the sentiment and charm, the quaintness and picturesqueness, of a New Orleans long gone to decay. This idea seems, indeed, to some extent, to have been shared by the public who read Cable, that public for whom taste and intellect were represented by Richard Watson Gilder, the editor of the *Century Magazine*. When George Cable was presented with an honorary degree of Master of Arts by Yale, it was "with the desire of recognizing publicly the eminent success which you have achieved in embalming in literature a unique phase of American social life which is rapidly passing away." Yet Cable himself had no idea that he was engaged in embalming anything: he supposed himself to be dealing with the realities of contemporary life—and, in the work of his best years, this was true.

The New Orleans of George Cable's time—and even the New Orleans of today—is a laboratory where certain American situations present themselves, if not in a form necessarily more acute than elsewhere, at least in more vivid colors. Louisiana, originally French, was transferred in 1762 to Spain, with the result of arousing extreme hostility between the French and the Spanish inhabitants. At the beginning of the nineteenth century, it was transferred back from Spain to France, and then sold by Napoleon to the United States, with the result of provoking a new kind of hostility, this time between the original Latin Americans, Spanish and French, on the one hand, and the Anglo-Saxon Americans who had come in to take possession, on the other. At the same time, the mingling of the whites with the large Negro element of the population had resulted in a class of mulattoes who constituted a special problem. Thus, one found in New Orleans simultaneously in a concentrated field and in intensified form, the conflict of European nationalities, as between the Spanish and the French; the conflict of the Latins and the Anglo-Saxons; and the conflict of two totally different races, as between the Negroes and the whites. Add to this the sectional conflict at the time of the Civil War, of the American South with the North, a conflict felt so much more painfully and for so much longer a time after the war by the South than by the North. The whole American problem of diversity and unity was here, and no writer ever studied it more thoroughly or thought about it more intelligently than George Washington Cable did.

For Cable was essentially a sociologist. He was not in the least a fancier of lavender and old lace. He was a good deal closer to Upton Sinclair than he was to Myrtle Reed. He had a real sense of beauty, but there was too much of the Puritan in him—his mother had been a New Englander, and it was only comparatively late in life that Cable was able to make up his mind that the theater was not immoral—to allow him much to cultivate his sensibility. Though his books have their own sort of atmosphere, which seems to have enchanted his readers, it is certainly not the atmosphere of Cable's novels which appears most successful today. Compare one of Cable's Louisiana descriptions with a description of the same region by Lafcadio Hearn. The lush background that Hearn is so good at investing with color and glamor has a way of turning flat in Cable. Beneath the floridity of the Southerner and his courteous and affable manner, we catch a glimpse of William Wetmore Story and his statue of Cleopatra. And so, though Cable had a most remarkable, an almost unexcelled ear for human speech, though he reported it with the most scrupulous accuracy, he did little to make it attractive. Just as he listened with attention

to the songs of birds and transcribed them into musical notation, so he studied the different varieties of the French, Spanish
and Negro Creole dialects and the language of the Acadians,
both English and French, with a scholarly exactitude that must
be as valuable to the phonetician as it is forbidding to the ordinary reader. This rendering, with pitiless apostrophes, of these
special pronunciations was complained of even in the period of
Cable's greatest popularity, and it constitutes a formidable ob-
stacle to appreciating him today.

Cable's own conception of his craft comes out plainly in certain of the letters included in this biography. Of *The Grandissimes*, he writes that the editors of *Scribner's*, in which it first
appeared, did not know "that the work I should by and by
send them was going to have any political character. But that
was well-nigh inevitable. It was impossible that a novel written
by me then should escape being a study in the fierce struggle
going on around me, regarded in the light of that past history
—those beginnings—which had so differentiated Louisiana civilization from the American scheme of public society. I meant
to make *The Grandissimes* as truly a political work as it has ever
been called. . . . My friends and kindred looked on with disapproval and dismay, and said all they could to restrain me.
'Why wantonly offend thousands of your own people?' But I
did not intend to offend. I wrote as near to truth and justice as
I knew how, upon questions that I saw must be settled by calm
debate and cannot be settled by force or silence."

The Grandissimes was the first full-length instalment of
Cable's anatomy of Southern society. He prepared at about the
same time for the United States Census of 1880 a report on the
"social statistics" of New Orleans which was specially commended by the authorities; and it was this blending of what
may perhaps be taken as a New England respect for facts with
a humanism quite alien to New England which left Louisiana,
in Cable's writings, perhaps the most satisfactorily studied of
nineteenth-century American communities. For Cable, who
had never been in France, had read and spoken French all his
life and who, brought up as a Presbyterian, had come to manhood in a Catholic community, could penetrate Louisiana in
every layer and all directions.

In *The Grandissimes* Cable incorporated a story that he had never been able to sell to the "family" magazines of the period and that had consequently not been included in the popular *Old Creole Days*. The reason for rejecting this manuscript that had been given by George Parsons Lathrop, writing for William Dean Howells, then editor of the *Atlantic Monthly*, was "the unmitigatedly distressful effect of the story." This was the *Story of Bras-Coupé*, the adventures of an African king sold into slavery in the United States. When Bras-Coupé is brought to Louisiana and taken into the fields, and he first comes to understand that it is intended for him to work with common Negroes, he hits the foreman over the head with his hoe, picks up one of the other slaves and bites him in the leg and throws him away, and raises havoc till the overseer shoots him down. A woman slave, who speaks his language, is brought to interpret to him, and he instantly falls in love with her and allows himself to be ruled through her. He demands to marry her; and, on the night of his wedding, gets drunk and forgets his status; he knocks down his master, who has already resented being treated by him as king to king. He is brutally hunted to death. As a study of what man can make of man, of the deformation of human relations by unnatural social institutions, the story of Bras-Coupé is as powerful in its smaller scope as *Uncle Tom's Cabin* itself. With the story of Mme. Lalauré in *Strange True Stories of Louisiana* and some other detached episodes, it almost puts Cable in the class of the great Russian chroniclers of serfdom.

For it is not the love stories in Cable's fiction that really interest Cable: it is the social and political situations. It is human life throttled in the web of society that arouses all his emotion, at the same time that he can trace with nicety every one of the tangled strands and explain the necessities that have strung it. One of the features of this biography is a hitherto unpublished account by Cable of the development of his political ideas. He had fought in the Confederate Army, but had afterwards come to unorthodox conclusions in regard to the Negro question and the relations of the North and the South. About the time that he began to give public expression to his opinions on these subjects, he moved his family from New Orleans to New England. The real occasion for this change of residence was the ill-health of Cable's wife; but, in spite of the fact that he made it a rule never to publish an opinion in the North which he had not first put forward in person from a public platform in the South, returning there expressly for the purpose, there can be no doubt that Cable's native city was no longer very comfortable for him. He was one of the clearest-minded Americans of his time, and in the South, after the Civil War, so detached and realistic an intelligence was uncommon and unwelcome. It was not common or welcome anywhere. Cable understood both South and North; the American and the European; the white man and the Negro; and he would not become the partisan of any of them. What he believed in were democratic principles of the kind that he understood the American Republic to have been founded to put into practice; and he devoted all his study and art to the attempt to impress their importance on a public that were occupied for the most part—during our period of industrial development after the Civil War—with aims that ran counter to these. The moral of Cable's stories is always that distinctions between human beings on social or national or racial grounds must be regarded as merely provisory; that there can never be a true equilibrium, that there can only be conflict and agony, where such discriminations are used as pretexts for unequal privilege.

February 13, 1929

Virginia Woolf and the American Language

A N ARTICLE BY Virginia Woolf in the *New Republic* of February 13, 1929, started a controversy that went on for months, in the correspondence columns of that magazine, about the differences between British and American English. The first three of these letters appeared in the issue of April 24 of the same year:

Sir: In her article *On Not Knowing French*, Virginia Woolf says, "Thus a foreigner with what is called a perfect command of English may write grammatical English and musical English—he will, indeed, like Henry James, often write a more elaborate English than the native—but never such unconscious English that we feel the past of the word in it, its associations and attachments."

Just as a matter of curiosity, I am interested to know what she considers the native language of Henry James—Choctaw, perchance!— since he came from the wilds of Boston.

I am quite familiar with that "certain condescension" which the English display towards us poor benighted Americans, but it is a surprise to learn that we are looked upon as newcomers to the English language.

Harriot T. Cooke

Cannes, France

To this Mrs. Woolf replied:

Sir: I hasten to submit to your correspondent's correction and to retract my opinion that because Henry James was born in Boston he therefore did not write English like a native. I will do my best to believe that the language of Tennyson and the language of Whitman are one and the same. But may I explain that the responsibility for my error rests with Walt Whitman himself, with Mr. Ring Lardner, Mr. Sherwood Anderson, and Mr. Sinclair Lewis? I had been reading these writers and thinking how magnificent a language American is, how materially it differs from English, and how much I envy it the power to create new words and new phrases of the utmost vividness. I had even gone so far as to shape a theory that the American genius is an original genius and that it has borne and is bearing fruit unlike any that grows over here. But in deference to your correspondent I hasten to cancel these views and will note for future use that there is no difference between England and America; climate and custom have produced no change of any sort; America is merely a larger England across the Atlantic; and the language is so precisely similar that when I come upon words like *boob, graft, stine, busher, doose, hobo, shoe-pack, hiking, cinch* and many others, the fact that I do not know what they mean must be attributed to the negligence of those who did not teach me what is apparently my native tongue.

Having thus admitted my error, may I "just as a matter of curiosity" ask to be enlightened on another point? Why, I wonder, when I say that Henry James did not write English like a native, is it assumed that I intend an insult? Why does your correspondent at once infer that I accuse the Bostonians of talking Choctaw? Why does he allude to "condescension" and refer to "us poor benighted Americans" and suppose that I look upon them as "newcomers to the English language" when I have said nothing of the sort? What have I done to make him angry? Lowell's essay *On a Certain Condescension in Foreigners* (for such he apparently thought the English) should, I think, have for pendant *On a Certain Touchiness in*—dare I say it?—*Americans*. But may I implore you, Sir, if I use that word, not to infer that I thereby imply that you wear a pigtail and paint your forehead red? If I speak of "Americans" it is merely because our common ancestors some centuries ago agreed, for reasons best known to themselves, to differ.

Virginia Woolf

London, England

I had been told by Elinor Wylie, after one of her trips to London, of a meeting with Virginia Woolf which—though Elinor may have distorted a little—had sounded rather disagreeable. Mrs. Woolf, she declared, had asked her why she tried to write literary English; she had told Elinor that it would be much more interesting if she let herself go in her native American and tried something in the line of Ring Lardner. I was goaded to the following intervention:

Sir: I deplore the tone of this controversy. It is true that Mr. Cooke is touchy, but it is also true that Mrs. Woolf takes rather a perverse view. No one will dispute that English is spoken and written differently in England and in the United States, but English English and American English are not so different as Mrs. Woolf—and as certain American writers themselves—would like to have us believe. If they were as different as all that, the *New Republic* would never be able to publish Mrs. Woolf's articles. As a matter of fact, American writers do write as "unconsciously" as English ones (does Mrs. Woolf suppose that Walt Whitman learned the language he wrote in like Latin?)—

and one does "feel the past of the word . . . its associations and attachments" in what they write. The difference is simply that, in the case of American writing, the attachments and associations are partly those which, during the past two or three hundred years, have been acquired in North America instead of in the British Isles. Behind both English and American English lies the much longer past of English literature and speech which Americans and Englishmen have in common. Thus, for example, though there is so much that is Yankee in the accent and vocabulary of Emerson, there is at least as much of the Elizabethan poets whom he seems to have been always reading; and even Mr. H. L. Mencken, our most conspicuous champion of an "American language," owes a good deal of his peculiar flavor and humor to his combination with American slang of a curious literary vocabulary that sounds as if it had been derived from Restoration comedies and eighteenth-century novels.

What is the use of pretending that the English spoken by Englishmen and the English spoken by Americans are actually two different languages? There are quite enough different languages already, and they have caused quite enough trouble. The so-called American language is partly American slang (a good deal of which is taken over by the English, as we take over a good deal of theirs), and partly illiterate English written in the United States. Ring Lardner, for example, is merely an expert in different kinds of American illiteracy and slang, and in his stories about New York actors, Western baseball players, etc., he is doing exactly the same sort of thing that Kipling has done in those stories of his which are supposed to be told by Irish soldiers or Scotch engineers. I do not know whether Mrs. Woolf supposes that all the different characters and authors of all the different American books that she reads are speaking the same picturesque tongue, and that this is "American." But I can assure her that, in the United States as elsewhere, there is a good deal of difference between North and South, East and West, rich and poor, town and country, etc., and that the speech of one kind of American may often seem as strange to another as Burns or William Barnes must to a Londoner. In the meantime, there is a standard English intelligible all over the United States, and intelligible also, apparently, to English people—so that it is possible for Mrs. Woolf and Mr. Cooke to carry on a correspondence without referring to a grammar or a dictionary. (Incidentally, Henry James was born, not in Boston, but in New York, and bitterly resented being taken for a New Englander.)

Mrs. Woolf's only comment on this, in a letter not intended for publication, was that for her what Whitman wrote was American and that she was content to let the controversy rest.

From the several letters that followed, I add one by Professor George E. G. Catlin that appeared in the issue of May 8,
because it makes a point that I omitted, in calling attention to
the fact that the differences between British and American English were due precisely to the fact that "the past of the word,"
whether for better or worse, has in many instances been longer
preserved in the United States than in England:

Sir: As an Englishman resident during part of each year in America,
will you permit me to comment on Mrs. Virginia Woolf's thesis that
the English and American languages are different tongues and that the
Americans must suffer from an inferiority complex if they are not
proud of that fact?

Except in the case of slang, the meaning of which is frequently unknown to many of my American friends themselves, but the origin of
which is often to be found in the English sporting papers of the last
century, I have never found that I failed to understand what was said
to me in America. The use of "guess" may sound novel until I recall
Chaucer; of "some" until I recall Aubrey; of "candy" until I recall the
"candie shoulder" of James I; of "sure" until I recall Milton; of
"gotten" until I recall the Bible. In Yorkshire, on the other hand, I
only sometimes understand what is said to me; in Ayrshire, I seldom
understand; while nowhere are my ears assailed by such debased English as in London. There are more differences to be found between
the popular speech of two English counties than between the speech
of the literate in Oxford and Harvard or in Ely and Seattle.

These things are, of course, commonplace knowledge to Mrs.
Woolf. Were her thesis correct, there would be, not only an American
but a Canadian and an Australian language. There are, however,
many British subjects in the European section of the Empire who are
desperately anxious to take out a patent for the English language. The
cause of their evident annoyance when the patent is infringed, I leave
to those psychoanalysts to discover who are curious about the significance of "correct speech" as a symbol. But I do not doubt that it is
very vexatious to a literary group when the living flood of popular
speech sweeps over the deadening breakwaters of purism.

I heartily agree with Mr. Wilson that there are more than enough
languages already; they do not need to be multiplied inside the
English-speaking world. It may be that the place of honour ("honor,"
wrote King James) in that world is now on this side of the Atlantic; I
do not know. Kant (an old-fashioned liberal) said that diversity of language was one cause of war: whether that be true I do not know. But
I do suggest (with all respect to a fascinating and distinguished

writer) that Mrs. Virginia Woolf should reflect whether her view is not untenable in literature, pernicious in politics and evil in its cultural consequences.

George E. G. Catlin

Cornell University,
Ithaca, New York

But this correspondence left untouched the large problems of the future of English in the English-speaking countries. The situation of English in the United States was at that time and afterwards in a continual state of crisis. We did not have, and we do not have now, any generally accepted standards of vocabulary, grammar or spelling for the language in which we write. Every American writer has had to decide for himself how much he would try to retain of academic traditional English and how far he would allow himself to exploit this or that form of the American vernacular. The English, in the meantime, were drawing up, for the first time in the history of their literature, a set of rules for correct usage. Their great authority, the Fowlers' *Modern English Usage*, could hardly have been conceived by Ben Jonson, the author of the first English grammar, who, in spite of his preoccupation with the inflected classical languages, wrote habitually, like other Elizabethans, such phrases as "between you and I"—a misuse condemned as an Americanism in an English article quoted by one of the *New Republic* correspondents; and, in his section on the inflection of pronouns, fails even to mention this question. The result of this process in England (though not in the case of Virginia Woolf) was to weaken and impoverish the language by assuming as an ideal for good prose a mere linking of accredited formulas.

Some later discussions of this subject will be found under *Talking United States.* Neither Professor Catlin nor I tackled squarely the question of American usages that are neither illiterate nor slang and that have since been compiled on an enormous scale in the *Dictionary of American English* and the *Dictionary of Americanisms*, both published by the University of Chicago.

Dos Passos and the Social Revolution

JOHN DOS PASSOS'S *Airways, Inc.*, was produced in March as the last play of the season of the New Playwrights' Theater, and almost entirely failed to attract attention. This was due, principally, I believe, to the fact that by that time the critics had become rather discouraged with the revolutionary drama of Grove Street and that the New Playwrights themselves were so low in funds that they could not afford proper publicity. None the less, *Airways, Inc.*, was a remarkable play, perhaps the best that the New Playwrights have done; and though this is not the place to speak of the merits of the Grove Street production, which I thought were considerable, the published text of the play demands attention as a work of literature.

Airways is, like the group's other plays, a social-political-economic fable; but Dos Passos is more intelligent than most of his associates—he is able to enter into more points of view —and he is a much better artist. His play is neither a naturalistic study nor a vaudeville in the manner of John Howard Lawson, though it has some of the elements of both; it is rather a sort of dramatic poem of contemporary America. With great ingenuity, Dos Passos had assembled on a single suburban street-corner representatives of most of the classes and groups that go to make up our society. We concentrate upon the life of a single middle-class household, but this is submerged in a larger world: its fate is inextricably bound up with a current real-estate boom; a strike that eventually gives rise to a Sacco-Vanzetti incident; and the promotion of a commercial aviation company. Nor, as is likely to be the case in this kind of play, are the social types merely abstractions which never persuade the imagination. Dos Passos has succeeded in producing the illusion that behind the little suburban street-corner of the Turners lies all the life of a great American city—all the confusion of America itself; and *Airways* made the meager stage of the bleak little Grove Street Theater seem as big as any stage I have ever seen. Dos Passos has also given the household of the Turners an extension in time as well as in space: he has provided a chorus of two old men, an American inventor and a

Hungarian revolutionist, whose role is to relate what we see to what has gone before in history and to what may be expected to come after.

It is in the construction of this sort of sociological fable that Dos Passos particularly excels. The strength of his novel, *Manhattan Transfer*, lay in the thoroughness and the steady hand with which he executed a similar anatomy on the city of New York as a whole. As a dramatist he is less expert; and *Airways* suffers in certain ways from comparison with *Manhattan Transfer*. Dos Passos sometimes interrupts his action with long passages of monologue, which, though they might go down easily in a novel, discourage our attention in the theater; and his last act, though the two separate scenes are excellent in themselves, fails to draw the different strands together as we expect a third act to do. But, on the other hand, *Airways*, at its best, has an eloquence and a spirit that *Manhattan Transfer* largely lacked. It is one of the best-written things that Dos Passos has so far done—perhaps freer than any other of his productions both from rhetoric doing duty for feeling and from descriptions too relentlessly piled up. Dos Passos is probably only now arriving at his mature prose style.

So much for the purely artistic aspect of *Airways*. It is impossible to discuss it further without taking into account Dos Passos's political philosophy. Dos Passos is, one gathers from his work, a social revolutionist: be believes that, in the United States as elsewhere, the present capitalistic regime is destined to be overthrown by a class-conscious proletariat. And his disapproval of capitalist society seems to imply a distaste for all the beings who go to compose it. In *Manhattan Transfer*, it was not merely New York, but humanity that came off badly. Dos Passos, in exposing the diseased organism, had the effect, though not, I believe, the intention, of condemning the sufferers along with the disease; and even when he seemed to desire to make certain of his characters sympathetic, he had a way of putting them down.

Now, in *Airways*, there are several characters whom Dos Passos has succeeded in making either admirable or attractive, but these are, in every case, either radicals or their sympathizers. His bias against the economic system is so strong that it extends beyond its official representatives to all those human beings whose only fault is to have been born where such a system prevails and to be so lacking in courage or perspicacity as not to have allied themselves with the forces that are trying to fight it. In Dos Passos, not only must the policeman not fail to steal the money with which the street-kids have been playing craps; but even the young people of *Airways* who, however irresponsible and immoral, might be expected to exhibit something of the charm of youth—become uglier and uglier as the play proceeds, till they finally go completely to pieces in a drunken restaurant scene which is one of Dos Passos's masterpieces of corrosive vulgarity. It is especially curious to note the treatment which the American aviators receive at the hands of both Dos Passos and Lawson. The aviator is one of the authentic heroes that our American civilization now produces. But for Lawson or Dos Passos, an aviator cannot be an authentic hero, or even, apparently, a genius, because he is not on the side of the revolution. The truth is, of course, that the aviator of the type of Lindbergh or Byrd never troubles himself with these questions at all and, even when, as in the case of Lindbergh, he is exploited for a time by the government, he exists and performs his achievements in a world independent of politics. But to a Lawson or a Dos Passos, he is suspect: they cannot let him get away with anything, and eventually, in what they write, they succeed in destroying or degrading him. In Lawson's play, *The International*, another New Playwrights production, the Lindbergh character appears as a drunken taxi-driver—or perhaps as a drunken bum in a taxi—amid the débâcle of the capitalist state; and in *Airways*, the young aviator is sent up by the agents of his capitalist employers to scatter leaflets on a strikers' meeting. He is drunk, and falls and breaks his back.

Now, the life of middle-class America, even under capitalism and even in a city like New York, is not so unattractive as Dos Passos makes it—no human life under any conditions can ever have been so unattractive. Under however an unequal distribution of wealth, human beings are still capable of enjoyment, affection and enthusiasm—even of integrity and courage. Nor are these qualities and emotions entirely confined to class-conscious workers and their leaders. There are moments in reading a novel or seeing a play by Dos Passos when one finds oneself ready to rush to the defense of even the American bathroom, even the Ford car—which, after all, one begins to reflect, have perhaps done as much to rescue us from helplessness, ignorance and squalor as the prophets of revolution. We may begin to reflect upon the relation, in Dos Passos, of political opinions to artistic effects. Might it not, we ask ourselves, be possible—have we not, in fact, seen it occur—for a writer to hold Dos Passos's political opinions and yet not depict our middle-class republic as a place where no birds sing, no flowers bloom and where the very air is almost unbreathable? For, in the novels and plays of Dos Passos, everybody loses out: if he is on the right side of the social question, he has to suffer, if he is not snuffed out; if he is on the oppressors' side, his pleasures are made repulsive. When a man as intelligent as Dos Passos—that is, a man a good deal more intelligent than, say, Michael Gold or Upton Sinclair, who hold similar political views—when so intelligent a man and so good an artist allows his bias so to falsify his picture of life that, in spite of all the accurate observation and all the imaginative insight, its values are partly those of melodrama—we begin to guess some stubborn sentimentalism at the bottom of the whole thing, some deeply buried streak of hysteria of which his misapplied resentments represent the aggressive side. And from the moment we suspect the processes by which he has arrived at his political ideas, the ideas themselves become suspect.

In the meantime, whatever diagnosis we may make of Dos Passos's infatuation with the social revolution, he remains one of the few first-rate figures among our writers of his generation, and the only one of these who has made a systematic effort to study all the aspects of America and to take account of all its elements, to compose them into a picture which makes some general sense. Most of the first-rate men of Dos Passos's age—Hemingway, Wilder, Fitzgerald—cultivate their own little corners and do not confront the situation as a whole. Only Dos Passos has tried to take hold of it. In the fine last speech of *Airways*, he allows the moral of his play to rise very close to the surface. The spinster sister of the Turner household has just received the news that the strike leader, with whom she has been in love and who has been made the victim of a frame-up, has finally been electrocuted: "Now I'm beginning to feel it," she says, "the house without Walter, the street without him, the city without him, the future that we lived in instead of a honeymoon without him, everything stark without him. Street where I've lived all these years shut up in a matchwood house full of bitterness. City where I've lived walled up in old dead fear. America, where I've scurried from store to subway to church to home, America that I've never known. World where I've lived without knowing. What can I do now that he is gone and that he has left me full of scalding wants, what can I do with the lack of him inside me like a cold stone? The house I lived in wrecked, the people I loved wrecked, around me there's nothing but words stinging like wasps. Where can I go down the dark street, where can I find a lover in the sleeping city? At what speed of the wind can I fly away, to escape these words that burn and sting, to escape the lack that is in me like a stone?"

It is true that the lack of real leadership is felt by us today as a stone. It is Dos Passos's recognition of this—his relentless re-iteration of his conviction that there is something lacking, something wrong, in America—as well as his insistence on the importance of America—that gives his work its validity and power. It is equally true, of course, of H. L. Mencken that he finds something lacking and something wrong; but the effect of Mencken on his admirers is to make them wash their hands of social questions. Mencken has made it the fashion to speak of politics as an obscene farce. And Dos Passos is now almost alone among the writers of his generation in continuing to take the social organism seriously.

April 17, 1929

T. S. Eliot and the Church of England

*F*or *Lancelot Andrewes* by T. S. Eliot contains essays on Lancelot Andrewes and John Bramhall, two seventeenth-century English divines, and on Machiavelli, F. H. Bradley, Baudelaire, Thomas Middleton, Crashaw and Irving Babbitt. They all display the author's unique combination of subtle and original thinking with simple and precise statement, and will be read by everybody interested in literature. T. S. Eliot has now become perhaps the most important literary critic in the English-speaking world. His writings have been brief and few, and it is almost incredible that they should have been enough to establish him as an intellectual leader; but when one tries to trace the causes of the change from the point of view of the English criticism of the period before the war to the point of view of our own day, one can find no figure of comparable authority. And we must recognize that Eliot's opinions, so cool and even casual in appearance, yet sped with the force of so intense a seriousness and weighted with so wide a learning, have stuck oftener and sunk deeper in the minds of the post-war generation of both England and the United States than those of any other critic.

For *Lancelot Andrewes*, however, is not, like *The Sacred Wood*, a book merely of literary criticism. The essays which it contains have been selected by Eliot for the purpose of indicating a general position in literature, politics and religion. This position, he tells us in his preface, "may be described as classicist in literature, royalist in politics, and Anglo-Catholic in religion"; and it is further to be expounded in "three small books," called respectively *The School of Donne*, *The Outline of Royalism* and *The Principles of Modern Heresy*.

Mr. Eliot's ideas, in *For Lancelot Andrewes*, appear chiefly by implication; and we run the risk of misrepresenting them in attempting to discuss them on the basis of this book. Still, Eliot has invited us to read this slender collection of essays as a prelude to the trilogy mentioned above, and it is difficult to know how else to deal with it. The clearest and most explicit statement on the subject of religion I can find is the following from the essay in which Eliot points out the deficiencies of Irving Babbitt's humanism: "Unless by civilization you mean material progress, cleanliness, etc. . . . if you mean a spiritual and intellectual coördination on a high level, then it is doubtful whether civilization can endure without religion, and religion without a church." One recognizes a point of view which is by way of becoming fashionable among certain sorts of literary people, yet this usually presents itself merely as a sentiment that it would be a good thing to believe rather than as a real and living belief. And, though Eliot lets us know that he does believe, his faith, in so far as we find it expressed in these essays and in his recent poems, seems entirely uninspired by hope, entirely unequipped with force—a faith which, to quote his own epigraph, is merely "ready to die."

Now, no one will dispute that, at the present time, our society is in need of the kind of ideals which the churches were once able to supply; but the objection to Eliot's position is simply that the churches are now out of the question as a solution to our present difficulties, because it is so difficult to get educated people to accept their fundamental doctrines—and that, even if a few first-rate ones can convince themselves that they do, one does not see how they can possibly hope for a revival general enough to make religion intellectually important again. I agree that, without a church, you cannot have a real religion; and I sympathize with Mr. Eliot's criticism of certain substitute religions, like that of H. G. Wells, which try to retain the benefits of faith while doing away with the necessity of believing. You cannot have real Christianity without a cult of Jesus as the son of God. But since it has plainly become anachronistic to accept the prophet Jesus in this role, it seems that we must reconcile ourselves to doing without both the churches and religion. The answer to Mr. Eliot's assertion that "it is doubtful whether civilization can endure without religion" is that we have got to make it endure. Nobody will pretend that this is going to be easy; but it can hardly be any more difficult than persuading oneself that the leadership of the future will be supplied by the Church of England or by the Roman Catholic Church or by any church whatsoever.

Nothing seems to me more sadly symptomatic of the feeble intellectual condition of a good many literary people, of their unwillingness or incapacity to come to terms with the world they live in, than the movement back to Thomas Aquinas—or, in Eliot's case, back to Bishop Andrewes. It is not, of course, a question of the wisdom or the spiritual authority of Aquinas or Andrewes in his own day, when it was still possible for a first-rate mind to accept the supernatural basis of religion. But to argue, as in the literary world one sometimes finds people doing, that, because our society at the present time is badly off without religion, we should make an heroic effort to swallow medieval theology, seems to me utterly futile as well as fundamentally dishonest. If the salvation of our civilization depends on such religious fervor as our writers are capable of kindling —if it depends on the edifying example of the conversion of Jean Cocteau and the low blue flame of the later Eliot—then I fear that we must give up hope.

I was writing last week of John Dos Passos and his mirage of a social revolution. It seems to me that T. S. Eliot is a case of much the same kind: Eliot, like Dos Passos, is a highly culti-vated American who does not care for contemporary America; but, instead of escaping from the American situation by way of Greenwich Village radicalism and the myth of a serious-minded and clear-eyed proletariat, as Dos Passos attempts to do, Eliot has gone to England and evolved for himself an aristocratic myth out of English literature and history. Eliot's classicism, royalism and Anglo-Catholicism, from the notion I get of them in his recent writings, seem to me as much academic at-titudes, as much lacking in plausibility, as Dos Passos's cult of the class-conscious proletariat: it is as hard to imagine royalty and the Church becoming more instead of less important, even in England, as it is to imagine the American employees becoming less instead of more middle-class. Most Americans of the type of Dos Passos and Eliot—that is, sensitive and widely read literary people—have some such agreeable fantasy in which they can allow their minds to take refuge from the perplexities and oppressions about them. In the case of H. L. Mencken, it is a sort of German university town, where people drink a great deal of beer and devour a great many books, and where they respect the local nobility—if only the Germany of the Empire had not been destroyed by the war! In the case of

certain American writers from the top layer of the old South, it
is the old-fashioned Southern plantation, where men are high-
spirited and punctilious and women gracious and lovely, where
affectionate and loyal Negroes are happy to keep in their place
—if only the feudal South had not perished in 1865! With Ezra
Pound, it is a medieval Provence, where poor but accomplished troubadours enjoy the favors of noble ladies—if only
the troubadours were not deader than Provençal! With Dos
Passos, it is an army of workers, disinterested, industrious and
sturdy, but full of the good-fellowship and gaiety in which the
Webster Hall balls nowadays are usually so dismally lacking—if
only the American workers were not preoccupied with buying
Ford cars and radios, instead of organizing themselves to overthrow the civilization of the bourgeoisie! And in T. S. Eliot's
case, it is a world of seventeenth-century churchmen, who
combine the most scrupulous conscience with the ability to
write good prose—if it were only not so difficult nowadays for
men who are capable of becoming good writers to accept the
Apostolic Succession!

Among these, the writers like Dos Passos and Mencken stay
at home and denounce America, while the writers like Eliot
and Pound go abroad and try to forget it. It is peculiarly hard
for such men to get an intellectual foothold in our world: New
York, in particular, just now, is like the great glass mountain of
the *Arabian Nights*, against which the barques of young writers
are continually coming to grief. And this is true not merely of
the United States, but more or less of the whole Western
world. Industrially, politically and socially, Europe itself is
becoming more and more like America every day; and the catastrophe of the war has demoralized America, too. It is up to
American writers to try to make some sense of their American
world—for their world is now everybody's world, and, if they
fail to find a way to make possible in it what T. S. Eliot desider-
ates: "a spiritual and intellectual coördination on a high level,"
it is improbable that any one else will be able to do it for them.
That world is a world with a number of religions, but not
amenable to the leadership of a single church—and it is a
world in which, whatever reorganization one may prophesy for
the democratic state, the restoration of the monarchic principle seems improbable to the last degree. It is a world in which

Eliot's program would not appear very helpful. We shall certainly not be able to lean upon the authority of either Church or King, and we shall have to depend for our new ideals on a study of contemporary reality and the power of our own imaginations.

April 24, 1929

Dahlberg, Dos Passos and Wilder

I N *The Woman of Andros*, Thornton Wilder has turned
Terence's *Andria* into a fable of the world without Christianity. At some indeterminate date before the birth of Christ,
the son of a well-to-do merchant on the Greek island of Brynos
falls in love with the sister of an hetaira and gets her with child.
But it has been arranged for him by his family to marry a girl
of his own class, and he is in doubt as to what to do about his
mistress. The intelligent and sympathetic father leaves it up to
the young man, who seeks enlightenment in a religious fast
and vigil. In the meantime, however, the hetaira's household
—the hetaira herself having died—has been sold to a visiting
pimp, and by the time the father has succeeded in buying
Glycerium back and the son has returned from the temple with
his mind firmly made up to marry her, the poor girl has been
overcome by the strain of her situation, and both she and her
baby die.

Thornton Wilder has achieved his effect with accomplished
technical skill: he has induced us to follow his story with sympathy and suspense, but he has kept us from understanding the
full significance of the incidents we have been witnessing until
we read the final sentence of the book, which is repeated from
the first paragraph, where it has seemed to have only a casual
interest, but which now retrospectively illuminates all that has
come between: "But behind the thick beds of clouds the moon
soared radiantly bright, shining upon Italy and its smoking
mountains. And in the East the stars shone tranquilly down
upon the land that was soon to be called Holy and that even
then was preparing its precious burden." Looking back, we
now understand that we have been watching a world in half-
darkness: these people have been groping and perplexed—they
have as yet known no revelation, they can depend upon no authority, to justify their impulses toward charity, toward putting
the instinct of brotherhood before those of convention and interest. We see now that the cultivated hetaira—who, in conformity with the tradition of Wilder's novels, is secretly and

hopelessly in love with the boy—in her acceptance of disappointment and death, and her final philosophical reflections: "I want to say to someone . . . that I have known the worst that the world can do to me, and that nevertheless I praise the world and all living. All that is, is well. Remember some day, remember me as one who loved all things and accepted from the gods all things, the bright and the dark"—we see that Chrysis is supposed to represent the highest culture and moral wisdom which, before the coming of Christ, the pagan world could attain, and that she has already, in making her house an asylum for simpleton, pauper and cripple, anticipated a new and deeper morality. We see that the asceticism of the priest of Apollo anticipates that of the Christian priesthood, that the merchant and his son are groping for principles that only the gospel of Christ can supply, and that the dead mother and child are a symbol for the death of the pagan world, which another mother and child, in "the land soon to be called Holy," are to waken to another life.

This moment before the advent of Christianity has already been exploited as a theme for fiction; it has even been a favorite theme. Its popularity has been due, I suppose, partly to the influence of Renan, who, in his *Origines du Christianisme*, subtly creates the impression that the Graeco-Roman culture was itself tending independently toward all that was best in Christianity, and that it had, also, virtues of its own that were more attractive than most of the Christian ones. Pater's *Marius the Epicurean* seems to have taken its subject and mood from the final volume of the series, which describes the reign of Marcus Aurelius; but Pater slightly shifted the emphasis: he gave Christianity a certain advantage. The Gospel is with Pater, as with Wilder, the word for which humanity has been waiting, the only thing needful that the ancient world has lacked. Anatole France followed Renan, also, but, with a livelier malice than Renan's, he tipped the scales against Christianity, and delighted, in *Sur la Pierre Blanche*, in showing how Paul before Gallio at Corinth had not really, as Renan had said, represented in his unprepossessing person the imminent future of Europe, of which the cultivated Roman had no suspicion, but had been merely the fanatical product of a semi-barbarous

interlude—since, when Europe should have recovered from
the Middle Ages, she was to aim, in her civilization, at Gallio's
ideals, not Paul's.

Now, Wilder has picked up this pagan-Christian theme and,
tipping the balance, as Pater did, in favor of Christ again, has
written a book which belongs to the period of Pater and Anatole France. *The Woman of Andros*, though it is very well done,
strikes me as being a kind of thing that there is no longer much
point in doing. I am sure that, in revisiting the ancient world,
the author has intended to tell us, as every writer must do,
something interesting about our own. We gather from Wilder's
play *The Angel That Troubled the Waters* that he himself is a
believer in the Christian creed, and I assume that in *The Woman
of Andros* he is trying to show us the sorrows and doubts that
we ourselves must experience if we live without the Christian
religion. There is behind many a page of this book a broken-
hearted Proustian sob which has welled up, all too unmistakably, from the peculiar sentimentality of our own time and not
from any state of mind that one can associate with the Greeks;
and there are also some admirable passages that speak to us
directly of ourselves: "From time to time she peered into
her mind," Wilder writes of the dying hetaira, "to ascertain
what her beliefs were in regard to life after death, its judgments or its felicities; but the most exhausting of all our adventures is that journey down the long corridors of the mind
to the last halls where belief is enshrined." But the further
Thornton Wilder withdraws into the past, the more imitative
he becomes. This ought not necessarily to be true; but the fact
is that, ever since the romantic revival set the fashion of recreating the past, the writers have been ringing the changes on the
Christian-pagan theme, loading the dice for one or the other,
and that dealing with the past, for Wilder, means not merely
going back to Greece, not merely going back to Terence, but
going back to the Paris of yesterday. His new book, for all the
charm of its style, the grace of narrative and the spare firm outline which Wilder never fails of, as it is paler than his other
books, comes closer to seeming mawkish. Wilder announced,
or made his hero announce, at the conclusion of *The Cabala*
that he was returning with high hopes to New York. But he
was next heard from in Cluxambuqua, and he now hails us

with rather a far faint voice from a Greek island of some vague date B.C. One always reads with pleasure and edification anything that Thornton Wilder writes—but just because he is evidently a first-rate man, one would like to see him more at home.

Edward Dahlberg, the author of *Bottom Dogs*, is, on the other hand, very close to us—he is closer to us, indeed, than we quite care to have literature be. *Bottom Dogs* is the back-streets of all our American cities and towns. Mr. Dahlberg, as a writer, has nothing in common with the consummate sophistication of Thornton Wilder, and his narrative is sometimes dull; but what he has brought in from the obscurer sections of Los Angeles, Cleveland, Kansas City is something more than an interesting document—it is a work of literature that has the stamp of a real and original gift. The prose of *Bottom Dogs* is partly derived from the language of the streets itself, but to say this may give a misleading impression: Dahlberg's prose is primarily a literary medium, hard, vivid, exact and racy, and with an odd kind of street-lighted glamor. I do not agree with D. H. Lawrence, who has written for this sordid story a curious and suggestive introduction, that the dominating feeling of the book is repulsion. It would be easy for a writer of another kind to make Dahlberg's kind of experience repulsive, but I do not feel that Dahlberg has done so: the temperament through which he has strained his orphan homes, his barber shops and bakeries, his dance-halls and Y.M.C.A.'s, though he is always realistically observant, seems a gentle and unassertive, and, consequently, an unembittered one. We read the book, at any rate, with wonder to see how the rawest, the cheapest, the most commonplace American material may be transmuted by a man of talent, so submerged in it that he can only speak its language, yet acting upon it so strongly, so imbuing it with his own tone and color and texture, that he can make it yield a work of distinction.

Now, John Dos Passos, in *The 42nd Parallel*, has consciously and deliberately worked out a medium similar to Dahlberg's. *The 42nd Parallel*—which it seems to me Dos Passos's publishers have made a serious mistake in not announcing for what it is: the first section of a large-scale novel—is to deal with the role of the United States in relation to the rest of the world during the early years of the present century; but though it is written from the point of view of an unusually internationally minded American of unusually wide culture, the author has been able to immerse himself in the minds and the lives of his middle-class characters, to identify himself with them, to a degree that must astonish any reader of Dos Passos's other novels. In this respect, *The 42nd Parallel* is quite different from *Manhattan Transfer* and marks a striking advance beyond it. *Manhattan Transfer*, after all, might almost have been written by a very intelligent and very well-documented foreigner: the characters are seen from the outside and do not always seem organically human. But in this new work of fiction, Dos Passos has abandoned the literary baggage that encumbered his exploration of New York. Here one finds no elaborate backdrops and no Joycean prose-poems. For the method of *The 42nd Parallel*, Dos Passos has perhaps gone to school to Ring Lardner and Anita Loos; he is, at any rate, the first of our writers—with the possible exception of Mark Twain—who has successfully used colloquial American for a novel of the highest artistic seriousness. This has enabled him to keep us close to the characters as we never were in *Manhattan Transfer*. He still has moments of allowing his people to contract into two-dimensional caricatures of qualities or forces he hates; but, in general, we live their lives, we look at the world through their eyes.

These characters of *The 42nd Parallel* belong mostly to the white-collar class. Almost all of them begin as obscure and more or less mediocre-appearing people, who, from the ordinary American point of view, are anxious to improve their condition. Neither the gentle spinster stenographer from Washington, the amiable publicity director from Wilmington nor the sharp woman interior decorator from Chicago, has an intimation of any other values than those of the American business office, of the American advertising game, of the American luxury trade, out of which they make their salaries and in terms of which they conceive their ambitions. Only the nephew of the radical Irish printer reacts against the habits of the white-collar class and tends to identify his interests with those of a proletariat. The author introduces separately each one of his five principal characters—we have of each a continuous history from childhood. For this, he has invented a narrative method which enables him to cover a great deal of ground with astonishing rapidity and ease, yet to give us the illusion of finding out all about his people's lives: their friends and the members of their families, their amusements and their periods of stagnation, the places where they work and how much they get, the meals they eat, the beds they sleep in. And without any explicit commentary, each of these sequences of data and incident is made to create a character. Eleanor Stoddard's cold-blooded shrewdness and passionate appetite for refinement or J. Ward Moorhouse's unconscious charlatanry is presented entirely in terms of *things*. And when these commonplace individuals, who have first been presented to the reader independently of one another, are finally brought together, they take on a further significance—we realize that what we have been witnessing is the making of our contemporary society. And as Dos Passos can indicate in masterly fashion the shift from one city to another, so that we understand, without having been overtly told, the difference between the way people behave and feel in Chicago and the way they behave and feel in New York, in Washington, Minneapolis, Pittsburgh or Mexico City; so—also, apparently, without being told—we at last seem to understand the national character of America. The author has sandwiched in, between the sections of the life-histories of his characters, what he labels as "newsreels"—that is, medleys of newspaper-clippings—that give us a picture of the public consciousness running parallel with the private events of the lives that are narrated in detail; as well as a series of brief biographies (very well done) of eminent contemporary Americans, all shown as hampered, stunted or perverted by that same commercial society in which the characters of the novel are submerged. And at the end of this first instalment, with the entrance of the United States into the war and the appearance of the last of the characters, a young garage man from North Dakota, who in his wanderings has fallen in with a rich and drunken cracker from Okeechobee City and been persuaded by him that he ought to go over and get a load of the fun in Europe "before the whole thing goes belly-up"—Dos Passos, in the perfectly aimed final paragraphs, reveals this character suddenly as a symbol for the American people, adventurous and well-intentioned but provincial and immature, voyaging out from its enormous country into a world of which it knows nothing.

This novel, when it has been completed, may well turn out to be the most important that has yet been produced by any American of Dos Passos's generation. Dos Passos seems the only one of the novelists of this generation who is concerned with the large questions of politics and society; and he has succeeded in this book in bridging the gap, which is wider in America than anywhere else and which constitutes a perpetual problem in American literature and thought, between the special concerns of the intellectual and the general pursuits and ideas of the people. The task of the intellectual is not merely to study the common life but to make his thoughts and symbols *seem* relevant to it—that is, to express them in terms of the actual American world without either cheapening them or rendering them vapid. Dos Passos, who has read as much and traveled as widely as Wilder, does not always avoid spinning literature—especially in the first section, which has a flavor of *Huckleberry Finn*; and, in consequence, he is sometimes flimsy, where Dahlberg, in dealing with a similar subject, would be authentic and dense. But, though in neither intensity nor skill is Dos Passos superior to Hemingway, *The 42nd Parallel* seems to me, from the point of view of its literary originality and its intellectual interest, by far the most remarkable, the most encouraging American novel that I have read since the end of the war.

March 26, 1930

Notes on Babbitt and More

T HE FOLLOWING notes deal with the essays by Irving Babbitt and Paul Elmer More which appeared in the humanist symposium called *Humanism and America.*

Humanism: An Essay at Definition
By Irving Babbitt

(1) *The law of measure on which it [humanism] depends becomes meaningless unless it can be shown to be one of the "laws unwritten in the heavens" of which Antigone had the immediate perception, laws that are "not of to-day or yesterday," that transcend in short the temporal process.*

This seems to me a grotesque misapplication of the famous speech from Sophocles. Let me point out, in the first place, that what Antigone says is "ἄγραπτα κἀσφαλῆ θεῶν νόμιμα" —"unwritten and unfailing laws of the gods"—and that Professor Babbitt, in changing "gods" to "heavens" (which is particularly inappropriate in this case, since Antigone has just specified the gods of the underworld), is following the Victorian tradition of Jebb and Jowett, who, by substituting such Christian words as "God" and "heaven" for the pre-Christian conceptions of the Greeks, almost succeeded in giving Sophocles and Plato the aspect of pious English dons. But Babbitt has turned Sophocles into something worse and even more alien to his true nature: he has turned him into a Harvard humanist. In the scene in question, Aritigone is not talking about the law of measure or anything remotely resembling it—she has disobeyed Creon's edict by performing funeral rites for her brother and she is justifying herself for her insubordinate conduct. There is no self-control about Antigone's behavior: she has committed an act of passionate personal loyalty, regarded as excessively rash and wrong-headed by everybody else in the play, including her own sister, whose "inner check" is more highly developed than Antigone's. When Creon demands how Antigone has dared to break the law, she answers fiercely that such a law as his edict is contrary to the laws of the gods.

The romantic might, in fact, turn this scene against the humanist with more appropriateness than the humanist can use it against the romantic. Antigone has the same hasty insolent intemperate nature as her father Oedipus—we are told so explicitly in the play—and she is asserting her individual will in defiance of law and expediency—she is making an impulsive and desperate gesture. Aristotle—"a true humanist," according to Babbitt—says of this passage, in showing the distinction between conventional and natural law, that Antigone vindicates the latter in asserting "ὅτι δίκαιον, ἀπειρημένον, θάψαι τὸν Πολυνείκη, ὡς φύσει ὂν τοῦτο δίκαιον,"—that her act, though it violated the prohibition, had the sanction of natural right, was "right according to nature." Now Antigone, of course, is not a nineteenth-century romantic, and Aristotle does not mean by "nature" quite the same thing that Rousseau does. But what Rousseau means does have something in common with what Aristotle means that Antigone means, whereas what Antigone means can't by any possible stretch be associated with Babbitt's "law of measure." Babbitt grossly misrepresents Sophocles when he applies Antigone's speech in this way: "The laws unwritten in the heavens" is one of Babbitt's favorite quotations: he has used it again and again in order to give us the impression that Sophocles has endorsed the humanist "will to refrain." Yet, as I say, if it is a question of slinging classical texts, the old-fashioned romantic who is Babbitt's bugbear—if there be any such still alive—might turn Antigone's outburst against Babbitt—and, relapsing into the truculence of the age of Bentley, which the manners of the humanists invite, might add, as Antigone does:

> σοί δ' εἰ δοκῶ νῦν μῶρα δρῶσα τυγχάνειν,
> σχεδόν τι μώρῳ μωρίαν ὀφλισκάνω.

Babbitt elsewhere in this essay says that Sophocles "ranks high among occidental humanists," though he admits—making reservations in regard to the opinion of Matthew Arnold—that "perfect poise is no doubt impossible; not even Sophocles succeeded in seeing life steadily and seeing it whole." I don't know in precisely what respect Professor Babbitt considers Sophocles to have fallen short of perfect poise; but it is certainly true that Sophocles' characters are usually remarkable for anything but poise—they are as violent and as harsh as the people in the plays of Eugene O'Neill. Where the "law of measure" comes in is certainly not in connection with the conduct of Sophocles' people—the hot-headed overconfident Oedipus; the "fierce child of a fierce father," Antigone; the relentless and morbid Electra, etc.—but in Sophocles' handling of his material—the firmness of his intellectual grasp, the sureness of his sense of form, the range of psychological insight which enables him to put before us the rages, the ambitions, the loyalties, of so many passionate persons, that spend themselves against one another and expire in the clear air, leaving only with the echo of their tirades the vibration of the taut verse. In a world dominated by the law of measure, there would, however, be no humanist masterpieces such as the tragedies of Sophocles—since Babbitt claims them, with reservations, as humanist masterpieces—because there would be no violent passions to write about. This might be a good thing—perhaps we ought to be glad to do without the Sophocleses if we could get rid of the unruly passions. But, on the other hand, we ought perhaps to think twice before letting ourselves in for a world where the sole masterpieces were humanist symposia.

(2) *It would not be easy to argue with any plausibility that the typical modernist is greatly concerned with the law of measure; his interest, as a glance at our newspapers should suffice to show, is rather in the doing of stunts and the breaking of records, in "prodigies, feats of strength and crime," the very topics that, according to the traditional report, Confucius banished from his conversation.*

In this respect, our age is no worse than any other. What is done today for the people by the newspapers was done formerly by the composers of ballads, and ballad literature has always been occupied with prodigies, feats of strength and crime. The *Iliad* itself was presumably made out of ballads— and, in any case, there can be no question that it deals with prodigies, feats of strength and crime. The Greek dramatists, including Sophocles, got their themes from Homer or similar sources. It is true that the genuine poet is able to do with such stories something that the simple reporter is not usually able to do, but the material that he deals with is the same. And the general run of the ballads of any age has been as crude as newspaper stories. The sages of our own time—Professor Babbitt, for example—are, I should say, as little preoccupied with the prodigies and crimes of the newspapers as Confucius was with the common gossip.

(3) *In the case of such encroachments [of naturalism upon the domains of humanism or religion] there is not only a quarrel between the naturalist and the humanist, but a quarrel of first principles. When first principles are involved the law of measure is no longer applicable. One should not be moderate in dealing with error.*

It has apparently never occurred to Professor Babbitt that one's moderation ought to extend to not being too sure that one is absolutely right and that others are absolutely wrong—though Mr. More, in his companion essay, quotes from Whitehead, against the dogmatists of Darwinism, Cromwell's, "My brethren, by the bowels of Christ I beseech you, bethink you that you may be mistaken!" We might have thought that if the law of measure were valuable anywhere, it would be valuable in the domain of ideas, where the failure sufficiently to respect it has notoriously bred war and oppression since the beginning of the world. Babbitt surely did not learn from Plato, whom he invokes in the next paragraph, that we should feel so sure of our own opinions that we need not be moderate with other people who happen to have different ones. The hero of Plato's novel of ideas is, of course, Socrates, but Plato's dialogues are a novel, none the less, and the impression, I think, that most people get from them, though they may be persuaded by Socrates' opinions, is that the world has a good many aspects and that there is a good deal to be said on all sides. The people in Plato who follow Babbitt's precept that we "should not be moderate in dealing with error" are the judges of Socrates. I doubt whether even Aristotle was so sure that he was right as Babbitt. If Mr. Babbitt wants to find a tradition for his policy in dealing with error, he must look not to the Academy and the Lyceum, but to the councils of the Inquisition, the revolutionary tribunal of the Terror and—to come closer to

Professor Babbitt's home—Dedham Courthouse and Boston State House.*

(4) *Positively one may define it [the higher will] as the higher immediacy that is known in its relation to the lower immediacy —the merely temperamental man with his impressions and emotions and expansive desires—as a power of vital control* (frein vital).

So Paul Elmer More asserts (in *Aristocracy and Justice*) that if a man "retires into himself and examines his own motives and the courses of his self-approval and discontent . . . he will discover that there is a happiness of the soul which is not the same as the pleasure of fulfilled desires, whether these be for good or for ill, a happiness which is not dependent upon the results of this or that choice among our desires, but upon the very act itself of choice and self-control."

Now, why on earth is virtue, with the humanists, always made to reside exclusively in what Babbitt calls the "will to refrain"? "Humanism," says Professor Babbitt, in making a distinction between humanism and religion, "is not primarily enthusiastic." So far as I can see, it is not enthusiastic at all. Professor Babbitt goes on to say that the humanist, though he "cannot afford to be an enthusiast in Rousseau's sense, on the other hand should not neglect the truth of Rousseau's saying that 'cold reason has never done anything illustrious.'" But the writings of the humanists strike us with a chill even more mortal than that of reason. And how can one be seriously impressed by a philosophy which enjoins nothing but negative behavior?—as if humanity were not, now as always, as much in need of being exhorted against coldness and indifference and routine as against irresponsible exuberance—especially Anglo-Saxon humanity. As if it were not obvious that Boston and New York, Manchester and London, were not suffering rather from a lack of normal human fellowship and normal human hope and joy than from any demoralizing effects of unbridled "humanitarian" sympathies, indiscriminate emotional "expansiveness" or universal orgiastic dissipation—as if our clerks, our factory workers and our respectable professional and business

*This refers to the Sacco-Vanzetti case.

classes were all in danger of falling victims to the rhapsodical enthusiasm and the lawless individualism of romanticism! If it is merely a question of refraining, these people are all good humanists: they have either been compelled by society to refrain from most of the enjoyments, from the exercise of most of the faculties, that make the amenity of human life, or they refrain because their education has been too limited to enable them to conceive their own aesthetic and emotional possibilities, or because their natures are too poor to have any.

As a matter of fact, however, Professor Babbitt, as I have noted above, has managed to exempt his own professional activities from the law of measure, the duty to refrain. He makes it plain that, in "dealing with error," we are no longer obliged to be moderate; and as Professor Babbitt, in his writings, hardly ever deals with anything but error, he is rarely obliged to be moderate. Professor Babbitt—and the other humanists —are permitted to drop their ideal of decorum the moment they put pen to paper. It is not decorous to look for nothing but mistakes in the writings of your contemporaries; it is not decorous always to call attention to these mistakes with a sneer; it is not decorous to take a word like humanism, which has formerly been applied to the great scholars, philosophers, satirists and poets of the Renaissance, and to insist that it ought to be regarded as the property of a small sect of schoolmasters so fatuous that they do not hesitate to assign schoolmasters' A's, B's and C's in humanism to "Homer, Phidias, Plato, Aristotle, Confucius, Buddha, Jesus, Paul, Virgil, Horace, Dante, Shakespeare, Milton, Goethe, Matthew Arnold, Emerson and Lowell" (I quote a list of their preferred great figures); it is not decorous to assume that you yourselves are the only persons who have taken seriously the vices and woes of your own time and that everybody except yourselves is engaged either perversely or stupidly in trying to make them worse. The exercise of decorum by the humanists is evidently confined to their private lives, where the public cannot benefit by it.

(5) *This movement has, from the eighteenth century and in some respects from the Renaissance, been marked by a growing discredit of the will to refrain. The very word renunciation has*

been rarely pronounced by those who have entered into the move-
ment. The chief exception that occurs to one is Goethe (echoed at
times by Carlyle). Any one who thinks of the series of Goethe's love
affairs, prolonged into the seventies, is scarcely likely to maintain
that his Entsagung *was of a very austere character even for a*
man of the world, not to speak of a saint.

It seems to me that assumptions are here being made in regard to sexual morality which require a good deal of proving
on Professor Babbitt's part. He goes on to say, a little further,
that "the real humanist consents, like Aristotle, to limit his desires only in so far as this limitation can be shown to make for
his own happiness." If one disapproves of Goethe's love affairs,
but if the end to be achieved is happiness, one would have to
show first that these love affairs failed to make Goethe happy.
It seems to me that Mr. Babbitt should shoulder this burden of
proof and argue that it did not do Goethe good at the same
time that it did the ladies no harm for him to fall in love after
he was seventy. But these are questions which Babbitt and
More will never consent to argue, as to which they simply make
assumptions—just as they assume that virtue is identical with
the will to refrain—for the reason that these opinions are not
really conclusions from evidence, but the mere unexamined
prejudices of a bigoted Puritan heritage which these gentlemen—for all their voyaging through the varied realms of the
mind—have never succeeded in sloughing off, and which they
persist in mistaking for eternal and universal laws, because—
they have put this forward as an overwhelming justification—
when they look into their own natures, they find them there.

The Humility of Common Sense
By Paul Elmer More

(1) *It is a nice question to ask whether belief in the absolute ir-*
responsibility of the artistic temperament has engendered the
modern ideal of absolute art, or the contrary. . . . The point I
would make is the falseness and futility of the logical deduction
that art can . . . dispense with the stuff of humanity or nature,
or can weigh anchor and sail off into a shoreless sea of unreality.

In the first part of Mr. More's essay, marked by his usual
intellectual arrogance, which he incongruously entitles *The*

Humility of Common Sense, he is occupied with the old "art for
art's sake" doctrine as it has recently been formulated by some
of its champions. Now, one may agree with Mr. More that the
artist should not be irresponsible and that he cannot dispense
with humanity and nature—one may even agree that "art for
art's sake" has given rise to a good deal of nonsense, as indeed
what doctrine has not? But it is obvious that Mr. More fails to
see how this point of view is the natural and inevitable product
of a particular situation. Art is, of course, a profession like medicine, law or banking, a trade like market-gardening or carpen-
try, that supplies certain human needs; it is one of our human
devices for adjusting ourselves to the world and for mastering
it in a way that the other animals cannot do. It is preposterous,
certainly, for artists to talk as if they were able to work *in vacuo*
or as if it were possible for them to remain indifferent to the
effects of their work on human life. But in the course of the
nineteenth century, they were goaded into talking in this way,
into making a cult of art for its own sake, by the progress of
the industrial revolution and the rise of the middle class. It was
one of the fatal defects of industrial-commercial society that it
neglected or discouraged the appetites for which the artists
had formerly provided; and as the market value of art depreciated to the point where its practitioners found themselves
pushed almost into the role of outlaws, they became embittered and desperate. They swore, if they had any spirit, that
they were going to work at their craft even though nobody
wanted their wares, and they thus arrived at the slogan that has
irritated so many people. The fact that they should have felt
the necessity for asserting the value of what they were doing
was a sign of their maladjustment, of the abnormality of their
situation; but, given this situation, the very faith in aesthetic
values, the dogged devotion to art, not infrequently called
forth qualities of heroic endurance and self-denial. It was to
some extent true, of course—especially toward the end of the
century—that the isolation of the artist, his consciousness of
swimming against the current, had sometimes the effect of de-
forming his work. But what student of literature who is not
content naïvely to praise or blame while referring works from
different periods to the same ideal standards, what critic aware
of art in its relation to the other forces of the society in which

it is practised, will assert that even the poet of the fin de siècle could or should have done otherwise? In the generation of the middle century, even so great a man as Flaubert had found it possible to save his soul only through the cult of art. Yet the notion that the cynical Flaubert and the diabolistic Baudelaire could have exercised, in their novels and poems, the most exacting kind of self-discipline, exerted, in dealing with the materials supplied them by their imaginations, a rigorous will to refrain; that their work might thus fortify their readers as well as entertain them—this is something Mr. Paul Elmer More seems incapable of conceiving. He apparently believes that the only way in which it is possible for a reader or a writer to school himself in these bad days is to read or write literary criticism of the type of his own and Babbitt's, which, though based on thorough reading and distinguished by sound writing, has obviously not required a discipline a tenth as difficult as that which has gone to produce some of the works it so loftily castigates.

Even aside, however, from its meaning in this special situation, the slogan of "art for art's sake" has a meaning which would still remain valid even in an age which did not, as our own does, freeze out the artists and make them defiant. From this point of view, Mr. More's attitude is open to the same sort of criticism as that of the not insensitive but rather unintelligent socialist of the type of Upton Sinclair. Upton Sinclair disapproves of works of art which do not point explicitly a socialist moral, as Paul Elmer More disapproves of works of art which do not point explicitly the moral of self-control. Each insists on denouncing as irresponsible and evil or futile all the writers in which it is impossible for him to find his own particular moral stated in his own particular terms. Now, aside from the fact that reality presents a variety of aspects and may be expected to suggest more than one kind of moral, and aside from the fact that fine workmanship itself always contains an implicit moral, it should further be borne in mind that in the arts as in the sciences a certain freedom for experimentation is necessary: one must allow a good deal of apparently gratuitous, and even empty or ridiculous work, if one wants to get masterpieces. Gregor Mendel was dead eighteen years before anyone had even suspected that his hobby of interbreeding green peas was anything other than a harmless monastic diversion; Gauss's non-Euclidean geometry, which he had been too timid to publish, as well as Ricci and Levi-Civita's calculus, had seemed the idlest of mathematical exercises till Einstein found them just the tools he needed, ready to his hand. But, in general, the gratuitous experimentation of the scientific world is known only inside its own laboratories, whereas the corresponding work of the literary world is likely to be circulated more widely. When it happens to fall under the eye of an Upton Sinclair or a Paul Elmer More, he is infuriated by what seems to him its fatuity: he demands at once to know what these writers imagine they are good for. Well, they may not be good for anything, but, on the other hand, they may be valuable—one has to wait and see what comes of them, what other writers may get out of them. Virgil, a poet in high repute with Mr. More and the other humanists, had laid under contribution not merely Homer but also the romantic rebel Apollonius Rhodius, whose innovations, in Alexandria, had had no important results, but from whom, two and a half centuries later, Virgil was partly to derive his misty and subtle feeling for nature and human life. The Alexandrians—as, for different reasons, the poets of the end of the century—were denied participation in the life of a great society, and they cultivated art for art's sake. In view of their having kept alive the poetic tradition of Greece as well as having made contributions to the later poetry of Rome, will Paul Elmer More contend today that the work of these writers was futile?

(2) *They ["a few restless souls" among the "radical writers of to-day"] hold deliberation to be the foe of liberation. Hence the later theory, exemplified in English by James Joyce, that art shall not reproduce a picture of life as the humanist sees it, or even from the point of view of the realist, but for its subject matter shall descend to what they call the pure "stream of consciousness." The hero of fiction shall have no will, no purpose, no inhibition, no power of choice whether for good or evil, but shall be merely a medium through which passes an endless, unchecked, meaningless flux of sensations and memories and emotions and impulses.*

But Joyce does not exemplify anything of the sort: his characters are all going about their business like the characters of any other novelist. Bloom, Dedalus, Mrs. Bloom and the others do have their wills, their purposes, their inhibitions, and they make their moral decisions—indeed, these moral decisions are the crucial events of *Ulysses*. What has probably misled Mr. More is Joyce's method of dealing with the human mind, not by telling us what it does, but by trying to present it directly in the terms in which it is aware of itself from hour to hour, from moment to moment. The minds of the people in Joyce are sometimes relaxed or confused, at other times intent and lucid: it depends on the character and the situation. The principal way in which *Ulysses* differs from the kind of novel to which Mr. More is accustomed is not in Joyce's depriving his characters of moral sense or will, but simply in his showing us their consciousnesses as if they were beehives under glass, and of making us watch them through the whole of a day—it is a difference of technique, and of pace and scale. But I cannot suppose, as a matter of fact—from the extreme inappropriateness of Mr. More's remarks about Joyce—that he has ever done anything more than look into him, and I will venture to say that this high-handed habit on the part of the humanist critics of attempting to dispose of contemporary writers whom they obviously haven't read by supercilious classroom jeers is an even more serious scandal to their cause than their misrepresentation of the ancients, whom they have at least carefully studied. So Mr. More, in *The Demon of the Absolute*, has described Dos Passos's *Manhattan Transfer* as "an explosion in a cesspool" without apparently the faintest suspicion that Dos Passos intends his novel as an indictment of the same social conditions of which Mr. More himself has always taken so gloomy a view. But not only is Mr. More unable to recognize in *Manhattan Transfer* the work of a man who, like himself, has been "deafened," as he once wrote of his own state of mind, "by the 'indistinguishable roar' of the streets" and can "make no sense of the noisy jargon of the market place," and who finally causes his hero to escape from the modern American city with as much relief as ever Mr. More did when he went into his celebrated retreat at Shelburne; he has not even succeeded in informing himself from any other sources than this novel as to Dos Passos's general point of view. If Dos Passos had been a second-rate eighteenth-century essayist, Mr. More would know everything about him, including his political opinions—if he had been the most obscure New England poet (of the seventeenth century, that is), Mr. More would have read him through.

(3) *"The only way of mitigating mechanism,"* he *[A. N. Whitehead] says, "is by discovery that it is not mechanism." And so, instead of admitting humbly that mechanism is mechanism while beside it there exists something of a totally different nature, and that the ultimate nexus between these two fields of experience surpasses our comprehension, he must demonstrate mechanism out of the world altogether.*

But why *should* Whitehead admit humbly that mechanism is mechanism and that humanity exists beside it as something of a totally different nature? Why *should* he assume that the ultimate nexus between these two fields of experience surpasses our comprehension? I do not feel with Mr. More that the effect of Whitehead's metaphysics is to "make a travesty of the inorganic world," that it threatens "to deprive humanity of what is distinctly human." Why should Mr. More take for granted that to change our idea of humanity necessarily means to degrade it? There can be no advances in philosophy without the altering of old conceptions. And I cannot, for the life of me, see that Mr. More has any other real objection to Whitehead's ideas than that they would, as he believes—and I am not sure that he is right even here—tend to discredit the distinction between "man" and "thing" upon which his own humanistic philosophy is based. He makes no attempt to show that Whitehead's speculations are not justified, that his arguments are not sound; he makes no effort whatever to discuss the scientific findings—the conception of the "event," for example, as the ultimate unit of both the organic and the inorganic worlds—upon which Whitehead has based his metaphysics and which he did not himself invent. He merely asserts that Whitehead should never have undertaken at all to account for the relations between the organic and the inorganic worlds. He says that he "admits" this "humbly," but one gathers from his tone that he would, if he could, get out an injunction against all wanton metaphysics directed to this end, just as he would, if he could, get out an injunction against all experimentation in the arts. Yet it is plain that if the philosophers of the past had been content to accept so incuriously the apparent paradoxes of experience, we should not have any philosophy at all, and Mr. More would have no Plato and no Platonists to beguile his academic retirement. One cannot avoid the conclusion that the primary difficulty for Mr. More is to admit that it is possible for anyone, either in art or in science, to find out anything new, and I cannot explain this state of mind except on the hypothesis that Mr. More is really an old-fashioned Puritan who has lost the Puritan theology without having lost the Puritan dogmatism. Mr. More is more certainly than Professor Babbitt a man of some imagination; he is able, up to a point, to follow the thought of the modern world, as appears from his not unintelligent and often sensitive expositions of the ideas of other writers (if they are not absolutely contemporaries); but some iron inhibition seems inevitably to come into play to restrain Mr. More from agreeing with anything in modern philosophy or from accepting anything in modern art. Everything he encounters here seems to have the effect of alarming him, even when, as in the case of Whitehead, one would think he ought to find it reassuring. One law for man and another law for thing is the whole of philosophy for More, as the will to refrain is the whole of morals. Outside these—anywhere, that is, except among the brave little band of humanists—he sees only perdition, chaos. It is as if Mr. More, on one of his sides, were capable of meeting on his own ground the great modern philosopher or poet, but as if some other element in his nature—which be tries to foist upon us, too, as the universal law of the "inner check"—had operated to make him shy away from philosophy and poetry themselves, so that, in spite of his vigorous intellect and his genuine sensibility, he is unable to allow himself to profit by any book not written sufficiently long ago to have acquired an academic sanction almost equivalent to a religious one.

A certain passage from Whitehead's *Science and the Modern World* is quoted by Mr. More as follows: "When Darwin or Einstein proclaim[s] theories which modify our ideas, it is a triumph for science." Mr. More is going on to criticize this passage, but in the meantime he has observed that Whitehead has been so indiscreet as to write "proclaim" as a plural verb after two subjects connected by "or," and where any ordinary critic would either have left Whitehead's sentence as he wrote it or have made him a present of the singular ending without calling the reader's attention to it, Mr. More has put it in brackets, as who should comment scornfully "[sic!]." Mr. More may not be able, or may not dare, to imagine, as Whitehead has done, a metaphysical explanation of the relations between the organic and the inorganic worlds, but he can, and, by Heaven, he will, correct this philosopher's grammar!

March 19, 1930

Sophocles, Babbitt and Freud

M R. SEWARD COLLINS has taken me to task in the October number of the *Bookman* for my remarks on Irving Babbitt and Sophocles published in the *New Republic* of March 19, and I see that Mr. Gorham B. Munson also considers me unsound on this point. I had objected to Professor Babbitt's advertising his "law of measure" as one of the authentic "unwritten laws of the gods" to which Antigone appeals in the scene where she defies Creon. It is plain that Professor Babbitt has never, in the name of his law of measure, attempted to induce anyone to defy any written law whatever; but Mr. Collins asserts that he is justified in his allusion to Sophocles' heroine, because Babbitt, like Antigone, is appealing to conscience. They are both vindicating moral principles that are not prescribed by the letter of the law, but that are matters, primarily, of individual insight. He refers me to a passage in *Oedipus Rex*, where the laws of the gods are also invoked. I have looked this passage up, and I find that the divine laws are mentioned here in quite a different connection. The chorus are frightened and worried, because things are looking bad for Oepidus: they are doing the Greek equivalent of crossing themselves, they hope that they may be kept pure in word and deed. If Babbitt wanted a tag from Sophocles, this passage would have been more to his purpose, but the fact is that he always uses *Antigone*. I also found in Jebb's text a note that referred to a passage in Book VII of Plato's *Laws*, and I looked this up, too. There the phrase is much closer to *Antigone* than the phrase in *Oedipus Rex*—ἄγραπτα νόμιμα, Sophocles; ἄγραφα νόμιμα, Plato—but it turned out that the "unwritten laws" in question were not the higher insights of conscience, but the ancient uncodified customs—in connection with education and the care of children—"commonly called unwritten laws." "Unwritten laws," then, was a common phrase used by Antigone for her own particular purpose. If it means to her what it means to Plato, she is referring merely to the traditional custom of sprinkling earth on the bodies of the dead, in which case it has obviously nothing in common with the moral revelations of

Babbitt. And if it is taken as a justification of her own moral revelations, it still seems to me that there is a grotesque discrepancy between Antigone standing up to Creon and Babbitt and Mr. Collins making themselves disagreeable over humanism. It still seems to me that Irving Babbitt is very far from understanding Antigone.

But of course Mr. Collins thinks that it is I who do not understand Antigone. He believes that, by describing her as "passionate" and "fierce," I have made her into "a Greenwich Village heroine." Well, first of all, I hadn't supposed that anybody denied that Antigone was fiery and insubordinate—Jebb certainly doesn't: see his introduction. Mr. Collins says that when I call her "fierce," I have only one word to go upon and that that represents in the text a momentary and erroneous opinion on the part of the troubled chorus; but actually the chorus again and again apply to Antigone such terms as "passionate" and "fierce," and the line that I quoted, "fierce child of a fierce father," indicates—what is otherwise plain from the way in which she behaves—that Sophocles intended Antigone to have inherited certain qualities from Oedipus. I suppose that even the humanists will not dispute that Oedipus was hasty and insolent—his deplorable ὕβρις is an academic cliché. The dramatist, as a matter of fact, represents the whole family of Oedipus, with the single exception of Ismene, as exceedingly bad-tempered and rash (see the brawl between Oedipus and his father, the quarrel between the brothers, and the cursing of his son by Oedipus). Bad-tempered people are Sophocles' specialty; his characters, as I said, resemble in this respect—and I said that they resembled in this respect only—the characters of Eugene O'Neill.

Granted, however, that Antigone is naturally impetuous and wilful, why does she make such an issue of performing the funeral rites for her brother, Polyneices? According to Mr. Collins, her insistence is merely a matter of "family piety and religious duty." Again, I did not know that anyone disputed that Antigone's motive was a special affection for her brother. But this raises an interesting question, which must be my excuse for prolonging this controversy. In the *Antigone* as it stands in the manuscripts, and as Sophocles presumably wrote it, one of the striking features of the heroine's behavior is the fact that, though she is engaged to be married, she never mentions this fact or her fiancé. In her anxiety for her dead brother, no thought of her living lover comes to make her hesitate a moment in her resolve to sacrifice herself. She does not even go to Haemon to complain about the edict, as a woman in love would be sure to do—especially since Haemon is Creon's son and it would have been natural for her to try to get him to intercede with his father. We, in fact, hardly hear about Haemon at all till he comes to intercede on his own account. When Antigone is about to be led away, she laments that she must die unmarried, but only in a general way and still without mentioning Haemon, who a little while before has rushed off in fury and desperation and who will kill himself after a vain effort to save her. She does, however, apostrophize Polyneices: she tells him that what she has done for him she would never have done for a child or a husband—for one can always get another child or husband, whereas a brother is irreplaceable.

This, as I say, is what happens in the *Antigone* as Sophocles presumably wrote it. But Richard Jebb, following certain other scholars, has found this version unintelligible and has proceeded to alter the text in such a way as, from his own point of view, to make Antigone more winning than human. His first intervention occurs in a scene in which Antigone's sister, the gentler and more conventional Ismene, remonstrates with her uncle Creon for robbing his son of a bride. Antigone is standing by, but, as is normal with Sophocles, only two persons speak in the dialogue. Now Jebb, with no textual justification, takes away one of Ismene's lines, in which she exclaims "O beloved Haemon, how thy father wrongs thee!" and assigns it to Antigone, and avoids making the dialogue more complicated still by attributing the next line to the chorus, who are immediately to take up the theme. Thus Antigone is given, as he says, a "solitary reference to her love" which "heightens in a wonderful degree our sense of her unselfish devotion to a sacred duty." Jebb's only attempt to make this tampering acceptable by adducing internal evidence consists of a single objection on the basis of a phrase in the line that follows, an objection that he himself invalidates by quoting from Sophocles' *Electra* an example of a similar phrase used precisely in the sense that he wants to discredit. And when he comes to the sixteen-line passage about dying for a brother rather than a husband, he rejects it altogether as spurious, in spite of the fact that Aristotle had it and that Jebb himself is forced to confess that he can hardly discover a shadow of a linguistic reason against it. The principal argument is that certain of these lines have a close resemblance to a passage in Herodotus; but may this not be merely a case of a common ancient saying which both Herodotus and Sophocles had heard and which Sophocles makes his heroine press into service naïvely to explain and defend her behavior, just as he makes her resort to the phrase about the "unwritten laws of the gods"? I am told by an English friend of a similar saying in England, which he heard as a child from his nurse, about the unique value of brothers as compared with lovers. Jebb, however, finds the scene incomprehensible, and he is able to invoke the authority of Goethe, who told Eckermann that this speech of Antigone's vitiated the whole play by assigning to the heroine an "unworthy" motive after she had "given the most admirable reasons for her conduct" and "shown the noble courage of a stainless soul." But this objection had never occurred to Aristotle, and can we suppose that it would have occurred to Goethe if he had lived late enough to have read Freud?

For it is not, I believe, due entirely to the accident of Sophocles' having written a play involving an incestuous relation that the Oedipus complex has been named after his hero. Mr. Collins has reproached me for showing myself "about as near to the true spirit of Sophocles as an Oedipus complex"; but if he will read the passage in *Oedipus Rex* in which Jocasta tries to reassure her son-husband by telling him that men often dream of sexual relations with their mothers, he will see that there is more in common between Sophocles and Freud than he supposes. And it seems to me plain that, in Antigone, the poet was consciously presenting a case of what we should call nowadays a brother-fixation. Sophocles did not call it that, and he did not consider it from our clinical point of view; but his comprehension of human motives was profound and realistic,

and it seems to me impossible not to conclude that he emphasized deliberately for his dramatic purpose the difference
between Antigone's attitude toward Haemon and her attitude
toward Polyneices.

When we compare Antigone with Electra, our suspicions are
further confirmed. Antigone and Electra are in certain ways
very different: Electra is ingrown and virulent whereas Antigone is candid and appealing. But they are in other ways
much alike: both are self-willed and ruthless, and both are
contrasted with weaker, more "feminine" sisters: Electra's
scenes with Chrysothemis are obvious counterparts to Antigone's scenes with Ismene. Jebb himself notes the closeness
of this parallel. Furthermore, both Electra and Antigone are
passionately attached to brothers. The first things that we learn
about Electra are that she bitterly hates her mother and broods
continually on the wrong done her father; she is morbid, vitu-
perative, harsh: we tend at first to find her unsympathetic. It is
only when she is told that her brother is dead and given the
urn that is supposed to contain his ashes that we really come to
understand her. She breaks down over the urn, and it is revealed to us for the first time how much tenderness, affection,
devotion has for years been subdued and perverted by a life
vowed entirely to vengeance. It has been only the memory of
Orestes, her brother whom she has nursed as a child, as dear to
her as to his mother, whom she had not allowed to be cared
for by the servants and who had called her alone among his sisters "Sister"—it has been only the memory of Orestes and the
hope of his eventual return that have kept her alive in the
hated household (Euripides' Electra is married, but Sophocles'
is not). Now Orestes appears and reveals himself—the brother
and sister are reunited for the first time in ten years: the
avengers drop their masks, and the most moving scene in the
tragedy occurs. Then Orestes, with the connivance of Electra,
goes in and kills Clytaemnestra.

Now, Seward Collins asserts that Antigone "is impelled primarily by religious conviction" and accuses me of being incapable of admitting that "the heroine of a Greek drama might
have acted from noble motives." But Electra also, for that
matter, is acting with a religious sanction. Has not Apollo

himself told Orestes to kill his mother? And how do the humanists stand in regard to the nobility of matricide and in regard to all the other outrageous things for which the characters in Greek tragedies claim a divine sanction? The chorus in *Electra* too, invokes the unwritten laws, in connection with her duty to her murdered father—and how can you get any humanism out of *Electra*? The moral philosophy that the humanists profess to derive from Sophocles seems to me pure boloney. Sophocles is essentially a dramatist, a presenter of character in conflict. If he happened to be a modern, a single blast of the black bitter pessimism of the choruses of *Oedipus Colonus* would have been enough to scare them off this poet for life. And his Freudian situations would have caused them to shudder with horror.

Apropos of these latter, has nobody ever written about the Freudian aspect of Antigone, in connection with this controverted passage? If the scholars have not yet done so, the analysts surely must have.

December 3, 1930

This article attracted the attention of Professor Walter R. Agard of the University of Wisconsin, who had been working on the problem of the controverted lines in the *Antigone*, and he later sent me a paper on the subject—*Antigone 904–20*, in the issue of *Classical Philology* of July, 1937—which defends the authenticity of this passage, analyzing the motives of Antigone and corroborating my view of her character:

"This rationalization [of her concern for her brother]," Mr. Agard writes, "admittedly unconvincing to any sober-minded person, is in keeping with the character of Antigone. She is not sober-minded. Not only in this play and in the *Oedipus at Colonus* of Sophocles, but also in the *Seven against Thebes* of Aeschylus and Euripides' *Phoenician Women*, Antigone is pictured as an emotionally high-strung girl, devoted above all else to her ill-fated father and brothers, with whom she closely identifies herself. Feeling rather than reason controls her actions, as the Chorus is frank in saying (383, 'captured in folly'; 471–72, 'passionate child of a passionate father, she does not know how to yield to misfortune'). Toward Polyneices this feeling is directed with special intensity. It is obviously more than religious duty that impels her to bury his body. She loves him passionately (Antigone 48, 'my own'; 73, 'I shall lie in death beloved, with him, my dear one'; 81, 'my dearest brother'; 503, 'my own brother')."

But it is probably unnecessary at this late date to insist that Antigone was not a humanist.

"H. C."*

ONE'S first encounters with Herbert Croly were likely to be rather baffling. It was never very easy for him to deal with people, and if the visitor himself were at all diffident, he would be likely to find the conversation petering out in a discontinuous series of remarks offered more and more haltingly by the visitor, to which Croly would mutter responses more and more fragmentary and more and more imperfectly audible. Eventually the visitor would lose heart and stop, and a terrible silence would fall: the atmosphere would become taut with panic. Croly would sit absolutely motionless, his eyes dropped on his hands, which would be clasped in his lap; his face was rather sallow, and to the visitor appeared hostile or morose. As the silence went on longer and longer and became more and more unbearable, the visitor would finally be driven to break it at any price by some absurd or irrelevant opening, to which Croly would be likely to return some equally wild reply; and the visitor, uncomfortable and puzzled, would conclude that the interview was over and that, brief and inconclusive though it might have been, he had already stayed too long. He would awkwardly take his leave and go away more mystified than ever as to the personality of the editor of the *New Republic*, who seemed to play so important a role in American political journalism without one's ever having been able to discover precisely what sort of man he was.

But on some other occasion, if one continued to see him, a contact would eventually be made. Something said would reach below the level on which ordinary conversation is conducted —a level at which it was almost impossible for Croly to carry on conversation at all—and he would respond with an earnestness which, with a minimum of emphasis, carried a maximum of conviction. He would lift his gaze and meet you directly: his eyes were clear, firm and green, and his look was one of the straightest I have ever known. One felt that one had looked

*This was written for an issue of the *New Republic* devoted to memoirs and appreciations of its late editor-in-chief, Herbert Croly, who had died on May 17, 1930.

into the eyes of an absolutely candid and honest person—that the public affairs of which one had been talking were things that mattered to Croly as deeply as our private affairs do to the rest of us. When he stood up, one became aware that his figure —he was an excellent tennis-player—was slender and erect. And as one had been surprised by the clear straight green gaze from those dim and meditative, those brooding eyes, so when thereafter one read his editorials, one had the sense of, behind their anonymity and their sometimes forbidding style, the absolute sincerity and seriousness which made him in the intellectual life of his time a figure so much more important and so much more interesting than many more brilliant writers and more picturesque personalities, even when they had succeeded in learning what Croly had to teach and had expressed it more strikingly than he could. Political journalism is, after all, even among radicals and liberals, much of the time merely a job like another, and may as easily become a matter of routine as a job of any other kind. But this it never became for Croly: a distant war, a scoundrel returned to office, which for most of us would be merely a subject for a disapproving editorial, would be for Croly events which touched his life, which, when he spoke of them, obviously gave him pain.

But one might be aware of all this and yet at first have no idea of the sensitivity, the intelligence and the intensity which his constraint so often masked. If he seemed impassive—and he sometimes impressed people as being as impassive as a Chinaman—it was not because he remained impervious to the things that went on around him, but because he felt them too much. He was, for example, extraordinarily perceptive of people's personal qualities and behavior, and he could see at once what most people were up to. This was one of the principal reasons for his value as a political critic: he was usually able with remarkable accuracy to calculate what sort of abilities any figure in public life would develop and how he would be likely to act. He was sometimes accused of serious mistakes, in politics as well as in journalism, in attributing his own integrity, his own liberal idealism, to persons who had nothing in common with him; but in cases of this sort, I usually felt that Croly had not so much been blind to the dubious aspects of the man in question as merely giving him the benefit of the doubt. He had, also, though he was sometimes criticized for a lack of aesthetic appreciation and though he believed himself deaf to music and incapable of enjoying poetry, something certainly of the sensibility that goes to make the artist. His imagination was easily touched, and he responded to atmospheres and scenes as readily as anyone I have ever known. I have heard him describe a Mexican landscape—the combination of dryness and vibrancy in the light and air of the high plateau and the strange exhilaration which had thrilled him with an unexpected sense of renewal and revelation—with the subtlety and the precision of one of those French novelists who specialize in *paysages*. And you would finally understand—what you might never, when you first knew him, have suspected—that he was one of those rare persons whom we prize because we can touch them at any time, in any mood, on any subject, and be sure of an instant and true response. The contrast between his real accessibility, his real range of intelligence and feeling, and his apparent lack of warmth, was one of the curious paradoxes of his character. If one had assumed, as one was likely to do, that he was inarticulate and indirect, he surprised one by openness and frankness; if one had supposed that he was withdrawn and introspective, he shocked one by clairvoyance and realism; and for all his inhibiting shyness, his almost excessive sensitiveness in both his public and his private relations, he could if necessary, be formidable and final.*

A similar contrast appeared in his writing. He once rather surprised me by telling me that he considered his culture mainly French—for, in spite of his years of study in Paris and his addiction to French political philosophy, it seemed to me at the time that nothing could be less French than his habitual long heavy sentences, than the Latin derivatives and vague abstract phrases, only occasionally relieved by some pungent American colloquialism, which tended to blur his thought. Yet

---

*Jane Addams of Hull House once told me later that she had known Herbert's mother, Jane Croly—who had an active career as a journalist and as one of the original organizers of the American women's clubs—and had sometimes gone to her house. Herbert, then a little boy, would get behind the curtains of the drawing-room and attract the attention of the company by bulging and flapping them about without allowing himself to be seen. She said that she had always thought of this as characteristic of him.

when I came to read him more carefully, I found that a paragraph in this plodding vein would often be picked up at last by some brief, clear and happy sentence which put the whole thing with a certain wit. I saw that it might be true that his mind was in some respects closer to the French than to the Anglo-Saxon, and when he told me that his father had been Irish, I understood whence these qualities had come. He was most sensible to qualities of style in other writers, though, in his editorial capacity, if an article came in which was badly written, he could never suggest how to improve it. Yet clumsiness, pretentiousness, vulgarity, in writing as in everything else, seemed actually to make him suffer. I remember meeting him once between the acts at the first night of Eugene O'Neill's *Welded*—that baldest of O'Neill's poorer plays—and feeling that I had never seen distress so nakedly displayed by a human face. He spoke of O'Neill's dialogue as if it had been a terrible accident that had happened to one of his friends—as indeed it actually was, for Stark Young had directed the production.

But as one came to know Croly better, one learned to pay less attention to these superficial aspects of his personality and to value the spirit they partly veiled: one could put it to oneself more clearly in what precisely consisted his peculiar superiority, his peculiar originality. I came to the conclusion that Croly was not primarily a political philosopher, that he had become an editor and journalist only, as it were, by accident. The last sentence of the last paragraph of his most important book, *The Promise of American Life*, reads as follows: "The common citizen can become something of a saint and something of a hero, not by growing to heroic proportions in his own person, but by the sincere and enthusiastic imitation of heroes and saints, and whether or not he will ever come to such imitation will depend upon the ability of his exceptional fellow-countrymen to offer him acceptable examples of heroism and saintliness." Now, it seems strange that a writer on politics should estimate the promise of American life from its possible capacity for producing saints; yet it was natural for Herbert Croly, because he himself was a kind of saint, and it is not at all difficult to imagine him becoming, in some other period, not a writer on public affairs, but, say, the founder of a religious order. Not that, meeting him in New York, one would have recognized him as a type of ascetic. On one of his sides, he was a man of the world. He loved the city and was never long happy away from it—he loved London and Paris; he liked the theater, liked going to lively places, enjoyed meeting clever people. He not infrequently went in for gay waistcoats, and always carried and smoked his own cigars. And in spite of the fact that considerable trouble had been taken over the lunches at the *New Republic*, the cuisine at last came so to bore him that it was difficult to induce him to eat there except on the two crucial days of the editorial week—though the smile with which he used to confess this had a shade of that sadness which would cloud his spirit at the general failure even of things connected with idealistic causes to live up to a high level of distinction. He had also a strong taste for gambling and was addicted to both poker and bridge, for which his face, with its effect of drawn blinds, must especially have qualified him.

Yet, essentially, he was one of the most unworldly men that I have ever known. It may have been partly due to his parents having been born in Europe and their having been deeply imbued with the ideas of the eighteenth-century Enlightenment in the forms in which it had persisted into the nineteenth century, that, looking out upon the beginning of the American twentieth, it had troubled him to be forced to recognize that our very American democratic ideal of unhampered individual enterprise had resulted, with the rise of industrialism, in a society where the richest men were generally regarded as the most admirable and their money and their ways of getting it as not to be criticized or tampered with, no matter what bankruptcy and degradation this involved for other sections of the population or what corruption and stultification for themselves. It may be, as I say, that this tendency had been partly derived from his parents, both professional British "intellectuals" who had come to the United States (the elder Croly, to whom Herbert dedicated *The Promise of American Life*, had himself written a book called *Glimpses of the Future*). Yet one came to feel that Herbert was the kind of man who in any civilization at any time would have found himself dissatisfied with society. From *The Promise of American Life*, which Theodore Roosevelt had laid under contribution, to the signing of the Treaty of Versailles, he had—for all his skepticism and shrewdness about practical politicians—fixed his hopes on political programs. He had had the *New Republic* back Wilson when he took us into the war, in the expectation that Wilson would justify this by the peace he would be able to make. After the peace conference, the *New Republic* was obliged to disavow the peace treaty; it maintained its sedate and self-confident tone, and continued as a political journal; but for Croly, with his scrupulous nature, his sense of personal responsibility, the outcome of the war was a source of actual anguish and humiliation. During those days, he despaired of politics and really never quite took them seriously again; and from the moment he turned away from politics, he gravitated toward religion. Herbert's parents had been followers of Auguste Comte—he had been the first child in the United States to be christened in the Positivist faith, that dryest, least seductive or inspiring of all the de-supernaturalized sects —and his whole training had been rationalistic. He seemed now to be making an effort to reconcile with this inculcated rationalism some profound mystic feeling that was natural to him.

It was this, I think, that had given him, from the beginning, his peculiar spiritual authority. I never knew Herbert Croly intimately, except in so far as any contact with such a man is more intimate, because it touches us at a deeper level, than many close associations with ordinary people; and I can write only a series of impressions which to those who knew him better may appear misleading. Yet I feel that Croly's personality was of a kind that must present a certain mystery even to those who knew him best. We learn to recognize, as we grow older, the same elements and motives in others with which we have become all too familiar in our experience with ourselves; but in men like Herbert Croly there seems to emerge in a pure and intensified form a virtue that arrests our attention and that is ultimately able to command us because we cannot understand it, cannot analyze it or explain it away. And I believe that Croly's later writings represented an attempt on his own part to explain to his rational intelligence this wellspring of spiritual power. He was attempting to assign it somehow to a God of more vitality and majesty than Comte's Supreme Being, to a more acceptable version of that Deity in whom he had been taught not to believe. To a friend and associate even less a believer than he, it did not seem that he was ever successful. But to such an associate, of a younger generation, and so at a further remove from the God of the ancient faith, it was plain —and especially of late, at a time, during the period of his illness, when one could see him only rarely and briefly—that he was one of those who make it possible for us to maintain that faith in life itself which, in the United States of our day, the brutalized, the comfortable, the timid, the hopeless and pleasure-drugged, the fatigued and machinery-driven, seem pressing on every hand, and within ourselves, to destroy. He was one of those who, quite without dogmatism and though he seemed all his life to be seeking truth in collaboration with others rather than telling people what to think, somehow manage to establish the enduring values which argument in itself is impotent to prove or disprove; and, aside from one's personal affection for him, his death may disturb one, for a time at first, as if it were a blow at those values themselves—as if we found ourselves more at the mercy of the blindness and confusion of life.

July 16, 1930

The Nietzschean Line

NORMAN DOUGLAS has been aroused by *Mother India* to write an attack on Western civilization called *Good-bye to Western Culture: Some Footnotes on East and West* (the English title is *How about Europe?*). His notes on the tyrannies and manias of European as contrasted with Hindu life make an entertaining book; but they represent a line of criticism which is no longer so impressive as it once was.

The oppression of our laws, in the West, says Douglas, is much worse than that of an oriental despot. The latter "is uncertain," (he is here quoting another writer) "and leaves to the oppressed chances and hopes of escaping it; it varies with the individual; and those who suffer, if not benefited, are, at least, consoled by the vengeance that, sooner or later, overtakes the guilty. The tyranny of law is a dead and immovable weight, that compresses at once the activity of the limb and the energy of the mind; leaves no hope of redress, no chance of escape; is liable to no responsibility for its acts or vengeance for its crimes." And in Europe, "an air of pointless preoccupation hangs about like influenza, infecting the sanest and most self-possessed of us. You encounter it in every walk of life and every grade of society: complications and glumness, with feverish streaks in between; in a word, fluster. There is as much grace and dignity in a European existence just now as there is in a fat bourgeoise running after an omnibus. The Americanization of life on this continent may have contributed its share; it has infused a note of impermanence. Gregarious and homeless, fearing solitude as never before, our European is losing his idiosyncrasy. Hustle is his opiate, his refuge from self. . . . Hindus are not afflicted with the fidgets. . . . They do not imagine, like Europeans, that they are driving a machine because they happen to be tangled up in its works." "Why," he finally demands, "does one belong to such a race, so sad and yet so ferocious?"

So far we may heartily agree; but Norman Douglas's farewell to Europe is like Clive Bell's book on "Civilization" and the tirades of H. L. Mencken (both of whom Mr. Douglas invokes). We ask, What then?—and we get no answer. What does Mr. Douglas want to do with Western society? How does he propose to bring it back to those virtues which it has abandoned and which he is still able to admire in the East? Mr. Douglas would reply, I suppose, that he does not propose to do anything: he is content to live in Capri and keep away from it all. He is content to occupy himself with the animals and the birds of the Greek anthology, about which he has written a learned book. So Clive Bell merely wants to be let alone to enjoy beautiful pictures and fine wines; and so Mencken asks for nothing but his Brahms, his beer and his books, and the hilarious spectacle of his neighbors. When we look for a central point of view in Douglas, we find much the same thing that we do in Mencken: a diluted and inconsistent Nietzscheanism (he has a good deal to say about Nietzsche, and his book is dedicated to Oscar Levy, Nietzsche's English translator). Like Mencken, Norman Douglas believes that the illiterate should be left illiterate; that the poor should be left poor; that the socially inferior should be kept in their places. The caste system is one of the things that he most approves of in India; and, like Mencken, he has a good deal to say about the scarcity in Europe of "gentlemen." (Mencken, of course, as an American, thinks that Europe is full of gentlemen, but Norman Douglas, being a European, thinks the gentlemen are all in the East.) For Mr. Douglas, one of the great merits of the caste system seems to be that it unfailingly provides for European gentlemen travelling in the East devoted, efficient and handsome servants.

Here are Douglas's final conclusions as to what is wrong with the Western world: "I become more and more convinced, with increasing years, that the roots of the mischief lie far back, in the Roman point of view. The shoddiness of our ideals—the shoddiness of all our ideals, social and political—is a heritage from those unimaginative Roundheads, with their ingrained vulgarity, their imperialism, their pernicious doctrine of the *raison d'état*, and the welcome they gave, as vulgarians naturally would give, to imported pinchbeck like Christianity." The religious wars and the Spanish Inquisition have "consumed our mental fiber to this day, and blunted our apperception of finer issues"; and Christianity has led to "our cult of those fetid 'masses' whom, in accordance with New Testamentary injunctions, we are now breeding as carefully as if they were Pekingese spaniels, and who, in return, have imposed on us by law their own fatuous and degrading aspirations." The pernicious political results of Rome are, first, that "that tiresome standardizing mania of theirs [has] destroyed the more delicate tissues in the national character of people subject—however superior intellectually—to themselves"; and second, that "the state idolatry of the Romans, their toga tomfoolery, has converted European races into a pack of mongrels snarling at each other."

It will be seen that the vein is a familiar one. Norman Douglas, who writes so clearly, does not think any more clearly than any other dilettante of epicurean tastes who desires to figure as a champion of all the moral and aesthetic values without being willing to deal with the problem of how these values are created or lost. The passages I have quoted are full of such words and phrases as "shoddiness," "ingrained vulgarity," "vulgarians," "pinchbeck," "coarsened our mental fiber," "our apperception of finer issues," "those fetid 'masses'," "destroyed the more delicate tissues,"—phrases which are calculated to convince us of Norman Douglas's "ingrained" refinement and to establish between him and us—Mencken and Clive Bell do the same thing—a genial understanding that he and we belong to a rare superior order of beings; that we are, in fact, "aristocratic," and that the other people don't matter. The way in which writers of this kind persuade us to accept their opinions is precisely similar to the methods by which "quality" advertising is conducted—by which a picture, for example, of a smart-looking woman eating paté de foie gras and a smart-looking man with a monocle, with some smartly printed text about "these charming people" who are "always so casually yet successfully pioneering in the realm of enjoyment," is used as a bait to make people spend their money on "menthol-cooled cigarettes." If the reader can be induced to imagine himself one of these charming people, he may not even know whether or not he enjoys cigarettes that are flavored with menthol, just as the reader of Norman Douglas may fail to notice that vulgarity and delicacy, fetidness and refinement, are treated as if they were God-given qualities, independent of other factors—as if they had no relation to questions of money and education. But what makes people "vulgar" or "fine?" And in a civilization like our present one—the creation of a single class, the middle class, of that eighteenth-century society whose passing Mr. Douglas laments, in the course of the exploitation of a single human aptitude, mechanical invention, for the purpose of getting rich—in a civilization like our own, how can you tell whether they are fine or not? From the island of Capri, it may not be possible to see them very clearly; and from the point of view of one engrossed in the birds and the beasts of the Greek anthology, it may not be easy to appreciate the peculiar sort of refinement—refinement in the various mechanical and scientific techniques—that our industrial society has certainly achieved.

The Nietzschean of Norman Douglas's type is moreover always trying to have it both ways: he always attempts to combine a ruthless and contemptuous attitude toward those aspects of ordinary humanity that happen to be distasteful to him with a sympathetic and even sentimental one toward those aspects that happen to appeal to him. Mr. Douglas, for example, is all against our cult of "those fetid 'masses' whom," in accordance with New Testamentary injunctions, he alleges we are now "breeding as carefully as if they were Pekingese spaniels." Very well: should he not, as a Nietzschean, be willing to let them die? Yet in an earlier part of the book, he made a point of wringing our hearts with an account of the wretched children in English and French reformatories. These children do not, as a rule, belong to Mr. Douglas's class: they belong to "those fetid 'masses'." So why should Mr. Douglas worry about them? If it is true that the "filthy and damp walls exude misery and vice," this is a condition appropriate to the fetid. If it is true that young girls are put in straitjackets and made to lap up their food from the floor, a punishment from which they sometimes suffocate—this certainly does not err in the direction of breeding them like Pekingese. Why on earth should Mr. Douglas care whether the reformatories are cleaned up or not? If it is true, as he says, that there are six thousand French convicts "rotting in French Guiana" and that "the whole [penal] system is riddled with cruelties and abuses and absurdities," what should that matter to a resolute Nietzschean, who elsewhere refers to the unemployed as "scum" and objects to paying taxes for poor relief?

The few constructive suggestions that are offered by Mr. Douglas, with a great air of realism and common sense, appear to me more or less frivolous. "In England we build 165,000 new houses every year, and yet, in London alone, there are said to be 130,000 persons living in insanitary dens. An ex-Mayor of Manchester has lately written a book on *How to Abolish the Slums*. I have not read it, but can suggest a solution of the problem that would cost not a half-penny: stop this breeding. And the point to notice is this, that the breeding would stop automatically were it not officially encouraged." What makes Mr. Douglas so sure of this? "They manage these things better, out East," he declares. You think that he is going on to tell us that in India they exterminate the poor; but it turns out that he is thinking of the fact that the East is full of beggars and that begging is there a recognized profession. But how can you make English working people beg even when they are out of work? And do they deserve, for their reluctance to do so, to be described by Mr. Douglas as "dregs," inferior to the beggars of the East?

In spite of Mr. Douglas's denunciations of the meddlesomeness and absurdity of law-making, it is curious to note that, the moment it is a question of anything that he himself has an interest in seeing done or not done, he is as prompt to appeal to legislation as any other modern European. He protests against some English by-law which makes it necessary to get a license for a dog-kennel, but later on he becomes equally indignant over the lax enforcement of another by-law which makes "the fouling of footways by dogs" an offense liable to a fine. Only eight people, it seems, have so far been convicted. "When eighty thousand have been fined," says Douglas, "that downcast look of the cockney will begin to disappear." This is a matter about which he feels strongly, so call in the police by all means.

I have considerable respect for Norman Douglas. His career has been an honorably independent one. He has lived in a variety of countries and is not easily intimidated by the conventions of his own place and time. But the kind of social criticism represented by *Good-bye to Western Culture*—and, as I say, we have had a good deal of it—seems to me essentially trivial.

October 22, 1930

The Literary Consequences of the Crash

A CHANGE of tone and of point of view will be noted in my articles of the early thirties.

Even before the stock market crash of October, 1929, a kind of nervous dissatisfaction and apprehension had begun to manifest itself in American intellectual life. The liberating movement of the twenties had by that time accomplished its work of discrediting the gentility and Puritanism of the later nineteenth century; the orgy of spending of the Boom was becoming more and more grotesque, and the Jazz Age was ending in hysteria. The principal points of view of this period I tried, after the crash, to sum up in an article of March 23, 1932:

The attitudes of the decade that followed the war, before the depression set in, already seem a long way off:

The attitude of the Menckenian gentleman, ironic, beer-loving and "civilized," living principally on the satisfaction of feeling superior to the broker and enjoying the debauchment of American life as a burlesque show or three-ring circus; the attitude of old-American-stock smugness, with its drawing aloof from the rabble in the name of old Uncle Gilead Pilcher who was Governor of Connecticut or Grandfather Timothy Merrymount who was killed in the Civil War—though the par-venus kept crashing the gate so fast, while the prosperity boom was on, that it was becoming harder and harder to get one's aloofness properly recognized; the liberal attitude that American capitalism was going to show a new wonder to the world by gradually and comfortably socializing itself and that we should just have to respect it in the meantime, taking a great interest in Dwight W. Morrow and Owen D. Young; the attitude of trying to get a kick out of the sheer size and energy of American enterprises, irrespective of what they were aiming at; the attitude of proudly withdrawing and cultivating a refined sensibility or of losing oneself completely in abstruse intellectual pursuits—scholastic philosophy, symbolic logic or metaphysical physics; the attitude of letting oneself be carried along by the mad hilarity and heartbreak of jazz, living only for the excitement of the evening; the attitude of keeping one's mind and morals impregnably disinfected with the feeble fascism-classicism of humanism.

I have in one mood or another myself felt some sympathy with all of these different attitudes—with the single exception of humanism; and they have all, no doubt, had their validity for certain people, for special situations. Yet today they all look rather queer: they are no use in our present predicament, and we can see how superficial they were. We can see now that they all represented attempts on the part of the more thoughtful Americans to reconcile themselves to a world dominated by salesmen and brokers—and that they all involved compromises with the salesman and the broker. Mencken and Nathan laughed at the broker, but they justified the system which produced him and they got along with him very well, provided he enjoyed George Moore and had pretensions to a taste in liquor; the jazz-age romantics spent the broker's money as speedily and wildly as possible and tried to laugh off the office and the factory with boyish and girlish jokes; the old-American-stockers sniffed at him, but though they salved their consciences thus, they were usually glad to get in on any of his good things that were going; the liberals, who had been vaguely unhappy, later became vaguely resigned and could never bring themselves to the point of serious quarrelling with him; the poets and philosophers hid from him—and the physicists grew more and more mystical in the laboratories subsidized mainly by the profits from industrial investments; the humanists, in volume after volume, endeavored by sheer hollow thunder to induce people to find in the stock exchange the harmony and dignity of the Parthenon.

I did not include in this catalogue a cult that was spreading in New York and that had converts in and around the *New Republic*: that of the Russo-Greek charlatan Gurdjieff, who undertook to renovate the personalities of discontented well-to-do persons. He combined making his clients uncomfortable in various gratuitous ways—such as waking them up in the middle of the night and training them to perform grotesque dances—with reducing them to a condition of complete docility, in which they would hold, at a signal, any position, however

awkward, that they happened to be in at the moment. They
were promised, if they proved themselves worthy of it, an ultimate initiation into the mysteries of an esoteric doctrine.
Gurdjieff's apostle in the United States was the English ex-
journalist A. R. Orage, a funereal and to me a distasteful person, who drilled his pupils, not in dancing, but in a kind of
dialectic and who acquired at one time a considerable influence over the mind of Herbert Croly, whose inhibited personality and unsatisfied religious instincts laid him open to the
lures of a cult that pretended to liberate the mind and to put
one in touch with some higher power. But Croly was a fastidious man, and in the long run he found Orage grating. I was
myself the object of several attempts to recruit me to the Orage group, but the only interchange of influence that took
place between Orage and me consisted of my once persuading
him to go to the National Winter Garden (described under
Burlesque Shows above); when I next saw him, he told me with
a severity that suggested a sense of outrage that he had not enjoyed it at all. Gurdjieff, however, whom I never met, had apparently a rogue's sense of humor. A young man in the office,
a bishop's son who had lost his faith and was groping for
something to take its place, told me of the banquets of roast
sheep or goat, served in great pots in the Caucasian style and
eaten with the fingers, to which Gurdjieff would invite his disciples and at which he would have read aloud to them a book
he had written called *A Criticism of the Life of Man: Beëlzebub's
Tale to His Grandson.* "It sounds as if it had been written," said
this neophyte, "just on purpose to bore you to death. Everybody listens in silence, but every now and then Gurdjieff will
suddenly burst out laughing—just roaring—nobody knows
about what."

I did not read *Beëlzebub's Tale*, but I did read *Das Kapital*.
Not that I want to compare the two works, but there *was* a
certain similarity in the way in which people then approached
them; and I was surprised to find that an apparently social
evening that would turn out to be a conspiracy to involve one
in some Communist organization resembled a dinner I had
once attended at which I was chilled to discover that the
springes of Orage had been laid for me—and these both recalled to me an earlier occasion on which a literary conversa-

tion, in the rooms of the proselytizing rector of the Episcopal Church at Princeton, had been prodded by amusing remarks in the direction of the Christian faith. People did want faiths and churches badly, and though I am good at resisting churches, I caught a wave from the impulsion of the Marxist faith.

The stock market crash was to count for us almost like a rending of the earth in preparation for the Day of Judgment. In my articles of the months just before it, I had often urged writers to acquaint themselves with "the realities of our contemporary life," to apply themselves to "the study of contemporary reality," etc. I myself had not exercised enough insight to realize that American "prosperity" was an inflation that was due to burst. I had, however, become aware that we liberals of the *New Republic* were not taking certain recent happenings so seriously as we should. The execution of Sacco and Vanzetti in August, 1927, had made liberals lose their bearings. During the months while the case was working up to its climax, Herbert Croly had been away in Honolulu attending a conference called by the Institute of Pacific Relations. When he returned, I was surprised to learn that he did not entirely approve of the way in which we had handled the case. Croly's method of commenting on current events was impersonal and very abstract; and, in his absence, we had given way to the impulse to print certain articles which were certainly, for the *New Republic*, unusually concrete and militant. I first became aware of a serious divergence between my own point of view and Croly's when I was talking with him one day about a leader called *A Nation of Foreigners* that I wrote for the paper in October. He did approve of this editorial, but for reasons that put me in a false position. My article had dealt with the futility of attempting to identify "Americanism" with the interests and ideas of the Anglo-Saxon element in the United States, pointing out that, in this case, the Irish, who had been snubbed by the Anglo-Saxon Bostonians, had combined with them in the most wolfish way to persecute the immigrant Italians; and I discovered that Croly was pleased at my treating the subject from this angle rather than from that of class animosities. This class aspect he wanted to deny; it was one of the assumptions of his political thinking—I had not then read *The Promise of American*

Life—that the class struggle should not, and in its true form did not, occur in the United States.

I had been running the literary department, and this was my first excursion on the political side of the paper, which Croly had kept strictly in line with his own very definite ideas. Sometime in the later months of 1928, he had the first of several strokes, and was never able again to perform his full functions as editor-in-chief. When he died in May, 1930, the paper was carried on by the editors as a group, with no one in Croly's position, and we had—rather difficult with men of conflicting opinions and temperaments, with nobody to make final decisions—to work out a policy of our own. I had been troubled by another incident that took place in the autumn of 1929. The bitter and violent Gastonia strike of the textile workers in North Carolina had been going on ever since spring. It was the first major labor battle conducted by a Communist union. Sixteen union members, including three women, were being tried for the murder of a chief of police, who had invaded without a warrant the tent-colony in which the strikers had been living; and the death penalty was being asked for all of them except the women. Feeling on both sides had been roused to the point of ferocity—we were not then familiar with the Communists' habit of manufacturing martyrs—and, after the execution of Sacco and Vanzetti, one was apprehensive of another judicial lynching. John Dos Passos and Mary Heaton Vorse both asked the *New Republic* to send them to report on Gastonia, but both were thought to be too far to the Left to be reliable from our point of view. "The liberals," Dos Passos said to me, "are all so neurotic about Communists!" This was perfectly true; and the pressure on us to do something about Gastonia had at the time almost no effect. The young man who had been hooked by Orage—who had had no experience of labor disputes—was going down to a fashionable wedding at Asheville, not far from Gastonia, and he was asked to drop in at the seat of trouble. When he came back, this young man reported that there was nothing of interest going on. I do not know whom he could have talked to. He had been in Gastonia on the very day, September 14, when the hostilities were coming to a climax. In an attempt to prevent a union meeting, an armed mob had fired on unarmed strikers and had killed a woman named Ella May Wiggins, a widow with five children, who had written songs for the strikers and was extremely popular among them. Her death gave the Communists a battle-cry and the strikers an unforgettable grievance. It was obvious that the *New Republic*, which was supposed to cover labor sympathetically, was falling down on this part of its program.

The next month the slump began, and, as conditions grew worse and worse and President Hoover, unable to grasp what had happened, made no effort to deal with the breakdown, a darkness seemed to descend. Yet, to the writers and artists of my generation who had grown up in the Big Business era and had always resented its barbarism, its crowding-out of everything they cared about, these years were not depressing but stimulating. One couldn't help being exhilarated at the sudden unexpected collapse of that stupid gigantic fraud. It gave us a new sense of freedom; and it gave us a new sense of power to find ourselves still carrying on while the bankers, for a change, were taking a beating. With a businessman's president in the White House, who kept telling us, when he told us anything, that the system was perfectly sound, who sent General Douglas MacArthur to burn the camp of the unemployed war veterans who had come to appeal to Washington, we wondered about the survival of republican American institutions; and we became more and more impressed by the achievements of the Soviet Union, which could boast that its industrial and financial problems were carefully studied by the government, and that it was able to avert such crises. We overdid both these tendencies; but the slump was like a flood or an earthquake, and it was long before many things righted themselves.

*The Economic Interpretation of Wilder**

PERHAPS no other literary article published in the *New Republic* has ever aroused so much controversy as Michael Gold's on Thornton Wilder in the issue of October 22. We have received, and are still receiving, dozens of letters about it, and most of these letters are earnest protests.

Now, this magazine has, of course, no prejudice against Thornton Wilder—his books have been often enough praised in its pages to invalidate this charge. But, on the other hand, it considers Michael Gold also an important writer whose critical opinions have a special interest, since he is one of the only American critics of any literary ability who writes about books from the Marxist point of view. Most of our critics, like most other Americans, have no central point of view—they are in the habit of merely sampling different kinds of books and writing down the various thoughts that come into their heads. Does not the very outcry which Mr. Gold has provoked show up the insipidity and pointlessness of most of our criticism?

For the harsh and scurrilous things that Mr. Gold says about Mr. Wilder can hardly account in themselves for the disturbance his review has created. Criticisms equally scurrilous have been printed about other writers: witness Hemingway's satire on Sherwood Anderson in his burlesque novel *The Torrents of Spring* or the amenities of the humanist controversy. Yet, so far as we know, no article, review or editorial on a literary subject has ever recently aroused such an uproar as Gold's economic analysis of Wilder; and it seems to us, in spite of the possible objections which might be made to the manner of Mr. Gold's essay, that he has raised a fundamental issue and that there is a good deal to be said on his side.

First, however, for what is to be said against it. The Marxist critic of the type of Michael Gold must assume that the character of the literature produced during any period is determined by the economic position of the class for whom it is written. That economic and social factors do play a much larger

*This appeared in the *New Republic* as an unsigned editorial.

part in molding people's ideals, and consequently in coloring their literature, than most people are willing to admit, we are perfectly ready to agree. Yet there are groups which cut through the social classes, and these tend to have an independent existence. The writers make a group of their own; the painters make a group of their own; the scientists make a group. And each of these groups has its own tradition, its own craft and body of doctrine which has been brought down to the present by practitioners that have come from a variety of classes through a variety of different societies. In dealing with a work of literature, we must consider it not only from the point of view of its significance in the social system, but also from the point of view of its craft. A Communist critic who, in reviewing a book, ignores the author's status as a craftsman is really, for purposes of propaganda, denying the dignity of human work.

A typical example of this is to be found in Upton Sinclair's *Mammonart*: in this book, he appraises the literature of the world with the social-economic touchstone, but then goes on to glorify without reserve the physicists in the California laboratories. Yet if the people exploring the atom should be regarded as disinterested intellectuals, why may not the poets be? And if the works of the poets are influenced by feudal patrons and bourgeois audiences, why may not the discoveries of the physicists be conditioned—as they probably are—by the outlook of the capitalist society which has supplied them with the money for their laboratories? Has not the artist as good a chance as the scientist of living up to an impersonal ideal! Mr. Sinclair and Mr. Gold ought to think about this. The author of *Jews Without Money*, especially, ought to recognize and confess how much he has in common with the author of *The Bridge of San Luis Rey*—sensitiveness to human contacts, a love of picturesque detail, a gift for molding firm prose into short comprehensive units, and even a touch of sentimentality.

Not, however, that the author or scientist—except, rarely, at some extreme limit—can ever be *completely* disinterested, can ever detach his mind from the social community, the organism, to which his body belongs, to function as if in a vacuum. The various guilds of the arts and sciences do *tend* to become independent, but they never can quite succeed; and it is true that a social situation is implied in every product of human

thought, no matter how remote from society its propositions
or images may be or how impersonal the technique that presents them. Now, the furious protest raised by Michael Gold's
attack on Wilder suggests that there is somewhat more point
to the Marxist objection to that writer than one had before
suspected. It has already been pointed out in these pages that
Thornton Wilder owes a good deal to Proust—in fact, without
being aware of it and though he is a writer of real originality,
he has in a sense been a popularizer of Proust. He has tapped
the main of Proust's rich, luxurious, intoxicating sentimentality and brought a pipe-line to every American home. For Proust
is surely the writer who, more even than any of the romantics, has made heartbreak a protracted pleasure: the romantics'
hearts broke against desolate backgrounds but Proust's heart
breaks at the Ritz. Now, Wilder in *The Cabala* is also at the
Ritz, and he sticks, in his subsequent books, to a decorative
Parisian antiquity that amounts to the same thing. The malaise,
the frustration, the misery, with which he and Proust both deal
are the illnesses of the cultivated people in a capitalistic society,
which neither the luxuries of the Ritz nor the up-to-date fragments of the past—which Anatole France was always collecting
—to be found in the fascinating antique shops and galleries
can do more than deaden a little. The pathos in Proust, after
all, is merely the more presentable side of the impotence, the
creeping corruption, the lack of the will to live. And so in
Wilder the pathos and the beauty derived from exotic lands of
the imagination may be, as Michael Gold suggests, a sedative
for sick Americans. The sedative and the demand for it are
both products of the same situation: a people disposed to idealism, but deprived of their original ideals and now making
themselves neurotic in the attempt to introduce idealism into
the occupations—organizing, financing, manufacturing, advertising, salesmanship—of a precarious economic system the
condition for whose success is that they must profit by swin-
dling their customers and cutting one another's throats.

November 26, 1930

Schnitzler and Philip Barry

A FRAIL, sensitive and lovely woman in a Middle Western town is married to a good and dull young man, who breeds horses and loves college reunions, but who cannot give her a child. There arrives in town on a lecture tour a brilliant psychologist: he stays with them and makes love to the wife. Then he goes, and the woman has a child by him without the husband's suspecting that it is not his own. But the mother unintentionally antagonizes the boy against his supposed father, who, in spite of the child's fear of horses, insists upon making him ride. The boy has a bad fall and sinks into a neurotic stupor, from which it is impossible to rouse him. At this moment the voice of the lover is heard on the radio lecturing in Chicago. The mother flies to the phone and summons him, and the doctor, alone in the room with the child, finds a lever to lift the psychological obstruction and bring him back to normal consciousness. The doctor's first impulse is to put an end to the whole distressing situation by taking both the child and his mother away; but the situation has gone on too long— the blow would be too hard for the husband. And, besides, the psychologist is a congenital bachelor; he has been dependent for years on the support of an adoring assistant, who jealously looks after him and keeps him out of trouble. He takes his leave again. The doctor is a man of genius, who is able to illuminate the woman's life, give her a gifted child and, by exercising his professional art, liberate the child's mind, but he is also a relentless egoist, absorbed in his own career as an inspired scientific spellbinder and with the weaknesses of such a man. He could never take, as the husband does, the lifelong responsibility for either the child or the mother—he can only come and go; and it is the husband who, in the end, has the care of both woman and child, while the psychologist must return to his eternally maladjusted life, leaving the woman as much as ever in love with him. "Not changed. Complete!" she exclaims about him almost joyfully, as she watches him from the window.

If this is the story that Mr. Philip Barry means to tell in his new play *Tomorrow and Tomorrow*—and I am not quite sure that it is, so uncertain is Mr. Barry's touch—he has, I think, started out with a promising theme, out of which a first-rate comedy might have been made. The best parts of *Tomorrow and Tomorrow* are, in fact, very good comedy—for example, the relations between the silver-tongued doctor and his devoted but hard-boiled secretary. This secretary, Gillespie, played perfectly by Osgood Perkins, is the only person in the play through whom Mr. Barry allows himself to exercise his skill at the American humorous "line." The psychologist and his secretary have just been making the inevitable social rounds in the university town.

"HAY. Bring a chair, Gillespie.

"GILLESPIE. Not me. I ate Mrs. William A. Plant's chicken salad and drank her cocoa.

"HAY. I was wiser.

"EVE. I think you behaved beautifully, both of you.

"GILLESPIE. Why's she called 'Mrs. William A. Plant'? Is there another Mrs. Plant? A William H.? Or Willy K.—?

"EVE. Not that I know of.

"GILLESPIE (*thoughtfully*).—And still always Mrs. William A. Plant. H'm.—Oh, well, why not?

"*He goes out again into the library, with the books, sweater, hat and brief-case.*"

The best scene in the play, it seems to me, is that in which the psychologist says good-by for the last time: he pulls out his watch to see how near it is to train time and finds that the crystal has come out again. It has been coming out for years, he says—he is always hoping that it will break so that he can get a new crystal, but all it does is come out. Why? asks Eve. Because it doesn't fit. She asks him for the first time how he lives and, speaking for the first time matter-of-factly, he tells her that he lives in hotels, that he works almost all day and that he doesn't sleep at night. Then he and Gillespie catch the train.

The greater part of *Tomorrow and Tomorrow* is, however, unfortunately, not like this. Mr. Barry has here set out to do a bang-up serious play, and he is acutely conscious of the fact. He has aimed at austerity and brevity, and the effect is extremely unnatural. For example, it is not very long after Gillespie has gone out of the room and left Eve and the doctor together in the scene from which I have quoted above that Eve remarks to the doctor: "I have been at such pains about this little supper." This might be a bad translation of Ibsen or Strindberg—some of Eugene O'Neill sounds like this, too, and it may be by way of O'Neill that Philip Barry has caught this way of talking; but it is not what an American woman like Eve would be likely to say about a little supper. Most of the dialogue is in this vein. Even admitting that Doctor Hay is supposed to have an element of ham, the scenes between him and Eve—finely played though they are by Herbert Marshall and Zita Johann—are romantic in a banal way that makes it impossible to take them seriously at the same time that none of the lines is ever clearly underlined as comic: "HAY. It [the wine] tastes of sun and rain and earth. EVE. Good things to taste of."—"Is the laurel in bloom, Eve." etc.

It is curious to see Arthur Schnitzler's *The Affairs of Anatol* after *Tomorrow and Tomorrow*. The Austrian is always perfectly sure of the effect he will produce with his characters: he knows how to make them ridiculous and sympathetic at the same time, and the one sentimental scene is sentimental to just the right degree, so that it does not jar with the rest. One speculates as to what Schnitzler might have done with Eve and Dr. Hay; one can imagine how he would have made us laugh at the lecturer's easy poetry and his weakness and at Eve's naïveté without losing either the romance of their meetings or the pathos of their farewells. Yet the trouble is not simply that Philip Barry is an inferior dramatist to Schnitzler: Schnitzler himself is, after all, no giant; but he does have the considerable advantage of a sounder culture behind him. It is precisely in this department of high comedy deriving from character—or lightly handled tragedy—that the Americans show up worst. The case of Philip Barry is strikingly like that of Clyde Fitch: Clyde Fitch's straight comedy was excellent—original and authentically American; but as soon as he set out to be serious, he was stilted, commonplace, insupportable. He suffered evidently from a deep-seated assumption that being serious and being comic were two entirely different things; he was unable to realize that comedy does not have to be mere refined horseplay, that it may be serious in itself, and that, if it isn't, no amount of stage rhetoric, no injections of sentimentality, can ever make it so. The plays of Philip Barry, like certain other products of New York—like the songs of Cole Porter, like a good deal of the *New Yorker* magazine—have the deftness and a glimmering of the comic sense that are cultivated in a high civilization, but, like other things of the kind in New York, they remain imperfect, uncertain, rather unsatisfactory, because they have no stable social system behind them and consequently no fixed code of manners or definite point of view. They flicker and float on the surface of the shifting heterogeneous city; are at their best when they reflect its queer mixtures and its disconcerting surprises. But to write a really first-rate comedy, you ought to have a set of standards, even if those of a small class or group, to refer people's behavior to. Eugene O'Neill, for all his faults, has these for the whole of humanity; Arthur Schnitzler has them for the sophisticated pre-war Viennese. But Philip Barry, who writes for a sophisticated class with little social tradition and little real education—this play has no more to do with the Indiana town in which it is laid than Cole Porter's new musical show—has a very hard time getting hold of anything that will enable him to take a clear line in regard to all the curious things that he sees going on about him.

February 4, 1931

Joseph de Maistre

WHEN literary people, hard pressed by the threat of democratic reforms, feel the need for a reactionary authority, they are likely to resort to Joseph de Maistre.

De Maistre was one of the few really distinguished writers who spoke for the Catholic reaction in the period after the French Revolution; and he has always been especially useful to conservative-minded intellectuals, because, in reading or remembering him, they are able to tell themselves that in that era all the brilliant brains were not on the subversive side. I have so often had de Maistre thrown at my head as an antidote to modern radicalism that I recently decided to look into him; and my report is that the "prophet of reaction" is by no means so formidable a thinker as he has sometimes been represented.

There was of course after the French Revolution a role for a critic like de Maistre. By the time the Revolution had run its course, it was not difficult to perceive the extravagance of the eighteenth-century doctrines which had led up to it. Rousseau had said that people were naturally good and that it was only institutions which had perverted them. Well, Robespierre had been Rousseau's disciple, and by the time the Republic had foundered in the blood of its quarrelling leaders and given way to the Emperor Napoleon, it did not look as if the people were so naturally good or so amenable to the reforms of the Goddess of Reason as the Rousseaus and Condorcets had asserted.

De Maistre wrote, in his *Essai sur le Principe Générateur des Constitutions Politiques*: "One of the great errors of a century that confessed all the errors was the belief that a political constitution could be written and created a priori, when reason and experience agree in showing that a constitution is a divine production and that precisely the most fundamental and most essentially constitutional part of a nation's laws is something that can never be written." It was impossible, de Maistre insisted, that the work of the Revolution should last: the new system was a purely theoretical one which had been artificially imposed by cranks. De Maistre makes merry over the efforts of the cranks to dignify their work with classic names. It is use

and use alone, he says, that can dignify and fill with meaning
the names of places and buildings—the Tuileries, for example
—that were originally commonplace. And you cannot prop up
something ephemeral by giving it a grandiose name. The
Odéon, for example: for all the pretentious Greek label, it
couldn't last! And then, the Olympic Games, so presumptu-
ously inaugurated, of which an enthusiastic contemporary had
asserted that "the day would come when they would attract
the whole of Europe to the Champ de Mars"—how preposterous that was! De Maistre's instances were not well-chosen, and
his arguments do not sound so good today as they may have
done in 1809. There is something in what he says: you cannot
invent a new social system and get people to accept it overnight. But that did not mean that in France the old régime had
been preferable or that the new, in spite of Napoleon, had not
taken a very strong hold—which were the conclusions de
Maistre drew.

Joseph de Maistre was a petty noble—very proud of his connections with the French aristocracy—from a family of Savoyard magistrates. He had had his first education at the hands of
the Jesuits and then had gone to study law at the University of
Turin. He worked hard at mastering French, but he never allowed himself to read any book without first writing home for
permission from his parents. He sat afterwards in the Savoyard
senate, of which his father was president.

De Maistre in his early phase entertained somewhat liberal
views. He even belonged for a time to a Reform Lodge and
was considered by the authorities a dangerous character. But
when the French Revolution was threatening, he was delegated by his fellow-members to report to the King of Sardinia
that the lodge had been dissolved. When the armies of the Republic invaded Savoy, de Maistre fled with his family. He could
have saved his property from confiscation, after Savoy had
been annexed by the French, by taking the oath of allegiance
to the new government; but he had brothers on the other side,
and he refused to contribute to the support of the revolutionary army. After some years of knocking about rather miserably
—at one time he and his wife were reduced to their last pieces
of silver plate—he was finally, in 1803, sent to St. Petersburg, as
envoy extraordinary and minister plenipotentiary to the King

of Sardinia. Separated from his wife and children, he remained there for fifteen years. By this time he was an embittered reactionary, and he occupied the long days of his exile by writing books to expound his position.

What is impressive about Joseph de Maistre is what is impressive about most sincere reactionaries from Dr. Johnson to Dostoevsky: his vision of human sin.

The great radical is likely to be one who either is free from a sense of guilt or has evolved a psychological mechanism which enables him to turn moral judgments against himself into moral judgments against society. A man like Kropotkin is himself so guileless, so benevolently disposed toward his fellowmen, that it is impossible for him to imagine that other people, if left to themselves, may not all be as pure as he. A Rousseau, with the elements much more mixed, was able, at the moment of his revelation, to put off all the humiliating experiences which had hindered him and rankled with him on an iniquitous social system, quite alien to the natural man, from which he could dissociate himself.

The reactionary, on the other hand, is likely to start from a profound conviction of the evil of the natural man. Instead of worrying because people do not get enough freedom, he is obsessed by the need for police—authority, discipline, order. How else can you keep the Devil under control? Dr. Johnson, who would not let Garrick take him behind the scenes of his theater for fear of the demoralizing effect on him of the bare necks and arms of the actresses, was all for Church and King; Dostoevsky, who, when the peasants had murdered his father, felt a kind of common guilt with the murderers and who behaved as if he were expiating in Siberia crimes with which he had never been charged, came back full of loyalty to Church and Tsar. De Maistre, who was able to justify the apparent injustice of the days when he and his wife and children had been exiled, homeless and starving, by the sins he knew his soul must answer for before the tribunal of God, defended the divine right of kings and the infallibility of the Pope; and he thus most commands our respect when he is insisting on the evil of life as something which cannot be avoided, which reason can never abolish or rhetoric conjure away. Injustices, from our human point of view, do certainly occur, he says (in *Les Soirées de Saint-Pétersbourg*); people suffer for crimes that they never committed. But if you take mankind in the gross, as God does, you will see that we all share in human sin. This sin is our common inheritance, our common debt; not one of us is free from it; and we must all of us contribute to paying it. De Maistre repudiates, he tells us, the snobbish point of view of that queen who was supposed to have said, "You may be sure that God thinks twice about damning our sort of people!" No: not one of us is innocent! That Elizabeth of France, the King's sister, should have had to die by the guillotine just as the monster Robespierre did, does not prove that God is unjust: "Every man, in his quality of man, is subject to all the ills of humanity." We are subject to unjust executions just as we are to apoplexy. But if we look at things in the large, we shall see "that the greatest mass of happiness, even temporal happiness, goes, not to the virtuous man, but to virtue." Because, if this were not true, the whole moral order would be wrong—which is absurd.

This leads de Maistre to one of his most famous performances. The whole moral order is *not* wrong, and in reality our human justice is acting in behalf of the divine. The executioner, therefore, in spite of the fact that all the world avoids him, is a man appointed by God, "created like a world" and set apart. How else is it possible to account for him?—how else is it possible to explain that a man can be found to accept the job? Yet the executioner does exist and carries out his terrible orders. De Maistre tells you about it:

"A somber signal is given: an abject minister of justice comes to knock at his [the executioner's] door and let him know that he is needed. He sets out; he arrives at the public square, which is crowded with an eager excited throng. A prisoner or a murderer or a blasphemer is given over to him. He seizes him and stretches and ties him on a horizontal cross; he lifts his arm and a horrible silence falls. Nothing is heard but the cry of the bones cracking under the heavy rod and the howlings of the victim. Then he unties him and carries him to the wheel: the shattered limbs get twisted in the spokes; the head hangs; the hair stands out; and from the mouth, gaping open like a stove, come only now a few bloody words which at intervals beg for death. Now the executioner has finished: his heart beats, but it is for joy; he applauds himself, he says in his heart: 'Nobody is better at the wheel than I!' He comes down and holds out his blood-stained hand, and the Law throws into it from a distance some gold pieces which he carries away with him through a double hedge of people, who draw away in horror. He sits down to table and eats; then he gets into bed and goes to sleep. When he wakes up the next day, he begins to think about something quite different from the work he has been doing the day before. Is he a man? Yes: God receives him into his temples and allows him to pray. The executioner is not a criminal; yet no tongue is willing to say, for example, that he is 'virtuous,' that he is 'a good fellow,' that he is 'estimable,' etc. No moral commendation fits him, because any such commendation assumes some sort of bond with mankind, and the executioner has none.

"And yet all grandeur, all power, all discipline are founded on the executioner. He is the horror of the human association and the tie that holds it together. Take out of the world this incomprehensible agent, and at that instant will order give way to chaos, thrones fall and society vanish. God, who is the source of all sovereignty, is, therefore, the source of all punishment, too."

It has been objected to de Maistre that he is hard. The truth is that he is not hard enough. As he says, a professional executioner is incomprehensible to him. In his earlier days, as a matter of fact, he had resigned from the senate of Savoy, which had judiciary functions, precisely because he could not bring himself to sentence people to death. And, although he was willing to face the fact that everything he valued in the world depended on that horrible wheel, he evaded this uncomfortable situation as much as he possibly could. If, according to the divine arrangement, the virtuous must sometimes suffer, then the innocent must sometimes get tortured. What about Jean Calas, the Protestant merchant who had been persecuted by a Catholic mob for a crime he had perhaps never committed and who had been broken on the wheel?—Calas, whom Voltaire had defended and whose name he had made a symbol for the savagery of religious intolerance? Well, the truth is, de Maistre replies, that Calas was probably guilty. The chief thing

that makes de Maistre think so is the flippancy displayed by
Voltaire while he was agitating in Calas' defense—this flippancy having been exemplified by a remark in one of Voltaire's
letters: "You find my memoir too hot, but I am working on
another one for you which is going to be a scorcher." Nothing
can be more probable than that God Himself, in a case like
this, makes a point of helping the police so that they won't fail
to get the right person; and, besides, there is always the chance
that, even if a man is executed for a crime which he did not
commit, he may deserve to be punished for something else.
And yet, even where the victim is certainly guilty, an execution
like that of Calas, by "torture ordinary and extraordinary" and
by breaking alive on the wheel, is unquestionably a distasteful
affair. Even when we can reconcile ourselves to contemplating
the agonies of the wicked, how can we contemplate the state
of mind imposed on the executioner? We can get around this
haunting difficulty by no less heroic a piece of sophistry than
excluding the executioner from the human race! De Maistre
has to invent for this man a character as frankly inhuman as
that of a goblin or a djinn in a fairy-tale. (One is not even convinced by de Maistre's description that he has ever actually witnessed an execution.) He is obliged to tell himself that Jack
Ketch is *not* really a man like himself, that he is a different kind
of being altogether from the fellow whose humane sensibilities
compelled him to resign from the Senate.

I know of no more striking example of the lengths to which
an intelligent man can go to escape the disagreeable implications of a position he has an interest in maintaining. The
Boston lawyers who steadily maintained that, though Sacco
and Vanzetti might well be innocent, it was necessary to have
them executed, in order to uphold the authority of the Massachusetts courts, though they are less sympathetic than Joseph
de Maistre, were really arguing more soundly than he, as they
were arguing more soundly than the thousands of their respectable and kindly fellow-townsmen who, like de Maistre,
did their best to convince themselves that, in spite of the dubious evidence, the accused were very likely guilty, or that, if
they didn't deserve death for murder, they did for political
heresy.

You find this wanting to have it both ways all through *Les Soirées de Saint-Pétersbourg*. So with those other earthly evils—cancer and war. After describing with some vividness their horrors, he tries to show us they are, after all, not so horrible; religion and self-discipline are stimulated in time of war; and as for cancer, there is a girl in St. Petersburg whom cancer has gradually converted into a model of pious devotion. Even in regard to the Revolution, de Maistre is not really so uncompromising as he is sometimes assumed to be. He could not extirpate his early liberalism, and this weakened his royalist position. He was too serious and too intelligent not to realize and deplore the corruption and incompetence of the old régime. But the Revolution was "a great and terrible sermon which Providence has preached to men—a sermon with two morals. Revolutions are made by abuses: this is the first moral, and it is addressed to sovereigns. Nevertheless, it is infinitely better to have abuses than revolutions: this is the second moral, and it is addressed to peoples." And he accepted the French Republic in so far as he believed it the only thing which could hold France together against her enemies.

Not a very satisfactory position. Knowing well that on that quarrelsome continent, where the nations were well engaged in the path that was to lead to 1914, no sovereign could ever bring unity, he advocated setting up a body which should derive its authority from the Pope and keep peace by imposing its decisions. The truth was that Joseph de Maistre had himself been irremediably influenced by the rationalism and humanitarianism of the bourgeois philosophers he patronized. His class bias was, of course, very strong; we see it even in his attempts at justice. The worst crime that de Maistre could imagine was the guillotining of the King's sister. Calas was far from mattering so much. But why, then, should he have mattered at all? From de Maistre's point of view, he was a heretic in any case. Voltaire, against whom, from the St. Petersburg of Alexander I, de Maistre is always railing, has got him worried about Calas after all. And why bother about the fates of common soldiers? A thoroughly hard-boiled aristocrat ought to have taken all that for granted. But Joseph de Maistre's attitude is never really hard-boiled and realistic, but, on the contrary, sophistical and literary. It is an affair of ingenious reasoning and elegiac rumination in a limbo between two worlds. When de Maistre died, Talleyrand said of him: "The prophet of the past has fallen asleep in the bosom of eternity, with his memories which he takes for premonitions."

August 24, 1932

An Appeal to Progressives

THE FOLLOWING article appeared in the *New Republic* of January 14, 1931. It was announced as "the first of a series . . . discussing the position of the contemporary progressive, . . . the outcome of conversations among the editors, which have been occurring for several months." The editor-in-chief, Herbert Croly, had died on May 17, 1930.

It seems to me that the time has come for liberals seriously to reconsider their position. The liberalism which the *New Republic* has represented in the past was derived primarily from Herbert Croly's book *The Promise of American Life*, written more than twenty years ago. This book was an original interpretation of American political and social history, which in its field set a new standard of realism. In the earliest days of the Republic, the strong centralization policy of Hamilton had been established for the protection of the propertied classes, and the reaction led by Jefferson was intended as a democratic antidote. But Mr. Croly showed that when the Jeffersonians got into power, they took over the Hamiltonian structure practically intact, though at the same time they refused to abandon their democratic pretensions, thus, as he says, beginning "that career of intellectual lethargy, superficiality and insincerity which ever since has been characteristic of official American political thought." The American democratic ideal was thus more or less disingenuous from the beginning: the actual purpose of the government was one thing and the rhetoric of politics was another. It got to be stock procedure to claim as a democratic "right" the freedom to pursue any course that happened to promote one's own interests. The institution of slavery, for example, was guaranteed by the Constitution, though it violated in the most shocking manner the spirit of the Declaration of Independence: the Southerners claimed their legal "rights," and the Abolitionists claimed natural "rights." The contradictions involved in our government and the ideals associated with it gave rise to a double rebellion—the rebellion of the South against the government and the rebellion of the

North against the Constitution. The Civil War ensued, and, as a result, both the Constitution and the social structure of the South became altered in important respects. The machine and the ideal were now repaired and started on their way again.

Herbert Croly goes on, however, to show that the industrial development of the country had then produced a second critical situation as serious as that which had brought on the war. Our society transformed itself: the masters of industry and commerce came rapidly to constitute a special and supremely powerful class; the lawyers, who had formerly run the government, were turned into another special class that prospered by keeping the bankers and business men out of trouble; politics was left to a third specialized class, the bosses and professional office-holders—the labor unions grew up as a fourth, engaged (at first) in fighting the other three. The old machine and ideal, even in their amended form, failed to meet the needs of the new American world by as much as the Bethlehem steel works, the Grand Central Station and the Singer Building were unlike Mount Vernon, Monticello or the log cabin where Lincoln was born. A readjustment as drastic was required as that which had cost us the Civil War. "The time may come," Croly wrote, "when the fulfilment of a justifiable democratic purpose may demand the limitation of certain rights, to which the Constitution affords such absolute guarantees; and, in that case, the American democracy might be forced to seek by revolutionary means the accomplishment of a result which should be attainable under the law." Croly did, however, still believe that this result might be attained under the law—that the wholesale corruption of politics, the shameless exploitation of labor, the ruthless wrecking by competitive business of thousands of honorable careers and the general degradation of the national standards in everything except technical skill might be dealt with at a not too distant date by our machinery of representative government. He conceived this new democratic goal as a return to Hamiltonian centralization, but in the interests not merely of the propertied class but of the American people as a whole—a new machinery and a new objective which he says he is not afraid to have called "socialism." Everyone, in the United States, had again been claiming as some sort of "right" the freedom to do whatever he pleased—the business men, the lawyers, the politicians and the labor organizers. What was needed was a frank confession that, if we were to save the democratic ideal, we must discard the illusion of unlimited freedom and work out a systematic curtailment of the rights of everyone in the interests of all.

Yet Croly still believed that this result might eventually be accomplished by an orderly series of reforms. In spite of his unsparing criticism of our official political ideals and even of our political reformers, he still had faith in American politics—or rather, perhaps, in an American democratic spirit able to control life through politics, a spirit embodied for him by Lincoln, the man who had changed the state and preserved it, too. Herbert Croly differed from the out-and-out socialist of his time by encouraging the idea of nationalism—not the imperialistic nationalism of Great Britain and of the late German Empire, but a nationalism which did impel him to support the entrance of the United States into the European War. He expressly repudiated the notion of an international working-class movement dedicated to fighting international capitalism. It was still possible for Herbert Croly to feel that the United States was a kind of mystical entity—something isolated, self-contained and self-perpetuating—that could be counted on to solve its own problems and eliminate its own diseases. And to the extent that he believed in the United States, he thus believed not only in nationalism but in capitalism as well. He thought that the American spirit would be strong enough to compel American capitalism to restrain and reform itself.

That Herbert Croly came to lose hope as time went on—though he never abandoned his original position—is proved by his acute distress over the failure of Woodrow Wilson at Paris and by his increasing skepticism about politics. It seems to me impossible today for people of Herbert Croly's general aims and convictions to continue to believe in the salvation of our society by the gradual and natural approximation to socialism which he himself called progressivism, but which has more generally come to be known as liberalism. That benevolent and intelligent capitalism on which liberals have always counted has not merely not materialized to the extent of accepting socialism—it has not even been able to prevent a national economic disaster of proportions which neither capitalists nor liberals foresaw and which they both now profess themselves unable to explain. There are today in the United States, according to the census director, something like nine million men out of work; our cities are scenes of privation and misery on a scale which sickens the imagination; our agricultural life is bankrupt; our industry, in shifting to the South, has reverted almost to the horrible conditions, before the Factory Acts, of the England of a hundred years ago, and the fight of the unions there for recognition is all to begin again; so many banks are failing that the newspapers do not dare to print the truth about them. And when we look to South America or to the European countries west of Russia, we see only the same economic chaos, the same lack of capacity or will to deal with it, and the same resultant suffering. May we not well fear that what has broken down, in the course of one catastrophic year, is not simply the machinery of representative government but the capitalist system itself?—and that, even with the best intentions, it may be henceforward impossible for capitalism to guarantee not merely social justice but even security and order? May we not fear lest our American society, in spite of its apparently greater homogeneity, be liable, through sheer inefficiency, the heritage of political corruption, to collapse in the long run as ignominiously as the feudal regimes of old France and Russia?

The capitalist Americans of the twentieth century are certainly more kindly and democratic than the landlords of the feudal age; but, on the other hand, the capitalist system makes it very much easier for people not to realize what they are doing, not to know about the danger and the hardship, the despair and the humiliation, that their way of life implies for others. The feudal lord might flog or kill his serfs, but he was dealing directly with the human realities as the stockholder or the banker is not. The feudal master might be arrogant and cruel, but his arrogance and cruelty were open, accepted as necessities imposed or enjoyed as privileges conferred by superior social position. But the chivalrous Southerner whose interest is mounting up in the bank that lends money to the textile mill is no more conscious that he has helped pull the trigger that murdered Ella May Wiggins* than the cultivated Bostonian knows that the money that reaches his pocket from the shares in the South Braintree shoe company in which his broker has recommended his investing has on its way helped turn on the switch that electrocuted Sacco and Vanzetti. Mr. Lawrence Dennis, late of Seligman, has recently written in this magazine of the queer and unenviable lot of the bond salesmen, who, taking over their bonds on trust from the bankers and selling them to customers who take them on trust, do not assume any professional responsibility and never touch at any point the realities of the things with which they are dealing. Not only are the people in a capitalist society very often completely ignorant as to what their incomes come from; it is actually sometimes impossible or very difficult for them to find this out. And as long as a fair proportion of the bankers, the manufacturers, the middle men, the merchants and the workers whom their capital and machines keep busy are able to make a little more money than before, no matter how unscrupulously or short-sightedly, we are able, as a nation, to maintain our belief in our prosperity and even in our happiness.

That is what has been happening in the period which has just now come to a close. The liberal Stuart Chase tried to make us see this situation in his little book called *Prosperity: Fact or Myth?* published in 1929, on the eve of the stock-market crash. Between 1922 and 1928, he tells us, the average income in the United States was increased twenty percent, but this left the average annual wage in 1929 "well below $1,500." Through this whole period the coal, textile, shoe, leather, shipbuilding and railroad-equipment industries were all doing more or less badly and the people employed in them were hanging on to the bare edge of subsistence; the farmers became more and more impoverished; the mergers and the new machinery were throwing more and more people out of work; and the radio and motor industries, on which the illusion of prosperity depended, were prospering at the expense of selling these articles to many people who didn't need them. The salesmen and advertisers had had to begin to break down the

*See page 405.

"sales resistance" of their public: it was no longer a question merely of persuading people of the attractiveness of one's wares but of combating a positive antagonism to them. The sales departments resorted to both inspirational and scientific methods, but when the public began to come to from the industrial opium-dream, the motor-car industry was suddenly sunk and the rest of American business went with it. May we not ask ourselves whether it is possible, in the conditions of our capitalist society, for any further spectacular appearance of revival to be anything more than a spurt depending on the overinflation, equally senseless and mischievous, of some other inessential industry?—an inflation just as sure to end in another abject disaster?

In any case, American optimism has taken a serious beating; the national morale is weak. The energy and the faith for a fresh start seem now not to be forthcoming: a dreadful apathy, unsureness and discouragement is felt to have fallen upon us. It is as if we were afraid to go on with what we were doing before or as if we had no longer the heart for it. I want to suggest that the present depression may be nothing less than one of the turning-points in our history, our first real crisis since the Civil War. The Americans at the present time seem to be experiencing not merely an economic breakdown but a distinct psychological change. From the time of the Civil War on, all our enthusiasm and creative energy went into the development of our tremendous resources. This development had two aspects: one was the exploration of the continent and the engineering feats involved in reclaiming it; the other the amassing of gigantic fortunes. Today the discoveries have all been made: we no longer look toward the West, as the Europeans once looked to America, as to a world of untold treasures and wonders—and the excitement of mastering new seacoasts, new rivers, forests, prairies and mountains seems now completely spent. This was already true at the time of the European War (when, incidentally, we were running into a business depression), but the war gave us a new objective—new discoveries, the discovery of Europe; new heroic stunts of engineering, the transportation of our army to France. Since the end of the war, however, we have, as a people, had nothing to carry us along except the momentum of money-making. We have been trying still to find in it the exhilaration of the money-making of our earlier period, which had been largely the exhilaration of the wildness and size of the continent—the breaking it in to the harness of the railroads, the stumbling upon sudden riches. But during these last years our hope and our faith have all been put behind the speed of mass production, behind stupendous campaigns of advertising, behind cyclones of salesmanship. Our buoyancy had been becoming hysterical. And the reaction from an hysterical exhilaration is a slump into despondency and inertia. What we have lost is, it may be, not merely our way in the economic labyrinth but our conviction of the value of what we were doing. Money-making and the kind of advantages which a money-making society provides for money to buy are not enough to satisfy humanity—neither is a system like ours in which everyone is out for himself and devil take the hindmost, with no common purpose and little common culture to give life stability and sense. Our idolization of our aviators—our extravagant excitement over Lindbergh and our romantic admiration (now beginning to cool off) for Byrd—has been like a last desperate burst of American idealism, a last impulse to dissociate our national soul from a precipitate progress that was taking us from automobiles and radios straight through electric refrigerators to Tom Thumb golf-courses.

The old American ideal and legend of the poor boy who gets to be a millionaire, which gradually came to take the place of the poor boy who got to be President, has today lost almost all its glamor. Not only do people not hope to be Hoover—they do not even hope so often as they did to be Carnegie or Henry Ford. The romance of the legend of the poor boy was the romance of the old democratic chance, of the career open to the talents—but the realities of a millionaire society have turned out to be the monstrosities of capitalism: the children of the successful poor boy get lazy and sick on their father's money, and the poor boys who afterwards arrive on the scene discover that—with the crippling of the grain market, the elimination of the factory worker by the development of the machine and the decimation of the white-collar class, even though sometimes apparently well on their way to getting in on the big money themselves, by enormous business mergers—the career is no longer open to the extent that had originally been hoped. What began as the libertarian adventure of eighteenth-century middle-class democracy seems to have ended in the cul de sac of an antiquated economic system. And capitalist-minded as the Americans have now become, they seem to feel they are in a cul de sac. It is as if they did not dare to go on. In spite of the fundamental absurdity of so much of what we have lately been doing, we are considerably better educated and more intelligent than we once were, and since the war we have been closer to Europe. The Buicks and Cadillacs, the bad gin and Scotch, the radio concerts interrupted by advertizing talks, the golf and bridge of the suburban household, which the bond salesman can get for his money, can hardly compensate him for daily work of a kind in which it is utterly impossible to imagine a normal human being taking satisfaction or pride—and the bond salesman is the type of the whole urban office class. The brokers and bankers who are shooting themselves and jumping out of windows have been disheartened by the precariousness of their profession—but would they be killing themselves if they loved it? Who today, in fact, in the United States, can really love our meaningless life, where the manufacturer raises the workers' wages only in order to create a demand for the gadgets which for better or worse he happens to have an interest in selling them, while agriculture goes hang, and science and art are left to be exploited by the commercial laboratories, the market for commercial art illustration and the New York publishers' racket, or to be fed in a haphazard way by a dole from the fortunes of rich men who have been conscience-stricken or simply overpowered at finding themselves at the end of their careers with enough money on their hands to buy out an old-fashioned empire?

We liberals have professed not to love it, yet we have tried to believe in it, none the less. In a country where money changes hands so often and social position fluctuates so easily, where the minds of the working class have seemed largely to have been absorbed into the psychology of the middle class, we have been unable to believe in the Marxist doctrine that capitalism must eventually give rise to class warfare, and we have perhaps never taken sufficiently seriously Karl Marx's prediction that for many years to come the stupid automatic acquisi-

tive instinct of humanity would still be so far ahead of its capacity for intelligent and disinterested behavior that the system
of private enterprise would never even be able to run itself with
foresight enough to avoid a wreck. It used to be pointed out
that in America our support of this system was indestructible,
since the stock market made it possible for anybody who had
been able to save a little money to become a capitalist himself,
with interests presumably identical with those of J. P. Morgan
and Charlie Schwab. But can we expect that to be true in the
future?—and even if people persist in aspiring to be stock-
market capitalists, should they be encouraged in this or even
left to their luck? Should they not rather be shown that their
interests are incompatible with capitalism itself?

Yet the truth is that we liberals and progressives have been
betting on capitalism—and that most of our heroes and allies,
heterodox professors like Dewey and Beard, survivors of the
old republican tradition like Woodrow Wilson and Justice
Holmes, able and well-educated labor organizers like the
officers of the Amalgamated, intelligent journalists like Lippmann and Chase, though all sincere and outspoken democrats,
have been betting on capitalism, too. And now, in the abyss of
starvation and bankruptcy into which the country has fallen,
with no sign of any political leadership which will be able to
pull us out, our liberalism seems to have little to offer beyond
a discreet recommendation of public ownership of water
power and certain other public utilities, a cordial feeling that
labor ought to organize in a non-social-revolutionary way and
a protest, invariably ineffective, against a few of the more obviously atrocious of the jailings, beatings-up and murders with
which the industrialists have been trying to keep the working
class docile.

Doesn't this program today seem rather inadequate? We
liberals have always insisted on the desirability of a planned
society—the phrase "social control" has been our blessed
Mesopotamian word. If this means anything, does it not mean
socialism? And should we not do well to make this plain? It
may be said that at the present time it is utopian in America to
talk about socialism; but with the kind of administrations that
the country has lately been getting, do not all our progressive
proposals, however reasonable or modest, seem utopian? Is it

not obvious, as was lately made plain by an article in this magazine, that a government like our present one is incapable of acting in good faith in even the simple matter of preserving the water power which is supposed to be operated for the general benefit from being exploited by private profiteers? Our society has finally produced in its specialized professional politicians one of the most useless and obnoxious groups which has perhaps ever disgraced human history—a group that seems unique among governing classes in having managed to be corrupt, uncultivated and incompetent all at once. We know that we are not even able to depend on them today to protect us against the frankly disreputable race of blackmailers, thieves and assassins who dominate our municipal life. We know that we cannot even complain that the racketeers are breaking the laws which are supposed to be guaranteed by the government, because the government differs little from the racketeers. How can we expect them, then, to check the relatively respectable scoundrels who merely rob us of the public utilities by more or less legalistic means?

Yet, as I say, it may be true that, with the present breakdown, we have come to the end of something, and that we are ready to start on a different tack. If we look back through the depressions of the last fifty years, we see that through every one of them there always remained something for which the Americans could still legitimately feel ambition or enthusiasm, something to challenge the national spirit and appeal to the national imagination. After 1885, there were still the West and the consolidation of the railroads; after the prolonged depression of the nineties, the final consolidation of great industries such as United States Steel as well as the crusade led by Theodore Roosevelt against these great corporations in the interests of the dangerously increasing number of those who were being injured by the process of consolidation, and the robustious Rooseveltian imperialism; after the slump of the early years of the European War, our entrance into the war; and after the slump that followed the war, the period of the glorification of the automobile and the airplane. Today the further consolidation of the big business units is ruining more people even than in Roosevelt's time, and there is no sign of a

Roosevelt or a Wilson to revive our political vision and to persuade the people who are out of luck that something is about
to be done for them. It may be that the whole money-making
and -spending psychology has definitely played itself out, and
that the Americans would be willing, for the first time now, to
put their traditional idealism and their genius for organization
behind a radical social experiment. The future is as blank in the
United States today as the situation is desperate: the President
seems so inhibited by dread of encouraging subversive forces
and by faith in the capacity of the capitalist system to right itself and survive that it is impossible for him to act, and when
he tries to, he is deadlocked by Congress; nor have the industrialists or the financiers come forward with any constructive
proposal. But this very blindness of the outlook may mean that
we are looking in the wrong direction and that help may be
coming from some other quarter. In the meantime, one gets
the impression that the people who don't deal in ideas are
doing more thinking at the present time than the professional
ideologues.

The minds of the general public have, furthermore, been
more affected by the example of Soviet Russia than is easily
grasped by anyone who has been in the habit of assuming that
it is only the radical or liberal who understands what Russia is
up to, and that the ordinary American citizen is bound to be
stupidly prejudiced against the Soviet system. During the NEP
period in Russia, the capitalist powers were relieved to feel that
the Russians had been forced to recognize the impracticability
of Communism and were quietly returning to laissez faire. But
with the inauguration of the Five-Year Plan to eliminate capitalist business in Russia, the aspect of things changed. The apparent success of the plan has had its effect on all classes in all
the rest of the world—on the Americans, surely, not least. In
the course of this winter of our capitalist quandary, the Soviets
have been emerging from the back pages of the New York newspapers and are now given much and prominent space—even to
interviews with Stalin's mother; and behind what one reads on
the subject in even the reactionary papers, one feels as much
admiration as resentment. After all, the great Communist project is distinguished by almost all the features that Americans
have been taught to glorify—the extreme of efficiency and

economy combined with the ideal of a herculean program—
like a Liberty Loan drive—to be put over by concerted action
to the tune of impassioned boosting. The Russians, furthermore, on their own side, have been studying American methods: they have imported a thousand American engineers and
put them at the head of enormous enterprises with practically
a free hand, and one would not be at all surprised to hear that
Mr. Edward L. Bernays had been in Moscow at the time of the
recent trial. We have already, in spite of the Treasury regula-
tion, been doing a good deal of trading with Russia, and an
important New York bank was at one time on the point of advancing to the Soviets the loan that has been advocated by this
magazine.

The Communists in the United States assume that, by their
very nature, neither our government nor our business is capable of learning anything from or of associating itself with the
Soviets. They believe that a war against Russia is inevitable.
They believe, moreover, that they themselves constitute a
trained compact minority which, at the moment when American capitalism shall have finally broken down completely and
been left helpless in its ignorance and anarchic selfishness, will
be able to step in and man the works. To liberals, this idea has
always sounded absurd, but who will say that it is entirely fantastic today when the machine is so badly in need of repairs,
and one can see no political group in any position of power
that has either a sensible plan or even good intentions? I
believe that if the American radicals and progressives who repudiate the Marxist dogma and the strategy of the Communist
Party still hope to accomplish anything valuable, they must
take Communism away from the Communists, and take it
without ambiguities, asserting that their ultimate goal is the
ownership by the government of the means of production. If
we want to prove the Communists wrong, if we want to demonstrate that the virtue has not gone out of American democracy,
if we want to confute the Marxist cynicism implied by "economic laws" the catastrophic outcome of which is, after all,
predicted only on an assumption of the incurable swinishness
and inertia of human nature—if we seriously want to do this,
an American opposition must not be afraid to dynamite the
old conceptions and shibboleths and to substitute new ones as

shocking as necessary. Who knows but they may seem less
shocking to the ordinary suffering public than to us shibboleth-
experts ourselves? When John Dos Passos proposed last summer that what was really needed in the United States was a
publicity expert like Ivy Lee to familiarize the public with the
idea of Communism and induce people at least to remain neutral toward Communist agitation instead of clapping all the
Communists in jail, the suggestion, to some, sounded comic.
Yet Dos Passos at once had a letter from a publicity man in San
Francisco, who said that the same idea had recently occurred
to him and that he would like nothing better than a chance to
carry it out. There are some signs that the liberals are having
ideas as well as the publicity men: Stuart Chase has said lately
that the past year may represent "the end of an epoch" and has
offered a set of suggestions for rescuing the economic structure, and John Dewey has just proposed to Senator Norris that
he lead a new political party. The extreme illiberalism of the
post-Wilsonian period has had the effect of discouraging liberals. We have gone on complaining and recommending, but
with a vigor that has tended to diminish in proportion as we
came to be conscious that people were not listening to us.
Who knows but, if we spoke out now with confidence and
boldness, we might find our public at last?

January 14, 1931

From the fall of 1930 to the spring of 1934, I spent a good
deal of time reporting political and industrial events, and
thereafter, till 1940, writing a study of Marxism and the Russian Revolution, so that I did not give the literary events of
these years as much attention as I had given to those of the
twenties or as I was afterwards to give to those of the forties.

The Literary Class War

IN THE FALL of 1930, a year after the stock-market crash, there appeared in the *New Republic* an attack by Michael Gold on Thornton Wilder. Michael Gold is, of course, a Communist, and his article was an attempt to arraign Mr. Wilder at the bar of the Communist ideology. He declared that Mr. Wilder's writings were the poetry "of a small sophisticated class that has recently arisen in America—our genteel bourgeoisie" and on a plane with "luxury hotels, golf, old furniture and *Vanity Fair* sophistication." *The Cabala* and *The Bridge of San Luis Rey* were among the things that helped this "parvenu class to forget its lowly origins in American industrialism"— providing them with "a short cut to the aristocratic emotions," disguising "the barbaric sources of their income, the billions wrung from American workers and foreign peasants and coolies" and encouraging them to "feel spiritually worthy of that income." Mr. Wilder's Christianity was merely "that newly fashionable literary religion that centers around Jesus Christ the First British Gentleman"; and his style a "neat tailormade rhetoric," whose serenity was "that of a corpse" and which, when pricked, would "bleed violet ink and *apéritif*." How, he asked, could "this discreet French drawing-room hold all the blood, horror and hope of the world's new empire? . . . Where are the modern streets of New York, Chicago and New Orleans? . . . Where are the cotton mills, and the murder of Ella May and her songs?* Where are the child slaves of the beet fields? Where are the stockbroker suicides, the labor racketeers or the passion and death of the coal miners?"

This assault provoked one of the most violent controversies which the literary world has lately known. The writer of the present article had felt, when he first read Gold's article, that the latter had overshot his mark and had read into Wilder's popularity a Marxist moral that it did not have. But as the letters began to shower in and kept up for months without

*See page 405.

abatement, he was finally forced to the conclusion that there *was* a class issue involved in the dispute. For equally severe attacks on other equally popular authors had never brought forth anything like this. The people who applauded Gold seemed to be moved by a savage animus; those who defended Wilder protested or pleaded in the tone of persons who had been shocked by the desecration of a dearly beloved thing. Strange cries from the depths arose, illiterate and hardly articulate.

The editors of the *New Republic* decided at last that the controversy called for some sort of official comment on the part of the magazine; and the writer produced a leader in which he justified Gold's attack—pointing out that Thornton Wilder obviously owed a good deal to Proust; that the pinings and dissatisfactions that were the dominant emotions in Proust represented the illness of the cultivated classes in a capitalistic society; and that Wilder, without intending it and though a writer of genuine merit, had popularized Proust for American readers.

The author of this leader was not in a position to take other writers to task too severely for coming under the influence of Proust, since he himself had not long before contributed to the same magazine a long and sympathetic essay on *A la Recherche du Temps Perdu* and had also published a novel not unflavored by the fumes of the cork-lined chamber. His editorial on the Gold-Wilder controversy had been written from the bourgeois point of view, as Michael Gold's article had been from the proletarian one. Yet it turned out to be too Marxist for many *New Republic* readers, who at once, in a revival of the controversy, transferred their indignation from Mr. Gold to myself, and so deluged us with letters that the editors were obliged to put an end to the discussion.

The situation was made more complicated by the fact that Mr. Gold, on his side, was under criticism from his own Marxist camp. He had just published and had been having considerable success with his book about the New York East Side, *Jews Without Money*, and the Communist critics were scolding him for having made this a volume of personal memories that centered around an individual, the official theory being that, in a Communist work of art, there ought not to be a protagonist, since the subject should be always the group. One of these

critics, Mr. Melvin Levy, in an otherwise appreciative review—
which also appeared in the *New Republic*—had insisted that
Jews Without Money was "written without reference to the
mass"; that "labor organizations and strikes" were "not mentioned," though they were "probably more a part of the life of
this group than any other in America"; that the big shirtwaist
makers' strike and the Triangle fire, for example, though they
had taken place during the period with which *Jews Without
Money* dealt, received no attention in it; and that the characters
were not proletarians at all, but "merely poor people" whose
sorrows and strivings were not the inevitable products of a
class situation, but individual accidents: if they had not happened to have hard luck, they might have turned into contented petty bourgeois. Yet it was evident that Mr. Melvin
Levy had not always been so clear himself about the duty of
the revolutionary writer: he had published not long before a
novel about Greenwich Village, which, I believe, did not deal
at all with the struggles of the proletariat; and, in a review of
an earlier book by Mr. Gold, he had complained that some of
the stories had been "tailored to meet a pattern of 'proletarian
literature' and propaganda." "It is not merely," wrote Mr.
Levy, "that they sacrifice artistic excellence for propaganda: if
they did that successfully, they would be justified. But they
have not the veracity and conviction that make good propaganda. They are distant and unreal: unmoving."

To the first of these reviews, Mr. Gold made an eloquent
reply:

"I think Comrade Levy [he wrote] is too dogmatic in his
application of the proletarian canon. There is nothing finished
or dogmatic in proletarian thought and literature. We cannot
afford it. We are pioneers. . . . It would be fatal for us to
have fixed minds. Proletarian literature is taking many forms.
There is not a standard model which all writers must imitate,
or even a standard set of thoughts. There are no precedents.
Each writer has to find his own way. All that unites us, and all
we have for a guide, is the revolutionary spirit. . . .

"To my mind, it is the task of each proletarian writer to describe that portion of proletarian life with which he is most saturated. . . . Comrade Levy . . . is disappointed because I
. . . did not include the Triangle fire and the great garment

strikes. Yet I could do nothing else honestly and emotionally at the time. I could only describe what I had seen with my own eyes. I did not want to falsify the emotional values and bring in material that I did not feel. I do not believe any good writing can come out of this mechanical application of the spirit of proletarian literature. In America, where everything is confused, we must begin humbly with the things we know best."

He then went on to make an interesting plea:

"It is difficult to write proletarian literature in this country, because all the critics are bourgeois. If a Thornton Wilder writes books in praise of the Catholic theology or if a Robinson Jeffers preaches universal pessimism and mass-suicide, that is art. But if a revolutionary writer, even by implication, shows the social ideals that are stirring in the heart of the working class, he is called a propagandist. This taunt which one meets on every side creates a powerful psychic force which proletarian writers will have to ignore. I will admit it had set up inhibitions in my own mind that I have not yet overcome. Perhaps Levy has perceived this in *Jews Without Money*, but I assure him that it is hard to overcome in a first book. It will take other books; it will take a group literature and collective experimentation before we can feel as easy in our proletarian world as every bourgeois writer feels in his. Meanwhile, let us not fear to be crude or propagandistic. We are going somewhere; the rest of literature is sinking into the arms of Catholicism, and death."

This whole controversy, in short, took place in an atmosphere of intellectual confusion—an atmosphere which has not yet cleared up. The results seem to have been that Michael Gold has taken to writing for the *New Masses* little Communist Sunday-school stories, in which the role of a proletarian hero is subordinated with effort and imperfect success to the conflicts of a social group; while Thornton Wilder, not unmoved, apparently, by the reproach of neglecting America, has brought out a volume of little plays several of which—and they are quite good—deal with American subjects, one of them transferring the Christian motif so obnoxious to his Marxist critics from the Greek island of *The Woman of Andros* to Trenton, New Jersey, and another presenting a Pullman car with a technique based, as Mr. Wilder explains, on the Japanese Noh plays, but with an effect faintly reminiscent of Dos Passos and John Howard Lawson in their New Playwrights' Theater days. He is said to have stated a belief that every enormously popular book has concealed in it some sentimentality.

There is no question that the Gold-Wilder case marks definitely the eruption of the Marxist issues out of the literary circles of the radicals into the field of general criticism. It has now become plain that the economic crisis is to be accompanied by a literary one.

May 4, 1932

C. L. Dodgson: The Poet Logician

I F THE Lewis Carroll centenary has produced anything of special interest, I have failed to see it. C. L. Dodgson was a most interesting man and deserves better of his admirers, who revel in his delightfulness and cuteness but do not give him any serious attention. "Frankly this is to be the book of Lewis Carroll," wrote John Francis McDermott in his introduction to Dodgson's collected verse, published three years ago, "and I have no intention here of allowing Charles Lutwidge Dodgson, a dull and uninteresting person, to intrude in it any more than is absolutely necessary." Richard Herrick, the editor of *The Lewis Carroll Book*, is so determined that we shall see in Dodgson nothing but an exponent of pure nonsense that he does not hesitate to mutilate his work. He reprints, out of *Rhyme? and Reason?*, only the poems that happen to please him; he suppresses, with the exception of a few stanzas, the long and elaborate *Phantasmagoria*, for the extraordinary reason that he believes it to have been spoiled by "Carroll's serious interest in psychic matters"; and he lops off the charming and significant epilogue to *Through the Looking Glass*, without which the book is incomplete:

> Still she haunts me, phantomwise,
> Alice moving under skies
> Never seen by waking eyes.

On the other hand, he includes some very amusing letters and a mathematical fantasia called *A Tangled Tale*. The whole book seems thrown together as a hasty publisher's job—there is not even a table of contents—and is typical of the careless handling that Lewis Carroll ordinarily gets.

The truth is that, if Dodgson and his work were shown as an organic whole, his "nonsense" would not seem the anomaly which it is usually represented as being. It is true that on one of his sides he was a pompous and priggish don. He used to write letters to friends the next morning after he had been having dinner with them and beg them never again in his presence to speak so irreverently of Our Lord as they had the

evening before, because it gave him infinite pain; and he wrote
to the papers in a tone of indignation worthy of Mr. Podsnap
protesting against the impiety of W. S. Gilbert in being whimsical about curates on the stage. But even this side of Dodgson
should not be kept out of the picture: the *Alice in Wonderland*
side has an intimate relation with it. Under the crust of the pious professor was a mind both rebellious and skeptical. The
mathematician who invented Alice was one of those semi-
monastic types—like Walter Pater and A. E. Housman—that
the English universities breed: vowed to an academic discipline
but cherishing an intense originality, painfully repressed and
incomplete but in the narrow field of their art somehow both
sound and bold. A good deal of the piquancy of the Alice
books is due to their merciless irreverence: in Alice's dreaming
mind, the bottoms dismayingly drop out of the didactic little
poems by Dr. Watts and Jane Taylor which Victorian children
were made to learn, and their simple and trite images are re-
placed by grotesque and silly ones, which have rushed in like
goblins to take possession. And in the White Knight's song
about the aged man a-sitting on a gate, a parody of Wordsworth's *Leech-Gatherer*, Lewis Carroll, in his subterranean
fashion, ridiculed the stuffed-shirt side of Wordsworth as savagely as Byron had ever done. Wordsworth was a great admiration of Dodgson's; yet as soon as he enters his world of
dreams, Lewis Carroll is moved to stick pins in him. This poem
in its original form, before it had been rewritten to adapt it to
Alice's dream, had been even more subversive of Victorian
conventions:

> I met an aged, aged man
>   Upon the lonely moor:
> I knew I was a gentleman,
>   And he was but a boor.
> So I stopped and roughly questioned him,
>   "Come, tell me how you live!"
> But his word impressed my ear no more
>   Than if it were a sieve.

It is curious what ordination as a clergyman of the Church
of England can do to an original mind. The case of Dodgson
is somewhat similar to those of Donne and Swift—though

Dodgson was shy and stammered and never took priest's orders; and he was closer, perhaps, to Swift and Donne than to the merely whimsical writer like Barrie or A. A. Milne, for Dodgson had a first-rate mind of a very unusual sort: he was a logician who was also a poet.

The poetry and the logic in Dodgson were closely bound up together. It has often been pointed out that only a mind primarily logical could have invented the jokes of the Alice books, of which the author is always conscious that they are examples of faulty syllogisms. But it also worked the other way: his eccentric imagination invaded his scholarly work. His *Symbolic Logic* (which had nothing to do with the subject called by the same name of which A. N. Whitehead and Bertrand Russell laid the foundation in their *Principia Mathematica*) contains syllogisms with terms as absurd as any in the Alice books:

> A prudent man shuns hyenas;
> No banker is imprudent.
> No banker fails to shun hyenas.

Dodgson's *Euclid and His Modern Rivals* had nothing to do with non-Euclidean geometry, but in the section called *A New Theory of Parallels* of his *Curiosa Mathematica* he grazed one of the conceptions of relativist theory; and is there not a touch of Einstein in the scenes in which the Red Queen has to keep running in order to remain in the same place and in which the White Queen gives a scream of pain before she has pricked her finger?

In literature, Lewis Carroll went deeper than his contemporaries realized and than he usually gets credit for even today. As studies in dream psychology, the Alice books are most remarkable: they do not suffer by comparison with the best serious performances in this field—with Strindberg or Joyce or Flaubert's *Tentation de Saint Antoine*. One of Alice's recent editors says that the heroine's personality is kept simple in order to throw into relief the eccentrics and monsters she meets. But the creatures that she meets, the whole dream, *are* Alice's personality and her waking life. They are the world of teachers, family and pets, as it appears to a little girl, and also the little girl who is looking at this world. The creatures are always snapping at her and chiding her, saying brusque and rude and

blighting things (as if their creator himself were snapping back
at the authorities and pieties he served); and she in turn has a
child's primitive cruelty: she cannot help mentioning cats when
she is swimming around with the mouse, and later on, with the
birds all around her, she comes out, as if naïvely, with, "Dinah's
our cat. And she's such a capital one for catching mice, you
can't think! And oh, I wish you could see her after the birds!
Why, she'll eat a little bird as soon as look at it!" But though
Alice is sometimes brutal, she is always well-bred; and, though
she wanders in a world full of mysteries and of sometimes disagreeable surprises, she is always a sensible and self-possessed
little upper-class English girl, who never fails in the last resort
to face down the outlandish creatures that plague her: she can
always bring the dream to an end by telling the King and
Queen and the Court that they're nothing but a pack of cards
or by picking up the Red Queen and shaking her. She can also
be sympathetic and sometimes—for example, with the White
Knight—exhibits a maternal instinct, but always in a sensible
and practical way. Lewis Carroll is never sentimental about
Alice, though he is later on to become so, in the messiest Victorian way, in the Sylvie and Bruno books. Yet *Sylvie and Bruno*,
too, has considerable psychological interest, with its alter-
nations of dream and reality and the elusive relationships
between them. The opening railway journey, in which the narrator is dozing and mixes with the images of his dream his
awareness of the lady sitting opposite him, is of an almost
Joycean complexity and quite inappropriate for reading to
children.

I do not, however, agree with Mr. Herrick, in the case of the
Alice books, that the Alice that grown-ups read is really a different work from the Alice that is read by children. The grown-
ups understand it better, but the prime source of the interest is
the same. Why is it that very young children listen so attentively to Alice, remember it all so well and ask to hear it again,
when many other stories seem to leave little impression? It is
surely the psychological truth of these books that lays its hold
on us all. Lewis Carroll is in touch with the real mind of childhood and hence with the more primitive elements of the mind
of maturity, too—unlike certain other writers who merely exploit for grown-ups an artificial child-mind of convention

which is in reality neither child-like nor adult. The shiftings
and the transformations, the mishaps and the triumphs of
Alice's dream, the mysteries and the riddles, the gibberish that
conveys unmistakable meanings, are all based upon relationships that contradict the assumptions of our conscious lives
but that are lurking not far behind them. In the "straight"
parts of *Sylvie and Bruno*, Lewis Carroll was mawkishly Victorian to the point of unintentional parody (having produced
in *The Two Voices* a masterpiece of intentional parody!), but in
the Alice books he quite got away from the upholstery and the
gloomy institutions of the nineteenth-century world. I believe
that they are likely to survive when a good deal of the more
monumental work of that world—the productions of the Car-
lyles and the Ruskins, the Spencers and the George Eliots—
shall have sunk with the middle-class ideals of which they were
the champions as well as the critics. Charles Dodgson who, in
morals and religion, in his attitude toward social institutions,
was professedly and as he himself believed, more conventional
than any of these, had over them the curious advantage of
working at once with the abstract materials of mathematical
and logical conceptions and with the irrationalities of dreams.
His art has a purity that is almost unique in a period so clut-
tered and cumbered, in which even the preachers of doom to
the reign of materialism bore the stamp and the stain of the industrial system in the hard insistence of their sentences and in
the turbidity of their belchings of rhetoric. They have shrunk
now, but Alice still stands.

I suggest to the Nonesuch Press that it would do well to get
out a definitive and comprehensive one-volume edition of
Dodgson, like their admirable editions of Blake and Donne.
The trouble about such collections as that which Mr. Herrick
has edited is that they are intended primarily for children.
There is no Charles Lutwidge Dodgson for grown-ups. *Sylvie
and Bruno*, which is never reprinted, ought to be made available; and there ought to be at least as many readers for the
Curiosa Mathematica and the *Dynamics of a Particle* as for
Donne's sermons or Blake's prophetic books. Dodgson's letters
should be included, his articles on local events at Oxford and
his journal of his trip to Russia; and there ought to be a good
memoir. The only biography of Dodgson is a conventional life

by a relative published in 1899. No writer, so far as I know, has ever done a serious portrait of him or made a real study of his work.

May 18, 1932

The needs pointed out in this article were very promptly supplied. In 1935, Mr. J. F. McDermott brought out a volume of the miscellaneous writings of Dodgson: *The Russian Journal and Other Selections from the Works of Lewis Carroll*; and in 1937 the Nonesuch Press did publish, as I had suggested, a well-produced omnibus volume, *The Complete Works of Lewis Carroll*, containing almost everything of Dodgson's (the Russian journal is not included) that a non-scholarly person could read. *Some Aspects of Pastoral* by William Empson (American edition called *English Pastoral Poetry*), published in 1935, includes an interesting study of the Alice books, which treats the cataclysmic finale of the dinner at the end of *Through the Looking-Glass* as the eruption of a repressed don, exasperated by dining with his colleagues.

The first full-length biography since *The Life and Letters of Lewis Carroll* by his nephew S. D. Collingwood appeared in 1945: *Victoria Through the Looking-Glass: The Life of Lewis Carroll*, by Florence Becker Lennon. This book has its unsatisfactory features. Mrs. Lennon presents her material in rather an untidy way: she nowhere, so far as I can find, for example, gives the date of Dodgson's birth—certainly not in the proper place; and the filling-in of the background, done from this side of the Atlantic, is synthetic and not easily assimilable. But this study is, nevertheless, the best thing that has yet been written about Lewis Carroll. The literary criticism is excellent; the psychological insight sometimes brilliant; and Mrs. Lennon has brought together, from the most scattered and various sources, a good deal of information. The impression that she actually conveys of what Dodgson's existence was like is more convincing than some of her theories. Mrs. Lennon believes that Charles Dodgson was intimidated by his clergyman father, so that he felt himself obliged to take orders and never dared question the creed of the Church. She seems to believe that he might otherwise have developed as an important original thinker. She also worries about what she regards as his frus-

trated sexual life: if he had only, she sighs, been capable of a
mature attachment for a woman which would have freed him
from his passion for little girls! (a penchant with which his position as elder brother of seven motherless sisters as well as the
strong feminine streak in him noted by Mrs. Lennon must
have had a good deal to do). What she does not understand, I
think, is that Dodgson, in terms of his age and place, was remarkably "well-adjusted." His enjoyment of the Oxford "Stu-
dentship," with its relatively agreeable work and exceptionally
comfortable quarters, which he won on his graduation was dependent on his acceptance of celibacy; and there is nothing to
show that this irked him much. His admiration and affection
for his father seem to have been complete; the rectory in which
he grew up was obviously as little as possible like that described by Samuel Butler in *The Way of All Flesh*; and with the
Dodgsons the church tradition was strong: Charles's father
and mother, who were cousins, had had the same Archbishop
for a grandfather. Since reading this biography and Collingwood's memoir, I am less disposed than I was when I wrote
the above article to assume that Charles Dodgson was seriously
cramped by his role. Mrs. Lennon insists that, in his photographs, he has the look of one "crucified," but she does not
produce any evidence that he actually suffered much. There is
mockery of course in Alice, who finds herself at odds with the
"creatures"; there are, as both Mrs. Lennon and Mr. Empson
suggest, outbreaks of contemptuous violence at the ends of
the Alice books and *Sylvie and Bruno*; but the forces of benev-
olence and common sense always triumph in what is not merely
the conventional Victorian happy ending, as they certainly did
in Dodgson's life. The conditions of teaching in an English
university in the middle of the nineteenth century may seem to
us today unnatural, but all social and professional situations involve their special disabilities, and in the position that Dodgson had chosen he seems to have functioned well. If a part of
his intelligence lived underground, if a part of his personality
was screened, it is plain that—Mrs. Lennon admits this—Alice
would never have gone down the rabbit-hole, would never have
walked through the mirror, if this had not been the case. Dodgson's work in mathematics and logic was somewhat eccentric,
too, and he sometimes, we are told, proposed problems, just as

his stories do, that probed into the depths of their subjects; but in these scientific fields as in fiction he seems to have given the world all that he was capable of. The author of *Sylvie and Bruno* was trying already for more than he could manage. Mrs. Lennon, has, I believe, been the first to point out the exact and complicated parallels between the dreams and the actualities that make this book psychologically interesting (my own references to these above have been added for the sake of completeness since the article was first written), but the novel for grown-ups is otherwise childish; and in mathematics and logic, according to the expert opinions cited by Mrs. Lennon, he either ignored or had never discovered the more advanced work in these fields, and did not perhaps get even so far as in his exploration of dreams.

It is one of the pioneering merits of *Victoria Through the Looking-Glass* that Mrs. Lennon has looked up these authoritative estimates of Dodgson's mathematical and logical work; and, a poet, she is able herself to provide an expert opinion on his poetry. The only aspect of his varied activity to which she does not seem quite to do justice is his achievement as an artist-photographer; but this subject has been dealt with since in a book called *Lewis Carroll Photographer* by Helmut Gernsheim (1950). Mr. Gernsheim considers Dodgson "the most outstanding photographer of children of the nineteenth century" and, after Julia Margaret Cameron, "probably the most distinguished amateur portraitist of the mid-Victorian era." In this field he was eccentric and perfectionist as he was in everything else. He showed the real reckless artist's passion in his pursuit of his two favorite kinds of subjects: celebrities and little girls. The former he besieged unabashedly, undaunted by occasional snubs and not afraid to arrive before breakfast, with all his apparatus in a cab, so that his prospects would not have a chance to escape. In his search for attractive little girls, he attended such incongruous functions as archery meetings and Freemason's fêtes, and spent part of his vacations at the seaside, supplied always with safety-pins in case he should find "a little girl hesitating to paddle in the sea for fear of spoiling her frock." His trophies repaid him for his risks and ordeals. A few of his portraits were reproduced in the Collingwood *Life and Letters*, but these do not give an adequate idea of the interest and scope of these plates. There was, it seems, an enormous body of work, of which twelve albums are known to survive. The sixty-four plates from three of them that Mr. Gernsheim includes in his book show a dramatic sense of personality—in the posing, the arrangement of the backgrounds and the feeling for facial expression—that one would not have suspected in Dodgson from his letters and his literary work and that reminds one of his love of the theater (which, in taking Holy Orders at Oxford, he made sure that he would not be expected to renounce). Here, humanly appealing and vivid, you have the troubled Elizabethanism of Tennyson; the jaunty, almost rakish bohemianism of Tom Taylor, the editor of *Punch*; the contemptuous independence of Rossetti; the serious and challenging young-womanhood of the eighteen-year-old Ellen Terry; the healthy Victorian attractiveness of Alexander Munro and his wife; and the morbid Victorian intensity of "Mrs. Franklin and her daughter Rose." There is a liveliness and a humor in these pictures that sometimes suggest Max Beerbohm. It is, one supposes, unlikely that Max could have seen these albums at the time he did his drawings of *Rossetti and His Circle*, but the photographs of the Millais's and the Rossettis seem to anticipate these. As for the pictures of children, they, too, are extremely varied and provide a new revelation of Lewis Carroll's special genius for depicting little English girls that is as brilliant in its way as Alice.

Lytton Strachey

IT IS sometimes the case with first-rate people that their lives seem to come to an end—sometimes very suddenly—just when they have finished performing their function. This was the case with Lytton Strachey. Lytton Strachey's chief mission, of course, was to take down once for all the pretensions of the Victorian Age to moral superiority. His declaration in the preface to *Eminent Victorians*, "Je n'impose rien; je ne propose rien: j'expose," was certainly not justified by the book that followed. His irony here was so acid that it partly dehumanized his subjects. The essays on Manning and Dr. Arnold, though the technique gives an effect of detachment, have a force of suppressed invective; and the essays on Florence Nightingale and Gordon, written with the same metallic accent, make the subjects less sympathetic than they probably deserve to be. In attempting to destroy, for example, the sentimental reputation that had been created for Florence Nightingale, he emphasized her hardness to such a degree as to slight her moral seriousness and the deep feeling for suffering that drove her. Only at moments does he let these appear: "O Father," he quotes her as writing, "Thou knowest that through all these horrible twenty years, I have been supported by the belief that I was working with Thee who wast bringing everyone, even our poor nurses, to perfection"; and "How inefficient I was in the Crimea, yet He raised up from it trained nursing." Such a woman must have been more than the mere demon of energy that Lytton Strachey tried to make her appear.

But from *Eminent Victorians* on, the ferocity of Strachey abates. Queen Victoria is already a different matter. In this book, both Victoria and Albert become human and not unattractive figures. He is said to have approached them originally in the mood of *Eminent Victorians* and then found himself relenting. Victoria is not caricatured as Florence Nightingale is: she is presented simply as a woman, living, for all her exalted position and her public responsibility, a woman's limited life. To Strachey's Victoria, the role of queen is a woman's personal experience, a matter of likes and dislikes, of living up to social obligations. This is the force of the famous deathbed scene, which has been imitated so often by people who have tried to reproduce the cadences without understanding the point: that Victoria has lived through the Victorian Age, has stood at the center of its forces, without knowing what it was all about.

But in Strachey's next biography, *Elizabeth and Essex*, he produces a somewhat similar effect without the same ironic intention. *Elizabeth and Essex* seems to me the least satisfactory of Strachey's books. His art, so tight and so calculated, so much influenced by the French, was ill-suited to the Elizabethan Age. His Elizabeth, though a fine piece of workmanship like everything he did, is worse than metallic, it is wooden. It concentrates so narrowly on the personal relation between the Queen and her favorite that we wonder, glancing back to the earlier book, whether it really was Victoria who lacked interest in the politics and thought of her time, whether it was not perhaps Strachey himself. Certainly Elizabeth lived in a larger intellectual world than Victoria, yet we get almost none of it in Strachey. In general, we do not feel that the individual fates of the characters are involved with the larger affairs of history. The personal story is told with insight, but then, after all, Michelet tells a thousand such stories, taking them in his stride. And we here, for the first time with Strachey, become disagreeably aware of the high-voiced old Bloomsbury gossip gloating over the scandals of the past as he ferrets them out in his library. Lytton Strachey's curious catty malice, his enjoyment of the discomfiture of his characters, is most unpleasantly in evidence in *Elizabeth and Essex*. His attitude toward women —Florence Nightingale, Mme. du Deffand, Queen Victoria or Queen Elizabeth—was peculiar in this, that he was fascinated by their psychology without feeling any of their attraction, and rather took pleasure in seeing them humiliated. The feminine subjects he chose were certainly lacking in feminine charm, and he seemed to do everything possible to make them unappetizing. His study of Queen Elizabeth in the light of modern psychology brings her character into sharper focus, but the effect of it is slightly disgusting; it marks so definitely the final surrender of Elizabethan to Bloomsbury England.

The revolt against Victorian pretences thus ends in faintly scabrous psychology; and in his next book Lytton Strachey recapitulates his view of history—a view with which Flaubert and Anatole France, Henry Adams and T. S. Eliot have already made us familiar and which assumes that modern society, in relation to the societies of the past, represents some sort of absolute deterioration. In *Portraits in Miniature*, which seems to me one of Strachey's real triumphs, he gives glimpses, through a series of thumb-nail sketches of for the most part minor historical and literary personages, of the evolution of modern society from the Elizabethan to the Victorian Age. These personages, by very reason of their special interest or small capacity, supply cultures particularly clear of the social and intellectual bacteria at work during the periods in which they lived. The first specimen is Sir John Harrington, the Elizabethan inventor of the water-closet; then we are shown some seventeenth-century types: an amateur scientist, a truculent classical scholar, an ambitious university don, the leader of an uncouth Protestant sect, and a few eighteenth-century types: a French abbé who consorted with the philosophers, a French magistrate and country gentleman who insisted on his rights, a lady of sensibility; and we end with Mme. de Lieven, whose liaison with the bourgeois Guizot marks for Strachey the final surrender of the splendid aristocratic qualities he had admired in Queen Elizabeth. A second series of miniatures reviews the British historians from the eighteenth-century Hume to the Victorian Bishop Creighton, and suggests a similar moral. The industrial, democratic, Protestant, middle-class world is a come-down, says Strachey by implication, from Queen Elizabeth, from Racine, from even Voltaire (these last two are favorites of Strachey's, on whom he has written more than once). When one considers the great souls of the past, the present seems dreary and vulgar—the Victorian Age in particular, for all its extraordinary energy, was a disgrace to the human spirit. This is the whole of the message of Strachey; and when he had said it as pointedly as possible in the fewest possible words, he died.

*

But not only did Strachey in his writings point an historical moral: he illustrated one himself. In his gallery of English historians, he himself should fill out the series. Certainly one of the best English writers of his period, he makes us feel sharply the contrast between Shakespeare's England and his. Shakespeare is expansive and untidy and close to the spoken language. Lytton Strachey, whose first-published book was a history of French literature, is so far from being any of these things that one of his chief feats consists in having managed to achieve in English some of the effects of French. His biographical method, though novel in England, was already an old story in France. Sainte-Beuve was the great master of it, and Strachey's ironic tone has something in common with his. The weaknesses as well as the virtues of Strachey's style are the result of his imitation of French models. He is lucid and cool and precise, but he is terribly given to clichés. The penalty of trying to reproduce in English the chaste and abstract vocabulary of French is finding one's language become pale and banal. No wonder the age of Shakespeare turned rigid and dry in Strachey's hand. And by the time he had reached *Portraits in Miniature*, he was importing belatedly to England a point of view that since the middle nineteenth century had become a commonplace in France.

The real force and audacity of Lytton Strachey are therefore seen best, as I have indicated, at the beginning of his career. In *Eminent Victorians*, which was published just at the end of the war, he stripped forever of their solemn upholstery the religion, the education, the statesmanship and the philanthropy of the society which had brought it about. The effect in the English-speaking countries was immediate and swiftly pervasive. The biographers turned at once to the easy game of exposing accepted celebrities, and this soon became a bore and a nuisance. The harshness of *Eminent Victorians* without Strachey's wide learning and bitter feeling, the intimate method of *Queen Victoria* without his insight into character, had the effect of cheapening history, something Strachey never did— for, though he was venomous about the Victorians, he did not make them any the less formidable. He had none of the modern vice of cockiness; he maintained a rare attitude of humility, of astonishment and admiration, before the unpredictable spectacle of life, which he was always finding "amazing" and "incredible." But neither the Americans nor the English have ever, since *Eminent Victorians* appeared, been able to feel quite the same about the legends that had dominated their pasts. Something had been punctured for good.

September 21, 1932

The Satire of Samuel Butler*

THE GENIUS of Samuel Butler was a livid intense flash. It brought out the black darkness around it, then itself rather quickly dimmed out.

The child of a provincial English rectory, he grew up in the narrowest, the most snobbish, the most bigoted and the most ungracious atmosphere which the Protestant nineteenth century produced. He rebelled against it and broke away from it, and he damned it forever in his masterpiece, *The Way of All Flesh*, which is likely to survive as one of the classical accounts of how hateful life could become when the successful British middle class mixed avarice with religion. "I had to steal my own birthright," says Butler. "I stole it and was bitterly punished. But I saved my soul alive." The punishment had affected him more permanently than he knew. He had blasted Langar Rectory to eternity, but it had left upon him its blight. His soul was alive; but, as Bernard Shaw says, he had been maimed by his early training. Having begun as the bad boy of a pious family, he was never to outgrow his original reactions. The dread of his father's bullying rage and his mother's harrowing prayers could still inhibit his mental processes; and up to the day of his death he could never assert himself without something of the sulkiness of the adolescent child who blurts out that he doesn't believe the Bible, betraying by his excessive pugnacity the delusion that the world, like his family, was conspiring to keep him down.

The Freudian would be able to show how, even after Butler had escaped from the domination of his father, he was still forced to keep putting in his father's place other persons of high authority and, identifying himself with some lesser person, to insist on the latter's superior claims. Dante, Virgil, Bach, Beethoven and Darwin had all to play the role of old Butler, while Handel, Giovanni Bellini, Tabachetti and Gaudenzio Ferrari were one by one put forward as the snubbed young man. When he did admire accepted reputations, as in the case

*Written as an introduction to *Erewhon*.

of Shakespeare and Homer, he had to work up heretical theories that flew in the face of authority as to who they had really been and what they had really meant. And though in *Erewhon* and *The Way of All Flesh* his revolt against his father had inspired him to what is certainly his most brilliant work, his controversies with substitute fathers became less and less interesting as Butler grew older, and he himself ended as a kind of crank. The shadows of the rectory were closing on him. His wit had attracted attention when *Erewhon* had first come out, but his work was not to be accepted as a part of the general culture of the time till after Butler's death, when *The Way of All Flesh* was published, and Bernard Shaw, the great popularizer, introduced him to a larger public. Shaw points out that, though Butler had revolted against the intolerance of his parents and though he yearned all his life toward a world in which opinions were playful and manners easy, he became as intolerant about Darwin as his father had been about himself; and the elder Yeats has put on record that, if one happened to meet Butler on a railway journey, his aspect could be so forbidding that one did not dare to speak to him first.

Erewhon, however, which was written in Butler's late twenties and early thirties, has the freshness and the bravado of his first defiance of the rectory and of his escape from his father and from England; and it is consequently his most attractive though not perhaps his greatest book. While the young Samuel Butler, just up from Cambridge, had been preparing for ordination in London, his religious faith had been shaken by his discovery that, among the poor boys in a class he was teaching, the ones who had not been baptized were by no means, so far as he could see, morally inferior to the ones who had; and, to the tune of lamentation and fury on the part of his father and mother, he had decided that the Church was not for him. He had persuaded his father to send him to New Zealand; and there in less than five years' time he had nearly doubled the £4,400 with which his father had grudgingly equipped him. The adventures amid wild and beautiful landscapes which finally bring Butler's hero to *Erewhon* are simply Butler's own travels in New Zealand; and his satire has here the clear-headedness and the high spirits of freedom of a young man on his own a long way from home. When he comes back to England, his father will not fail to cloud this clearness by insisting that the publication of *Erewhon* has caused Samuel's mother's death; and when in later years he travels in Sicily, he will receive no more vital revelation than that of his unprovable theory of the feminine authorship of the *Odyssey*. But he enjoys, in his *Erewhon* period, something of true intellectual liberation. (Two of the best of his later books—*The Way of All Flesh* and *Life and Habit*—followed closely on *Erewhon*.) He comes into contact here more intimately than ever afterwards with that ideal race of healthy and natural beings, gay, good-mannered and with comfortable consciences, whom he had imagined as the antithesis of the rectory and who were to haunt him and make him wistful all his life. (It will still be the legend of such a race which will delight him so much in Homer; and the "authoress of the *Odyssey*" herself seems a fantasy of such an ideal mate as he might have hoped to find among them.) Here even the eternal antagonism that Butler felt toward his father loses some of its bitterness and strain. In the chapter on *The World of the Unborn*, there is a magnanimous, an almost tender, insight of a kind very rare in Butler. For the moment he is free not to hate; he can understand that parents have not chosen their children any more than their children have chosen them, and that the plight in which the situation places us may be equally cruel for both.

Butler's *Erewhon*, therefore, is not a production that can be compared with *Candide* or *Gulliver's Travels*. The book is not a definite expression of a satirical point of view based on mature experience: it is the brilliant first fling of an able and gifted young man. It does not pretend to either the logic of Swift or the singleness of intention of Voltaire. The narrative is simply a device for uniting an assortment of satirical notions—in some cases, reductions to absurdity of English conceptions and institutions; in other cases, whimsical suggestions for improving them by their own methods; in still others, flights of fantastic reasoning whose application is rather uncertain.

Of this last kind, *The Book of Machines* is a curious and interesting example. Here there seem to be several intentions involved. One recognizes at once a burlesque of the methods of theological controversy. Samuel Butler had been brought up on theology, and its sophistries had affected his habits of thought in such a way that, when he sets out to write mock apologetics in a later book, *The Fair Haven*, attempting to discredit the Resurrection by inventing a simple-minded churchman who defends it with fallacious arguments, he misses fire through working on too large a scale and sounding too much in earnest, whereas the arguments of *The Authoress of the Odyssey*, which he means to be taken seriously, coming after his insidious satires, only put us on our guard against his theory. *The Book of the Machines*, he asserted at first, was a parody of the famous *Analogy* of that Butler (unrelated to himself) who had tried to defend revealed religion against the attacks of the Deists by demonstrating that their objections could equally well be urged against the known constitution of Nature. In a discussion of *Erewhon* in a letter, not long after its publication, Butler says of what he calls his "obviously absurd theory that they [the machines] are about to supplant the human race and be developed into a higher kind of life": "When I first got hold of the idea, I developed it for mere fun and because it amused me and I thought would amuse others, but without a particle of serious meaning; but I developed it and introduced it into *Erewhon* with the intention of implying: 'See how easy it is to be plausible, and what absurd propositions can be defended by a little ingenuity and distortion and departure from strictly scientific methods,' and I had Butler's *Analogy* in my head as the book at which it should be aimed, but preferred to conceal my aim."

But he had also another book in mind. This disquisition, when it had first appeared as an article in a New Zealand paper, had been called *Darwin Among the Machines*; and though Butler denied in his preface that he had intended to make fun of Darwin's theory, he acknowledged later on that he *had* intended to criticize it. "With *Erewhon*," Butler declared in a letter of 1902, "Charles Darwin smelt danger from afar. . . . He knew very well that the machine chapters in *Erewhon* would not end there." The *Book of the Machines* is thus, also, the first thrust in the battle with Darwinism that Butler was fighting all his life. If man and the other animals could develop through natural selection, why could not machines do so likewise? Had not Darwin, in assuming that the animals were mechanical, made it unthinkable that life should be purposive? Had he not "banished mind from the universe"? Samuel Butler has put himself in the queer situation—which would be interesting to analyze—of attacking on moral grounds the man who had supplied the most damaging weapons to the assault on that orthodox religion against which Butler himself was a rebel. For Samuel Butler was a moral philosopher, to use the old-fashioned term: he never became a modern scientist. He stuck halfway in an anomalous position between science and traditional theology. It was again the shell of the rectory which Samuel the rebel could never shed—and perhaps he felt some envy of Darwin, who had been a pupil of his grandfather's, the Bishop Butler who had been head of Shrewsbury School. Yet, working in his cramped intellectual space, he was able to drive home his Lamarckian point with intensity and telling effect.

There is, of course, however, in the fantasy of the machines another satiric theme and one much more obvious to us today, though evidently not so obvious to Butler: the appalling possibilities of the enslavement of man by the machine. "Man's very soul," Butler writes, "is due to the machines; it is a machine-made thing; he thinks as he thinks, and feels as he feels, through the work that machines have wrought upon him, and their existence is quite as much a *sine qua non* for his, as his for theirs." Nor does he fail to note the relation between the development of machinery and the competitive industrial system: "It is for neglecting them [the machines] that he [man] incurs their wrath, or for using inferior machines, or for not making sufficient exertions to invent new ones, or for destroying them without replacing them. . . . The machines, being of themselves unable to struggle, have got man to do their struggling for them: as long as he fulfills this function duly, all goes well with him—at least he thinks so; but the moment he fails to do his best for the advancement of machinery by encouraging the good and destroying the bad, he is left behind in the race of competition; and this means that he will be made uncomfortable in a variety of ways, and perhaps die."

How did Butler, five years after *Das Kapital*, eighteen years after Dickens' *Hard Times*, fail to satirize the profit-motive, which was turning the machine into a tyrant? He was far from approving the kind of civilization that the middle class had brought with it in its rise. He envied, on the one hand, the

civilized primitives of the world of the Homeric poems (who
lived before the machines) and of Erewhon (where they had
destroyed them); and, on the other hand, the worldly upper
class as represented by Townley in *The Way of All Flesh*. When
he makes Ernest in *The Way of All Flesh* turn shopkeeper and
marry the housemaid whom his mother has turned away and
send his children to be brought up by simple people such as
his own great-grandfather had been, Butler is criticizing the
evolution of his own family. The Butlers, taking flight from the
linen-draper who had been the father of Bishop Butler, had accumulated in two generations the education, the religion and
the snobbery which they had unloaded on the unhappy Samuel.
He understood very well the preoccupation of the Victorians
with money; and in his use of money as a comic motivation he
ran true to the satiric school of his time. For the Elizabethan
dramatists, the Barabases and the Volpones were still more or
less exceptional monsters. But for Dickens, the Jonas Chuzzlewits, the Bounderbys, the Smallweeds and the Grides were
common types of the dominant class. And with such comedies
of Gilbert's as *Engaged* and the plays of the Marxist Shaw,
money comes to play a similar role to that of gallantry in
Wycherley and Congreve. Samuel Butler could not even write
a classical oratorio on the idyllic theme of Narcissus without
yielding to an impulse to ridicule it with such program notes as
the following:

> An aged lady taken ill
> Desires to reconstruct her will;
> I see the servants hurrying for
> The family solicitor;
> Posthaste he comes and with him brings
> The usual necessary things.
> With common form and driving quill
> He draws the first part of the will,
> The more sonorous solemn sounds
> Denote a hundred thousand pounds, etc.

It is the entanglement of quarrels about money with disputes
about religion that makes the conflict between Ernest and his
father in *The Way of All Flesh* so comic and so ignoble.

Yet Butler, though he could be most amusing about people's

mercenary motives, was too much a middle-class man himself to analyze the social system, in which, for all his financial diffi-culties, he occupied a privileged position. As soon as he got back from New Zealand, he invested all the money he had made there in a group of new joint stock companies, which a banker friend of his had financed and in which he was induced to become a director. These companies were manufacturing steam-engines, patent gas-meters, tanning extracts and other commodities produced by the menacing machines. The com-panies all failed, and Butler lost most of his money. He had felt bound in honor to buy back the shares of friends who had in-vested in them at his advice. Then, almost as badly off as before he had gone to New Zealand, he threatened to make certain claims against an interest in a family estate to which he believed his father had induced him, while still a minor, to sign away his rights—the case of the youth in *Erewhon* who "was charged with having been swindled out of a large property by his guardian"—and compelled the old man to make him an allowance. "If in my books," wrote Butler late in life, "from *Erewhon* to *Luck or Cunning?* there is something behind the written words which the reader can feel but not grasp—and I fancy that this must be so—it is due, I believe, to the sense of wrong which was omnipresent with me, not only in regard to Pauli, the Darwins and my father, but also in regard to my ever-present anxiety about money."

When the elder Butler died, however, Samuel inherited his interest in the estate and lived comfortably the rest of his life. For all his satiric insight, he had basically the psychology of the *rentier*. One of the things that had nagged him most all his life was the fact that he had not had the family income to which he thought himself entitled; and when he did finally get it, he promptly sat down to write the Life and Letters of his grandfather, Bishop Butler, whom he had satirized in *The Way of All Flesh*. Later he described himself, in the preface to his last book, *Erewhon Revisited*, as "a member of the more ad-vanced wing of the English Broad Church."

May 24, 1933

André Malraux

NOBODY on our side of the Atlantic has yet written anything, so far as I know, about André Malraux, the French novelist; and, though I have read only two of his half-dozen books and am unable to deal with his work in any thoroughgoing fashion, I want to bring this fascinating and profitable writer to the attention of American readers. If the recent apotheosis of André Gide has been tending to discourage you with French literature, you will be glad to see the French genius cropping up again in a field where you would least expect it. A fault of much French writing lately has been that it has all seemed to be steeped in the atmosphere of the literary world of Paris, with its smug and self-conscious dependence on the French literary tradition. But M. André Malraux turns up a long way from Paris, and he nowhere—at any rate, in either of the books I have read—pays his pious respects to Racine.

M. Malraux first visited the orient at the age of twenty-three as head of an archeological expedition to Indo-China; but he presently dropped the cultural problems of ancient Cambodia for the political problems of the present. The orient that Malraux writes about is not the orient of *Madame Butterfly*. He published in 1928 a novel called *Les Conquérants*, which dealt with the events of the Chinese revolution in 1925. The reader who picked up this book was dazzled by an unhoped-for searchlight into a region which had previously seemed distant and dim. Here was a picture, based evidently on intimate knowledge, of the conflict of forces in modern China, with every figure, oriental or European, thrown into brilliant relief, every Chinese water-front or street—junks and steamers, pagodas, bars and banks—made distinctly and solidly visible. And here was something even more remarkable—something one had not yet found in contemporary fiction to the same degree: the psychological atmosphere of stress, with its own peculiar passions and moralities, its tense and sustained attitudes, which is coming to be felt throughout the world.

A translation of *Les Conquérants* (*The Conquerors*)—made, I am told, at Aldous Huxley's suggestion—has been brought out in England, but seems to have had no success at all. I do not know whether the odious role that is played in the book by the British has had anything to do with this. The novel has done no better here. Harcourt, Brace brought over sheets and sold only eight hundred copies. Yet I urge American and English publishers—especially now that reviewers are beginning to take Jules Romains as solemnly as he takes himself—to consider bringing out a translation of Malraux's new and even more important novel, *La Condition Humaine.*

I have spoken of Malraux's achievement in conveying the sense of strain produced by the antagonisms of modern society. The publication of *Les Conquérants* was followed, in *La Nouvelle Revue Française*, by a controversy between Malraux and Trotsky. (Trotsky's two papers are included in his *Problems of the Chinese Revolution.*) It was Trotsky's complaint that Malraux, though he had chosen a revolutionist for hero, had "introduced into his observations a small note of blasé superiority, seeming to excuse himself for his transient contact with the insurrection of the Chinese people, as much perhaps to himself as to the academic mandarins in France and the traffickers in spiritual opium." This is putting it a little too strongly; but it is true that Malraux's hero, Garin, has a certain alloy of old-fashioned romanticism. There are moments when he gives the impression of being simply another René or Manfred, somber, tortured, terrifying, a solitary savage rebel, seeking in the revolution what René had sought in the American forests, grasping at his bureau of propaganda with the same sort of desperation that Byron had brought to Greece. Part Swiss and part Russian, formerly an anarchist, Garin hates the bourgeoisie without real fellow-feeling for the masses: "'I don't love humanity. I don't love even the poor, the people—those, in fact, for whom I am fighting.' 'But you like them better than the others.' . . . 'I like them better, but only because they're beaten. Yes: on the whole, they have more feeling, more humanity, than the others—they have the virtues of the beaten. What's absolutely certain, however, is that I have nothing but hatred and disgust for the bourgeoisie from which I come. But as for the others, I know very well that they'd become quite abject as soon as we'd conquered together. We have our struggle in common—that's clear, at any rate.'" His dominant passion, he admits, is for power, and in the final scenes of the story, worn out with his work and dying of malaria and dysentery, he declares in his delirium that he now regrets having chosen to serve the Communists instead of England, since it is England that commands the real power. Yet in spite of his doubt and his egoism, he sticks by the revolution and is receiving, on the final page, the dispatches that bring the news of victory. Trotsky has expressed the opinion that what Garin needed was "a good inoculation of Marxism." Malraux retorted to this that there was something of Garin in Trotsky— pointing out that when you read in Trotsky's autobiography "the moving account of his fall, you forget that he is a Marxist, and perhaps he forgets it himself." He also protested that *La Condition Humaine* was not—what Trotsky had called it—a "novelized chronicle" of the Chinese revolution. "The principal emphasis," he says, "is on the relation between individuals and a collective action, not in the collective action alone." "The book," he explains, "is first of all a presentation of the human situation (*une accusation de la condition humaine*)."

André Malraux's new novel has this phrase for its title, *La Condition Humaine*, and it develops in a more explicit way the ideas implicit in *Les Conquérants*. *La Condition Humaine* is a much more ambitious and a more remarkable book than *Les Conquérants*. In the latter, Garin pretty well holds the spotlight, and there is an "I" who plays the role of Dr. Watson, deeply agitated by his hero's every utterance and standing by, indefatigably wide-eyed, while Garin receives portentous telegrams. He also plays the role of Conrad's Marlow. He is, in fact, our old friend the fictional observer who, from a more or less conventional point of view, looks on at a mystery or a moral problem. In this new book, however, the novelist gets rid of his European observer and, meeting Trotsky's challenge, attacks the revolution directly. Dealing with cultures the most diverse, moral systems the most irreconcilable, he establishes a position outside them which enables him to dispense with the formulas alike of the "academic mandarins" and of the orthodox Communists. I do not know of any modern book which dramatizes so successfully such varied national and social types. Beside it, even E. M. Forster's admirable *A Passage to India* appears a little provincial; you even—what rarely happens nowadays to the reader of a French novel—forget that the author is French. You see juxtaposed the old Buddhist China and its half-Europeanized children; the vaporing imagination of ruined aristocratic Europe and the single-minded will to money of the European business king; the American Calvinist missionary unwittingly building the character of the young Chinese terrorist; and—growing up under all the rest like the elm that splits the pavement—the new world of the revolutionary Marxist which is reorienting all the moralities. Nor is this handled in the manner of the journalist, as Paul Morand might have done it. The personalities of Malraux's characters are organically created and thoroughly explored. We not only witness their acts and see them in relation to the forces of the social-political scene: we share their most intimate sensations.

The handling of this huge and complicated subject must have given the author a good deal of trouble. He evidently sat down like an engineer to the problem of designing a structure that would meet a new set of conditions; and an occasional clumsiness of mechanics appears. The device of presenting in dramatic scenes the exposition of political events, to which we owe Garin and his eternal dispatches, here appears as a series of conversations so exhaustive and so perfectly to the point in their function of political analysis as—in spite of the author's efforts to particularize the characters—occasionally to lack plausibility. And we are sometimes thrown off the track when a thesis that deals with psychology comes butting into a paragraph devoted to explaining the "objective conditions" or when a description that had seemed as external as a colored picture postcard of Shanghai takes sudden subjective turn.

Yet, on the whole, the author has met these problems with amazing originality and skill. He has a genius for effects of contrast. The opening of *La Condition Humaine*, which follows the activities of a Communist group—a Chinese, a half-breed Jap, a Belgian and a Russian—the night before the insurrection, is a masterly dramatization. The initial inability of Tchen to bring himself to murder the man from whom he must steal the orders for the guns and his immediate realization afterwards of his terrorist's vocation; Baron Clappique's romances in the night club and his subsequent revelation of his ignoble trade; the confession of Kyo's wife that, on the eve of the insurrection, she has been unfaithful to him, and its repercussions on revolutionary solidarity; Tchen's report of what he has done and felt to his Buddhist-sociologist master, Gisors, and Gisors' prompt liquidation of his own anxiety and horror in an opium dream, in which the ripples from a boat on a lake full of water-lilies spread out to sweep all horror and anxiety into the purity and peace of the Divine—followed immediately by the spectacle of the real boat putting out in the Shanghai harbor to steal the guns for the insurrection: each one of these shocks is a flash that illuminates the conflicts and anomalies of the tense international city.

I have spoken of Malraux's success in avoiding conventional formulas. Where, however, is his own center? What is his frame of reference? What he wants to show us, he says, is the human situation. What is his view of the human situation? What every human being wants, he makes his philosopher Gisors explain, is not the object of his ambition itself, but to escape from the conditions of life, to give oneself the illusion of being God. Gisors attains this through opium; Tchen through assassination —an act in which he immolates himself, is the destroyed as well as the destroyer; Ferral, the French business man, tries to reach it through his sexual relations, in which he imagines himself in the roles of both possessed and possessor; even the rickety Baron Clappique finds it at the gambling table, where he identifies himself with the roulette ball, the master of both gain and loss; Kyo, the Japanese, rises above life when, for the sake of the revolution, he commits hara-kiri with cyanide; and Katov, the Russian Communist, gives his cyanide to brother Communists whose morale is weaker than his, when they have all been condemned to be burnt in the furnace of a locomotive. Tchen, Malraux lets us know, has saved his soul; Kyo has saved his, and more nobly; and Katov most nobly of all, because he can only fulfil himself by sacrificing himself to others.

There is, then, something else in the book besides the mere theme of escape from the human situation. The events described in *La Condition Humaine*, which occurred in 1927, must still have been going on while *Les Conquérants* was being written. At the end of the earlier novel, the Chinese revolution—there presented as the work of Garin as well as of Chiang Kai-shek—is assumed to be already victorious; in the later, the Communists fail, sold out by Chiang Kai-shek to the interests of Western capital and paralyzed by the faulty policy of the Comintern itself. Malraux seems, in line with Trotsky's advice, to have made some progress in Marxism. His interpretation of recent events seems now essentially Marxist—though he never, as I have said, slips into the facile formulas; and though the criticism his characters make of the line of the Comintern is more or less that of Trotsky, he maintains in relation to Trotsky, too, an attitude of independence. Marxism, Gisors observes, is not a doctrine but a will; and it is simply that, in Malraux's world, the only men he respects are animated by the Marxist will. *La Condition Humaine* ends with Gisors, who has lost his son Kyo, sinking back into the culture of the East and lighting up the opium pipe, while May, Kyo's widow, sets out for Moscow.

August 9, 1933

M. Malraux, on reading this article, wrote me the following letter:

n.r.f.

Le 2 oct.

Monsieur—Je trouve à mon retour à Paris l'article que vous voulez bien me consacrer.

Comme je vous réponds en suivant cet article permettez-moi d'abord quelques précisions. Je n'ai publié, en plus des livres que vous avez lus, qu'un livre et une plaquette (que je vous envoie)—le reste est très court et sans importance. D'autre part, mon père n'etait pas fonctionnaire en Indochine.* Je suis allé en Asie à 23 ans, comme chargé de mission archéologique. J'ai alors abandonné l'archéologie, organisé le mouvement Jeune-Annam, puis suis devenu commissaire du Kuomintang en Indochine et enfin à Canton.

Il y a du vrai dans ce que dit Trotsky de Garine, et dans ce que vous en dites vous-même. Peut-être faudrait-il pourtant tenir compte d'une certaine objectivité. Que ce personnage soit marxiste, certes non. Peut-être a-t-il tort, mais c'était ainsi. Il y avait à Canton en 1927 (ce fut très différent en 1927) singulièrement plus d'aventuriers

*This corrects an erroneous statement that I had made in the original version of my article.

révolutionnaires que de marxistes. Et lorsque Borodine discutait avec Sun-Yat-Sen, il n'était jamais question de lutte de classes.—Je ne voudrais pas faire de cela un argument, mais une nuance. Car il est fort vrai que le rôle joué dans mes livres par l'objectivité n'est pas de premier plan, et que *Les Conquérants* sont un roman "Expressioniste" comme, toutes proportions gardées, *Wuthering Heights* ou les *Karamazoff.*

Vous dites très justement que *La Condition humaine* développe certaines idées implicites dans *Les Conquérants*. Et aussi que le livre est meilleur (à la verite, du moins, c'est le seul que j'aime). Ma construction, en effet, ne pourrait rejoindre celle d'un écrivain comme Morand: ses types reposent sur l'observation ironique, le mien sur le besoin de traduire à travers des personnages un certain ordre de valeurs éthiques.

Ne voyez en ce semblant de discussion qu'un moyen de remercier plus longuement le premier critique, en Amérique, qui s'intéresse à ce que j'écris et croyez, je vous prie, Monsieur, à ma sympathie artistique, car je suis depuis longtemps l'effort de la *New Republic.*

André Malraux

Gertrude Stein Old and Young

I. 27, rue de Fleurus

GERTRUDE STEIN has written her memoirs. But she has attributed them to her friend and companion of twenty-five years and has called them *The Autobiography of Alice B. Toklas.* Her book is thus something rather different from the ordinary volume of memoirs. It is Gertrude Stein's imaginative projection of how she and her life and her circle must look to Alice B. Toklas. Miss Toklas is presented as the enthusiastic admirer and the obedient shadow of Miss Stein; she turns toward her as the sunflower toward the sun. Yet Miss Toklas's personality is by no means indistinguishable from Miss Stein's: Miss Stein has created her as an individual. And *The Autobiography of Alice B. Toklas* has something of the character and charm of a novel—a novel of which the subject is the life that Miss Stein and Miss Toklas have made for themselves in Paris, the salon over which they have presided, the whole complex of ideas and events of which they became the center: a social-artistic-intellectual organism.

It is an instructive and most entertaining book. The chapters which deal with the period before the European War are perhaps the most interesting part: here Miss Stein tells about her discovery of Picasso and Matisse, what they were like in their early phases, the gradual taking-shape as a movement of the tendencies of isolated artists, the development of her own literary methods. There is a good deal of wisdom about art and artists, literature and writers: "As Picasso once remarked, when you make a thing, it is so complicated making it that it is bound to be ugly, but those that do it after you they don't have to worry about making it and they can make it pretty, and so everybody can like it when the others make it." All this part of the book has the excitement of artistic adventure, which Gertrude Stein skillfully points up by making the narrator, Miss Toklas, come into the Stein world from the outside without knowing at first what it is all about. These chapters, with their stories of Matisse's insulted portrait, Gertrude Stein's

posing for Picasso, Braque's assault on the picture expert and
the dinner for the douanier Rousseau, are moving in their quiet
understatement. It was what Jean Cocteau called "the heroic
age," and Gertrude Stein's account of it evokes a nostalgia for
the days when the independent shows and the little magazines
were matters of prime importance, when everybody was serious about art and it was possible for American spinsters in
Paris to coöperate in perfect understanding with revolutionary
poets and painters. At the banquet for the douanier Rousseau,
Marie Laurencin "sang in a thin voice some charming old norman songs"; Rousseau, "blissful and gentle, played the violin"
and talked about his memories of Mexico; and Guillaume
Apollinaire invited Miss Stein and Miss Toklas "to sing some
of the native songs of the red indians" (to follow Miss Stein's
usage). André Salmon got drunk and chewed up Miss Toklas's
new hat; but she did not resent it long, as he "woke up very
charming and very polite" and it was all by way of homage to
the douanier.

The high heart of this period, however, was shaken by the
death in the war of Guillaume Apollinaire; the movement had
collided with historical events. The later chapters of the book
are less exciting. The painters have all arrived; the writers are
all arriving. Everybody, as Gertrude Stein intimates, is bent on
his own career. Miss Stein and Miss Toklas become more
waspish. "Gertrude Stein liked him [Ezra Pound] but did not
find him amusing. She said he was a village explainer, excellent
if you were a village, but if you were not, not." "There was
also Glenway Wescott but Glenway Wescott at no time interested Gertrude Stein. He has a certain syrup but it does not
pour." And they are pretty hard on Ernest Hemingway: "Gertrude Stein and Sherwood Anderson are very funny on the
subject of Hemingway. The last time that Sherwood was in
Paris they often talked about him. Hemingway had been
formed by the two of them and they were both a little proud
and a little ashamed of the work of their minds. . . . And
then they both agreed that they have a weakness for Hemingway because he is such a good pupil. He is a rotten pupil, I
protested. You don't understand, they both said, it is so flattering to have a pupil who does it without understanding it, in
other words he takes training and anybody who takes training

is a favorite pupil. They both admit it to be a weakness. Gertrude Stein added further, you see he is like Derain. You remember Monsieur de Tuille said, when I did not understand why Derain was having the success he was having that it was because he looks like a modern and smells of the museums."

It is true that, as one reads this book, one is more forcibly struck than ever by Hemingway's debt to Gertrude Stein. Such passages as the following suggest that he has been influenced by her conversational as well as by her literary style (I hardly dare suggest that the writing of Miss Stein may in turn have been somewhat affected by the conversations of Hemingway's characters): "It was about this time that the futurists, the Italian futurists, had their big show in Paris and it made a great deal of noise. Everybody was excited and this show being given in a very well known gallery everybody went. Jacques-Emile Blanche was terribly upset by it. We found him wandering tremblingly in the garden of the Tuileries and he said, it looks alright but is it. No it isn't, said Gertrude Stein. You do me good, said Jacques-Emile Blanche." Or: "He and I always say that he and I will be the last people of our generation to remember the war. I am afraid we both of us have already forgotten it a little. Only the other day though Elmer announced that he had had a great triumph, he had made Captain Peter and Captain Peter is a breton admit that it was a nice war. Up to this time when he had said to Captain Peter, it was a nice war, Captain Peter had not answered, but this time when Elmer said, it was a nice war, Captain Peter said, yes Elmer, it was a nice war."

Yet one feels that Miss Stein, in her criticism of certain of her friends and disciples, as expressed at any rate in this book, is affected by two unavowed considerations which tend to bias her judgment. In the first place, she is the ruler of a salon: there is something of Mme. Verdurin about her. You get the impression that when her protégés go elsewhere or cease to need her, she can no longer believe in them quite so strongly. She seems, for example, to hint that the virtue began to pass out of Matisse as soon as he became popular and prosperous and, moving away from Paris, no longer could come to her dinners. In the second place, she is a writer who has herself had some difficulty in getting published and who has not yet received the recognition to which she considers herself entitled. Her only references to Joyce in this book are (1) a mention of a project to bring him to see her that never came to anything and (2) the report of a derogatory remark that Picasso made about his work. Herself Miss Stein describes as "in english literature in her time . . . the only one." Success, for her, seems to imply some imposture or deterioration. Yet it is hard to tell how much deliberate irony there may be in the presentation of all this through the medium of Alice B. Toklas. There is evidently a certain amount of pure mischief in her treatment of Hemingway, as to whom a distinct difference is indicated between Miss Stein's and Miss Toklas's opinions. And it is hardly imaginable that the creator of Miss Furr and Miss Skeene can be insensible to the humors of Miss Toklas and Miss Stein. A cool and pervasive irony has always been one of the characteristics of Gertrude Stein's writing; and there is certainly, in this portrait of two ladies, more artistic impersonality than most of the comments I have heard will allow. When you have read it, you take away an impression of Miss Stein and Miss Toklas in Paris that is not in the least like anything you get from the memoirs, say, of Margot Asquith or of Isadora Duncan, but, rather, like your recollection of one of the households of Jane Austen.

The Autobiography of Alice B. Toklas, though not Gertrude Stein's most important book, is likely to prove her most popular. It is the only thing she has published since *Three Lives* which, from the ordinary point of view, is very easily readable. And she explains here, or makes Alice B. Toklas explain, in simpler language than heretofore, what she has subsequently been trying to do in the experiments that, beginning with *Tender Buttons*, have stimulated and troubled the literary world.

Let us hope that the *Autobiography*, with its wisdom, its distinction and its charm, may persuade the general public to recognize Gertrude Stein for what she is: one of the remarkable women of her time and, if not "in english literature the only one," at least one of the original ones. Hitherto, though her influence has always been felt at the sources of literature and art, her direct communications with this public have been intermittent and blurred, and, on the whole, neither the readers of modern books nor the collectors of modern painting have realized how much they owe her. When she was lecturing at Oxford and was asked by her hecklers why she "thought she was right in doing the kind of writing she did," she replied "that it was not a question of what anyone thought but after all she had been doing as she did for about twenty years and now they wanted to hear her lecture. This did not mean of course that they were coming to think that her way was a possible way, it proved nothing, but on the other hand it did possibly indicate something." The interest in the publication of these memoirs from quarters in which she has been scoffed at or ignored is a tribute of the same kind.

October 11, 1933

II. *Things As They Are*

The Banyan Press of Pawlet, Vermont, has published, in an edition of five hundred and sixteen copies, a very early manuscript of Gertrude Stein's: a short novel, to which the author had given the title *Quod Erat Demonstrandum* but which the editor, making use of a phrase from the story, has retitled *Things As They Are*. The manuscript is dated October 24, 1903, when the author was twenty-nine, and it must have been written before *Three Lives*, the first of her published books, which came out in 1909. Like *Three Lives*, it is quite comprehensible, and it does not even show any tendency toward the Steinian repetitiousness that already appears in *Three Lives*. It is a production of some literary merit and of much psychological interest. The reviewer had occasion some years ago to go through Miss Stein's work chronologically, and he came to the conclusion at that time that the vagueness that began to blur it from about 1910 on and the masking by unexplained metaphors that later made it seem opaque, though partly the result of an effort to emulate modern painting, were partly also due to a need imposed by the problem of writing about relationships between women of a kind that the standards of that era would not have allowed her to describe more explicitly. It

seemed obvious that her queer little portraits and her mis-
chievously baffling prose-poems did often deal with subjects of
this sort. Now the publication of *Things As They Are* comes to
confirm this theory. It is a story of the tangled relations of
three Lesbian American girls of the early nineteen-hundreds,
told with complete candor and an astonishing lack of self-
consciousness.

When one says that it is told with candor, one does not
mean that it has much in common with those case-histories of
Havelock Ellis that, published in his *Studies in the Psychology of
Sex* between 1897 and 1910, did a good deal to clear the air. In
this document of Gertrude Stein's, there is nothing in the least
scandalous (unless the subject itself be considered so), and the
whole thing is done with a sobriety, even an abstractness of
language, that recalls the French classical novels of the type of
Adolphe and *La Princesse de Clèves*. (The author's geometrical
title was, in fact, so perfectly appropriate that one wonders why
the editor should have wanted to change it.) Yet this study has
behind it something of the modern scientific temper and
brings us back to the brilliant young woman who, at Radcliffe,
took psychology with William James and was called by him his
best woman pupil, and who went through—though she did
not graduate—five years of medical school at Johns Hopkins.

Gertrude Stein went to Europe in 1903, after she had
dropped her medical work, and the heroine of *Things As They
Are*, a college graduate named Adele, is first seen on a ship
bound for Europe. She has given herself up in her steamer
chair "to a sense of physical weariness and to the disillusion-
ship [sic] of recent failures" when she is approached by a handsome girl, well-to-do and college-bred like herself, whose
obvious interest in her has the result of suddenly awakening
her from a "long emotional apathy." This girl, whose name is
Helen, tactfully pays her court, and Adele, though with a certain passivity, more or less responds to her attentions. But
Helen has another friend, Sophie, an intimate of long standing, who is also a friend of Adele's and who later explains to
Adele, when they are back in the United States, the nature of
her (Sophie's) relations with Helen. Adele is at first filled with
horror but, goaded by Helen's challenge, eventually herself
succumbs. This gives rise to something in the nature of the

heterosexual ménage à trois, but with differences that come out distinctly in the report of an observant woman who is not much disturbed by emotion. The homogeneity of sex seems in some ways a stabilizing influence, yet the intrusion of a masculine element on the part of the women themselves and the difficulty they have in keeping it up are uncertain and upsetting factors. Adele will assert of Sophie that "it was not that she had the manners of a perfect hostess but the more obtrusive good manners of a gentleman," and will try to assure herself that, in her attitude toward the trusting and deceived Sophie, she has not behaved like "a cad"; but at other moments strained relations collapse into feminine cattiness and lead to bitter altercations that seem almost to reach the hair-pulling stage. This inevitably becomes faintly comic, as if one were witnessing a triangle between three mislaid empty gloves, all intended for the left hand, and one cannot be sure that Gertrude Stein is not already treating the situation with irony. One does feel some personal animus on the part of the author toward Sophie, and the triangle results in an impasse that is painful for all three of the ladies—since Helen, of whom her family disapprove and who is kept by them on short rations, is obliged to do her travelling at Sophie's expense (Europe is a necessity for all of them), and Adele, realizing at last that she cannot break up the pair, finds it too much for her pride always to be following Helen and stealing moments from her intimacy with Sophie. Yet the smiling detached Gertrude Stein is already emerging in *Things As They Are* from the perplexities and the trying adjustments of the young woman intellectual who insists that she is loyal to the middle-class virtues. You are reminded in certain passages of the comedy of Miss Furr and Miss Skeene, that touching pair of left-hand gloves who are the heroines of another story.

This latter detachment of Gertrude Stein's is seen in its beginnings in *Things As They Are*, not only in the author's tone but also in the character of Adele. Adele is self-centered and rather inert; she does not readily give herself; she likes to be alone and ruminate, to feel that she is "her own man." Helen and Sophie, with their passions and reproaches, stimulate but also annoy her; her involvement with them hampers her movements. "Much as I wanted you," she says to Helen,

"I was not eager [to see you again] for after all you meant to me a turgid and complex world, difficult yet necessary to understand, and for the moment I wanted to escape all that, I longed only for obvious, superficial, clean simplicity." Her impulse, when she is faced with a problem, is not to see it through, for which Helen sometimes scolds her, but simply to drop it and go away and turn her attention to something else —as the young Gertrude Stein had declined to take William James's examination, explaining that she was very sorry but did not feel like an examination that morning. James gave her an A just the same, but she fared worse at Johns Hopkins, where her peculiar insouciance had to contend with hostile instructors who had not been convinced, in that era, that women should be admitted to medical schools. One feels, in *Things As They Are*, that Adele might have bucked Sophie if she had not so determinedly insisted on deserting the "strapped" Helen and going abroad again by herself. The mature Gertrude Stein later on—in her literary personality—went up on a high mountain, where she could dwell, when she chose, in a cloud. The already well-marked egoism of her heroine Adele is brought out by the comments of Adele's companions. It had grown, by the time of *Three Lives*, to that of the egoism of "Miss Mathilda," about whom revolve like satellites the three respectful maids, the Good Anna, Melanctha and the Gentle Lena, who give their names to the stories; and it had swollen to monstrous proportions by the time of *The Autobiography of Alice B. Toklas*, in which Miss Mathilda of Bridgepoint becomes frankly Miss Stein of Paris, an Olympian known only remotely through the impressions of an admiring high priestess.

The frustration of the young Adele, at the end of *Things As They Are*, is a matter, one feels, less of tragic loss than of failure of domination. Gertrude Stein, in her subsequent career, did partially succeed in dominating, through her salon, her collection, her wide reputation, her influence on certain writers; and in so far as she failed to carry off her pretentious claims, she seems to have concealed this—to add a third suggestion to the two I have already made to explain her later impenetrability—by putting herself, once for all, out of the reach of uncomfortable criticism. This reviewer met Miss Stein only once, but he received, in the course of that interview, an agreeable first impression of a quick and original intelligence dealing readily from the surface of the mind with the surfaces presented by life—the responses so direct and natural, the surfaces seen so unconventionally, that one did not at first feel anything wrong; but a chilling second impression of (to resort to an overworked metaphor) a great iceberg of megalomania that lay beneath this surface and on which, if one did not skirt around it, conversations and personal relations might easily crash and be wrecked. This iceberg—heavy and hard as the stone that her name brings to mind—must have been forming in an emotional solitude, and it now held her two-thirds submerged. I doubt whether the obscurity that hid it—the function of which seems to me quite different from that of Joyce or Virginia Woolf—will interest future readers as much as the limpidity of *Things As They Are.*

In any case, we must not leave *Things As They Are* without a glance at the attractive figure of the young independent girl in the costume of 1900, "the cut of whose shirt-waist alone betrayed her American origin" and of whom her friends, meeting her in Rome, exclaimed that she "looked as brown and white and clean as if [she] had just sprung out of the sea"; who liked to sit "in the court of the Alhambra watching the swallows fly in and out of the crevices of the walls, bathing in the soft air filled with the fragrance of myrtle and oleander and letting the hot sun burn her face and the palms of her hands" and who enjoyed making friends with a young Spanish girl whose language she could not speak and from whom she parted "as quiet friends part," turning again and again and "signing a gentle farewell" as long as they could see one another; who came back to "the white snow line of New York harbor," from the damp of a London winter, delighted to see the American flag, "the clean sky and the white snow and the straight plain ungainly buildings all in a cold and brilliant air without spot or stain," and who wandered for days about the Boston streets, "rejoicing in the passionless intelligence of the faces." She would be able, she must already have begun to feel, eventually to do without passion.

September 15, 1951

I may have exaggerated in this review the Lesbian aspect of Gertrude Stein's obscurity. At any rate, the first volume of her unpublished writings in the Yale University Library—brought out since this article was written—which consists of prose portraits composed in the years 1908–1912, does not seem to bear out my theory. One feels rather that the ruminative dimness is the result of an increasing remoteness in her personal relationships.

Mr. Wilder in the Middle West

A FEW YEARS AGO, Thornton Wilder was the center of a controversy on Marxism and literature. He was challenged by Michael Gold and others to come away from his first-century Greek islands and his imaginary eighteenth-century Perus and turn his attention to the United States. Mr. Wilder seems to have taken up this challenge in his new novel called *Heaven's My Destination*, and though, in the course of the polemical battle, he was sometimes unfairly treated, the episode should not be regretted if it is true, as has been reported, that it stimulated Mr. Wilder to attack this American subject.

Heaven's My Destination seems to me much Mr. Wilder's best book. It is as brilliant and sharp as *The Woman of Andros*, which seems to me his weakest novel, was comparatively mawkish and pale. The effect, in fact, on Mr. Wilder of taking his opponents' advice—if that is really what happened—has been so vividly to bring him to life that they are likely to experience a shock. In the first place, he has applied to the smoking-cars, the summer camps and the boarding-houses of the Middle West that gift for social observation that he exercised in *The Cabala* on an aristocratic international society, but on which in his intervening novels he has not had much occasion to call; and Oklahoma City, Kansas City and Ozarksville become much more entertaining places than even his Roman drawing-rooms. Besides this, Mr. Wilder has created in his central character, George Brush, a religious textbook salesman, a more complete and living person than any in his other books. And the pathetic Proustian cadences, here, have vanished from Mr. Wilder's style; his sentimentality is nowhere in evidence. The tone is always comic or matter-of-fact—with the result that Mr. Wilder's vision of an imperfect and suffering humanity comes through a good deal more tellingly than in any of his earlier novels. Finally—what makes *Heaven's My Destination* unique in its Middle Western field—he has handled his Sinclair Lewis material with his characteristic elegance of form and felicity of detail, his Mozartian combination of lightness and grace with

seriousness. (The Keatsian and Mozartian affinities of Wilder
were what his opponents in the Michael Gold controversy
tended to leave out of account; but he is probably the only
contemporary American whom it is possible to mention in
connection with such names.)

George Brush, Mr. Wilder's hero, though professionally a
textbook salesman, is by vocation a saint. "Of all the forms of
genius," Mr. Wilder quotes on the title-page from *The Woman
of Andros*, "goodness has the longest awkward age." When we
first encounter George Brush, he is attempting to save souls in
the smoking-car and annoying hotel managers by writing
Bible texts on the blotters. He comes from a farm in Michigan,
he has graduated from Shiloh Baptist College, where he has
been converted by a child evangelist, hopped up with morphine. But he has thought out his own principles of righteousness, and he has become many kinds of a crank. He is
unworthy, he believes, to go into the church, on account of
having once fornicated with a farmer's daughter at a farm
where he was spending the night. He has been looking for her
ever since to marry her. He is always getting arrested, as a result of his unconventional behavior in his attempts to live up
to his principles. He insists upon riding in a Jim Crow car,
because he believes in the equality of the races; draws all his
money out of the bank and tries to give the bank the interest,
because he believes in "voluntary poverty"; and makes a point
of allowing a hold-up man to collect from him more money
than he needs to, in order to show the thief that "he's really a
beggar at heart." In the course of his twenty-fourth year, the
period covered by the story, he makes himself absurd and obnoxious in an extraordinary variety of ways. In the course of
his adventures as a travelling salesman, he encounters a variety
of human types: the conscientious and desperate man, the cynical and desperate man (the story takes place during the depression), the intelligent man caught in a routine, the brilliant
man embittered by pride, the professional prostitute and the
professional minister of the Gospel, the criminal and the policeman. They reason with George Brush, remonstrate with him,
play jokes on him, insult him, rob him, beat him up, jail him;
but, in a sense, they are all powerless against him, because he is

a genuinely virtuous man, sustained by the knowledge that he wants to do right. Although his program for edifying people is almost completely wrong, he manages to do them good in ways that he has not planned simply by being what he is: a man who takes his obligations to the rest of humanity so seriously that he never thinks at all of his own interest.

At last he succeeds in finding the girl whom he feels he is bound to marry. She is more or less unattractive and doesn't in the least want to marry him; but he finally induces her to do so. For her, the marriage is not a success. He has to go out on the road again, and she lets him know that she wants to leave him. (This marriage is the only part of the story that seems to me incomplete and a little unconvincing. Why did Roberta, when George Brush turned up again, find him so completely distasteful? Why, when they were married, did he not proceed with his program of producing the half dozen children that he considered essential to an American home?) He loses his faith on the road and falls ill. He is desolated by the idea that his life has been all a failure, that everything he has done has been stupid and that everybody has come to hate him.

But an incident now occurs that, slight though it may seem in itself, has strangely important results. There has been living in Kansas City a Polish priest named Father Pasziewski. We have heard almost nothing about him except that he has been at death's door with gallstones, that he has then recovered and gone on with his work, that he is "an awful disappointed man" because the boys and girls of his parish—"the Knights of St. Ludowick" and "Mary's Flowers"—to whom he has devoted himself, have been turning into gangsters and dance-hall girls. He and George Brush have never met, but each has always inquired about the other: each has recognized the other's vocation. George Brush has been deeply moved by the news that Father Pasziewski was praying for him on Fridays. Now Father Pasziewski has died, and he has sent George one of his silver spoons (is this a symbol of apostolic succession?). George Brush recovers from his illness, and goes on trying to do people good and getting into new kinds of trouble.

Mr. Wilder has told this story with great skill and has made it on the surface extremely funny. A gift of humor one might not have suspected is another of Mr. Wilder's resources that has suddenly emerged in this book. But his real theme is George Brush's development, the education he derives from his misfortunes; and the remarkable feat Mr. Wilder performs is to make us end by liking and respecting his hero.

I do not see any reason that the radical reviewers who have been nagging at Thornton Wilder to write about his native country should not find *Heaven's My Destination* acceptable. Mr. Wilder, through Father Pasziewski, has tied up George Brush with the Church. But the act of divine intervention—I suppose that Mr. Wilder intends it as such—the arrival of the silver spoon, is not in itself, like the well-timed collapse of the Bridge of San Luis Rey, implausible to the non-believer. And in the meantime we have been given something more than a brilliant and veracious picture of an American variety of religious experience. George Brush, as I have said, is the type of saint, and he is therefore a universal character. The saint is a very special kind of person, but he turns up in other fields besides the religious one. The radical movement, too, has its saints, and they are people fundamentally akin to George Brush. Upton Sinclair in his early phases resembled him in some ways quite closely and committed some of the same sort of absurdities.

The radical's real objection to *Heaven's My Destination* would be that George Brush's creator never allows him to encounter a radical. What about the next generation of Father Pasziewskis? I happen to know the child of a family of Polish priests who has become an energetic Communist. And what about George Brush in ten years? We leave him at twenty-four: what is to be the rest of his education? He has evidently already discarded the fundamentalism that he affirmed at twenty-three. We are apparently intended to understand that he has finally investigated Darwin and no longer accepts the Garden of Eden. But is he not almost sure to go farther in the rationalistic criticism of his beliefs? What is to prevent him, with his pacifist principles, from discovering, as did A. J. Muste, that other religious pacifist, with whom, also, George Brush has something in common, that the causes of war are involved with the social-economic system—and becoming a labor organizer?

From the tenor of Mr. Wilder's other work, I assume that, when George Brush gets well and goes on trying to live up to his principles, he has recovered his faith in God. But this is actually left rather ambiguous, and perhaps Mr. Wilder ought to be challenged once more to make it clear just what George Brush's point of view is when he goes out on the road again.

January 6, 1934

The Literary Worker's Polonius

A Brief Guide for Authors and Editors

Nature of Magazines and Editors

THE PRIMARY FACT to be grasped about editors is that they are not independent agents, but function as parts of the larger organisms known as magazines. Magazines, like other living organisms, develop according to certain laws and pass through regular life-cycles. These cycles may vary in length from a few to many years; but they all complete the same cycle (unless they meet untimely ends); they have a youth, a maturity and an old age. In its earliest years, a magazine may seem spontaneous, novel and daring; but by the time it has reached its maturity it has, as the French say, "taken its fold," and it succumbs to a force of inertia against which the youngest and freshest editor is as powerless as the oldest and stalest. Thereafter, it grows old, declines and dies.

Magazines derive their principle of being from a relation between some part of the mind of the editor and some part of the mind of the public. They rarely represent the whole of the editor or the editor at his best; and they do not usually give the public all it wants. But the relationship, once established, apparently cannot be altered. Both editor and reader may be bored by the contents of the magazine; but at this point it will be impossible to introduce any real novelty or to make any serious new departure. To his readers as well as to his contributors, the editor may seem timid, pedantic, unimaginative, obsessed by formulas. But anyone who has had anything to do with magazine offices knows that there is always a Higher Power which decides all important issues: the magazine as an entity in itself. And this entity takes on eventually a purely metaphysical character: it has nothing to do with commercial considerations. It can often be demonstrated that a drastic change in policy would increase the circulation of the magazine; but such a change is no more possible to effect than the transformation, by grafting on wings or claws, of one kind of animal into another.

Magazines cannot be born again. The most that can be done with a magazine is to subject it to a sort of face-lifting process, which, though it may improve its look at long distance, only exposes it, on closer examination, in a more hideous state of senility. Or, as in the case of the old *Dial*, a magazine can be deliberately killed off, and the name taken over for a new one. But, otherwise, the most that can be hoped is that a magazine may pass its old age in something like comfort and peace without lapsing from its original standards. All too often it must linger on in a dotage or a cheapened form which disgusts its former readers.

Duties of the Editor to the Contributor

The scope within which it is possible for the editor to exercise independent volition is thus seen to be narrowly circumscribed. It is limited, in fact, to the purely business aspects of his dealings with his contributors. The selection of material is determined by the higher will of the magazine; but the editor can be more or less prompt in registering and conveying to the contributor the decisions thus arrived at. And the prompt communication of decisions is one of the editor's prime duties to his writers. The editor has a regular job; the writer very often has not, and he may even depend for the necessities of life on selling what he has written. He usually wants an immediate decision even though it may be adverse; such a decision would at least make it possible for him to send his manuscript elsewhere.

Some editors are efficient about this: Mencken and Nathan, for example, were remarkable for the definiteness and promptness of their decisions. But many editors are either the victims of badly organized offices or lack consideration for writers, and cause by their negligence or irresolute stalling an immense amount of depression, exasperation and sometimes even actual privation.

A piece of writing, once accepted, should be paid for on the nail (if the finances of the paper permit it); and, once accepted, it should be printed. In the first connection, the ideal method is that of one of the New York weeklies, which sends the check with the letter of acceptance. In the matter of printing, it ought to be said that there are sometimes extenuating circumstances, which the writer should understand and allow for. One of the editors may have pressed a decision in favor of accepting a manuscript which one or more of the other editors may afterwards consciously or unconsciously sabotage; or an editor may sabotage a manuscript which he has been responsible for accepting himself. Allowing, however, a certain small margin for sincere doubts and differences on the part of editors, it must be asserted, as a general thing, that the writer has just cause for complaint when an editor accepts his manuscript and then suppresses it by leaving it in the "barrel."

Connected with this is another matter which has probably caused between the editor and the writer more misunderstanding and bitterness than any other aspect of their relations, and which has often for the writer, and sometimes for the editor, resulted in serious loss. This is the question of ordering things in advance. The problem of making these decisions clear and afterwards keeping them straight is entirely in the hands of the editor, and it is sometimes not the least difficult of his problems, since the writer, through his eagerness for the order, will sometimes unconsciously do his best to mistake an expression of possible interest for a commitment to buy what he writes; but any editor with a primary grasp of the duties of his position will school himself never to leave any doubt as to whether or not an article is ordered and to stick by his engagement, once it has been made. If the manuscript turns out too badly, he is not absolutely bound to print it; but he is certainly bound to pay for it and to give it back to the writer, so that the latter may have a chance of publishing it elsewhere.

Duties of the Writer to the Editor

On the other hand, the writer should allow the editor a reasonable length of time in which to decide and should not pester him with letters and telephone calls till a maximum of, say, two weeks has elapsed.

The writer should always have his manuscript typed, and he should never send it in to the magazine accompanied by a long letter, or, unless he knows one of the editors, by any letter at all. In the first place, these letters are rarely read; and, in the second place, they usually have the effect of prejudicing the editor against the piece instead of stimulating his interest in it. This prejudice may sometimes result in unfairness on the part of the editor, if the writer is inexperienced and has thought it the natural thing to address himself directly to the editor— since he is used to being addressed by the editor, in the editorial department of the magazine, in a friendly and even confidential manner. But such writers should be warned that manuscript-reading is one of the most trying of an editor's tasks and that the notion of reading long letters in addition is one that he rejects with impatience. Manuscripts must speak for themselves; letters can never help them. If the writer should happen to know one of the editors, who he imagines may be sympathetically disposed toward him, he may address his manuscript to this editor (though some magazines have tried to bar this): he may possibly get prompter consideration. But he should never write more than a line.

Nature of Authors

The relations between authors and reviewers are a constant source of anxiety to authors. To understand why this should be so, we must first examine the nature of authors.

Authors in the main are persons who are preoccupied with constructing and peopling individual intellectual worlds. They may be roughly divided into three classes:

1. *Fiction-Writers.* Novelists and short-story writers are writers who make up fantasies about imaginary people. Such writers may in certain instances be on fairly good terms with one another, but the imaginary worlds they inhabit tend to be mutually exclusive. As a result, they seem ungenerous to one another, and it is sometimes superficially concluded that they are exceptionally vain and envious people. This is, however, not always the case. The pure type of fiction-writer who merely reacts to the stimuli of life with no broad philosophical or

historical interest will feel naturally that the work of another such writer, especially if he is dealing with the same material, is a monstrous misrepresentation or even a deliberate imposture.

2. *Poets.* Poets are today imaginative writers who use the technique of verse. This technique, though employed by the ancients for almost every form of utterance and record, from songs to dramas and epics, from legal codes to medical treatises, has come to be confined in our epoch to functions of a specialized kind. Where the novelist deals in character, adventure and situation, the poet is usually limited to the expression of emotion and mood or to the simple description of people and objects. As a consequence, being a poet is rarely a full-time job, and the poet has large spaces in his life which are not filled by his literary activity proper and in which he is likely to occupy himself with a kind of professional politics. Poets form into groups, which in their combinations, disruptions and recombinations, their debates, practical jokes and fierce battles, tend to keep them in a state of excitement. In this group instinct they somewhat resemble painters—though painters, by reason of the fact that they practise a genuine handicraft instead of a purely intellectual métier, have a certain amount of physical work to tire them and are not so erinaceous as poets. The reactions of groups of poets toward one another may be said to correspond more or less to the reactions of individual novelists.

3. *Scientific, philosophical and critical writers.* This class includes all those writers who are occupied with the attempt to present or to interpret known events, or to investigate the nature of reality. They are sometimes capable of a kind of collaboration hardly known among novelists and poets, for the reason that, where the materials are facts themselves, it usually requires more than one person to ascertain what the facts are and to organize them, and where the field is that of mathematical or metaphysical theory, a staff of several persons may be enlisted to develop the ramifications of a subject. But though it is possible for a number of experts to work together on some special subject, it not infrequently happens that monopolies are attempted by the groups themselves or by powerful authorities in some department, and these may lead to stupendous combats like the brawlings of Leviathan and Behemoth. It should

be added that literary critics may develop the worst characteristics of any of these other classes of writers.

(It may be suggested that the writers of fictionized biography and history constitute a fourth class, which should be
listed between classes 1 and 2; but the truth is that producers of
books of this type are not genuine writers at all, but merely a
kind of chimera believed in during the Boom by publishers.)

It will be seen, then, that all classes of authors tend to assume
that their personally created worlds have some kind of general
validity, and that they are likely to be disturbed when an attempt
is made by anyone else to question or upset this assumption.

The author is most often upset in this way by the people
who review his books. For an author, the reading of his reviews,
whether favorable or unfavorable, is one of the most disappointing experiences in life. He has been laboring for months
or for years to focus some comprehensive vision or to make
out some compelling case, and then finds his book discussed
by persons who not only have not understood it, but do not
even in some instances appear to have read it. In twenty-two
reviews out of two dozen, either the reviewer has attempted
nothing more than to give a description of the contents of the
book, not even doing this correctly (and these reviews are
often copied word for word from one another), or his comments, either praise or blame, seem to the author to have little
or no relevance to the book he believes he has written. The
reading of his reviews, indeed, is so likely to let the author
down after the excitement and satisfaction of finishing his book
that there is a good deal to be said for the practice of those
writers who go off on trips to remote parts of the world as
soon as their last proofs have been corrected.

In order to understand why the reviewer thus disappoints
the author, we must inquire as to who reviewers are and under
what circumstances they do their work.

Nature of Reviewers

Reviewers may be classified under five heads:

1. *People who want work.* Every magazine office is a clearing-
house for people who need money or jobs: the waiting-rooms

are always full of college graduates, indigent radicals, escaped débutantes and wives, young boys who have just bummed their way from the Coast, and many other types of persons who want to write or to associate themselves with writing, as well as personal friends of the editors in difficulties. These people should be given considerate attention, if only because it sometimes turns out that there is a really good writer among them; and it is customary on magazines with literary sections to try them out on writing book reviews. These book reviews are often very bad and not far, if at all, removed from school exercises. But the editor will want to pay for them if he knows that the writer needs money, and when he has paid for them, he will feel that he ought to print them if by any means they can be made presentable. The best solution to this problem is probably that adopted by one of the New York weeklies. This magazine sells the extra books which come into the office for review and provides a permanent fund for the relief of needy writers, thus rendering it unnecessary to purchase from them reviews which may turn out to be either unprintable or printable only at the expense of a great deal of drudgery on the part of the editor.

To the groups mentioned above should be added the impoverished novelist or poet who, though gifted and expert in his own field, may have no aptitude for or practice in reviewing.

2. *Literary columnists.* The writer of a newspaper literary column has to read and talk about one or more books a day for five or six days of the week. To go through all these books conscientiously and comment upon them thoughtfully is a task beyond human capacity; and, in consequence, it is not to be expected of these writers that they should give us much serious criticism. Not all of them are interested in books: some are literary columnists merely by accident; others may be well-equipped persons who have to write so much and so fast that they are not able to do themselves justice. But in any case one should judge these writers, not as essayists or critical authorities, but as chroniclers of the literary news, who are managing more or less sensibly and more or less entertainingly to give, by a selection of excerpts or a swift résumé of a book's con-

tents, a more or less adequate idea of the events of the publishing season.

Where the newspaper reviewer is most likely to go wrong is in explaining the purport or the significance of a book. A short and concentrated piece of writing such as one of Ernest Hemingway's short stories is very quickly read (these reviewers are naturally delighted when they strike something easy to get through), and the chances are that the reviewer will miss many things that the author has worked hard to make implicit in it, that he will, in fact, miss the point. And in the case of a long book, he is likely to be forced to skip through it, and so not only mistake the author's intention, but make blunders as to what has been said. When André Malraux's *Man's Fate* came out in English, for example, the newspaper accounts of the characters and the story seemed to me so different from what I remembered from reading it in French that I was driven to look up the translation. But the translator had in general been accurate: it was the reviewers who had sometimes been confused from having had to deal hurriedly and briefly with so crowded and complex a work. Yet it is also true that even in the case of Thornton Wilder's *Heaven's My Destination*, one of the newspaper reviewers managed to mix up the characters. It may perhaps be demanded of the newspaper reviewer that he avoid this sort of literal inaccuracy, but even that is demanding a good deal and the most, probably, that one should expect.

3. *People who want to write about something else.* Book-reviewing is frequently exploited, especially by the young, as a pretext for writing an essay of one's own on the subject dealt with by the book or for neglecting the book altogether and writing an essay on some other subject. Such reviews are often bitterly resented both by authors and by conscientious critics; but anyone who has ever been an editor must regard them, if they are interesting in themselves, with a certain amount of leniency: it is so relatively rare for an editor to get really interesting articles of any kind that he cannot afford to discourage them even on those occasions when they displace proper reviews. The author may console himself with the thought that the review he might otherwise have had would probably have been as poor as most reviews.

We may also treat under this head the problem of young people in general. Should a brilliant but inexperienced young writer be allowed to treat a mature writer unfairly in a brilliant but uncomprehending review? The young must be given a chance, and their point of view is sometimes important, even when what they say is entirely aside from the mark. Older writers have sometimes to resign themselves to being mistreated by youth. And there are also, of course, the embittered old who are irked at being driven to write reviews and who take it out in putting the young in their places and in undermining their more prosperous contemporaries.

4. *Reviewer experts.* The so often unsatisfactory results of having books of poetry reviewed by persons who have never written verse, works of philosophy by persons with no philosophical training, and so forth, have led editors to try to get poets to write about poets, philosophers to write about philosophers. The trouble with this, however, is that the philosopher or the poet is likely to belong either to the same school or to some opposing school, so that in either case the review may be biased and produce for the outside reader a misleading impression of the book.

5. *Reviewer critics.* These are extremely rare. Most people who are capable of first-rate criticism do not want to interrupt their other work for jobs as unremunerative as book reviews. Exceptional cases were Van Wyck Brooks and H. L. Mencken; but the former was rather narrowly specialized, and the latter has always tended to use book-reviewing as a way of putting over his own personality and his opinions on all sorts of subjects. The only American writer who has tried recently to do this kind of thing the way, ideally, it ought to be done was a second-rate man, Stuart P. Sherman. Such a reviewer should be more or less familiar, or be ready to familiarize himself, with the past work of every important writer he deals with and be able to write about an author's new book in the light of his general development and intention. He should also be able to see the author in relation to the national literature as a whole and the national literature in relation to other literatures. But this means a great deal of work, and it presupposes a certain amount of training. Sainte-Beuve had to work all week— hardly taking time out for lunch—for each of his *Causeries du*

Lundi. But Sainte-Beuve was perhaps a unique case. Has there ever been another example of a man of Sainte-Beuve's abilities devoting so large a part of his life to weekly articles on miscellaneous subjects?

I want to suggest, however, that it might be a profitable idea for some editor to get a really able writer on literature and make it worth his while to do a weekly article. For a man who should combine a sound education with intelligence and literary ability he would probably best go to the universities, where the *Herald Tribune* got Stuart Sherman and the *New Masses* Granville Hicks. Let him take, say, a Newton Arvin or a Haakon Chevalier, impose upon him no duties that would impede his weekly articles—Burton Rascoe's articles evidently suffered, when he ran the *Herald Tribune* book section, from his having too much to do—and pay him enough to live on. He should not be expected to cover what is published, but to write each week of a man or a book. I believe that such a feature would prove valuable to the magazine that installed it and an excellent thing for the literary world in general.

Attitude of the Author toward the Reviewer

It will thus be seen that the author has no justification for expecting serious criticism from reviewers, and that, in becoming elated or indignant over anything that is written about his books, he is wasting his nervous energy.

His reviews, if he knows how to read them, may have for the author a certain interest; but he will not be able to find out from them very much about the value of his work. For this he will have to depend on other sources, such as remarks made in casual conversation and evidences of his effect on other writers—always bearing in mind, however, that the true excellence or badness of what he has written may never really be grasped during his lifetime—a hazard for which we must all be prepared. And in the meantime he should read his reviews, not as the verdict of a Supreme Court of critics, but as a collection of opinions by persons of various degrees of intelligence who have happened to have some contact with his book. Considered from this point of view, there is occasionally something to be learned from them.

Special Psychology of Reviewers

The reviewer, like other kinds of writers, has his ego; and, since he is continually occupied with other people's books, it is somewhat peculiarly difficult for this ego to assert itself. One of the best ways in which a reviewer can give himself a vicarious sense of creation is by encouraging and presenting new writers who have previously been unknown; but when a writer is already known, the reviewer may procure the sensation of power by making the gesture of putting him down. This psychology must always be reckoned with. In the literary world in the last few years, one has seen a number of writers cried up at the time when they were still obscure, by the more discerning critics, and then afterwards disparaged by them. This has happened in turn to Eugene O'Neill, Edna St. Vincent Millay, Ernest Hemingway and Thornton Wilder. It is the rarest thing in the world at the present time to find a word of intelligent critical comment on any of these important writers. And the unfortunate Mr. Saroyan has been put through the cycle in record time. He was first discovered by the editors of *Story* and acquired a reputation among its readers. Then, when his book was published, he got some prompt enthusiastic reviews. But he had now been triumphantly brought out, and after this there was nothing left for the later reviewers of his books but to try to make him ashamed of himself.

Duties of the Reviewer to the Author

On the other side, however, the reviewer has certain obligations in relation to the author.

I have recommended lenience toward reviewers who use the books they are supposed to be reviewing as pretexts for expressing themselves; but only in cases where their articles—what happens comparatively rarely—are interesting in themselves. There is no excuse at all for an uninteresting review that tells nothing about the book. The reviewer, at the very least, should be expected to supply information. The retelling of the story of a novel, the summary of an historical or philosophical book, the selection of representative passages and the attempt to communicate the quality of a poet, is the most boring part of the reviewer's business, but it is an absolutely essential part. The reader should be given a chance to judge whether or not he would be interested in the book, irrespective of what the reviewer may think of it; and it is an indispensable discipline for the reviewer, or any critic, to give the gist of the book in his own words. The reviewer, when he sets about this task, is quite likely to find that there is more in the book, or less in it, or something different in it, than he imagined when he first went through it. If the author is incoherent or woolly, the critic will be able to detect it. If the reviewer is incompetent, his incompetence will be evident to his more acute readers when they find out he cannot tell them what is in the book.

The failure to follow this procedure is one of the factors responsible for those opaque pretentious essays, aesthetic, metaphysical or social, that, especially in the highbrow reviews, are sometimes hung on the titles of books. The reader has no means of knowing, if he has not himself read the books, whether they prove the critic's points or not: the titles play the role of counters to which, from the reader's point of view, no value has been assigned. It is as vitally important for the critic to establish definite identities for the books that he discusses in an essay as it is for the novelist to establish them for the characters who figure in his story.

Attitude of the Author toward His Public

Another class of persons toward whom the poised author should adopt an unemotional attitude are the people who write him letters. Most of these fall into the following categories:

1. *Insane people and cranks.* The author should be able to spot these and should remember that people in abnormal states of mind are likely to be set off by anything.

2. *Lonely women and persons in provincial isolation.* Of these, even when they are sane, very much the same thing may be said: the fact that they write authors letters shows merely that they need to communicate with somebody and does not necessarily imply any interest or merit in the author's books.

3. *Young people who want the author to read their manuscripts.*

4. *People who want the author's autograph.* These, for the

most part, either want it for a collection, and have no interest in the author's books, or want it in order to sell it.

Along with a good many of these, the author will receive a few letters from people who are interested in what he has written and have something to say to him about it. But, in general, it may be assumed that the letters written to authors mean nothing. No writer who has been an editor can ever take letters so seriously as is often done by writers who have had no such experience. Every editor has seen almost incredible evidence that one cannot publish anything in a magazine so bad that some reader will not write in to say that it has changed his life, or so good that it will not cause someone to cancel his subscription.

Duty of the Public toward the Author

One should never send manuscripts to authors. They have enough to do writing their books. If authors read the manuscripts sent them, they would never be able to do anything else. The author of a manuscript who desires advice should send it to a publisher or editor: they pay people for this kind of work.

Duty of Authors to Other People

The author should not make a practice of sending out to his friends, or to persons whom he admires but does not know, large quantities of his books, inscribed. In the first place, he will be out of pocket if he exceeds the publisher's quota of free copies. In the second place, inscribed books from authors are likely to prove a nuisance: the person to whom the book has been sent is likely to feel that he ought to read it and yet at the moment may not be able to; he will go around having it on his conscience that he ought to have written to the author. And when he does get around to reading it, he may feel that the flattering or affectionate inscription obliges him, whether he likes it or not, to say something nice about it. Such a present is really a bribe that is likely to prevent the reader from coming out with the candid opinion which the author imagines he values.

Duty of the Novelist to the Public and the Profession

The novelist should never put at the end of his novel a date of the following kind:

Boulogne-sur-Mer–Hoboken
December 1934–*January* 1935

This kind of thing has been in fashion ever since Joyce dated Ulysses:

Trieste–Zurich–Paris 1914–1921

but it is rarely justified. In Joyce's case, the book took seven years, and the date has a special point, for Stephen Dedalus in 1904 is made to tell the Dubliners of the novel that he will produce something important in ten years' time. But it is usually a mistake for other writers to imitate this, for the reasons that, in the first place, it is dangerous to suggest a comparison with Joyce; and, in the second place, that such dates are irrelevant. In the case of a poem, date and place may in certain instances be in order if they add something that helps in understanding it and that cannot be conveniently put into the poem. But if a novelist is really successful, he will have interested us in characters and happenings that are supposed to have nothing to do with himself; he will have induced us to accept their reality, and it is therefore an impertinence to his own creation to remind us of himself and where he has worked. If the novelist has been unsuccessful, the reader, when he has got through the book, will not care to be reminded of the author and his sojourn at Boulogne-sur-Mer.

June, 1935

The Classics on the Soviet Stage

IN 1935, I spent five months in the Soviet Union. While there, I was invited to contribute an article to an English-language paper published in Russia, the Moscow *Daily News*. I settled upon the only subject in the contemporary cultural field in Russia upon which it would be possible for me to write without saying anything unacceptable: the current productions of classical plays (I did not want to discuss the new Soviet plays). This was approved at first; but then my dossier was no doubt consulted, and it was discovered that I had, in New York, been associated with Max Eastman, at one time an admirer of Trotsky and a critic of the Soviet Union, on the advisory board of the *Modern Monthly*, a non-Stalinist magazine. There was a tradition in Russian Communism—inaugurated, I fear, by Lenin—of making people who had come over to Bolshevism denounce publicly their previous non-Bolshevik connections. When D. S. Mirsky had returned to Russia to pursue a Soviet literary career, he had been forced to publish a book, *The Intelligentsia of Great Britain*, unmasking, as it was then called, the English writers among whom he had been living in exile. I was now called upon to write for the *Daily News* a formal repudiation of Max Eastman. This I refused to do, and I induced them to accept the following article.

———

We used to hear a good deal in America about Soviet suppression of the classics. We were told that whenever a pre-revolutionary play was produced on the Soviet stage, it was caricatured out of all recognition. It is true, I believe, that in a recent production of *Hamlet*, some startling innovations were made to bring it into line with Marxist ideology. But one of the things that have most struck me since I have been here has been, not only the excellence of the theater, but in respect to the drama and music of the past, the freedom and scope of its range.

I had expected something rather different. My attitude when I first arrived may be indicated by the experience of an American friend of mine who attempted soon after her arrival to see

Meyerhold's production of *Camille*. She had heard much of this brilliant director who did daring and original things with the classics, and she had understood that everything on the Russian stage was given a strong revolutionary emphasis. When, therefore, before the curtain went up, two sailors came out and shook hands, she was not in the least surprised. And then afterwards when, instead of a Paris salon, she was confronted with the deck of a ship and when it turned out that Camille was a sort of woman sailor and that, instead of having but two or three serious admirers, she was evidently worshipped by the whole crew, my friend continued to set it all down to the new proletarian interpretation of the bourgeois Dumas *fils*. Nor was she seriously troubled at the end, when the lady of the gardenias was shot down on deck with her shoes on instead of dying of "consumption" in bed. It was only as she was leaving the theater that my friend found out that what she had been witnessing was not Meyerhold's production of *Camille*, but Taïrov's production of *The Optimistic Tragedy*, a play of the Civil Wars, which dealt with the Baltic fleet and had a brave woman commissar for heroine.

In a somewhat similar state of mind, the night of my own arrival in Russia, I went to hear Verdi's *Otello* and was surprised to find simply an admirable but, it seemed to me, quite traditional operatic production. Later, I saw Meyerhold's version of the Pushkin-Chaikovsky opera *The Queen of Spades*, and felt afterwards that I understood better both the pre-Soviet Russian soul and the romantic nineteenth century. I could not see that the story had been used to point a revolutionary moral. *The Cherry Orchard* seemed the same as ever, aristocratic nostalgia and all. And *The Pickwick Club* at the Second Art Theater gave the impression of being actually too gay and mild. I thought that it had failed rather regrettably to make the most of certain opportunities for "propaganda" that Dickens himself had supplied. After seeing Ostrovsky's *Talents and Admirers*, I did, to be sure, learn that the original ending had been changed; but I confess that the new one—in which the poor young student, abandoned by the ambitious actress, justifies himself and his work in a more or less revolutionary speech instead of committing suicide as Ostrovsky had intended him to do seemed to me the best scene in the play.

Of course, it is true that the Soviet point of view does pervade in one way or another the whole of the Russian theater. I can see, looking back on the Dickens play, that not only is Sam Weller made to figure as the real hero (as he actually becomes in the novel), but that he is also made to emerge from the devoted subordination to his master which allowed the Victorian audience to approve of him in spite of his audacities, and to assert himself with more force and rudeness. And I suppose that Verdi's *Otello* may partly owe its present popularity to the Soviet attitude toward race problems. But the theater of every place and age has been stamped by the interests and purposes of the society which has paid to see its shows; and I cannot see that the Soviets at the present time can be accused of mistreating the classics. Take even a case—the only one I have seen—where the handling of an old play had obviously been strongly affected by the special preoccupations of the moment: the production of *Romeo and Juliet* by the Theater of the Revolution. This was plainly a *Romeo and Juliet* inspired by and designed for the Komsomol. Lots of energy—sometimes rather self-conscious, sometimes misapplied, as when Romeo and Juliet and the Nurse were continually throwing themselves around and rushing up and down steps and ladders. And it surely does some violence to Shakespeare's intention to play the balcony scene in such a way as to make the audience laugh —in order, I was told, to fall in with the unromantic attitude toward love of the younger generation. Yet when I compared this Soviet production, with its seriousness, its large scope and its elaborate attention to detail, with a production of *Romeo and Juliet* which I had seen in New York last winter, it must be admitted that the Soviets had still very much the best of it. Shakespeare, in the Soviet production, whatever liberties had been taken with him, had the Komsomol to bring him to life. In New York, he had nobody at all. I remembered that the actress who played Juliet in New York had been so dreary in the scene in the bedroom in which she drinks the sleeping potion that, responding to the idea of the narcotic rather than to the terror and passion that the poet had tried to convey, I had actually myself gone sound asleep—an accident of which I was not in danger at the Theater of the Revolution, though the production lasted five hours.

We English-speaking audiences should look ridiculous complaining of the damage done to Shakespeare by the Soviet productions of his plays when we have ourselves been tolerating for two centuries all sorts of arrangements and adaptations, which bowdlerize him, sentimentalize him and make hash of him—until we have finally even come to believe that the gags that Colley Cibber wrote into *Richard III* are Shakespearean masterstrokes. In nothing more conspicuously, in fact, does the vitality, the imagination and the significance of the Soviets' own great role appear than in this power to make real and to throw into relief the symbolic fables of the stage. Today, when the cultural tradition of Russia, interrupted for a time by the Revolution, has been resumed, and resumed with fresh interest, keener scrutiny and bolder enthusiasm, the Soviet theater takes its place as, I suppose, the most brilliant in the world: one of the few real artistic glories of these artistically barren years.

July 2, 1935

———

It was true, at the time I was there, that the Soviet theater was splendid. Though this was after the murder of Kirov and the political purges had already begun, the cultural life of the Soviet Union was still in its relatively liberal phase, when the "directive" was that artists should not hesitate to learn from the art of feudal past and from the bourgeois art of the present. The great theatrical producers were still very important figures, with whom it was difficult to interfere, and their theaters, whose personnel enjoyed more personal freedom and a higher standard of living than perhaps any other group, came as near as had ever been possible for any institution under the Soviet system to functioning in an autonomous way. This privileged domain of the theater has recently been described, in a book called *Taming the Arts*, by a Russian violinist, Mr. Juri Jelagin, now in the United States. He tells, also, how, the year after my visit, the terror caught up with the arts, and the government began breaking up these theaters and censoring productions of the classics. The cultural tyranny of Stalin ended by imposing everywhere a type of propaganda drama that dealt only in idealized characters so different from anything that actually existed that, in order to make the actors believe in them, it was necessary, says Mr. Jelagin, artificially to create for them living conditions that approximated to those represented on the stage. Meyerhold's theater was closed, and he was charged with the crime of "formalism"; when he protested against the new policy, he was arrested and disappeared. His wife, an actress, was killed in her apartment, and found, Mr. Jelagin says, with seventeen knife-wounds in her body.

Letter to the Russians about Hemingway

WHEN I visited the Soviet Union, I was assigned as a guide and advisor by the cultural liaison organization VOKS Sergei Tretyakov, then a well-known literary figure. I knew him already as the author of an effective melodrama, which had been done in New York under the title *Roar, China!* He was tall, very sober and a little rigid; he wore spectacles and had shaved his gray hair; and he rather resembled, as was sometimes said of him, a professor or a Protestant pastor. But in literature he was earnestly Leftist. He was a great participator in groups. He had passed through futurism and the group called LEF, in both of which—he was very proud of this—he had been associated with Mayakovsky. He was at that time one of the great champions of "fact literature" as distinguished from "plot literature"; he declared that the Soviet newspaper was the *War and Peace* of the present, and he was engaged in writing a novel about the collective farms, which was a matter of pure documentation that took him into the country on fact-gathering excursions. Though Tretyakov was theoretically one of the most intransigent of Soviet writers, who had declared his scorn of fellow-travellers, I found him both mild and polite. He did his best to be helpful to me, and I ate some good dinners in his apartment, where he would show me the old files of the LEF magazines. On one occasion, he prepared me for meeting his father by saying, "He's a real peasant!.," but when I was presented to the elder Tretyakov, he seemed to me a well-bred old gentleman, whose mustaches and small Van Dyke beard must always have been carefully tended.

I wanted to buy books. There was some difficulty about this, due to restrictions and my lack of money; and Tretyakov suggested that I contribute an article to the Russian edition of *International Literature* and have the Writers' Union pay me in books. There was a considerable excitement about Hemingway in the Soviet Union then, and it was agreed that I should write about his latest book, which had not yet been translated. Just before I left Moscow, Tretyakov took me to a bookseller in the ancient Tverskaya, now rechristened Ulitsa Gorkovo, who dealt in pre-Soviet books. To enter it was something of a shock, for one seemed to step out of the new Russia and land in a pocket of the past. The proprietor, with his skull-cap, his ivory pallor, his tarnished green velvet jacket, his archaic fringe of red beard that ran under his chin from ear to ear, might have been a contemporary of Gogol's. These old books, especially in good editions, were rather rare in the Soviet Union, and it was forbidden to take them out of the country, unless one bought them for valuta at Intourist emporiums and could show a certificate for them; but the amiable Tretyakov, with his slightly complacent official air, promised to arrange all this. I chose a set of Turgenev that was rather expensive and several other things, and I left with the bookseller some books that I had already acquired elsewhere and that I wanted to have sent with the others, including a large-paper two-volume edition of Taine's *Théorie de l'Intelligence,* which had been given me by a friend in Leningrad. Few of these I ever saw again, either my old books or the new purchases. When a package finally reached me in America, I found, instead of the set of Turgenev, one very badly battered volume of a Soviet edition on cheap paper: Volume XII, the last, which contained a miscellaneous collection of Turgenev's reviews and speeches. The only thing I had ordered that they sent me was a volume of Mayakovsky's drawings. The Taine had disappeared. So not only have I never been paid for the article that follows by the Soviet periodical that ordered and ran it, but I was robbed of my Taine on account of it. Poor Tretyakov vanished in the purge, along with almost everyone else who represented the Leninist tradition of socialist idealism. His obstinate loyalty to it may well have seemed to his inquisitors stupid. He had staked his whole career on the iconoclasm—which was bound to be for Tretyakov not an uproarious but a solemn matter—of his brilliant ally Mayakovsky; he had sworn on Marx and Lenin a lifelong devotion to the doctrine that an up-to-date report on industrial work in progress was the highest form of literature. I felt very badly about him. It outrages one's sense of justice that a man should be encouraged by the government to maintain an official attitude and then punished for doing so when this attitude is repudiated by the government. Such people as Tretyakov, industrious, pious and a little absurd, have been among the most pathetic victims of Stalin's soul-destroying reign.

———

Letter to the Russians about Hemingway

I have been very much disappointed by the new book by Ernest Hemingway. *Green Hills of Africa* is certainly far and away his weakest book—in fact (leaving out of consideration the burlesque *Torrents of Spring*), the only really weak book he has written.

Green Hills of Africa is a narrative of an actual hunting expedition, in which "the writer has attempted," as Hemingway says, "to write an absolutely true book to see whether the shape of a country and the pattern of a month's action can, if truly presented, compete with a work of the imagination." In my opinion, he has not succeeded. The sophisticated technique of the fiction-writer comes to look artificial when it is applied to a series of real happenings; and the necessity for sticking to what really happened prevents the writer from supplying the ideal characters and incidents which give meaning to a work of fiction. The book is thus an instructive experiment: it brings out very clearly the difference between actual experience and the imaginary experience of fiction, but it is a warning of reefs to steer clear of.

Aside from this—or perhaps for the very reason that he has chosen to treat his material in the wrong way—the literary personality of Hemingway here appears in a slightly absurd light. He delivers a self-confident lecture on the high possibilities of prose-writing, with the implication that he himself, Hemingway, has realized or hopes to realize these possibilities; and then produces what are certainly, from the point of view of prose, the very worst pages of his life. There is one passage which is hardly even intelligible—the most serious fault for a writer who is always insisting on the supreme importance of lucidity. He inveighs with much scorn against the literary life and the professional literary men of the cities; and then manages to give the impression that he himself is a professional literary man of the most touchy and self-conscious kind. As a newspaper reviewer has said of Hemingway, he went all the way to Africa to hunt, and then when he thought he had found a rhinoceros, it turned out to be Gertrude Stein—an old friend and admiration of Hemingway's, who wrote of him disparagingly in her recent autobiography and upon whom, in *Green Hills of Africa*, he has taken the opportunity to revenge himself. He affirms in accents of defiance his perfect satisfaction with the hunter's life and his passionate enthusiasm for Africa; and then turns out the only book I have seen that makes Africa and its animals seem dull.

When the Soviet critic, I. Kashkin, who has contributed to the English edition of *International Literature* a very able essay on Hemingway—what is, in fact, perhaps so far the only serious full-length study of him that has yet been made—when Kashkin comes to read *Green Hills of Africa*, he will no doubt find much confirmation for his theory that the author of *In Our Time* has been becoming more sterile in proportion as he has become more detached from the great social issues of the day. And it is true that one of the things which strikes us most and which depresses us as we read *Green Hills of Africa* is the apparent drying-up in Hemingway of his interest in his fellow-beings. Wild animals can, of course, be made extremely interesting; but the animals in this book are not interesting. We do not learn very much more about them than that Hemingway wants to kill them. Nor do we learn much about the natives: there is, to be sure, one fine description of a tribe of marvellous runners, but the principal impression we carry away is that the Africans were simple people who enormously admired Hemingway. Nor do we learn much more about his hunting companion than that the latter had better luck than Hemingway and inspired Hemingway with envy; nor much more about Mrs. Hemingway than that she is fond of Hemingway. Nor does the author seem, in any really serious way, even to take very much interest in himself; the self-dramatized Hemingway we get has the look of having been inspired by some idea of what his public must expect after reading his rubbishy articles in the men's-wear magazine, *Esquire*.

Yet I am not by any means sure that—as Kashkin perhaps would conclude—it is Hemingway's material which is here at fault. It is not the fact that, in *Green Hills of Africa*, he is dealing with an African hunting expedition instead of with the

Can it not be said that on the highest plane of imaginative literature, the plane on which Hemingway must be considered, what is written about an old bull-fighter is written, also, about other kinds of men? Is not real genius of moral insight a motor that will start any engine? The non-Marxist who reads a banal Marxist fable, written without real insight or feeling, does not feel or imagine anything. The Marxist who reads a story presenting a dramatic conflict, though the conflict may be as far from the class struggle as the battle between a man and a bull, will surely, if the story is written with sympathy, passion and skill, identify himself with the hero. Do we not translate what moves us in literature into terms of whatever we do in our lives?

But that, Kashkin might reply, is an extremely dangerous doctrine. Suppose the hero of the story in question is frankly a counter-revolutionary. How can we be sure that the reader will translate counter-revolutionary courage into terms of revolutionary activity? How do we know that he will not be persuaded to admire the counter-revolution? We cannot know this, of course. But we may be assured that wherever the main current of human hope and progress runs, the readers will get out of all kinds of literature the kind of inspiration they need for their own particular activities, the kind of consolation they require for their own particular defeats. That the Soviets assume this to be true is indicated by the fact that they are at present translating wholesale the classics both of antiquity and of the modern world and republishing their own classics with pious care. I observed, when I was recently in Russia, that even the novels of the counter-revolutionary Dostoevsky were still of interest to Soviet readers and that the government was bringing out his note-books. And surely there is something more to the increasing popularity of Shakespeare in Russia than a desire on the part of the Soviet audiences to study the failures of feudal princes. Individuals in Russia still fail; they still suffer their griefs and frustrations; and people still go to the theater to have their souls purged through pity and terror.

I feel that Soviet critics, as well as many Marxist critics elsewhere, sometimes underestimate the positive qualities of the modern non-Marxist masters. A writer like Kashkin might answer that today the only positive forces are those which are

working for the destruction of the rotten old capitalist world
and for the liberation through socialism of stunted and cramped
human powers. I can only adduce, as an example of the law of
moral interchangeability which I would invoke on behalf of
Hemingway, that on my recent visit to Russia the passage from
contemporary literature that I found came most often to
mind, that seemed to me to express most eloquently the effect
of the Revolution on all kinds and conditions of people in the
Soviet Union, was from the writings of that arch-bourgeois,
arch-snob, arch-aesthete and arch-decadent, Marcel Proust. It
is that passage at the end of the section describing the death of
the novelist Bergotte in which Proust speaks of the moral obligations that make themselves felt in spite of everything, and
that seem to have reached humanity from some source outside
its own wretched self—obligations "invisible only to fools—
and are they really even to them?" Proust was speaking here of
the artist's obligations—for him, in his world of dissolving values, art was the only element which seemed to keep its validity
and last. But when I was travelling in the Soviet Union, these
words would come back into my mind, and I would find that
the obligations involved in the ideal of the Leninist tradition,
permeating even those parts of society, motivating even those
individuals, by whom at first sight it seemed least to be felt,
had substituted themselves for the obligations involved in
Marcel Proust's ideal of art. "Invisible only to fools—and are
they really even to them?"

December 11, 1935

———

This article, which came out in the *New Republic* on the
date given above, appeared later in Russian in issue No. 2 for
1936 of *Internatsionalnaya Literatura* (the two texts are slightly
different). It was accompanied by an editorial rejoinder, which
I here translate (the italics are the writer's):

We are glad to print the interesting article by Edmund Wilson written by him especially for Soviet readers. Wilson is one of the most
considerable critics who have appeared in the post-war generation of
American literature. He has of recent years taken an active part in the
Left movement of the intelligentsia, and though be has not arrived in

the camp of revolutionary literature, stopping halfway, he has nevertheless accomplished a significant evolution toward the Left. The article written by E. Wilson, after a visit (last summer) to the Soviet Union, constitutes a new link in the development of Soviet-American literary relations.

It would be out of place here to attempt a general discussion with Wilson on the fundamental problems of Marxist criticism, especially since, in formally replying to the article on Hemingway by I. Kashkin, Wilson is actually arguing against very primitive theses that he has picked up somewhere or other and that sound rather like a *parody* of Marxist criticism. Over these theses E. Wilson is able to score an easy enough victory.

What interests us more is the positive part of E. Wilson's article. In connection with this we shall allow ourselves to make two observations.

Hemingway's book before the last, *Winner Take Nothing*, was met with fixed bayonets by the American bourgeois critics. Hemingway, they said, was "repeating himself," and this fact annoyed them extremely. When *Green Hills of Africa* came out, a book that was really bad, a regular Witches' Sabbath took place in the literary departments of the newspapers and magazines. The critics, frothing at the mouth, demonstrated that Hemingway was "finished." They could not have been more anxious about this if they had been the hired agents of publishing houses who were competing with Hemingway's publisher.

The article by E. Wilson does not belong to this *vulgarly commercial* type of criticism. On the contrary, it is obvious that Wilson likes and esteems Hemingway and that he is saddened by his creative collapse. All the more striking, then, is *the shirking of the task of analysis of the contradictions in Hemingway's work* which constitutes, as it were, the invisible axis of Wilson's article.

That Hemingway has lost the ability to embody the contradictions by which he is torn in harmonious artistic form, has unmistakably been shown by Wilson. Wilson cannot be suggesting seriously that the central problem by which Hemingway is confronted is the recovery of his lost artistic quality on the basis of his former contradictions. Now, come: is this really possible? Has E. Wilson read Hemingway's article on the veterans,* in which the writer speaks in the first person, as he does in *Green Hills of Africa,* and is no less "intense and severe" than in the best of his artistic productions.

Not to speak out about these questions amounts to a betrayal of

---

*An article by Hemingway called *Who Killed the War-Veterans in Florida?* which appeared in *Internatsionalnaya Literatura,* No. 12, 1935.

the fact that one takes even less interest in Hemingway's fate than the malice-breathing newspaper critics. To limit oneself to a consideration of the "aesthetic factors" means to alienate oneself from the living processes of literature, to dissociate oneself from political and moral responsibility for the artist's fate in the disintegrating bourgeois world. An article by Granville Hicks which we read in the *New Masses* not long ago on the same subject as Wilson's article expressed a deep concern for the artist and did its best to discover ways by which Hemingway might escape from his creative blind alley. Here you may see at once the advantage of Marxist criticism over the passively contemplative kind.

And now, one more observation.

The attempt to judge artistic questions *sub specie aeternitatis* has the defect that, even when accompanied by good intentions about dealing with the facts, it must lead to excessive generalizing. Thus Wilson is correct in pointing out that *courage* is one of the elements in Hemingway's "moral code." But his further discussion of the role of Hemingway's creative activity under conditions of socialist culture is definitely not correct. The courage of Hemingway's heroes is the *courage of despair*. It may inspire the respect, even the admiration, of the Soviet reader, but it is powerless to awaken in him any valid social and psychological conceptions, because it is entirely lacking in the *dynamic optimism* that constitutes the *fundamental characteristic of the courage of the socialist world-view in life and in art*.

The "over-all" theory of the psychology of the mechanism of response to art which is involved in Wilson's idea that the reader identifies himself passively with *any* fully realized character in an artistic production, independently of this character's intellectual content, is *absolutely false*.

In the response to works of art, as in the creation of works of art, there is always an intellectual and moral element; the Marxist reader, in his approach to bourgeois literature, pits himself against it, actively selecting the feelings and ideas that he recognizes as close to his own, and rejecting the alien and hostile ones.

This does not mean that the Soviet publishers bring out the works of Hemingway or Proust for the sole purpose of demonstrating "bourgeois decay." Every genuine work of art—and such are the productions of Hemingway and Proust—enriches the reader's knowledge of life and heightens his artistic sensibility and his emotional culture—in a word, it figures in the broad sense, as a factor of educational value. Liberated socialist humanity inherits all that is beautiful, elevating and sustaining in the culture of previous ages. Such are the laws of historical development.

———

I do not know which now seems more touching: my conviction that the Leninist idealism was sure to command universal respect in the Soviet Union of the thirties or my critic's belief that their "liberated humanity" would be allowed to help itself freely to the cultural treasures of the past.

Talking United States

THE ARTICLES razzing the New Deal which have been appearing in the *American Mercury* over the name of H. L. Mencken have been sounding so much like the compositions supposed to be transmitted from the other world by the spirits of Mark Twain and William James that it is reassuring to have at last from Mencken's authentic living hand a new edition of *The American Language.*

This fourth edition of Mr. Mencken's *Inquiry into the Development of English in the United States* is more than twice as long as the *Preliminary Inquiry* of 1919. In this new version, little survives of the original tentative essay: the work has been brought to maturity—reorganized, filled out and deepened, and it presents itself in its present form as one of the few recent books of which it is possible to say that it ought to be in every American library and that it ought to be read by every foreigner who wants to understand the United States. What is most remarkable about it is that a work which covers so much ground and which illustrates with copious examples so many philological phenomena should remain for eight hundred pages so uniformly entertaining. It is rarely that a student of language is also a literary artist: Mr. Mencken has collected his Americanisms and exhibits them in the pages of this book with the loving appreciation of a naturalist mounting butterflies or ticketing new fishes. Yet even this image is too pedantic. One is made to feel throughout *The American Language* the movement and the pressure of the American people, vindicating their independence, filling out their enormous country, attracting and consolidating with themselves the peoples of older nations, inseminating that older world itself with their habits of thought and their speech. We listen to their voices here, as they change the intonations of English, develop a new vocabulary, break the language into a new syntax—from the accents of Noah Webster, sedulously carrying through, in the department of spelling and punctuation, the recent revolution against England, to those of the latest arrivals in the back streets of the "foreign" sections of cities, where old tongues lose their primitive inflections under the influence of the easy new speech, yet, in the process of deliquescence, shoot their particles into the air around.

There are certain significant differences to be noted between this latest edition and the earlier editions of Mr. Mencken's study. Seventeen years ago, Mr. Mencken was still uncertain as to whether American usage would come eventually to dominate English or whether the two dialects would simply drift apart. But today he seems to have no doubt that English is destined "to become, on some not too remote tomorrow, a kind of dialect of American, just as the language spoken by the American was once a dialect of English." At the end of the first edition, he ventured the following prophecy: "Given the poet, there may suddenly come a day when our *theirns* and *would'a hads* will take on the barbaric stateliness of the peasant locutions of Old Maurya in *Riders to the Sea*. They seem grotesque and absurd today because the folks who use them seem grotesque and absurd. But that is a too facile logic and under it is a false assumption. In all human beings, if only understanding be brought to the business, dignity will be found, and that dignity cannot fail to reveal itself, soon or late, in the words and phrases with which they make known their high hopes and aspirations and cry out against the intolerable meaninglessness of life." This passage has now been omitted. The prophecy is already coming true. Since the first *American Language* of 1919, we have had Sinclair Lewis and Eugene O'Neill, Sherwood Anderson and Carl Sandburg, Hemingway and Dos Passos, Ring Lardner and Mencken himself in his more colloquial works.

Looking back today, we can see that this first edition of *The American Language* marked a stage in the development of our literature. It marked the moment when the living tide of American had mounted so high along the sands of "correct English" that some formal recognition was necessary. Six years later, in 1925, the review *American Speech* was started, and Sir William Craigie, one of the compilers of the big Oxford dictionary, sailed for the United States to begin work on a dictionary of American. To many readers of Mencken's first edition, the chapter on the syntax of "the common speech," in which he was bold enough to suggest that we should eventually conjugate the past indicative of the verb *to be* with *was* for all persons and numbers, must have seemed entirely frivolous. To-day it makes more impression; we are not so sure of the grammar of the future; and, in any case, we must give Mencken credit for one of the really valuable services performed in our own day by American criticism for American writing. For the period of literary activity which reached its height just after the war, two critics of importance stand out: Mencken and Van Wyck Brooks. Brooks exposed the negative aspects of our literary tradition and urged us to get away from our governesses. Mencken showed the positive value of our vulgar or colloquial heritage; and he did more than anyone else in his field to bring about that "coming of age" for which Brooks had sounded the hour. The publication of Mencken's *Book of Prefaces* in 1917, with its remarkable essay on Dreiser and its assault on "Puritanism as a Literary Force," was one of the cardinal events for the new American literature. Mencken did not discover Dreiser, but he was the first critic to focus him clearly as a figure to be taken seriously, because he was able to appreciate, and to stimulate in us a certain appetite for, the Americanism of Dreiser in all its rawness. This *positive* treatment of Dreiser —so different from the negative attitude with which even sympathetic critics had so often in the past approached Mark Twain —was really the weight that tipped the scales; and the appearance of *The American Language* gave Mencken's position a scholarly base which the academically minded—a group to which most of our critics belonged—did not find it easy to brush aside.

Mr. Mencken has invited corrections and suggestions, so I will mention the following points:

It seems to me that Mr. Mencken has underestimated the recent influence of fashionable English slang on the smart patter of the United States. There exists a kind of blended Anglo-American jargon in the insouciant British tradition, which I believe to be mainly the creation of the Englishman P. G. Wodehouse, who lived for years in the United States and whose American musical comedies, written with Jerome Kern, have been as popular as his English novels. This patter has not been confined, as Mr. Mencken thinks such things are, to "consciously elegant circles," but has seeped down through middle-class youth in general to an extent hitherto unknown for any slang tinged with Briticism. . . . In his discussion of English and American "honorifics," I think that Mr. Mencken should mention the difference between the English usage, which prefers a single Christian name or, if there is a middle name, two simple initials (C. K. Ogden, H. G. Wells), and the usage in the United States, where we go in for family middle names (Harriet Beecher Stowe, Richard Grant White—I pick them at random from Mencken's pages). This habit represents no doubt a desire to store up and transmit distinction in a society where titles are impossible, an attempt to weave a net of prestige, to establish a solidarity, for the property-owning classes, among kaleidoscopic mixtures of stock and across the gaps of enormous spaces.

Mr. Mencken describes Henry James as "a violent Anglophile" and quotes criticisms of American habits of speech uttered by him late in life when he had long been living in England. The truth is, however, that the early Henry James who wanted to be the American Balzac, was well aware of the possibilities of American. I quote the following from *An Animated Conversation* (included in *Essays in London*, but first published in 1889). The imaginary dialogue is taking place between English people and Americans:

OSWALD (*to Clifford*). What do you mean by my language?
CLIFFORD. I mean American.
OSWALD. Haven't we a right to have a language of our own?
DARCY. It is inevitable.
CLIFFORD (*to Oswald*). I don't understand you.
BELINDA. Already?
CLIFFORD. I mean that Oswald seems at once to resent the imputation that you have a national tongue and to wish to insist on the fact that you have it. His position is not clear.
DARCY. That is partly because our tongue itself is not clear as yet. We must hope that it will be clearer. Oswald needn't resent anything, for the evolution was inevitable. A body of English people crossed the Atlantic and sat down in a new climate on a new soil, amid new circumstances. It was a new heaven and a new earth. They invented new institutions, they encountered

different needs. They developed a particular physique, as people do in a particular medium, and they began to speak in a new voice. They went in for democracy, and that alone would affect—it *has* affected—the tone immensely. *C'est bien le moins* (do you follow?) that that tone should have had its range and that the language they brought over with them should have become different to express different things. A language is a very sensitive organism. It must be convenient—it must be handy. It serves, it obeys, it accommodates itself. . . .

BELINDA. . . . I listen to Darcy with a certain surprise . . . for I am bound to say I have heard him criticize the American idiom.

DARCY. You have heard me criticize it as neglected, as un-studied: you have never heard me criticize it as American. The fault I find with it is that it's irresponsible—it isn't American enough. . . .

BELWOOD. You have the drawback (and I think it a great disadvantage) that you come so late, that you have not fallen on a language-making age. The people who first started our vocabularies were very *naïfs*. . . . New signs are crude, and you, in this matter, are in the crude, the vulgar stage.

DARCY. That no doubt is our misfortune. . . . But we have always the resource of English. We have lots of opportunity to practise it.

CLIFFORD. As a foreign tongue, yes.

DARCY. To speak it as the Russians speak French.

CLIFFORD. The Russians are giving up French.

DARCY. Yes, but *they've* got the language of Tolstoy. . . . Our great writers have written in English. That's what I mean by American having been neglected.

Lastly, I wish that Mr. Mencken would add a chapter, or even write a companion volume, on the development of style in America. How have the different rhythm and tempo of Amer-ican speech, how have the different values given the English vowels, affected the writing of poetry? And how is it that the prose-styles of writers so different from one another as, say, Mark Twain, Henry James and Dreiser are all, in their several ways, modes of expression characteristically American which could never have been produced by the English? Two things, certainly, would be plain from such a study. First, that at a time when prose-style in England was growing more and more ornate or elaborate (Ruskin, Carlyle, Meredith: even Dickens suffers badly from the upholstery of the period, except when his characters are talking), American prose was reverting to something more like the colloquial directness of the writing of the seventeenth century. If it is not true, as Ernest Hemingway has said, that "all modern American literature comes from *Huckleberry Finn*," it is certain that one stream of it does. It would be impossible to bring the language of literature any closer to the language of ordinary talk than has been done by Mark Twain and his successors. Some of the best of American fiction has been written as a series of simple statements connected only by *and*.

Another feature of our literature has been its comparative neglect of the English heritage proper and its readiness to resort to other sources. The influence of French culture in America, which goes back to the Francophile Jefferson and Franklin, has certainly been very much greater than it has, during the same period, in England (setting aside the Irishmen George Moore and James Joyce, and the Pole Joseph Conrad). The American fiction of the last generation was profoundly affected by the French novel—from the influence of Flaubert and his school on Henry James and Edith Wharton to the influence of Zola on Frank Norris; and the poetry of our own generation has been pretty well permeated by French symbolism. Our culture is polyglot in its elements: in spite of the English basis of our language, we are culturally almost as close to the other European countries as to England. The stray French and Spanish words which fluttered into Whitman's poems were harbingers of more sweeping migrations. Mencken's burlesque denunciations certainly come straight from the German as do Dreiser's long doleful and laboring sentences. And lately the patterns of our fiction have been shaken by reverberations from Russia.

One wishes that Mr. Mencken would bring out, also, with specimens and commentary, a study of American writing.

July 15, 1936

In reviewing, on August 25, 1945, the first volume of Mencken's *Supplement to The American Language*, I noted that he promised for the second volume an appendix on American prose-style (for which, however, he was not to find space); and I discussed this subject again:

Every American writer, more than ever today, has to struggle with a problem of language in choosing between current American and traditional literary English. Henry James, in his own time so much under suspicion of infatuation with England, actually mixed Americanisms with Anglicisms—along with a sprinkling of colloquial French—to produce an international style. Relatively uneducated writers like Ring Lardner and Mark Twain have had so poor a literary vocabulary that they were likely to seem bald or thin when they attempted straight English prose, and they could only express themselves adequately by having their story told by a character who spoke some form of illiterate dialect or special slang. Dos Passos, in *U.S.A.*, met the problem by using the third person for the life-stories of several characters but telling each in the special idiom of his locality, occupation and stratum, and interweaving them in such a way as to achieve, through parallel and contrast, a larger drama and a symphonic effect. Writers like Fitzgerald and Faulkner, whose prose has a basis in lyric verse and who have needed the vocabulary of literature, have suffered sometimes, in weaving their spells, from unintentionally setting the teeth on edge by their imprecise use of words. A writer like Elinor Wylie, whose mastery of literary English was accurate, complete and brilliant, suffers a little, on the other hand, from the effect of artificiality that we are likely to feel in America in the presence of any collection of precious objets d'art from abroad. Mr. Mencken himself, in his early writings, invented a bold combination of literate traditional English with alive-and-kicking native slang and the robustious tone of German polemics. The first edition of *The American Language* was written, however, in a more sober style. One remembers a British reviewer's pointing out that, in arguing for American, Mr. Mencken was content to write mainly in orthodox British English. That reproach can no longer be made. In this supplement, Mr. Mencken has succeeded in adapting the American idiom to the requirements of philological exposition.

The truth is that, since 1919, when Mr. Mencken merely

ventured to suggest that the vernacular might someday be accepted as a medium for serious writing, the American form of English has been rapidly coming into its empire—absorbing, for the purposes of literature, more and more of the idiom of daily life, redeeming it from its comic and plebeian connotations, blending it with the language of books, and pouring it into well-rounded molds for work that may prove enduring.

It will be noted that, though there is no basic contradiction between the opinions expressed in these articles and my views of 1929 that are to be found under *Virginia Woolf and the American Language*, there is a definite shift of emphasis. In the earlier letters to the *New Republic*, the other correspondents and I were arguing against Mrs. Woolf for the historical right of Americans to claim as their own the English language; later on, I was defending our right to do with it what we liked.

American Critics, Left and Right

I. Communist Criticism

I QUOTE the following from Maurice Baring's *Outline of Russian Literature*, written before the Russian Revolution:

"The didactic stamp which he [Belinsky] gave to Russian aesthetic and literary criticism has remained on it ever since, and differentiates it from the literary and aesthetic criticism of the rest of Europe, not only from that school of criticism which wrote and writes exclusively under the banner of 'Art for Art's sake,' but from those Western critics who championed the importance of moral ideas in literature, just as ardently as he did himself, and who depreciated the theory of Art for Art's sake just as strongly. Thus it is that, from the beginning of Russian criticism down to the present day, a truly objective criticism becomes a political weapon. 'Are you in my camp?' If so, you are a good writer. 'Are you in my opponent's camp?' Then your god-gifted genius is mere dross.

"The reason of this has been luminously stated by Professor Bruckner: 'To the intelligent Russian, without a free press, without the liberty of assembly, without the right to free expression of opinion, literature became the last refuge of freedom of thought, the only means of propagating higher ideas. He expected of his country's literature not merely aesthetic recreation; he placed it at the service of his aspirations. . . . Hence the striking partiality, nay unfairness, displayed by the Russians toward the most perfect works of their own literature, when they did not respond to the aims or expectations of their party or their day. . . .'

"Herein lies the great difference between the Russian and Western critics, between Sainte-Beuve and Belinsky; between Matthew Arnold and his Russian contemporaries. Matthew Arnold defined the highest poetry as being a criticism of life; but that would not have prevented him from doing justice either to a poet so polemical as Byron, or to a poet so completely unpolitical, so sheerly aesthetic as Keats; to Lord Beaconsfield as a novelist, to Mr. Morley or Lord Acton as historians, because their 'tendency' or their 'politics' were different from his own. The most biassed of English or French critics is broadminded compared to a Russian critic. Had Keats been a Russian poet, Belinsky would have swept him away with contempt; Wordsworth would have been condemned as reactionary; and Swinburne's politics alone would have been taken into consideration. At the present day, almost ten years after Professor Bruckner wrote his *History of Russian Literature*, now that the press is more or less free, save for occasional pinpricks, now that literary output is in any case unfettered, and the stage freer than it is in England, the same criticism still applies. Russian criticism is still journalistic. There are and there always have been brilliant exceptions . . . but as a rule the political camp to which the writer belongs is the all-important question; and I know cases of Russian politicians who have been known to refuse to write, even in foreign reviews, because they disapproved of the 'tendency' of those reviews, the tendency being non-existent—as is generally the case with English reviews—and the review harboring opinions of every shade and tendency. You would think that narrow-mindedness could no further go than to refuse to let your work appear in an impartial organ, lest in that same organ an opinion opposed to your own might appear also. But the cause of this is the same now as it used to be, namely that, in spite of there being a greater measure of freedom in Russia, political liberty does not yet exist; liberty of conscience only partially exists; the press is annoyed and hampered by restrictions; and the great majority of Russian writers are still engaged in fighting for these things, and therefore still ready to sacrifice fairness for the greater end—the achievement of political freedom."

Russian literary criticism, then, runs to party politics, just as French criticism runs to ideas; and this tendency has probably been intensified since the Marxist revolution. At any rate, it has penetrated through the Communist movement to the criticism of other countries. We have been suffering in America for a long time, in the critical writing of the Left, from a virulent infection with it. It is not merely a question of criticism

written from a social point of view, or even of Marxist criticism; but of criticism dominated by the quarrels of Russian
factional politics.

And, due to the turn which Stalinism has been taking, this
has now become a serious nuisance. As Stalin has been rousing
against him more formidable political enemies and has been
resorting to more violent methods of silencing them, the literary criticism of the Stalinist press has become, not more perhaps, but more conspicuously, diverted from its proper objects
to playing the role of special pleader for Stalin. There was a
time when literary Communists were few and when they were
the spokesmen for a most important point of view which had
hardly got into the liberal weeklies, let alone the old family
monthlies. One could count on Michael Gold, for example, to
stand outside the bourgeois literary world and to give its illusions no quarter. But today, when half that world has turned
Leftist, the Communist point of view is no longer a rarity, and
we have a right to call its exponents to account.

One of the worst drawbacks of being a Stalinist at the present time is that you have to defend so many falsehoods. Not
only has the whole role of Trotsky been travestied or suppressed to suit Stalin's purpose, but, on account of Lenin's relations with Trotsky and his criticism of and conflicts with
Stalin, it has even been made impossible to write a real biography of Lenin or even to publish his later correspondence. The
great Marxist scholar D. Rzyanov, the head of the Marx-Engels
Institute and the collector and editor of the complete Marx
and Engels, whose only sin in the field of Marxist research had
been a too zealous desire to justify Marx against any possible
kind of criticism, was never allowed to finish his work but sent
to die in prison, on political charges of which one of the most
serious seems to have been his failure to feature Stalin sufficiently in his commentary. The trials which have followed the
assassination of Kirov have thrown up a nightmare structure of
accusations and imputations—including the assertion, rather
strange on the part of a socialist government, that the defen-
dants had "lost the characteristics of human beings"—in which
it is difficult to separate the true from the false but of which a
good deal must certainly be false; and the condemnation of
Zinoviev and Kamenev has involved the authorities in the fur-

ther rewriting of Bolshevik history at their expense. The death of Gorky and the recent imprisonment of Radek, already himself badly compromised by his compliance under pressure with the official myths, were like the extinction of the final sparks of intellectual light connected with the Stalinist dictatorship.

This is not to disparage the executive abilities of Stalin or the practical achievements of the Soviets, but a political group which adopts as a policy the suppression of opinion and the falsification of history on the scale and with the unscrupulousness of the Stalinists is hardly a beneficent influence for the production of literature or ideas. I cannot see that the new United Front is making a bit of difference. This change in the Communist tactics has coincided with a period of bitter struggle between Stalin and his political opponents and with a tightening of the terror; and, from behind the anxious affability of the Communist literati toward writers who do not seem likely to offend because they do not yet know anything about Communism, there appears, at any suggestion of criticism, the nervousness, which now seems verging on panic, of the satellites of a jealous boss who does not brook the least doubt or disrespect. One is shocked to find writers whom one has known before as sober and conscientious reviewers quoting passages out of their context in such a way as to give them a different meaning, inventing passages which do not exist, trumping up counter-revolutionary charges and misrepresenting the author's plain drift in a way that implies not, perhaps, necessarily a deliberately dishonest intent but rather, due to the influence of fixed ideas, an actual misreading of the text. The Stalinist intelligentsia at the present time are like chickens that have been mesmerized by a chalk-line drawn from their beaks: they stand paralyzed with their beaks on the line, they cannot look away from the line, and at the end of the line there is nothing.

One can feel, at this stage, very little hope that any intellectual health will ever come out of Stalinist Communism. It is the old problem of gathering figs from thistles—and what is that saying of Krylov's, in the fable of the peasants and the river, that the young will never be corrected where the old are committing the same sins? How can you expect the pupils to report reliably on the books they review when the masters are corrupting whole libraries? Stalinist criticism, then, is doubly suspect: in being Stalinist and in being Russian. As for the Trotskyists, they are often more intelligent, and they are freer to think and to say what they think. But they suffer, also, from the Russian defects in being the obverse of the Stalinist coin. They, too, tend to turn everything into a factional issue and are likely to proceed to a literary discussion with all the polemics of a party unmasking. The whole thing reached a high pitch of comedy when a writer in the *New Masses* the other day, on the evidence of an editorial in the *Nation* on the subject of the Zinoviev trials and the signature of two *Nation* editors to a petition intended to procure for Trotsky the right to defend himself, made an effort to force the *Nation* to acknowledge itself a Trotskyist journal, "the organ of a band of counterrevolutionary conspirators and assassins"; while at the very same moment an attempt was made by a writer in the *Modern Monthly* to represent the *New Republic* as Stalinist. From the point of view of the Communist groups, the whole world of the political Left is divided into Stalinist, Trotskyist and Lovestonite, and it seems absolutely inconceivable to them that it is possible for anyone not to belong to one or another of these factions.

Now, all this is straight Russian, and it would make no sense in the United States, even if the politics involved were not those of the Soviet Union. Mr. Baring, in the passage I have quoted, does no doubt exaggerate a little in speaking of English reviews which have no political tendency; yet it is certain that such tendencies as they and the *Nation* and the *New Republic* represent are of a general non-factional kind. In respect to literary criticism, we have never developed the fierce partisanship of the Russians because we have never, except locally or briefly, found ourselves in the same situation as they. We can afford to leave party politics out of our literary discussion, and even out of our political discussion, because we are free to express ourselves in speeches and editorials as the Russians have never been able to do. The great English critics like Johnson and Coleridge have been men of wide range and independent judgment. They had strong political opinions; and Johnson has been accused of allowing his—in the case of Milton, for example—to bias his literary judgment. But Johnson on Milton seems magnanimous if we compare it with, say, Joseph Freeman on Trotsky's

History of the Russian Revolution or on the murals that Diego Rivera has been painting since he associated himself with Lovestone. And even the American critics, Van Wyck Brooks and Vernon L. Parrington, whose work has social implications, are never partisan in the Russian sense. It is absurd for Communist literary men to play, in the United States, at living in a world of veiled propaganda and conspiratorial movements—or in a world in which their group has seized power and can excommunicate and suppress. (For the Russian revolutionaries persisted, even after their victory, in regarding literature and the other arts as branches of party politics. Hence the efforts of repressive groups like RAPP to invest themselves with official authority, and the continual meddling of the government, as in the Shostakovich incident, with the natural development of the arts. A new revolutionary dictatorship, not yet sure of its position, can hardly be expected to countenance direct counterrevolutionary propaganda; but the relation at the present time between the Soviet government and Soviet literature is something specifically Russian which would be quite abnormal elsewhere. In all the fuss we have been hearing lately about the right and the wrong party-line in literature, it never seems to have occurred to anybody to say: "Party-lines in literature are nonsense! Literature will get along quite well without the interference or guidance of even the most brilliant politicians. Even a socialist government will have concerned itself quite enough with these matters when it has secured for the public interest the profits of the publishing business." The contrary policy in Russia has resulted in a situation where not only are the writers and artists forbidden to criticize the administration, but they are always in danger of being suddenly pilloried and told, as in the case of poor Shostakovich, that they will have to change their style of writing, since they are not supplying tunes that can be easily hummed by the head of the government.)

This tendency is also quite alien to the practice of Marx and Engels, who in general enjoyed art for what it was worth and pursued their political-economic analysis, even when applied to art, as something belonging to a different department. Even Lenin, who was troubled by the exaltation that he felt in listening to Beethoven, because it made him forget the crimes of society, manifested in his contacts with literature no such pettiness of party solicitude—see his attitude toward Gorky, for example—as the Communist Intellectuals that speak in his name.

The real problem has been brought out into the open in an article in *Partisan Review* by Mr. Louis Kronenberger:

"There is really no fundamental dilemma," he says. "It is more necessary for us to interest ourselves in an important subject treated without much merit than in an unimportant subject treated with considerable merit. *Culture herself* demands that we put the right social values ahead of the right literary values; and whenever we encounter people who want to keep art dustproof, who bewail the collapse of 'aesthetic values,' it is our duty to ascertain just how far their indignation is a screen for reactionary and unsocial thinking.

"The obverse of this—which is the cultural coarsening inevitable to a period of stress—is on the other hand a very serious problem for the critic. As men of thought tend increasingly to approximate the psychology of men of action, as the business of saving civilization increasingly ousts from their minds the idea of enriching it, there must follow all along the line a relaxation of standards, both ethical and aesthetic. The amenities decline, the non-utilitarian aspects of culture decrease, tolerance ceases to be feasible, and reason to be altogether sufficient. It is less important that the search for truth should survive than that the cancers of society should be cut out; but it is important enough. The critic therefore must act with a full sense of authority and responsibility toward what, when the crisis is over, we shall want to come back to; culture of that kind is like a cathedral where, just now, we cannot often pray but which we must preserve from bombardment. And culture of that kind has its uses in any program of protest. It must not stop men from fighting to restore order to the world, but it may give them a sense of what order signifies and stands for."

Mr. Kronenberger has attacked this subject with a good deal more seriousness and candor than it usually gets in that quarter (I take it that *Partisan Review* is edited by Stalinist Communists); but it seems to me that he still leaves things somewhat unclear. What course would you follow, precisely, in order to maintain the attitude recommended by Mr. Kronenberger? Mr. Kronenberger himself works on *Fortune,* writes book reviews for the *Nation*, translates La Rochefoucauld and edits anthologies of light verse and of English eighteenth-century literature. Does this fill the bill?—or what? What precisely is involved in the "relaxation of standards, both ethical and aesthetic"? At what point does the "search for truth," which is "important enough," become less important than "that the cancers of society should be cut out"? Does this mean that it is all right to assert on the word of the Stalin administration that Trotsky is a species of Fascist, who has been working in conspiracy with the Nazis to assassinate the Soviet leaders? Or does it mean that one can go merely so far as to misrepresent the contents of a book which contains some criticism of Stalin? Or does it mean merely that we may "put the right social values ahead of the right literary values"? And does this mean that, in your role of book-reviewer, you ought to caricature a good novel by Hemingway or Wilder and glorify an indifferent one about a textile strike? Or merely that you ought to neglect the one and respectfully notice the other. The root of the difficulty here may be seen, in the passage I have just quoted, in Mr. Kronenberger's use of the word "right." What he really ought to arrive at is a point of view from which it would be possible for him to say that, for himself, certain things are right and certain other things wrong. But he is only able to get so far as to assert that culture herself demands that social values be put ahead of literary values, and yet at the same time to talk about them both as "right." Right for whom, doing what? How can you take part in the civil war and at the same time preserve the cathedral?

The times, it is true, are confusing. It is not always easy to know what to do. But one thing that is certainly not worth doing is formulating theoretical positions. One has to make up one's mind in what capacity one is going to function. And from the moment one is not trying to function as an organizer or an active politician (and agitational literature is politics), one must work in good faith in one's own field. A conviction that is genuine will always come through—that is, if one's work is sound. You may say, This is no time for art or science: the enemy is at the gate! But in that case you should be at the gate: in the Spanish International Brigade, for example, rather than engaged in literary work. There is no sense in pursuing a

literary career under the impression that one is operating a
bombing-plane. On the one hand, imaginary bombs kill no actual enemies; and, on the other, the development of a war psychology prevents one's real work from having value. When
you "relax the aesthetic and ethical standards," you abandon
the discipline itself of your craft.

January 20, 1937

II. Bernard De Voto

As for the literary Right, it hardly exists any more. Irving
Babbitt is dead, and Paul Elmer More writes little. It is unfortunate that there is nobody nowadays to uphold the conservative point of view. The academic background of the older
critics had certain decided advantages. They had the scholarly
habit, for one thing, of doing a thorough and careful job, and
could never have adapted themselves to the kind of miscellaneous monthly reviewing that even the better-grade critics—
such as Mary M. Colum in the *Forum* and John Chamberlain
in *Scribner's*—have recently been reduced to: a kind that can
have little weight because it imposes the necessity of grouping
together a number of books that may have nothing whatever
in common except simultaneity of publication. The featured
reviewer who dealt regularly, from a definite point of view,
with subjects of serious interest seemed to have become extinct.

Then a conspicuous exception appeared in the shape of Mr.
Bernard De Voto, the new editor of the *Saturday Review of
Literature.*

Mr. De Voto is evidently something new, and he deserves
our respectful attention. First of all, it must be said that it is
pleasant to find regular weekly reviewing done by a man who
can write, who ranges widely and observes acutely, who studies
an author's whole work and attempts to sum it up, and who is
truculently independent. Mr. De Voto has already succeeded
in making the *Saturday Review* quite interesting. The whole
magazine is coming to bear the stamp of the new editor's ideas
and special interests, and it gets from them a force and an accent that it never has had before. Mr. De Voto is a Westerner
who has been trained at Harvard but who has never repudi-

ated the West. On the contrary, he has stuck to it stubbornly, making use of the lessons he has learned from it in dealing with the rest of the world, and championing its cultural importance. He has written some interesting papers on Mormonism (Utah is his native state); and in his book on *Mark Twain's America*, he has thrown some new light on the life of the frontier and on Mark Twain's literary sources. Among the literary phenomena of his own time, he has maintained a toughness of mind that has become more and more uncommon. No popular reputation passes current with him till he has attempted to assay its worth for himself; and he seems to shed fashionable shibboleths as easily as a really good raincoat sheds water. Furthermore, he has the academic training which has enabled him, for example, to clean up without remorse on the psychoanalytical biographers who have been aping Lytton Strachey. We must, therefore, be thankful for Mr. De Voto. He is trying to do something in the *Saturday Review* that nobody else has been doing, and he has qualifications for doing it well.

Yet precisely because Mr. De Voto has undertaken this kind of responsible criticism, we expect of him more than he has given us yet. We expect of him an intelligible basis of taste and an intelligible general point of view. He *sounds* as if he were being discriminating in his discussion of the relative merits of books, yet the standards by which he judges them remain obscure; he *sounds* as if his strictures on other people's doctrines were based on some solid philosophy of which he was very certain; and yet, though we keep on reading him in the interested expectation of being told what that philosophy is, its outlines never appear. On the surface, Mr. De Voto is positive and plainspoken, but when we try to go below the surface, we find ideas that seem confused and erratic.

Mr. De Voto as a critic may be examined most satisfactorily in his book on *Mark Twain's America*, which is the most elaborate of his literary studies and typical of his methods and habits of mind. This "essay in the correction of ideas" somewhat labors under the disadvantage of being one of those books that have been written, not primarily to present the author's own view, but to combat somebody else's. This is characteristic of Mr. De Voto, who always seems to approach his subjects

with a chip on his shoulder. In this case, the writer with whom
Mr. De Voto is trying to pick a quarrel is Mr. Van Wyck Brooks,
the author of *The Ordeal of Mark Twain*. Now, it is true that
Mr. De Voto is able to correct some minor errors on the part
of Mr. Brooks, and at least one serious one: the assumption
that, in the last century, when the country was full of communities organized by socialist and religious groups, Americans
had taken no part in the movements represented, as Mr. Brooks
says, by "the Tolstoys and the Marxes, the Nietzsches and the
Renans, the Ruskins and the Morrises." And he is able to correct the lugubrious picture that Mr. Brooks painted of the old
Far West by filling in the more cheerful aspects. But one ends
by deciding that Mr. Brooks is a kind of King Charles's head for
Mr. De Voto: an obsession which is not altogether rational.

For, after all, by the time Mr. De Voto is done, he seems to
have supplied evidence himself for most of Mr. Brooks's points:
that the life of the frontier was savage and taxed the pioneer's
endurance and that Mark Twain's humor (as a consequence of
this, according to Mr. Brooks—Mr. De Voto deplores the phenomenon but he does not attempt to explain it) tends to run
to the disgusting and the horrible; that the genteel tradition of
the East had an emasculating influence on letters and that, for
Mark Twain, this influence, as represented by Boston and Hart-
ford and Olivia Clemens, imposed an ordeal of another sort.
Where Mr. De Voto attempts to ignore Van Wyck Brooks's
findings, he obviously exposes himself. He is, for example,
quite ready to throw out all the literary deadwood that is the
basis of Brooks's contention that Mark Twain did not mature
as an artist; but he hardly touches at all on the rankling indignation at institutions which is Brooks's very striking evidence
that there was an undeveloped social prophet in Mark Twain.
And, though Brooks's psychoanalytic interpretations may
sometimes seem a little far-fetched, he does at least try to establish a relation between Mark Twain's choice of subjects and
his methods of treating them and his character and social background; whereas De Voto is content to exclaim that Mark
Twain was a great artist and a fine old boy, and, aside from
tracing some of his sources, to leave his relation to his work
unexplained.

It may possibly be true that Mr. Brooks has attached too

much importance to the incident related by Mark Twain's biographer, in which the young Sam, much given to mischief, is made to swear by his mother at his father's deathbed that he will always thereafter be a good boy. But the duality that Mr. Brooks attributes to Mark Twain is there in his work as plain as day—in the antagonism, for example, represented for Huckleberry Finn by Miss Watson and her world, on the one hand—to which Tom Sawyer is more or less committed—and the Nigger Jim and the raft, on the other; and this duality does account, as Mr. De Voto scarcely attempts to do, and scoffs, in fact, at the notion of doing, for the dualities of *Pudd'nhead Wilson* and the Siamese twins in *Those Extraordinary Twins.*

What is more serious is that Mr. De Voto completely evades the central question which Mr. Brooks is most impressive in illuminating: the question of Mark Twain's pessimism. Mr. De Voto's explanation of this pessimism is simply that Mark Twain had seen a good deal of life and that, being no fool, it had made him gloomy. But so had Dickens and Dostoevsky and a great many other people, who did not, nevertheless, become pessimists. The pessimism of Mark Twain is surely one of the blackest cases on record. Such documents as his thoughts on the death of his daughter, which Mr. De Voto does not mention, are rare in the history of Western civilization. We know that there were special causes for the pessimism of a Swift or a Leopardi; and Mr. Brooks is certainly well advised in looking for a special cause for the pessimism of Mark Twain. He is perfectly convincing, it seems to me, in finding it in causes similar to those that evidently operated in the cases of Leopardi and Swift: in a crippling insurmountable frustration. Involved with all this is Mr. De Voto's failure to give an adequate account of *Huckleberry Finn.* Mr. Brooks may have praised that book too scantily, but he did put his finger on its meaning; whereas, if you believe Mr. De Voto, it is simply a marvellous story about floating down the Mississippi. Mr. De Voto devotes eleven pages to *Huckleberry Finn* and yet manages never to mention the theme which gives the book its emotional force and makes it something more impressive than a mere picaresque novel: the contrast between Huck's natural instincts and the distortions of civilization.

The truth is that Mark Twain's books, though funny, are in

general, sad—just as that other great Westerner, Lincoln, who was also funny, was sad; and Mr. De Voto never explains or even faces this fact. Of course, the Far West of the sixties and seventies was more hilarious and more exciting than Mr. Brooks, in his earlier and dolorous phase, was able to represent it, and Mr. De Voto's correction is in order; but the kind of whooping it up for the good old days that Mr. De Voto attempts in his chapter called *Washoe* is just as emotional and just as "literary," that is to say, just as poetic, as Mr. Brooks's bitterness. In one of the essays in his collection called *Forays and Rebuttals,* Mr. De Voto denounces literary "fantasy," which he opposes to historic "fact": "The fantasies of the literary historian are frequently beautiful and nearly always praiseworthy, but they are a form of protection or of wishful thinking, a form of illusion and even of delusion," etc. Yet in what sense is Mr. De Voto's vision of a mining-town in Mark Twain's day "fact" that would make Mr. Brooks's vision "fantasy"? Mr. De Voto's book is full of rhetoric—the "incandescence" of the West, for example, which is always being brought in to do duty for more exact description. Parts of it sound, in fact, as if they had been written for declamation. There are moments when it suggests a Hollywood picture made from a novel by Fannie Hurst. Mr. De Voto is even capable of throwing out Mark Twain's own testimony (page 124) when it does not fall in with his own conception; and at one point he seems to be wanting us to accept bear-and-badger-baiting as evidence that the life of the pioneer was not devoid of gaiety and charm. (Observe, also, that in the above quotation, he is trying to psychoanalyze somebody— though one of his great objections to Brooks is that Brooks tried to psychoanalyze Mark Twain.)

As for Mr. De Voto's main grievance, it seems to me largely unfounded. He complains that American criticism has written down Mark Twain as a failure and insufficiently appreciated his work; whereas the fact surely is that the period he complains of has been that in which Mark Twain has been appreciated most. The older critics tended to exclude him from serious literature; but, beginning with William Lyon Phelps's essay and going on through John Macy and Mencken, the respect for Mark Twain has been growing. Stuart P. Sherman's chapter on him in *The Cambridge History of American Literature*, published in 1921, though rather uninspired, certainly takes Mark Twain seriously. Even Brooks does not belittle Mark Twain: he dignifies him by making him tragic; and the negative influence of Brooks and those who have followed his line has been negligible in comparison with the influence of Mark Twain's writings themselves. Ernest Hemingway and Sherwood Anderson have amply acknowledged their debt to Mark Twain; and the main stream of American humor has followed the channel he deepened. It is certainly not true in general that the Croly-Brooks view of the frontier has dominated in the writing of our period. On the contrary, the folklore and romance of the West have, if anything, been overdone. Haven't we all heard enough by this time about Sutter and Paul Bunyan and Billy the Kid? The Wild Bill Hickoks and Calamity Janes are now the heroes and heroines of Hollywood; and the demand for American folk humor has actually now reached a point where the author of *Caleb Catlum's America* has found it profitable to produce it synthetically.

What, then, is Mr. De Voto's real grievance? This indignation at other people's errors which seems to prevent him from stating his own case, this continual boiling-up about other people's wild statements which takes a form not merely wild but hysterical, have been characteristic of all his criticism.

Well, this may be partly due to the Westerner's grudge against the Easterner; and I should say that a certain amount of it was due to the peevishness of the literary professor against the writer outside the academic enclosure. Stuart Sherman behaved in very much the same way till he himself came to work in New York. It is a combination of disapproval, often on sound enough grounds, of what seems to them cheap and superficial in the work of writers ignorant of the classics and with no training in the standards of scholarship, and of envy of the freedom of the non-academic. The critic who is or has been a teacher cannot seem to help adopting toward his readers the tone he has acquired in the classroom. That Bernard De Voto has been somewhat conditioned by the academic environment is indicated, I think, by the fact that, in his essays on education, where he is dealing with a world in which he has lived, whose difficulties and hopes he has shared and whose victories he has helped to win—even in criticizing that world severely—he gives out both heat and light; but that whenever he encounters, for example, the graduates or denizens of Greenwich Village, which has also had its hopes and its hardships, its ignominies and its victories, he stiffens with the distrust of a stranger.

Yet De Voto, I should say, fundamentally, has nothing of the supercilious professor. There is evidently some other reason for his attitude toward his contemporaries; but the difficulty is to imagine from what point of view it is possible to charge them all with a common guilt. In his review of Carl Van Doren's *Three Worlds*, he seemed to sweep them all together and accuse them of "misrepresenting" America; he seemed to ascribe to each one all the opinions of all the others. He must have mastered some precious secret which the rest of us badly need if he is not to be included himself in this general potpourri (he belongs to the same generation as the writers of the twenties he denounces, and he has been publishing novels for years)—if he can claim the privilege of standing apart and knowing that he is saved, while he looks on at the plunge of the Gadarene swine.

But what *is* this point of view, this secret? Mr. De Voto never lets us know. He only hints, and on the basis of his hints one is unable to construct anything that hangs together. One gathers that he is definitely opposed to certain tendencies that he regards as prevalent and which he characterizes variously as "progressive," "Utopian" and "religious." These tendencies evidently have to do with the desire to see the economic system modified in such a way as to safeguard human society against the social inequalities, depressions and wars which, visibly in Europe, as Mr. De Voto writes, are destroying civilization itself. Mr. De Voto's antagonism to Mr. Brooks seems, in fact, to have been primarily inspired by the latter's concern about these problems. Well, of the people that Mr. De Voto lumps together, some are no doubt Utopians; but others are Marxists, and Marx and Engels exploded Utopian socialism almost a century ago.* Yet all of them, one gathers from Mr.

*I have had to let this statement stand in order not to be in the position of suppressing my own past errors while perpetuating Mr. De Voto's. I was later to discover that in this connection Mr. De Voto could have made out a very

De Voto, have in some way been untrue to America. And not only the ones who want to get rid of capitalism—equally those who, like Sinclair Lewis, simply stayed at home and criticized. All the works of this period, apparently—Lewis's caricatures, Hemingway's idyls, Brooks's diagnoses, O'Neill's tragedies, Dos Passos's social webs, Fitzgerald's drinking-parties, Sherwood Anderson's waking dreams, Edna Millay's lyrics—had it in common that they betrayed America.

But in the interests of what is Mr. De Voto speaking? Who or what has been betrayed? A group, so far as one can gather, that Mr. De Voto calls the middle class. These middle-class people, it seems, have been going about their business, taking care of the country's essential work and maintaining its moral soundness, while our writers of the twenties and thirties have been jeering at them and leaving them in the lurch and attempting to bemuse them with Utopian visions. It is hard to understand why this solid middle class should have bought and read so many copies of the books of the above-named writers, who have blasphemed their American heritage.

What then? All is dim after that. Fitful chinks in the clouds of words show principles leaning at unexpected angles, which seem to change between the chinks. For example: "Revolutions are always struggles between special groups; only propaganda tries to make them seem the will of the people in action. The people remain mostly unharried by them, neither willing nor acting, and in the end pay tribute to the old group, victorious, or to the new one which has cast it out. Even agrarian revolt has little to do with the agrarians in a mass." Then another barrage against the intellectuals, under cover of which no troops seem to advance. Then a vision—very vivid and convincing, this one—of the rise of the Mormon community in Utah: we are shown how, beginning with something that was in some ways very similar to communism, it developed a privileged hierarchy and succumbed, in the long run, to the financial and industrial interests. From this, some kind of moral seems supposed to be drawn. But what is it? Something about

---

good case, and that the scientific pretences of Marxism smuggled in a Utopian element which has made possible, in the Soviet Union, one of the hugest impostures of history. See *Marxism at the End of the Thirties.*

dictatorship and how all dictatorships must take the same course? Something about the enslaving effects of capitalism? Does he mean to suggest that Salt Lake City exhausts the possibilities of human society? One would think that the absorption of the communism of the Mormons in the expansion of the capitalist system precisely proved the Marxists' case. There are any number of questions that we should like to put to Mr. De Voto. Since we do not understand his premises, it is difficult to know how to debate with him. He seems content to tear his hair and, lumping us all together like one of those composite pictures that does not resemble anybody, pretend he is arguing with us.

I am sure that I am being unfair to Mr. De Voto, but I have written in the hope of smoking him out. He has been influenced by the Italian sociologist Vilfredo Pareto, and, since I have not myself read Pareto, I haven't this key to his system. I *have* read the number of the *Saturday Review* that Mr. De Voto devoted to Pareto, but the articles, including his own, threw very little light on the subject. I gather that the discipline of Pareto enables you to detach yourself from social groups and to study them objectively and dispassionately. Is that what Mr. De Voto is trying to do when he becomes so madly excited about the life of the American frontier?

Let him stand and unfold himself. What does he want? If he does not believe in the improvement of society, to what does he look forward, then?—and where do the values of literature come in? Let him not merely refer us to Pareto. Let him not merely tell us we are Easterners (especially since a good many of us are Westerners) who will never understand the frontier. It is a long time since anybody new in this field has really had anything to say to us; and if Mr. De Voto has something to say, he may be sure of an attentive audience.

February 3, 1937

It's Terrible! It's Ghastly! It Stinks!

I HAVE laughed a good deal in reading a new book—*The Great Goldwyn* by Alva Johnston—about Sam Goldwyn, the Hollywood producer. It is fun to hear how Mr. Goldwyn, when told that a script was "too caustic," said: "To hell with the cost! We'll make it anyway!"; and how he brought Maeterlinck to Hollywood in a private car and then, after seeing his first script, rushed out of the room screaming: "My God, the hero is a bee!" Alva Johnston, who is an adept at this kind of personal sketch, has handled his subject with deftness. He has turned out a good piece of light reading, through which the Goldwyn gags are sprinkled in such a way as to give the whole story a certain comic sparkle.

And yet this book makes one slightly sick. It has the slave-brand of Hollywood upon it. Instead of being able to present Sam Goldwyn as the rich humorous character he undoubtedly is, with whatever credit for energy and enterprise he deserves, Mr. Johnston seems to feel forced to flatter him. Mr. Johnston does not, to be sure, offer up his homage to Goldwyn with quite the piety of denizen of the studios. He is used to writing "profiles" for the *New Yorker*, and he makes a point of turning his paeans off with quick winks and light changes of tone. But the flattery is there just the same. One gets very definitely the impression that Mr. Johnston has written his sketch in such a way that Mr. Goldwyn will be able to read it or to have certain selected passages read to him and imagine that he has been apotheosized by Mr. Johnston, while at the same time Mr. Johnston will be let out with his friends in New York by the delicate irony which he has aimed in their direction but which may not be perceptible to Mr. Goldwyn. Or it may be all a special kind of publicity designed to give more serious weight to Mr. Goldwyn by scaling down his colossal vanity and ignorance, and what sounds from Mr. Johnston's account like a lack of ordinary sportsmanship and decency, to the proportions of amusing foibles which only endear him the more to his friends.

I will quote only two examples—the whole book is written

in the same way. "It has been said," says Mr. Johnston, "that if Shakespeare were alive today, Goldwyn would have him. It is an interesting notion; some of the bad plays, like *Cymbeline*, *Troilus and Cressida* and *Pericles*, might have been tightened up into great dramas if the playwright had had a producer over him to tell him, 'It stinks, Wagspeare. It's lousy. It's terrible. It's ghastly. You're ruining me, Wagstaff.'" Very funny about Goldwyn talking to Shakespeare; but what is Mr. Johnston's object in asserting that the defective plays of Shakespeare could have been converted by Mr. Goldwyn into "great dramas"? Mr. Johnston must know as well as anybody that Mr. Goldwyn would not be able to do anything for the least of Shakespeare's plays except turn it into something different and worse. And here is the conclusion of *The Great Goldwyn*: "Last year was Sam's twenty-third in the movie business; his press department at that time spotted him two years and celebrated the completion of his quarter-century in the business. Next year is Sam's real silver jubilee. It is something for everybody to feel patriotic about. The U.S.A. leads the world by a wider margin in pictures than anything else, and one of the chief reasons is the Great Goldwyn."

Well, I for one will be damned if I will feel patriotic about Sam Goldwyn's silver jubilee, which his agents have been unable to restrain themselves from celebrating two years too early. In what sense does the United States lead the world in moving pictures? We make more of them than any other country and are, I suppose, more proficient technically, but have we ever turned out anything that was comparable artistically to the best German or Russian films? I can think of nothing except Charlie Chaplin, who is his own producer and produces simply himself. There was a time—up to, say, 1930—when our pictures seemed to be improving. There were new actors brought in from Europe and from the speaking stage in New York; there was mechanical experimentation and an aesthetic attention to photography; intelligent directors were given their chance.

But then the depression fell; the producers were frightened and forced to retrench; and the whole movie business seemed to harden into something immovably banal. It nailed down its favorite formulas in all their vulgarity and falsity, and almost entirely abandoned any attempt to make the old situations seem lifelike or to point them up with novel direction. The actors who were brought to Hollywood were handled with extreme stupidity, and, if they stayed there, almost invariably ruined. A lot of talent has been fed into the studios, and what have our pictures to show for it? How shall we ever know now, for example, whether Katharine Hepburn—or, for that matter, Greta Garbo—ever really had anything in her? They set the talented Emil Jannings to performing over and over again wretched parodies of his German masterpieces, with everything that had given them reality and made them human and moving bleached out by the insipid Hollywood sun, until he could stand it no longer and departed. Charles Laughton has also escaped and has returned to England and the Old Vic. Marlene Dietrich, who must have had some ability at least as a night club singer, because she has made marvellous phonograph records in German, has been turned into something in the nature of one of those loose-jointed dolls designed to be propped up against the pillows in boudoirs with sateen bedspreads, and has been made to appear in pictures so foolish, so unsightly and of such horrible taste that the most beautiful woman in the world could not play in them without looking ridiculous. But the only mirrors, apparently, in which film actors can look at themselves are the magazines that exploit the glamor of the trade and are edited for adolescent schoolgirls. That able Soviet actress Anna Sten the Great Goldwyn was unable to use at all; and I see that she is now making for another producer pictures with such titles as *Love Me Again, Gorgeous* and *Orchid Girl.* Mae West, whose peculiar attraction was that she worked up her own material and created a legendary world of her own, now has to have savorless imitations written for her by Hollywood hacks, who have quickly converted her fantasies into run-of-the-mill goods. The vultures of the Coast get them all. A director like King Vidor who has serious aspirations ends by turning out the worst kind of monstrosity: the bad serious picture. The shimmering polish of Lubitsch ends as a veneer on the awful old formulas. We have actually got to a point where features like Tarzan and Charlie Chan are the most satisfactory things one can go to. They are absurd, they are fairy tales; but they do have a certain independent existence.

The other day, after long abstinence from the movies, the result of having seen nothing but bad films for a year, I went to one for the first time in months. I had assumed that the Marx brothers were indestructible. True, I had been reading the publicity stories about their new picture, *A Day at the Races*: how it had first been taken all over the country in the form of a stage entertainment, with a view to weeding out every gag that could not be immediately appreciated by the audience of the average town of over two or three thousand inhabitants. (This was partly, apparently, the work of Mr. George S. Kaufman, who, years ago, after his first experience of Hollywood, wrote *Once in a Lifetime* as a satire on it but later went back to learn the trade.) But I hadn't foreseen that the result of this would be to deprive the Marx brothers of all their natural vitality and spontaneity. As if even popular comic art, if this is really to capture the public, were not more a matter of putting over on an audience (as Charlie Chaplin and Walt Disney have) something from one's own imagination than of finding an infallible formula to provoke its automatic reactions! The idea of establishing and exploiting the lowest common denominator of audiences has finally killed the movies. They are absolutely sterile and static. And even the Marx brothers are no longer the Marx brothers. Their corporate élan has been deadened by unnatural selection of their dullest gags; and they now fall asunder helpless. It would be amusing if *A Day at the Races*, after all the special trouble taken with it, should turn out to be a total flop.

And the writers. Before the vultures have picked the bones of theatrical talent, the big white worms of the studios have grown fat on the decaying flesh. But the vultures get the worms, too. Have we not all had needy friends who have gone West with a smile on their lips and who have never returned again?—from whom we have ceased to hear and whose names we no longer mention, whom we remember as young people of promise, wondering what they have found to do and never thinking to connect them with the processed stuff we hear croaked out, between kisses and pistol-shots, by the smooth-faced gigantic phantoms, when we are foolish enough to go to the movies? It is true, as Mr. Johnston tells us, that Sam Goldwyn always wants the best writers; and there they are out on the Golden Coast, cooped up in their little cells, like school children in study-hour. Teacher is the supervisor, and one hopes to be teacher's favorite. There they are, blowing in their money on goofy Los Angeles houses and on ostentatious cocktail parties, at which they talk about their salaries and their options and always speak of their superiors with admiration, while they submit to being spied upon and having their correspondence opened. Those who do not care to admit surrender pretend to be uncompromising Leftists, getting together in little groups to give three discreet cheers for Stalin and to shed a tear for Republican Spain. But when the Writers' Guild was organized, it took only one woof from Schulberg to send them running like prairie-dogs—leaving the job to the technicians and the actors. And now the blacklisted leaders are creeping back, having become so profoundly habituated to high salaries for low work that, no matter how radical they claim to be, they don't know how to get along without them.

I remember only one American critic who has seemed to me to do full justice to this subject of the Hollywood producers: Mr. George Jean Nathan in the *Smart Set*. Mr. Nathan had the rich and reckless language for it; I am sorry that my own powers are relatively feeble. That was ten years or more ago; but it is plain that today's producers, including the Great Goldwyn and the late lamented Irving Thalberg, are the same megalomaniac cloak-and-suit dealers that their predecessors were. You have only to look at their products. You have only to look at their staffs. From the servant you may know the master. Mr. Johnston can have had only a brief submergence, and look at the book he has written.

July 21, 1937

1961. When this article first appeared in the *New Republic*, Mr. George S. Kaufman wrote in to complain of its inaccuracy in regard to himself. I had forgotten about his letter when I reprinted the piece in this book, but I came upon it later and I now want to make the correction. "In my entire life," Mr. Kaufman wrote, "I have spent something like three months writing for the movies; I did not write *A Day at the Races*, with which Mr. Wilson so gleefully credits me, and it is untrue that I 'went back for more' after *Once in a Lifetime*, because up to that time I had never seen the place, and neither had Moss Hart."

The Oxford Boys Becalmed

I CONFESS to feeling somewhat less enthusiasm than usual for the two new books of W. H. Auden: *On This Island*, a volume of poems, and *The Ascent of F-6*, a play written with Christopher Isherwood. It looks as if the group to which Auden belongs—the school of young Oxford poets which includes C. Day Lewis, Stephen Spender and Louis MacNeice—had lapsed, after their first lift of enthusiasm for the clean sweep that communism promises, the first exhilaration of repudiating the world to which they belonged, into a period of relaxation, of cooling down and marking time.

Mr. Auden himself has presented the curious case of a poet who writes an original poetic language in the most robust English tradition, but who seems to have been arrested at the mentality of an adolescent schoolboy. His technique has seemed to mature, but he has otherwise not grown up. His mind has always been haunted, as the minds of boys at prep school still are, by parents and uncles and aunts. His love poems seem unreal and ambiguous as if they were the products of adolescent flirtations and prep-school homosexuality. His talk about "the enemy" and "their side" and "our side" and "spying" and "lying in ambush" sounds less like anything connected with the psychology of an underground revolutionary movement than like the dissimulated resentments and snootiness of the schoolboy with advanced ideas going back to his family for the holidays. When this brilliant and engaging young student first came out for the class struggle so strongly, it seemed an audacious step; but then he simply remained under the roof of his nice family and in the classroom with his stuffy professors; and the seizure of power he dreams of is an insurrection in the schoolroom: "I should like to see you make a beginning before I go, now, here. Draw up a list of rotters and slackers, of proscribed persons under headings like this. Committees for municipal or racial improvement—the headmaster. Disbelievers in the occult—the school chaplain. The bogusly cheerful—the games master—the really disgusted—the teacher of modern languages. All these have got to die without issue. Unless my memory fails me there's a stoke hole under the floor of this hall. The Black Hole we called it in my day. New boys were always put in it. Ah, I see I am right. Well look to it. Quick, guard that door. Stop that man. Good. Now boys hustle them, ready, steady—go."

With all this—and at times out of all proportion to the interest of what he has had to say—Mr. Auden's imagery and language have been remarkable for an energy, a felicity, a richness, a resource, a nerve, which have made him a conspicuous figure. He certainly has more of what it takes to become a first-class poet than anybody else of his generation in England or, so far as I can think, in the United States. And in one department Mr. Auden is entirely and brilliantly successful: he has invented a new satire for the times. The most satisfactory part of his work seems to me that which includes such skits as *The Dance of Death*, with its cheap and weary rhythms; the satiric-elegiac choruses of *The Dog Beneath the Skin*; and such poems as the one, in this new collection, in which he describes the Cambridge intellectuals,

> Who show the poor by mathematics
> In their defense
> That wealth and poverty are merely
> Mental pictures, so that clearly
> Every tramp's a landlord really
> In mind-events.

He is especially good at calling the roll of the lonely, the neurotic, the futile—of all the queer kinds of individuals who make up the English upper classes. No one else has given us just this sense, at once pathetic and insipid, of the slackening of the social organism and the falling apart of its cells.

But, once having taken their stand, once having put themselves on record, we get the impression that Mr. Auden and his associates are at a loss as to what to do next. In some ways they appear to be retrograding. Thus the idiom of Auden in this latest book seems to me to be actually less personal than it was in his earlier poetry. He had revived in that earlier work the great idiom of English poetry at its most vigorous, its liveliest and freest, telescoping the whole tradition, from the emphatic alliteration of Anglo-Saxon through the variety and ease of the

Elizabethans to the irony and bizarre imagination of the generation just before his own. But in *On This Island* it seems to me that the rhythms of the lyrical and reflective poems let one down by approximating too closely to the deliberate looseness of the satirical ones; and the off-rhymes begin to get on one's nerves. (Near-rhymes and negligent rhythms are, I suppose, a symptom of blurred emotions. There are moments when Louis MacNeice sounds like a serious Ogden Nash.)

It has come to be a depressing feature of the literary scene at the present time—noticeable also in this country—that writers who had hitherto seemed able to stand on their own feet have begun flopping over on one another and imitating one another's idiom—without there necessarily being any question of the normal attraction of the weaker toward the stronger. Thus Auden, whose voice we have known and liked, disconcerts us by suddenly falling into the accents of Housman or Yeats or the palest of the later Eliot. Thus Louis MacNeice, who seems to me perhaps (except Auden himself) the most gifted of the Auden group, the master of a lyric impressionism that differs from the work of the rest, appears, in a recent number of the English magazine *New Verse*, to have toppled over on Auden and to have become almost indistinguishable from him.

The second of the Auden and Isherwood plays, *The Ascent of F-6*, is certainly very much inferior to *The Dog Beneath the Skin*. *The Dog Beneath the Skin* had its shortcomings: a good deal of its satire was banal—it sounded as if the clever schoolboys had just discovered some of the stalest jokes of Marxism and worked them up for a school entertainment. But the first part, at any rate, was very funny; and the choruses, as I have said, were certainly of Auden's best. *The Ascent of F-6* suffers even more from the flimsiness of amateur theatricals; and here Marxism has been forgotten for a relapse into Freudianism. The theme is a sort of psychoanalytic version of a career like that of Colonel Lawrence. This piece has the annoying defect of appearing to be padded in tiresome way and yet at the same time to be too short and not to exploit the possibilities of its subject.

Not, however, that Auden and his group are any worse off than other Left intellectuals. They have, in fact, an advantage over most of them in having been able to give expression to their plight and their time more brilliantly and with fewer false attitudes. The combination of communism with homosexuality, of an England suburbanized and Americanized in the peculiarly dreary English way with an English university culture as rich as the richest fruitcake, is something quite new in literature, which it took some courage and genius to manage. MacNeice and Auden are only thirty; C. Day Lewis is thirty-two; Stephen Spender is twenty-eight. They are remarkable, at that age, in having been able to say so well something that had not yet been said at all:

> So in this hour of crisis and dismay,
> What better than your strict and adult pen
> Can warn us from the colors and the consolations,
> The showy arid works, reveal
> The squalid shadow of academy and garden,
> Make action urgent and its nature clear?
> Who give us nearer insight to resist
> The expanding fear, the savaging disaster?
>
> This then my birthday wish for you, as now
> From the narrow window of my fourth-floor room
> I smoke into the night, and watch reflections
> Stretch in the harbor. In the houses
> The little pianos are closed, and a clock strikes.
> And all sway forward on the dangerous flood
> Of history, that never sleeps or dies,
> And, held one moment, burns the hand.

February 24, 1937

Prize-Winning Blank Verse

THERE is perhaps not much point, at this time and in this place, of writing a depreciation, merely for the sake of a depreciation, of the plays of Mr. Maxwell Anderson. Mr. Anderson is by no means pretentious about his work. It is the donors of the Pulitzer Prize, who gave a prize to *Both Your Houses*, and the members of the Drama Critics' Circle, who have twice in succession chosen plays of his for their award, that have made his work appear pretentious. And Mr. Stark Young has already discussed in these pages the various productions of Mr. Anderson's plays and dealt admirably with their literary as well as with their theatrical qualities. I see, moreover, that Mr. V. F. Calverton and Mr. George Jean Nathan have chosen this moment to light into him. There are, however, certain things to be said about Maxwell Anderson's general aims that none of these critics has said, so I shall lay on with the rest.

Toward the end of the season last year, when *Winterset* had been covering itself with glory, I went around to see what I understood from the reports of it I had heard to be a great American poetic drama on the theme of Sacco and Vanzetti. What I was actually confronted with was a belated disembodied shadow of the productions, so unpopular in their day—universally neglected by the critics—of the old New Playwrights' Theater in Grove Street. There were the Jews out of Em Jo Basshe's *The Centuries*; the street scene, with its agitators and policemen, out of Dos Passos's *Airways, Inc.*; and a general influence of the stagecraft—the set that accommodates a variety of scenes—of John H. Lawson. During the first act, I became quite interested, for it seemed to me that the writers of the New Playwrights might have founded a school, after all, and I was hoping that Mr. Anderson might have succeeded in improving on his originals. But as the play went on, I was baffled at discovering that the New Playwrights' characters were expressing themselves in blank verse of an hypnotic monotony and imagery of a dismal banality. The revolutionary social content had been extracted from the New Playwrights entirely. *Winterset* was indeed that wonderful coffee which enables you to sleep like a child. I did, in fact, fall asleep in the course of the last act and only woke up again when somebody fired a gun. All the characters were now being killed in an ending which was Elizabethan at least in its wholesale slaughter; but I was left quite unmoved by the fate of stage fictions who talked Mr. Anderson's blank verse.

I afterwards made a point of reading the text of *Winterset* in order to find out what I had missed. But the play seemed to me even feebler than it had when I had seen it on the stage. The production and the acting had invested some of the scenes with something like imagination; but in the text I could not discover anything that seemed to me in the least authentic as emotion, idea or characterization. Mr. Anderson is dealing with the after-effects of such a tragedy as the execution of Sacco and Vanzetti. He makes the son of an anarchist father, executed for another's crime, fall in love with the sister of the real criminal, whom he has devoted his life to pursuing. The young man gives up his revenge, sparing the girl's brother and allowing himself to fall into the hands of the gang. Miriamne has come to represent for him "all hope and beauty and brightness drawn Across what's black and mean"; he wishes to emerge from "this everglades of old revenge" and "forget to hate," perhaps at last to forgive. But it is too late. The gangsters kill them both. The Talmudic old Jewish father closes the play by announcing the "masterless might" of the universe, and declaring that only the human "cry toward something dim In distance, which is higher than I am" makes man the "emperor of the endless dark even in seeking."

> this is the glory of earth-born men and women,
> not to cringe, never to yield, but standing,
> take defeat implacable and defiant,
> die unsubmitting.

But what is the point of this? Mr. Anderson's hero, Mio, has just given up his life's purpose. In what sense is his defeat "implacable and defiant"? He is supposed to be the son of an anarchist, a class-conscious victim of the class war, and such a man would scarcely have regarded the exposure of the real culprit and the vindication of his father's innocence as merely a matter of private revenge. Yet Mr. Anderson makes him succumb to his interest in a little girl whose supposed sweetness of character is made to manifest itself in speeches that sound as if they had been written under the influence of a favorite English teacher and published in the school magazine by a young daughter of the bourgeoisie; and then gives him a funeral speech—of a kind, by the way, not especially appropriate to the mentality of a Talmudic Jew—which suggests some Promethean champion of the human mind and will.

I have also read—not having seen them—*The Masque of Kings* and *High Tor*, and they make upon me the same impression of pointlessness and mediocrity. The protagonist of *The Masque of Kings* gives up his revolutionary purpose just as Mio gives up his revenge; the protagonist of *High Tor* gives up the noble stand he has taken against the vandalism of industrial development. Mr. Anderson's heroes are always retiring: they become disillusioned with their own designs before instead of after they have realized them, and this makes his dramas rather disappointing. There is never any real fight. When everything is over, some sententious character gives expression to the thought "*Sic transit gloria mundi!*" in more or less hackneyed terms, and Mr. Anderson's performance is finished.

For the rest, Mr. Stark Young has analyzed these plays as much as it is profitable to do, and he has even, I feel, sometimes been led by skillful production or acting to give them a little more credit than they deserve. He is quite kindly about *High Tor*, which seems to me—among plays that make any claim to serious consideration—one of the silliest I have ever read. I agree with Mr. Young when he says that some of the bursts of Mr. Anderson's poetic eloquence "sound like a Stephen Phillips version of an Arthur Symons translation of a decadent German versifying of a lax translation of Euripides."

Yet Maxwell Anderson's writing is not all so bad as that. The point is that in his blank verse he is seen at his worst. The prose parts of his plays are much better. And in the days when he wrote prose altogether—in *What Price Glory?* and in the hobo play that he made from Jim Tully's *Beggars of Life*—he showed a gift for vernacular dialogue much richer and more original than anything that has appeared in his verse.

*

Mr. Anderson has, however, a positive conviction that plays should be written in verse. He has explained in his preface to *Winterset*. "Those," he says, "who have read their literary history carefully know that now is the time for our native amusements to be transformed into a national art of power and beauty. It needs the touch of a great poet to make the transformation, a poet comparable to Aeschylus in Greece and Marlowe in England. Without at least one such we shall never have a great theater in this country, and he must come soon, for these chances don't endure forever. I must add, lest I be misunderstood, that I have not mistaken myself for this impending phenomenon. I have made my living as teacher, journalist and playwright and have only that skill as a poet which may come from long practice of an art I have loved and studied and cannot let alone."

This assumption of Mr. Anderson's seems to me quite mistaken. It is true that verse has been passing out as a technique for writing plays; but is it true that it is really needed? After all, verse-technique has also passed out in all sorts of other departments of literature to which no one would now think of restoring it. In the last century, it was still used for novels; in the eighteenth century, for essays. Before that, in the ancient world, it was used for prophecies, laws, science, history and manuals of agriculture. Whatever the reasons for its falling into disuse, it is undeniable today that pure verse-technique has come to be employed—and is almost never otherwise effectively employed —in a narrow and specialized field: that of lyric poetry. The modern writers who come closest to the great writers of epics and the great dramatic poets of the past—the Flauberts and Tolstoys and Ibsens and Shaws and Prousts—have almost invariably written prose. At most, there is a blending with prose of something of the technique of verse: in certain writers one can see the transition quite clearly. For example, the long poems of Robinson Jeffers show a tendency to disintegrate into prose; and the prose novels of James Joyce contain vestiges of the rhythms of verse. Isn't it true that if Synge and O'Neill, of whom Mr. Anderson speaks, had lived in Otway's time, they would have still been writing their tragedies in verse? And is Mr. Maxwell Anderson prepared to assert that the plays of

Molière, for example, which, through an accident purely chronological, happen partly to have been written in verse, would be the worse for having been written in prose? The mere literary technique itself is not the issue here: the technique is determined by the rhythms of speech, and it changes with these rhythms, which in turn are determined by the pace of life and, basically, by man's relation to his environment, which changes from age to age. One sees this very plainly in Ibsen, who began by writing plays in verse, of which his countrymen say he was one of their great masters, but who, outgrowing the influence of the romantic era, became later a master of prose. Does Maxwell Anderson consider that *The Wild Duck* and *Hedda Gabler* are less successful than *Brand* and *Peer Gynt*, and can he imagine them written in verse? And what could be more synthetic than the costume-dramas of Rostand, the chief practitioner of modern poetic drama?

Mr. Anderson, it seems to me, in his own plays, has presented the most striking example of the obsolescence of verse-technique. He is capable of writing well—in prose, and when he is close to American speech. But in these recent verse-plays he writes badly—not, I think, because he is technically incompetent, but rather because English blank verse has no longer any relation to the tempo or tongue of our lives, and so can provide no vehicle for his genuine gift of dialogue: the old rhythms can inspire him to nothing but a flavorless conventional imagery that was already growing trite in our grandfathers' time. When Mr. Anderson makes an effort to combine blank verse with the language of everyday speech, he gets something, as in *Winterset*, which is neither, and dreadful. (It is true that T. S. Eliot, in *Murder in the Cathedral*, has done better with the verse-drama than Maxwell Anderson; but, to my mind, the best scenes in this play are the prose ones: the sermon and the speech of the assassins.)

I am inclined to believe, furthermore, that it is Maxwell Anderson's infatuation with blank verse that has aborted his talents all around. Along with the rhythm goes not only the imagery, but the attitude, the point of view. Instead of any sentiments that any real people might conceivably feel today in connection with the events he depicts, the commentators in Mr.

Anderson's plays can only proffer the dimmest echoes of the sentiments of the Elizabethans in connection with events of quite a different character. A technique ought to grow out of the material; but Mr. Anderson is trying to impose on his a technique that has nothing to do with it. Instead of getting deeper into reality as he progresses in his artistic career, he is carried by his blank verse farther away.

June 23, 1937

"Give That Beat Again"

THE NEW BOOK by Miss Edna St. Vincent Millay I have found a little disappointing. For the first twenty-five pages or so, *Conversation at Midnight* is stimulating. Seven men of different kinds are brought together and made to talk about love, religion, communism, fascism, war and other subjects of current interest—with interludes on hunting, fishing, racing and mushroom-collecting. The poet is plunging with her ready intelligence into the confusion of cross-currents of the time, and the reader is put on the qui vive: he is expecting a revelation. But the discussion doesn't come to much. It covers familiar ground, and the people—the stockbroker, the Communist, the liberal, the Roman Catholic, the artist, the sensualist, the advertising man—say many of the clever things that people usually say without arriving at very many of the illuminating things which people do not usually say but which the poet ought to make them say. We expect the conversation to gather momentum, but in the latter part it rather bogs down. At the very end, it mounts to a climax with an increasingly acrimonious altercation between the stockbroker and the Communist—each of whom accuses the other of submitting slavishly to regimentation—to which the liberal host puts an end by offering both parties a drink.

But the dialogue is rarely allowed to penetrate to the fundamentals of the problems on which it touches. There are insights of considerable vividness—the picture of secularized man howling at night over the grave of God, the picture of the atheistic Communist rejecting the advances of Faith when he confronts it in its familiar form only to yield to it when it comes in a different guise; but the really great forces that are upsetting the world somehow do not get squarely on the stage. What is really involved, for example, in such an argument as that between the radical and the stockbroker is the conflict between the classless and the class ideal, and Miss Millay has sidestepped this by making the pretenses of both parties ridiculous.

It may be that this part of the discussion has been blurred as a result of the accidental burning of Miss Millay's first manuscript and of her having had to write the poem over. The worst developments of the Stalin dictatorship in Russia, with the new phase of the Stalin-Trotsky quarrel, which figure in this second version, had not yet taken place when the first was written; and it may be that Miss Millay has been goaded by this to make her imaginary Communist more fanatical and less convincing in his desire to see his fellows happy and free than he had been in the original version. In one of her most revealing flashes, she makes the liberal address the Communist as follows:

> Russia under Lenin is so many light-years away,
> Its noble beam approaches you but now;
> You stand transfigured in the golden light today
> Of a star that, even while you bask in its bright ray,
> Blackens, and disappears.
> We must allow,
> Perhaps another nineteen years,
> Before you see what's happening in Russia now.

The debate in *Conversation at Midnight* cannot have failed to be confused by all this. Yet there are larger issues involved in these questions of religion and socialism, fascism and democratic ideals, which go deeper than the passing events of politics, as they go deeper than the prejudices and emotions of such persons as Miss Millay presents; and one cannot see that Miss Millay has kept these issues in sight. For her, the whole upshot of the matter seems to be that both the stockbroker and the radical hanker only after the status of obedient cogs in a smoothly running machine. But is this what they are fighting about in Spain? Miss Millay probably does not really think so, since she has lately contributed to a volume of translations of Spanish poems, for the benefit of the Loyalist cause; but you would never find this out from *Conversation at Midnight*. Nor, failing to dramatize the issue of the democratic versus the capitalist society, does she focus the various opinions and types from any other clear point of view.

I believe that the fundamental trouble here is that Miss Millay is rather lacking in the dramatic imagination—that is, that it is not quite natural for her to identify herself with imaginary characters. Of her plays, *Aria da Capo* was an eclogue, highly charged and deeply disturbing, like all her best work of that time; but the characters—as was suitable—were pure abstractions. *The King's Henchman*, which had some beautiful poetry in it, was a dramatic poem rather than a play, as the plays of Yeats are poems. But in *Conversation at Midnight*, Miss Millay has tried to animate and keep distinct a number of different people, with their characteristic points of view; and her own point of view, so personal, so strongly created in her other poetry, turns out not to lend itself easily to this kind of dissociation. She is attempting a sort of thing not unlike some of Bernard Shaw's plays and very much like G. Lowes Dickinson's *A Modern Symposium*; but, failing their expertness in the analysis of ideas, she ought to, and tends to, get out of such a subject effects of emotional conflict of a kind quite alien to Dickinson or Shaw. Yet these chemical emotional reactions do not, to my mind, quite occur. What does happen is that, on the one hand, Miss Millay is either satirizing her characters' banalities or commenting on them from a long way off, while, on the other hand, her own peculiar pessimism, with its noble magnanimity and bitterness, is always trying to rise to the surface but is never allowed to emerge. We keep listening instinctively through the chatter and chaff for the voice we are accustomed to hear, and now and then we think it is speaking:

Ricardo said, "Whatever the case for God, the splendor
   of Man
Cannot be questioned."
This Music, this proud edifice erected
Out of reach of the tide
By drowning hands,
This deathless, this impeccable, projected
By peccant men, who even as they labored sank and died,
Irrefutable witness to that splendor stands.
It speaks more loud
Than the waves that batter
The wild bluff:
There is no God.
But it does not matter.
Man is enough.

But compare this to Miss Millay's sonnet, *On Hearing a Symphony of Beethoven*. For anyone capable of that, this was hardly worth doing at all. And in the meantime, the dramatized points of view of Miss Millay's fictitious personalities never give rise to any conflict half so real as the conflicts within the poet herself, as she has expressed them directly in her own person:

> Pity me that the heart is slow to learn
> What the swift mind beholds at every turn.

A good deal of the interchange of *Conversation at Midnight* falls into a vein of banter, worldly and witty and sometimes cute, which has not been exploited by Miss Millay since her prose sketches and dialogues of about fifteen years ago, published under the pseudonym of Nancy Boyd. To handle this kind of badinage in verse, she has developed a new semi-verse medium which is something like a combination of Ogden Nash and Robinson Jeffers, but which, in her hands, is much more flexible, as it follows a play of the intelligence that is quicker and subtler than either of theirs. *Conversation at Midnight is* really very witty; and the imagery, as is usual with Edna Millay, provides an element of excitement and surprise through its power to intensify realistic observation presented with a daring baldness:

> Corruption, too, is a kind of development—it depends
>   on the viewpoint. . . .
> To the buzzard under his shabby wings appraising the
>   beach from above, the whip-ray
> Till he be stranded and the land soldier-crabs have
>   taken his eyes out
> Has not achieved maturity.

But Nancy Boyd is not Edna Millay; and this group of ventriloquial figures does not bring her much closer to being so. Not, of course, that Nancy Boyd isn't good in her way; not that this book isn't more or less brilliant. But the best of the impersonal poems in the volume called *The Buck in the Snow* are more truly philosophical than the whole of this long symposium.

*

As for the verse, this reviewer has been prophesying for years about the obsolescence of verse-technique and the gradual victory of prose; but now he finds himself a little dismayed at the rapidity with which the process is going forward. Little did we think in our youth, when the Miltonic line seemed irrefrangible and when, our innocence, we used to laugh, as the poet intended us to do, at W. S. Gilbert's rhymed but meterless Bab Ballad of *The Lost Mr. Blake*, that we should live to see the day when its interminable lines that look and sound like paragraphs of prose would be the type of much serious poetry. The old strong beat of English verse has by this time been so broken, sprung, muted, loosened, that it might almost as well be abandoned altogether. Compare MacNeice and Auden with Yeats and Housman; Robinson Jeffers with John Masefield; Eliot's *Murder in the Cathedral* with his earlier work; Ogden Nash with Franklin P. Adams. And now Edna St. Vincent Millay, one of the sole surviving masters of English verse, seems to be going to pieces, too. She was beginning to indulge a loose hand with her metrics in the volume called *The Buck in the Snow*—quite successfully in some of the lyrics; and she went even further in this direction in a later book, *Wine from these Grapes*. But it was not till her translations from Baudelaire that the ravages of the mischief became alarming. Instead of rendering Baudelaire's alexandrines in English meters equally ringing, she fell into what seemed a fallacy entirely uncharacteristic in assuming that the effect of the French could be conveyed by slurring over the English stress and producing a line completely fluid. But the result was not a bit like Baudelaire: it was merely inferior verse for Edna St. Vincent Millay.

Now in *Conversation at Midnight*, you see metrics in full dissolution. The stress is largely neglected; the lines run on for paragraphs; sometimes the rhymes fade out. Occasionally poor little sonnets, like souls from the Platonic overworld that want to be born again, flutter in and are carried along by the all-liquefying flux, filling up quickly with its varied content, to which their form has no special appropriateness, in which it is difficult for them to crystallize a pattern. This is all something quite distinct from the *vers libre* of the early nineteen-hundreds, which, though proselike, was often redeemed by a lapidary sharpness and precision or had the rhythms of the

Whitmanesque chant. But the rhythms are weary now. They and the near-rhymes, as Mr. Max Eastman has said, almost amount to a joke on disciplined writing itself.

I do not complain of this state of affairs: I know that it is all on the cards. And *Conversation at Midnight* is, in any case, a highly entertaining interlude in Miss Edna Millay's work. Miss Millay at her most relaxed is livelier than most of our poets at their brightest. Yet I miss her old imperial line.

July 28, 1937

Dream Poetry

THE OTHER NIGHT I made up a poem in my sleep and remembered it after I woke up, and it has set me thinking about dream poetry.

The outstanding examples of imitation dream poetry are, of course, those of Lewis Carroll and James Joyce. Everybody knows the dream gibberish of *Jabberwocky* and the familiar classics gone wrong of *You are old, Father William* and *Sitting on a Gate*. And James Joyce's new book,* which is all a dream, contains some equally amusing examples. At one point the sleeping hero imagines himself coming out of a public house with a party of convivial companions. They insist on somebody's singing a ballad, which turns out, however, when it is finally heard, to be a pitiless exposé of the hero (a man named H. C. Earwicker, who has a tendency, in inferior-feeling moments, to associate himself with earwigs):

Have you heard of one Humpty Dumpty
How he fell with a roll and a rumble
And curled up like Lord Olaga Crumple
By the butt of the Magazine Wall,
Of the Magazine Wall,
Hump, helmet and all.

He was one time our King of the Castle
Now he's kicked about like a rotten old parsnip.
And from Green Street he'll be sent by order of His Worship
To the penal jail of Mountjoy
To the jail of Mountjoy!
Jail him and joy.

He was father of all schemes for to bother us
Slow coaches and immaculate contraceptives for the populace,
Mare's milk for the sick, seven dry Sundays a week,

Finnegans Wake had not come out in book form and did not as yet have a name. The ballad was quoted from one of the instalments that appeared in the magazine *transition*, in the form in which it there appeared. Its final form was somewhat different.

Openair love and religion's reform,
And religious reform,
Hideous in form . . .

'Tis sore pity for his innocent poor children
But look out for his missus legitimate!
When that frew gets a grip of old Earwicker
Won't there be earwigs on the green?
Big earwigs on the green,
The largest ever you seen, etc.

These are, however, the creations of comic art. Before going on to true dream composition, one may note that there exists, also, a sort of unintentional pseudo-dream poetry. T. S. Eliot suggests that the poetry of Swinburne really belongs in this category:

> Before the beginning of years
>> There came to the making of man
> Time with a gift of tears:
>> Grief with a glass than ran . . .

"This is not merely 'music,'" says Eliot. "It is effective because it appears to be a tremendous statement, like statements made in our dreams; when we wake up, we find that the 'glass that ran' would do better for time than for grief, and that the gift of tears would be as appropriately bestowed by grief as by time." But the poetry of Swinburne seems to me to be alcoholic, rather than dream, poetry; and alcoholic poetry is a distinct department. A better example of involuntary dream poetry is the verse of the late George Russell, who signed himself AE. I remember coming home very tired one night and picking up what I thought was a volume of Yeats, with the intention of reading myself to sleep. I had an experience that gave me the creeps for a moment. Something strange seemed to have happened to the familiar poems. They sounded like Yeats all right, but were suffused with an uncanny iridescence which made everything insubstantial, somehow slightly unpleasant and, so far as I could see, meaningless. The poems were not Yeats's but AE's, which had been brought out by the same publisher in a format almost identical with the collected Yeats. It was a copy sent for review that I had put in my bookcase and forgotten about. I had never looked into it before, and it had given me for a few moments the illusion that I was dreaming.

But these are not the real thing. There is perhaps only one great classic of well-authenticated dream poetry: Coleridge's *Kubla Khan*, which was begun in an opium trance and interrupted by somebody's knocking at the door, so that the poet, with his waking mind, was never able to finish it. Here the opium must have intensified the vision and speeded up intellectual activity. A more normal example is the well-known set of verses called *Dominus Illuminatio Mea*, which the novelist R. D. Blackmore, the author of *Lorna Doone*, is said to have composed in a dream:

> In the hour of death, after this life's whim,
> When the heart beats low, and the eyes grow dim,
> And pain has exhausted every limb—
>   The lover of the Lord shall trust in Him. . . .

This piece seems to have been a great favorite with Sir Arthur Quiller-Couch, who included it in two of the Oxford anthologies; but, interesting though it is as a specimen of what can be done by the sleeping mind, I have never been able to feel any enthusiasm for it. It is characteristic of dream poetry, as Eliot says, that it never means as much as it seems to.

A distinguished American poet* once told me that he had dreamt of composing a poem which had seemed to him in his dream the consummation of his whole career, if not the highest triumph of literature—a work of supreme beauty which also gave utterance to the profoundest thought ever compassed by a poet's mind. When he woke up, he still knew the poem, which turned out to run as follows:

> It's white to be snow,
>   It's cold to be ice,
> It's windy to blow,
>   And it's nice to be nice.

My own verses were of this gnomic character. I had dreamed that I was taking a cruise along the west coast of Italy. The principal stops were Cologne, Brescia, Rome and Santiago. We

---

*The late Ridgely Torrence.

were playing a game like bouts rimés with very peculiar conditions, of which one was that the words "the mandrake shrieks" were to appear in every poem. With enormous labor, but, as it seemed to me, great brilliance, I produced the following stanza; then decided to leave the ship and go back to Paris, because I was afraid I should fall down in the contest by not having time enough to supply another stanza equally remarkable:

> The human heart is full of leaks;
>> The human head is full of vapors.
> The crows disband; the mandrake shrieks;
>> The scandal was in all the papers.

Some crows were actually making a racket and had evidently penetrated my dream without being able to wake me.

But the most remarkable specimen of dream poetry which I have ever personally encountered was composed by a lady of my acquaintance.* The curious thing is that the other verse of hers I have seen, written during her waking hours, is distinctly inferior to this dream poem, which seems to me quite delightful and a little in the vein of *Kubla Khan.*

> And you, my love, and you, my sweet,
> The beauty of the morning greet,
>> For me it's end of day.
> Unclosed my eyes, unclosed the night;
> I saw star-clusters reel and right
> And nothing was that was the same
> As it had been ere this night came:
>> The moon knelt down to pray.
> I went back through the hidden door
> Where no sane man had gone before;
> I saw the beauties, touched the dross;
> I drank the wine and kissed the cross
>> And gave your love to pay,
> That I might touch eternity
> A moment's space, now you are free,
>> Long gone, long lost, away.

It is true, of course, that one of the main currents of modern poetry has been tending toward something like a condition of

*Mrs. William McFee.

dream since Mallarmé, and even since Poe. Modern life seems to have had the effect of driving the old kind of lyric feeling, which used to embrace the world, into the depths of the private consciousness; and the deliberate formulas and attitudes derived from the study of external reality which the younger poets are trying to impose on their poetry have a way of yielding nothing but rhetoric. Who knows but we may not, in the long run, have to depend on our dreams for lyrics?

July 31, 1937

This article brought me several letters with specimens of poetry written in dreams.

Mr. George V. Lockard, writing from Lancaster, Pennsylvania, sent me the following verses:

> The evening ends in noise and folly,
> Speeches beneath the one bright star
> Changing to sleepers on the trolley,
> Electric jolting of the car.
>
> Who seemed an Artemis on background green
> Mantling the darkness in Virgilian airs
> Decides to let her wit be seen,
> Dwindles to Millamant and public stares.

Mr. George W. Lyon, writing from Pittsburgh, sent me a copy of a letter published in the New York *Times Saturday Review of Books* of March 19, 1910, in which he told of composing a poem in a dream and gave the text of the poem, with a gloss which he had later added:

Two Voices

> Out of the atoms of earth we come,
> Back to the atoms of earth we go;
> Out of the dark of earth to light,
> Back to the dark of earth and night.
> Life is a problem and death is its sum—
> Out of the atoms of earth we come,
> Back to the atoms of earth we go.

This is the Voice of abysmal gloom and utter hopelessness.

> Out of the clod is sped the soul,
> Back to the Giver of Life to go;

This is the Voice of triumphant hope and regeneration.

Out of the shade of earth and night,
Back to the glow of realms in light.
Free is the wine from the clay of the bowl—
Out of the clod is sped the soul,
Back to the Giver of Life to go.

Mrs. Marjorie Bell, writing from New York, sent me the following poem, with an explanation of the circumstances under which it had been composed: "My father went to bed one night woozy with the high temperature of an oncoming cold, for which he had dosed himself with aconite. He always credited the verses to this combination of circumstances. He woke suddenly with an exalted sense of creative achievement, and managed to write down the lines word for word as he dreamed them, before they eluded him." The title, she says, "came with the poem, but doesn't quite fit."

The Jealousy of Taurus

A mighty ox with trenchant horn
Thrust at the earth when it was born
He made a gash both deep and wide—
"By Jove," he cried, "'tis red inside!"

And since that day, that mighty gash
With fire and smoke and lightning flash
Pours forth a flood of liquid flame—
And thus it was Mount Etna came.

Mr. John Chamberlain tells me that he once composed a sonnet in a dream, from which, when he awoke, he was able to remember the first two lines of the sestet:

And even though the tall giraffes were tough,
And even though the tough giraffes were tall . . .

Mr. E. M. Forster, in an essay called *An Outsider in Poetry* in his book *Two Cheers for Democracy*, says that he composed in a dream his only two lines of "modern poetry":

I will put down Hastings, you shall see
Companion to India as a boat gnawed.

He calls these lines modern, he says, "because they are obscure and minatory."

"Cousin Swift, You Will Never Be a Poet"

SWIFT'S VERSE has for some years been out of print. The last edition was that of William Ernst Browning, published in 1910, which was neither very adequately annotated nor very well arranged. Mr. Harold Williams has now prepared and the Oxford Press produced a scholarly and handsome edition— *The Poems of Jonathan Swift*—in three volumes. There seems, however, to hang a sort of curse over the indexes to editions of Swift's poetry, which prevents one's being able to use them. The Browning edition had indexes in the fronts of the volumes which listed the poems in their printed order, but no alphabetical index and no index of first lines. The Williams edition includes, at the beginning of each volume, an index of the three volumes that lists the poems in groups of "political," "personal," etc., but no index by titles of all the pieces, and an alphabetical index that covers all three of the volumes, but proves to be a nuisance in a different way, due to the fact that the three are consecutively paged and it is usually difficult to know in which volume to look for a given poem. One of the good features of the Williams edition is three facsimiles of manuscripts of Swift's in his firm and clear and beautiful hand.

It is to be hoped that the Oxford Press will eventually bring this edition out in a single volume at a lower price. I hasten to express this hope, yet I fear that even a cheap edition would fail to do very much to make the poetry of Swift more popular. His cousin John Dryden told him, on seeing one of his early pindaric odes, that he would never become a poet; and many people will not admit that he ever did. Yet the question of whether or not Swift is a "poet" comes down, as Leslie Stephen said in his English Men of Letters volume, to "a question of classification." "Swift's originality appears in the very fact that he requires a new class to be made for him." Leslie Stephen, it seems to me, is even too niggardly in the space that he devotes to Swift's verse. My own conviction is that it is almost as remarkable as his prose, and that a good deal of his very best writing is to be found among these five hundred or so pieces. This writing is not merely a versification of the prose of his satires and pamphlets. For there is a strong sensuous side to Swift—though, like Huysmans, he is sensitive mainly to ugly or disagreeable impressions. This comes through in the realistic similes which give a good deal of their flavor to his prose writings, and when he is dealing with certain congenial subjects such as the coins of the *Drapier's Letters*, which we seem to see and hear and handle. Swift had always a feeling for money: it stimulated his imagination, and he raised to a kind of poetry his tracts on financial questions.

But there is much more of this in his verse, and it makes him a poet of a special kind. He is inferior to Dryden and Pope in variety of color and delicacy of ear. He was too great a master of prose to be able to command entirely, though he was able to do so partly, the resources of the other technique. The sobriety and restraint which give his prose its distinction seem sometimes to impoverish his verse; his habit of hitting the nail on the head that makes the arguments of a pamphlet compelling, may produce a monotonous emphasis that deadens a development in verse.

This granted, we must recognize that Swift does successfully work in his poetry a vein hardly touched in his prose. He is here one of the most vivid portrayers of the life of the eighteenth-century city. *Morning* and *A City Shower*—of the latter of which he was rightly proud—the terrible panels of *The Progress of Virtue*, *The Progress of Beauty*, etc., which only Swift's strong drawing and his classic severity make tolerable—these are the products of a sharp observation hardly found in the novelists of the period. They are closer to Hogarth's engravings. Later on, he was to do Ireland superbly. *Helter Skelter*, the circuit ride of the attorneys, is a masterpiece of social caricature; so is *The Grand Question Debated*, with its picture of country-house life; so are even the *Verses Made for Women Who Cry Apples, etc.*, with Swift's feeling, sad and comic, for the lives of the women and his savoring of the wares they sell. Swift had, like Huysmans, an actual appetite for homely or sordid detail. When he is obliged to wait for the boat at Holyhead, he sits down to describe his bad accommodations, the "muddy ale and moldy bread"; when Stella is about to return from a visit, he describes to her, as if with relish, how the shabby surroundings of her home must take the place of the luxuries of the gentry:

> But now arrives the dismal day:
> She must return to *Ormond Key*:
> The coachman stopt, she lookt, and swore
> The Rascal had mistook the Door:
> At coming in you saw her stoop;
> The Entry brushed against her Hoop:
> Each Moment rising in her Airs,
> She curst the narrow winding stairs:
> Began a Thousand Faults to spy;
> The Ceiling hardly six Foot high;
> The smutty Wainscot full of Cracks,
> And half the Chairs with broken Backs . . .

Yet all through Swift's life there reëchoes a chagrin that had preyed upon him in the poverty of his youth. The great spirit subjected to indignity will dignify that indignity itself. And so, condemned to his deanship in Dublin, he gives the misery of the Irish a kind of grandeur. The poems that he wrote in Ireland supplement his political writings: they illustrate his economic arguments with a picture of the physical degradation of the people.

Besides this, there are flights of a macabre fantasy—*Death and Daphne* and *On Cutting Down an Old Thorn*—to which he does not give scope in the matter-of-fact extravagances of his prose. And there are many pieces, always interesting and sometimes very moving, that deal directly with his personal life. Swift's self-dramatization in his poems is really one of his most brilliant achievements—whether in the pièce de résistance on the reception of the news of his death and the well-known verses on Stella and Vanessa or in the less well-known Market Hill poems and the imitations of Horace, in which he writes of his relations with Harley. The best of these poems sometimes rise to the kind of tragic irony that one finds in his prose but which has here a special personal accent: the joke that is only a joke but of which the effect is crushing:

> Deaf, giddy, helpless, left alone,
> To all my Friends a Burthen grown,
> No more I hear my Church's Bell,
> Than if it rang out for my Knell:
> At Thunder now no more I start,

Than at the Rumbling of a Cart:
Nay, what's incredible, alack!
I hardly hear a Woman's Clack.

There is nothing else quite like this in literature. The curses
and sneers of Swift created a new kind of lyric.

December 8, 1937

Peggy Bacon: Poet with Pictures

I N NO FIELD have fashions and cliques come to play a more important role than in that of verse-reviewing. A writer who belongs to no group and has no connection with any current trend is likely not to get much noticed, let alone given a place in the anthologies. It would not be true to say that Peggy Bacon has not been appreciated and praised: her caricatures, her prints and her children's books have brought her a considerable reputation; but her volumes of pictures and verse, which contain some of the best of her work, have received almost no attention.

Miss Bacon has published two of these collections: *Animosities* and *Cat-Calls*. Here the verses help the drawings out, and we feel that we are getting her essence, as with her prints, her pastels and her paintings, we do not always do. The best of her prints and her bigger drawings are of course incomparable: she is, I suppose, the first woman artist successfully to invade the field of Hogarth, Goya and Daumier. But she sometimes attempts elaborate subjects that stagger a very feminine talent: where Hogarth is able to organize a complicated crowded print about a center of point and light that throws the whole picture into perspective, the larger groups of Peggy Bacon sometimes seem to get beyond her control and to coalesce in dark indistinctness; and in those of her larger productions where only a few figures are framed, she sometimes leaves great spaces of baldness that overbalance the wit of the rest. But these small drawings which illustrate her verses seem to me almost always quite perfect. They are as compact as medals of Pisanello, as clear as tiny plates by Callot.

Her verses have not always quite this sharpness. They are sometimes a little amateurish. But they are original both in accent and in pattern. They possess the immense distinction of not having been produced synthetically, as so much contemporary poetry is. And the work in her second volume shows an improvement over that of the first: in *Cat-Calls* there begin to appear, among the epigrams and ironic sketches, short lyrics—*Autumn Burden* and *Illusion*—which, in spite of some inexpert passages that a little more care would correct, find new words for personal moods. All the work in these books of Miss Bacon's has the mark of the authentic artist in that it does not derive from the desire to produce an impression for its own sake but pursues as its primary object what the writer really feels and thinks.

At first glance, these pictures and verses may seem waspish and a little morose. But, reëxamining them, one comes to appreciate their marvellous delicacy and fancy, their dryness, their elegance, their point—till they have become permanent sources of pleasure. This is the poetry of the ugly, the inadequate, the sordid, the ridiculous, the sad, but all distilled to a new felicity; it is the poetry of the pastoral suburban, the middle-class domestic and the human and animal young, but never kewpified or jollified or arch. The children are untidy and tend to be bad; the pets are dogs and cats, nothing more: they are not complicated by human attributes, but nobody has ever been more sensitive than Peggy Bacon is in catching the various phases of real cat and dog nature. Mamma and Poppa are none too handsome and none too smartly dressed, and the sitting-room where they read in the evenings is furnished in none too good taste. At the evening party, the women get rather silly, and the men are rather wistful old stuffed shirt-fronts. In the city, the houses are dingy, the kids dirty and the cats thin; an old horse has his nose in a feed-bag while the sparrows pick up the crumbs. In the towns, there are timid young ladies who peek out through the slits in the shutters and disdainful old parties in antiquated mansions who think nobody else lives on their street. In the country, the sun is rising on people asleep in their houses, who, on waking, will be rather astonished to find themselves confronted with one another and will make an effort to refocus their sight. In the fields, an old stump, an old shack falling down, a scarecrow with a woman's old dress and hat that seems to attract the crows. A tumbler and pills on a sick person's table; abandoned blocks and dolls on the floor; a pet bird that has turned up its toes and that will have to be buried in a candy-box. The old deformed and run-down shoes on the shelf in the cobbler's shop; the bald tailor, intent in his basement, driving his needle into somebody else's coat:

> The blackmailer
> slew the jailer
> —some distress
> and a scrap of crêpe—
> there is no jailer
> to watch the tailor,
> but nevertheless
> he can't escape.

In the midst of all this, one finds posted, as a beacon of a sort, here and there, some simple and wholesome object: a fine little glass of red wine in the center of a scalloped doily; a narrow old-fashioned clock with slender mahogany columns; a good plate of meat, peas and potatoes, with the heel of a loaf of white bread, a napkin and a mug of milk; a toy top, tipping but fixed, spinning on a point like an etcher's tool; and a hand with long craftsman's fingers, deliberately threading a needle or holding a spiky shell. Against all that is imperfect and dismal, such symbols of soundness stand: the symbols of food and work, of steadiness opposed to the flux of time, to the futile fatigue of movement.

This is what the life of art ought to be. What it ought not to be is rhetoric, personal or aesthetic. The trifles of Peggy Bacon, like the fables of La Fontaine, wear well and come to mean more the longer we know them.

April 27, 1938

Twilight of the Expatriates

The Tropic of Cancer, by Henry Miller, was published in Paris four years ago, but nobody, so far as I know, has ever reviewed it in the United States, and it seems to me to deserve some notice.

Every phase of literary opinion is responsible for its critical injustices. During the twenties, this book would have been discussed in the *Little Review*, the *Dial* and *Broom*. Today the conventional critics are evidently too much shocked by it to be able to bring themselves to deal with it—though their neglect of it cannot wholly have been determined by the reflex reactions of squeamishness. A book bound in paper and published in Paris has no chance against a book bound in cloth and brought out by a New York publisher, who will buy space to announce its appearance. The conservative literary reviews have not been so easily outraged that they would not give respectful attention to John O'Hara's *Butterfield 8* or squander space on the inferior Hemingway of *To Have and Have Not*. As for the Left-Wingers, they have ignored *The Tropic of Cancer* on the ground that it is merely a product of the decadent expatriate culture and can be of no interest to the socially minded and forward-looking present.

Expatriate Mr. Miller certainly is: he is the spokesman, par excellence, for the Left Bank; but he has produced the most remarkable book which, as far as my reading goes, has come from it in many years. *The Tropic of Cancer* is a good piece of writing; and it has also a sort of historical importance. It is the epitaph for the whole generation of American writers and artists that migrated to Paris after the war. The theme of *The Tropic of Cancer* is the lives of a group of Americans who have all more or less come to Paris with the intention of occupying themselves with literature but who have actually subsided easily into an existence almost exclusively preoccupied with drinking and fornication, varied occasionally by the reading of a book or a visit to a picture exhibition—an existence for which they muster the resources by such expedients as pimping for travellers, playing gigolo to rich old ladies and sponging on one another. The tone of the book is undoubtedly low; *The Tropic of Cancer*, in fact, from the point of view both of its happenings and of the language in which they are conveyed, is the lowest book of any real literary merit that I ever remember to have read; it makes Defoe's Newgate Calendar look like Plutarch. But if you can stand it, it is sometimes quite funny; for Mr. Miller has discovered and exploits a new field of the picaresque.

The disreputable adventures of Mr. Miller's rogues are varied from time to time with phosphorescent flights of reverie devoted to the ecstasies of art or the doom of European civilization. These passages, though old-fashioned and rhetorical in a vein of late romantic fantasy reminiscent of *Les Chants de Maldoror*, have a youthful and even ingenuous sound in queer contrast to the cynicism of the story. And there is a strange amenity of temper and style which bathes the whole composition even when it is disgusting or tiresome. It has frequently been characteristic of the American writers in Paris that they have treated pretentious subjects with incompetent style and sordid feeling. Mr. Miller has done the opposite: he has treated an ignoble subject with a sure hand at color and rhythm. He is not self-conscious and not amateurish. And he has somehow managed to be low without being really sordid.

The last episode of *The Tropic of Cancer* has a deadly ironic value. A friend of the narrator called Fillmore, who is unique among these cadgers and spongers in enjoying a small regular income, becomes entangled in an affair with a French girl, who is pregnant and declares him responsible. Poor Fillmore first drinks himself into an insane asylum; then, emerging, falls straight into the clutches of the girl and her peasant family. They reduce him to utter abjection: he is to marry her, set her father up in business. The girl quarrels with him every night over dinner. The narrator suggests to Fillmore that he run away and go back home. For the latter, the glamor is all off Paris: he has been up against the French as they really are (in general these émigrés see nobody but one another); he realizes at last that the French regard Americans as romantic idiots; and he is weepily homesick for America. He allows himself to be sent off on a train, leaving the narrator a sum of money to provide for the girl's accouchement.

But as soon as Fillmore is gone, the helpful hero, left to himself, with the money for the girl in his pocket, decides that good old Paris, after all, is a wonderful place to be. "Certainly never before," he thinks, "had I had so much in my fist at one time. It was a treat to break a thousand-franc note. I held it up to the light to look at the beautiful watermark. Beautiful money! One of the few things the French make on a grand scale. Artistically done, too, as if they cherished a deep affection even for the symbol." Ginette need never know about it; and, after all, suppose her pregnancy was all a bluff. He goes for a drive in the Bois. Does he want to take the money, he asks himself, and return to America too? It is the first opportunity he has had. No: a great peace comes over him now. He knows that for half an hour he has money to throw away. He buys himself an excellent dinner and muses on the Seine in the setting sun. He feels it flowing quietly through him: "its past, its ancient soil, the changing climate." It is only when they are looked at close-to that human beings repel one by their ugliness; they become negligible when one can put them at a distance. A deep feeling of well-being fills him.

In retelling this incident from *The Tropic of Cancer*, have I made it more comic than it is meant to be? Perhaps: because Mr. Miller evidently attaches some importance to the vaporings of his hero on the banks of the Seine. But he presents him as he really lives, and not merely in his vaporings or his poses. He gives us the genuine American bum come to lead the beautiful life in Paris; and he lays him away forever in his dope of Pernod and dreams.

March 9, 1938

Mr. Miller, in reply to this review, wrote the *New Republic* the following letter, which appeared in the issue of May 18. I regret that I am unable to restore a passage cut by the editors.

Sir: There are several inaccuracies in Mr. Wilson's review of *Tropic of Cancer* . . .

First of all, I should like it to be known that the book has been reviewed before, by Professor Herbert West. It has been mentioned numerous times in a sensational manner by so-called reputable magazines in America. . . . The theme of the book, moreover, is not at all what Mr. Wilson describes: the theme is myself, and the narrator, or the hero, as your critic puts it, is also myself. I am not clear whether, in the last paragraph of his review, Mr. Wilson meant to imply that Fillmore is the genuine American bum, or myself. If he means the narrator, then it is me, because I have painstakingly indicated throughout the book that the hero is myself. I don't use "heroes," incidentally, nor do I write novels. I am the hero, and the book is myself. . . .

Perhaps the worst mistake which the eminent critic makes in his review is to say that because a book is bound in paper and published in Paris, it has no chance against a book bound in cloth and sold in New York. This is the very contrary of the truth. Without any hocus-pocus of the American publicity agents, almost entirely by word-of-mouth recommendations, *Tropic of Cancer* has already gone into several editions at a price which for Europe is prohibitive. It is now being translated into three languages. It may be procured at leading bookstores in practically every important city of the world excepting those of America, England, Germany and Russia. It has been reviewed enthusiastically by some of the foremost critics of Europe. If it has not yet brought me riches, it has at any rate brought me fame and recognition. And, whether it is given notice by American reviewers or not, Americans coming to Europe buy it, as they once bought *Ulysses* and *Lady Chatterley's Lover*.

A conspiracy of silence, like censorship, can defeat its own ends. Sometimes it pays *not* to advertise. Sometimes the most effective, realistic thing to do is to be impractical, to fly in the face of the wind. The Obelisk Press took my book on faith, against all commercial wisdom. The results have been gratifying in every way. I should like to add that the Obelisk Press will publish any book of quality which the ordinary commercial publisher refuses, for one reason or another, to handle. Any writer with guts who is unable to get a hearing in America might do well to look to Paris. And damn all the critics anyway! The best publicity for a man who has anything to say is silence.

Henry Miller

Paris, France

The Pleasures of Literature
By a Book Lover

WITH how sure an expectation of solace, amid the turmoil and perplexities of our time, do I turn, when the fires of evening are lit, to my silent companions of the library! Here the din of the city dies away; here the feverish antagonisms of men reveal themselves *sub specie aeternitatis*. Here may I be rapt as by a magic carpet to those miraculous isles of Greece—"lily on lily, that o'erlace the sea"; or to journey with the returning Ulysses among the enchantments and terrors of Homer's golden day; or I may bid imagination run riot with Shakespeare and his carnival fellows of the spacious days of great Elizabeth, assuming the motley of their bawdy humors, the purple of their splendid passions, the mourning of their fantastic revenges; or I may prowl with Dickens or Balzac among the mysteries of the dark modern cities or lurch with George Borrow along the hedgerows; or I may revel in the thousand and one tales, more enthralling than the *Arabian Nights*, of Voragine's *Golden Legend*, Vasari's *Lives of the Painters* or Havelock Ellis's *Psychology of Sex*.

What a sovereign remedy is a book for the distempers both of the mind and of the body! How it protects us against sordidness and boredom! Shall I ever forget the exquisite delights of my first perusal of Congreve's plays, as I rode back and forth on the elevated, the subway or the electric car, in my days as a "cub reporter" on one of our great metropolitan dailies—an exercise which, I like to believe, had the effect of tempering my style against the pressures of newspaper writing? Or the ecstasy of my discovery at college, and at almost the same moment, of Dante, the greatest poet, and Plato, the greatest proseman, of all time?—how, cycling alone in the Princeton lanes, leafy and fragrant with May, I would declaim the ringing tercets of the former!—how, to the fluttering of the pages of my lexicon, the paragraphs of the *Symposium* or the *Phaedo* would commence to grow incandescent with a radiance that seemed steadily to glow more brightly till the radiance of morning itself made luminous the Jersey murk!

With what relish—nay, what famished appetite!—did I con-
sume in my rare leisure moments the only book I read at
Plattsburg in the summer of 1916, Anatole France's *Thaïs*—the
enjoyment of which and the bottles of milk that we drank after
our parching perspiring marches, as well as of my conversations with the Eli-bred Charles R. Walker, then at the peak of
his early brilliance and his eye, as his comrades were wont to
say, "in a fine frenzy rolling," are my only agreeable memories
of an experience which could but convince me that, though I
might perhaps do something with literature, I should never
make an acceptable soldier. How Michelet's *History of France*
later peopled the hills and the fields of Lorraine with the
armies of Charles the Bold as I plodded among them in khaki
—making them seem so eroded and worn, so patinated and
yet so blighted, by that history of traditional quarrels which
was still going on at the time and in which I found myself involved that I felt, with how poignant a pull!, the advantages of
my own America, where we were not oppressed so much by
history. Did I not shoulder the thick volumes of Renan in my
burdensome blanket-roll and lug them to German Trier, considerably hampering my movements, but maintaining uninter-
rupted my access to an admirable spirit, international and
humanistic, at a time when such qualities were by no means in
evidence either among his countrymen or in the nation he had
more or less regarded as his intellectual fatherland?

O indispensable books! O comforting alternative worlds,
where all discords are finally resolved, if not by philosophy,
then by art—how without you should we reconcile ourselves
to this troublesome actual world? How right is Mary M.
Colum when she tells us that one of the most terrible wounds
that have been dealt to the human spirit by the hand of dictatorship is its constriction of the dream-life of humanity! For
how should the palaces of statesmanship flourish where the
cathedrals of thought are forbidden?

At least that is the way I am getting to feel as I read, in the
more serious-minded reviews, the current discussions of literature. They are driving me right back into the arms of Charles
Lamb and Walter Pater and John Addington Symonds: old

bookworms whom a diet of belles-lettres had rendered a little bit boozy, but who did promote the appreciation of literature.

In my youth, we used to read James Huneker, who, chaotic and careless though he was, made you ravenous to devour his favorite writers. Later on, we read T. S. Eliot, who, though as sober as Huneker was boisterous, still stimulated the appetite for poetry and made the poets seem full of exciting surprises. But Eliot's criticism was completely non-historical. He seemed to behold the writing of the ages abstracted from time and space and spread before him in one great exhibition, of which, with imperturbable poise, he conducted a comparative appraisal. This was of course an intellectual triumph, and his essays had their very great value; but it was a feat that could only be performed at the cost of detaching books from all the other affairs of human life; and the author of this complaint used at that time to try to encourage the practitioners of literature to interest themselves in the development of society and in the larger events of the world—as most great literature, after all, has done. Even the non-moral and non-doctrinal Shakespeare, whose detachment seems so bafflingly consummate, presents issues—as Orson Welles's *Julius Caesar* has recently emphasized—of which, if you had read only Eliot on Shakespeare, you could never have had any notion. The economic disasters of the thirties have had, therefore, a useful effect in compelling attention to the "social significance" of novels, poems and plays. But the trouble is that social significance has now become an obsession. Today one is confronted by the spectacle of a philosophico-social criticism of a character purely analytic, which almost invariably comes to negative conclusions, and a politico-social criticism which, without making even the attempt of the other to ascertain the position of the writer in the bigger historical frame, is content to give him a high or low grade corresponding to the degree of his readiness to subscribe to the mechanical slogans of this or that political faction.

The young, usually subject to exaggerated enthusiasms, are today not enthusiastic—not enthusiastic, that is, about books: they merely approve or disapprove when a book does or does not suit their politics. But, seriously, I think it a pity that they do not learn to read for pleasure. They may presently find that an acquaintance with the great works of art and thought is the only real insurance possible against the barbarism of the time.

So back, I say, to the Renaissance, with its hunger and thirst for books! Back to Matthew Arnold and the "best that has been thought and felt in the world"! Back to John Keats first looking into Chapman's Homer! Back to Karl Marx reading Aeschylus through every year!

Edmund Wilson (not Christopher Morley)

January 29, 1938

Cold Water on Bakunin

M R. E. H. CARR is an odd phenomenon—perhaps a symptom of the decay of Great Britain. A former member of
the English diplomatic service, with an unusual equipment of
languages, he now uses his knowledge of Europe to write the
biographies of nineteenth-century revolutionists. These biographies have certain indisputable merits, to which I shall revert
in a moment; but what is odd is that Mr. Carr should choose
to write them. He has obviously had no first-hand experience
of revolutionary movements or revolutionaries, and he seems to
feel very little sympathy with them. Yet, on the other hand, he
does not condemn them; he seems merely to regard them as
futile. But, even in depicting them as wrong-headed and ineffective, he does not seem, even by implication, to be criticizing their revolutionary theories from any contrasting point
of view—even one of universal irony. There is, to be sure, a
slight accent of irony discernible in his treatment of his subjects, but the tone is mainly one of amused condescension. We
wonder sometimes why Mr. Carr should have gone to the
trouble of exploring these inaccessible materials and getting up
these complicated subjects—he has written books on Marx,
Bakunin and Herzen, as well as one on Dostoevsky—merely in
order to lift the eyebrow over them; and we ask ourselves
whether Mr. Carr may not be simply a Foreign Office Englishman who has been led more or less accidentally, through
his knowledge of German and Russian, to do some work in an
historical field hitherto not much worked in English.

In his new book, *Michael Bakunin*, Mr. Carr has written the
best of his biographies. It has the faults of his other books—
the dependence on colorless clichés, which makes impossible
any vividness of evocation; the never intermitting British chill,
which is always putting Bakunin in his place and which gets on
one's nerves with its characterization of all Bakunin's projects
as "interesting," all his ideas as "remarkable": "On the day of
Bakunin's arrival in Lyons, municipal elections were held, and
the short-lived and rather ridiculous Committee of Public
Safety abdicated in favor of the new municipal council." . . .

"Bakunin decided on the creation of a new revolutionary organ which was called, with singular inappropriateness, the Committee for the Saving of France." . . . "One other decision of the Bâle Congress had a certain piquant interest." . . . "The stalwarts of Le Locle had recently begun to publish a fortnightly journal entitled *Progrès*, devoted to the propagation of the aims of the International." . . . "The defunct Committee of Public Safety had, in a moment of enthusiasm, followed the famous though short-lived precedent of 1848 and turned the local factories into national workshops. The Municipal Council inherited this blessing from the Committee." Bakunin did sometimes conceive designs which might be characterized as "singularly inappropriate"; and revolutionary organizations do certainly have their humors. But why should it be assumed that there is something intrinsically absurd about the movement for national workshops, the decisions of the International or the agitation in favor of that body carried on by the Jura watchmakers?

Here, as in his book on Marx, Mr. Carr tells us everything about his subject except what it is all about. If one had no independent knowledge of Marx and Bakunin, one might almost wonder, after reading these biographies, why Mr. Carr had thought the subjects important enough to write about. Even when he indicates their importance, he does nothing to make us understand it; for he has accomplished the singular feat of telling the stories of the leaders of working-class movements without dealing with those conditions of working-class life under pressure of which they came into existence. For Mr. Carr, the labor movements of the nineteenth century tend to present themselves merely in terms of a more or less inept parliamentary politics. Nor does he really understand the psychology of these men who have chosen the working-class side, who have rejected the whole complex of organized society yet who have to continue to live in it when they no longer want to be of it; who must work underground, who spend decades in exile, always in danger of prison and wasting their emotions and their energies in sterile political quarrels and the bickerings of émigré life.

Yet this writer, it must be said, through his very detachment from the struggle, is in a position to perform certain services

which biographers who are socialists or anarchists themselves
are not always able to get around to. For one thing, he is careful and impartial in checking up on matters of evidence. Old
party traditions and loyalties mean nothing to him. And for
another thing, he devotes to the personal aspects of the careers
of his revolutionists an attention that they do not usually get at
the hands of the narrowly political biographer, who is interested only in the movement and systematically disregards the
family life and the love affairs of his hero. Mr. Carr has brought
out facts about Bakunin which are important and unfamiliar.
He is at his best in the first part of this book, in which he is
dealing with Bakunin's life in Russia. Mr. Carr has a special
knowledge of Russia, and he is here occupied with a milieu not
alien to him: the country life of a landowner's family. The
story of the Bakunin household, with their susceptibility to
tender emotion and to mad intoxication by ideas, sounds
much like Tolstoy or Turgenev. Mr. Carr seems to have established incontrovertibly that the "behavior-pattern" of all
Bakunin's life was fixed by his family relationships. Michael
Bakunin was the oldest boy of a family of ten boys and girls: he
dominated his brothers through his age and his sisters by reason of his sex. He was, on his own confession, in love with one
of his sisters, and he seems to have been jealous of them all. He
was always inciting the children to rebellion against their father.
When his sisters began to have admirers and marry, Michael
would exert himself to spoil their relations with their suitors
and husbands. Later in life, he did the same thing with other
women; but he never became any woman's lover. He was apparently impotent all his life. In Siberia, when he was forty-
four, he married an eighteen-year-old girl, who eventually,
while still living with Bakunin, had two children by another
man.

One cannot tell whether Mr. Carr is aware of the obvious
connection between Bakunin's incurable impotence and his
orgiastic passion for destruction, though he does see that
Bakunin's hatred of the State was a prolongation of his quarrel
with his father, and seems to suggest that his playing at con-
spiracies which did not exist outside his imagination was carried
over from the plots of his childhood, as his pathological borrowing was a survival of infantile dependence. I am not sure,

however, that Mr. Carr really explains Bakunin's conversion to the cause of revolution. Bakunin, during his youth in Russia, had been a loyal subject of the Tsar; when he had left it for western Europe it had been simply to see the world; he seems to have been nearly thirty before he began moving toward the Left with the Young Hegelian movement in Germany; he did not declare himself an atheist till he was fifty; and he did not come to believe in the revolutionary role of the working class or to formulate the creed of anarchism until 1866, when he was fifty-two. It may be that Bakunin was driven by the logic of politics and ideas to take each of the later steps of this progress: the last of them followed on his disillusion, as the result of the defeat of the Poles, with insurgent nationalism as a democratic revolutionary force. But what were really the determining factors in his taking that first step which counts? At what moment, so relatively late in life, was the attitude formed in the household at home transferred to contemporary society?

With the comic aspects of Michael Bakunin's career Mr. Carr is appreciative and skillful. How Bakunin unwittingly enrolled as an ally the Tsar's principal agent in Switzerland and sent him to Russia to report for him on revolutionary activities and to intercede with Bakunin's family in his efforts to induce them to surrender to him his share of the family estate, and how he finally compelled this agent, who was masquerading as a retired Russian general, to help him out with a considerable sum of money, which the man actually obtained from the Tsar as expenditure in the line of duty; how Bakunin persuaded one of his Italian followers, who had just inherited a fortune from his father, to allow him to blow it in, with no calculation of means or costs, on a magnificent house and estate designed to be a home for Bakunin and an asylum for revolutionists, how Bakunin wrote his wife to join him, as he was now in a position to keep her in comfort, how the money was all swallowed up before the place was finished, how the young Italian was horrorstruck and indignantly repudiated Bakunin, how, when poor Antonia arrived, Bakunin could not bear to tell her that the place was not really his and that the owner did not want them to live in it, and how he finally ran away rather than face this—these are enchanting and fabulous stories, which Mr. Carr has handled well.

Yet even here one a little resents the tone. After all, there must have been something in Bakunin—something great-visioned and noble—which enabled him to command such sympathy, to excite people with such extravagant dreams. As Mr. Carr does not show us the need which goaded the proletariat to go to Bakunin for leadership, so, though he calls Bakunin a "genius" and "great," he never gives us a sense of the power which he was able to devote to their service. The anarchist movement, after all, has long survived its prophet; and if it owes its founder Bakunin something of its lack of common sense, it owes him, also, something of its energy, its audacity and its humanity. Even such imprudent bravery as that of Bakunin in the Dresden revolution, hopeless, inconsistent politically and paid for by long and terrible years of prison, has had a value for the human spirit in its struggle against the timid self-interest perpetuated in human institutions. This exploit of Bakunin's was the kind of mistake that Marx would never have made; but it was prompted by a kind of exuberance, an irrepressible magnanimity, that gave Bakunin, in this one respect, a real superiority over Marx.

December 7, 1938

Shut Up That Russian Novel

THE Soviet Union is an immense expanse of territory, including the extremes of geographical contrast and inhabited by some hundred and seventy-five million people of varying races, social antecedents and degrees of education. These people, like people elsewhere, are compelled to make considerable exertions in order to survive in their environment; and when they are not eating, drinking or starving, quarrelling or copulating, idling or amusing themselves, they devote a certain amount of attention to organizing representative bodies for the purpose of safeguarding their social groups and to elaborating disciplines and devices to make possible their higher development.

These statements seem obvious enough; but if all that you knew about Russia were derived from our political press, you would hardly have gained any inkling of them. The name of the Soviet Union, for all the millions of souls it comprises, has ceased to signify a real section of the earth. It has become a battle-cry, a term of abuse, a counter in a political game. All this is because in this area an attempt has been lately going forward to vary the forms of social organization in such a way as to make it possible for the whole population to share in the facilities for higher human development instead of allowing these facilities to be controlled by certain specialized members of the community who enjoy them at the expense of the rest.

During the period just after the Russian Revolution, the USSR was a bugbear: all the hundred and forty million Russians were supposed to be what were called Communists—that is, greedy and murderous barbarians who wanted to take people's Ford cars away from them. Then gradually the Soviet Union came to mean for the American Left intellectuals the realization of the ideal modern community: American democracy and technical efficiency plus socialist elimination of unearned profits. For a great many Jews, it has figured the fulfillment of their millennial hopes; for the Stalinists, it has come to be the war-cry of a kind of international patriotism with which they have deafened themselves; for the Trotskyists, a lost fatherland, which would be wonderful if Trotsky were only there; for the Communists in general, a slogan in the struggle against the capitalist world; for the Marxists in general, the keystone of a thesis—that is, of an intellectual construction which enables one to feel safe and smug without studying contemporary realities or involving oneself in them in any way. More recently it has come more and more, on the part of dissatisfied middle-class persons, to be a pretext for making oneself disagreeable, for feeling comfortably superior to one's neighbors or for enjoying a vicarious sadism. For the liberals, it has always been a piece in a game as simple as checkers—a game which takes place in the liberals' minds. The checkers in this game are either white or black—that is, either desirable or undesirable. In the case of the Soviet Union, it has at times been a little bit difficult to make sure whether the checker representing it should be assigned to the liberals' side or to that of the liberals' opponents. At first, it was supposed to be definitely black; but later it was thought to be definitely white. Just now it is causing trouble by becoming more and more unmanageable for the appropriate moves of a white checker: some continue to try to play the game on the assumption that the piece is still white; others have decided to call it black. And in the meantime the one hundred and seventy-five million people, who know as well as you or I that they are people and not a bogey, a utopia, a millennium, a slogan, a thesis, a neurosis or a checker either black or white, are experiencing the same sensations that make other human beings contented or wretched and taking part in a social drama of immense importance and interest.

For what has been happening in Russia *is* important and interesting; but it is a pity that so very few people really exert themselves to look into it. There are, it is true, certain difficulties in the way; but it is possible to find out a good deal more than you might gather from reading the political journals. The truth is that most of the people who like to talk about Russia would much rather cherish their myths than give attention to such reports as are available and try to draw from them objective conclusions.

We have lately had a number of adverse reports—by Fred

Beal, Eugene Lyons and Victor Serge—which have been valuable because they contained a certain amount of new information, but which, taken without reference to anything else, have simply produced a fresh myth: the myth of the False Revolution. The writer of the present article has even been taken to task by Mr. Lyons in the *Saturday Review of Literature* for describing a statue of Lenin in the lobby of an opera-house in Leningrad as having "a look both piercing and genial, at once as if he were giving back to labor what it had made and inviting it to share for the first time in its heritage of human culture, and as if he were opening out to humanity as a whole a future of which for the first time they were to recognize themselves the masters, with the power to create without fear whatever they had minds to imagine." These ideas, asserts Mr. Lyons, are certainly not "Mr. Lenin's" but "Mr. Wilson's." Yet these ideas *were* certainly Lenin's: he was expounding them all his life. And the statue for its purpose was a good one, in which the sculptor had succeeded in expressing some such feeling as I put into words.

What, then, is now causing Mr. Lyons to talk as if this Lenin had never existed, as if the Bolshevik Revolution had never seemed to offer anything that the world might have been glad to have? If the Bolsheviks had not announced, from the moment of their coming to power, the aims that I have imputed to Lenin, Mr. Lyons would never have gone, as he did, to live in the Soviet Union, would never, as he so earnestly did, have propagandized in its behalf. His reaction now from one-hundred-percent loyalty takes the form of one-hundred-percent disapproval. His attitude seems to be that he has simply made a dreadful mistake. In other words, he is as biassed as before. His recent book, *Assignment in Utopia*, interesting though it is, is a monody of complaint. There is very little attempt—and this is true of Mr. W. H. Chamberlin, too—really to understand the Russians, to explain in terms of Russian character and wider historical analogy the development of the Bolshevik Revolution. Mr. Lyons is disappointed and angry and won't play with the Russians any more. He does not care to make any effort to form a realistic opinion. It will take centuries, he tells us (I quote him from memory), for humanity to digest such an event. Well, that may be true for the longview historian; but for the rest of us at the present time, the Soviet Union is part of our lives, one of the phenomena of the world in which we find ourselves; and we must not only be as well-informed as possible about it, we must try to judge it as coolly as possible.

One enlightening piece of evidence on recent conditions in Russia is a book called *Un Mineur Français Chez les Russes* by a French trade unionist named Kléber Legay, who visited the Soviet Union in the autumn of 1936. M. Legay is a militant labor leader, who is not, however, a Communist and who had been critical of the so-called Stakhanovist methods adopted for increasing production in Russia. He was induced by his Communist colleagues to go and see for himself, and he was promised full freedom to travel where he pleased and to talk personally with the Russian miners. But the moment Legay arrived, he was taken in hand by a guide, and he was kept for eight days in Moscow and compelled, very much against his wish, to march in a parade reviewed by Stalin. The French delegates, however, asserted their independence by refusing either to sing or to keep in step. He was allowed to visit some factories, where he discovered that the accounts of rates of pay which had been given him by the guides and officials were invariably contradicted by the testimony of the workers; and that, as soon as the authorities became aware of the persistency with which he was checking, they put an end to his investigations.

At last he was taken, as had been agreed, on a tour of the Don Basin; but when he had got there, he was not allowed to leave the train on which he lived and slept, except under the usual escort. The same discrepancy between fact and publicity appeared. Contrary to what he had been told by his guide, he found women at the bottom of the mines engaged in the heaviest kind of work. This underground work by women has been forbidden, he tells us, in all other, including the fascist, countries. At the mouth of the mine, young men with guns were standing guard over these women and over men of sixty; in the depths were more men with guns, who were squatting in the darkness of a corner and seemed to be trying to conceal themselves from the visitors. A mine worker's home which he insisted upon exploring revealed an appallingly low standard of living. The family told him that they earned more money but lived considerably worse than before the Revolution; and one of the officials put a stop to this by glaring fiercely and speaking sharply to the husband. Later, Legay's guides explained that the man had been drunk, though he had not observed any signs of it. As for the Stakhanovists, they had been raised out of the rank and file and had been given, like Ford service men, the pro-management point of view of employees on the fringes of the governing groups. They were the equivalent of our "loyal workers." M. Legay was at pains to ascertain how wages and programs of work were determined. He discovered, he says, that the mine administration makes out a budget for each mine and that if the workers find in practice that the fraction allotted them does not amount to a living wage, their only redress is to prove to the management that money can be saved from other expenses—in which case they may take the difference. If they cannot establish this to the mine administration's satisfaction, they must simply go to work at the wages prescribed. They have, of course, no right to strike; and the young men with guns are there to prevent them from attempting to do so. In the matter of planning production, the Party officials and the union officials are apparently all-powerful and final; they are themselves controlled by the Party. The engineers have little to say; but they are made entirely responsible for the carrying out of the program. If the program proves impossible of execution, they are charged with sabotage and shot.

Before he had been allowed to visit the mines, M. Legay had been subjected to a good deal of determined pressure in an effort to extract from him a general endorsement of the achievements of the Soviet Union. But he refused to give out statements or make speeches, and even insisted, at banquets, on drinking his toasts in water.

Yet even here, where we do have unquestionably an expert foreign opinion on workers' conditions in Russia, M. Legay—like Mr. Chamberlin and Mr. Lyons—tends to judge what he saw in the Soviet Union on the basis of the standards of the more advanced countries plus an ideal of socialist society. In France, he declares, whole departments which had been devastated during the war were reconstructed under the capitalist system in less than ten years' time, whereas in Russia the roads were still bad, the houses crude and the people dirty, after twenty years of what was supposed to be socialism. The point is that complaints of this kind are out of order in connection with Russia. This tone is natural enough in view of the Soviet pretensions, but one ought to get past one's impatience. One ought to take into account what Russia was like before the Revolution. The roads were always bad; the people were always dirty. They had no standards to restore like the French. And so with the new social structure of Russia, which turns out, for people like Kléber Legay, to present so different an aspect from that which he had been led to expect. It is quite obvious that the Soviet Union has developed a new class-stratification; but this phenomenon should be studied, not denounced. Why was such a development inevitable? What conclusions should we draw from it about Marxist theory?

Marx and Lenin predicted correctly that the old class-stratifications would carry over into socialist society in the shape of inequality of privilege and the varying rates of pay which it would not be easy to eliminate in view of the varying abilities and habits of people who had been bred under the old system. In other words, the socialist rulers would find that they could not persuade, say, a physician or the director of a theater to contribute to the creation of the communist humanity if they fed him and lodged him like a peasant. Karl Marx had given most of his thought to the future of the Western countries, in which bourgeois democracy and industry had already run their full course. In his last years, he was making special efforts to study the case of Russia, at the instigation of Russian revolutionists who had asked him whether a mainly feudal country like theirs might not skip some of the stages of Marxist development, and go straight from Russian village communism to socialist collectivism. Later on, Lenin did try to skip them, but was soon forced, with bitter laments over the shortcomings of his countrymen, to allow capitalist commerce some further scope through the measures of the New Economic Period. Yet he never seems to have foreseen the danger that, in a society just struggling out of feudalism and only beginning to master machinery and to claim the career open to the talents, a natural tendency to reproduce the history of the bourgeois countries might prove stronger than socialist principles. In the Soviet Union today, twenty years after the Bolshevik Revolution, they seem to have ended by evolving, much as we have done in the United States, a system of government by political bosses and an industrial and financial exploitation of those who have only muscle by those who have clever wits, and to have subsided to the low general level of intelligence in regard to public affairs which is inevitable for a community in which most of the people have only recently learned to read and write and have never had a chance to own anything.

One ought not to be indignant about this. One should look, not for villains, but for natural causes. Evasion of responsibility is one of the Russian vices: the Russians so dread making decisions that they usually pass them on, if possible, to the authorities higher up; they thus create their own despots. And closely involved with this habit is the national tendency to lie, which verges upon and merges into the oriental. The difficulty that they seem always to have had in meeting a situation squarely, in responding with a straight answer to a straight question, even in trusting their own constancy of purpose, has greatly complicated both their industry and their politics. The shifting moods and susceptible imaginations which have enabled them to produce their great novelists and poets, their great composers and actors, have not fitted them for statesmanship or organization. This gives rise to brutality in the governing groups; but those groups—though our critics of the Soviet Union no longer mention the fact—have always had their heroic element: the public spirit of those more conscientious, more constructive or more energetic persons who have tried to make themselves responsible for seeing to it that things do sometimes get done. How such persons are faring at the present time in relation to the racketeers of the Revolution, it is impossible for a foreigner to know; but one must not forget that such people have played a great role in Russia and that even the purges of Stalin can hardly have made them extinct.

One must also remember that the Soviet Union has suffered terribly for her socialist principles; and that her political ills have been aggravated by the ostracism or suspicion on the part of the rest of the world that the announcement of those principles has incurred. Here the Russian imagination has been playing a role of a kind which might perhaps have been impossible for a more prosaic or practical people: if the Soviets have been bogging down, at this very bad moment for all the world, through Russian executive incompetence and mechanical ineptitude, if they have been betrayed by Russian bureaucratism and their habit of passing the buck, they have at least been the first to introduce into the domain of actual statesmanship, to impress ineffaceably on the mind of the world, the ideal of the classless society. But it has, of course, been partly the fault of this very imagination that we have made the Soviet Union a myth. We have fallen under the spell of the often brilliant Soviet publicity just as we used to do under that of the Russian novel. Yet what we need at the present time is to try to see the Soviets realistically. We should not, for example, be drawn into supporting a war against Japan in order to defend a myth called "the Workers' Fatherland" any more than we should spend our energy fighting a mythical monster called "Stalin." The Russians, after taking as many losses in the interests of ideal revolutionary ends as any people can be expected to do, have, it seems, settled down for the present to a new kind of stratified society dominated by a new kind of governing class. The situation deserves sympathetic but soberly sociological attention. So long as we persist in imagining those one hundred and seventy-five million people as either a nightmare or a New Jerusalem, we shall never be able to deal with them. Let us shut up that Russian novel.

April 6, 1938

Marxism at the End of the Thirties

MARXISM is in relative eclipse. An era in its history has ended. It may be worth while at this moment to look back and try to see what has happened.

Let us begin by asking ourselves what we mean, whether we really mean anything definite and fixed, when we casually use the word "Marxism."

The Marxism of Karl Marx himself was, in its original form, a mixture of old-fashioned Judaism, eighteenth-century Rousseauism and early nineteenth-century utopianism. Marx assumed that capitalist society had corrupted the human race by compelling it to abandon spiritual values for the satisfactions of owning things: he believed that the day would arrive when the spirit would come back into its own, when humanity would destroy its false idols and the sheep be set off from the goats: this could only be accomplished by communism—i.e. the common ownership of the means of production which would make possible a society without classes.

Friedrich Engels, the son of a Rhineland manufacturer, who had worked in the Manchester branch of the family textile business and been horrified by the misery of the working class, turned Marx's attention to political economy and supplied him with data on the industrial system. They had both come to the conclusion that the economic factor was of fundamental importance in the development of human society; and, taking over from the philosophy of Hegel his principle of revolutionary change, they evolved a picture of history in which the machinery of progress was represented as a process of continual class conflict. Every important change in the methods providing the necessaries of life gave rise to new social-economic classes, which had to struggle with the obsolete classes in order to get control of the machine. The bourgeoisie had contended with and disposed of the feudal system, which was obstructing the freedom of the merchant to trade and the freedom of the worker to hire himself that were necessary for the successful functioning of the early competitive phases of capitalism; and the industrial proletariat would, in turn, do the same thing to the capitalist system, when this, in its later phases, should prove obstructive to the logical development of large-scale industry and financial monopoly into the single centralized system which could only be run by the state.

Marx and Engels, therefore, did what they could to promote the success of labor organizations which aimed at the enfranchisement of the working class or at procuring better pay or conditions: the English Chartist movement and the Communist League of the forties, the Workers' International of the sixties and seventies; and they tried to convince the members of these movements that they, the representatives of the working class, were enacting leading roles in the Marxist drama of history.

This drama, as imagined by Marx on the eve of the revolution of 1848, was to move swiftly to a catastrophic climax which would be followed by something in the nature of a millennium. Engels was envisaging the future in terms of the French Revolution plus the Apocalypse. But when, later, parliamentary machinery was set up in that feudal Germany which had made the background for the thought of both men, the German socialists who had been trained on Marx but who were now able to get themselves elected to the Reichstag began to decide that there was nothing inevitable about the social-economic impasse and the class-war Armageddon which Marx had been predicting. Since the pressure of the working class had been effective in securing certain reforms, there was perhaps, after all, no reason to believe that the socialist aims might not be accomplished by orderly and gradual legislation. And Marx himself in his later years began to concede that in democratic countries such as England, the United States and Holland, the socialist revolution might be effected through peaceful parliamentary methods—though he thought this would be likely to stimulate a revolt of the outvoted reactionaries.

Karl Marx sometimes praised the achievements of the democratic countries, as when he backed the cause of the North during the American Civil War; but more often—it represents the bent of his own somber and savage personality—he talks in terms of Armageddon, and Armageddon is what he leads us to expect. He even applauded the Commune, when the workers and soldiers of Paris rose against the bourgeois government and held the city two months—though the procedure of the Commune was a good deal more drastic than that which he had contemplated. He had never believed in the possibility of simply abolishing bourgeois institutions and setting up socialist ones in their place, which was what the Communards had attempted, but had expected that the proletarian dictatorship would begin by taking over the machinery of the existing bourgeois state.

It ought, also, to be noted here that one can find in the whole immense work of Marx and Engels a considerable variety of attitudes toward the main problems with which they were concerned. In the first place, there are two personalities involved, and their emphasis is somewhat different. Engels left to himself, as he was after Marx's death, was more tolerant and flexible politically, and insisted somewhat less on the materialistic side of what they called their Dialectical Materialism; and Karl Marx had within his own nature tendencies so strongly divergent that his formidable machinery of logic never succeeded in making them consistent: he was at the same time a moralist and prophet, who wanted to blast a generation of vipers, and a scientific student of history, who aimed at an objective analysis of economic processes. Add to this that the points of view of Marx and Engels, both, varied in relation to the apparent imminence or the apparent improbability of a revolutionary working-class movement in which they could take an active part; and that the young fighters of '48, who saw the industrial worker on one side of the barricades and the capitalist exploiter on the other, never quite came to terms with the elderly observers of the years of their exile in England, who were forced now to take account of the unexpected situations to which the capitalist system gave rise in its later and more complicated phases.

The writings of Marx and Engels thus lend themselves to being exploited, very much as the Scriptures have been, to furnish texts for a variety of doctrines; and there have even been different Marxist canons prepared by the different creeds. The German Social Democrats did not hesitate to tamper with the texts themselves; and the Russians of the Marx-Engels Institute, in publishing these texts as they were written, were at pains to provide a commentary which supplied the "correct" interpretation.

II

Marxism first reached Russia as early as 1868, when a translation of *Das Kapital* was published there, and it began to take hold in the eighties, after the Terrorist movement had culminated in the assassination of Alexander II. But as the Germans had made Marxism respectable, academic and parliamentarian, so in Russia, of necessity an outlawed movement, it became, in its most effective form, narrow, concentrated, grim and cruel. In Russia, the first problem of the radical was to get rid of a feudal autocracy which would not even hear of a constitution and which excluded the bourgeois liberals from its institutions of learning.

Vladimir Ulyanov, who called himself Lenin, belonged to a section of the professional classes which hid been hard hit in the eighties. His father, the director of schools for the province of Simbirsk on the Volga, had made his own career, an energetic and honorable one, which had earned him a patent of nobility, during the period of the educational reforms inspired by Alexander II, and had been prematurely retired from his post and forced to see his work undone when the reaction of Alexander III came to punish the murder of his predecessor. Lenin's elder brother, a student at the University of St. Petersburg, became involved in a plot to carry on the work of the Terrorists by assassinating Alexander III, but was caught by the police and hanged. The older Ulyanov had just died of a stroke, perhaps partly as a result of chagrin, and Vladimir was now head of the family. He profoundly admired his mother, who found herself everywhere ostracized as a result of her son's execution; and the succession of family misfortunes caused the iron to enter his soul. During his first eager years of young manhood, he was to find his own progress brutally blocked. As the result of a student demonstration in which he had played no important part, he was dismissed from the University of Kazan on suspicion as the brother of the Terrorist; and he was

forbidden to study a profession either at home or abroad. In
this period of frustration, he read Marx.

The harshness of the Tsarist autocracy inevitably called forth
harshness on the part of the groups who were fighting it; and
Russian Marxism took on some of the characteristics of the
Terrorist movement of the seventies. The band of trained and
dedicated revolutionists projected by Lenin in *What Is To Be
Done?*, his pamphlet of 1902, and afterwards realized by him in
the Bolshevik and Communist parties is a conception not to be
found in Marx, who had never got much further as an organizer than drafting programs and presiding at meetings for the
Communist League and the Workers' International. Lenin,
confronted with the ignorance of the illiterate Russian masses,
had frankly to propose that they should be directed by a nu-
cleus of revolutionary intellectuals; and, confronted with the
ineffectual loquacity of the common run of Russian intelligentsia, he had to insist that these upper-class leaders of the
proletarian movement should not be merely talkers or even
thinkers, but persons who would work actively for the Party
and who would be ready to take real responsibility. The springs
of Lenin's own activity were profound, irresistible, instinctive.
His prime motivations were probably the overpowering hatred
of suffering of which Gorky so emphatically speaks, combined
with a passion for combat that took a curiously impersonal
form and made him regard himself as a naked historical force
pitted against other such forces. He had disciplined himself in
such a way that the emotion always fed the conviction, and the
conviction always led to action. This process was brought to a
climax when the Tsarist regime involved Russia in the long
devastation and slaughter of what Lenin insisted on character-
izing as the Imperialist War.

The fact that the Provisional Government of Kerensky desired to continue the war and that it did not seem at all disposed to distribute land or food to the starving Russian masses
would thus in itself have been almost enough to make Lenin
resolve to overthrow it, even without the mesmeric driving
force provided by the Marxist conception of history. People
like the Menshevik Martov quite correctly pointed out that
Lenin was throwing overboard the procedure expressly prescribed by Marx and formerly accepted by Lenin himself, in

not waiting till a bourgeois "democratic" state had made the transition from the Tsarist autocracy to the socialist state of the workers. When Marx had been questioned by young Russians as to whether it would be possible for Russia, with its ancient peasant communes, to pass straight to a socialist economy without traversing all the stages of large-scale capitalist exploitation, he had, despite his earlier approval of the Commune, expressed himself as very doubtful.

But Lenin, for all his endless polemics, was little worried by Marxist theory: he was preoccupied not with ideas, but with actual current events, watching intently for the break, any break, that might make possible the destruction of the Tsardom. When the moment did come during the war, he saw the flimsiness and the impracticability of the bourgeois Provisional Government, and he supplanted it with a new kind of government based on the councils (*soviets*) of workers, peasants and soldiers which, as soon as the grip of the Tsar was relaxed, had been gravitating in 1917, as they had done in 1905, to unofficial positions of authority. But though Lenin disregarded the letter of Marx, he was true to the Armageddon spirit; and it had always been his habit to act first and look up later, when he had the leisure—what, as I have said, is not usually difficult—supporting texts in Marx and Engels.

Lenin's ultimate aims were of course humanitarian, democratic and anti-bureaucratic; but the logic of the whole situation was too strong for Lenin's aims. His trained band of revolutionists, the Party, turned into a tyrannical machine which perpetuated, as heads of a government, the intolerance, the deviousness, the secrecy, the ruthlessness with political dissidents, which they had had to learn as hunted outlaws. Instead of getting a classless society out of the old illiterate feudal Russia, they encouraged the rise and the domination of a new controlling and privileged class, who were soon exploiting the workers almost as callously as the Tsarist industrialists had done, and subjecting them to an espionage that was probably worse than anything under the Tsar. What Lenin had actually effected was a kind of bourgeois revolution; the situation had, in a sense, worked out according to Marx; but it was not at all what Lenin had intended. Lenin himself died, after only six years of power, in great perplexity and anguish of mind, outmaneuvered by one of his lieutenants who knew how to distribute patronage and had no scruples about deceiving the public.

At first, under the dictatorship of Stalin, a serious attempt was made to bring the economy of Soviet Russia up to the level of the capitalist nations, so that socialism might become a reality; but when, due to the mechanical ineptitude and the administrative inefficiency of the Russians, this seemed to be definitely failing, Stalin quickly buried the Leninist ideals, executed or otherwise suppressed all the people who were still disposed to defend them, and consolidated the position of those groups of officials who were doing their best to give Russia the strong bourgeoisie she had lacked and who have ended, it may be, by dominating the dictator Stalin himself.

In the meantime, the short circuit in the capitalist system which Karl Marx had so confidently predicted had actually taken place in Germany, but with results very different from those he had expected. Instead of the processes of capitalism giving rise automatically to a crisis in which a dispossessed proletariat was left facing a small group of capitalists, with nothing to do but to expropriate the expropriators, a new kind of middle class, as in Russia, came out of the petty bourgeoisie and did not find the slightest difficulty in enlisting ambitious members of the working class. This group succeeded in setting up a new kind of state socialism, in which the government planned and directed in the interests of the new governing class, without actually taking over the industrial plant, but eliminating the big capitalists, if necessary, and seeing to it that the working class were well enough off so that they did not become seriously recalcitrant.

III

Karl Marx had arrived at his vision of the working class expelling the capitalists by way of two false analogies. One of these was a probably unconscious tendency to argue from the position of the Jew to the position of the proletarian. The German Jews in Karl Marx's time were just escaping from the restrictions of the ghetto, which meant also the system of the Judaic world; and in this case the former victims of a social and economic discrimination, with their ancient religious discipline and their intellectual training, were quite easily able to take over the techniques and the responsibilities of the outside modern world. The proletariat, however, unlike the Jews, had no tradition of authority; they were, by their very position, kept ignorant and physically bred down. The country—industrial England—in which Marx prophesied that the widening gulf between the owning and the working classes would first bring about a communist revolution, had turned out to be the country where the progressive degradation of the underprivileged classes had simply had the effect of stunting them and slowly extinguishing their spirit. The other false analogy of Marx was his argument from the behavior of the bourgeoisie in the seventeenth and eighteenth centuries to the behavior to be expected of the working class, in their turn, in relation to the bourgeoisie. The European middle classes who finally dispossessed the feudal landlords were, after all, educated people, accustomed to administering property and experienced in public affairs. The proletariat, the true ground-down industrial workers on whom Marx was basing his hopes, were almost entirely devoid of any such experience or education; and what we now know invariably happens when the poor and illiterate people of a modern industrial society first master advanced techniques and improve their standard of living, is that they tend to exhibit ambitions and tastes which Karl Marx would have regarded as bourgeois. We have seen it in the United States, where we have produced what is really the earliest example of that new kind of bourgeoisie that they have been getting in Germany and Russia. But ours is a more highly developed, that is, a more democratic, version; and when I say that it is more democratic, I am using the words not in any loose sense, but in the definite sense that, with us, individual responsibility, the ability to make decisions, is a good deal more evenly distributed than it is in these other countries.

Is there nothing left of Marxism, then? Are there no basic Marxist ideas that may still be accepted as true?

I have above, at the risk of banality, discussed it in terms of its historical origins, because it seems to me that the shifting generalities to which the liberal mind is addicted still need to be constantly corrected by the facts of socialist history. But there is, of course, common to the Marxism of Marx and of Engels, of Lenin and of Trotsky, a technique which we can still use with profit; the technique of analyzing political phenomena in social-economic terms. There was this much in the claims of Marx and Engels that they had been able to make socialism "scientific": they were the first to attempt in an intensive way to study economic motives objectively. This does not, of course, mean, however, that we should try to find the key to the events of our time in the conclusions which these men of another time drew from the events of theirs. The Marxist method can get valid results only if applied afresh by men realistic enough to see, and bold enough to think, for themselves.

As for the aims and ideals of Marxism, there is one feature of them that is now rightly suspect. The taking-over by the state of the means of production and the dictatorship in the interests of the proletariat can by themselves never guarantee the happiness of anybody but the dictators themselves. Marx and Engels, coming out of authoritarian Germany, tended to imagine socialism in authoritarian terms; and Lenin and Trotsky after them, forced as they were to make a beginning among a people who had known nothing but autocracy, also emphasized this side of socialism and founded a dictatorship which perpetuated itself as an autocracy.

When all this is said, however, something more important remains that is common to all the great Marxists: the desire to get rid of class privilege based on birth and on difference of income; the will to establish a society in which the superior development of some is not paid for by the exploitation, that is, by the deliberate degradation of others—a society which will be homogeneous and coöperative as our commercial society is not, and directed, to the best of their ability, by the conscious creative minds of its members. But this again is a goal to be worked for in the light of one's own imagination and with the help of one's own common sense. The formulas of the various Marxist creeds, including the one that is common to them all, the dogma of the Dialectic, no more deserve the status of holy writ than the formulas of other creeds. To accomplish such a task will require of us an unsleeping adaptive exercise of reason and instinct combined.

February 22—March 1—March 8, 1941

Epilogue, 1952: Edna St. Vincent Millay

ONE is grateful to Mr. Vincent Sheean for having written the memoir of Edna Millay that he calls *The Indigo Bunting*, because, since this extraordinary woman's death, no adequate tribute has been paid to either her work or her personality, and Mr. Sheean, though he saw her only a few times in the later years of her life, has been able to bring to the subject his almost novelistic gift for dramatizing contemporary personalities. What sets Mr. Sheean off from the ordinary writer of memoirs, who depends on mere big names or on gossip, is his ardent sense of human greatness. Nothing, for example, could be more different from the way in which celebrities are usually described than the way of Mr. Sheean in such a book as *Between the Thunder and the Sun*. In his account of a house-party on the Riviera, he can give you the colors and contours of Maxine Elliott and Winston Churchill—like a portrait painter in the best old tradition—in such a way as to make them impressive without relinquishing a strong sense of character and personal idiosyncrasy. It is the special Irish faculty, no doubt—which one finds in Yeats's autobiography—for seeing people in their most human, and sometimes in their comic aspects, and yet making them walk the earth like the creatures of heroic legend. In Edna Millay, who had herself so much Irish, Mr. Sheean has an ideal subject, since one needed no romantic temperament, no predisposition to hero-worship, to recognize in her an exceptional being. It is one of the themes of his portrait that she exercised over wild birds what seemed to him a special attraction. This, he says, she pooh-poohed herself—she was not a sentimental or mystical person—explaining that they came to her window or circled about her head simply because she fed them; but what he tells us does show unmistakably that she exercised an enchantment for Vincent Sheean and induced him, for the first time in his life, to become acutely aware of birds, of which he seems hitherto to have been subnormally ignorant. One never forgot the things *she* noticed, for she charged them with her own intense feeling. This power of enhancing and ennobling life was felt by all who knew her.

It was probably a mistake, however, for Mr. Sheean to try to make a small book out of his necessarily slender memoirs. There is a whole chapter on birds in general, which seems little to the purpose and reads like padding—though I believe it is true, as he says and as the following pages will confirm, that Edna Millay had some special affinity with birds; and he runs later to speculations along the lines of his recent interest in Hindu religion, in which she does not seem to have been eager to follow him—not surprising, in view of her exclusive preoccupation with the actual human world. (God never, I think, appears in her works, after such early poems as *God's World* and *Renascence*, except as a mythological property, and her vision of man and the universe is expressed in her *Epitaph for the Race of Man*.) But *The Indigo Bunting* has a certain importance, for Mr. Sheean has recognized and been able to convey something of Edna Millay's qualities, and he has given the lead for others who knew her better and longer and to whom her work has meant more (Mr. Sheean says he read her poetry only after he met her in the forties) to supplement what he has written of his visits to the Boissevains at Austerlitz, New York, and on the island in Maine where they spent their summers. I propose to take advantage of this cue, with apologies to Mr. Sheean for using *The Indigo Bunting* as a pretext for a kind of counter-memoir. I hope that others who knew Edna Millay will also write about her. There ought to be a memorial volume. The wonder is, one realizes with shame, that none of those who were especially indebted to her—with the exception of Mr. Rolfe Humphries, who registered a brief protest in the *Nation* against the stupidity or indifference with which the news of her death was received—has done anything to commemorate this great writer. It is the proof of Mr. Sheean's instinct for spotting and his talent for celebrating what is really important in his own time that he first should have broken the silence.

I

I first met Edna Millay sometime early in 1929, but I had already known about her a long time. A cousin of mine, also a poet, Carolyn Crosby Wilson (now Carolyn Wilson Link), had been in Edna's class at Vassar, 1917, and when I had visited her at college in the spring of 1916, she had given me the April number of the *Vassar Miscellany Monthly*, of which she was one of the editors. I had read it coming back on the train and had been rather impressed by the leading feature, a dramatic dialogue in blank verse called *The Suicide*, by Edna St. Vincent Millay. Sometime later in 1916, my cousin sent me a copy of *A Book of Vassar Verse*, an anthology of poems from the *Miscellany* in which I found *The Suicide* and another similar poem by Miss Millay called *Interim*. I was then a fifteen-dollar reporter on the New York *Evening Sun* and was sometimes allowed to do book reviews. I tried to give the Vassar girls a little publicity —it must have been sometime in December—by the following two-paragraph notice, which, in view of later developments, has a certain ironic interest:

"The imaginative development exhibited in *A Book of Vassar Verse*, published by the *Vassar Miscellany Monthly*, bears out the editors' prefatory boast that the book has 'a certain significance of symbolism,' which makes apparent 'the widening range of the college girl's emotional and intellectual interest and the quickening of her contact with reality.' The poems which represent the last six years of the last century and the first six of this one seem a little pale and diffident, even when they are ecstatic, but the contemporary verse sounds a new note of frankness, intensity and dramatic feeling. Such things as *The Suicide*, *The Dragon Lamp* and Miss Ruth Pickering's fresh songs are original poems not unworthy of the American generation which has produced Miss Reese and Miss Teasdale.

"But it is, perhaps, still on the side of paleness and shyness that these lyrics err. It is of moonlight and the sound of the wind that they are fondest of singing, and of the wistful moods of sadness or joy which evaporate before we can examine them. That the Vassar poets have succeeded in giving some of these beautiful expression is not the least merit of a fine collection."

In 1917, when Miss Millay's book *Renascence* came out, I was in France with the A.E.F., and my cousin sent me a copy of the book, which impressed me much more than the Vassar poems. In 1920, when I was back in America again, I read in the March issue of the new literary magazine, the *Dial*, a sonnet called *To Love Impuissant*, which I immediately got by heart and found myself declaiming in the shower:

> Love, though for this you riddle me with darts,
> And drag me at your chariot till I die,—
> Oh, heavy prince! Oh, panderer of hearts!—
> Yet hear me tell how in their throats they lie
> Who shout you mighty: thick about my hair,
> Day in, day out, your ominous arrows purr,
> Who still am free, unto no querulous care
> A fool, and in no temple worshiper!
> I, that have bared me to your quiver's fire,
> Lifted my face into its puny rain,
> Do wreathe you Impotent to Evoke Desire
> As you are Powerless to Elicit Pain!
> (Now will the god, for blasphemy so brave,
> Punish me, surely, with the shaft I crave!)

The fascination that this poem had for me was due partly to its ringing defiance—at that time we were all defiant—but partly also to my liking to think that one who appreciated the poet as splendidly as I felt I did might be worthy to deal her the longed-for dart. This was a different, a bolder voice than the brooding girl of *Renascence*. How I hoped I might some-day meet her!

This was finally brought about—sometime in the spring of that year—by Hardwicke Nevin (the nephew of Ethelbert Nevin, the composer), whom my friend John Peale Bishop had known at Princeton. He had further excited my interest by his description of Edna's enchanting personality, and he had in-vited John and me to an evening party at his apartment in Greenwich Village, to which Edna came, late, from the theater, where she was acting with the Provincetown Players. I think it was just before this that I had seen the double bill there: a play of Floyd Dell's, in which she had acted, and her own *Aria da Capo*, in which her sister Norma played Columbine. I was thrilled and troubled by this little play: it was the first time I had felt Edna's peculiar power. There was a bitter treatment of war, and we were all ironic about war; but there was also a less common sense of the incongruity and the cruelty of life, of the precariousness of love perched on a table above the corpses that had been hastily shoved out of sight, and renewing its eternal twitter in the silence that succeeded the battle. In any case, it was after the theater that Edna came to Hardwicke Nevin's. She complained of being exhuasted, but was persuaded to recite some of her poems. She was dressed in some bright batik, and her face lit up with a flush that seemed to burn also in the bronze reflections of her not yet bobbed reddish hair. She was one of those women whose features are not perfect and who in their moments of dimness may not seem even pretty, but who, excited by the blood or the spirit, become almost supernaturally beautiful. She was small, but her figure was full, though she did not appear plump. She had a lovely and very long throat that gave her the look of a muse, and her reading of her poetry was thrilling. She pronounced every syllable distinctly; she gave every sound its value. She seemed sometimes rather British than American—in her quick way of talking to people as well as in her reading of her poems, and I have never understood how her accent was formed. I suppose it was partly the product of the English tradition in New England, and no doubt—since she had acted from childhood —of her having been taught to read Shakespeare by a college or school elocutionist. She had probably also been influenced by the English Mitchell Kennerley—Kennerley had been her first publisher—who had taken her up when she was still a girl, and, in a more important way, by the English dramatist Charles Rann Kennedy, who, with his wife Edith Wynn Matthison, the actress, had also been interested in her and had tried to persuade her to go on the stage. In any case, the trueness of her ear made it possible for her to write verse which was really in the English tradition. I believe that our failure in the United States to produce much first-rate lyric poetry is partly due to our flattening and drawling of the vowels and our slovenly slurring of the consonants; and Edna spoke with perfect purity. It may have been partly her musical training, which came out also in her handling of her voice. Among poets whose phonograph recordings I have heard, it seems to me that Edna Millay and E. E. Cummings and James Joyce give conspicuously the best performances. Joyce, like Edna Millay, is a musician with a well-trained voice; Cummings has, like Edna, the New England precision in enunciating every syllable. All three are masters of tempo and tone. If you play the recording of *Renascence*, you will hear how the *r* in the first line gets just the right little twist—so different from the harsh or the slighted *r*'s of the American regional accents; and how the vowels in *long* and *wood* are correctly made, respectively, short and long. If you play *Elegy*, you will hear in the closing lines her characteristic cadences that are almost like song. I do not remember whether she recited this poem the night that I met her first. If she did not, I heard it soon after. It was one of a series she had written for a girl-friend at Vassar who had died, which I thought among the finest of the things that she showed me then. What was impressive and rather unsettling when she read such poems aloud was her power of imposing herself on others through a medium that unburdened the emotions of solitude. The company hushed and listened as people do to music—her authority was always complete; but her voice, though dramatic, was lonely.

My next move was to cultivate her acquaintance by way of *Vanity Fair*, in the editorial department of which magazine John Bishop and I were both working then. She had at that time no real market for her poems; she sold a lyric only now and then to the highbrow *Dial*, on the one hand, or to the trashy *Ainslie's*, on the other. She was hard-up and lived with her mother and sisters at the very end of West Nineteenth Street. When I would go to get her there or take her home in a cab, the children that were playing in the street would run up and crowd around her. It was partly that she gave them pennies and sometimes taxi-rides, just as she later put out food for the birds, but it was also, I think, the magnetism that Vincent Sheean felt. We published in *Vanity Fair* a good deal of Edna's poetry and thus brought her to the attention of a larger public. This was the beginning of her immense popularity. Frank Crowninshield, the editor of *Vanity Fair*—a clever and extremely entertaining man—was in some ways rather shallow as well as unreliable, but he did have—as it were, as a heritage from his distinguished Boston family—a true instinct about painting and writing and a confidence in his own taste. He deserves a good deal of credit for featuring Edna Millay's poetry and for enabling her later to go abroad. There was nobody else in the publishing world who was both qualified to appreciate her work and in a position to do something to help her in a financial and practical way. As for John Bishop and me, the more we saw of her poetry, the more our admiration grew, and we both, before very long, had fallen irretrievably in love with her. This latter was so common an experience, so almost inevitable a consequence of knowing her in those days, that it is possible, without being guilty of personal irrelevancies, to introduce it into a memoir of this kind. One cannot really write about Edna Millay without bringing into the foreground of the picture her intoxicating effect on people, because this so much created the atmosphere in which she lived and composed. The spell that she exercised on many, of the most various professions and temperaments, of all ages and both sexes, was at that time exactly that which Vincent Sheean imagines she cast on the birds. I should say here that I do not believe that my estimate of Edna Millay's work has ever been much affected by my personal emotions about her. I admired her poetry before I knew her, and my most exalted feeling for her did not, I think, ever prevent me from recognizing or criticizing what was weak or second-rate in her work. Today, thirty years later, though I see her in a different "context," my opinion has hardly changed. Let me register this unfashionable opinion here, and explain that Edna Millay seems to me one of the only poets writing in English in our time who have attained to anything like the stature of great literary figures in an age in which prose has predominated. It is hard to know how to compare her to Eliot or Auden or Yeats—it would be even harder to compare her to Pound. There is always a certain incommensurability between men and women writers. But she does have it in common with the first three of these that, in giving supreme expression to profoundly felt personal experience, she was able to identify herself with more general human experience and stand forth as a spokesman for the human spirit, announcing its predicaments, its vicissitudes, but, as a master of human expression, by the splendor of expression itself, putting herself beyond common embarrassments, common oppressions and panics. This is man who surveys himself and the world in which he moves, not the beast that scurries and suffers; and the name of the poet comes no longer to indicate a mere individual with a birthplace and a legal residence, but to figure as one of the pseudonyms assumed by that spirit itself.

This spirit so made itself felt, in all one's relations with Edna, that it towered above the clever college girl, the Greenwich Village gamine and, later, the neurotic invalid. There was something of awful drama about everything one did with Edna, and yet something that steadied one, too. Those who fell in love with the woman did not, I think, seriously quarrel with her or find themselves at one another's throats and they were not, except in very small ways, demoralized or led to commit excesses, because the other thing was always there, and her genius, for those who could value it, was not something that one could be jealous of. Her poetry, you soon found out, was her real overmastering passion. She gave it to all the world, but she also gave it to you. As in *The Poet and His Book*—at that time, one of my favorites of her poems—with its homely but magical images, its urgent and hurried movement—she addressed herself, not to her lover, by whom, except momentarily, she had never had the illusion that she lived or died, but to everyone whose pulse could throb quicker at catching the beat of her poetry. This made it possible during the first days we knew her for John and me to see a good deal of her together on the basis of our common love of poetry. Our parties were in the nature of a sojourn in Pieria—to which, in one of her sonnets, she complains that an unworthy lover is trying to keep her from returning—where it was most delightful to feel at home. I remember particularly an April night in 1920, when we called on Richard Bennett, the actor, who had been brought by Hardwicke Nevin to the Provincetown Players, in the cheerful little house halfway downtown where he lived with his attractive wife and his so soon to be attractive daughters. I sat on the floor with Edna, which seemed to me very Bohemian. On some other occasion, we all undertook to write portraits in verse of ourselves. John's, under the title *Self-Portrait*, appeared in *Vanity Fair*, and we wanted to publish Edna's, but one of her sisters intervened and persuaded her that it wouldn't do. There was also a trip on a Fifth Avenue bus—we were going to the Claremont for dinner, I think—in the course of which Edna recited to us a sonnet she had just written: "*Here is a wound that never will heal, I know.*" For me, even rolling up Fifth Avenue, this poem plucked the strings of chagrin, for not only did it refer to some other man, someone I did not know, but it suggested that Edna could not be consoled, that such grief was in the nature of things.

I used to take her to plays, concerts and operas. We saw Bernard Shaw's *Heartbreak House* together, when it was first done in New York, in the November of 1920. I had not liked it much when I read it and had told her that it was a dreary piece on the model of *Misalliance*. But the play absorbed and excited her, as it gradually did me, and I saw that I had been quite wrong: *Heartbreak House* was, on the contrary, the first piece of Shaw's in which he had fully realized the possibilities of the country-house conversation with which he had been experimenting in *Getting Married* and *Misalliance*. At the end of the second act, Edna became very tense and was rather upset by the scene in which Ariadne—who had just said, "I get my whole life messed up with people falling in love with me"—plays cat-and-mouse with the jealous Randell; and when the curtain went down on it, she said: "I hate women who do that, you know." She must have had, in the course of those crowded years, a good many Randells on her hands, but her method of dealing with them was different from that of Bernard Shaw's aggressive Ariadne. She was capable of being mockingly or sternly sharp with an admirer who proved a nuisance, but she did not like to torture people or to play them off against one another. With the dignity of her genius went, not, as is sometimes the case, a coldness or a hatefulness or a touchiness in intimate human relations, but an invincible magnanimity, and the effects of her transitory feminine malice would be cancelled by an impartiality which was amiably humorous or sympathetic. It is characteristic of her that, in her sonnet *On Hearing a Symphony of Beethoven*, she should write of the effect of the music,

> The spiteful and the stingy and the rude
> Sleep like the scullions in the fairy-tale.

Spitefulness and stinginess and rudeness were among the qualities she most disliked and of which she was least willing to be guilty.

Between John Bishop and me relations were, nevertheless, by this time, becoming a little strained. Frank Crowninshield was complaining that it was difficult to have both his assistants in love with one of his most brilliant contributors. There was a time when, from the point of view of taking her out, I was more or less monopolizing Edna, and John, who, between the office and his perfectionist concentration on his poetry—which he recited in the bathroom in the morning and to which he returned at night—had collapsed and come down with the flu. I went to see him, and afterwards told Edna—no doubt with a touch of smugness—that I thought he was suffering, also, from his frustrated passion for her. The result of this—which I saw with mixed feelings—was that she paid him a visit at once and did her best to redress the balance. I knew that he had some pretty good poetry to read her, and this did not improve the situation.

But her relations with us and with her other admirers had, as I say, a disarming impartiality. Though she reacted to the traits of the men she knew—a face or a voice or a manner—or to their special qualifications—what they sang or had read or collected —with the same intensely perceptive interest that she brought to anything else—a bird or a shell or a weed—that had attracted her burning attention; though she was quick to feel weakness or strength—she did not, however, give the impression that personality much mattered for her or that, aside from her mother and sisters, her personal relations were important except as subjects for poems; and when she came to write about her lovers, she gave them so little individuality that it was usually, in any given case, impossible to tell which man she was writing about. What interests her is seldom the people themselves, but her own emotions about them; and the sonnets that she published in sequences differed basically from Mrs. Browning's in that they dealt with a miscellany of men without —since they are all about *her*—the reader's feeling the slightest discontinuity. In all this, she was not egotistic in any boring or ridiculous or oppressive way, because it was not the personal, but the impersonal Edna Millay—that is, the poet—that preoccupied her so incessantly. But she was sometimes rather a strain, because nothing could be casual for her; I do not think I ever saw her relaxed even when she was tired or ill. I used to suppose that this strain of being with her must be due to my own anxieties, but I later discovered that others who had never been emotionally involved with her were affected in the same way. She could be very amusing in company, but the wit of her conversation was as sharp as the pathos of her poetry. She was not at all a social person. She did not gossip; did not like to talk current events; did not like to talk personalities. It was partly that she was really noble, partly that she was rather neurotic, and the two things (bound up together) made it difficult for her to meet the world easily. When Mr. Sheean met her, late in her life, she at first, he tells us, seemed tongue-tied; then puzzled him extremely by thanking him, as if it had happened yesterday, for his having, in some official connection about which he had completely forgotten, sent her some flowers five years before; then analyzed, with a closeness he could hardly follow, a poem by Gerard Manley Hopkins, the sense of which she insisted, with bitterness and an "animation" that brought out "her very extraordinary beauty—not the beauty of every day but apart," had been spoiled by Hopkins' editor Robert Bridges' having put in a comma in the wrong place. But although Edna sometimes fatigued one, she was never, as even the most gifted sometimes are, tyrannical, fatuous or vain. She was either like the most condensed literature or music, the demands of which one cannot meet protractedly, or like a serious nervous case—though this side of her was more in evidence later—whom one finds that one cannot soothe.

What was the cause of this strain? From what was the pressure derived that Edna Millay seemed always to be under? At that time I was too young and too much in love to be able to understand her well, and I afterwards saw her only at intervals and in a much less intimate way. But I had found, when I had come into contact with the formidable strength of character that lay behind her attractiveness and brilliance, something as different as possible from the legend of her Greenwich Village reputation, something austere and even grim. She had been born in Rockland, Maine, and had grown up in small Maine towns. I heard her speak of her father only once. He and her mother had not lived together since the children were quite small, and her mother, who had studied to be a singer, supported them by district nursing without ceasing—as I learn from Mr. Sheean—to train the local orchestra and write out their scores. They were poor; the mother was away all day, and the three girls were thrown much on themselves. To Edna, her sisters and her poetry and music must have been almost the whole of life. Such suitors as she had had in Maine she did not seem to have taken seriously. By her precocious and remarkable poem, *Renascence*, written when she was hardly nineteen, she had attracted, at a summer entertainment, the attention of a visitor, Miss Caroline B. Dow, the New York head of the National Training School of the Y.W.C.A., who raised the money to send her to college. She did not graduate, therefore, till she was twenty-five, when she at last emerged into the freedom of a world where her genius and beauty were soon to make her famous, to bring all sorts of people about her, with an intellect and a character that had been developed in solitude and under the discipline of hard conditions. Her human emotional life had, it seemed to me, in her girlhood been rather cramped, but she had herself given her emotions their satisfaction through the objects—the poems—she was able to create, and this life of the mind, this life of art, by which she had triumphed in a little Maine town that offered few other triumphs, was to remain for her the great reality that made everything else unimportant. It is all in the astonishing *Renascence*, which is a study of claustrophobia (as well as, of course, a great affirmation of the stature of the human spirit). Hemmed in between the mountains and the sea of Camden on Penobscot Bay, the girl is beginning to suffocate; she looks up, and the sky seems to offer escape, but when she puts up her hand, she screams, for she finds it is so low that she can touch it, and Infinity settles down on her—she can hear the ticking of Eternity; she is beset by a new ordeal, for she begins to feel all human guilt, experience all human suffering, and this, too, becomes an oppression which is killing her; she now sinks six feet into the ground, and she feels the weight roll from her breast; her tortured soul breaks away, and the comforting rain begins to fall; but she is dead now and she wants to escape from the grave, which itself has become a prison, for she imagines how beautiful the world will be as soon as the rain is over; she prays to God for the rain to wash away the grave, and a storm comes and sets her free to those beauties of the world she has longed for; she springs up, embraces the trees, hugs the ground, feels that nothing can ever hide her from God again; the world, she now knows, is as wide as the heart, the heavens as high as the soul, but East and West will close in and crush you if you do not keep them apart, and the sky will cave in on you if your soul is flat. This poem gives the central theme of Edna Millay's whole work: she is alone; she is afraid that the world will crush her; she must summon the strength to assert herself, to draw herself up to her full stature, to embrace the world with love; and the storm—which stands evidently for sexual love—comes to effect a liberation. Her real sexual experience, which came rather late, was to play in her poetry the role of this storm, for it gives her the world to embrace, yet it always leaves her alone again, alone and afraid of death. Withdrawal is her natural condition: she was always, as Mr. Sheean indicates—and this made itself felt as a part of the strain— extremely shy of meeting people; and she was terrified by New York, of which I do not think she saw much, for she would not cross a street alone. She feels that she is "caught beneath great buildings," and she longs to be back in Maine—though the Maine she is homesick for is never in the least idealized, but, on the contrary, a meager country with threadbare interiors, wizened apples and weedy mussels on rotting hulls. One of her poems of this time that impressed me most was the long *Ode to Silence*, in which she celebrates an inner sanctuary that is like the grave of *Renascence*—a garden which lies "in a lull," like it, "between the mountains and the mountainous sea."

Of the household in which Edna grew up I had a glimpse, in the summer of 1920, when I went at her invitation—she had John Bishop and me on different weekends—to visit her at Truro, near the tip of Cape Cod. It was already dark when I got there—there was in those days a train that went all the way to Provincetown, shuffling along so slowly that it might have been plodding through the sand—and though I was met by a man with a cart, he did not, for some curmudgeonly Cape Cod reason, drive me all the way to the house, but dropped me some distance away from it, so that I somehow got lost in a field and dragged my suitcase through scrub-oak and sweet-fern in the breathless hot August night. At last I saw a gleam— a small house—which I approached from the fields behind it, and there I found the Millays: Edna, with her mother and her two sisters, none of whom I had met. The little house had been lent them for the summer by George Cram Cook (always known as "Jig"), the organizer of the Provincetown Players, who with Susan Glaspell lived across the road. It was bare, with no decoration and only a few pieces of furniture; a windmill that pumped water and no plumbing. Norma has told me since that, when it rained the first night they got there, before they knew they had neighbors who could see them, they had all taken a shower under the spout from the roof. They gave me a dinner on a plain board table by the light of an oil-lamp. I had never seen anything like this household, nor have I ever seen anything like it since. Edna tried to reassure me by telling me that I mustn't be overpowered by all those girls, and one of the others added, "And *what* girls!" Norma, the second sister, was a blonde, who looked a little like Edna; Kathleen, the youngest, was different, a dark Irish type. Edna was now very freckled. All were extremely pretty. But it was the mother who was most extraordinary. She was a little old woman with spectacles, who, although she had evidently been through a good deal, had managed to remain very brisk and bright. She sat up straight and smoked cigarettes and quizzically followed the conversation. She looked not unlike a New England schoolteacher, yet there was something almost raffish about her. She had anticipated the Bohemianism of her daughters; and she sometimes made remarks that were startling from the lips of a little old lady. But there was nothing sordid about her: you felt even more than with Edna that she had passed beyond good and evil, beyond the power of hardship to worry her, and that she had attained there a certain gaiety. The daughters entertained me with humorous songs—they sang parts very well together—which they had concocted in their girlhood in Maine. Here are the words of one that I remember, of which Norma has supplied me with an accurate version:

Song to Men

Kathleen, soprano; Vincent, baritone; Norma, tenor
Let us sing a little song
To the men we've loved so long—
And to those we've only loved
A little while
Tenor solo:　　　　A lit-tle while.

Ti de dee and ta dee da,
We must take them as they are—
  Let them spoof us
  For they love so
  To beguile.

Baritone solo: Let them beguile.

    Chorus
  Oh, darling men!

Baritone: Oh, men, men, men.
Oh, men alluring,
Waste not the hours—

Tenor: Sweet idle hours—
In vain assuring,
For love, though sweet,

Tenor: Love though tho thweet—
Is not enduring.
Ti de da! Ti da dee da!

Shall we have a smoke? We can—
Oh, a man is just a man
But a little old Fatima
  Burns so snug.

Baritone: She burns so snug.
Should we have another drink,
Do you think? (*Spoken*) Oh, let's not think!
  Pour another
  From the little
  Earthen jug—(*Sound of cork*) gug-
    gug-gug
  gug-gug-gug-gug-gug.

    Chorus
  Oh, darling men!
  Oh, men, men, men, etc.
(*Ending*)
  Ti de da! Ti da dee da!
  So there you are.

Edna had been turning into verse, for a collection called *Folk Songs of Many Peoples*, prose translations of some European peasant songs, and she sang me her versions, which

enchanted me—especially one from Esthonia, with a merry
and poignant tune:

> Piper, pipe a tune, call the dancers out!
> Oh, the happy bag-pipes, the laughing shout!
> Now the merry step we are treading!
> Health to all, and joy bless this wedding!
> Tra la la! Tra la la! Youth is all pleasure!
> Let the beating foot strike the time of the measure!

> Now the master's son, riches spurning,
> Weds the farmer maid of his yearning;
> Now the girl the rose garland covers,
> Leaves her father's house for her lover's.
> Tra la la! Lonely my heart, dream laden.
> Would that I the bridegroom were, of so sweet a maiden.

The word *lonely* in the second stanza was given a dramatic emphasis by being put in the place of the second *tra la la*, in such a way that the first syllable was prolonged in the two drooping notes.

Since there were only two rooms on the first floor, with no partition between them, the only way for Edna and me to get away by ourselves was to sit in a swing on the porch; but the mosquitoes were so tormenting—there being then no mosquito control—that we soon had to go in again. I did, however, ask her formally to marry me, and she did not reject my proposal but said that she would think about it. I am not sure that she actually said, "That might be the solution," but it haunts me that she conveyed that idea. In any case, it was plain to me that proposals of marriage were not a source of great excitement.

The next morning she sat on the floor and recited a lot of new poems—she rarely read her poetry, she knew it by heart. The Millays were rather vague about meals and only really concentrated on dinner, but they never apologized for anything. We played the Fifth Symphony on a primitive old phonograph that had been left with them by Allan Ross Macdougall. She was committing the whole thing to memory, as she liked to do with music and poems; and, raspy and blurred though it sounded, the power of its bold or mysterious motifs came through to me—surcharged with her power—as it never had done before. Jig Cook and Hutchins Hapgood dropped by and sat on the edge of the porch. The conversation was light but learned, and I was rather astonished when Jig quoted a poem in Sanskrit: I did not know at that time that he was a liberated Greek professor. But the things that remain with me most vividly—because she called my attention to them—are the vision of Jig Cook's daughter, Nilla, a handsome and sturdy little girl in a bright red bathing-suit walking along the beach, as we looked down from the cliff above; and a gull's egg we found on the sand—gulls do not build nests—which made Edna stop and stare. It came back to me seven years later when, going up to Cape Cod in the early summer, I found myself alone in Provincetown:

Provincetown

We never from the barren down,
    Beneath the silver-lucid breast
Of drifting plume, gazed out to drown
    Where daylight whitens to the west.

Here never in this place I knew
    Such beauty by your side, such peace—

These skies that, brightening, imbue
    With dawn's delight the day's release.

Only, upon the barren beach,
    Beside the gray egg of a gull,
With that fixed look and fervent speech,
    You stopped and called it beautiful.

Lone as the voice that sped the word!—
    Gray-green as eyes that ate its round!—
The desert dropping of a bird,
    Bare-bedded in the sandy ground.

Tonight, where clouds like foam are blown,
    I ride alone the surf of light,
As—even by my side—alone
    That stony beauty burned your sight.

For I was not "the solution," nor was anyone else she knew;
and she had come to a crisis in her life. "I'll be thirty in a
minute!" she said to me one day. She moved from the apartment she had shared with her family and where, she complained, the sewing-machine had interfered with her writing,
and took two rooms and a bath on West Twelfth Street, where
Kathleen eventually joined her. But this made her more accessible and exposed her to the importunities of her suitors, who
really besieged her door. She did not want to marry any of
them, and, having tried two Greenwich Village ménages, she
no longer had any illusions about extra-marital arrangements
that were supposed to leave the parties free but, since somebody was always jealous, actually made their relations intolerable. And even with her literary career, she had lately been
running into difficulties of a most discouraging kind. Her new
book, *Second April*, had been set up a long time before—she
showed me the proofs when I first knew her—but Mitchell
Kennerley, who was having financial troubles, did not bring
the book out and would not even communicate with her. Besides this, her benefactress, Miss Dow, to whom she had dedicated *Second April*, did not approve of her recent work—just
as James Joyce's patron, Miss Harriet Weaver, was scandalized

by *Ulysses**—and this worried her very much, for she could not write differently to please Miss Dow, and did not know how to answer her letters. She had one or two depressing illnesses. Her apartment was poorly heated, and I brought her an electric heater. I remember how miserable she seemed— though she never lost a certain liveliness—wrapped up in an old flannel bathrobe and bundled in shabby covers. Above the bed was a modern painting, all fractured geometrical planes that vaguely delineated a female figure, which the Millay girls called *Directions for Using the Empress*.†

It was decided she should go abroad. She had never been in Europe, and she wanted to get away from the Village. She had begun to do for *Vanity Fair* the satirical dialogues and sketches which were published under the pseudonym "Nancy Boyd," and this made it possible for Crowninshield to pay her a regular allowance. He did his best to induce Edna to sign these pieces with her own name—he offered her, in fact, more money; but she never would compromise about her work. No matter how confused her life became, she was always clear about this. If one compares the contents of *Figs from Thistles*, written in the same year as the poems in *Second April*, with the contents of the other book, one can see that she imposed on herself a pretty rigorous critical standard. She would not mix with her serious work any of the merely cute feminine pieces that had something in common with the songs that the sisters made up for their own amusement, nor any of the easier lyrics that reflected the tone of the women's magazines. This serious work, never loosely written, was tragic, almost pessimistic (though the best of her lighter verse had the same sort of implications). It was natural that Hardy and Housman should have been among her admirers. From Housman she partly derived (Mr. Sheean, in asserting that Edna Millay owed nothing to any

---

*See page 640.

†This, I learn from Norma Millay (Mrs. Charles Ellis), was the painter's own name for the picture, which was painted by Charles Ellis. "It was shown," she writes me, "at the Independent Artists' Show and was reviewed under this startling title." The picture, she says, was "an abstract portrait of Vincent's mechanical dressform, the Empress, which gained and lost weight by an intricate system of adjusting nuts and screws. When we later learned that the inventor of the Empress had killed himself, we understood it perfectly."

other poet since Shakespeare, has neglected this important exception), and she was closer to this masculine stoicism than to the heartbreak of Sara Teasdale. It was this tough intellectual side combined with her feminine attraction that made her such a satisfactory companion, and that persuaded so many men that they had found their ideal mate. She was quite free from the blue-stocking's showing-off, but she did have a rather schoolmarmish side—which rapped Mr. Sheean's knuckles when he put out a cigarette in his coffee-cup. In just this way I have heard her complain of the vandalisms of Greenwich Villagers who made a point of scorning bourgeois sanctions. And so she reprimanded me once when I tried to fulfil my editorial function by urging her to sign her name to her Nancy Boyd articles. Her attitude was: "Don't you know it's impolite to the teacher and reflects on the home you come from to throw chalk around in class?"

I tried to help her get on with these sketches, at the time when she was not yet well, by typing to her dictation, but she was anything but a facile writer and she insisted on putting in as comic lines remarks I had just made in earnest. We had at this time some wonderful conversations, at which quite a lot of bootleg gin was drunk, and, even in that dreadful form, this exhilarating bitter liquor has always kept for me a certain glamor that others have not acquired. On one of these occasions, she recited to me the fragments of a long poem she had started, called *Epitaph for the Race of Man*. This was something quite different from the sonnet sequence that she published in 1934. It was written, like *Renascence*, in iambic tetrameter; but it was equally evolutionary: there were monkeys, though not yet, I think, dinosaurs. It surprised me, for it was purely philosophical, and it gave me a new idea of her range. One evening we set out to talk French in preparation for her coming trip. I remarked that her ex-admirers ought to organize an alumni association—to which she answered with promptness and point: "*On en parle toujours, mais on ne le fait jamais.*" John Bishop and I, who had realized that we were both quite out of the running without, however, we thought, having yet been superseded by a serious rival, had renewed our good relations and spent an evening with her together, just before she left, on our old high and festive basis. But neither of us saw her off. I think that we were both afraid of the possible unknown others we might have to confront on the pier.

That I missed her may be seen from the following poem. I had read the *Georgics* of Virgil in the summer of 1922, and the phrase *in luminis oras*—which he uses in connection with the sprouting plants that reach upwards to "the shores of light"—though a conventional Latin formula that had appeared in the older poets, had echoed in my head with the accent of pathos that haunts even fertility in Virgil, and eventually gave me a motif.

Shut out the Square!
Though not for grayness and the rainy path—
For that intolerable aching air
Of meetings long resolved to silences
And absences like death—
For the throat a moment lifted, the wide brow shaken free,
Where there was neither leaf nor wind
A dryad by her tree—
Against the narrow door that closed the narrow hall,
Blank then but for a night that now for all
With blankness wounds the mind.

Gaze out with steady glare!
Present the tough unbroken glove!
For suddenly you heard to-night
Your voice that speaks and saw your hands that write,
Yet never speak nor write the name they love—
And knew the hours were waves that wash away
Farther each day to sea the summer sound
Of children shrill and late, of summer hours that run
Late, late, yet never sleep and never tire
Before they meet the sun.

We spoke the sudden words, the words already known—
We spoke, and spoke no more, for tongues were fire.
Now, watching from this shore at last, alone
I seem to wait the turning of that tide
That ebbs for ever.
                    Children, waking to the day,
Cry out for joy.

My stubborn heart to-night
Divines the fate of souls who have not died,
Buried in sullen shadows underground—
That reach for ever toward the shores of light.

II

I saw her in Paris in the summer of 1921. She had made new friends and, both there and in England, was having, I think, a very good time. I had the impression that Europe frightened her less than New York, but she must have continued to live with considerable recklessness, for, at the end of two years abroad, she was in very bad shape again. Returned home at the beginning of 1923, she married, in July, Eugen Boissevain, just before she went to the hospital for a serious operation. She had met him at Croton since she had come back from Europe, and had first got to know him in a round of charades. He was a Dutchman with an Irish mother, the son of the editor of the largest Dutch newspaper and himself a coffee importer, with offices in New York. He had been married to Inez Milholland, a Vassar girl who had practised law and become a famous public champion of labor causes and women's rights, who had died in 1916. He was a gentleman and had once been quite well-to-do. Max Eastman, in his autobiographical *Enjoyment of Living*, describes him at the time of his first marriage as "handsome and muscular and bold, boisterous in conversation, noisy in laughter, yet redeemed by a strain of something feminine that most men except the creative geniuses lack." With no particular talent or bent of his own, it was possible for him only vicariously to express this imaginative and sensitive side, and he was led, as it were, to the special vocation of assisting the careers of gifted women. He was twelve years older than Edna, and, although, as Max Eastman says, he had "the genius, the audacity and the uncompromising determination to enjoy the adventure of life," he made one feel that he had always behind him a stout background of Dutch burgher stability. She had made a very sound choice. He took her on a trip to the Orient and then bought a large farm at Austerlitz, New York, where they settled in 1925 and lived for the rest of their lives.

I used to see and correspond with her occasionally. I have a memory of calling on her once in January, 1924, in the tiny little house in Bedford Street, 75½, where they lived before they went to the country. I found her absorbed in a paint catalogue, of which she made the special shades of color and their often delightful names start into a relief that seemed almost as vivid as the voices of the Fifth Symphony when she had played it on the phonograph in Truro. From a note-book of 1928—it must have been early in the year, since *The Buck in the Snow* had not yet come out—I learn that she "summoned me to the Vanderbilt to talk about her bobolink poem," about which I seem to have been only moderately enthusiastic. "You mean you think it sounds like Mary Carolyn Davies!" I find she replied to my criticisms. "I said," my record continues, "that, when she had written *Second April*, she had been under so many kinds of pressure that the people who read her poems hardly thought about them as literature at all: there had been an element of panic about them. She said, 'Yes, and I still want to knock 'em cold!' For two cents she would tear up the bobolink proof and not let the *Delineator* have it. . . . She looked quite beautiful, very high pink flush, and brown dress that brought out her color." I noted, also, Boissevain's "protective attitude" and his saying that her recent work was "more objective." He was right, and the volume of lyrics called *The Buck in the Snow*—the first she had published since *The Harp-Weaver* of 1923—which came out later that year, contained work of a much less desperate, a more contemplative kind, which included, along with the bobolink, several of her finest poems: *Dawn, The Cameo, Sonnet to Gath, On Hearing a Symphony of Beethoven.*

This book contained also a piece that I read with both pleasure and embarrassment, for I recognized it—she afterwards confirmed this—as an account of an evening we had spent together (it must have been sometime that same winter), when I had been living in a little room on West Thirteenth Street opposite a taxi-garage and just around the corner from Greenwich Avenue. I had read her the Latin elegiacs that A. E. Housman had prefixed to his Manilius and a translation of them I had made; some of Yeats's latest poems, which she had not seen; James Joyce's *Pomes Penyeach*, as to which I thought her rather old-fashioned for objecting that the title cheapened them, as if he had let them go as the work of some "Nancy Boyd." I do not remember behaving as she describes (as people seem so often to say). I think she must have combined this occasion with some memory from our earlier phase, but it is painful to me to reread this poem today and to feel again, in retrospect, how much I must have hated to part from her.

Portrait

Over and over I have heard,
As now I hear it,
Your voice harsh and light as the scratching of dry leaves
        over the hard ground,
Your voice forever assailed and shaken by the wind from the
        island
Of illustrious living and dead, that never dies down,
And bending at moments under the terrible weight of the
        perfect word,
Here in this room without fire, without comfort of any kind,
Reading aloud to me immortal page after page conceived
        in a mortal mind.
Beauty at such moments before me like a wild bright bird
Has been in the room, and eyed me, and let me come near it.

I could not ever nor can I to this day
Acquaint you with the triumph and the sweet rest
These hours have brought to me and always bring,—
Rapture, coloured like the wild bird's neck and wing,
Comfort, softer than the feathers of its breast.
Always, and even now, when I rise to go,
Your eyes blaze out from a face gone wickedly pale;
I try to tell you what I would have you know,—
What peace it was; you cry me down; you scourge me
        with a salty flail;
You will not have it so.

    She had said to me in the course of this evening that the only bad feature of Austerlitz was its not being near the sea, of which she had a permanent need, that the hills and the woods walled her in and sometimes made her feel imprisoned (this was, as I now can see, one of the phases of her recurrent claustrophobia). I suppose it was to remedy this that they later bought their island in Maine. In the May of 1928, I had a wire from her inviting me to Austerlitz for a week-end. I went, and it was pleasant, as I learn from my notes—the prospect of seeing her again must, as usual, have stimulated my perceptions —to find myself on the train, in the widening landscape of up-state New York, with its dark and thick-bristling hills, today blurred with mist at the tops and misted at the bases with fruit-blossoms; and, in intervals of reading Proust's letters to Mme. Sheikévitch, I looked out on the long roads leading over these hills, the white houses and little red cabins and large-looming tarnished barns, the stone fences that lay in loose meshes, the small faded rural hotels that so often stood opposite the stations —with the soddenly wet gray day superimposed rather queerly on the freshest greenness of spring. There were desolate yellow freightcars trailing along the route, and the timbery marshes were studded with the rank green of skunk-cabbage leaves. The ponds and the streams had a dark smooth luster even under the rain, but the foam of the apple-blossoms, like some dirty sheep in a pasture, seemed yellowed by the turbid weather. A growth of squarish whitish houses in the bowl of one of the valleys seemed almost a product of the damp like the skunk-cabbage in the swamp. At Austerlitz—hirsute hills—the over-cast sultry weather seemed brooding like a mother-bird over the not yet quite opening beauties of spring, the little pink fruit-tree buds that were just on the point of bursting. The birds themselves seemed subdued, and Edna, when I reached the Boissevains' place, said that she imagined the farmhands— "ominously silent," also—perched somewhere with their heads under their wings. I had, on my side, been saving for her a simile and remarked that on one of the lawns I had passed the dandelions had looked like grated egg on spinach. We were neither of us, perhaps, at our best, but we always made a certain effort. Above the Boissevains' house—called Steepletop—a big densely green tree-grown hill, with the flat effect of a tap-estry, was stitched with distinct white birch.

Gene Boissevain, when I arrived, was planting a border of pansies with a gardener's intent application; but his attention seemed soon to flag, for he began singing cockney songs at the top of his voice. Then he addressed himself to oiling the lawnmower; then suddenly dropped it and proposed a drink. There was a comfortable living room, in which, as one first came into it, one was startled at being confronted by a dark human head staring fixedly and almost fiercely from eyes that had black irises and glowing whites: a bronze bust of Sappho, painted black, on an immense marble pedestal, which an admirer had sent Edna from Italy. There were also hangings from India, golden birds on a background of green, that she had brought back from her first trip to London. We did a good deal of leisurely drinking, all in the gamut of apple products, on which people who lived in the country much depended under Prohibition: apple brandies and apple wines that ranged in color from citron to amber. Edna was interesting herself in the local animals and birds and trees, which were beginning to turn up in *The Buck in the Snow*; but we decided not to go for a walk, as it had been earlier proposed to do. They had a sensitive German police-dog, who, when Boissevain had given her a scolding, would drag herself into the room, bumping against the chairs, as if her hind legs were paralyzed. They thought she was a case for Freud.

There was a piano in the living room, and the next morning I asked her to play. I had not heard her since years before, when she had taken off her rings and left them on the piano in my apartment in Sixteenth Street, and I had found in my mailbox the next morning a note dated "Three p.m. (out to get food)"—since she lived only a few blocks away—asking me to bring them back. She had now, she told me, taken up music again and was trying to work regularly at it. She was studying a sonata of Beethoven and played parts of it with her bright alive touch, dropping them, however, with impatience at the raggedness of her own performance. Then she got out a lot of new poems, over which we had a long session. It brought her back to her old intensity. She was desperately, feverishly anxious not to let her standard down. She sometimes kept a poem for decades before she got it into satisfactory form. I remember one ambitious piece called *Pittsburgh Rose*, on which she had been working that summer, that impressed me very much at the time but that she never got to the point of publishing —also *Menses*, which was not printed till *Huntsman, What Quarry?* in 1937. I would try to relieve the strain that was inevitably set up between us by talking about current ideas and books—to which at that time she paid little attention—and by telling her a gag of Joe Cook's, which I had also been saving for her, because it was a little in her own vein. Cook, in his latest show, had exhibited to the audience two shower-baths and explained they were his own invention: the remarkable thing about them was that you could have a complete shower without taking off your clothes and without getting them wet. He introduced to the audience two men in full evening-dress, wearing silk hats. They stepped into the showers and pulled the curtains—the sound of water was heard. Joe Cook then jerked open the curtains, and the gentlemen emerged drenched. Cook turned to the audience and said, "I have never been more embarrassed in my life!" But even as I was telling this and Edna was laughing at it, I was chilled by the awful seriousness of the implications it was taking on.

The next summer I was visiting near Austerlitz and called on the Boissevains one afternoon. While we were talking, it began to grow dark, and the living room was half in shadow. There were a number of people there, and the conversation was general. I had a curious and touching impression, as Edna sat quiet in a big chair, that—torn and distracted by winds that had swept her through many seas—she had been towed into harbor and moored, that she was floating at anchor there.

It was difficult for the romantics of the twenties to slow down and slough off their youth, when everything had seemed to be possible and they had been able to treat their genius as an unlimited checking account. One could always still resort to liquor to keep up the old excitement, it was a kind of way of getting back there; the old habit of recklessness was hard to drop, the scorn for safe living and expediency, the need to heighten the sensations of life. Edna had now been led back to something like the rural isolation of her girlhood, and in her retreat she had no children to occupy her, to compel her to outgrow her girlhood. Though I did not see much of her through all these years, I got the impression that she was alternating between vigorously creative periods when she produced the firm-based strong-molded work that represented her full artistic maturity—*Fatal Interview* and *Epitaph for the Race of*

Man—and dreadful lapses into depression and helplessness that sometimes lasted for months. I did not encourage her to talk about these; but I remember her telling me on one occasion, not very long after her marriage, when she had apparently spent weeks in bed, that she had done nothing but weep all the time; and on another, she startled me by saying, in the midst of showing me her poetry: "I'm *not* a pathetic character!" This must have been in 1928, at the time when she was still a romantic figure and a fabulously popular poet, imitated, adored and envied all over the United States, who was able to make large fees by reading her poems in public. Through all this, Eugen Boissevain must have been inexhaustibly patient, considerate and comprehending. He had given his whole life to Edna. He dropped his business and seriously worked the farm. He accompanied her on the triumphs of her reading tours and saw her through the ordeals of her hospitals. He arranged for her a social life—it is reflected, I suppose, to some extent, in *Conversation at Midnight*—of a kind that she could never have made for herself, which afforded her more "human" contacts than were possible in the exhausting relationships that were natural to her passionate spirit. Yet she continued, from time to time, to follow her old pattern of escape by breaking away from her domestic arrangements. The sequence of sonnets called *Fatal Interview*—certainly one of her most successful works and one of the great poems of our day—was evidently the product of such an episode. It is, I think, unique among her poems in representing the lover as wanting to end the affair before the poet is willing to let him go.

I did not see her for nineteen years after my call of 1929. It was not till 1944 that I seem even to have written her again. I had been astonished and worried by the poetry she had been publishing during the war, on a level of wartime journalism of which I had not imagined her capable. I tried to explain it as partly due to the natural anxieties of Eugen when Holland was seized by Hitler, and I remembered Henry James's description, in his life of William Wetmore Story, of Mrs. Browning's "feverish obsession" with the Italian Risorgimento. "It is impossible," says James, "not to feel, as we read, that to 'care,' in the common phrase, as she is caring is to entertain one's convictions as a malady and a doom. . . . We wonder why so much disinterested passion . . . should not leave us in a less disturbed degree the benefit of the moral beauty. We . . . end by asking ourselves if it be not because her admirable mind, otherwise splendidly exhibited, has inclined us to look in her for that saving and sacred sense of proportion, of the free and blessed *general*, that great poets, that genius and the high range of genius, give us the impression of even in emotion and passion, even in pleading a cause and calling on the gods." I concluded that when women of genius got carried away by a cause, this was the kind of thing that deplorably sometimes happened. But I thought that, since she had come to that pass, she probably needed artistic encouragement; the reviewers were giving her plenty of scolding. So I wrote her a letter in which I refrained from mentioning her war-verse at all but congratulated her on the album of her recordings, which, although it had been made some time before, in 1941, I had only recently bought. One of the poems she had recorded was *The Harp-Weaver*, for which I had not much cared when it first appeared. I had told her that it was one of her poems that belonged in a woman's magazine, and was surprised when she defended it strongly, as she did not always do with her work when it verged on the sentimental. I had known that it was about her own mother, and the volume was dedicated to Cora Millay. During the years when Edna had been living in Europe, she had arranged to bring her mother over—which, with her own meager resources at that time, could not have been easy to manage; and I knew how devoted she was to the debonair hard-bitten old lady who had worked for her and educated her. But I did not know with how much effectiveness she had put it into the Harp-Weaver poem—or, at least, into her reading of it, for it is better to hear than to read: the loneliness, the poverty, the unvalued Irish heritage, the Spartan New England self-discipline, the gift of artistic creation and intellectual distinction—she had taught her to write verse at four and to play the piano at seven—that the mother had been able to transmit. She had made of it something dramatic and almost unbearably moving, a record of the closest relationship that Edna, up to then, I suppose—that is, up to her marriage —had ever known. I wrote her something of this, and I told her that John Bishop had died that spring. I heard nothing from her for two years; then, in the summer of 1946, I received from her this strange letter:

> Steepletop,
> August, 1946.
>
> . . . It is two years now since I received your letter. You had bad news to tell me: the death of John Bishop. Even now, that seems unlikely. How you must have missed him that summer, and how you still must miss him, is something that I would rather not go into in my mind. For it would make me ache, only to think of it, and I don't like aching, any more than anybody else.
>
> You told me also, in that letter, that you liked my recorded readings from my poems. That pleased me enormously. I had felt pretty sure, myself, that they were good, but your verdict was like an Imprimatur to me.
>
> Your letter reached me at a time when I was very ill indeed, in the Doctors Hospital in New York. I was enjoying there a very handsome—and, as I afterwards was told, an all but life-size—nervous breakdown. For five years I had been writing almost nothing but propaganda. And I can tell you from my own experience, that there is nothing on this earth which can so much get on the nerves of a good poet, as the writing of bad poetry. Anyway, finally I cracked up under it. I was in the hospital a long time.
>
> This does not explain, of course, why, when I got out and came home, after I got well and strong again, still I did not write you. But here, happily for me, and for you, I can save ourselves the cumbersome explaining, by reminding you of a letter of Gerard Hopkins. In this letter he makes apology—I forget to whom; possibly to Robert Bridges, although, somehow, I think not—for having been so slow in answering. And he states—not in these words at all, but this is the meaning of it—: that the driving of himself by himself to make the beginning of a letter, is almost more than his strength can support. When once he has forced himself to begin the letter, he says, the going is not so bad. Well, I, too, suffer from that disease. For it is a disease. It is as real, and its outlines are quite as clear, as in a case of claustrophobia, or agoraphobia. I have named it, just in order to comfort myself, and to dignify this pitiful horror with a name, epistolaphobia. I say, "I, too, suffer from that disease." But I think I have it very much worse than he had. For after all, he did write many letters. And I don't. It is sheer desperation and pure panic—lest, through my continued silence, I lose your friendship, which I prize—that whips me to the typewriter now. I don't know where you are. But I think, and I think it often, "Wherever he is, there he still is, and perhaps

some day I shall see him again, and we shall talk about poetry, as we used to do."

I have just finished learning by heart Matthew Arnold's *Scholar Gypsy*,—such a lovely poem. I had wanted for years to know it by heart, but it had always looked a bit long to me. It is not at all difficult, however, to learn by heart, stanza by stanza; it is so reasonable. I have also learned by heart *The Eve of St. Agnes* and *Lamia*. *Lamia*, let me tell you, is a very long poem. And Keats, in both these poems, makes it as tricky as possible for you, by shifting all the time from "thou" to "you," and by whisking you suddenly from the past tense into the present tense. To get these passages into your memory, and exact, is really quite a chore. I have learned by heart, of Shelley, not only *To the West Wind*—and surely the second stanza of that poem is as fine a thing as ever was written in English—but also the *Hymn to Intellectual Beauty*—a devil to learn by heart. Anyway, I have them all now. And what evil thing can ever again even brush me with its wings?

With love, as ever,
Edna

. . . I am sending you, here—enclosed, three new poems of my own.* I hope, of course I hope very much, that you will like them. But don't—oh, for God's sake, don't for one moment—feel that you must write me something about them, or, indeed, in any way acknowledge this letter at all. I would not put so great a burden upon the shoulders and upon the brain of the person that in all the world I hated the most. I do not need your answer. I am happy enough as it is. For I have at last, after two years of recurring spiritual torment, been able to flog myself into writing a very simple letter to a dear and trusted friend.

E.

I forgot to tell you, even though I was speaking of Father Hopkins, that I have also learned by heart at least one third of his published poetry. Have you ever tried to learn him by heart?—It is great fun, very exciting, difficult.

In the August of 1948, I was attending the Berkshire Music Festival and, discovering that Austerlitz was not far away, I called up the Boissevains and went over with my wife to see them. I had not seen them for nineteen years, and when I had

*These were *Ragged Island*, *To a Snake* and a sonnet beginning *Tranquillity at length, when Autumn comes* . . . , which have since appeared in periodicals, but have not yet been collected in a book.

inquired about them of such friends of theirs as I happened to meet, they had not seemed to know much about them either. As we drove through the long tunnel of greenery that led to the Steepletop house, I felt, as I had not done before, that Edna had been buried out there. Gene Boissevain came out in his working-clothes. He shuffled in his leather moccasins, he had aged: he was graying and stooped. It seemed to me that he was low in morale. "I'll go and get my child," he said. I did not realize at first that this meant Edna. I found in the living room most of the things that had been there in 1929: the scaring Ethiopian Sappho, the golden birds on the "Tree of Life." But the birds were paler, their background was gray; the couches looked badly worn; the whole place seemed shabby and dim. I had the feeling that it was so long ago that they had set up keeping house together that they had ceased to notice the room, that they never did anything to freshen it up. One saw, standing outside the window, three rusty old tin oil-barrels, on which Edna could put food for birds without having it stolen by the squirrels. In one corner, a litter of copy-books covered table, couch, chair and floor.

In a few minutes, Edna came in, wearing slacks and a white working shirt, open at the neck. It was a moment before I recognized her. She had so changed in the nineteen years that, if I had met her unexpectedly somewhere, I am sure I should not have known her. She had become somewhat heavy and dumpy, and her cheeks were a little florid. Her eyes had a bird-lidded look that I recognized as typically Irish, and I noticed for the first time a certain resemblance to her mother. She was terribly nervous; her hands shook; there was a look of fright in her bright green eyes. Eugen brought us martinis. Very quietly he watched her and managed her. At moments he would baby her in a way that I had not seen him use before but that had evidently become habitual, when she showed signs of bursting into tears over not being able to find a poem or something of the kind. My wife said afterwards that Gene gave the impression of shaking me at her as if I had been a new toy with which he hoped to divert her. She said that she had been writing in the last two months and was very much excited about it, because, for two years before that, she had not been able to work. She talked about her wartime poetry as an error that she frankly confessed to. She knew that she had deserved the reviews she got, but had been hurt by them, nevertheless. She said that she had been dismayed when this handful of political verses—under the title *Make Bright the Arrows*—had been issued in the same format as her other books, as if she meant it to stand beside them, for she had intended a paperbound pamphlet that could circulate quickly and be thrown away. I was confirmed in my supposition that these poems had been inspired by loyalty to Eugen, when he talked about his family in Holland. One of his cousins had been tortured and killed; others had had hairbreadth escapes. Edna now constantly sent them packages. She always spoke of "our relatives," and one could see that she was very much attached to them. She had visited them in Holland and had even learned the language. My wife knows Holland and understands Dutch, and Edna, for her benefit, produced and read a poem she had written in Dutch. She showed us a good deal of her poetry, much of it in an unfinished state. It was of an almost unrelieved blackness. I could see that she was just emerging from some terrible eclipse of the spirit. I had difficulty in adjusting myself to Edna in her present phase. There was something more distressing than the old anxiety that she had shown before in discussing her verse: a pressure that she now put upon you for assurance, approval, praise, and, even in those moments when she sounded like a good-natured healthily laughing elderly woman, this, too, was a person I did not know, and these moments, as it were interpolated, seemed to leave her more nervous still. But the nervousness wore off with the drinks, as did my feeling of strangeness about her. This was, after all, the girl, the great poet, I knew, groping back *in luminis oras* from the night of the underworld. She had tackled Catullus's bitter poem, *Si qua recordanti benefacta priora voluptas* . . . ; and I could see that the last lines,

> Ipse valere, opto et taetrum hunc deponere morbum.
> O di, reddite mi hoc pro pietate mea!

had for her a special and desperate meaning. She was afraid that the translation she had sketched would not do the poem justice; and she told us that, when she had sat on the judges' committee for the Guggenheim fellowships, she had not been able to bring herself to vote for Horace Gregory, in spite of his list of distinguished supporters, on account of the badness of his translations of Catullus. But she had had some misgivings since—wasn't it better, perhaps, that the Latinless public should be able to get Catullus, even in an imperfect version? Eugen pulled her up: "Remember," he said, "that was the kind of thing you thought about your war poetry—that it was important to rouse the country." I thought this was very shrewd of him. We talked about John Bishop's poetry, of which I had sent her the collected volume, brought out after his death. She said that his poems had "more overtones" than those of any other contemporary poet: "It's like a row of poplars on a river, with another row reflected in the river." I told her how impossible it had been for me, though John had talked about his illness, to realize that the gloom of his poetry had a real and serious cause or to guess that it announced the approach of death. "Yes: he was despairing," she said.

I was reminded of the little Esthonian folk-song that I had loved so when she sang it in Truro, and I asked her about the anthology in which it had appeared. She didn't know where to find it, but, after reflecting a moment, she was able to recover the song, with its sweet little plaintive tune and her own bittersweet words. I inquired about the original version of the *Epitaph for the Race of Man*—I had been surprised by its coming out in such a different form from that of the version I had heard in 1920; and she told me that she had lost her first draft, of which she could now recall only scraps. Wanting Elena to hear her read, I asked her to recite *The Poet and His Book*. As she did so, the room became so charged with emotion that I began to find it difficult to bear. I could not weep, I did not want her to weep, and, though Elena thought we ought to have stayed, I soon insisted on leaving.

I told myself that Edna was even more fatiguing than she had been in her younger days, and I reasserted my middle-aged indifference. It was too much for me, at fifty-three, to go back to that old state of mind, so demandingly, imprisoningly personal. The whole thing was like one of those dreams that I had never quite ceased to have, in which I found myself with Edna again—though in these dreams she had sometimes seemed faded and shrunken, never ruddy and overblown as I saw her now. The gap of the almost two decades was

something that, encountering the real woman, I could not accept or take in. I had found them there, Edna and Eugen, just
as I had left them in 1929, and this latest visit connected itself
with my glimpses of that summer long past, not with anything
that had happened between. It became like the fears and desires, the revived emotions, of sleep; and the changes in her
were like the old images of dreams that come to us exaggerated, distorted, swollen with longing or horror. So she was
still, although now in a different way, almost as disturbing to
me as she had ever been in the twenties, to which she had so
completely belonged—for she could not be a part of my present, and to see her exerted on me a painful pull, as if to drag
me up by the roots, to gouge me out of my present personality and to annihilate all that had made it. My own life was now
organized and grounded, I had children to worry and divert
me; and from my present point of view, besides, it disturbed
me to find Edna and Eugen haunting like deteriorated ghosts
their own comfortable old house in the country. I tried to
imagine their lives. They were evidently very hard-up—a certain income that Gene had from Java had ceased at the time of
the war, and Edna could no longer give readings; they never
seemed to see anyone or go anywhere. When we asked them
to come to Tanglewood—an hour's drive away—and go with
us to one of the concerts, I was astonished to find that Edna,
who loved music so, had no idea at all of what the festival had
become and assumed that the concerts were still held under
canvas as they had not been since the very first years. We could
not persuade her to go. Gene had said that he would ask us to
dinner, but "I'm the only thing in the house—I'm the cook
and bottlewasher and maid,"—so I assumed that he attended
to the house as well as—with little help nowadays—the farm,
and cooked all the meals for Edna. But I could not conceive
what their daily existence, month after month, had been like or
what it would be like in the future. It did not occur to me, as
it had not done in connection with John Bishop, that they
were both very soon to die. What had desolated and frightened
me there was death, to which Eugen was wearily resigned but
against which Edna, when I saw her, with the draughts of her
unfinished Erebean poems, was making her last fierce struggle.

Eugen Boissevain died in the autumn of 1949. I had wondered already, at the time of our visit, what would happen to Edna if he should die first. All I was able to learn about her was that she was still living out at Steepletop. The night of October 20, 1950, I had a long dream about Edna. It began with a kind of revival of the longing I had had for her in the twenties, and she came to me in her old dream-shape, which was so much more familiar to me than that in which I had seen her last; but then it turned into a conversation that was taking place in the present. I was telling her about John Bishop's relations with another contemporary poet, who had sat at his feet and learned from him, then later had become better known than John and treated him, I had thought, rather shabbily. The next evening I heard of her death, which had taken place the day before, apparently very early on the morning of the nineteenth (Mr. Sheean gives the erroneous impression that she died the morning of the twenty-first). She had been living alone in the house and had evidently sat up all night reading the proofs of Rolfe Humphries' translation of the *Aeneid*, which were found in the living room on the floor around the chair in which she worked, with her notes on the table beside it. She must have been going upstairs at dawn and have felt faint and sat down on a step. She had set down on the step just above her a glass of wine she was carrying. A man who came in to do the chores found her there the next afternoon.* My dream was probably prompted by Sartre's book on Baudelaire, which I had been reading that night in bed and which must have led me to Edna by way of the translation of the *Fleurs du Mal* that she and George Dillon had made, which I had recently reread and thought better of than at the time of my review of *Conversation at Midnight*. My dream was partly motivated, no doubt, by my wanting, in my sleep, to have somebody to listen to my literary gossip and somebody from old times to talk to, but partly, I believe, also, by the impulse to console her in this

---

*She had at first, I learn, collapsed, after Eugen's death; then had sent away the friends who had come to be with her and insisted on living at Steepletop alone. Her letters show that, as autumn arrived, she had dreaded the winter there. Her sister writes me that when she came there after Edna's death, she found the house "in perfect and beautiful order: the floors were waxed; furniture polished; couches and chairs newly and brightly recovered."

vicarious way for the neglect that she, too, had been suffering. And I may have had some sort of intuition about what had happened the morning before. I do not mean anything supernatural, but the kind of sympathetic sense of the rhythms of another's life that may sometimes persist in absence, as I had had, in 1944, the feeling that she needed support, at the time of her nervous breakdown.

And she was to speak to me after her death, for the writing of this memoir had a curious sequel. Edna's sister has sent me two letters which Edna had written to me but which I had never seen. The first was dated March 5, 1929, and discussed a novel of mine that I had given her in manuscript. She had not said much about the book the last time I had seen her before she had written, but had promised to send me some notes on it. The letter with these notes had been addressed to a place I had already left and was forwarded to a wrong address, so that it came back to Steepletop when Edna and Gene were abroad and was never sent again. If I had had it, I should have answered it as she asked me to do and might not so completely have lost touch with her for almost twenty years. I thought that she had been offended by a character that was partly derived from her or had so much disliked the book that she had not wanted to write me about it. I now find that she had made careful and copious notes and had good-naturedly undertaken to rewrite in what she thought a more appropriate vein the speeches assigned to the character partly based on herself.

The second letter was an earlier unfinished draught of the one I have given above, which she had written, apparently, the year before and which was in some ways quite different from the one she eventually sent:

. . . I miss you very much. I wish I could see you and talk with you. Not see you just once, and pour out my heart to you, nothing like that. I wish I could see you every once in a while and talk with you, not about war and peace and depressing things like that, but about poetry, which is never depressing, because no matter how many people have done it badly, a few have done it well, and you can't get around that.

Your letter reached me a year ago last summer in Doctors Hospital in New York, where, after years of Painstaking and Pious Prostitution of Poetry to Propaganda, I was relaxing in a complete and handsome nervous breakdown.

("O di, reddite mi hoc pro pietate mea!")

You said in your letter that you liked the recordings of my poems which I had made for Victor. That came at just the right time . . . ; it helped me get well.

I wish I could see you. But if I can't see you, I wish I could write letters. It's too bad you haven't known all this time how much your letter meant to me. That is, if you would have cared, and I think you would have. But I can't write letters. Only when the moon is in perigee and the sun is in at least partial eclipse, can I seem to write a letter. But perhaps you're like that, too. After all, I haven't been hearing from *you* so very often, either, now that I come to think of it.—It's a real sickness, though, and no joking, this dread of writing letters, "Hard for the non-elect to understand," and the fact that one has, infrequently, a lucid interval, makes it no less a mania. Or rather, a phobia: *Epistolaphobia*—quite as real as *agora*, and much more of a nuisance—much more of a public nuisance, anyway.

Did you know that the line I just quoted ("Hard for the non-elect to understand") is from *Lamia?*—I would never have known it, except that I have just finished learning *Lamia* by heart. I am letter-perfect in it now; you can't fault me. It is something of a job, learning *Lamia* by heart; not because it is a long poem, although it is really a rather long poem, nor because Keats is difficult to memorize, for he isn't, except in the few places—and it is astonishing how few those places are, in a poem like *Lamia*—where obviously he could not make up his mind just how to say it, and so you can't make up your mind just how to remember it—but because Keats, like all the other boys then, had such an off-hand inconsequential, irritating way of changing from *thee* to *you* in the flicker of a lid-lash, and of swapping tenses mid-phrase.

> And I neglect the holy rite for thee.
> Even as you list, invite your many guests.
> *Lamia*

> . . . Meantime, across the moors,
> Had come young Porphyro, with heart on fire
> For Madeline; beside the portal doors,
> Buttressed from moonlight stands he, and implores—
> *The Eve of St. Agnes*

. . . The stately music no more breathes,
The myrtle sickened in a thousand wreaths.
Lamia

Nor suffer thy pale forehead to be kissed
By nightshade, ruby grape of Proserpine,
Weave not your rosary of yewberries
Ode to Melancholy

Go, for they call you, shepherd, from the hill,
Go, shepherd, and untie the wattled cotes;
No longer leave thy wistful flock unfed
The Scholar Gypsy

The quotation from Catullus shows that the poem I found her translating in 1948 was already much in her mind. The quotations from Keats at the end illustrate the "swapping" of tenses and the inconsistent use of *thou* and *you*, but they seem, also, to echo her own mood. She has written them all down from memory, with variations on the original punctuation, and in the fourth has unconsciously changed *make* to *weave*.

At the time I was writing this memoir, I happened one day, in the country, at Wellfleet on Cape Cod, where I live, to meet my neighbor from Truro, Phyllis Duganne. We talked about Edna Millay, and she told me of a memory she had of seeing her years ago in Greenwich Village running around the corner of Macdougal Street, flushed and laughing "like a nymph," with her hair swinging. Floyd Dell, also laughing, pursued her. Phyllis said she had always remembered it; and I leave this image here at the end to supplement my firsthand impressions—a glimpse of Edna as the fleeing and challenging Daphne of her *Figs from Thistles* poem—from the time when I did not yet know her, when she had first come from Vassar to the Village.

1961. James Joyce's correspondence with Harriet Weaver, which has been published since this book first appeared, shows that my reference to her on page 619 gives rather an unfair impression. She loyally saw Joyce through not only *Ulysses* but also *Finnegans Wake*.

AXEL'S CASTLE

*A Study in
the Imaginative Literature of 1870–1930*

Dear Christian Gauss:

You will see how these essays have grown out of your lectures of fifteen years ago. But it is not merely on that account that I have felt I owe you a debt in connection with them. It was principally from you that I acquired then my idea of what literary criticism ought to be—a history of man's ideas and imaginings in the setting of the conditions which have shaped them. And though this book is only a very limited and a very incomplete attempt at that sort of history, I have wanted to dedicate it to you in acknowledgment of the kindness and instruction which, beginning when I was at college, have continued ever since, and as a tribute to a master of criticism who has taught much in insisting little.

Yours as ever,

Edmund Wilson.

CONTENTS

I. Symbolism

I T is my purpose in this book to try to trace the origins of certain tendencies in contemporary literature and to show their development in the work of six contemporary writers. To persons already familiar with the field, my explanations in this first chapter will seem rudimentary; but I believe that it is still true in general, for reasons which I shall suggest, that the sources and fundamental principles of many of the books which have excited most discussion during the period since the War are singularly little understood. It is not usually recognized that writers such as W. B. Yeats, James Joyce, T. S. Eliot, Gertrude Stein, Marcel Proust and Paul Valéry represent the culmination of a self-conscious and very important literary movement; and even when we have become aware that these writers have something in common, that they belong to a common school, we are likely to be rather vague as to what its distinguishing features are.

We do, however, to-day as a rule have a pretty clear idea of the issues which were raised by the Romantic Movement of the beginning of the nineteenth century. We still debate Classicism and Romanticism, and when we attempt to deal with contemporary literary problems, we often tend to discuss them in those terms. Yet the movement of which in our own day we are witnessing the mature development is not merely a degeneration or an elaboration of Romanticism, but rather a counterpart to it, a second flood of the same tide. And even the metaphor of a tide is misleading: what we have to-day is an entirely distinct movement, which has arisen from different conditions and must be dealt with in different terms.

Romanticism, as everyone has heard, was a revolt of the individual. The "Classicism" against which it was a reaction meant, in the domain of politics and morals, a preoccupation with society as a whole; and, in art, an ideal of objectivity. In "Le Misanthrope," in "Bérénice," in "The Way of the World," in "Gulliver's Travels," the artist is out of the picture: he would consider it artistic bad taste to identify his hero with himself and to glorify himself with his hero, or to intrude between the reader and the story and give vent to his personal emotions. But in "René," in "Rolla," in "Childe Harold," in "The Prelude," the writer is either his own hero, or unmistakably identified with his hero, and the personality and emotions of the writer are presented as the principal subject of interest. Racine, Molière, Congreve and Swift ask us to be interested in what they have made; but Chateaubriand, Musset, Byron and Wordsworth ask us to be interested in themselves. And they ask us to be interested in themselves by virtue of the intrinsic value of the individual: they vindicate the rights of the individual against the claims of society as a whole—against government, morals, conventions, academy or church. The Romantic is nearly always a rebel.

In this connection, it is illuminating to consider the explanation of the Romantic Movement given by A. N. Whitehead in his "Science and the Modern World." The Romantic Movement, Whitehead says, was really a reaction against scientific ideas, or rather against the mechanistic ideas to which certain scientific discoveries gave rise. The seventeenth and eighteenth centuries were in Europe the great period of the development of mathematical and physical theory; and in the literature of the so-called Classical period, Descartes and Newton were influences as important as those of the classics themselves. The poets, like the astronomers and mathematicians, had come to regard the universe as a machine, obeying logical laws and susceptible of reasonable explanation: God figured merely as the clockmaker who must have existed to make the clock. People applied this conception also to society, which, from the point of view of Louis XIV and of the American Constitution alike, had the character of a planetary system or a well-regulated machine; and they examined human nature dispassionately, in the same lucid and reasonable spirit, to find the principles on which it worked. Thus the theorems of the physicist were matched by the geometrical plays of Racine and the balanced couplets of Pope.

But this conception of a fixed mechanical order came eventually to be felt as a constraint: it excluded too much of life— or rather, the description it supplied did not correspond to actual experience. The Romantics had become acutely conscious of aspects of their experience which it was impossible to analyze or explain on the theory of a world run by clockwork. The universe was not a machine, after all, but something more mysterious and less rational.

> "The atoms of Democritus,
>   And Newton's particles of light
> Are sands upon the Red Sea shore,
>   Where Israel's tents do shine so bright!"

Blake had already contradicted contemptuously the physical theory of the eighteenth century. And to Wordsworth, the countryside of his boyhood meant neither agriculture nor neo-classic idylls, but a light never seen on land or sea. When the poet looked into his own soul, he beheld something which did not seem to him reducible to a set of principles of human nature such, for example, as La Rochefoucauld's "Maxims": he saw fantasy, conflict, confusion. And he either set himself, like Wordsworth and Blake, to affirm the superior truth of this vision as compared to the mechanical universe of the physicists; or, accepting this mechanical universe, like Byron or Alfred de Vigny, as external to and indifferent to man, he pitted against it, in defiance, his own turbulent insubordinate soul.

In any case, it is always, as in Wordsworth, the individual sensibility, or, as in Byron, the individual will, with which the Romantic poet is preoccupied; and he has invented a new language for the expression of its mystery, its conflict and confusion. The arena of literature has been transferred from the universe conceived as a machine, from society conceived as an organization, to the individual soul.

What has really taken place, says Whitehead, is a philosophical revolution. The scientists of the seventeenth century who presented the universe as a mechanism had caused people to draw the conclusion that man was something apart from nature, something introduced into the universe from outside and remaining alien to all that he found. But a Romantic poet like Wordsworth has come to feel the falsity of this assumption: he has perceived that the world is an organism, that nature includes planets, mountains, vegetation and people alike, that what we are and what we see, what we hear, what we feel and what we smell, are inextricably related, that all are involved in the same great entity. Those who make fun of the

Romantics are mistaken in supposing that there is no intimate connection between the landscape and the poet's emotions. There is no real dualism, says Whitehead, between external lakes and hills, on the one hand, and personal feelings, on the other: human feelings and inanimate objects are interdependent and developing together in some fashion of which our traditional notions of laws of cause and effect, of dualities of mind and matter or of body and soul, can give us no true idea. The Romantic poet, then, with his turbid or opalescent language, his sympathies and passions which cause him to seem to merge with his surroundings, is the prophet of a new insight into nature: he is describing things as they really are; and a revolution in the imagery of poetry is in reality a revolution in metaphysics.

Whitehead drops the story at this point; but he has provided the key to what follows. In the middle of the nineteenth century, science made new advances, and mechanistic ideas were brought back into fashion again. But they came this time from a different quarter—not from physics and mathematics, but from biology. It was the effect of the theory of Evolution to reduce man from the heroic stature to which the Romantics had tried to exalt him, to the semblance of a helpless animal, again very small in the universe and at the mercy of the forces about him. Humanity was the accidental product of heredity and environment, and capable of being explained in terms of these. This doctrine in literature was called Naturalism, and it was put into practice by novelists like Zola, who believed that composing a novel was like performing a laboratory experiment: you had only to supply your characters with a specific environment and heredity and then watch their automatic reactions; and by historians and critics like Taine, who asserted that virtue and vice were as much the products of automatic processes as alkalis and acids, and who attempted to account for masterpieces by studying the geographical and climatic conditions of the countries in which they had been produced.

Not, however, that the movement known as Naturalism arose directly from "The Origin of Species." There had already set in, about the middle of the century, quite independent of the theory of Evolution, a reaction against the sentimentality and the looseness of Romanticism, and in the direction of the objectivity and the severity of Classicism again; and this reaction had already been characterized by a kind of scientific observation which closely corresponded to that of biological science. This reaction is seen most clearly in France. The Parnassian group of poets, who made their first appearance in the fifties—Gautier, Leconte de Lisle, Hérédia—seemed to have taken it for their aim merely to picture historical incidents and natural phenomena as objectively and accurately as possible in impassive perfect verse. Leconte de Lisle's elephants crossing the desert is a celebrated example: the elephants appear and disappear with a certain classical dignity and grandeur, and the poet leaves it at that.

It is less easy, in English poetry, to give clear examples of the reaction toward Naturalism: the English did not, after the Romantic Movement, take much interest in literary methods till toward the end of the nineteenth century. But the tendency toward what we call realism had set in, none the less: Browning, though he had, of course, nothing of the classical form of the Parnassians, was addicted to historical reconstruction of a kind more pedantic and less flamboyant than that of the true Romantics, and when he dealt with contemporary life, did so at least as realistically as any of the Victorian novelists—themselves going in Zola's direction without quite being aware of the fact. And we can see very plainly in Tennyson, who was much preoccupied with the doctrines of Evolution, something of the same exactitude of description combined with something of the same severity of verse—though with less hardness and more grace—that we find in the French poets.

> "Nor wilt thou snare him in the white ravine,
> Nor find him dropt upon the firths of ice,
> That huddling slant in furrow-cloven fells
> To roll the torrent out of dusky doors:
> But follow; let the torrent dance thee down
> To find him in the valley; let the wild
> Lean-headed eagles yelp alone."

And it is interesting to compare Tennyson, in this connection, with Pope on the rare occasions (though not so rare as people sometimes suppose) when he is describing natural objects:

> "The silver eel, in shining volumes roll'd,
> The yellow carp, in scales bedropp'd with gold."

These lines have the technical perfection and the precise observation of Tennyson, but they are heavier and more metallic. Pope is often, as a matter of fact, very close to the French Parnassians. The latter represent, in reality, a second classical-scientific movement, the counterpart to that represented by Pope.

But the highest developments of Naturalism took place, not in poetry, but in prose. The plays of Ibsen and the novels of Flaubert are the masterpieces of this second period of modern classicism, as Racine and Swift are of the first. The art of Flaubert and Ibsen is again, like the art of the seventeenth-century writers, scrupulously non-personal and objective, and it insists upon precision of language and economy of form. Compare the lucidity, the logic and the limited number of characters of such a tragedy of Ibsen's as "Rosmersholm" with the rigorous conventions of Racine; or compare "Gulliver's Travels" with "Bouvard et Pécuchet" or "L'Education Sentimentale." Yet, though the earlier works resemble the later ones in many obvious ways, they differ from them in this: where a seventeenth-century moralist like La Rochefoucauld would have sought to discover and set forth the universal principles of human behavior, a nineteenth-century writer like Ibsen or Flaubert has begun to study man in relation to his particular environment and time. The method of approach in both cases, however, may be described as "scientific," and it tends to lead us to mechanistic conclusions.

Now Flaubert and Ibsen both had been suckled on Romanticism. Flaubert had begun by writing a Romantic "Saint-Antoine" before he chastened it and cut it down to the more sober one which he published; and Ibsen had written in verse his Faustian "Brand" and "Peer Gynt" before he arrived at his realistic plays in prose. Each, beginning in Romanticism, had evolved for himself a new discipline and developed a new point of view. For "Madame Bovary" is not merely arranged and written differently from a novel by Victor Hugo: it also constitutes an objective criticism of a case of Romantic personality; and Ibsen was occupied all his life with situations produced by the conflict of the essentially Romantic conception of one's duty to one's own personality with the conception of one's duty to society.

But in the later prose plays of Ibsen, the trolls and ghosts of his early dramatic poems have begun to creep back into the bourgeois drawing-rooms: the Naturalist has been finally compelled to make cracks in his own mold. All that vaporous, confused and grandiose world of Romanticism had been resolutely ordered and compressed; but now the objective point of view of Naturalism, the machine-like technique which went with it, begin to cramp the poet's imagination, to prove inadequate to convey what he feels. The reader begins to chafe at the strain, and the artist begins to betray it. Huysmans described Leconte de Lisle as "the sonorous hardware man": we remember Wordsworth's strictures on Pope. Literature is rebounding again from the scientific-classical pole to the poetic-romantic one. And this second reaction at the end of the century, this counterpart to the Romantic reaction of the end of the century before, was known in France as Symbolism.

Now in attempting to write literary history, one must guard against giving the impression that these movements and counter-movements necessarily follow one another in a punctual and well-generalled fashion—as if eighteenth-century reason had been cleanly put to rout by nineteenth-century Romanticism, which then proceeded to hold the field till it was laid by the heels by Naturalism, and as if Mallarmé and Rimbaud had then blown up Naturalism with bombs. What really happens, of course, is that one set of methods and ideas is not completely superseded by another; but that, on the contrary, it thrives in its teeth—so that, on the one hand, Flaubert's prose has learned to hear, see and feel with the delicate senses of Romanticism at the same time that Flaubert is disciplining and criticizing the Romantic temperament; and so that, on the other hand, certain members of a school, unaffected by new influences abroad, will continue to practise its methods and to exploit its possibilities further and further, when nearly everybody else has abandoned it.

I have here purposely been selecting writers who seemed to represent some tendency or school in its purest or most highly developed form. We must, however, now consider some

Romantics who, in certain ways, carried Romanticism further than even Chateaubriand or Musset, or than Wordsworth or Byron, and who became the first precursors of Symbolism and were afterwards placed among its saints.

One of these was the French writer who called himself Gérard de Nerval. Gérard de Nerval suffered from spells of insanity; and, partly no doubt as a result of this, habitually confused his own fancies and feelings with external reality. He believed, even in his lucid periods—and no doubt Whitehead would approve his metaphysics—that the world which we see about us is involved in some more intimate fashion than is ordinarily supposed with the things that go on in our minds, that even our dreams and hallucinations are somehow bound up with reality. And in one of his sonnets he outdoes Wordsworth, with his "Presences of Nature in the sky" and his "Souls of lonely places," by imagining shuttered eyes coming to life in the very walls and "a pure spirit under the bark of stones."

But a more important prophet of Symbolism was Edgar Allan Poe. It was in general true that, by the middle of the century, the Romantic writers in the United States—Poe, Hawthorne, Melville, Whitman and even Emerson—were, for reasons which it would be interesting to determine, developing in the direction of Symbolism; and one of the events of prime importance in the early history of the Symbolist Movement was the discovery of Poe by Baudelaire. When Baudelaire, a late Romantic, first read Poe in 1847, he "experienced a strange commotion." When he began to look up Poe's writings in the files of American magazines, he found among them stories and poems which he said that he himself had already "thought vaguely and confusedly" of writing, and his interest became a veritable passion. In 1852, Baudelaire published a volume of translations of Poe's tales; and from then on the influence of Poe played an important part in French literature. Poe's critical writings provided the first scriptures of the Symbolist Movement, for he had formulated what amounted to a new literary programme which corrected the Romantic looseness and lopped away the Romantic extravagance, at the same time that it aimed, not at Naturalistic, but at ultra-Romantic effects. There was, of course, a good deal in common between Poe's poetry and such Romantic poetry as Coleridge's "Kubla Khan," as there was between his poems in prose and such Romantic prose as that of De Quincey. But Poe, by insisting on and specially cultivating certain aspects of Romanticism, helped to transform it into something different. "I *know*," we find Poe writing, for example, "that indefiniteness is an element of the true music [of poetry]—I mean of the true musical expression . . . a suggestive indefiniteness of vague and therefore of spiritual *effect*." And to approximate the indefiniteness of music was to become one of the principal aims of Symbolism.

This effect of indefiniteness was produced not merely by the confusion I have mentioned between the imaginary world and the real; but also by means of a further confusion between the perceptions of the different senses.

"Comme de longs échos qui de loin se confondent . . .
    Les parfums, les couleurs et les sons se répondent,"

wrote Baudelaire. And we find Poe, in one of his poems, *hearing* the approach of the darkness, or writing such a description as the following of the sensations which follow death: "Night arrived; and with its shadows a heavy discomfort. It oppressed my limbs with the oppression of some dull weight, and was palpable. There was also a moaning sound, not unlike the distant reverberation of surf, but more continuous, which beginning with the first twilight, had grown in strength with the darkness. Suddenly lights were brought into the room . . . and issuing from the flame of each lamp, there flowed unbrokenly into my ears a strain of melodious monotone."

This notation of super-rational sensations was a novelty in the forties of the last century—as was the dreamlike irrational musical poetry of "Annabel Lee" and "Ulalume"; and they helped to effect a revolution in France. For an English-speaking reader of to-day, Poe's influence may be hard to understand; and even when such a reader comes to examine the productions of French Symbolism, it may surprise him that they should have caused amazement. The medley of images; the deliberately mixed metaphors; the combination of passion and wit—of the grand and the prosaic manners; the bold amalgamation of material with spiritual—all these may seem to him quite proper and familiar. He has always known them in the English poetry of the sixteenth and seventeenth centuries—Shakespeare and the other Elizabethans did all these things without theorizing about them. Is this not the natural language of poetry? Is it not the norm against which, in English literature, the eighteenth century was a heresy and to which the Romantics did their best to return?

But we must remember that the development of French poetry has been quite different from that of English. Michelet says that in the sixteenth century the future of French literature had hung in the balance between Rabelais and Ronsard, and he regrets that it was Ronsard who triumphed. For Rabelais in France was a sort of equivalent to our own Elizabethans, whereas Ronsard, who represented to Michelet all that was poorest, dryest and most conventional in the French genius, was one of the fathers of that classical tradition of lucidity, sobriety and purity which culminated in Molière and Racine. In comparison with the Classicism of the French, which has dominated their whole literature since the Renaissance, the English Classicism of the eighteenth century, the age of Dr. Johnson and Pope, was a brief ineffective deviation. And from the point of view of English readers, the most daring innovations of the Romantic revolution in France, in spite of all the excitement which accompanied them, must appear of an astonishingly moderate character. But the age and the rigor of the tradition were the measure of the difficulty of breaking out of it. After all, Coleridge, Shelley and Keats—in spite of Pope and Dr. Johnson—had only to look back to Milton and Shakespeare, whose dense forests had all along been in view beyond the formal eighteenth-century gardens. But to an eighteenth-century Frenchman like Voltaire, Shakespeare was incomprehensible; and to the Frenchman of the classical tradition of the beginning of the nineteenth century, the rhetoric of Hugo was a scandal: the French were not used to such rich colors or to so free a vocabulary; moreover, the Romantics broke metrical rules far stricter than any we have had in English. Yet Victor Hugo was still very far from the variety and freedom of Shakespeare. It is enlightening to compare Shelley's lyric which begins, "O World! O Life! O Time!" with the poem of Alfred de Musset's which begins, "J'ai perdu ma force et ma vie." These two lyrics are in some ways curiously similar: each is the breath of a Romantic sigh over the passing of the pride of youth. Yet the French poet, even in his wistfulness, makes epi-grammatic points: his language is always logical and precise; whereas the English poet is vague and gives us images unre-lated by logic. And it will not be till the advent of the Symbol-ists that French poetry will really become capable of the fantasy and fluidity of English.

The Symbolist Movement broke those rules of French met-rics which the Romantics had left intact, and it finally suc-ceeded in throwing overboard completely the clarity and logic of the French classical tradition, which the Romantics had still to a great extent respected. It was nourished from many alien sources—German, Flemish, modern Greek—and especially, precisely, from English. Verlaine had lived in England, and knew English well; Mallarmé was a professor of English; and Baudelaire, as I have said, had provided the movement with its first programmes by translating the essays of Poe. Two of the Symbolist poets, Stuart Merrill and Francis Vielé-Griffin, were Americans who lived in Paris and wrote French; and an Amer-ican, reading to-day the latter's "Chevauchée d'Yeldis," for ex-ample, may wonder how, when Symbolism was new, such a poem could ever have been regarded as one of the movement's acknowledged masterpieces: to us, it seems merely agreeable, not in the least revolutionary or novel, but like something which might not impossibly have been written by Thomas Bailey Aldrich if he had been influenced by Browning. We are surprised to learn that Vielé-Griffin is still considered an im-portant poet. But the point was that he had performed a feat which astonished and impressed the French and of which it is probable that no Frenchman was capable: he had succeeded in wrecking once for all the classical Alexandrine, hitherto the ba-sis of French poetry—or rather, as an English reader at once recognizes, he had dispensed with it altogether and begun writing English metres in French. The French called this "*vers libre*," but it is "free" only in the sense of being irregular, like many poems of Matthew Arnold and Browning.

What made Poe particularly acceptable to the French, how-ever, was what had distinguished him from most of the other Romantics of the English-speaking countries: his interest in æsthetic theory. The French have always reasoned about litera-ture far more than the English have; they always want to know what they are doing and why they are doing it: their literary criticism has acted as a constant interpreter and guide to the rest of their literature. And it was in France that Poe's literary theory, to which no one seems to have paid much attention elsewhere, was first studied and elucidated. So that, though the effects and devices of Symbolism were of a kind that was familiar in English, and though the Symbolists were sometimes indebted to English literature directly—the Symbolist Movement itself, by reason of its origin in France, had a deliberate self-conscious æsthetic which made it different from anything in English. One must go back to Coleridge to find in English a figure comparable to the Symbolist leader, Stéphane Mallarmé. Paul Valéry says of Mallarmé that, as he was the greatest French poet of his time, he could also have been one of the most popular. But Mallarmé was an unpopular poet: he taught English for a living, and wrote little and published less. Yet, ridiculed and denounced by the public, who reiterated that his poetry was nonsense and yet were irritated by his seriousness and obstinacy, he exercised, from his little Paris apartment, where he held Tuesday receptions, an influence curiously far-reaching over the young writers—English and French alike—of the end of the century. There in the sitting-room which was also the dining-room on the fourth floor in the Rue de Rome, where the whistle of locomotives came in through the windows to mingle with the literary conversation, Mallarmé, with his shining pensive gaze from under his long lashes and always smoking a cigarette "to put some smoke," as he used to say, "between the world and himself," would talk about the theory of poetry in a "mild, musical and unforgettable voice." There was an atmosphere "calm and almost religious." Mallarmé had "the pride of the inner life," said one of his friends; his nature was "patient, disdainful and imperiously gentle." He always reflected before he spoke and always put what he said in the form of a question. His wife sat beside him embroidering; his daughter answered the door. Here came Huysmans, Whistler, Degas, Moréas, Laforgue, Vielé-Griffin, Paul Valéry, Henri de Régnier, Pierre Louys, Paul Claudel, Remy de Gourmont, André Gide, Oscar Wilde, Arthur Symons, George Moore and W. B. Yeats. For Mallarmé was a true saint of literature: he had proposed to himself an almost impossible object, and he pursued it without compromise or distraction. His whole life was dedicated to the effort to do something with the language of poetry which had never been done before. "Donner un sens plus pur," he had written in a sonnet on Poe, "aux mots de la tribu." He was, as Albert Thibaudet has said, engaged in "a disinterested experiment on the confines of poetry, at a limit where other lungs would find the air unbreathable."

What, then, was this purer sense which Mallarmé believed he was following Poe in wishing to give to the words of the tribe? What, precisely, was the nature of this experiment on the confines of poetry which Mallarmé found so absorbing and which so many other writers tried to repeat? What, precisely, did the Symbolists propose? I have called attention, in speaking of Poe, to the confusion between the perceptions of the different senses, and to the attempt to make the effects of poetry approximate to those of music. And I should add, in this latter connection, that the influence on Symbolist poetry of Wagner was as important as that of any poet: at the time when Romantic music had come closest to literature, literature was attracted toward music. I have also spoken, in connection with Gérard de Nerval, of the confusion between the imaginary and the real, between our sensations and fancies, on the one hand, and what we actually do and see, on the other. It was the tendency of Symbolism—that second swing of the pendulum away from a mechanistic view of nature and from a social conception of man—to make poetry even more a matter of the sensations and emotions of the individual than had been the case with Romanticism: Symbolism, indeed, sometimes had the result of making poetry so much a private concern of the poet's that it turned out to be incommunicable to the reader. The peculiar subtlety and difficulty of Symbolism is indicated by the name itself. This name has often been complained of as being inadequate for the movement to which it was given and inappropriate to certain of its aspects; and it may prove misleading to English readers. For the symbols of Symbolism have to be defined a little differently from symbols in the ordinary sense—the sense in which the Cross is the symbol of Christianity or the Stars and Stripes the symbol of the United States. This symbolism differs even from such symbolism as Dante's. For the familiar kind of symbolism is conventional and fixed; the symbolism of the Divine Comedy is conventional, logical and definite. But the symbols of the Symbolist school are usually chosen arbitrarily by the poet to stand for special ideas of his own—they are a sort of disguise for these ideas. "The Parnassians, for their part," wrote Mallarmé, "take the thing just as it is and put it before us—and consequently they are deficient in mystery: they deprive the mind of the delicious joy of believing that it is creating. To name an object is to do away with the three-quarters of the enjoyment of the poem which is derived from the satisfaction of guessing little by little: to suggest it, to evoke it—that is what charms the imagination."

To intimate things rather than state them plainly was thus one of the primary aims of the Symbolists. But there was more involved in their point of view than Mallarmé here explains. The assumptions which underlay Symbolism lead us to formulate some such doctrine as the following: Every feeling or sensation we have, every moment of consciousness, is different from every other; and it is, in consequence, impossible to render our sensations as we actually experience them through the conventional and universal language of ordinary literature. Each poet has his unique personality; each of his moments has its special tone, its special combination of elements. And it is the poet's task to find, to invent, the special language which will alone be capable of expressing his personality and feelings. Such a language must make use of symbols: what is so special, so fleeting and so vague cannot be conveyed by direct statement or description, but only by a succession of words, of images, which will serve to suggest it to the reader. The Symbolists themselves, full of the idea of producing with poetry effects like those of music, tended to think of these images as possessing an abstract value like musical notes and chords. But the words of our speech are not musical notation, and what the symbols of Symbolism really were, were metaphors detached from their subjects—for one cannot, beyond a certain point, in poetry, merely enjoy color and sound for their own sake: one has to guess what the images are being applied to. And Symbolism may be defined as an attempt by carefully studied means—a complicated association of ideas represented by a medley of metaphors—to communicate unique personal feelings.

The Symbolist Movement proper was first largely confined to France and principally limited to poetry of rather an esoteric kind; but it was destined, as time went on, to spread to the whole western world and its principles to be applied on a scale which the most enthusiastic of its founders could scarcely have foreseen. Remy de Gourmont, who was eventually to become the most distinguished critical champion of the movement, tells of his excitement, one afternoon in the eighties, at discovering the new poetry in a little magazine which he had picked up at a book-stall in the Odéon: "As I looked through it, I experienced the little æsthetic thrill and that exquisite impression of novelty which has so much charm for youth. I seem to myself to have been dreaming rather than reading. The Luxembourg was pink with early April: I crossed it toward the Rue d'Assas, thinking a great deal more about the new literature which was coinciding for me that day with the renewal of the world than about the business which had brought me to that part of Paris. All that I had written up to that time inspired me with profound disgust. . . . In less than an hour my literary orientation was radically modified." And Yeats wrote in 1897: "The reaction against the rationalism of the eighteenth century has mingled with a reaction against the materialism of the nineteenth century, and the symbolical movement, which has come to perfection in Germany in Wagner, in England in the Pre-Raphaelites, and in France in Villiers de L'Isle-Adam and Mallarmé and Maeterlinck, and has stirred the imagination of Ibsen and D'Annunzio, is certainly the only movement that is saying new things."

We do not talk about symbolism to-day in dealing with English literature; we do not even, as Yeats did at the end of the last century, think of the writers whom he mentions as all belonging to a "symbolical movement"; yet the influence of Mallarmé and his fellow poets was felt widely and deeply outside of France, and it is difficult to understand certain of the things which have been happening lately in English literature without some knowledge of the Symbolist school. I believe, in fact, that if English and American criticism have sometimes shown themselves at a loss when confronted with the work of certain recent writers, it is partly because the work of these writers is the result of a literary revolution which occurred

outside English literature. The case of the Romantic Movement was different: Wordsworth's prefaces were English manifestoes; Lockhart's attack on Keats and Byron's attack on
Jeffrey were blows struck in an English civil war. But in spite of
the Pre-Raphaelites, who were launched by an impulse somewhat similar to that of the Symbolists, and in spite of the English "æsthetics" and "decadents," who for the most part
imitated the French without very much originality, the battle
of Symbolism has never properly been fought out in English.
So that whereas French writers like Valéry and Proust who
have grown out of the Symbolist Movement, are well understood and appreciated by French literary criticism, the critics
of the English-speaking countries have often seemed not to
know how to deal with writers such as Eliot and Joyce. Even
when these writers have brought back into English qualities
which are natural to it and resources which it originally possessed, these elements have returned by way of France and have
taken on the complexion of the French mind—critical, philosophical, much occupied with æsthetic theory and tending
always to aim self-consciously at particular effects and to study
scrupulously appropriate means.

It has perhaps been peculiarly easy for certain of the leaders
of contemporary English literature—that is, of the literature
since the War—to profit by the example of Paris, because they
have themselves not been English. Of the writers in English I
shall discuss in this book, Yeats is an Irishman who turns
almost as easily toward Paris as toward London; Joyce an Irishman who has done most of his work on the Continent and
who has scarcely lived in England at all; and T. S. Eliot and
Gertrude Stein are Americans living abroad. The work of these
writers has been largely a continuance or extension of Symbolism. Yeats, the ablest of the *fin de siècle* group who tried in
London to emulate the French, managed to make Symbolism
flourish triumphantly by transplanting it to the more favorable
soil of Ireland. T. S. Eliot in his earliest poems seems to have
been as susceptible to the influence of the Symbolists as to that
of the English Elizabethans. Joyce, a master of Naturalism as
great as Flaubert, has at the same time succeeded in dramatizing Symbolism by making use of its methods for differentiating between his various characters and their varying states of

mind. And Gertrude Stein has carried Mallarmé's principles so far in the direction of that limit where other lungs find the air unbreathable as perhaps finally to reduce them to absurdity. It is true, however, that under proper conditions, these principles remain valid; and both the strength and the weaknesses characteristic of much of the literature since the War derive naturally from the Symbolist poets and may already be studied in their work. The literary history of our time is to a great extent that of the development of Symbolism and of its fusion or conflict with Naturalism.

II. W. B. Yeats

BORN in Dublin in 1865, William Butler Yeats was the son of an Irish Pre-Raphaelite painter, who had given him, at "fifteen or sixteen," Rossetti and Blake to read. Yeats's earliest verse was Pre-Raphaelite and Romantic: his long poem, "The Wanderings of Oisin" (1889), on a subject from Irish mythology, stains a kind of Shelleyan fluidity with a Keatsian richness of color. But, during the nineties, Yeats met Mallarmé in Paris, and though he knew at that time little French, was instructed in the doctrines of Symbolism by his friend Arthur Symons. "I think," he says, "that Symons's translations from Mallarmé may have given elaborate form to my verses of those years, to the latter poems of 'The Wind among the Reeds,' to 'The Shadowy Waters.'" And we have seen that he wrote of Symbolism as "the only movement that is saying new things."

If we do not ordinarily think of Yeats as primarily a Symbolist poet, it is because, in taking Symbolism to Ireland, he fed it with new resources and gave it a special accent which lead us to think of his poetry from the point of view of its national qualities rather than from the point of view of its relation to the rest of European literature.

It is easy, however, to see how close Yeats is, even in his later years, to the French poetry of the end of the century, in such a comparatively recent poem as "On a Picture of a Black Centaur":

"Your hooves have stamped at the black margin of the wood,
 Even where horrible green parrots call and swing.
 My works are all stamped down into the sultry mud.
 I knew that horse play, knew it for a murderous thing.
 What wholesome sun has ripened is wholesome food to eat
 And that alone; yet I, being driven half insane
 Because of some green wing, gathered old mummy wheat
 In the mad abstract dark and ground it grain by grain
 And after baked it slowly in an oven; but now
 I bring full flavoured wine out of a barrel found
 Where seven Ephesian topers slept and never knew

When Alexander's empire past, they slept so sound.
Stretch out your limbs and sleep a long Saturnian sleep;
I have loved you better than my soul for all my words,
And there is none so fit to keep a watch and keep
Unwearied eyes upon those horrible green birds."

Compare this with a characteristic sonnet of Mallarmé's:

"Le vierge, le vivace et le bel aujourd'hui
Va-t-il nous déchirer avec un coup d'aile ivre
Ce lac dur oublié que hante sous le givre
Le transparent glacier des vols qui n'ont pas fui?

Un cygne d'autrefois se souvient que c'est lui
Magnifique mais qui sans espoir se délivre
Pour n'avoir pas chanté la région où vivre
Quand du stérile hiver a resplendi l'ennui.

Tout son col secouera cette blanche agonie
Par l'espace infligée à l'oiseau qui le nïe,
Mais non l'horreur du sol où le plumage est pris.

Fantôme qu'à ce lieu son pur éclat assigne,
Il s'immobilise au songe froid de mépris
Que vêt parmi l'exil inutile le Cygne."

The centaur, the parrots, the wheat and the wine are, like the
swan, the lake and the frost, not real things (except that the
centaur is something Yeats has seen in a picture), but merely
accidental images which, by an association of ideas, have come
to stand for the poet's emotion. But where the French poets
were obliged to depend almost exclusively upon such symbols,
which tended to become more bewildering as they became
more heterogeneous, Yeats found in Irish mythology, unfamiliar even to Irish readers, and in itself rather cloudy and vague,
a treasury of symbols ready to his hand. He had thus perhaps a
special advantage. The Danaan children, the Shadowy Horses
and Fergus with his brazen cars—those mysterious and magical beings who play so large a part in Yeats's verse—have little
more objective reality than the images of Mallarmé: they are
the elements and the moods of Yeats's complex sensibility. But
they have a more satisfactory character than such a French
Symbolist mythology as Mallarmé's—though Mallarmé does

occasionally draw on the Old Testament or the classics for a Salome or a faun—because they constitute a world of which one can to some extent get the hang, where one can at least partly find one's way about.

And, as we follow the progress of Yeats's poetry, this world becomes less dim and iridescent. In "The Wind among the Reeds," which appeared in 1899, we still find "the flaming lute-thronged angelic door" and "the heaven's embroidered cloths —enwrought with golden and silver light" of the earlier Pre-Raphaelite Yeats. But sometime about the beginning of the century, the poet became dissatisfied, he tells us, and set out rigorously to eliminate from his poetry both Romantic rhetoric and Symbolistic mistiness.

The development of Yeats's later style seems to coincide with a disillusionment. The younger Yeats has lived much in fairyland: the heroes of his short stories and poems—Oisin, Red Hanrahan, the Man Who Dreamed of Fairyland—are always deserting the real world for the world of the Sidhe, the fairies. The real world is a sad unsatisfactory place: in one of the very first of Yeats's poems, the fairies warn the child they are stealing away—

> "Come away, O human child!
> To the waters and the wild
> With a faery, hand in hand,
> For the world's more full of weeping than you can
>   understand."

And the mortals who escape to fairyland find eternal love-making and laughter: they dance on twilit lawns to strange music. The Irish fairies of Yeats are not, like the fairies of the ordinary fairy-story, merely smaller human beings like ourselves, possessed of special supernatural powers: they are a different order of beings altogether, existing, as it were, in different dimensions. This strangeness, this real other-worldliness of the fairyland of Yeats's poetry, derives partly, no doubt, it would appear from the fascinating anthology of Irish fairy-tales which Yeats compiled and edited, from Irish folk-lore itself. The Sidhe were the natural creation of the dreaming and mocking Irish mind amid the illusory uncertain lights and mists of the Irish countryside. But Yeats has made of this Irish fairyland something which puts upon us a stronger spell than the spell even of the folk-tales in his anthology. Yeats's fairyland has become a symbol for the imagination itself. The world of the imagination is shown us in Yeats's early poetry as something infinitely delightful, infinitely seductive, as something to which one becomes addicted, with which one becomes delirious and drunken—and as something which is somehow incompatible with, and fatal to, the good life of that actual world which is so full of weeping and from which it is so sweet to withdraw. There is nothing sinister about the Sidhe in themselves: they are non-moral and relieved of mortal cares; for them, there is not even time; and from our human point of view, their fairy point of view is unseizable. But to the mortal who has lived among the fairies, who has lost the sense of human laws in their world, the consequences may be terrible— for he has preferred something else to reality—he has escaped the responsibilities of human life and he must fail of its satisfactions. The Man Who Dreamed of Fairyland, in one of the most beautiful of Yeats's early poems, had

> ". . . stood among a crowd at Drumahair;
> His heart hung all upon a silken dress,
> And he had known at last some tenderness,
> Before Earth made of him her sleepy care;
> But when a man poured fish into a pile,
> It seemed they raised their little silver heads,
> And sang how day a Druid twilight sheds
> Upon a dim, green, well-beloved isle,
> Where people love beside star-laden seas;
> How Time may never mar their faery vows
> Under the woven roofs of quicken boughs:
> The singing shook him out of his new ease.
>
> He wandered by the sands of Lisadill;
> His mind ran all on money cares and fears,
> And he had known at last some prudent years
> Before they heaped his grave under the hill;
> But while he passed before a plashy place,
> A lug-worm with its gray and muddy mouth
> Sang how somewhere to north or west or south,
> There dwelt a gay, exulting, gentle race;

And how beneath those three times blessed skies
A Danaan fruitage makes a shower of moons,
And as it falls awakens leafy tunes:
And at that singing he was no more wise."

And so with all our human needs and passions—the man who
dreamed of fairyland is always being distracted from them by
intimations of a world outside our world; and even when he is
dead, he can find "no comfort in the grave." So in another
poem, the joys of the "Happy Townland" where "boughs have
their fruit and blossom at all times of the year," where "rivers
are running over with red beer and brown beer" and where
"queens, their eyes blue like the ice, are dancing in a crowd,"
are irreconcilable with real life: the enchanted Happy Townland is also "the world's bane."

In the prose stories of Yeats's early period, this fairyland appears under its real aspect as the life of revery and imagination
—and of solitude. The narrator of "Rosa Alchemica" exiles
himself from the world in a house where tapestries, "full of the
blue and bronze of peacocks . . . shut out all history and activity untouched with beauty and peace," and where he is able
to find in "antique bronze gods and goddesses . . . all a
pagan's delight in various beauty . . . without his terror at
sleepless destiny and his labor with many sacrifices." Another
solitary, Michael Robartes, lives on the lonely Irish coast in a
house which he calls "the Temple of the Alchemical Rose" and
where by night the immortal spirits of beautiful long-dead men
and women from Egypt and from Greece come to dance in a
mosaic-lined room, with a great rose in mosaic on the ceiling.
It was characteristic of the *fin de siècle* writers to want to stand
apart from the common life and live only in the imagination. I
have said that the battle of Symbolism was never properly
fought out in English; but there was one writer in England
who played a rôle somewhat similar to that of Mallarmé in
France. Walter Pater was, like Mallarmé, a man of much intellectual originality who, living quietly and writing little, had a
profound influence on the literature of his time. More nearly
than anyone else, he supplied, in his literary criticism, an English equivalent to the Symbolist theory of the French. When
Pater says that experience gives us, "not the truth of eternal

outlines, ascertained once for all, but a world of fine gradations and subtly linked conditions, shifting intricately as we
ourselves change," he is stating a point of view exactly similar
to that of the Symbolists. But it was less in the field of æsthetic
theory than in that of the appreciation of life that Pater developed this point of view. The famous conclusion to "The Renaissance" fixed the ideal of a whole generation: "To regard all
things and principles of things as inconstant modes or fashions
has more and more become the fashion of modern thought.
. . . The service of philosophy, of speculative culture, towards
the human spirit, is to rouse, to startle it to a life of constant
and eager observation. Every moment some form grows perfect in hand or face; some tone on the hills or the sea is choicer
than the rest; some mood of passion or insight or intellectual
excitement is irresistibly real and attractive to us—for that moment only. Not the fruit of experience, but experience itself, is
the end. A counted number of pulses only is given to us of a
variegated, dramatic life. How may we see in them all that is to
be seen in them by the finest senses?" "We looked consciously
to Pater for our philosophy," Yeats wrote of himself and his
friends; and the tapestried house, the Alchemical Temple, had
been invented as ideal abodes where this philosophy might be
put into practice—as Yeats's fairyland itself had been but one
of the imaginary domains of the *fin de siècle* mind.

But just as Yeats's early poetry presents the fascination of
fairyland as something inimical to life in the real world, so
these stories of the life of ecstatic revery, unlike the typical
writings of the *fin de siècle* æsthetes, are edged with a consciousness of dangers and temptations inescapably involved in such a
life. In Yeats, we find the æstheticism of Pater carried through
to its consequences. What *is* the consequence of living for
beauty, as beauty was then understood, of cultivating the imagination, the enjoyment of æsthetic sensations, as a supreme end
in itself? We shall be thrown fatally out of key with reality—we
shall incur penalties which are not to be taken lightly. There is
a conflict here which cannot be evaded; and Yeats, even in his
earliest period, is unceasingly aware of this conflict. But still he
prefers to dwell most of the time in fairyland or among the
dancers of the Alchemical Temple. He would even transport
his human love, his human desire, into the climate of that

immortal world, where nothing that is ugly can jar and where
nothing that is beautiful fades:

"All things uncomely and broken, all things worn out and old,
 The cry of a child by the roadway, the creak of a lumbering
      cart,
 The heavy steps of the ploughman, splashing the wintry
      mould,
 Are wronging your image that blossoms a rose in the deeps
      of my heart.
 The wrong of unshapely things is a wrong too great to be
      told;
 I hunger to build them anew and sit on a green knoll apart,
 With the earth and the sky and the water, remade, like a cas-
      ket of gold
 For my dreams of your image that blossoms a rose in the
      deeps of my heart."

But now, in the period inaugurated by "The Green Helmet"
(published in 1912), the balance is to dip on the other side. In
the frustration of early love, apparently, he has paid the price of
escaping to fairyland, and the memory of it is bitter: he still
champions, he still puts above everything, the nobility and
splendor of the imagination; but he must face life's hard conditions. And the consciousness of inexorable limits has brought
his art to a sharper focus—the unbinding of "youth's dreamy
load" has made him a better poet. No longer content with the
ice-eyed queens of fairyland at the same time that he no longer
hopes from real life any satisfaction other than the triumph of
imagination through art, he applies to poetry all the vigor of
his intellect and all the energy of his passion. He would reduce
his verse to something definite and hard—at the same time
more severe and more passionate. Now the soap-bubble colors
vanish; the music of fairyland dies away; we behold only,
earthly and clear, the bare outlines of "cold Clare rock and
Galway rock and thorn."

In a poem which is at once a description of this style and an
admirable example of it, he tells how,

                "Maybe a twelvemonth since
                 Suddenly I began

> In scorn of this audience
> Imagining a man,
> And his sun-freckled face,
> And gray Connemara cloth,
> Climbing up to a place
> Where stone is dark under froth,
> And the down turn of his wrist
> When the flies drop in the stream:
> A man who does not exist,
> A man who is but a dream;
> And cried, 'Before I am old
> I shall have written him one
> Poem maybe as cold
> And passionate as the dawn.'"

Yeats inhabits, in this phase, a world of pure intense emotions expressed in distinct fine images. His words, no matter how prosaic, are always somehow luminous and noble, as if pale pebbles smoothed by the sea were to take on some mysterious value and become more precious than jewels or gold. He is less prodigal now of symbols and names, and his visions have a new austerity:

> "I call to the eye of the mind
> A well long choked up and dry
> And boughs long stripped by the wind,
> And I call to the mind's eye
> Pallor of an ivory face,
> Its lofty dissolute air,
> A man climbing up to a place
> The salt sea wind has swept bare."

When he returns to the heroic world of Irish mythology, he describes it with a new homeliness of detail. And more and more steadily he fixes his attention upon the actual world about him. He has come to desire above everything, as he says in another part of the poem about the fisherman,

> "To write for my own race
> And for the reality."

And again, in another poem:

> "Through all the lying days of my youth
> I swayed my leaves and flowers in the sun;
> Now I may wither into the truth."

He finds his subjects now in the events of his own life, no longer transposed into romantic convention, and in the public affairs of Ireland. And he succeeds in dignifying such subjects, as perhaps no other contemporary poet has done, at the same time that he never ceases to deal with them without sentimentality and in the plainest language. He can even challenge comparison with Dante—whom he now describes as "the chief imagination of Christendom"—by his ability to sustain a grand manner through sheer intensity without rhetorical heightening. He assumes, indeed, a kind of Dantesque mask. How he suggests the compactness and point of Dante's two- or three-line allusions in such a passage as,

> "Traders or soldiers who have left me blood
> That has not passed through any huxter's loin,
> Pardon, and you that did not weigh the cost,
> Old Butlers when you took to horse and stood
> Beside the brackish waters of the Boyne
> Till your bad master blenched and all was lost" . . .

and Dante's epigrammatic bitterness in,

> "Why should I blame her that she filled my days
> With misery, or that she would of late
> Have taught to ignorant men most violent ways,
> Or hurled the little streets against the great,
> Had they but courage equal to desire?"

And he has also a Dantesque exaltation—an exaltation no longer the opium dream of fairyland, but such as life has to offer within its limits: the admiration for ancestor or friend, the pride in honor kept or work well done, the wild memory of early love:

> "And what of her that took
> All till my youth was gone
> With scarce a pitying look?
> How should I praise that one?
> When day begins to break

I count my good and bad,
Being wakeful for her sake,
Remembering what she had,
What eagle look still shows,
While up from my heart's root
So great a sweetness flows
I shake from head to foot."

II

With the development of this maturer style, it became impossible any longer to regard Yeats merely as one of the best of
the English lyric poets of the nineties. The author of "The
Lake Isle of Innisfree," which had so delighted Robert Louis
Stevenson, had grown, in an interval of ten years during which
nobody outside of Ireland had apparently paid much attention
to him, to the unmistakable stature of a master. No other poet
writing English in our time has been able to deal with supreme
artistic success with such interesting and such varied experience.
No other writer has been able to sustain the traditional grand
manner of the poet with so little effect of self-consciousness.

And in spite of the immense amount of poetry published
and read to-day, the personality truly and naturally poetic
seems to be becoming rarer and rarer. It may be true that the
kind of dignity and distinction which have been characteristic
of the poet in the past are becoming more and more impossible in our modern democratic society and during a period
when the ascendancy of scientific ideas has made man conscious
of his kinship with the other animals and of his subjection to
biological and physical laws rather than of his relation to the
gods. It was easy for the lyric poet, from Wyatt's age to Waller's,
to express himself both directly and elegantly, because he was a
courtier, or, in any case, a member of a comparatively small educated class, whose speech combined the candor and natural-
ness of conversation among equals with the grace of a courtly
society. It was possible for him honestly to take up a residence
in an intellectual world where poetic images stood for actualities because the scientific language and technique for dealing
with these actualities had not yet come to permeate thought.
But the modern poet who would follow this tradition, and

who would yet deal with life in any large way, must create for
himself a special personality, must maintain a state of mind,
which shall shut out or remain indifferent to many aspects of
the contemporary world. This necessity accounts partly, I suppose, for Yeats's preoccupation in his prose writings with what
he calls the Mask or Anti-Self, a sort of imaginary personality,
quite antagonistic to other elements of one's nature, which
the poet must impose upon himself. It is hard to imagine a
seventeenth-century poet being driven to such a theory—a
theory which makes one's poetic self figure as one of the halves
of a split personality; and it seems true that Yeats himself has
not been able to keep up his poetic rôle without a certain effort. We find, at any rate, in his criticism and his autobiographical writings a remarkably honest and illuminating account of
the difficulties of remaining a poet during the age in which we
live.

Yeats seems to be conscious from the first of an antagonism
between the actual world of industry, politics and science, on
the one hand, and the imaginative poetic life, on the other. He
tells us, in his autobiography, that a vital issue seemed to be
raised for him, in his boyhood, by the then popular and novel
realism of Bastien-Lepage and Carolus Durand as against the
mysticism of the Pre-Raphaelite painters. Bastien-Lepage's
"clownish peasant staring with vacant eyes at her great boots"
represented already to the young Yeats that Naturalistic, scientific vision which contradicted and warred with his own. And
he takes up from the beginning, in his criticism, a definite and
explicit position in regard to Naturalism: he will stand apart
from the democratic, the scientific, modern world—his poetic
life shall be independent of it; his art shall owe nothing to its
methods. His principles in literature are those of the Symbolists, but he formulates them more clearly and defends them
with more vigor than anyone else has yet done in English.

"There is," he asserts in his early essay on the symbolism of
Shelley, "for every man some one scene, some one adventure,
some one picture, that is the image of his secret life, for wisdom
first speaks in images and . . . this one image, if he would but
brood over it his whole life long, would lead his soul, disentangled from unmeaning circumstance and the ebb and flow
of the world, into that far household, where the undying gods

await all whose souls have become simple as flame, whose bodies have become quiet as an agate lamp." All great literature, says Yeats, is created out of symbols: observations and statistics mean nothing; works of art which depend upon them can have no enduring value. "There is something," he says, "of an old wives' tale in fine literature. The makers of it are like an old peasant telling stories of the great famine or the hangings of '98 or from his own memories. He has felt something in the depth of his mind and he wants to make it as visible and powerful to our senses as possible. He will use the most extravagant words or illustrations if they will suit his purpose. Or he will invent a wild parable, and the more his mind is on fire or the more creative it is, the less will he look at the outer world or value it for its own sake. It gives him metaphors and examples, and that is all. He is even a little scornful of it, for it seems to him while the fit is on that the fire has gone out of it and left it but white ashes. I cannot explain it, but I am certain that every high thing was invented in this way, between sleeping and waking, as it were, and that peering and peeping persons are but hawkers of stolen goods. How else could their noses have grown so ravenous or their eyes so sharp?"

And in all his activity as playwright and journalist in connection with the Abbey Theatre, Yeats is leading a reaction against Naturalism. This reaction, which, by way of Germany and under the name of Expressionism, has attracted so much more attention since the War, had not, at the time of the founding of the Abbey Theatre, manifested itself very vigorously on the Continent. Symbolism did not play yet in the theatre the rôle that it was playing in poetry. Yet its seeds had already sprouted here and there. August Strindberg, returning from Paris to Sweden, wrote between 1899 and 1902 the Symbolistic "To Damascus" and "Dream Play," the prototypes of the German Expressionistic drama; and Maeterlinck, with vague, pale and suave images, quite different from Strindberg's lively, queer and dissonant ones, had created quite a little theatre of Symbolism. Now Yeats, in his own dramatic works, has produced a theatre somewhat similar to Maeterlinck's. The productions of a greater poet, equipped with a richer and more solid mythology, these plays do, however, take place in the same sort of twilit world as Maeterlinck's—a world in which the characters are less often dramatic personalities than disembodied broodings and longings. Yeats's plays have little dramatic importance because Yeats himself has little sense of drama, and we think of them primarily as a department of his poetry, with the same sort of interest and beauty as the rest. But Yeats, the director and propagandist of the Abbey Theatre, does have considerable importance in the history of the modern stage. The Abbey Theatre itself, of recent years, with the Gorky-Chekhovesque plays of Sean O'Casey, has taken a Naturalistic turn which Yeats never contemplated or desired; but his long and uncompromising campaign for a revival of poetic drama contributed much to contemporary efforts to break up the rigid technique and clear the stage of the realistic encumbrances of the Naturalistic drama. Yeats's greatest contribution to the theatre has been, not his own plays, but those of Synge, whom in 1896 he discovered stagnating in Paris and induced to return to Ireland. Synge succeeded, on a small scale, during the few years before he died, in creating for the Abbey Theatre perhaps the most authentic example of poetic drama which the modern stage has seen.

Yeats at this period, the period of the founding and the first battles of the Abbey Theatre, is both active and effective. There has always been more of the public figure and more of the pugnacious Irishman about him than his philosophy invites us to believe. But this philosophy never ceases to insist upon the irreconcilable opposition between the life of self-assertion in the practical world and the life consecrated to the recovery and contemplation of the precious symbol, which, "if he [the poet] would but brood over it his whole life long, would lead his soul, disentangled from unmeaning circumstance and the ebb and flow of the world," into the presence of the gods. Yeats recurs again and again to the necessity of mortifying the will: "Every visionary knows that the mind's eye soon comes to see a capricious and variable world, which the will cannot shape or change, though it can call it up and banish it again"; "We must find some place upon the Tree of Life for the Phœnix nest, for the passion that is exaltation and the negation of the will"; the style of the dialogue in Synge's plays "blurs definition, clear edges, everything that comes from the will, it turns imagination from all that is of the present, like a gold background in a religious picture, and it strengthens in every emotion whatever comes to it from far off, from brooding memory and dangerous hope," etc.

For the rest, Yeats's prose, in its beginnings, when he is most under the influence of the Pre-Raphaelites and Pater, is a little self-consciously archaic—it has a Renaissance elaborateness and pomposity; and it is a little too close to the language of poetry—the meaning is often clotted by metaphor. But Yeats's prose, like his verse, has, with time, undergone a discipline and emerged with a clearer outline. Yeats is to-day a master of prose as well as a great poet. He was already magnificent in his intermediate period—the period of "Per Amica Silentia Lunae" (1917): "We make out of the quarrel with others, rhetoric, but of the quarrel with ourselves, poetry. Unlike the rhetoricians, who get a confident voice from remembering the crowd they have won or may win, we sing amid our uncertainty; and, smitten even in the presence of the most high beauty by the knowledge of our solitude, our rhythm shudders. I think, too, that no fine poet, no matter how disordered his life, has ever, even in his mere life, had pleasure for his end. Johnson and Dowson, friends of my youth, were dissipated men, the one a drunkard, the other a drunkard and mad about women, and yet they had the gravity of men who had found life out and were awakening from the dream; and both, one in life and art and one in art and less in life, had a continual preoccupation with religion. Nor has any poet I have read of or heard of or met with been a sentimentalist. The other self, the anti-self or the antithetical self, as one may choose to name it, comes but to those who are no longer deceived, whose passion is reality. The sentimentalists are practical men who believe in money, in position, in a marriage bell, and whose understanding of happiness is to be so busy whether at work or at play, that all is forgotten but the momentary aim. They find their pleasure in a cup that is filled from Lethe's wharf, and for the awakening, for the vision, for the revelation of reality, tradition offers us a different word—ecstasy."

This is perhaps still a little *too* magnificent, still a little too much like poetry. But in his autobiography, "The Trembling of the Veil" (1922), Yeats has achieved a combination of grandeur with a certain pungency and homeliness which recalls the more lightly and swiftly moving writers of the seventeenth century rather than the more heavily upholstered ones of the earlier Renaissance. The prose of Yeats, in our contemporary literature, is like the product of some dying loomcraft brought to perfection in the days before machinery. The qualities of a good prose style in English to-day are likely to be those of a sound intellectual currency, clipped out by a sharp cutter and stamped by a solvent mint; Rudyard Kipling, Bernard Shaw and T. S. Eliot, however else they may differ, have these characteristics in common. Of Samuel Butler, Shaw's master, Yeats has written that he was "the first Englishman to make the discovery that it is possible to write with great effect without music, without style, either good or bad, to eliminate from the mind all emotional implication and to prefer plain water to every vintage, so much metropolitan lead and solder to any tendril of the vine." The style of the seventeenth century, on the other hand—the style of Walton's "Lives" or Dryden's prefaces—was a much more personal thing: it fitted the author like a suit of clothes and molded itself to the natural contours of his temperament and mind; one is always aware that there is a man inside, whereas with Kipling, Eliot or Shaw, the style seems to aim at the effect of an inflexible impersonal instrument specially designed to perform special functions. Yeats's prose is, however, still a garment worn in the old-fashioned personal manner with a combination of elegance and ease, at the same time that it is unmistakably of our time by virtue of a certain modern terseness and of a characteristically modern trick—we shall encounter it later in Proust—of revealing by unexpected juxtapositions relations of which one had not been aware—"He had been almost poor," writes Yeats of Wilde in the period before his disaster, "and now, his head full of Flaubert, found himself with ten thousand a year"—or of effecting almost startling transitions from the particular to the general and back again. For Yeats has become a critic now not merely of literature, but of human life and society in general: compare the passage on Johnson and Dowson which I have quoted above from "Per Amica Silentia Lunae," with the realistic and subtle analysis, in "The Trembling of the Veil," of the causes for the final breakdown of that "tragic generation."

III

Yeats has shown himself, in his prose writings, a man of both exceptionally wide information and exceptional intellectual curiosity; but, for all the variety of his interests and the versatility of his intelligence, he has, in rejecting the methods of modern science, cut himself off in a curious way from the general enlightened thought of his time. Yet his mind is so comprehensive and so active that he has felt the need of constructing a system: and, finding it impossible to admit the assumptions upon which most modern systems are based, he has had recourse to the only science which his position has allowed him to accept, the obsolete science of Astrology. As a young man, Yeats frequented clairvoyants and students of Astrology and Magic; Madame Blavatsky, the necromantic Theosophist, seems to have made upon him a considerable impression. And in 1901 he was led to formulate, in an essay on Magic, the following set of beliefs, to which he still apparently adheres:

"(1) That the borders of our mind are ever shifting, and that many minds can flow into one another, as it were, and create or reveal a single mind, a single energy.

"(2) That the borders of our memories are as shifting, and that our memories are a part of one great memory, the memory of Nature herself.

"(3) That this great mind and great memory can be evoked by symbols."

What Yeats was really approaching here was some such systematic study of the symbolism of myths, trances, dreams and other human visions as psychoanalysis and anthropology were attempting from a different direction. And despite the obvious charlatanism or naïveté of most of his instructors and fellow investigators, Yeats's account of his researches is interesting. For it is not merely that Yeats loves the marvellous: he is also intent upon discovering symbols which may stand for the elements of his own nature or which shall seem to possess some universal significance. The results of this research are very curious. When we read Yeats's account of his adventures among the mediums, it becomes plain that, in spite of his repudiation of science, he has always managed to leave himself a margin of scientific doubt. Like Huysmans, he betrays an instinct to scrutinize and check up on the supernatural which is disastrous to genuine mysticism. Just as in Huysmans's case, we always feel that the wistful student of Satanism has too much solid Dutch common sense really to deceive himself about his devils, so in Yeats—he himself has confessed it—the romantic amateur of Magic is always accompanied and restrained by the rationalistic modern man. "He and I often quarrelled," Yeats writes of himself and A. E., "because I wanted him to examine and question his visions, and write them out as they occurred; and still more because I thought symbolic what he thought real like the men and women that had passed him on the road." Yet Huysmans went so far as to claim—or at least to make one of his characters claim—as genuine examples of demoniacal possession those very hysteria cases of Charcot's which at that moment were leading Charcot's young pupil Freud to his first great discovery of the principle of emotional repression; and Yeats attributes to a sort of supernatural being designated as "Anima Mundi" precisely such universal symbols as are studied by such psychologists as Jung. What is most curious is that Yeats should at last have constructed out of these symbols an elaborate mystical-metaphysical system.

This system was set forth in "A Vision," a work which occupied Yeats for many years and which he published privately in 1926. "A Vision" presented an elaborate theory of the variation of human personality, of the vicissitudes of human history and of the transformations of the soul in this world and the next. This theory was worked out with geometrical diagrams and set forth in terms of such unfamiliar conceptions as *daimons, tinctures, cones, gyres, husks* and *passionate bodies.*

Yeats asserts that human personality follows the pattern of a "Great Wheel." That is, the types of personality possible constitute a kind of closed circle—they are regular stages in a circular journey to and fro between complete objectivity at one pole and complete subjectivity at the other; and this journey may be represented by the orbit of the moon, to which it corresponds. Let the moon represent subjectivity and the sun, objectivity: then the dark of the moon, when it is closest to the sun, is the phase of complete objectivity; and the full moon, which is farthest from the sun, is the phase of complete subjectivity. At these two opposite poles of the circle, human life is impossible: there exist only antipodal types of supernatural beings. But along the circumference of the circle, between these two ultra-human poles, there occur twenty-six phases which cover all possible types of human personality.

Yeats's theory of the variation of these types is extremely complicated. He begins by assigning to "incarnate man" four "Faculties": the Will, "by which is understood feeling that has not become desire . . . an energy as yet uninfluenced by thought, action or emotion"; the Mask, which means "the image of what we wish to become, or of that to which we give our reverence"; the Creative Mind, "the intellect . . . all the mind that is consciously constructive"; and the Body of Fate, "the physical and mental environment, the changing human body, the stream of Phenomena as this affects a particular individual, all that is forced upon us from without." The Will is always opposite the Mask: "it looks into a painted picture." The Creative Mind is opposite the Body of Fate: "it looks into a photograph; but both look into something which is the opposite of themselves." We follow the Will around the clock, and by combining it with the other elements according to geometrical laws we calculate the characters of the different phases. Starting at the right of the objective pole, the soul passes first through varieties of almost purely physical life—Yeats takes his examples here from the Bacchuses and shepherds of the poets. It is moving toward subjectivity, however—Walt Whitman, Alexandre Dumas: it is seeking itself, and as it progresses, it becomes more beautiful. The ultra-human subjective phase, which apparently includes Christ, is described as "a phase of complete beauty," where "Thought and Will are indistinguishable, effort and attainment are indistinguishable—nothing is apparent but dreaming Will and the Image that it dreams." This is preceded and followed by phases which include Baudelaire and Beardsley; Keats and Giorgione; Blake and Rabelais; Dante and Shelley; and presumably Yeats himself: men who have withdrawn from the life of the world in order to live in their dream. But once the all-subjective phase is past, the soul

". . . would be the world's servant, and as it serves,
Choosing whatever task's most difficult

Among tasks not impossible, it takes
Upon the body and upon the soul
The coarseness of the drudge. Before the full
It sought itself and afterwards the world."

And it is now leaving beauty behind and headed toward deformity:

"Reformer, merchant, statesman, learned man,
Dutiful husband, honest wife by turn,
Cradle upon cradle, and all in flight and all
Deformed because there is no deformity
But saves us from a dream."

The soul has now come full circle: the three final human phases
before the phase of complete objectivity are the Hunchback,
the Saint and the Fool.

Yeats has worked all this out with great care and with considerable ingenuity. He has described each of the twenty-eight
phases and supplied us with typical examples. What we find in
this part of the book is Yeats's familiar preoccupation with the
conflict between action and philosophy, reality and imagination. (It is amusing and characteristic that, according to his
system, the side of humanity closest to the sun—that is, closest
the objective nature—should be the side that is bathed in darkness, whereas the side which is furthest from the sun—that is,
nearest the subjective nature—should be the side that is bright!)
Now this is a subject which has hitherto, in Yeats's prose as
well as in his verse, usually inspired him well; the symbols of
the Mask, the Sun and Moon, etc., if they have sometimes been
a little disconcerting when we encountered them in his critical
writings, have created just the right impression of significance
in mystery for Symbolistic poetry. And there are, to be sure,
certain passages of "A Vision" as brilliant as Yeats at his best.
He writes, for example, of the phase of "the Receptive Man,"
to which he assigns Rembrandt and Synge: "The man wipes his
breath from the window pane, and laughs in his delight at all
the varied scene." And of the phase of "the Obsessed Man," to
which he assigns Giorgione and Keats: "When we compare
these images with those of any subsequent phase, each seems
studied for its own sake; they float as in serene air, or lie hid-

den in some valley, and if they move it is to music that returns always to the same note, or in a dance that so returns upon itself that they seem immortal." And, in what is perhaps the most eloquent passage in the book, he returns to a certain type of beautiful uncontemplative woman who has already haunted his poetry: "Here are born those women who are most touching in their beauty. Helen was of this phase; and she comes before the mind's eye elaborating a delicate personal discipline as though she would make her whole life an image of a unified *antithetical* (that is, subjective) energy. While seeming an image of softness, and of quiet, she draws perpetually upon glass with a diamond. Yet she will not number among her sins anything that does not break that personal discipline, no matter what it may seem according to others' discipline; but if she fail in her own discipline she will not deceive herself, and for all the languor of her movements, and her indifference to the acts of others, her mind is never at peace. She will wander much alone as though she consciously meditated her masterpiece that shall be at the full moon, yet unseen by human eye, and when she returns to her house she will look upon her household with timid eyes, as though she knew that all power of self-protection had been taken away, and that of her once *primary Tincture* (that is, objective element) nothing remained but a strange irresponsible innocence. . . . Already perhaps, through weakness of desire, she understands nothing, while alone seeming of service. Is it not because she desires so little and gives so little that men will die and murder in her service?" And there is a strange imaginative power in the conception behind the final sequence of the Hunchback, the Saint and the Fool.

Yet "A Vision," when we try to read it, makes us impatient with Yeats. As a rule, he expounds his revelations as if he took them seriously—that is, as if he believed that *masks* and *husks* and *daimons* and *passionate bodies* were things which actually existed, as if they were as real as those visions of A. E.'s which had been as real to A. E. as the people in the street, but which Yeats had tried to induce him to question; and indeed one would think that to elaborate a mystical system so complicated and so tedious, it would be necessary to believe in it pretty strongly. Yet now and then the skeptical Yeats reasserts himself and we are startled by an unexpected suggestion that, after all, the whole thing may be merely "a background for my thought, a painted scene." If the whole thing, we ask ourselves, has been merely an invented mythology, in which Yeats himself does not believe, what right has he to bore us with it—what right has he to expect us to explore page after page of such stuff as the following description of the habits of the soul after death: "The *Spirit* first floats horizontally within the man's dead body, but then rises until it stands at his head. The *Celestial Body* is also horizontal at first but lies in the opposite position, its feet where the *Spirit's* head is, and then rising, as does the *Spirit*, stands up at last at the feet of the man's body. The *Passionate Body* rises straight up from the genitals and stands in the centre. The *Husk* remains in the body until the time for it to be separated and lost in *Anima Mundi.*"

In "A Packet for Ezra Pound" (1929) a new light is thrown on "A Vision." We learn that Yeats's wife is a medium, and that the theories set forth in this book were communicated through her by supernatural beings. Yeats tells us how, four days after their marriage in 1917, Mrs. Yeats surprised him by attempting automatic writing. "What came in disjointed sentences, in almost illegible writing, was so exciting, sometimes so profound, that I persuaded her to give an hour or two day after day to the unknown writer, and after some half-dozen such hours offered to spend what remained of life explaining and piecing together those scattered sentences. 'No,' was the answer, 'we have come to give you metaphors for poetry.' The unknown writer took his theme at first from my just published 'Per Amica Silentia Lunae.' I had made a distinction between the perfection that is from a man's combat with himself and that which is from a combat with circumstances, and upon this simple distinction he built up an elaborate classification of men according to their more or less complete expression of one type or the other. He supported his classification by a series of geometrical symbols and put these symbols in an order that answered the question in my essay as to whether some prophet could not prick upon the calendar the birth of a Napoleon or a Christ." Yeats describes the manifestations which accompanied these revelations: the perfumes, whistlings, smells of burnt feathers, bursts of music, apparitions of great black birds and of "persons in clothes of the late sixteenth century and of the seventeenth." On one occasion, when an owl was hooting in the garden, the dictating spirit asked for a recess: "Sounds like that," the spirit explained, "give us great pleasure." And there were also mischievous obstructive spirits who attempted to mislead the Yeatses and who were designated as "Frustrators"; "the automatic script would deteriorate, grow sentimental or confused, and when I pointed this out the communicator would say 'from such and such an hour, on such and such a day, all is frustration.' I would spread out the script and he would cross all out back to the answer that began it, but had I not divined frustration he would have said nothing."

We learn also, by the way, a fact which might, for a psychologist, throw a good deal of light on the development of Yeats's personality. It appears that not only has Yeats always succeeded in steering clear of science: he has never till recently read philosophy. "Apart from two or three of the principal Platonic Dialogues I knew no philosophy. Arguments with my father, whose convictions had been formed by John Stuart Mill's attack upon Sir William Hamilton, had destroyed my confidence and driven me from speculation to the direct experience of the Mystics. I had once known Blake as thoroughly as his unfinished confused Prophetic Books permitted, and I had read Swedenborg and Boehme, and my initiation into the 'Hermetic Students' had filled my head with Cabalistic imagery." Now, however, he wants to study philosophy as an aid to understanding the "system." The spirits ask him to wait till they have finished. At the end of three years, when the supernatural revelations have ceased, and "A Vision" is actually in proof, Yeats takes down from Mrs. Yeats, who, it appears, did not share her husband's ignorance, a list of the philosophers she had read. For four years, Yeats applies himself to these, and what he finds makes him uneasy about "A Vision": he feels that he must partly have misinterpreted what the spirits have told him. But the spirits themselves intervene to put an end to this disquieting situation: they make him stop his philosophical studies.

As we read all this, we say to ourselves that Yeats, growing older, has grown more credulous. But we come, at the end, to the following passage: "Some will ask if I believe all that this book contains, and I will not know how to answer. Does the word belief, used as they will use it, belong to our age, can I think of the world as there and I here judging it?" And he intimates that, after all, his system may be only a set of symbols like another—a set of symbols, we recognize, like the Irish myths with which he began.

Into the personal situation suggested by Yeats's account of his revelations, it is inappropriate and unnecessary to go: the psychological situation seems plain. When Yeats, at the crucial period of his life, attempted to leave fairyland behind, when he became aware of the unsatisfying character of the life of iridescent revery, when he completely recreated his style so as to make it solid, homely and exact where it had formerly been shimmering or florid—the need for dwelling with part of his mind—or with his mind for part of the time—in a world of pure imagination, where the necessities of the real world do not hold, had, none the less, not been conjured away by the new artistic and intellectual habits he was cultivating. Where the early Yeats had studied Irish folk-lore, collected and sorted Irish fairy tales, invented fairy tales for himself, the later Yeats worked out from the mediumistic communications of his wife the twenty-eight phases of the human personality and the transformations of the soul after death. Yeats's sense of reality today is inferior to that of no man alive—indeed, his greatness is partly due precisely to the vividness of that sense. In his poetry, in his criticism and in his memoirs, it is the world we all live in with which we are confronted—the world we know, with all its frustrations, its defeats, its antagonisms and its errors—the mind that sees is not naïve, as the heart that feels is not insensitive. They meet reality with comprehension and with passion—but they have phases, we are astonished to discover, when they do not seem to meet it at all. Yet the scientific criticism of supernatural phenomena is actually as much a part of the reality of Yeats's world as it is of that of most of the rest of us. And when Yeats writes of his supernatural experiences, this criticism, though it may be kept in the background, is nevertheless always present—his realistic sense is too strong, his intellectual integrity too high, to leave it out of the picture. Though he is much addicted to these fantastic imaginings, though he no doubt needs their support to enable him to sustain his rôle of great poet—yet when he comes to write about his spirits and their messages, he cannot help letting us in on the imposture. He believes, but—he does not believe: the impossibility of believing is the impossibility which he accepts most reluctantly, but still it is there with the other impossibilities of this world which is too full of weeping for a child to understand.

It is interesting to compare "A Vision" with that other compendious treatise on human nature and destiny by that other great writer from Dublin: Bernard Shaw's "Guide to Socialism and Capitalism." Here we can see unmistakably the differences between the kind of literature which was fashionable before the War and the kind which has been fashionable since. Shaw and Yeats, both coming as young men to London from eighteenth-century Dublin, followed diametrically opposite courses. Shaw shouldered the whole unwieldy load of contemporary sociology, politics, economics, biology, medicine and journalism, while Yeats, convinced that the world of science and politics was somehow fatal to the poet's vision, as resolutely turned away. Shaw accepted the scientific technique and set himself to master the problems of an industrial democratic society, while Yeats rejected the methods of Naturalism and applied himself to the introspective plumbing of the mysteries of the individual mind. While Yeats was editing Blake, Shaw was grappling with Marx; and Yeats was appalled by Shaw's hardness and efficiency. "I hated it," he says of "Arms and the Man"; "it seemed to me inorganic, logical straightness and not the crooked road of life and I stood aghast before its energy." And he tells us that Shaw appeared to him in a dream in the form of a sewing machine, "that clicked and shone, but the incredible thing was that the machine smiled, smiled perpetually."

In his Great Wheel of the twenty-eight phases, Yeats has situated Shaw at a phase considerably removed from his own, and where the individual is headed straight for the deformity of seeking, not the soul, but the world. And their respective literary testaments—the "Vision" and the "Guide"—published almost at the same time, mark the extreme points of their divergence: Shaw bases all human hope and happiness on an equal distribution of income, which he believes will finally make impossible even the pessimism of a Swift or a Voltaire; while Yeats, like Shaw a Protestant for whom the Catholic's mysticism was impossible, has in "A Vision" made the life of humanity contingent on the movements of the stars. "The day is far off," he concludes, "when the two halves of man can divine each its own unity in the other as in a mirror, Sun in Moon, Moon in Sun, and so escape out of the Wheel."

IV

Yet, in the meantime, the poet Yeats has passed into a sort of third phase, in which he is closer to the common world than at any previous period. He is no longer quite so haughty, so imperturbably astride his high horse, as during his middle Dantesque period. With the Dantesque mask, he has lost something of intensity and something of sharpness of outline. In "The Tower" (1928), certain words such as "bitter," "wild," and "fierce," which he was able, a few years ago, to use with such thrilling effect, have no longer quite the same force. He writes more loosely, and seems to write more easily. He has become more plain-spoken, more humorous—his mind seems to run more frankly on his ordinary human satisfactions and chagrins: he is sometimes harsh, sometimes sensual, sometimes careless, sometimes coarse.

Though he now inhabits, like Michael Robartes, a lonely tower on the outermost Irish coast, he has spent six years in the Irish senate, presiding at official receptions in a silk hat, inspecting the plumbing of the government schools and conscientiously sitting through the movies which it is one of his official duties to censor. He is much occupied with politics and society, with general reflections on human life—but with the wisdom of the experience of a lifetime, he is passionate even in age. And he writes poems which charge now with the emotion of a great lyric poet that profound and subtle criticism of life of which I have spoken in connection with his prose.

We may take, as an example of Yeats's later vein, the fine poem in "The Tower" called "Among School Children." The poet, now "a sixty year old smiling public man," has paid an official visit to a girls' school kept by nuns; and as he gazes at the children there, he remembers how the woman he had loved had told him once of some "harsh reproof or trivial event" of her girlhood which had changed "some childish day

to tragedy." And for a moment the thought that she may once
have looked like one of the children before him has revived the
excitement of his old love. He remembers the woman in all her
young beauty—and thinks of himself with his present sixty
years—"a comfortable kind of old scarecrow." What use is philosophy now?—is not all beauty bound up with the body and
doomed to decay with it?—is not even the divine beauty itself
which is worshipped there by the nuns inseparable from the
images of it they adore?

> "Labor is blossoming or dancing where
> The body is not bruised to pleasure soul,
> Nor beauty born out of its own despair,
> Nor blear-eyed wisdom out of midnight oil.
> O chestnut tree, great rooted blossomer,
> Are you the leaf, the blossom or the bole?
> O body swayed to music, O brightening glance,
> How can we know the dancer from the dance?"

Here the actual scene in the convent, the personal emotions it
awakens and the general speculations which these emotions
suggest, have been interwoven and made to play upon each
other at the same time that they are kept separate and distinct.
A complex subject has been treated in the most concentrated
form, and yet without confusion. Perceptions, fancies, feelings
and thoughts have all their place in the poet's record. It is a
moment of human life, masterfully seized and made permanent, in all its nobility and lameness, its mystery and actuality,
its direct personal contact and abstraction.

III. Paul Valéry

PAUL VALÉRY first met Mallarmé in 1892, when Valéry was twenty-one: he became thereafter one of the most faithful and serious of Mallarmé's disciples. Valéry wrote little at this time and did not even collect his verses in a book; yet the Symbolists of what was then the younger generation seem to have acknowledged his supremacy from the beginning. What we find in these poems to-day is chiefly the chaste-celestial, the blue-and-white mood of such poems of Mallarmé's as "Apparition" in what seems a thinner diluted form. Paul Valéry, like his master, is "haunted" by the "azure"; but that azure is less a pure blue realm and more a rarefied upper air. Here and there in these early poems, however, the later Valéry is plainly recognizable: it is his characteristic interest in method apart from matter which leads him to publish two versions of the same sonnet; and in the uncompleted "Profusion du Soir," perhaps the most remarkable of these poems, by a confusion peculiar to Valéry the sunset which the poet is watching is assimilated to his state of mind until it seems sometimes only a set of images for a complex of emotions and thoughts.

Valéry has given us a curious description of his attitude toward Malllarmé at this time:

"When I began to see Mallarmé, I had almost entirely lost my interest in literature. Reading and writing were becoming dull work for me, and I confess that they still bore me a little. The study of myself for its own sake, the comprehension of that attention itself and the desire to trace clearly for myself the nature of my own existence, almost never abandoned me. This secret disease alienates one from letters, despite the fact that it has its source in them.

"Mallarmé figured, however, in my private system as the representative of the most accomplished art, as the highest phase of the loftiest literary ambition. In a deep sense, I had his mind for a companion, and I hoped that, despite the difference in our ages, and the immense disparity of our gifts, the day would come when I should not be afraid to lay before him my difficulties and my special ideas. It was not in the least that he intimidated me, for no one was ever more kindly or more charmingly simple than he; but I felt, at that time, a sort of contrast between the practice of literature and the pursuit of a certain rigor and of a complete intellectual sincerity. The question is infinitely delicate. Should I attempt to induce Mallarmé to discuss it? I was fond of him and valued him above everybody, but I myself had renounced the adoration of that which he had adored all his life, and to which he had offered up everything, and I could not bring myself to let him know it.

"I could, however, see no more genuine homage than to lay my thought before him, and to show him how much his researches, and the very fine and precise analysis from which they proceeded, had in my eyes transformed the literary problem and had led me to give up the game. The point was that Mallarmé's efforts, which were quite opposed to the doctrines and aims of his contemporaries, were tending to order the whole domain of letters through the general consideration of forms. It is remarkable in the extreme that, through the exhaustive study of his art and with no scientific education, he should have arrived at a conception so abstract and so close to the most abstruse speculations of certain of the sciences. He never discussed his ideas except figuratively. Explaining anything explicitly was strangely repugnant to him. His profession, which he detested, counted for something in that aversion. But, in attempting to sum up to myself his tendencies, I allowed myself to formulate them in my own way. Ordinary literature seemed to me comparable to an *arithmetic*, that is to say, to an attempt to obtain particular results in which it was difficult to distinguish the principle from the example: but the kind of literature which he had conceived seemed to me analogous to an *algebra*, for it assumed the intention to emphasize, to conserve and to develop the forms of which language is capable.

"But from the moment, I said to myself, that a principle has been recognized and grasped by someone, it is quite useless to waste one's time applying it. . . .

"The day I was awaiting never came."

Mallarmé died in 1898. But Paul Valéry had already passed through a personal crisis as a result of which he had ceased to write verse. This moral and intellectual crisis was precipitated, Valéry Larbaud tells us, by an unhappy love affair. Through sleepless nights Valéry struggled with his emotions: "the will was driven back on itself, schooled itself to leap clear, to break idols, to free itself, at no matter what cost, from those false-hoods: literature and sentiment. The supreme crisis, the costly victory took place during a stormy night—one of those storms of the Ligurian coast [he was at Genoa] which are not accom-panied by very much rain, but during which the lightning is so frequent and so bright that it gives the illusion of broad day-light. From that night none of the things which had hitherto made up the life of the young man mattered any longer. He left Montpellier [where he had studied at the university] and went to live in Paris, where he would be able, when he chose, to shut himself away in solitude, in order to give himself up to that 'penetration of himself,' which has now become his only concern."

During the twenty years that follow, Valéry works in the Ministry of War and in the Havas news agency, and produces no more verse. The "study of oneself for its own sake, the com-prehension of that attention itself and the desire to trace clearly for oneself the nature of one's own existence" is the only thing which interests him now. During these years he writes his "In-troduction to the Method of Leonardo da Vinci" and invents his mythological character, M. Teste. Both Leonardo da Vinci and M. Teste (Mr. Head, a companion creation to Rabelais's Messer Gaster, Mr. Belly) are, for Valéry, symbols of the pure intellect, of the human consciousness turned in upon itself. The mind of Leonardo in itself is something immeasurably greater than any of its manifestations in particular fields of activity—painting, writing, engineering or strategy. Action cramps and impoverishes the mind. For by itself the mind is able to deal with an infinite number of possibilities—it is not constrained by the limitations of a field. The mind by itself is omnipotent. And consequently the method, the theory, of doing anything is more interesting than the thing done. For the method may be applied so much more widely—may be uni-versally applied. When a principle, in fact, "has been recog-nized and grasped, it is quite useless to waste one's time applying it."

And M. Teste, unlike Leonardo, does disdain to apply his method to anything. His whole existence is given up to the examination of his own intellectual processes. He is a symbol of the human consciousness isolated from "all the opinions and intellectual habits which spring from the common life and our external relations with other men," and disembarrassed of "all the sentiments and ideas which are engendered or excited in man by his misfortunes and his fears, his terrors and his hopes; and not freely by his sheer observations upon the world and upon himself." M. Teste is, in fact, as his creator admits, frankly a monster. And though he exerts upon us a certain fascination, we resent him—he gives us the creeps. We sympathize with Mme. Teste, who is made uneasy by M. Teste's preoccupation, by his way of entering a room as if he did not see it, by his addressing her as "Being" or "Thing." Yet though she fears him, though she does not understand him, she has never ceased to adore him—she does not envy other women who have married ordinary men. And he, when he awakes from his meditations, sometimes seizes upon her brusquely, as if with relief, appetite and surprise. M. Teste and Mme. Teste are, after all, indispensable to each other.

In 1917, Valéry marries a lady of Mallarmé's circle. And at the end of twenty years, he begins writing again. André Gide has finally persuaded him to allow his early poems to be collected and published, and he has had the idea of adding to them a new poem of from twenty-five to fifty lines—the last, perhaps, which he will ever write. But, in the meantime, during his period of retirement, he has studied psychology, physiology, mathematics—he has become preoccupied with questions of method. "Twenty years without writing verse, without even attempting to write it, almost even without reading any! . . . Then, these problems presenting themselves again; and one's discovering that one did not know one's trade; that the little poems one had written long ago had evaded all the difficulties, suppressed what they did not know how to express; made use of an infantile language." For his new poem, he imposes upon himself "laws, constant requirements, *which constitute its true object*. It is an exercise, indeed—intended as such, and worked and reworked: a production entirely of deliberate effort; and then of a second deliberate effort, whose hard task is to mask the first. He who knows how to read me will read an autobiography, in the form. The *matter* is of small importance."

And this poem, which was to have filled but a page, occupies Valéry for more than four years and runs finally to five hundred and forty verses. At the last moment, when it is just about to be printed (1917), Valéry finds for it the title, "La Jeune Parque." But, in spite of its title, its heroic grand manner and its reverberating alexandrines, "La Jeune Parque" is no conventional French poem on a subject from Greek mythology. Valéry speaks of the "rather monstrous copulation of my system, my methods and my musical exigencies with the classical conventions." And it is certain that this mysterious poem represents a genre which has never appeared in literature before. Mallarmé's Hérodiade and his Faun are the precursors of Valéry's young Fate: they have already a certain ambiguity and seem at moments less imaginary personages than names attached to metaphysical reveries. But Valéry has carried the subtleties of conception, the complexities of presentation, of this characteristically Symbolist form much further than Mallarmé. Is "La Jeune Parque" the monologue of a young Fate, who has just been bitten by a snake? Is it the revery of the poet himself, awakening early one morning in bed and lying more or less awake till dawn? Is it the voyage of the human consciousness testing out all its limitations, exploring all its horizons: love, solitary thought, action, sleep, death ?—the drama of the mind which would withdraw from the world and rise superior to it but which is inevitably pulled back into life and involved in the processes of nature? It is all of these—yet the various strata, "physical, psychological and esoteric," as Francis de Miomandre describes them, are not overlaid one upon the other as in a conventional allegory or fable. They are confused and are always melting into one another—and it is this which makes the obscurity of the poem. The things that happen in "La Jeune Parque" and in Paul Valéry's other mythological monologues —the Narcissus, the Pythoness and the Serpent of the rich period of poetic activity which followed immediately upon "La Jeune Parque"—are never, on the one hand, quite imaginable as incidents which are actually taking place and never, on the other hand, quite reducible merely to thoughts in the poet's mind. The picture never quite emerges; the idea is never formulated quite. And for all the magnificences of sound, color, and suggestion which we find in these poems stanza by stanza, it seems to me that they are unsatisfactory because they are somehow not assimilable as wholes.

Yet Paul Valéry, when we put him beside Mallarmé, whom he echoes in these poems so often, is seen to possess the more vigorous intellect and the more solid imagination. Mallarmé is always a painter, usually a water-colorist—he wrote verses for ladies' fans as he might have painted little figures and flowers on them. He has his brightness and relief, but it is only such brightness and relief as is possible to someone working in the flat—whereas Valéry's genius is sculptural rather: these mythological poems have a density of cloud-shapes heavily massed—if they were not clouds, we should call them marmoreal. He gives us figures and groups half disengaged—and he runs to effects less of color than of light: the silvery, the sombre, the sunny, the translucent, the crystalline. And his verses carry off with the emphasis of an heroic resounding diction reminiscent of Alfred de Vigny the fluid waverings, the coy ambiguities and the delicately caught nuances which he has learned from Mallarmé. If Mallarmé was to supply subjects for Debussy, Valéry, outliving Debussy's vogue, was to be inspired in "La Jeune Parque" by Gluck. Valéry is, indeed, a sort of masculine of an art of which Mallarmé is the feminine. The elements in Mallarmé which made it possible for him to edit a woman's magazine and to write with his characteristic daintiness about styles in women's clothes is complemented, in Valéry, by a genius more powerful and stout which has a natural affinity with that of the architect.

And there is more substance in Valéry than in Mallarmé. In spite of his insistence that it is only the form, only the method in his work which interests him, Valéry's poetry has a certain dramatic quality. He is preoccupied with a particular conflict—the conflict between that part of man's existence which is represented by the abstraction of M. Teste and that part which is submerged in the sensations, distracted by the accidents, of the everyday world. If one were to read only "M. Teste"—though M. Teste is presented with some humor—or if one were to read only Valéry's prose, one might take him for one of the dryest and one of the most relentlessly abstract of minds. And it is true that the point of view of M. Teste figures conspicuously in the poetry of Valéry, as it predominates in his prose—that none of his characters is ever allowed to have a life independent of the intellectual world where at any moment he may appear as an abstraction, and that we suspect Valéry of preferring to human subjects, or at least of finding more satisfactory, the marble columns and stately palms which he makes the heroes of certain of his poems. It is true that even in love he tends to seek to suspend sensual satisfaction and keep his mistress in the timeless imminence which is for him a rival satisfaction— begging the woman in "Les Pas" not to hasten, for he enjoys awaiting her as much as her kiss, and making his Serpent say to Eve, when she is on the point of tasting the fruit of the tree:

> "Que si ta bouche fait un rêve,
> Cette soif qui songe à la sève,
> Ce délice à demi futur,
> C'est l'éternité fondante, Eve!"

He seems, in fact, to prefer women asleep, or fatigued, because he can think of them then, as in "Dormeuse," as forms of pure abstraction, from which the personality has departed, or because he can reflect, as in "La Fausse Morte," that the satiety of love is a kind of death; he likes to imagine them, as in "Intérieur," insubstantial transparent presences who pass before the eyes of the mind like glass through the beams of the sun. Yet there has perhaps never been a poet who enjoyed the sensuous world with more gusto than Valéry or who more solidly bodied it forth. In the reproduction, in beautiful verses, of shapes, sounds, effects of light and shadow, substances of fruit or flesh, Valéry has never been surpassed. Of the summer cicada, he writes:

> "L'insecte net gratte la sécheresse" . . .

of a cemetery by the sea:

> "Où tant de marbre est tremblant sur tant d'ombres" . . .

of the pool of Narcissus, when it is evening in the forest—"une tendre lueur d'heure ambiguë existe"—and the water is smooth as a mirror:

> "Onde déserte, et digne
> Sur son lustre, du lisse effacement d'un cygne" . . .

of a rough sea:

> "Si l'âme intense souffle, et renfle furibonde
> L'onde abrupte sur l'onde abbatue, et si l'onde
> Au cap tonne, immolant un monstre de candeur,
> Et vient des hautes mers vomir la profondeur
> Sur ce roc" . . .

And his human figures are like heroic statues which have yet a vibrancy and a soft envelopment. His Serpent puts before us an Eve of Michael Angelo:

> "Calme, claire, de charmes lourde,
> Je dominais furtivement,
> L'œil dans l'or ardent de ta laine,
> Ta nuque énigmatique et pleine
> Des secrets de ton mouvement!"

And later, when she is tempted:

> "Le marbre aspire, l'or se cambre!
> Ces blondes bases d'ombre et d'ambre
> Tremblent au bord du mouvement!"

And in one marvellous line of "Dormeuse," he reveals a whole recumbent figure:

> "Ta forme au ventre pur qu'un bras fluide drape."

Valéry's poetry is then always shifting back and forth between this palpable and visible world and a realm of intellectual abstraction. And the contrast between them, the conflict implied between the absolute laws of the mind and the limiting contingencies of life, opposites impossible to dissociate from one another, is, as I say, the real subject of his poems. Rather an unpromising subject, one might suppose—one, at any rate, entirely remote from the emotions of Romantic poetry. Yet this queer antagonism has inspired Valéry to some of the most original poetry ever written, to some of the indubitably great poetry of our time. We may take as an example of this theme treated on Valéry's full scale his most popular and perhaps most satisfactory poem, "Le Cimetière Marin," which celebrates Valéry's return to poetry after his long period of inactivity. Here the poet has stopped at noon beside a graveyard by

the sea: the sun seems to stand still above him; the water looks
as level as a roof on which the boats are doves walking. The external world at the moment seems to figure that absolute
toward which Valéry is always turning, with which he has been
for so many years obsessed. Yet, "O Noonday!" he cries, "for
all your immobility, I am the secret change in you—I am the
flaw in your enormous diamond!"—But the dead, there below, they have gone to join the void—they have become a part
of inanimate nature. And suppose he himself, the living man,
has, alive, merely the illusion of movement—like the runner or
the arrow of Zeno's paradoxes?—"But no!" he exhorts himself. "Break up that brooding, that immobility, which has all
but absorbed you!" The salt wind is already rising to break up
the tranquil roof of the sea, and to dash it against the rocks.
The world enters into movement again and the poet must go
back to life!

It is quite impossible, however, in other language, to provide a scenario for one of Valéry's poems: in doing so, one must
leave out almost all that is most characteristic of Valéry. In
trying to clear up his meaning, one clears it up too much. The
truth is that there are no real ideas, no real general reflections,
in such a poem as "Le Cimetière Marin": Valéry presents, even
more completely than Yeats in such a poem as "Among School
Children," the emotion merged with the idea and both embedded in the scene where they have occurred. It is the aim
and the triumph of the Symbolist poet to make the stabilities
of the external world answer to the individual's varying apprehension of them. It is, indeed, his effect, if not his purpose, to
lead us to question the traditional dualism which would make
them out to be two separate things. In such a poem as "Le
Cimetière Marin," there is no simple second meaning: there is
a marvellously close reproduction of the very complex and
continually changing relation of human consciousness to the
things of which it is conscious. The noonday is inorganic Nature, but it is also the absolute in the poet's mind, it is also his
twenty years of inaction—and it is also merely the noonday itself, which in a moment will no longer exist, which will be no
longer either tranquil or noon. And the sea, which, during
those moments of calm, forms a part of that great diamond of
nature in which the poet finds himself the single blemish,

because the single change, is also the image of the poet's silence, which in a moment, as the wind comes up to lash the sea, will give way to a sudden gust of utterance, the utterance of the poem itself. World and poet are always overlapping, are always interpenetrating, as they might in a Romantic poem; but the Symbolist will not even try, as the Romantic would be likely to do, to keep their relations consistent. The conventions of the poem's imagery change as quickly and as naturally as the images passing through the poet's mind.

II

Since "Charmes" (1922), Paul Valéry has published no more poetry, but a good deal of miscellaneous prose. Valéry's prose, in spite of the extravagant respect with which it is treated by his admirers, is by no means so remarkable as his verse. In the first place, it seems doubtful whether Valéry has ever really mastered a prose style. There are many admirable things in his essays, passages of a fine terseness, tightness and wit, but the prose is always liable to get snarled in a knot of words which balks the understanding at the same time that it exasperates the taste.

The opacities of Valéry's prose are usually attributed by Valéry's admirers, who in this only follow the intimations of the master himself, to the originality and profundity of his ideas. But the truth is that, when we go through Valéry's essays, we are unable to find many ideas. We find simply, as we do in his poetry, the presentation of intellectual situations, instead of the development of lines of thought. A French critic has already taxed Valéry with being a philosopher who won't philosophize; and it is true that the "rigor" of which he is always talking is rather an artistic effect of his prose, produced by certain devices of style like the artistic effects of his poems, than a quality of his logic. In spite of his passion for method, Valéry seems to have taken singularly little trouble to sort out or set in order his ideas: like M. Teste, he is occupied rather with savoring his intellectual sensations and in coining more or less mixed metaphors to convey them. And though it is possible to a certain extent to share his enjoyment of this pastime, in the long run we find it dreary and even repellent. What, we ask, has Valéry-Teste succeeded in dredging up by that abysmal self-scrutiny of his? Why, not much more than the realization, which he is hardly the first to have arrived at, that all forms of intellectual activity—even those which seem on the surface very different: poetry and mathematics, for example—are fundamentally the same sort of thing, merely arrangements or organizations of selected elements of experience. In so far as Valéry really deals in ideas, he is, in fact, a sort of super-dilettante, who, though he has many passages of pungent writing and stimulating insight, is just as likely, with groans of heavy labor, to unload a ponderous platitude. Most of Valéry's reputation for profundity comes, I believe, from the fact that he was one of the first literary men to acquire a smattering of the new mathematical and physical theory. Valéry has, it is true, made interesting use of this, but one wishes sometimes that he would either go further with it or leave philosophy alone. He never seems to have gotten over his first excitement at reading Poincaré, and he is still rather snobbish about it: he is always telling us how difficult it is going to be to make us understand this or that, and then the portentous thought, when it comes, turns out to be one of the commonplaces of modern scientific philosophy—the sort of thing which J. W. N. Sullivan, for example, has had no difficulty in explaining lucidly in the short popular essays of his "Aspects of Science."

As a literary critic, however, Valéry has both interest and importance. He is perhaps the principal exponent in France of a peculiar point of view about poetry which has gained currency with the progress of modern Symbolism. The Romantics thought of a poem as primarily a piece of self-expression—a gushing forth of emotion, a bursting into song. The conception fashionable to-day is quite different: the doctrines of Symbolism were in some ways closely analogous to the doctrines of Romanticism, but in this respect the later Symbolists are at the opposite pole from the Romantics. Paul Valéry's attitude toward poetry is both more esoteric and more scientific than that of Romantic criticism.

Valéry had already in 1894, in his "Introduction to the Method of Leonardo da Vinci," defined a work of art as "a machine intended to excite and combine the individual formations" of a particular "category of minds." And from the time of "La Jeune Parque," he has never ceased to insist that a poem is an intricate intellectual problem, a struggle with self-imposed conditions—that it is, above all, something *constructed*. Or, according to a favorite simile of Valéry's, a poem is like a heavy weight which the poet has carried to the roof bit by bit—the reader is the passer-by upon whom the weight is dropped all at once and who consequently receives from it in a moment an overwhelming impression, a complete æsthetic effect, such as the poet has never known in composing it. "Enthusiasm," says Valéry, "is not an artist's state of mind." And also: "Genius is a habit which certain people acquire." "X wants us to believe that a metaphor is a communication from Heaven. A metaphor is what occurs when one looks at things in a certain way, as getting dazzled is what occurs when one looks into a sun. When one looks at things in what way? You feel it, and some day it will perhaps be possible to explain it in the most precise terms. Do this and that—and you have all the metaphors in the world."

This apparently cool and analytic attitude, however, is accompanied, curiously enough, by an excessively esoteric conception of poetry. This conception is most clearly stated and its weakness, it seems to me, made most clearly manifest in a preface which Valéry has just contributed to a commentary on his own "Charmes" by the French essayist Alain (this scholastic layer upon layer of commentary is itself very characteristic of the contemporary criticism of poetry). Here we find, as usual, the scientific approach—which it occurs to us, as we read, is largely a matter of scientific similes: "There are certain rather mysterious bodies which physics studies and which chemistry uses: I always think of them when I reflect upon works of art." These are the catalytic agents, which precipitate chemical changes without being affected themselves. So the work of art, says Valéry, acts upon the mind into which it is introduced. Even when chemically considered, then, the work of art remains something "mysterious." And by "works of art," it further appears that, in the department of literature, Valéry means poetry exclusively. Prose, he says, has "sense" for its sole object —but the object of poetry is something not only more mysterious, but also apparently more occult: "There is absolutely no question in poetry of one person's transmitting to another something intelligible that is going on in his mind. It is a question of creating in the latter a state whose expression is precisely and uniquely that which communicates it to him. Whatever image or emotion is formed in the amateur of poems, it is valid and sufficient if it produces in him this reciprocal relation between the word-cause and the word-effect. The result is that the reader enjoys a very great freedom in regard to ideas, a freedom analogous to that which one recognizes in the case of the hearer of music, though not so intensive."

It seems to me that a pretense to exactitude is here used to cover a number of ridiculously false assumptions, and to promote a kind of æsthetic mysticism rather than to effect a scientific analysis. In the first place, is it not absurd to assert that prose deals exclusively in "sense" as distinguished from suggestion, and that one has no right to expect from poetry, as Valéry says in another passage, "any definite notion at all"? Is verse really an intellectual product absolutely different in kind from prose? Has it really an absolutely different function? Are not both prose and verse, after all, merely techniques of human intercommunication, and techniques which have played various rôles, have been used for various purposes, in different periods and civilizations? The early Greeks used verse for their histories, their romances and their laws—the Greeks and the Elizabethans used it for their dramas. If Valéry's definitions are correct, what becomes of Homer, Virgil, Dante, Shakespeare and Goethe? They all of them deal in sense as well as suggestion and aim to convey "definite notions." These definitions have, however, obviously been framed to apply to the poetry of Valéry himself and of Mallarmé and the other Symbolists. Yet it does not really apply even to them. As we have seen, Valéry's poetry does make sense, it does deal with definite subjects, it does transmit to us "something intelligible that is going on inside his mind." Even though in calling his book of poems "Charmes," he has tried to emphasize its esoteric, magical, non-utilitarian character, we cannot admit that it is anything but an effort like another of articulate human speech. What happens when we communicate with each other, in literature as well as in curses and cries for help, and in verse as well as in prose—what part is played by "sense" and what part is played by suggestion, and whether sense and suggestion are different and separable—are questions which take us far and deep: I shall return to them in a later chapter. But Valéry has already let us see—it is even one of his favorite ideas—that he understands the basic similarity between the various forms of intellectual activity; he has taken pride in pointing out the kinship between poetry and mathematics. And if the function and methods of poetry are similar to those of mathematics, they must surely be similar to those of prose. If Valéry resembles Descartes, as he seems willingly to indulge himself in imagining, then it is impossible to make a true distinction between a philosophical or mathematical treatise and however Symbolistic a poem. Valéry betrays himself here, it seems to me, as a thinker anything but "rigorous"; and he betrays also, I believe, a desire, defensive no doubt at the same time as snobbish, to make it appear that verse, a technique now no longer much used for history, story-telling or drama and consequently not much in popular demand, has some inherent superiority to prose. He has not hesitated even to assure us elsewhere that "poetry is the most difficult of the arts"!

III

With all respect for Valéry's intelligence, for his candor and independence, it must be admitted that he is taken too seriously —and perhaps takes himself too seriously—as a universal sage. "Stupidity is not my forte," he says—and though we are willing to agree, we should prefer not to hear him say it. A great poet, we should prefer not to have him continually explaining what superhuman labor it has cost him to compose his poems and intimating that, in comparison with his own work, the poetry of other poets is mostly facile and superficial— especially when we remember his replying to a correspondent who had complained of some awkward inversion in "La Jeune Parque" that the reader had happened to hit upon precisely one of those passages in the poem which Valéry had "literally improvised in the hasty lassitude of finishing it up."

The pretentious and snobbish side of Valéry was seen at its worst on the occasion of his election to the French Academy, when he succeeded to Anatole France's chair and had to deliver an address upon his predecessor—an incident which is

worth dwelling upon, however, because it has a certain historical importance. Valéry behaved on this occasion in a highly
unconventional manner. In the first place, it appears that at the
Academy the uniforms are passed on from generation to generation and that a new member fits himself as best he can from
such old uniforms as are available—as American college graduates at commencement rent old graduation gowns. Paul Valéry,
however, is reported to have astounded the Academicians by
appearing in a smart brand-new uniform which he had had
made for him by a fashionable tailor. The address on Anatole
France which he then read is said to have been received with
consternation. It has always been the custom for the newly
elected member to compose an "*éloge*" on the man he is succeeding; but, instead of the usual complimentary obituary,
Valéry delivered himself of a piece of criticism which can hardly
be described as anything less than an attack. Anatole France
had been unfriendly to Symbolism in the days when it had
been new and unpopular: he had said that he could "never
believe in the success of a literary school which expressed difficult thoughts in obscure language." He had made fun of Mallarmé and spoken contemptuously of Rimbaud. And in his
own writing he had represented that French tradition of classical lucidity and simplicity against which the Symbolists were
rebelling. Now Paul Valéry is only the second Symbolist to
have been admitted to the French Academy, and his election
was like a final official recognition of the literary party which
had once been outlawed. His funeral sermon on Anatole France
is composed in the mood of a none too generous victor, at
once complaining and cocky. Valéry adopts the general tone of
desiring in a patronizing way to say something kindly and appreciative about France, but everything that he says turns out
to sound disparaging. He takes up *seriatim* all the charges
which have been made against France since his death—such as
the meaningless gossip to the effect that, if it had not been for
Mme. de Caillavet, he would never have accomplished anything
—and, with the air of mitigating their seriousness, somehow
succeeds in giving them weight. He speaks of France's "sinu-
osity" and prudence in such a way as to convey the impression
that he was timid and insincere (since, though France had invited popular hatred, had sacrificed his place in the Academy

and had embroiled himself with his friends, in defending the innocence of Dreyfus, he had failed to understand and champion Symbolism); and he concludes that, in view of France's humble origins (he was the son of a bookseller on the quais), he had really done very well indeed. Valéry furthermore refrains throughout in a marked and insulting manner from mentioning France's name—a perfectly innocuous pseudonym derived from a family nickname for Anatole-François—and makes upon it the following comment: "He himself would not have been possible, would scarcely have been conceivable, except in France, whose name he assumed. Under that name, so difficult to carry off, and which it required so much assurance to adopt, he won the favor of the universe. He presented it, indeed, with a France possessing all those specious qualities with which, if she herself were to remain satisfied, the universe would suffer; but which were agreeable to him and to which he did not feel any objection." Valéry goes on to speak at length of France, the nation (Valéry himself is half Italian, and a tendency to think in Italian is evidently at the bottom of some of the peculiarities of his style), and ends his address on a high note of patriotism.

Now one would naturally not expect Paul Valéry to go against his convictions, or even politely to conceal them with evasions, merely because he had happened to succeed to the place of a writer of whom he disapproved. Furthermore, with Valéry's criticisms of France it is partly possible to agree. It is not without reason that Anatole France has come to represent to many French literary people all that is elegantly second-rate in the writing of the previous generation. France was the last great writer of a tradition and in his work the peculiar weaknesses of the tradition became, in consequence, especially conspicuous. It is true that before he died, he had lived long enough to have produced certain books which, for their empty unctuousness and suavity, their mechanical neatness of form, do tend to discourage us rather with Renanian irony and pity and with classical symmetry and clearness. It was time that those formulas should be discarded—there was nothing more to be done along those lines. And Valéry is one of those who have abolished them. Yet, with all faith in the methods of Symbolism, with all enthusiasm for its achievements, as one reads this patronizing and feline paper one cannot help rebelling against what appears to be Valéry's assumption that it is impossible at the same time to be profound and to write as lightly and lucidly as France did. Valéry himself seems deliberately on this occasion to have avoided writing attractively or clearly: though his subject is not in the least metaphysical, though there is nothing in the least difficult about what he is saying, this address is perhaps his masterpiece of bad writing. Never have Valéry's viscous prose, his masses of clotted abstractions, his hindside-foremost presentations of thought, been managed to worse advantage. To say that the author of "Le Jardin d'Epicure" would have turned in his grave if he could have heard Valéry's paper would be to understate the situation: France's bitterest clerical enemies could have wished him no more horrible punishment than to have had to listen to them in Hell.

In any case, Valéry's advent to the Academy, in suggesting a contrast between Valéry and France, marks even more sharply than the divergence between Yeats and Bernard Shaw the difference between the new methods and attitudes of the typical literature of the period since the War and those of the literature of the period which the War ended. Anatole France was a popular writer: he aimed to be persuasive and intelligible—he used frankly to remind his secretary, Brousson, that they were "working for a bourgeois clientèle. That is the only one that reads. Do not tear away the veil of the temple. Pluck it off a little at a time. Riddle it with sly little holes. . . . Leave to your reader the easy victory of seeing further than you." His books were sold on all the bookstalls of France and known all over the civilized world. Whereas Paul Valéry disregards altogether the taste and intelligence of the ordinary reader: instead of allowing his reader the easy victory, he takes pride in outstripping him completely. And he is read chiefly by other writers or by people with a special interest in literature: his poems are always out of print and his other writings are always being published in editions so expensive and limited as practically never to circulate at all. Anatole France was voluminous: he supplied his public with a whole literature of romance, history, criticism, satire, drama, poetry, philosophy, political pamphlets, newspaper articles and speeches. Paul Valéry publishes little: his whole genius has been concentrated to the production of a few magnificent poems—beyond these, he has written almost nothing but a few volumes of miscellaneous notes. Anatole France was essentially a rationalist: he did not deny the incongruities and incoherences of experience, but he attempted to write about them, at least, in a simple, logical and harmonious style. Paul Valéry has set himself, on the contrary, the task of reproducing by his very language all the complexities and confusions of our interacting sensations and ideas. The phenomena with which France usually deals are the events of life as it is lived in the world; with Valéry the object of interest is the isolated or ideal human mind, brooding on its own contradictions or admiring its own flights. When France turns away from literature, he occupies himself naturally with politics—he goes on the stump for Dreyfus, allies himself with the Socialist party, writes editorials for its paper, addresses meetings of working men and finally declares himself a Communist. But Valéry concerns himself little with politics, and then only as a detached intelligence—his extra-literary pursuits are scientific. And whereas for France, science meant exclusively a conventional nineteenth-century mechanism, with which he had become so deeply imbued that he was haunted all his life by nightmares of the dizziness of space, the extinction of the sun, the fatally automatic character of human loves and ambitions, the reversion of mankind to barbarism through a reversal of the evolutionary process—Paul Valéry has emerged into an era when the scientific point of view no longer implies this determinism. (France's attitude toward modern science was like his attitude toward Symbolism: when in his old age he met Einstein in Berlin and Einstein tried to explain to him his theories, France had no patience to listen: "When he told me that light was matter, my head began to swim and I took my leave.") For the modern scientific thought which colors Valéry's speculations has extricated itself from the conception of ineluctable laws of nature, relentless chains of cause and effect. Valéry discusses in one of his most interesting essays the oppression and panic felt by Pascal at his vision—a typically seventeenth-century vision of the scientific imagination—of the silent abysses of space. Such imaginings drove a Pascal into fanatical piety—the equivalent conceptions of two centuries later drove

France to a habit of despair which came largely to counteract and invalidate his hopes for human society. To Pascal and France alike, man seemed ignominious and insignificant. But Valéry can laugh at both: he has caught already the first lights of an age in which our increasing knowledge of the universe will have come to change "not merely our ideas, but certain of our immediate reactions" and "what one might call 'Pascal's reaction' will be a rarity and a curiosity to psychologists." Man is no longer to be a tiny exile, pitting himself amidst vast space against matter: what he has been thinking of as his soul, the exclusive possession of human beings, is somehow bound up with that external nature which he has been regarding as inanimate or alien, and his mind, which has lately seemed as feeble as a spark of phosphorescence on a midnight ocean, turns out to have constructed its own universe.

It is particularly illuminating to compare Valéry's M. Teste with France's most celebrated creation, M. Bergeret of the "Histoire Contemporaine." M. Bergeret is a social being, polite, agreeable and fond of company: though sadly harassed in the community where he lives by many elements which he feels to be hostile or undesirable, the common interests of that community and of the civilization it represents are what he has chiefly at heart. He is always discussing this civilization with his neighbors, and when an important political issue arises, he is positive and prompt to take sides. But M. Teste is outside society, he has almost succeeded in dissociating himself from human relations altogether: "He neither smiled, nor said good-day nor good-bye; and seemed not to hear one's how-do-you-do"—he goes to bed and goes to sleep in the presence of a guest, and his effect on Mme. Teste is to make her feel that she is non-existent. He is ill-mannered, self-preoccupied, austere— the modern psychologists would probably diagnose him as introverted, narcissistic and manic depressive.

And in general it may be said that the strength of Anatole France's generation was the strength to be derived from a wide knowledge of human affairs, a sympathetic interest in human beings, direct contact with public opinion and participation in public life through literature. The strength of solitary labor and of earnest introspection is the strength of Valéry's.

IV. T. S. Eliot

I HAVE noted the similarity between the English seventeenth-century poets and the French nineteenth-century Symbolists. The poetry of T. S. Eliot has, in our own time, brought together these two traditions, as it is Eliot who, so far as I know, has for the first time called attention to their resemblance. "The form," he says, "in which I began to write, in 1908 or 1909, was directly drawn from the study of Laforgue together with the later Elizabethan drama; and I do not know anyone who started from exactly that point."

I have so far, in discussing the early Symbolists, spoken chiefly of Mallarmé. But T. S. Eliot derived, as he indicates, from a different branch of the Symbolist tradition. In 1873 there had appeared in Paris a book of poems called "Les Amours Jaunes," by a writer who signed himself Tristan Corbière. "Les Amours Jaunes" was received with complete indifference, and scarcely more than a year after it appeared, the author died of consumption. Only thirty at the time of his death, Tristan Corbière had been an eccentric and very maladjusted man: he was the son of a sea captain who had also written sea stories and he had had an excellent education, but he chose for himself the life of an outlaw. In Paris, he slept all day and spent the nights in the cafés or at his verses, greeting at dawn the Paris harlots as they emerged from the station house or the hotel with the same half-harsh, half-tender fellow-feeling for the exile from conventional society which, when he was at home in his native Brittany, caused him to flee the house of his family and seek the company of the customs-men and sailors—living skeleton and invalid as he was, performing prodigies of courage and endurance in the navigation of a little cutter which he sailed by preference in the worst possible weather. He made a pose of his unsociability and of what he considered his physical ugliness, at the same time that he undoubtedly suffered over them. Melancholy, with a feverishly active mind, full of groanings and vulgar jokes, he used to amuse himself by going about in convict's clothes and by firing guns and revolvers out the window in protest against the

singing of the village choir; and on one occasion, on a visit to
Rome, he appeared in the streets in evening dress, with a mitre
on his head and two eyes painted on his forehead, leading a pig
decorated with ribbons. And Corbière's poetry was a poetry of
the outcast: often colloquial and homely, yet with a rhetoric of
fantastic slang; often with the manner of slapdash doggerel,
yet sure of its own morose artistic effects; full of the parade of
romantic personality, yet incessantly humiliating itself with a
self-mockery scurrilous and savage, out of which, as Huysmans
said, would sometimes rise without warning "a cry of sharp
pain like the breaking of a 'cello string"—Corbière's verse
brought back into French poetry qualities which had been
alien to its spirit since François Villon's day.

So outlandish did Corbière appear even from the point of
view of the Romantics that he was dismissed, when he was noticed at all, as not merely unseemly but insane—till Paul Verlaine, in 1883, did him honor in a series of articles, "Les Poètes
Maudits," which was one of the important critical events in
the development of Symbolism. Verlaine himself, a more accomplished artist, but a less original and interesting personality, had been strongly influenced by "Les Amours Jaunes"—he
seems, indeed, to have caught over from Corbière, not only
certain artistic effects, but even something of his own poetic
personality, his peculiar accent of wistful naïveté: compare
Corbière's "Rondels pour Après" with Verlaine's sonnet which
begins, "L'espoir luit comme un brin de paille dans l'étable";
or "Paria" with "Casper Hauser."

But another French poet, Jules Laforgue, nineteen years
younger than Corbière, had independently developed a tone
and technique—poignant-ironic, grandiose-slangy, scurrilous-
naïve—which had much in common with Corbière's. Laforgue
was the son of a schoolmaster and, for all his nonchalance in
handling rudely the conventions of French poetry, much more
a professional man of letters than Corbière. Laforgue even errs
through preciosity in his fashion; what with Corbière seems a
personal and inevitable, if eccentric, manner of speech, in
Laforgue sounds self-conscious and deliberate, almost sometimes a literary exercise. He was tubercular, as Corbière was
also, and dead at twenty-seven—and his gentleness and sadness
are still those of a sick well-cared-for child; his asperities, his

surprising images, his coquetries, his cynicism, and his impudence, are still those of a clever schoolboy. Laforgue's friends procured him a post as reader to the Empress Augusta of Germany; and, falling under the spell of German philosophy, he brought its jargon into his verse, contributing thereby to Symbolism perhaps the one element of obscurity which it had lacked.

Yet Laforgue is a very fine poet and one of the most remarkable of the Symbolists. He and Corbière had introduced a new variety of vocabulary and a new flexibility of feeling. With Mallarmé, it may be said that, on the whole, it is the imagery, not the feeling, which is variable: though sometimes playful, he is classical in the sense (as Yeats and Valéry are) that he sustains a certain grandeur of tone. But it is from the conversational-ironic, rather than from the serious-æsthetic, tradition of Symbolism that T. S. Eliot derives. Corbière and Laforgue are almost everywhere in his early work. The emphatic witty quatrains of Corbière, with their sudden lapses into tenderness or pathos, are heard again in the satiric verse of Eliot: a poem like "Mr. Eliot's Sunday Morning Service" would hardly, one imagines, have been written without Corbière's "Rapsodie Foraine." And as "Conversation Galante" derives clearly from certain poems in Laforgue's "Complaintes" and "Imitation de Notre-Dame la Lune," so the more elaborate "Portrait of a Lady" and "The Love Song of J. Alfred Prufrock" follow closely the longer poems of Laforgue. Compare the conclusion of "Mr. Prufrock" with the conclusion of the early version of Laforgue's poem "Légende":

"I grow old . . . I grow old . . .
I shall wear the bottoms of my trousers rolled.

Shall I part my hair behind? Do I dare to eat a peach?
I shall wear white flannel trousers, and walk upon the beach,
I have heard the mermaids singing, each to each.

I do not think that they will sing to me.

I have seen them riding seaward on the waves
Combing the white hair of the waves blown back
When the wind blows the water white and black.

We have lingered in the chambers of the sea
By sea-girls wreathed with seaweed red and brown
Till human voices wake us, and we drown."

. . .

"Hier l'orchestre attaqua
 Sa dernière polka

Oh! L'automne, l'automne!
 Les casinos
 Qu'on abandonne
Remisent leurs pianos! . . .

Phrases, verroteries,
Caillots de souvenirs.
Oh! comme elle est maigrie!
Que vais-je devenir? . . .

Adieu! Les filles d'ifs dans les grisailles
Ont l'air de pleureuses de funerailles
Sous l'autan noir qui veut que tout s'en aille.

Assez, assez,
C'est toi qui as commencé.

Va, ce n'est plus l'odeur de tes fourrures.
Va, vos moindres clins d'yeux sont des parjures.
Tais-toi, avec vous autres rien ne dure.

Tais-toi, tais-toi,
On n'aime qu'une fois" . . .

Here it will be seen that Eliot has reproduced Laforgue's irregular metrical scheme almost line for line. Furthermore, the subject of Laforgue's poem—the hesitations and constraints of a man either too timid or too disillusioned to make love to a woman who provokes his ironic pity at the same time that she stirs gusts of stifled emotion—has a strong resemblance to the subjects of "Mr. Prufrock" and the "Portrait of a Lady." And in another poem, "La Figlia Che Piange," Eliot has adapted a line of Laforgue's: "Simple et sans foi comme un bonjour"—"Simple and faithless as a smile and shake of the hand." He has even brought over into English some of the unstressed effect of French verse: how different, for example, is the alexandrine of Eliot's just quoted from the classical English alexandrine "which like a wounded snake drags its slow length along" or "with sparkless ashes loads an unlamented urn." (In his exhaustive "Influence du Symbolisme Français sur la Poésie Américaine de 1910 à 1920," M. René Taupin has shown the influence of Gautier also in Eliot's satiric poems: "The Hippopotamus," it appears, is almost a transcript of a hippopotamus by Gautier, and the "Grishkin is nice" passage in "Whispers of Immortality" repeats a "Carmen est maigre" of Gautier.)

It must not be supposed, however, that Eliot is not original or that he is not the equal of either of his masters. Those longer and more elaborate poems—"Derniers Vers" in the collected edition—which Laforgue was constructing at the time of his death out of more fragmentary and less mature work are certainly his most important performances: through his masterly flexibility of vocabulary and metric, he has here achieved one of the definitive expressions of the pathetic-ironic, wordly-æsthetic moods of the *fin de siècle* temperament. Yet, though Eliot has, in certain obvious respects, applied Laforgue's formula so faithfully, he cannot properly be described as an imitator because he is in some ways a superior artist. He is more mature than Laforgue ever was, and his workmanship is perfect in a way that Corbière's and Laforgue's were rarely. T. S. Eliot's peculiar distinction lies, as Clive Bell has said, in his "phrasing." Laforgue's images are often far-fetched and inappropriately grotesque: his sins in this respect are really very closely akin to those of the English metaphysical poets; but Eliot's taste is absolutely sure—his images always precisely right. And the impression that Eliot leaves, even in these earliest poems, is clear, vivid and unforgettable: we do not subordinate him to his Symbolist predecessors any more than, when we find him, as in "Gerontion," writing in the rhythms of late Elizabethan blank-verse, we associate him with Middleton or Webster.

When we come to examine Eliot's themes, we recognize something which we have found already in Laforgue, but which appears in Eliot in a more intense form. One of the principal preoccupations of Flaubert—a great hero of Eliot's, as of Eliot's fellow-poet, Ezra Pound's—had been the inferiority of the

present to the past: the Romantics had discovered the possibilities of the historical imagination; with their thirst for boldness,
grandeur, and magnificence, they had located these qualities in
past epochs—especially the Middle Ages and the Renaissance.
And Flaubert, who shared with the Romantics this appetite for
the gorgeous and the untamed, but who constrained himself,
also, to confront the actual nineteenth-century world, pursued
two parallel lines of fiction which lent significance and relief to
each other. On the one hand, he reconstructed, in "Salammbô"
and in "La Tentation de Saint-Antoine," the splendid barbarities of the pagan world and the heroic piety of the early Christian; and on the other, he caricatured, in "Madame Bovary," in
"L'Education Sentimentale" and in "Bouvard et Pécuchet,"
the pusillanimity and mediocrity of contemporary bourgeois
France. This whole point of view of Flaubert's—summed up,
as it were, in "Trois Contes," where the three periods are contrasted in one book—was profoundly to affect modern literature. We shall find it later on in Joyce; but in the meantime we
must note its reappearance in the poetry of Eliot. Eliot, like
Flaubert, feels at every turn that human life is now ignoble,
sordid or tame, and he is haunted and tormented by intimations that it has once been otherwise. In "Burbank with a
Baedeker: Bleistein with a Cigar," the young American tourist
in Venice, superseded in his affair with the Princess Volupine
by a vulgar Austrian Jew, meditates on the clipped wings and
pared claws of the Lion of St. Mark's, the symbol of the old arrogant Venice and of the world where such a city was possible.
In "A Cooking Egg," the poet demands, after a call upon a
very mild, dull spinster: "Where are the eagles and the trumpets?" and himself returns the saddened answer: "Buried beneath some snow-deep Alps." In "Lune de Miel," the Middle
Western American travellers, stifled with the summer heat and
devoured by the bedbugs of Ravenna, are contrasted with the
noble crumbling beauty of the old Byzantine church less than
a league away, of which they are totally unaware and to which
they have apparently no relation; and in "Mr. Eliot's Sunday
Morning Service," the combined grossness and aridity of the
modern clergymen is contrasted with the pure and fresh religious feeling of a picture of the baptism of Christ by "a painter
of the Umbrian school." In the best and most effective of

these poems, "Sweeney Among the Nightingales," the poet, during a drowsy, idiotic and mildly sinister scene in some low dive, where two of the girls are supposed to be plotting against one of the men, remembers, at the sound of nightingales singing, the murder of Agamemnon in Æschylus:

> "The host with someone indistinct
> Converses at the door apart,
> The nightingales are singing near
> The Convent of the Sacred Heart,
>
> And sang within the bloody wood
> When Agamemnon cried aloud,
> And let their liquid siftings fall
> To stain the stiff dishonoured shroud."

The present is more timid than the past: the bourgeois are afraid to let themselves go. The French had been preoccupied with this idea ever since the first days of Romanticism; but Eliot was to deal with the theme from a somewhat different point of view, a point of view characteristically American. For T. S. Eliot, though born in St. Louis, comes from a New England family and was educated at Harvard; and he is in some ways a typical product of our New England civilization. He is distinguished by that combination of practical prudence with moral idealism which shows itself in its later developments as an excessive fastidiousness and scrupulousness. One of the principal subjects of Eliot's poetry is really that regret at situations unexplored, that dark rankling of passions inhibited, which has figured so conspicuously in the work of the American writers of New England and New York from Hawthorne to Edith Wharton. T. S. Eliot, in this respect, has much in common with Henry James. Mr. Prufrock and the poet of the "Portrait of a Lady," with their helpless consciousness of having dared too little, correspond exactly to the middle-aged heroes of "The Ambassadors" and "The Beast in the Jungle," realizing sadly too late in life that they have been living too cautiously and too poorly. The fear of life, in Henry James, is closely bound up with the fear of vulgarity. And Eliot, too, fears vulgarity—which he embodies in the symbolic figure of "Apeneck Sweeney"—at the same time that he is fascinated by it. Yet he chafes at the limitations and pretenses of the culture represented by Boston—a society "quite uncivilized," as he says, "but refined beyond the point of civilization." He has some amusing satiric poems about old New England ladies—in one of which he reflects on his way to the house of his Cousin Harriet, how

> ". . . evening quickens faintly in the street,
>   Wakening the appetites of life in some
>   And to others bringing the *Boston Evening Transcript.*"

And the "Portrait of a Lady," whether the scene be laid in Boston or in London, is essentially a poem of that New England society "refined beyond the point of civilization": from the Lady, who serves tea among lighted candles—"an atmosphere of Juliet's tomb"—with her dampening efforts at flattery and flirtation through the medium of cultured conversation—her slightly stale and faded gush about Chopin and her memories of Paris in the spring—the poet is seized with an impulse to flee:

> "I take my hat: how can I make a cowardly amends
>   For what she has said to me?
>   You will see me any morning in the park
>   Reading the comics and the sporting page.
>   Particularly I remark
>   An English countess goes upon the stage,
>   A Greek was murdered at a Polish dance,
>   Another bank defaulter has confessed.
>   I keep my countenance,
>   I remain self-possessed
>   Except when a street piano, mechanical and tired,
>   Reiterates some worn-out common song
>   With the smell of hyacinths across the garden
>   Recalling things that other people have desired."

But he is always debating things with his conscience: his incurable moral solicitude makes him wonder:

> "Are these ideas right or wrong?"

So Mr. Prufrock in the room where

> "... women come and go
> Talking of Michelangelo,"

wistfully asks himself:

> "Shall I say, I have gone at dusk through narrow
>   streets
> And watched the smoke that rises from the pipes
> Of lonely men in shirt-sleeves, leaning out of
>   windows?" ...

And Mr. Prufrock wonders also whether he should not put a question to his lady—but he never gets to the point of putting it.

II

But Eliot's most complete expression of this theme of emotional starvation is to be found in the later and longer poem called "The Waste Land" (1922). The Waste Land of the poem is a symbol borrowed from the myth of the Holy Grail: it is a desolate and sterile country ruled by an impotent king, in which not only have the crops ceased to grow and the animals to reproduce, but the very human inhabitants have become incapable of having children. But this sterility we soon identify as the sterility of the Puritan temperament. On the first pages we find again the theme of the girl with the hyacinths (themselves a symbol for the rearisen god of the fertility rites who will save the rainless country from drouth) which has already figured in "La Figlia Che Piange" and "Dans le Restaurant"—a memory which apparently represents for the poet some fulfillment foregone in youth and now agonizingly desired; and in the last pages it is repeated. We recognize throughout "The Waste Land" the peculiar conflicts of the Puritan turned artist: the horror of vulgarity and the shy sympathy with the common life, the ascetic shrinking from sexual experience and the distress at the drying up of the springs of sexual emotion, with the straining after a religious emotion which may be made to take its place.

Yet though Eliot's spiritual and intellectual roots are still more firmly fixed in New England than is, I believe, ordinarily understood, there is in "The Waste Land" a good deal more than the mere gloomy moods of a New Englander regretting an emotionally undernourished youth. The colonization by the Puritans of New England was merely an incident in that rise of the middle class which has brought a commercial-industrial civilization to the European cities as well as to the American ones. T. S. Eliot now lives in London and has become an English citizen; but the desolation, the æsthetic and spiritual drouth, of Anglo-Saxon middle-class society oppresses London as well as Boston. The terrible dreariness of the great modern cities is the atmosphere in which "The Waste Land" takes place—amidst this dreariness, brief, vivid images emerge, brief pure moments of feeling are distilled; but all about us we are aware of nameless millions performing barren office routines, wearing down their souls in interminable labors of which the products never bring them profit—people whose pleasures are so sordid and so feeble that they seem almost sadder than their pains. And this Waste Land has another aspect: it is a place not merely of desolation, but of anarchy and doubt. In our post-War world of shattered institutions, strained nerves and bankrupt ideals, life no longer seems serious or coherent —we have no belief in the things we do and consequently we have no heart for them.

The poet of "The Waste Land" is living half the time in the real world of contemporary London and half the time in the haunted wilderness of the mediæval legend. The water for which he longs in the twilight desert of his dream is to quench the spiritual thirst which torments him in the London dusk; and as Gerontion, "an old man in a dry month," thought of the young men who had fought in the rain, as Prufrock fancied riding the waves with mermaids and lingering in the chambers of the sea, as Mr. Apollinax has been imagined drawing strength from the deep sea-caves of coral islands—so the poet of "The Waste Land," making water the symbol of all freedom, all fecundity and flowering of the soul, invokes in desperate need the memory of an April shower of his youth, the song of the hermit thrush with its sound of water dripping and the vision of a drowned Phœnician sailor, sunk beyond "the cry of gulls and the deep sea swell," who has at least died by water, not thirst. The poet, who seems now to be travelling in a country cracked by drouth, can only feverishly dream of these things. One's head may be well stored with literature, but the heroic prelude of the Elizabethans has ironic echoes in modern London streets and modern London drawing-rooms: lines remembered from Shakespeare turn to jazz or refer themselves to the sound of phonographs. And now it is one's personal regrets again—the girl in the hyacinth-garden—"the awful daring of a moment's surrender which an age of prudence can never retract"—the key which turned once, and once only, in the prison of inhibition and isolation. Now he stands on the arid plain again, and the dry-rotted world of London seems to be crumbling about him—the poem ends in a medley of quotations from a medley of literatures—like Gérard de Nerval's "Desdichado," the poet is disinherited; like the author of the "Pervigilium Veneris," he laments that his song is mute and asks when the spring will come which will set it free like the swallow's; like Arnaut Daniel, in Dante, as he disappears in the refining fire, he begs the world to raise a prayer for his torment. "These fragments I have shored against my ruins."

"The Waste Land," in method as well as in mood, has left Laforgue far behind. Eliot has developed a new technique, at once laconic, quick, and precise, for representing the transmutations of thought, the interplay of perception and reflection. Dealing with subjects complex in the same way as those of Yeats's poem "Among School-Children" and Valéry's "Cimetière Marin," Eliot has found for them a different language. As May Sinclair has said of Eliot, his "trick of cutting his corners and his curves makes him seem obscure when he is clear as daylight. His thoughts move very rapidly and by astounding cuts. They move not by logical stages and majestic roundings of the full literary curve, but as live thoughts move in live brains." Let us examine, as an illustration, the lovely nightingale passage from "The Waste Land." Eliot is describing a room in London:

> "Above the antique mantel was displayed
>   As though a window gave upon the sylvan scene
>   The change of Philomel, by the barbarous king
>   So rudely forced; yet there the nightingale

> Filled all the desert with inviolable voice
> And still she cried, and still the world pursues,
> 'Jug Jug' to dirty ears."

That is, the poet sees, above the mantel, a picture of Philomela changed to a nightingale, and it gives his mind a moment's swift release. The picture is like a window opening upon Milton's earthly paradise—the "sylvan scene," as Eliot explains in a note, is a phrase from "Paradise Lost"—and the poet associates his own plight in the modern city, in which some "infinitely gentle, infinitely suffering thing," to quote one of Eliot's earlier poems, is somehow being done to death, with Philomela, raped and mutilated by Tereus. But in the earthly paradise, there had been a nightingale singing: Philomela had wept her woes in song, though the barbarous king had cut out her tongue—her sweet voice had remained inviolable. And with a sudden change of tense, the poet flashes back from the myth to his present situation:

> "And still she *cried*, and still the world *pursues*,
> 'Jug Jug' to dirty ears."

The song of birds was represented in old English popular poetry by such outlandish syllables as "Jug Jug"—so Philomela's cry sounds to the vulgar. Eliot has here, in seven lines of extraordinary liquidity and beauty, fused the picture, the passage from Milton and the legend from Ovid, into a single moment of vague poignant longing.

"The Waste Land" is dedicated to Ezra Pound, to whom Eliot elsewhere acknowledges a debt; and he has here evidently been influenced by Pound's "Cantos." "The Waste Land," like the "Cantos," is fragmentary in form and packed with literary quotation and allusion. In fact, the passage just discussed above has a resemblance to a passage on the same subject—the Philomela-Procne myth—at the beginning of Pound's Fourth Canto. Eliot and Pound have, in fact, founded a school of poetry which depends on literary quotation and reference to an unprecedented degree. Jules Laforgue had sometimes parodied, in his poems, the great lines of other poets—

> "O Nature, donne-moi la force et le courage
> De me croire en âge" . . .

And Eliot had, in his early poetry, introduced phrases from Shakespeare and Blake for purposes of ironic effect. He has always, furthermore, been addicted to prefacing his poems with quotations and echoing passages from other poets. But now, in "The Waste Land," he carries this tendency to what one must suppose its extreme possible limit: here, in a poem of only four hundred and three lines (to which are added, however, seven pages of notes), he manages to include quotations from, allusions to, or imitations of, at least thirty-five different writers (some of them, such as Shakespeare and Dante, laid under contribution several times)—as well as several popular songs; and to introduce passages in six foreign languages, including Sanskrit. And we must also take into consideration that the idea of the literary medley itself seems to have been borrowed from still another writer, Pound. We are always being dismayed, in our general reading, to discover that lines among those which we had believed to represent Eliot's residuum of original invention had been taken over or adapted from other writers (sometimes very unexpected ones: thus, it appears now, from Eliot's essay on Bishop Andrewes, that the first five lines of "The Journey of the Magi," as well as the "word within a word, unable to speak a word" of "Gerontion," had been salvaged from Andrewes's sermons; and the "stiff dishonoured shroud" of "Sweeney Among the Nightingales" seems to be an echo of the "dim dishonoured brow" of Whittier's poem about Daniel Webster). One would be inclined *a priori* to assume that all this load of erudition and literature would be enough to sink any writer, and that such a production as "The Waste Land" must be a work of second-hand inspiration. And it is true that, in reading Eliot and Pound, we are sometimes visited by uneasy recollections of Ausonius, in the fourth century, composing Greek-and-Latin macaronics and piecing together poetic mosaics out of verses from Virgil. Yet Eliot manages to be most effective precisely—in "The Waste Land" —where he might be expected to be least original—he succeeds in conveying his meaning, in communicating his emotion, in spite of all his learned or mysterious allusions, and whether we understand them or not.

In this respect, there is a curious contrast between Eliot and Ezra Pound. Pound's work *has* been partially sunk by its cargo of erudition, whereas Eliot, in ten years' time, has left upon English poetry a mark more unmistakable than that of any other poet writing English. It is, in fact, probably true at the present time that Eliot is being praised too extravagantly and Pound, though he has deeply influenced a few, on the whole unfairly neglected. I should explain Eliot's greater popularity by the fact that, for all his fragmentary method, he possesses a complete literary personality in a way that Pound, for all his integrity, does not. Ezra Pound, fine poet though he is, does not dominate us like a master imagination—he rather delights us like a miscellaneous collection of admirably chosen works of art. It is true that Pound, in spite of his inveterate translating, is a man of genuine originality—but his heterogeneous shorter poems, and the heterogeneous passages which go to make his longer ones, never seem to come together in a whole—as his general prose writing gives scrappy expression to a variety of ideas, a variety of enthusiasms and prejudices, some ridiculous and some valid, some learned and some half-baked, which, though valuable to his generation as polemic, as propaganda and as illuminating casual criticism, do not establish and develop a distinct reasoned point of view as Eliot's prose-writings do. T. S. Eliot has thought persistently and coherently about the relations between the different phases of human experience, and his passion for proportion and order is reflected in his poems. He is, in his way, a complete man, and if it is true, as I believe, that he has accomplished what he has credited Ezra Pound with accomplishing—if he has brought a new personal rhythm into the language—so that he has been able to lend even to the borrowed rhythms, the quoted words, of his great predecessors a new music and a new meaning—it is this intellectual completeness and soundness which has given his rhythm its special prestige.

Another factor which has probably contributed to Eliot's extraordinary success is the essentially dramatic character of his imagination. We may be puzzled by his continual preoccupation with the possibilities of a modern poetic drama—that is to say, of modern drama in verse. Why, we wonder, should he worry about drama in verse—why, after Ibsen, Hauptmann, Shaw and Chekov, should he be dissatisfied with plays in prose? We may put it down to an academic assumption that English drama ended when the blank verse of the Elizabethans ran into the sands, until it occurs to us that Eliot himself is really a dramatic poet. Mr. Prufrock and Sweeney are characters as none of the personages of Pound, Valéry or Yeats is—they have become a part of our modern mythology. And most of the best of Eliot's poems are based on unexpected dramatic contrasts: "The Waste Land" especially, I am sure, owes a large part of its power to its dramatic quality, which makes it peculiarly effective read aloud. Eliot has even tried his hand at writing a play, and the two episodes from "Wanna Go Home, Baby" which he has published in *The Criterion* seem rather promising. They are written in a sort of jazz dramatic metre which suggests certain scenes of John Howard Lawson's "Processional"; and there can be no question that the future of drama in verse, if it has any future, lies in some such direction. "We cannot reinstate," Eliot has written, "either blank verse or the heroic couplet. The next form of drama will have to be a verse drama, but in new verse forms. Perhaps the conditions of modern life (think how large a part is now played in our sensory life by the internal combustion engine!) have altered our perception of rhythms. At any rate, the recognized forms of speech-verse are not as efficient as they should be; probably a new form will be devised out of colloquial speech."

In any case, that first handful of Eliot's poems, brought out in the middle of the War (1917) and generally read, if at all, at the time, as some sort of modern *vers de société*, was soon found, as Wyndham Lewis has said, to have had the effect of a little musk that scents up a whole room. And as for "The Waste Land," it enchanted and devastated a whole generation. Attempts have been made to reproduce it—by Aldington, Nancy Cunard, etc.—at least a dozen times. And as Eliot, lately out of Harvard, assumed the rôle of the middle-aged Prufrock and to-day, at forty, in one of his latest poems, "The Song of Simeon," speaks in the character of an old man "with eighty years and no to-morrow"—so "Gerontion" and "The Waste Land" have made the young poets old before their time. In

London, as in New York, and in the universities both here and
in England, they for a time took to inhabiting exclusively barren beaches, cactus-grown deserts, and dusty attics overrun
with rats—the only properties they allowed themselves to work
with were a few fragments of old shattered glass or a sparse
sprinkling of broken bones. They had purged themselves of
Masefield as of Shelley for dry tongues and rheumatic joints.
The dry breath of the Waste Land now blighted the most amiable country landscapes; and the sound of jazz, which had formerly seemed jolly, now inspired only horror and despair. But
in this case, we may forgive the young for growing prematurely decrepit: where some of even the finest intelligences of
the elder generation read "The Waste Land" with blankness or
laughter, the young had recognized a poet.

III

As a critic, Eliot occupies to-day a position of distinction
and influence equal in importance to his position as a poet. His
writings have been comparatively brief and rare—he has published only four small books of criticism—yet he has probably
affected literary opinion, during the period since the War,
more profoundly than any other critic writing English. Eliot's
prose style has a kind of felicity different from that of his poetic
style; it is almost primly precise and sober, yet with a sort of
sensitive charm in its austerity—closely reasoned and making
its points with the fewest possible words, yet always even, ef-
fortless and lucid. In a reaction against the impressionistic criticism which flourished at the end of the century and which has
survived into our own time—the sort of criticism which, in
dealing with poetry, attempts to reproduce its effect by having
recourse to poetic prose—T. S. Eliot has undertaken a kind of
scientific study of æsthetic values: avoiding impressionistic rhetoric and *a priori* æsthetic theories alike, he compares works of
literature coolly and tries to distinguish between different orders of artistic effects and the different degrees of satisfaction
to be derived from them.

And by this method, Eliot has done more than perhaps any
other modern critic to effect a revaluation of English literature. We sometimes follow his literary criticism with the same

sort of eagerness and excitement with which we follow a philosophical inquiry. Professor Saintsbury has played in literature
much the same sort of rôle that he has played as a connoisseur
of wines, that of an agreeable and entertaining guide of excellent taste and enormous experience; Edmund Gosse, often
intelligent and courageous in dealing with French or Scandinavian writers, could never quite, when it came to English literature, bring himself to drop his official character of Librarian
of the House of Lords—his attitude was always a little that of
the Beef Eater in the Tower of London, who assumes the transcendent value of the Crown Jewels which he has been set to
guard and does not presume to form a personal opinion as to
their taste or their respective merits; and the moral passion of
Paul Elmer More has ended by paralyzing his æsthetic appreciation. But T. S. Eliot, with an infinitely sensitive apparatus for
æsthetic appreciation, approaching English literature as an
American, with an American's peculiar combination of avidity
and detachment and with more than the ordinary English
critic's reading in the literatures, ancient and modern, of the
Continent, has been able to succeed as few writers have done
in the excessively delicate task of estimating English, Irish and
American writers in relation to one another, and writers in English in relation to writers on the Continent. The extent of
Eliot's influence is amazing: these short essays, sent out without publicity as mere scattered notes on literature, yet sped
with so intense a seriousness and weighted with so wide a
learning, have not only had the effect of discrediting the academic clichés of the text-books, but are even by way of establishing in the minds of the generation now in college a new
set of literary clichés. With the ascendancy of T. S. Eliot, the
Elizabethan dramatists have come back into fashion, and the
nineteenth-century poets gone out. Milton's poetic reputation
has sunk, and Dryden's and Pope's have risen. It is as much as
one's life is worth nowadays, among young people, to say an
approving word for Shelley or a dubious one about Donne.
And as for the enthusiasm for Dante—to paraphrase the man
in Hemingway's novel, there's been nothing like it since the
Fratellinis!

Eliot's rôle as a literary critic has been very similar to Valéry's
in France: indeed, the ideas of the two men and their ways of

stating them have corresponded so closely that one guesses they must influence each other a good deal. Like Valéry, Eliot believes that a work of art is not an oracular outpouring, but an object which has been constructed deliberately with the aim of producing a certain effect. He has brought back to English criticism something of that trenchant rationalism which he admires in the eighteenth century, but with a much more catholic appreciation of different styles and points of view than the eighteenth century allowed. The Romantics, of course, fare badly before this criticism. Vague sentiment vaguely expressed, rhetorical effusion disguising bad art—these Eliot's laconic scorn has nipped. For him, Byron is "a disorderly mind, and an uninteresting one": Keats and Shelley "not nearly such great poets as they are supposed to be"; whereas the powers of Dryden are "wider, but no greater than those of Milton." Just as Valéry lately protested in a lecture that he was unable to understand the well known lines of Alfred de Musset:

> "Les plus désespérés sont les chants les plus beaux,
> Et j'en sais d'immortels qui sont de purs sanglots."

so Eliot, in an essay on Crashaw, has confessed, with a certain superciliousness, his inability to understand the following stanza from Shelley's "Skylark":

> "Keen as are the arrows
> Of that silver sphere
> Whose intense lamp narrows
> In the white dawn clear,
> Until we hardly see, who feel that it is there."

"For the first time, perhaps," says Eliot, "in verse of such eminence, sound exists without sense."

It will be seen that Eliot differs from Valéry in believing that poetry should make "sense." And he elsewhere, in his essay on Dante in "The Sacred Wood," remonstrates with Valéry for asserting that philosophy has no place in poetry. Yet Eliot's point of view, though more intelligently reasoned and expressed, comes down finally to the same sort of thing as Valéry's and seems to me open to the same sort of objection. Eliot's conclusion in respect to the relation of philosophy to poetry is that, though philosophy *has* its place in poetry, it is only as something which we "see" among the other things with which the poet presents us, a set of ideas which penetrate his world, as in the case of the "Divina Commedia": in the case of such a poet as Lucretius, the philosophy sometimes seems antagonistic to the poetry only because it happens to be a philosophy "not rich enough in feeling . . . incapable of complete expansion into pure vision." Furthermore, "the original form of philosophy cannot be poetic": the poet must use a philosophy already invented by somebody else. Now, though we may admire the justice of Eliot's judgments on the various degrees of artistic success achieved by Dante, Lucretius and others, it becomes plainer and plainer, as time goes on, that the real effect of Eliot's, as of Valéry's, literary criticism, is to impose upon us a conception of poetry as some sort of pure and rare æsthetic essence with no relation to any of the practical human uses for which, for some reason never explained, only the technique of prose is appropriate.

Now this point of view, as I have already suggested in writing about Paul Valéry, seems to me absolutely unhistorical—an impossible attempt to make æsthetic values independent of all the other values. Who will agree with Eliot, for example, that a poet cannot be an original thinker and that it is not possible for a poet to be a completely successful artist and yet persuade us to accept his ideas at the same time? There is a good deal in Dante's morality which he never got out of the Scholastics, as, for all we know, there may be a good deal in Lucretius which he never got out of Epicurus. When we read Lucretius and Dante, we are affected by them just as we are by prose writers of eloquence and imagination—we are compelled to take their opinions seriously. And as soon as we admit that prose writing may be considered on the same basis with verse, it becomes evident that we cannot, in the case of Plato, discriminate so finely as to the capacity of his philosophy for being "expanded into pure vision" that we are able to put our finger on the point where the novelist or poet stops and the scientist or metaphysician begins; nor, with Blake any more than with Nietzsche and Emerson, distinguish the poet from the aphorist. The truth is, of course, that, in Lucretius' time, verse was used for all sorts of didactic purposes for which we no longer consider it appropriate—they had agricultural poems, astronomical poems, poems of literary criticism. How can the "Georgics," the "Ars Poetica" and Manilius be dealt with from the point of view of the capacity of their material for being "expanded into pure vision"? To modern readers, the subjects of the "Georgics" —bee-keeping, stock-raising, and so forth—seem unsuitable and sometimes annoying in verse; yet for Virgil's contemporaries, the poem must have been completely successful—as, indeed, granted the subject, it is. Nor does it follow that, because we are coming to use poetry for fewer and fewer literary purposes, our critical taste is becoming more and more refined, so that we are beginning to perceive for the first time the true, pure and exalted function of poetry: that is, simply, as Valéry says, to produce a "state"—as Eliot says, to afford a "superior amusement." It is much more likely that for some reason or other, verse as a technique of literary expression is being abandoned by humanity altogether—perhaps because it is a more primitive, and hence a more barbarous technique than prose. Is it possible to believe, for example, that Eliot's hope of having verse reinstated on the stage—even verse of the new kind which he proposes—is likely ever to be realized?

The tendency to keep verse isolated from prose and to confine it to certain highly specialized functions dates in English at least from the time of Coleridge, when, in spite of the long narrative poems which were fashionable, verse was already beginning to fall into disuse. Coleridge defined a poem as "that species of composition which is opposed to works of science by proposing for its *immediate* object pleasure, not truth; and from all other species (having *this* object in common with it), it is discriminated by proposing to itself such delight from the *whole*, as is compatible with a distinct gratification from each component part." Poe, who had doubtless read Coleridge on the subject, wrote thirty years later that there was no such thing as a long poem, that "no very long poem would ever be popular again," etc. Eliot and Valéry follow Coleridge and Poe in their theory as well as in their verse, and they seem to me to confuse certain questions by talking as if the whole of literature existed simultaneously in a vacuum, as if Homer's and Shakespeare's situations had been the same as Mallarmé's and Laforgue's, as if the latter had been attempting to play the same sort of rôles as the former and could be judged on the same basis. It is inevitable, of course, that we should try to arrive at absolute values through the comparison of the work of different periods—I have just praised Eliot for his success at this—but it seems to me that in this particular matter a good many difficulties would be cleared up if certain literary discussions could be removed from the artificially restricted field of verse—in which it is assumed that nothing is possible or desirable but a quintessential distillation called "poetry," and that that distillation has nothing in common with anything possible to obtain through prose—to the field of literature in general. Has not such a great modern novel as "Madame Bovary," for example, at least as much in common with Virgil and Dante as with Balzac and Dickens? Is it not comparable from the point of view of intensity, music and perfection of the parts, with the best verse of any period? And we shall consider Joyce in this connection later.

With all gratitude, therefore, for the salutary effect of Eliot's earlier criticism in curbing the carelessness and gush of the aftermath of Romanticism, it seems plain that the anti-Romantic reaction is leading finally into pedantry and into a futile æstheticism. "Poetry," Eliot wrote in "The Sacred Wood," "is not a turning loose of emotion, but an escape from emotion; it is not the expression of personality, but an escape from personality. But, of course, only those who have personality and emotion know what it means to want to escape from them." This was valid, and even noble, in 1920 when "The Sacred Wood" was published; but to-day, after ten years of depersonalized and over-intellectualized verse, so much of it written in imitation of Eliot, the same sort of thing in the mouths of Eliot's disciples sounds like an excuse for *not* possessing emotion and personality.

Yet, in spite of the weaknesses of Eliot's position as he has sometimes been driven to state it dogmatically, he has himself largely succeeded in escaping the vices which it seems to encourage. The old nineteenth century criticism of Ruskin, Renan, Taine, Sainte-Beuve, was closely allied to history and novel writing, and was also the vehicle for all sorts of ideas about the purpose and destiny of human life in general. The criticism of our own day examines literature, art, ideas and specimens of human society in the past with a detached scientific interest or a detached æsthetic appreciation which seems in either case to lead nowhere. A critic like Herbert Read makes dull discriminations between different kinds of literature; a critic like Albert Thibaudet discovers dull resemblances between the ideas of philosophers and poets; a critic like I. A. Richards writes about poetry from the point of view of a scientist studying the psychological reactions of readers; and such a critic as Clive Bell writes about painting so exclusively and cloyingly from the point of view of the varying degrees of pleasure to be derived from the pictures of different painters that we would willingly have Ruskin and all his sermonizing back. And even Virginia Woolf and Lytton Strachey have this in common with Clive Bell that they seem to feel they have done enough when they have distinguished the kind of pleasure to be derived from one kind of book, the kind of interest to be felt in one kind of personality, from the kind to be found in another. One is supposed to have read everything and enjoyed everything and to understand exactly the reasons for one's enjoyment, but not to enjoy anything excessively nor to raise an issue of one kind of thing against another. Each of the essays of Strachey or Mrs. Woolf, so compact yet so beautifully rounded out, is completely self-contained and does not lead to anything beyond itself; and finally, for all their brilliance, we begin to find them tiresome.

Now there is a good deal in T. S. Eliot of this pedantry and sterility of his age. He is very much given, for example, to becoming involved in literary Houses-that-Jack-Built: "We find this quality occasionally in Wordsworth," he will write, "but it is a quality which Wordsworth shares with Shenstone rather than with Collins and Gray. And for the right sort of enjoyment of Shenstone, we must read his prose as well as his verse. The 'Essays on Men and Manners' are in the tradition of the great French aphorists of the seventeenth century, and should be read with the full sense of their relation to Vauvenargues, La Rochefoucauld and (with his wider range) La Bruyère. We shall do well to read enough of Theophrastus to understand the kind of effect at which La Bruyère aimed. (Professor Somebody-or-other's book on 'Theophrastus and the Peripatetics' gives us the clew to the intellectual atmosphere in which Theophrastus wrote and enables us to gauge the influences on his work—very different from each other—of Plato and Aristotle.)" At this rate (though I have parodied Eliot), we should have to read the whole of literature in order to appreciate a single book, and Eliot fails to supply us with a reason why we should go to the trouble of doing so. Yet against the background of the criticism of his time, Eliot has stood out unmistakably as a man passionately interested in literature. The real intensity of his enthusiasm makes us forget the primness of his tone; and his occasional dogmatism is redeemed by his ability to see beyond his own ideas, his willingness to admit the relative character of his conclusions.

IV

But if Eliot, in spite of the meagreness of his production, has become for his generation a leader, it is also because his career has been a progress, because he has evidently been on his way somewhere, when many of his contemporaries, more prolific and equally gifted, have been fixed in their hedonism or despair. The poet of "The Waste Land" was too serious to continue with the same complacence as some of his contemporaries inhabiting that godforsaken desert. It was certain he would not stick at that point, and one watched him to see what he would do.

This destination has now, however, become plain. In the preface to the new 1928 edition of "The Sacred Wood," poetry is still regarded as a "superior amusement," but Eliot reports on his part "an expansion or development of interests." Poetry is now perceived to have "something to do with morals, and with religion, and even with politics perhaps, though we cannot say what." In "For Lancelot Andrewes," published in the same year, Eliot declares himself a classicist in literature, an Anglo-Catholic in religion and a royalist in politics, and announces that he has in preparation "three small books" treating of these subjects and to be called respectively "The School of Donne," "The Principles of Modern Heresy," and "The Outline of Royalism." There follows a slender selection of essays, which hint quietly at what may be expected.

We must await the further exposition of Eliot's new body of doctrine before it will be possible to discuss it properly. In the meantime, we can only applaud his desire to formulate a consistent central position, at the same time that we may regret the unpromising character of the ideals and institutions which he invokes. One cannot but recognize in Eliot's recent writings a kind of reactionary point of view which had already been becoming fashionable among certain sorts of literary people—a point of view which has much in common with that of the neo-Thomists in France and that of the Humanists in America. "Unless by civilization," writes Eliot, "you mean material progress, cleanliness, etc. . . . if you mean a spiritual coordination on a high level, then it is doubtful whether civilization can endure without religion, and religion without a church." Yet you can hardly have an effective church without a cult of Christ as the son of God; and you cannot have such a cult without more willingness to accept the supernatural than most of us to-day are able to muster. We feel in contemporary writers like Eliot a desire to believe in religious revelation, a belief that it would be a good thing to believe, rather than a genuine belief. The faith of the modern convert seems to burn only with a low blue flame. "Our literature," Eliot has himself recently made a character in a dialogue say, "is a substitute for religion, and so is our religion." From such a faith, uninspired by hope, unequipped with zeal or force, what guidance for the future can we expect?

One cannot, however, doubt the reality of the experience to which Eliot testifies in his recent writings—though it seems to us less an Anglo-Catholic conversion than a reawakening of the New Englander's conscience, of the never quite exorcised conviction of the ineradicable sinfulness of man. Eliot admires Machiavelli because Machiavelli assumes the baseness of human nature as an unalterable fact; and he looks for light to the theologians who offer salvation, not through economic readjustment, political reform, education or biological and psychological study, but solely through "grace." Eliot apparently to-day regards "Evil" as some sort of ultimate reality, which it is impossible either to correct or to analyze. His moral principles seem to me stronger and more authentic than his religious mysticism—and his relation to the Anglo-Catholic Church appears largely artificial. The English seventeenth century divines whose poetry and sermons he admires so much, upon whom

he seems so much to depend for nourishment, exist in a richer,
a more mysterious, a more heavily saturated atmosphere, in
which even monumental outlines are blurred; Eliot himself is
stiffer and cooler, more intent, more relentless, more clear. He
has his own sort of graciousness, but he seems, as the phrase is,
a little thin-lipped. His religious tradition has reached him by
way of Boston.

In any case, Eliot's new phase of piety has brought with it a
new humility. He apologizes in his 1928 preface for the "assumption of pontifical solemnity" which he now detects in
"The Sacred Wood," and his recent little book on Dante (a
most admirable introduction) not merely surprises but almost
embarrasses us by the modesty with which Eliot professes to
desire nothing but to be of use to beginners and to tell us of a
few of the beautiful things which he has found in the great
poet. I will not say that this humility has enfeebled his poetry.
The three devout little poems which he has published as
Christmas cards since "The Hollow Men" announced the nadir
of the phase of sterility and despair given such effective expression in "The Waste Land," seem comparatively uninspired; but
the long poem or group of poems, "Ash-Wednesday" (1930),
which follows a scheme somewhat similar to that of "The Waste
Land," is a not unworthy successor to it.

The poet begins with the confession of his bankruptcy:

"Because I do not hope to turn again
Because I do not hope
Because I do not hope to turn
Desiring this man's gift and that man's scope
I no longer strive to strive towards such things
(Why should the agèd eagle stretch its wings?)
Why should I mourn
The vanished power of the usual reign? . . .

Because these wings are no longer wings to fly
But merely vans to beat the air
The air which is now thoroughly small and dry
Smaller and dryer than the will
Teach us to care and not to care
Teach us to sit still.

> Pray for us sinners now and at the hour of our death
> Pray for us now and at the hour of our death."

There follow passages in which the prayer is apparently answered: the poet's contrition and pious resignation are rewarded by a series of visions which first console then lighten his heart. We find an imagery new for Eliot, a symbolism semi-ecclesiastical and not without a Pre-Raphaelite flavor: white leopards, a Lady gowned in white, junipers and yews, "The Rose" and "The Garden," and jewelled unicorns drawing a gilded hearse: these are varied by an interlude which returns to the imagery and mood of "The Waste Land," and a swirling churning anguished passage which suggests certain things of Gertrude Stein's. At last the themes of the first section recur: the impotent wings of the agèd eagle seem to revive, as,

> "From the wide window toward the granite shore
> The white sails still fly seaward, seaward flying
> Unbroken wings.
> And the lost heart stiffens and rejoices
> In the lost lilac and the lost sea voices
> And the weak spirit quickens to rebel
> For the bent golden-rod and the lost sea smell
> Quickens to recover
> The cry of quail and the whirling plover
> And the blind eye creates
> The empty forms between the ivory gates
> And smell renews the salt savour of the sandy earth . . ."

The broken prayer, at once childlike and mystically subtle, with which the poem ends seems to imply that the poet has come closer to the strength and revelation he craves: grace is about to descend.

> "Blessèd sister, holy mother, spirit of the fountain,
>   spirit of the garden,
> Suffer us not to mock ourselves with falsehood
> Teach us to care and not to care
> Teach us to sit still
> Even among these rocks,
> Our peace in His will
> And even among these rocks

Sister, mother
And spirit of the river, spirit of the sea,
Suffer me not to be separated

And let my cry come unto Thee."

The literary and conventional imagery upon which "Ash-Wednesday" so largely relies and which is less vivid because more artificial than that of Eliot's earlier poems, seems to me a definite feature of inferiority; the "devil of the stairs" and the "shape twisted on the banister," which are in Eliot's familiar and unmistakable personal vein, somehow come off better than the jewelled unicorn, which incongruously suggests Yeats. And I am made a little tired at hearing Eliot, only in his early forties, present himself as an "agèd eagle" who asks why he should make the effort to stretch his wings. Yet "Ash-Wednesday," though less brilliant and intense than Eliot at his very best, is distinguished by most of the qualities which made his other poems remarkable: the exquisite phrasing in which we feel that every word is in its place and that there is not a word too much; the metrical mastery which catches so naturally, yet with so true a modulation, the faltering accents of the supplicant, blending the cadences of the liturgy with those of perplexed brooding thought; and, above all, that "peculiar honesty" in "exhibiting the essential sickness or strength of the human soul" of which Eliot has written in connection with Blake and which, in his own case, even at the moment when his psychological plight seems most depressing and his ways of rescuing himself from it least sympathetic, still gives him a place among those upon whose words we reflect with most interest and whose tones we remember longest.

V. Marcel Proust

MARCEL PROUST is the first important novelist to apply the principles of Symbolism in fiction. Proust had assimilated a great variety of writers from Ruskin to Dostoevsky, and he had acquired a remarkable technical virtuosity; but, born in 1871, he had been young in the eighties and nineties, when Symbolism was in the air, and the peculiar methods and form of his great novel certainly owed much to Symbolist theory. I have said that the influence on the Symbolists of Wagner was as considerable as that of any writer of books, and it is significant of Proust's conception of his art that he should have been in the habit of speaking of his "themes." His enormous novel, "A la Recherche du Temps Perdu," is, in fact, a symphonic structure rather than a narrative in the ordinary sense. The shifting images of the Symbolist poet, with their "multiplied associations," are here characters, situations, places, vivid moments, obsessive emotions, recurrent patterns of behavior.

The book begins with an overture: we must note and remember the opening chords. "*Longtemps, je me suis couché de bonne heure,*" is the first sentence of "A la Recherche du Temps Perdu," and it is followed by a second sentence in which the word "*temps*" is twice heard. We are in the vague world of sleep: the narrator, shut away in his darkened room, has lost all sense of external reality, all consciousness even of the room itself. He fancies himself in other places where, in the course of his life, he has slept: a child at his grandfather's in the country; a visitor in a country house; at a seaside hotel in summer; in winter in a military town where the young Frenchmen serve their term in barracks; in the midst of Paris; in Venice. "Ah, I've fallen asleep at last, even though Mother never came to say good-night!" This is the first theme to be developed: we find ourselves in the grandfather's house. M. Swann is coming to dinner, and the boy's father sends him to bed without his mother's good-night kiss. The child is sensitive and nervous: he cannot sleep till he has seen his mother. He sends her a note by the maid, but she refuses to answer it. The child is in anguish. He lies awake for hours, till he hears the door-bell ring and knows that M. Swann has left. Then he goes out into the hall-way and throws himself upon his mother, as she is coming up to bed. She is angry at first: she and his grandmother, who are already aware of his tendency toward morbid sensibility, have adopted with him a policy of firmness. But the father takes pity on him and induces the mother to go in and comfort him. She reads him to sleep with a novel of George Sand's and spends the night in his room.

Thereafter we are introduced to a variety of personages as-sociated with Combray, the small provincial town where the boy's grandfather lives: a hypochondriac aunt who refuses to stir from her bed; a provincial snob who longs to know the great people of the countryside, the Guermantes; an unhappy old music teacher, whom everybody pities because his daugh-ter has disgraced him. M. Swann has married beneath him and comes with his wife and daughter to stay at his estate outside the town. The memories of boyhood are suddenly dropped and Proust tells us at length about Swann's marriage: though rich and in smart society, he has fallen in love, rather late in life, with a stupid *cocotte* who has begun by driving him mad with jealousy. When "Du Côté de chez Swann" first appeared, even those who recognized its genius were worried by its apparent lack of direction. To-day, we can admire the ingenuity with which Proust, in these first pages of his book, has succeeded in introducing nearly every important character. And not merely every strand of his plot, but also every philosophic theme. We are able here to note already one feature which all his charac-ters have in common. All alike are suffering from some form of unsatisfied longing or disappointed hope: all are sick with some form of the ideal. Legrandin wants to know the Guer-mantes; Vinteuil is wounded in his love for his daughter; Swann, associating the beauty of Odette with that of the women of Botticelli, ridiculously and tragically identifies his passion for her with his neglected æsthetic interests. At the end of the history of Swann, we are back in the narrator's boyhood: he has himself conceived a romantic admiration for the beauti-ful Mme. Swann and he makes a practice of waiting to see her pass in one of the alleys of the Bois de Boulogne. This very November, he concludes—it is the end of the first movement of the symphony—he has happened to walk again in the Bois:

the trees were brilliant with autumn; he describes the cold
beauty of the day; but it is entirely a different beauty from the
beauty which intoxicated him in youth. "The reality which I
had known existed now no longer. Because Mme. Swann did
not arrive at the same time as when I was young and looking as
she had looked when I used to see her, the Avenue seemed
quite different. The places which we have known do not belong
to the world of space, where we locate them for convenience.
They were only a narrow slice among the other contiguous
impressions which made up our life of that time: the memory
of a certain image is only the regret of a certain instant; and
the houses, the roads and the avenues are fugitive, alas! like the
years."

Proust had at one time had the idea of dividing his novel into
three parts and calling them respectively: "The Age of Names,"
"The Age of Words" and "The Age of Things." We are now
in the Age of Names: we see everything—love, art and the
great—through the imagination of boyhood. "A l'Ombre des
Jeunes Filles en Fleur" is, as it were, one long adolescent revery.
It contains only one conspicuous episode. The boy makes the
acquaintance of Swann's daughter, a little girl with whom he
goes to play in the afternoons in the Champs-Elysées, and falls
desperately in love with her. But the hysterical over-eagerness,
the undisciplined need to lean excessively on other people, of
the spoiled child that he has become, now that his parents have
already begun to treat him like an invalid who must be hu-
mored and indulged, end by exasperating the little girl and
making her indifferent to him. She snubs him one day, and he
is still able to muster enough strength of will to satisfy his
wounded pride by breaking off with her: he betrays his weakness, however, by carrying his policy to the extreme of refusing
ever to see her again.

As I have said, we have been submerged through these
volumes—and for most tastes, have been submerged far too
long—in the reveries of adolescence. But people who have
stuck in the "Jeunes Filles en Fleur" and thus know only the
subjective Proust must acquire a false idea of what his genius is
like. We are now to be violently thrown forward into the life of
the world outside. The contrast between, on the one hand, the
dreams, the broodings and the repinings of the neurasthenic

hero, as we get them for such long stretches, and, on the other, the rich and lively social scenes, dramatized by so powerful an imagination, is one of the most curious features of the book. These latter scenes, indeed, contain so much broad humor and so much extravagant satire that, appearing in a modern French novel, they amaze us. Proust, however, was much addicted to English literature: "It is strange," he writes in a letter, "that, in the most widely different departments, from George Eliot to Hardy, from Stevenson to Emerson, there should be no other literature which exercises over me so powerful an influence as English and American." In the descriptive parts of the early volumes, we have recognized the rhythms of Ruskin; and in the social scenes which now engage us, though Proust has been compared to Henry James, who was deficient in precisely those gifts of vividness and humor which Proust, to such an astonishing degree, possessed, we shall look in vain for anything like them outside the novels of Dickens. We have already been struck, in "Du Côté de chez Swann," with the singular relief into which the characters were thrown as soon as they began to speak or act. And it seems plain that Proust must have read Dickens and that this sometimes grotesque heightening of character had been partly learned from him. Proust, like Dickens, was a remarkable mimic: as Dickens enchanted his audiences by dramatic readings from his novels, so, we are told, Proust was celebrated for impersonations of his friends; and both, in their books, carried the practice of caricaturing habits of speech and of inventing things for their personages to say which are outrageous without ever ceasing to be lifelike to a point where it becomes impossible to compare them to anybody but each other. As, furthermore, it has been said of Dickens that his villains are so amusing—in their fashion, so enthusiastically alive—that we are reluctant to see the last of them, so we acquire a curious affection for even the most objectionable characters in Proust: Morel, for example, is certainly one of the most odious characters in fiction, yet we are never really made to hate him or to wish that we did not have to hear about him, and we feel a genuine regret when Mme. Verdurin, with her false teeth and her monocle, finally vanishes from our sight. This generous sympathy and understanding for even the monstrosities which humanity produces, and Proust's capacity for galvanizing these monstrosities into energetic life, are at the bottom of the extraordinary success of the tragi-comic hero of Proust's Sodom, M. de Charlus. But Charlus surpasses Dickens and, as has been said, is almost comparable to Falstaff. In a letter in which Proust explains that he has borrowed certain traits of Charlus from a real person, he adds that the character in the book is, however, intended to be "much bigger," to "contain much more of humanity"; and it is one of the strange paradoxes of Proust's genius that he should have been able to create in a character so special a figure of heroic proportions.

Nor is it only in these respects that Proust reminds us of Dickens. Proust's incidents, as well as his characters, sometimes have a comic violence almost unprecedented in French: Mme. Verdurin dislocating her jaw through laughing at one of Cottard's jokes, the furious smashing by the narrator of Charlus's hat and the latter's calm substitution of another hat in its place, are strokes which no one but Dickens would have dared. This heightening in Dickens is theatrical; and we sometimes—though considerably less often—get the same impression in Proust that we are watching a look or a gesture deliberately underlined on the stage—so that Charlus's first encounter with the narrator, when the former looks at his watch and makes "the gesture of annoyance with which one aims to create the impression that one is tired of waiting, but which one never makes when one is actually waiting," and Bloch's farewell to Mme. de Villeparisis, when she attempts to snub him by closing her eyes, seem to take place in the same world as Lady Dedlock's swift second glance at the legal papers in her lover's handwriting and Mr. Merdle's profound stare into his hat "as if it were some twenty feet deep," when he has come to borrow the penknife with which he is to open his veins.—And there even seems distinguishable in the Verdurin circle an unconscious reminiscence of the Veneerings of "Our Mutual Friend": note especially the similarity between the rôles played by Twemlow in the latter and in the former by Saniette.

To return, however, the structure of the novel begins at this point to appear. Proust has made of these social episodes (often several hundred pages long) enormous solid blocks, cemented by, or rather embedded in, a dense medium of introspective

revery and commentary mingled with incidents treated dramatically on a smaller scale. Proust's handling of these complex social scenes is masterly: it is only in the intermediate
sections that we feel he has blurred his effects by allowing the
outline of the action to become obscured by the profusion of
the hero's reflections on it. We also become aware that these
main scenes follow a regular progression. In the early "flash-
back" to the story of Swann's marriage which has been described above, we have already assisted at two social scenes on
something less than the full scale. First of all, Swarm has gone
to dinner at the Verdurins', at whose house he first knows
Odette: the Verdurins are outside society altogether and pretend to think smart people "tiresome." They are self-assertive
and ill-bred bourgeois, who, however, have a furious appetite
for entertaining and patronizing artists, and other persons
whom they consider clever. Later on, we see Swann at an
evening party given by a Mme. de Saint-Euverte: a few smart
people go to Mme. de Saint-Euverte's, but they do so with a
clear consciousness of being kind to her. In the part of the
book at which we have now arrived, the part which is predominantly social, the narrator first attends an afternoon reception
at the house of Mme. de Villeparisis, an aunt of the Guermantes, who, though still on good terms with her family, has
none the less become rather *déclassée* by reason of a scandalous
past, but who is a rung above Mme. de Saint-Euverte, as Mme.
de Saint-Euverte is a rung above Mme. Verdurin; then, a dinner at the house of the Duchesse de Guermantes, who, though
one of the smartest hostesses in Paris, occupies not quite the
most exalted rank; and finally an evening reception held by the
Prince and Princesse de Guermantes, representatives of German royal families and not merely of the purest blood, but of
the most inviolable correctitude and dignity. In the latter part
of the book, we shall assist at three more of these scenes: in the
first two, we return to the Verdurins, into whose salon the
people from the upper strata have now, for one reason or another—the bourgeoisie is absorbing the old nobility—begun
to filter down; and in the last, which occurs in the last chapter,
we return to the top again, a matinée at the Prince de Guermantes's, where we encounter, not only Legrandin and the
Saint-Euvertes, but also Odette and Morel, the son of the

narrator's uncle's valet, and where the new Princesse de Guermantes turns out to be none other than Mme. Verdurin,
whom the Prince, ruined by the defeat of Germany, has married for her money.

In the meantime, to return again to the section we have been
discussing ("Le Côté de Guermantes" and the first part of
"Sodome et Gomorrhe"), which is principally concerned with
the "world" and with worldly people, we here begin also to
understand for the first time the author's moral attitude. We
find that each of these three major social episodes follows more
or less the same formula and points the same moral. The first,
the narrator's début at Mme. de Villeparisis's, is contrasted immediately with the death of the grandmother, which serves entirely to discredit the values of the snobs with whom the hero
has been consorting. The grandmother, who has been ill for
some time, takes the boy for a walk in the Champs-Elysées and
goes to the public toilet. During her absence, the boy overhears the woman who tends the toilet talking to the keeper of
the grounds: "I choose my clients," she explains, "I don't receive everybody in what I call my salons!" The grandmother
returns: she too has overheard the conversation: "It sounded
exactly like the Guermantes and the Verdurins," she says, as
they walk away; and she quotes, as is her habit, from Mme. de
Sévigné. But she keeps her head turned in order to conceal
from the boy that she has just had a paralytic stroke. In a flash,
by making us feel in this scene the goodness and pathos of the
grandmother, for whom any sort of meanness or malice, for
whom any wordliness or snobbery, is impossible, Proust has
swept down the whole web of social relations which he has just
been at such pains to spin. The next episode, the dinner at the
Duchesse de Guermantes's, is followed by Swann's going to
call on the Duc and Duchesse just as they are leaving for a costume ball. Swann, with one of those lapses of taste which we
have been told are characteristic of him, clumsily discloses the
fact that he has just been warned by the doctors that he is dying.
But the Guermantes are made to behave with cruelty as well as
tactlessness, for they are so much preoccupied with getting to
the ball, they take their social activities so much more seriously
than anything else, that they cannot even attempt to think of
anything human to say to a man who is an old friend of both

and whom the Duchesse, at least, admires. In the third episode, Swann appears at the reception of the Prince de Guermantes during the bitterest period of the Dreyfus case: Swann
is a Jew and has sided with the Dreyfusards; and he is not so
well received as formerly. The Prince takes him aside, and the
guests murmur that he has been asked to leave. But so far from
this having been the case, we learn at the end of the evening,
the Prince, whom Proust, with his masterly skill at what the
conjurors call "false direction," has allowed us to suppose not
only stiff but stupid, is, with his aristocratic sense of responsibility and his Teutonic seriousness of mind, the only person
present who has tried to form a just opinion: he has come to
the conclusion that Dreyfus is probably innocent and has
merely wanted to discuss it with Swann. (In the latter part of
the novel, this formula is twice repeated: first, when the narrator dines with the Verdurins in the country and, returning to
his hotel, hears the elevator-boy tell with pride how his sister,
who is kept by a rich man, excrementally exhibits her scorn of
the servant class from which she has risen; and finally when,
in the midst of the second reception at the Princesse de
Guermantes's—where the Princess is now the former Mme.
Verdurin—we are shown the daughter and son-in-law of the
great tragic actress "La Berma," who has shortened her life by
returning to the stage in order to finance their social career,
deserting their mother in her illness to go to the Guermantes's
matinée, to which they have not even been asked.)

In each of these cases, Proust has destroyed, and destroyed
with ferocity, the social hierarchy he has just been expounding.
Its values, he tells us, are an imposture: pretending to honor
and distinction, it accepts all that is vulgar and base; its pride is
nothing nobler than the instinct which it shares with the
woman who keeps the toilet and the elevator boy's sister, to
spit upon the person whom we happen to have at a disadvantage. And whatever the social world may say to the contrary, it
either ignores or seeks to kill those few impulses toward justice
and beauty which make men admirable. It seems strange that
so many critics should have found Proust's novel "unmoral";
the truth is that he was preoccupied with morality to the extent
of tending to deal in melodrama. Proust was himself (on his
mother's side) half-Jewish; and for all his Parisian sophistication,

there remains in him much of the capacity for apocalyptic moral indignation of the classical Jewish prophet. That tone of lamentation and complaint which resounds through his whole book, which, indeed, he scarcely ever drops save for the animated humor of the social scenes, themselves in their implications so bitter, is really very un-French and rather akin to Jewish literature. The French novelist of the line of Stendhal and Flaubert and Anatole France, with whom otherwise Proust has so much in common, differs fundamentally from Proust in this: the sad or cynical view of mankind with which these former begin, which is implicit in their first page, has been arrived at by Proust only at the cost of much pain and protest, and this ordeal is one of the subjects of his book: Proust has never, like these others, been reconciled to disillusionment. This fact is clearly one of the causes of that method which we find so novel and so fascinating of making his characters undergo a succession of transformations: humanity is only gradually revealed to us in its selfishness, its weakness and its inconsistency. Anatole France would probably, for example, have put before us the whole of Odette de Crécy in a single brief description—-a few facts exactly noted and two adjectives which, contradicting each other, would have pricked us with the contradiction of her stupidity and her beauty; Stendhal would have stripped her of romance in the first sentence in which he recorded the simplest of her acts. But with Proust, we are made to see her in a variety of different aspects through the eyes of the men who have adored her; and her mediocrity and moral insensibility, to Proust such a tragic matter, are never fully allowed to appear until the final pages of the novel, when for the first time we hear her express herself on her experience with her various lovers.

In that part of the book which we are discussing, we have fully emerged from the Age of Names and are well advanced with the Age of Things, that is, of realities; and we begin to understand why Proust finds these realities so inacceptable, as we become aware of the standards by which he judges them. These standards are supplied, on the one hand, by such artists as Bergotte, the novelist, and Vinteuil, the composer; but on the other hand, by Swann and by the narrator's mother and grandmother. I do not doubt that both of these latter were drawn, as Swann admittedly is, from Jewish originals; and it is plain that a certain Jewish family piety, intensity of idealism and implacable moral severity, which never left Proust's habits of self-indulgence and his worldly morality at peace, were among the fundamental elements of his nature. The world is different from Combray, not merely because Combray is provincial, but because the world is the world and occupied with the things of the world. It is really not Combray itself, but the example of his mother and grandmother, with their kindness, their spiritual nobility, their rigid moral principles and their utter self-abnegation, from which Proust's narrator sets out on his ill-fated adventures among men.

In the section which I have just been discussing, we have been shown the life of the worldlings and we have seen that it was vanity. Now we shall be shown the world of lovers and we shall find it an inferno. First, however, we may pause a moment to examine the architecture of the structure of which we now stand in the middle; and we find to our surprise that Proust, in spite of his apparent looseness, carelessness and prolixity, has both chosen his materials with economy and built with them monumentally. He is really careless and loose only in matters of detail; and his framework will bear the weight of all his longueurs and digressions. His running conversational tone has been made to serve as a device for covering up the calculated ingenuities of his drama and for rendering its sudden peripeties and its moments of passionate eloquence more effective because more unexpected. I have spoken of the regular progression of the social scenes: one can see now how consistently Proust has striven in a variety of other ways for close unity and significant order. Half the characters in the story are Guermantes; and almost all the rest are people whom the hero has known as a child at Combray (as the Guermantes, in a sense, also are). The Duc and Duchesse de Guermantes, Mme. de Villeparisis and Charlus's Jupien all live in the same building in Paris as the family of the hero himself. All the themes have been stated in the first volumes; and all the pieces are now before us. No new elements will be introduced: Proust has provided himself with the elements—and with those elements alone—which are needed for what he calls his "demonstration." We have now become aware that the characters of "A la

Recherche du Temps Perdu" all illustrate general principles and that they have been carefully selected by Proust to cover the whole of the world that he knows: Odette is all that is stupid in woman which, at the same time, arouses men's passions and enchants their dreams; Charlus, the struggle in one soul between the masculine and feminine, and beyond that, the cruel paradox of a fine mind and a sensitive nature at the mercy of instincts which humiliate them; Mme. de Guermantes, the best that a snob can hope to be without becoming a serious person, etc., etc. These colossal figures, without losing individuality—we hear the very sound of their voices—take on universal significance.

For it is only the presentation, and not the development, of Proust's characters which is discontinuous. They are designed, in Proust's own language, to illustrate certain laws; and though they appear to us in a succession of different aspects, as they are seen at different times and different places and by different observers, their behavior, their personalities, have a compelling logic. Proust's method of presenting them, however, so as to show only one aspect at a time is one of his great technical discoveries, and we must stop a moment to illustrate it. The more important characters in Proust are made to pass through so many phases that it would be impossible to trace briefly their histories. But we may note the transformations of one of the subordinate characters.

When we first meet Mme. de Villeparisis, it is at the seaside summer resort, Balbec: the narrator's grandmother has known her during their schooldays, but, with her characteristic modesty and good taste, taking it for granted that Mme. de Villeparisis belongs to a superior social class, has never since attempted to see her. Mme. de Villeparisis, however, recognizes her old school friend at Balbec and insists upon entertaining her. The old marquise takes the grandson out driving, and she seems to him the perfect type of great lady; she enchants him with anecdotes of the famous people who had been friends of her father's and whom as a child she had used to see at their house. When the boy has returned to Paris, however, she invites him to one of her receptions, and he learns now that her social position is by no means so brilliant as he had supposed: for some reason, she has lost caste; many people will not come to her

house. She is also a sort of blue-stocking: she paints and publishes memoirs, and has thereby ceased to be typical of her
class. She is envious, sometimes mean, a little stuffy and a little
pathetic. But the young man never ceases to wonder what
dreadful sin Mme. de Villeparisis can be guilty of to have war-
ranted such ostracism: he cannot imagine anything disgraceful
enough, anything which such a woman might have done
which such women did not do every day with impunity. He
makes an attempt to find out from her nephew, Charlus, but
only discovers that, so far as Charlus is concerned, Mme. de
Villeparisis is not *déclassée* at all: she is simply his aunt and a
Guermantes, and the opinion of the outside world has never
penetrated to him. He explains to the young man, however,
that the late M. de Villeparisis was a nobody, with no title of
his own, and that they had merely invented "de Villeparisis" in
order that she might still have one. But years afterwards, at
Venice, the narrator sees Mme. de Villeparisis in the dining-
room of the hotel where he is stopping, and he overhears her
conversation at table with the old diplomat, M. de Norpois,
who has been her lover for years. It is one of those banal and
laconic exchanges between persons who have lived long together and who have nothing new to say to each other: they
discuss their shopping, the stock market, the menu. Mme. de
Villeparisis is disfigured by some sort of eczema which has broken out on her face: she seems tired and old. When an Italian
prince comes over to their table, M. de Norpois watches her
relentlessly with a severe blue eye to see that she does not
commit any of the slips which, when they had both been
younger, had amused him. An ordinary novelist would have
left it at this. But with Proust, the point of the story is still to
come—in a final transformation which is retrospective. When
the narrator leaves the dining-room and rejoins his mother
outside, he finds also a Mme. Sazerat, an old, excellent and
rather boring neighbor from Combray. Mme. Sazerat, ever
since they have known her, has been living in very reduced circumstances. When the narrator happens to mention that
Mme. de Villeparisis is in the dining-room, Mme. Sazerat begs
him to point her out: it was for her sake, Mme. Sazerat explains, that her father had ruined himself: "Now that father is
dead," she adds, "my consolation is that he loved the most

beautiful woman of his time." The hero takes her into the dining-room and tries to show her Mme. de Villeparisis—but, "We can't be counting from the same place," Mme. Sazerat objects. "As I count, there's nobody at the second table but an old gentleman and a dreadful blowzy little hunched-up old woman." We realize with astonishment that what the young man had never been able to imagine was simply that Mme. de Villeparisis had once been beautiful, unscrupulous and cruel, had wasted lives and broken hearts, like Odette de Crécy herself. Proust's skill at producing these effects is one of the most amazing features of his art: as each successive revelation is made, we see perfectly that the previous descriptions of the character fit equally well our new conception, yet we have never foreseen the surprise. Behind the varied series of aspects, we are aware of the personality as a complete and unmistakable creation: the series, as Proust says, describes its curve.

To return, however, to the story where we left it, we now enter the inferno of the passions, of which we have previously only had glimpses. The hero's love affair with Albertine, which is balanced, near the beginning, by his childhood infatuation with Swann's daughter, is the culminating, and the most enormously elaborated, episode of the book. The narrator falls in love with a girl in almost every way the opposite of himself: she is lively, sensual, piquant. She is an orphan and has no money and is obliged to live with an aunt, who dislikes her and whom she dislikes. The aunt is a dull bourgeois, but there is about Albertine a good deal of the Parisian gamine. While his mother is away at Combray, the hero brings Albertine to stay in the family apartment, where, for the time, he is living alone. There commences between him and Albertine one of those fatal emotional see-saws which seem first to have been described by Stendhal in the love affair between Julien Sorel and Mathilde de la Mole. So long as Proust's hero is sure of Albertine, he finds himself indifferent to her and decides that he will not marry her; but as soon as he suspects her of infidelity, he becomes morbidly obsessed by jealousy. In the meantime, he has grown more self-indulgent, more lazy, more egoistic and more hypochondriacal. He lies in bed till noon every day and will not take Albertine out: he keeps her like a prisoner. He leans too hard upon her, just as he leaned too hard upon Gilberte, but with consequences far more serious, because he has by this time lost the self-control which might have enabled him to break off the relationship, as he had done in the former case. He becomes at last so exigent and so nagging that, after a jealous scene one evening, Albertine runs away the next morning before he has gotten up. During the night, he has heard her, in her room, violently throwing open a window—opening the windows at night was forbidden, because the air was supposed to be bad for his asthma—as who should say: "This life is smothering me! Asthma or no asthma, I must have air!" And he has been shaken by an agitation more profound than any he has known since that other night in his childhood when M. Swann had come to dinner and his mother had failed to kiss him good-night; and as he had done on that former occasion, he goes out into the hall and stands waiting, hoping—in vain—to attract Albertine's attention.

In the morning, he finds a letter which says: "I leave you the best of myself." She goes back to her aunt in the country; and only then does it occur to her lover that she is, after all, a *jeune fille à marier* and that he has taken advantage of her situation to put her in an impossible position. He makes frantic efforts to get her back; then suddenly receives the news that she has fallen from her horse and been killed. Immediately afterwards, a letter arrives which she has written just before her death and in which she tells him she wants to come back to him. He has suspected her of Lesbian propensities, and this is one of the things which has tortured him; but he is never now to know certainly how much of what he has suspected is the product of his imagination and how much is true. Some evidence, after she is dead, leads him to believe that she is innocent; other reports, that she was even more depraved than he had ever imagined, that she had finally come to believe herself suffering from a form of "criminal insanity" and that her accident had been more or less deliberate—she had allowed herself to be killed out of remorse for a suicide she had caused. In either event, he feels that he is to blame: if she was innocent, he has wronged her; if she was guilty, he has abandoned her to the perversity which she herself dreaded: "It seemed to me that, by reason of the fact that my love had been altogether selfish, I had allowed Albertine to die, just as I had killed my grandmother." In any case, this harrowing failure undermines his own morale. At last, he completely collapses and takes refuge in a sanitarium, where he remains for a number of years.

This episode with Albertine, upon which Proust put so much labor and which he intended for the climax of his book, has not been one of the most popular sections, and it is certainly one of the most trying to read. Albertine is seen in so many varying moods, made the subject of so many ideas, dissociated into so many different images, and her lover describes at such unconscionable length the writhings of his own sensibility, that we sometimes feel ourselves going under in the gray horizonless ocean of analysis and lose sight of the basic situation, of Proust's unwavering objective grasp of the characters of both the lovers which make the catastrophe inevitable. Furthermore, the episode of Albertine does not supply us with any of the things which we ordinarily expect from love affairs in novels: it is quite without tenderness, glamour or romance—the relation between Albertine and her lover seems to involve neither idealism nor enjoyment. But this is also its peculiar strength: it is one of the most original studies of love in fiction and, in spite of the rather highly special conditions under which it is made to take place, we recognize in it an inescapable truth. And it ends by moving us in a curious way, precisely when Proust seems indifferently to have neglected all the customary apparatus for getting effects of pathos out of themes of love and death. The tragedy of Albertine is the tragedy of the little we know and the little we are able to care about those persons whom we know best and for whom we care most; and the pages which tell how Albertine's lover forgot her after she was dead, by reason of their very departure from any other treatment of death that we remember in fiction, give us that impression of a bolder honesty, of a closer approach to reality, which we get only from deep and original genius. As in the case of Paul Valéry's "Cimetière Marin"—so characteristic of our own time and such a curious contrast to Gray's "Country Churchyard"—it is less the nostalgia for perished beauty and the pathos of wasted passions that move us than amazement at their obliteration.

This brings us, however, to Proust's central ideas, of which this episode is only the chief exemplification. We have already been shown the failure of Swann to satisfy with Odette his un-realized æsthetic longings. So the narrator's friend, Saint-Loup, has made himself miserable over a shifty little actress whom the hero has formerly known in a brothel, but who wears the as-pect for Saint-Loup of all the talents and all the charms. And so the narrator has now proved for himself the fatal impossibil-ity of finding our happiness in another individual. A woman will not, and cannot, live in the world in which we would have her—that is, the world in which we live, which we ourselves imagine; and what we love in her is merely the creation of our own imagination: we have supplied her with it ourselves. This tragic subjectivity of love is even more striking in the case of the sexual inverts (Proust supplements the normal love affairs of Swann and of the narrator with, as it were, homosexual an-nexes, consisting on the one hand, of Charlus and his friends, and, on the other, of Albertine and her Lesbian companions); for here, to the eyes of an ordinary person, there is nothing ro-mantic to be seen at all, and the grotesque disparity between the ideal which is exalting or tormenting the lover and the ob-ject in which he has located it becomes ludicrous or disgusting. In the case of a wholly noble and disinterested love, a devotion in which sex plays no part, such as the grandmother's love for the boy, the discrepancy is perhaps most hopeless of all: for the boy simply takes for granted all the grandmother's solicitude and attention, is too self-centred to be aware of her sufferings and scarcely thinks about her at all till after she is dead. And by one of his most brilliant strokes, Proust shows us finally that the raucous Mme. Verdurin has been a victim of the same mal-ady as the rest: her fierce despotism over her "little clan," her frenzied efforts to keep them together, her nagging them to come to her house and her persecuting them when they stay away, have been merely the symptoms of another variety of the same passion which has been torturing Swann, the narrator and Charlus: jealousy—but in this case transferred from an in-dividual to a group. Nor are the lovers the only persons who are baffled by fixing their hopes upon other human beings, by seeking to extend their own private reality to the external world. Legrandin, the provincial snob, lives to abandon his snobbery; when he comes to be invited everywhere, he no longer cares to go out. And, in a gruesome final episode, Proust shows us the whole futile comedy enacted in an unexpected form: Charlus, who has been steadily degenerating, has finally arrived at a phase where all his more human impulses have decayed and he has become perverse for the sake of perversity: vice itself has become the ideal. But his efforts to degrade himself are as ill-fated as the grandmother's efforts to sacrifice herself to the welfare of others: for the persons he pays to collaborate with him care nothing about being vicious: they only want to earn an honest penny and their heart is hopelessly not in their work. Even in pursuing evil, where satisfaction depends on others, man is doomed to disappointment.

Nor does Proust's pursuit of this theme stop here. The conviction that it is impossible to know, impossible to master, the external world, permeates his whole book. It is reiterated on almost every page, in a thousand different connections: Albertine's lies; the gossip about the heir-apparent of Luxemburg; the contradictory diagnoses of the doctors who are consulted about the grandmother's illness; the attractions of Rivebelle and Balbec, mutually invisible across the water; the ticking of the watch in Saint-Loup's room, which the visitor is unable to locate; the names in the railway time-table of the towns in the neighborhood of Balbec, which first rouse romantic images in the mind of the boy and whose etymologies are explained by the curé of Combray, then become for the young man simply the stations of the Balbec railway, and are later explained differently and authoritatively by Brichot, so that they take on an entirely new suggestiveness. And I have shown already how the characters change their aspect, as the point of view of the observer changes.

Proust has created in this respect a sort of equivalent in fiction for the metaphysics which certain philosophers have based on the new physical theory. Proust had been deeply influenced by Bergson, one of the forerunners of the modern anti-mechanists, and this had helped him to develop and apply on an unprecedented scale the metaphysics implicit in Symbolism. I have already suggested in the first chapter of this book that the defense by such a philosopher as Whitehead of the metaphysics of the Romantics should apply—and it should apply *a fortiori*—to the metaphysics of the Symbolists. For modern physics, all our observations of what goes on in the universe are relative: they depend upon where we are standing when we make them, how fast and in which direction we are moving— and for the Symbolist, all that is perceived in any moment of human experience is relative to the person who perceives it, and to the surroundings, the moment, the mood. The world becomes thus for both fourth dimensional—with Time as the fourth dimension. The relativist, in locating a point, not only finds its co-ordinates in space, but also takes the time; and the ultimate units of his reality are "events," each of which is unique and can never occur again—in the flux of the universe, they can only form similar patterns. And in Proust's world, just as the alleys of the Bois de Boulogne which the hero had seen in his youth under the influence of the beauty of Odette have now changed into something quite different and are as ir- recoverable as the moments of time in which they had had their only existence—just as his people, in spite of the logic of the processes by which they change, are always changing and will finally fade away, disintegrated by illness or old age; so love, of which we hope so much, changes and fails us, and so society, which at first seems so stable, in a few years has recom- bined its groups and merged and transformed its classes. And, as in the universe of Whitehead, the "events," which may be taken arbitrarily as infinitely small or infinitely comprehensive, make up an organic structure, in which all are interdepend- ent, each involving every other and the whole; so Proust's book is a gigantic dense mesh of complicated relations: cross- references between different groups of characters and a multi- plication of metaphors and similes connecting the phenomena of infinitely varied fields—biological, zoological, physical, æs- thetic, social, political and financial. (These similes seemed far- fetched and silly to the first readers of Proust's novel—but Proust insisted that one of his principal concerns was to dis- cover the real resemblances between things which superficially appeared different. And we remember that the far-fetched comparisons of the poetry of the age of Gongora and Crashaw, to which the poetry of the Symbolists seems akin, have been defended as indicating relations where none had previously been perceived.)

Proust has further, in a larger way, varied the color, tone and pace of his narrative to correspond to the various periods of the hero's life. To the shimmering reveries of boyhood succeed the chatter, the sociability and the vivacity of young manhood; and to these, with that extraordinary sunrise which brings to the hero, not the splendor of the morning, but the dawning of the realization of human corruption and cruelty, succeeds a nightmare of the passions, which at its climax, in the almost demoniacal scene where the Verdurins set Morel against Charlus, seems blasted with the dry breath of Hell. It is characteristic of Proust that, though the vices he here deals with fascinated him and though he extracts from them a good deal of comedy, he should have given to this part of his novel the Scriptural title "Sodom and Gomorrah," and that he should make us feel that all the characters are damned. The grandmother and Swann are now dead. Bergotte dies; and at his death it is intimated, as it has already been intimated in connection with the composer Vinteuil, that only in artistic creation may we hope to find our compensation for the anarchy, the perversity, the sterility and the frustrations of the world.

There is, however, yet another phase. After the death of Albertine, the fumes begin to clear away. When the narrator, after the War, finally emerges from his sanitarium, the world seems more sober, more level, less colorful, less troubling. He accepts—for the first time in years—an invitation to a reception at the Princesse de Guermantes's. Just as he is arriving, he is crowded off the roadway by one of the carriages going to the party, and as he steps up on to the kerb, he is visited by a strange sensation—the moment of stepping up seems to be charged with some mysterious significance. He has known such puzzling moments before: in the early part of the story he has told us of the inexplicable impression made upon him by the combination of certain church steeples which he had seen on a drive in his childhood and again, at a later age, by a clump of trees near Balbec. Why had these sights seemed to mean something special? Why had he derived from them a special satisfaction? To-day he resolves to get to the bottom of his feeling in connection with the kerb: he fixes his mind upon it and presently finds himself experiencing a whole series of similar sensations. In every case, he now comes to realize, some accident of the physical world—some odor, touch, taste or sound—has served to revive in his consciousness what he had felt at some moment of the past when a similar sense-impression had occurred—as the uneven steps of the kerb, by reminding his body of the water-steps of Venice, has brought back for an instant into his mind, divorced from the rest of Venice, the bright Venetian light and water. And these memories which move him so deeply, which spring back into his consciousness so promptly at the most irrelevant provocation, must possess some peculiar value. Are they not symbols for the fundamental truths of that internal world of our consciousness which is all we know of reality? Are they not alone among our experiences in having an existence outside Time?—in yielding us a kind of truth independent of Time's flux, independent of the incoherent and ever-changing succession of our other impressions? He must apply himself to deciphering their hieroglyphics.

When he finally goes in among the guests and after his long absence meets the people he has known, he feels acutely the passage of time, which has profoundly affected them all. Still haunted by the image of Albertine, as he had first seen her at the seaside at Balbec, he begs Gilberte Swann (who has since been married) to introduce him to some young girls. Gilberte brings her daughter over, and when he sees her, he knows fully at last that he himself is old. He has a vision of the time which he has lived and which he is still dragging with him in memory. While waiting in the library, he has happened to take down the same novel of George Sand with which his mother had read him to sleep that night, so many years ago, when he had lain awake so long because she had not come up to kiss him. And now, across all the years, he hears again the ringing of the bell which had announced M. Swann's departure, and is terrified suddenly to know that it must ring in his mind forever. From that night when his parents had first indulged him had dated the decline of his will. The slope on which he had started then has brought him to the debacle with Albertine and has left him, already old, with his wasted life, "le temps perdu"—a hypochondriac like his aunt Léonie, who had seemed to him so eccentric in his youth and whom he had never dreamed of coming to resemble. For Proust, in spite of his æstheticism and malingering, was, on one of his sides, as I have said, a merciless moralist—indeed, by the time we have finished his book, we have ceased to be surprised at his admiration for George Eliot, have come to see how much he has in common with her.

Proust's hero, at any rate, must now retrieve the defeat of his will—this sorry past which he now carries along with him, with no power to change it, to better it. He will turn, he vows, away from the world; but he is too selfish to live for others as his grandmother had done. Too selfish and too skeptical—for what had his grandmother ever found in those to whom she sacrificed herself but impervious egoism? and what had she ever earned but suffering? It is hopeless to seek happiness in others —in society or in love. One must turn in upon oneself—one finds the true reality only there: in those enduring extra-temporal symbols—incidents and personalities as well as land-scapes—which have been precipitated out by the interaction of one's continually changing consciousness with the continual change of the world. He will make of his life a book, and he will base it upon these symbols. So he may assert his will at last and retrieve his moral surrender—so he may turn at last to swim against the current of the undammed, unchannelled sensibility with which he has been drifting all his life—and at the same time master the world, rejoin the reality which has always seemed to elude him, and, opposing the flow of Time, estab-lish something outside it: a work of art.

For Proust, though all his observations seem relative, does, like Einstein, build an absolute structure for his world of ap-pearances. His characters may change from bad to good, from beautiful to ugly, as Einstein's measuring-rods shrink and elon-gate, his clocks become accelerated or retarded; yet as Einstein's mathematical apparatus enables us to establish certain relations between the different parts of the universe, in spite of the fact that we do not know how the heavenly bodies are moving in respect to one another and no matter from what point of view our measurements have been made—so Proust constructs a moral scheme out of phenomena whose moral values are always shifting. (Perhaps the narrator's grandmother may be taken as playing for Proust the same rôle that the speed of light does for Einstein: the single constant value which makes the rest of the system possible!)

These last pages of Proust's novel, like the death and forgetting of Albertine, make no appeal to any of the emotions in which novelists usually deal. They are occupied simply with the genesis of the book which we have just read. Yet they have a strange dramatic power, and they move us—as Proust is always able to do—just when there seems to be nothing more to be said. Through this queer exaltation of an artistic and intellectual passion divorced from every other source of human joy is heard the door-bell still ringing from Combray, more distinct because isolated now and with a new and sombre significance—as Edith Wharton says, like the knock of Fate at the door. And in the long last sentence of the book the word "Time" begins to sound, and it closes the symphony as it began it.

II

The fascination of Proust's novel is so great that, while we are reading it, we tend to accept it *in toto*. In convincing us of the reality of his creations, Proust infects us with his point of view, even where this point of view has falsified his picture of life. It is only in the latter part of his narrative that we begin seriously to question what he is telling us. Is it really true, we begin to ask ourselves, that one's relations with other people can never provide a lasting satisfaction? Is it true that literature and art are the only forms of creative activity which can enable us to meet and master reality? Would not such an able doctor as Proust represents his Cottard as being enjoy, in supervising his cases, the satisfaction of knowing that he has imposed a little of his own private reality upon the world outside? Would not a diplomat like M. de Norpois in arranging his alliances?— or a hostess like Mme. de Guermantes in creating her social circle? Might not a more sympathetic and attentive lover than Proust's hero have even succeeded in recreating Albertine at least partly in his own image? We begin to be willing to agree with Ortega y Gasset that Proust is guilty of the mediæval sin of *accidia*, that combination of slothfulness and gloom which Dante represented as an eternal submergence in mud.

For "A la Recherche du Temps Perdu," in spite of all its humor and beauty, is one of the gloomiest books ever written. Proust tells us that the idea of death has "kept him company as

incessantly as the idea of his own identity"; and even the water-
lilies of the little river at Combray, continually straining to
follow the current and continually jerked back by their stems,
are likened to the futile attempts of the neurasthenic to break
the habits which are eating his life. Proust's lovers are always
suffering: we scarcely ever see them in any of those moments
of ecstasy or contentment which, after all, not seldom occur
even in the case of an unfortunate love affair—and on the rare
occasions when they *are* supposed to be enjoying themselves,
the whole atmosphere is shadowed by the sadness and corrupted by the odor of the putrescence which are immediately
to set in. And Proust's artists are unhappy, too: they have only
the consolations of art. Proust's interminable, relentlessly repetitious and finally almost intolerable disquisitions on these
themes end by goading us to the same sort of rebellion that we
make against those dialogues of Leopardi in which, in a similar
insistent way, Leopardi rings the changes on a similar theme:
that man is never happy, that there is no such thing as satisfaction in the present. We have finally to accept with dismay the
fact that Leopardi is a sick man and that, in spite of the strength
of his intellect, in spite of his exact, close, sober classical style,
all his thinking is sick. And so with Proust we are forced to
recognize that his ideas and imagination are more seriously affected by his physical and psychological ailments than we had
at first been willing to suppose. His characters, we begin to
observe, are always becoming ill like the hero—an immense
number of them turn out homosexual, and homosexuality is
"an incurable disease." Finally, they all suddenly grow old in a
thunderclap—more hideously and humiliatingly old than we
have ever known any real group of people to be. And we find
that we are made more and more uncomfortable by Proust's
incessant rubbing in of all these ignominies and disabilities. We
begin to feel less the pathos of the characters than the author's
appetite for making them miserable. And we realize that the
atrocious cruelty which dominates Proust's world, in the behavior of the people in the social scenes no less than in the relations of the lovers, is the hysterical sadistic complement to
the hero's hysterical masochistic passivity. What, we ask, is the
matter with Proust?—and what is it that has happened to his
novel? The hero of "A la Recherche du Temps Perdu" is not

the same person as the author—the man who is supposed to
be telling the story represents only specially selected aspects of
the man who is actually composing the novel, and he is kept
strictly within certain limits. For further light on Proust's career and personality, we must go to his other writings and his
letters, and to the memoirs of his friends.

We learn from these that Proust's chronic asthma developed,
like that of his hero, very early; and that Proust himself was
aware from the beginning of the neurotic character of his ail-
ment. One specialist, to whom his friends, the Bibescos, had
insisted upon his going, told him that his asthma had "become
a nervous habit," and that the only way for him to be cured
was to go to a sanitarium in Germany, where they would break
him of the asthma habit ("because I shall certainly not go,"
says Proust, to explain his use of the conditional) "as morphine
addicts are cured of the morphine habit"; and another doctor
(perhaps the same) told Proust that he would prefer not to attempt to cure him, as even if he should be successful, Proust
would simply develop a different set of symptoms. Proust had
evidently come to use his illness as a pretext for escaping the
ordinary contacts with the world, for being relieved from the
obligations of punctuality and from embarrassing encounters.
His super-normal sensitiveness must have made the social life
which so fascinated him inordinately difficult for him; and his
illness gave him a sort of counter-advantage over people whom,
with the deep-rooted snobbery which coexisted with a bold
and searching intelligence, he imagined to possess some advantage over him. His illness enabled him to come late and, by
doing so, to attract attention; to attract attention and provoke
compassion by sitting at dinner in his overcoat; or not to come
at all and, by stimulating people's interest, to make them all
the more eager to entertain him. He had already, apparently,
reached the point at an early stage of his career of compelling
Prince Antoine Bibesco and his brother to come in late at night
and describe to him what had been going on at parties from
which he had stayed away. And when the Bibescos arranged to
have him meet their cousin, the Princess Marthe Bibesco, who
had written a clever book and whom he had expressed a great
desire to know, he appeared at the ball where she was to be present "livid and bearded" and constantly shivering, "his collar

turned up over his white tie" and "his body encased in a pelisse
which was too big for him," so that "he had the appearance of
having come with his coffin," and sat staring at her, as she
danced, "with great sad eyes"—until he had made her so self-
conscious and nervous, that, when she was finally introduced
to him, she snubbed him.

In 1896, when Proust was twenty-five, some men friends of
his own age put on a little amateur revue. Proust had then just
brought out his first book, "Les Plaisirs et les Jours," rather a
gaudy de luxe affair, for which, with his passion for smartness,
for combining fashion with art, he had succeeded in obtaining
a preface by Anatole France, pictures by Madeleine Lemaire
and musical settings for some of his poems by Reynaldo Hahn;
and one of the characters in the revue was made to protest to a
character made up as Proust about the high price of "Les
Plaisirs et les Jours"—to which Proust was made to reply with
hyperbolic politeness and abysmal self-depreciation. When
Proust saw this scene at a rehearsal, he went away mortally
wounded and would not come to any of the performances. And
at the time when he was much in love with a young lady—the
present Jeanne Pouquet and apparently one of the originals of
Gilberte—and was in the habit of going out to Neuilly to talk
to the girls and bring them refreshments while the young
men were playing tennis, he would be troubled by dark
suspicions—probably not, says Mme. Pouquet, unjustified—
when a tennis ball would be suddenly landed in the midst of
the conversation and lunch. The girl married Proust's friend,
Gaston de Caillavet, and Proust ceased for many years to see
them. Late one evening, however, at a time when Proust had
long been living as a recluse, he called at the Caillavets's without warning and, pouring forth a thousand apologies, insisting
that they were not to disturb themselves, asked the butler
whether he could see them. When Mme. de Caillavet and her
husband appeared, he begged to be presented to their daughter, who had grown up without his having known her (as the
narrator in his novel asks to meet the daughter of Gilberte). The
young girl had gone to bed, but Proust implored them to make
her come down. Mlle. de Caillavet was accordingly summoned
and appeared in a very bad humor—but ended by finding
Proust charming and talking to him for more than an hour.

One has heard much of Proust's exquisite politeness, but as we read his letters, we come gradually to sympathize with those inconsiderate friends of his youth who had kidded him about it in their revue. The interminable and finespun solicitude with which Proust caresses his friends in his letters all too often only serves to emphasize the fundamental lack of consideration which allows him to use his asthma as an excuse for holding them at his disposition without making definite appointments with them or for compelling them to wait upon him at inconvenient hours. Such a letter as the following to Mme. Scheikevitch is not merely polite to excess: it exhibits a peculiar kind of overcultivated and fundamentally unconvincing sensibility to which it would be hard to find anything equal even in the eighteenth century: "How distressing to learn that you have been ill, what an additional source of distress to learn it only now—not to have been able to be sad when you were suffering, because I knew nothing about it. How was it that I did not know? Probably because I have seen the Princess Soutzo so rarely and with so many people about—it is she who has just told me. It is in a retrospective manner, now that you are well again, that I must return in my imagination and mount your Calvary—sleep through, or rather, not sleep through, your nights of fever. So treacherously malignant is our human fate that, as if it were not painful enough for me to have to grieve about you with my friendship of to-day, the past of your suffering restores to me for a moment my more lively friendship of a year ago. It is with that friendship that I commiserate with you for all the distress that you have had and it makes me accord a maximum force of compassion at a time when the compassion which would be dictated by the present leaf of the calendar of my friendship would be already sorrowful enough." Later, when Mme. Scheikevitch had lost her money as a result of the Bolshevik revolution, Proust wrote—mentioning at the beginning of his letter that he was "very tired to write to you to-night"—to offer to share with her the proceeds from the sale of a part of his furniture which he was contemplating at the time—though "in my cardiac condition to-night I shan't be able to get up safely for two days." Mme. Scheikevitch declined this suggestion "with some vivacity," and Proust was infinitely grieved. He now advanced the even more inacceptable proposal that she should engage to supply *Le Temps* with a daily article and that Proust should write it for her.

"It is impossible," writes Jacques-Emile Blanche, "to understand his correspondence (his mania), letters of six or eight or ten pages to anybody at all, unless one divines the difficulty of establishing peaceful and normal interchanges with a person so remote and inaccessible, who, from politeness, *'gentillesse,'* smothered you with flowers."

Here we are still, however, dealing merely with the superficial aspects of Proust's life. For further insight into his personality, we must go to that early collection of stories and sketches which—remarkable as they are—because they are immature, expose as Proust's great novel does not do, his special fantasies and preoccupations. "Les Plaisirs et les Jours," written when Proust was between twenty and twenty-three, contains already all the characteristic motifs of "A la Recherche du Temps Perdu." We discover here, not without surprise and uneasiness, that the disillusionment and the valetudinarianism which we had supposed at least painfully earned by an arduous progress of the soul to maturity, had in reality already been present in a completely developed form in the gifted and well-to-do young man scarcely out of his teens. The hero of the first of these stories, "La Mort de Baldassare Silvande, Vicomte de Sylvanie," is a sensitive and accomplished nobleman who composes music and plays the violin, who is always accompanied when at home on his estate by two pet peacocks and a pet kid, and who values, with jealous vanity, the friendship and attentions of the Duke of Parma. But though the Vicomte is rich, brilliant, smart and usually successful in love, he is dying of general paralysis at the age of thirty-five: he will never see thirty-six. And in the knowledge that he is surely dying, Baldassare Silvande is truly happy for the first time in his life—he loves to lie in bed savoring the last moments of his life, foretasting the sad sweetness of last partings. The women whom he has easily possessed have meant comparatively little to the Vicomte, but he is madly in love with and furiously jealous of a little Syracusan princess who loves another and cares nothing about him. Now, however, that Baldassare is on the point of death, the little princess often comes to see him and treats him with tenderness.

But, after a time, to Baldassare's surprise, and to the surprise of the doctors who are attending him, he finds himself taking a turn for the better: he begins to walk again and is evidently on the point of getting well. But, faced with unexpected recovery, Baldassare is brought to the realization that he would much prefer to die: he had prepared to take leave of life and he no longer cares to bother with living—what he really enjoys is a dying condition. And, after a month of steady recovery, he begins to relapse into his invalid state and is soon unable to walk again. He summons the perverse Syracusan princess and begs her, as his dying request, for his sake to stay away from a ball where he knows that she is to lead the cotillion with her lover. "I cannot promise you that," she replies. "It is two months now since I have seen him, and I may never see him again." "Then remember me for a moment," he pleads—"for the little time that, if I were there, you might be obliged to spend with me in order to avoid the appearance of being too much with him." "I hardly dare promise you that," she answers, "the ball will last so short a time. Even if I am with him all the time, I shall hardly have time to see him. I will give you a moment every day afterwards." "That won't be possible, you will forget me, but if, in a year's time—or perhaps even longer, alas!—something sad that you might happen to be reading, a death or a rainy night, should make you think of me, what a kindness you would be doing me!" Baldassare arranges himself to die. In his last pathetic and exquisite moments, he watches from the window a ship setting sail for India and listens to the chime of a distant village "imperceptible and profound as a heartbeat." He remembers how his mother had used to kiss him good-night in bed, how she had chafed his bare feet in her hands and sat beside him when he could not sleep—and how, when his engagement to be married had been broken, only his mother had been able to console him. And amidst a sorrowing family, he expires—just as the Duke of Parma arrives.

It is easy to recognize in the hero of this preposterous story both the narrator of Proust's novel and Swann—especially as we first see Baldassare precisely, as we do Swann, through the eyes of a small boy, his nephew, who does not thereafter play any rôle in the story and whose sole office in it seems to be to swell the grandeur of the *grand seigneur* by showing him in the perspective of a child's imagination. It is, in fact, almost as if the half-romantic Vicomte were a projection of the child's imagination.

In another story, "La Confession d'une Jeune Fille," a young girl—who tells the story herself—has spent the sweetest hours of her life with her mother on a family estate; but at the age of fourteen, an "already very vicious" little cousin had taught her "things which made her thrill at once with voluptuousness and remorse." She had finally torn herself away, feeling a desperate need for her mother, whom she supposed to be still in Paris. Suddenly, however, as she was wandering through the grounds, she had found her mother sitting on a bench, smiling and holding out her arms. The young girl had thrown herself upon her and confessed, weeping, all that had happened. But at sixteen the girl was further corrupted by a "perverse and wicked" young man; and from that time on, "once the habit had been acquired, there was no lack of immoral young men to exploit it." By the time the girl has reached twenty, the mother's health has begun to fail and she wishes to see her daughter married. The girl, in order "to prove to her mother how much she loves her," agrees to marry "precisely the young man who was likely to have upon her the happiest influence." He had also the special qualification of being willing to come and live with the family so that the girl and her mother need not be separated. But almost on the very eve of the wedding, while the young girl's fiancé is out of town, her family entertain at dinner the man who has first led her astray. At the insistence of a convivial uncle and against her better inclination she permits herself to drink three glasses of champagne, whereupon, going into another room and locking the door, she and her evil genius fall into each other's arms. When they are about to join the company again, the girl looks at herself in the mirror and sees her "shining eyes, her flushed cheeks, her offered mouth—a sensual, stupid and brutal joy," with, beside them, "the mouth of Jacques, avid beneath its mustaches." Then, from the mirror, she becomes aware that her mother is standing behind them watching them from the balcony outside the window. The mother's heart is weak: she falls backwards and is instantly killed. The young girl, at the beginning of her confession, has declared that she is about to commit suicide.

The first thing that strikes us about this story is its similarity to that curious incident at the beginning of "A la Recherche du Temps Perdu," in which Mlle. Vinteuil is made to derive a sadistic satisfaction from allowing her Lesbian companion to spit on her father's picture. To what extent this improbable scene was the creation of Proust's imagination we learn from Mme. de Gramont, who, in her book of memoirs of Montesquiou and Proust, prints a letter in which Proust explains to her that the situation had been based on a real incident. Mme. de Gramont, however, tells us that she herself had heard the anecdote, and that, as a matter of fact, it was perfectly harmless and merely amusing: Proust had actually, either misunderstanding it or remembering it wrongly—distorting it at any rate in his own mind along the lines of his peculiar obsessions—substituted for the original story a sinister invention of his own. But, beyond this, we are able to identify in the incident of Mlle. Vinteuil and in its prototype, "La Confession d'une Jeune Fille," the embryo of which the long novel is only the growth into a larger organism. Not that the behavior itself of the narrator of "A la Recherche du Temps Perdu" is presented as corresponding entirely with the behavior of these two wayward young girls; but in the large design of the novel, the pattern is unmistakably repeated. In order to recognize it, however, we must first consider how the book is constructed and by what methods its meanings are conveyed.

The real elements, of course, of any work of fiction, are the elements of the author's personality: his imagination embodies in the images of characters, situations and scenes the fundamental conflicts of his nature or the cycle of phases through which it habitually passes. His personages are personifications of the author's various impulses and emotions: and the relations between them in his stories are really the relations between these. One of the causes, in fact, of our feeling that certain works are more satisfactory than others is to be found in the superior thoroughness and candor with which the author has represented these relations. We feel his world to be real and complete, not merely in proportion to the variety of elements it includes, but also in proportion as we recognize these elements as making up an organic whole. From this point of view, Dostoevsky is one of the most satisfactory of novelists;

Myshkin and Rogozhin thrill us because they are the opposite
poles of one nature; the three brothers Karamazov move us
because they are the spirit, mind and body of one man. And if
we ask ourselves why even so great a novelist as Dickens does
not make upon us so profound an impression as Dostoevsky,
we realize that it is because in the case of Dickens, wide and
varied as the world of his novels is, the novelist himself is not
sufficiently conscious of the significance of what happens there,
so that, except in the very best of them, he has admitted a
larger conventional element than the greatest novelists ordinarily allow and has been content to press into service melodramatic "good" characters and villains into whom he has
scarcely projected himself at all. Now if Dickens falls short of
Dostoevsky in this respect, Proust has passed a good deal
beyond him. In Dostoevsky, as in Dickens, though the characters are as much the embodiment of the novelist's impulses
and emotions as the images of a dream, there is always the
framework of the story to account for and carry them. But
there is hardly any such framework in Proust. I have said that
Proust's novel was a symphony, and I have indicated its relation to Symbolism—and I have explained Proust's special idea
of the kind of symbols which were valid for literature, the kind
of symbols of which his own novel was to be made. Like all the
graduates of the Symbolist school, Proust was a determined
opponent of Naturalism: in the last part of "A la Recherche du
Temps Perdu," when he explains the plan of his novel, he expresses himself emphatically and at great length on the futility
of trying to represent reality by collecting and organizing the
data of the external world, and he handles with what is evidently deliberate carelessness all those facts which a Naturalistic novelist would have been scrupulous to have consistent and
precise. What is more, there is no explicit logical connection
between the different elements of "A la Recherche du Temps
Perdu." There is a story, the story of the narrator, his illusions
and disillusions in connection with the world of snobbery and
his attachments for Gilberte and Albertine; yet what must have
been, what would by any other novelist be presented as having
been, some of the most important relations and experiences of
his life are scarcely touched upon at all. We hear much about

the narrator's grandmother, but almost nothing about his father and are never told precisely what his father does; we hear much about his holidays at the seashore, but nothing about his education; we are told at length about his visit to Saint-Loup when the latter is doing his year of military service, but nothing save through casual allusion about his own term in barracks. On the other hand, certain of the characters that figure most prominently in the novel have almost no relation to the hero at all—at least no relation which the story accounts for: Swann is merely a friend of the family whom the narrator has occasionally seen in his youth, Charlus a person he sometimes meets later on. Yet these two characters almost dominate, respectively, the earlier and the later parts of the book—and as we read, we never question their significance: it is only when we think to examine Proust's novel from the point of view of ordinary fiction that we become aware of their irrelevance to the main narrative. Then we perceive that "A la Recherche du Temps Perdu," which begins in the darkened room of sleep, stands alone as a true dream-novel among works of social observation. It has its harmony, development and logic, but they are the harmony, development and logic of the unconscious.

I do not mean, however, to suggest that Proust accomplished this result unconsciously. In retelling the stories from "Les Plaisirs et les Jours," which must inevitably sound rather absurd, I have perhaps made them seem more naïve than, as Proust writes them, they actually are. Proust is already, in his early twenties, not by any means unaware of the neurotic psychology of his characters—this is, in fact, in spite of his clothing their history in much lyric elegiac prose of the *fin de siècle* sensibility, one of the chief sources of his interest in them. We ask ourselves in surprise, as we finish one of these curious tales, whether Proust has not intended, after all, for all his apparent deliquescent Romanticism, to present us with a realistic case history. And so the more we meditate on his novel, the more clearly we come to realize that the shifting proportions and juxtapositions of its elements, the order in which they are introduced, tell a fuller and somewhat different story than the rather meagre and uneventful one of the narrator, whose own innocuous enough case is so soon extinguished in a sanitarium (to which, one remembers, Proust himself would not go). We recognize, on a prodigious scale, the pattern of the Vinteuil episode in "Swann" and of the "Confession d'une Jeune Fille." The rôle of Mlle. Vinteuil's father in the first of these, of the young girl's mother in the second, is played in the novel to some extent by the mother of the hero, but chiefly by the hero's grandmother. We know what place Proust's own mother had held in his life: he had lived with her up to the time of her death, when Proust was thirty-four, and in the same room he had had as a child. "The death of his mother," says Mme. Pouquet, "was for Marcel the greatest grief of his life, a veritable rending asunder. He had always remained for her a little child. She surrounded him with every attention, every vigilance. She knew how to look after him without ever imposing herself on him or importuning him. She cushioned his life. She accepted all Marcel's caprices as perfectly natural things." And we know from the "Sentiments Filiaux d'un Parricide" in the miscellany "Pastiches et Mélanges" that he bitterly and morbidly blamed himself for having saddened and perhaps shortened her life. Now the hero of the novel is represented as causing his grandmother and mother much anxiety and as reproaching himself extravagantly for doing so, but he is not made to sin against them— their simplicity, piety, rigor, their too protective affection—in the same perverse way in which the *jeune fille* and Mlle. Vinteuil do. Yet the impression we get is the same. About the middle of "A la Recherche du Temps Perdu," in a series of touching, wonderfully written, but exceedingly cruel scenes, the hero's grandmother is made to die; and immediately afterwards, the figure of Charlus begins to swell to enormous proportions: to the salute of a sulphurous overture, the most formidable set-piece in the book, the demon of homosexuality rises.

This subject does take on, in Proust, a truly demoniacal character: Proust does not try to sell us homosexuality by making it appear attractive and respectable, as André Gide, for example, does. The tone of the overture to "Sodome et Gomorrhe," which so sepulchrally groans and wails over the hard lot of the homosexuals, is gruesome rather than tragic; and as we read on, we become aware of something special and rather suspect about Proust's attitude toward this subject. It seems to me plain, in spite of all the rumors as to the ambiguity of Albertine's sex, that both Proust's hero and himself were exceedingly susceptible to women: we are certainly made to feel the feminine attraction of both Albertine and Odette, and the spell of their lovers' infatuation, whereas, on the other hand, none of the male homosexual characters is ever made to appear anything but horrible or comic. Proust had apparently, in his youth, been in love at different times with several women—Mme. Pouquet was evidently one of these—had fared rather badly with them and had never forgiven them to the end of his days. And he shows in "A la Recherche du Temps Perdu" more resentment against the opposite sex than enthusiasm for his own. Homosexuality figures in Proust almost exclusively under the aspect of perversity, and it is in general unmistakably associated, as in the incident of Mlle. Vinteuil, with another kind of perversity, sadism. The cruel and nasty side of Proust is the inevitable reaction against, the inevitable compensation for, the good-little-boy side which—see the letters quoted above to Mme. Scheikevitch—was a great deal too good to be human—or, more precisely, which remained rather puerile. Proust himself has given the key to the situation in his comment on Mlle. Vinteuil: "It was not that she derived pleasure from the idea of doing evil, that evil seemed agreeable to her. It was that pleasure seemed to her wicked. And since, whenever she gave herself up to it, it was accompanied for her by evil thoughts which were otherwise foreign to her virtuous nature, she ended by finding in pleasure something diabolical, by identifying it with Evil."

The grandmother, in the novel, dies in agony; and the demon Charlus pops up. The narrator, still in his mother's house, tortures himself over his inability to hold Albertine, whom he has brought there in his mother's absence, at the same time that he is never able to make up his mind whether he has ever really wanted her. When Albertine finally leaves him, the emotional life of the book becomes progressively asphyxiated by the infernal fumes which Charlus has brought with him—until such a large percentage of the characters have tragically, gruesomely, irrevocably, turned out to be homosexual that we begin for the first time to find the story a little incredible. Charlus is obviously a projection of the later Proust, an extension of the

history of the narrator, as Swann has been of the earlier and as
Baldassare Silvande seemed to be of the young nephew who
magnified him. We assist at Charlus's moral debacle and we
leave him finally in a state of semi-idiocy. And the ultimate
degradation of Charlus is followed immediately, with an effect
of recovery and contrast, by the narrator's heroic resolve to
retrieve the waste of his self-indulgent life by shutting himself away from the world and giving himself up to writing his
novel—a retirement by which, he strangely explains, he will
also punish himself for the anxiety he had caused his grandmother, for the suffering and illness which she had been forced
to endure in solitude.

The elements here of Proust's dependence on his mother; his
unsatisfactory relations with women; and his impulses toward
a sterile and infantile perversity, would, no doubt, be explained
in somewhat different ways by the different schools of modern
psychology: Proust is a perfect case for psychoanalysis. But
that there is a relation between these elements is plain. Proust
was never able to find any other woman to care for him as his
mother did. His friends have testified to the fact that it was impossible for any friend or inamorata to meet the all-absorbing
demands for sympathy and attention which he was accustomed
to having satisfied at home; and he was unwilling or unable to
make the effort to adjust himself to any non-filial relation. The
ultimate result was that strange state of mind which often disconcerts us in his novel: a state of mind which combines a
complacent egoism with a plaintive malaise at feeling itself
shut off from the world, a dismay at the apparent impossibility
of making connections with other human beings. We end by
feeling that, after all, he enjoys the situation of which he is
always complaining. Did he not prefer, after all, his invalid's
cell, with his mother ministering to him, to the give and take
of human intercourse? The death of his mother upset this situation and we probably owe his novel to it. Proust, with his nar-
cotics, his fumigations, his cork-lined chamber, his faithful
servants and his practice of sleeping all day, arranged for himself an existence as well protected as it had been during his
mother's lifetime; but lacking that one human relationship
which had sustained him, he was obliged to supply something
to take its place and for the first time he set himself seriously to

work. His need now to rejoin that world of humanity from which he had allowed himself to be exiled became much more pressing, and his book was a last desperate effort to satisfy it. But the book itself had been undertaken, if not quite, as he says, "on the eve of death, knowing nothing of my trade," at least late in life and with no experience of writing to be read, of putting himself into communication with his readers; and the penalties for this were the unassimilably long sentences and the tiresome repetitious analyses—self-indulgences on Proust's part even here—which sometimes make him so exasperating to read.

And it is further true that Proust's novel as a whole, superb as are the qualities of objective dramatic imagination which have gone into it, was never quite disengaged from his sick-room. "That work which I was bearing inside me," he calls it in "Le Temps Retrouvé"—he never entirely got it out. Is he telling us his own case-history with symbols? Is he presenting the world as he believes it to be? He is never perhaps quite sure himself. That he could doubt what seem to be the book's basic assumptions is indicated by one of his letters in which he confesses to having cut out a long passage of "A la Recherche du Temps Perdu" in which he had asserted that reciprocal love was not merely difficult and rare, but universally impossible—leaving only an expression of skepticism as to whether anyone was any better off than he. And I believe that those aspects of his novel which seem ambiguous or distorted are due to Proust's own uncertainty as to whether he is exemplifying universal principles of human conduct or projecting by images sometimes monstrous the elements of a personality which he knew to be morbid and special.

Proust's novel kept him up till he had finished it; but when he had finished it, he died. His mother died in 1905; and between 1906 and 1912, Proust had written the whole of a first version of "A la Recherche du Temps Perdu" (without the chapter about the War, which was added afterwards). The first volume was brought out in 1913; and thereafter, though his illness grew worse, though he seemed on the point of succumbing at last to that death which since his early twenties when he had written "La Mort de Baldassare Silvande" he had indulged himself continually in anticipating, he survived long enough to revise and supervise the publication of almost the whole. But he did not quite see it through. The last sections which he sent to the press were the volumes called "La Prisonnière"—the climax of the narrator's story, his struggle and failure with Albertine. After that, in the novel itself, there is nothing but demoralization and decay until the end, when the narrator makes a stand, in the only way which now seems possible, against the universal disintegration: by setting himself to reintegrate experience in a work of literature—the point, therefore, at which Proust himself had sixteen years earlier begun. He did not live to finish correcting the proofs of "La Prisonnière"—who will wonder that so neurotic a man was unable to remain alive to put in order the final chapters of so dispiriting a story? Early in the October of 1922 he caught a chill and ran up a high fever, but stubbornly refused to see a doctor. He worked at his novel harder than ever, as if he had been racing with the death which at the same time he was frankly inviting. As his fever grew continually worse, he ceased to take any nourishment except a little iced beer which he had brought in, in a pail, from the Ritz. When his brother, a doctor, came to see him, Proust, fearing to be dislodged from his apartment, threatened to jump out of the window if he were not let alone, but promised to allow medical treatment as soon as he had finished his work. The day of his death, in mid-November, he summoned his maid at three in the morning and dictated to her some supplementary notes on the death of the novelist, Bergotte—remarking when he had finished that he thought what he had added was good. It is at the death of Bergotte that Proust's narrator, in what is perhaps the noblest passage of the book, affirms the reality of those obligations, culminating in the obligation of the writer to do his work as it ought to be done, which seem to be derived from some other world, "based on goodness, scrupulousness, sacrifice," so little sanction can we recognize them as having in the uncertain and selfish world of humanity—those "laws which we have obeyed because we have carried their precepts within us without knowing who inscribed them there—those laws to which we are brought by every profound exercise of the intelligence, and which are invisible only—and are they really?—to fools." But at about this time, and perhaps as a result of the effort of dictating these revisions, an abscess burst in Proust's lung and the next day he was dead.

III

In spite of all the less reassuring or less agreeable aspects of Proust which appear more plainly in his letters and the memoirs of him than in "A la Recherche du Temps Perdu"—his self-coddling, his chronic complaining, his perversity, his overcultivated sensibility—we get the impression from them, as we do in his novel, of an intellect and imagination vigorous, comprehensive and deep. One of the things which strikes us most is his capacity for keeping in intimate touch with various circles of friends, as with various fields of activity, sympathizing with the emotions, understanding the interests, and following the affairs of each, though of the several groups already represented by the memoirs which have so far been published, all seem pretty well independent of each other and some scarcely at any point to overlap. And in spite of all his parade of weakness, in spite of all his masks and indirections, we remember him as a personality of singular magnanimity, integrity and strength. That he was capable of showing considerable spirit was shown by his behavior at the time of the Dreyfus case and by his fighting a duel with a journalist over a review of "Les Plaisirs et Les Jours." "There were in Marcel Proust," says Lucien Daudet, "all the elements of a spoiled child: he never actually became one, because his genius had the corrective effect of dissociating these elements—his genius, his personal dignity and also his sense of humor."

And so though we may regret the spoiled child in Proust, the spoiled child of rich parents who has never had to meet the world on equal terms and who has never felt the necessity of relating his art and ideas to the general problems of human society; though the tragedy of the Guermantes' light reception of Swann's announcement of his mortal illness may come to seem to us somewhat less tragic in retrospect—though we may come to feel a little impatient at having our pity so continually solicited for valetudinarian neurotics who are at least always provided with enough money to be neurotic in peace and comfort; though Proust's dramatic progressive revelation of the anomalies and miseries of the world may come to appear to us less profound when we begin to realize the extreme naïveté of some of the assumptions upon which he proceeds— snobbish naïveté in regard to the importance of social differences and naïveté in regard to sex and to human relations in general; none the less, we must recognize in Proust, it seems to me, one of the great minds and imaginations of our day, absolutely comparable in our own time, by reason both of his powers and of his influence, to the Nietzsches, the Tolstois, the Wagners and the Ibsens of a previous generation. He has recreated the world of the novel from the point of view of relativity: he has supplied for the first time in literature an equivalent on the full scale for the new theory of modern physics.

Imaginatively and intellectually, Proust is prodigiously strong; and if we feel an element of decadence in his work, it may be primarily due to the decay of the society in which he lived and with which his novel exclusively deals—the society of the dispossessed nobility and the fashionable and cultivated bourgeoisie, with their physicians and their artists, their servants and their parasites. We are always feeling with Proust as if we were reading about the end of something—this seems, in fact, to be what he means us to feel: witness the implications of the bombardment of Paris during the War when Charlus is in the last stages of his disintegration. Not only do his hero and most of his other characters pass into mortal declines, but their world itself seems to be coming to an end. And it may be that Proust's strange poetry and brilliance are the last fires of a setting sun—the last flare of the æsthetic idealism of the educated classes of the nineteenth century. If Proust is more dramatic, more complete and more intense than Thackeray or Chekov or Edith Wharton or Anatole France, it may be because he comes at the close of an era and sums up the whole situation. Surely the lament over the impossibility of ideal romantic love which Proust is always chanting on a note which wavers between the tragic and the maudlin announces by its very falling into absurdity the break-up of a whole emotional idealism and its ultimate analysis and readjustment along lines which Proust's own researches, running curiously close to Freud, have been among the first to suggest. "A la Recherche du Temps Perdu" subsumes, in this respect, "The Great

Gatsby," "The Sun Also Rises," "The Bridge of San Luis Rey," the sketches of Dorothy Parker, and how many contemporary European novels! Proust is perhaps the last great historian of the loves, the society, the intelligence, the diplomacy, the literature and the art of the Heartbreak House of capitalist culture; and the little man with the sad appealing voice, the metaphysician's mind, the Saracen's beak, the ill-fitting dress-shirt and the great eyes that seem to see all about him like the many-faceted eyes of a fly, dominates the scene and plays host in the mansion where he is not long to be master.

VI. James Joyce

JAMES JOYCE'S first work of fiction, the volume of short stories called "Dubliners," was finished in 1904 and was to have been brought out by a Dublin publisher; but for a combination of reasons, including the supposed impropriety of certain of the stories, the introduction by name of the Dublin shops, restaurants and pubs, and some disrespectful references to Queen Victoria and Edward VII on the part of one of the characters, the Irish publishers could never bring themselves to publish the book until it had first been brought out in England in 1914, ten years after it had been written. "A Portrait of the Artist as a Young Man" was published first in New York in 1916. Neither of these books had much in common with the English fiction then being written: the typical novelists of that time were H. G. Wells and Arnold Bennett, and Joyce was not in the least like either. In their recent literary renaissance the Irish had been closer to the Continent than to London; and James Joyce, like George Moore, was working in the tradition, not of English, but of French fiction. "Dubliners" was French in its objectivity, its sobriety and its irony, at the same time that its paragraphs ran with a music and a grace quite distinct from the taut metallic quality of Maupassant and Flaubert. And "A Portrait of the Artist as a Young Man," coming at a time when the public was already surfeited with the early histories of sensitive young men—the Edward Ponderevos, the Clayhangers, the Jacob Stahls, the Michael Fanes—not only was able to attract attention, but had the effect of making most of these books look psychologically superficial and artistically shoddy.

"Ulysses" was published in Paris in 1922. It had originally been conceived as a short story for "Dubliners," and was to have been called "Mr. Bloom's Day in Dublin" or something of the sort. But this idea was afterwards combined with the further history of Stephen Dedalus, the hero of the autobiographical "Portrait of the Artist as a Young Man." "Ulysses," however, in its final form as a volume of seven hundred-odd large pages, took shape as something entirely different from either of Joyce's earlier books, and it must be approached from a different point of view than as if it were merely, like the others, a straight work of Naturalistic fiction.

The key to "Ulysses" is in the title—and this key is indispensable if we are to appreciate the book's real depth and scope. Ulysses, as he figures in the "Odyssey," is a sort of type of the average intelligent Greek: among the heroes, he is distinguished for cunning rather than for exalted wisdom, and for common sense, quickness and nerve rather than for, say, the passionate bravery of an Achilles or the steadfastness and stoutness of a Hector. The "Odyssey" exhibits such a man in practically every situation and relation of an ordinary human life—Ulysses, in the course of his wanderings, runs the whole gauntlet of temptations and ordeals and through his wits he survives them all to return at last to his home and family and to reassert himself there as master. The "Odyssey" thus provides a classical model for a writer attempting a modern epic of the ordinary man—and a model particularly attractive to a modern writer by reason of the apparently calculated effectiveness, the apparent sophistication, of its form. By a device suggestive of some of the novels of Conrad, Homer has framed the wanderings of Ulysses between an introductory group of books in which our interest is aroused in the hero before we meet him by Telemachus's search for his lost father, and a culminating group of books which present dramatically and on a larger scale the wanderer's return home.

Now the "Ulysses" of Joyce is a modern "Odyssey," which follows closely the classical "Odyssey" in both subject and form; and the significance of the characters and incidents of its ostensibly Naturalistic narrative cannot properly be understood without reference to the Homeric original. Joyce's Telemachus of the opening books is Stephen Dedalus—that is, Joyce himself. The Dedaluses, as we have already learned from "A Portrait of the Artist as a Young Man," are a shabby-genteel family of Dubliners. Stephen's father, Simon Dedalus, has run through a great variety of employments to end up as nothing in particular, a drinker, a decayed sport, an amateur tenor, a well-known character of the bars. But Stephen has been given a good education at a Jesuit college, and we have seen him, at the end of the earlier novel, on the point of leaving for France to study and write. At the beginning of "Ulysses," he has been

back in Dublin a year: he had been summoned home from
Paris by a telegram that his mother was dying. And now, a year
after her death, the Dedalus family, already reduced to poverty,
has become completely demoralized and disintegrated. While
Stephen's young sisters and brothers have hardly enough to
eat, Simon Dedalus makes the rounds of the pubs. Stephen,
who has always resented his father, feels now that in effect he
has none. He is more isolated in Dublin than ever. He is
Telemachus in search of a Ulysses. His friend, the medical student, Buck Mulligan, with whom he is living in an old tower
on the coast and who believes himself to share Stephen's artistic tastes and intellectual interests, really humiliates him by patronizing him and turns to ridicule his abilities and ambitions.
He is Antinous, that boldest of Penelope's suitors, who, while
Ulysses is away, tries to make himself master of his house and
mocks at Telemachus. Stephen has announced at the end of
the earlier book that he is going forth "to forge in the smithy
of my soul the uncreated conscience of my race"; and now he
has returned to Dublin baffled and disinherited—his life with
Mulligan is dissolute and unproductive. Yet as Telemachus
finds friends and helpers, so Stephen is reminded by the old
woman who brings the milk for breakfast in the tower of that
Ireland whose uncreated conscience it is still his destiny to
forge: "Old and secret . . . maybe a messenger." She is
Athene in the guise of Mentor who provides Telemachus with
his ship; and the memory of Kevin Egan, an Irish exile in Paris,
is the Menelaus who speeds him on his way.

The scene now shifts, as it does in the "Odyssey," to the lost
Ulysses himself. Joyce's Ulysses is a Dublin Jew, an advertisement canvasser named Bloom. Like Stephen, he dwells among
aliens: a Jew and the son of a Hungarian father, he is still more
or less of a foreigner among the Irish; and a man of something
less than mediocre abilities, but of real sensibility and intelligence, he has little in common with the other inhabitants of
the lower middle-class world in which he lives. He has been
married for sixteen years to the buxom daughter of an Irish
army officer, a professional singer, of prodigious sexual appetite, who has been continually and indiscriminately unfaithful to him. They have had one daughter, who is already
growing up and apparently going the way of her mother; and

one son, of whom Bloom had hoped that he might resemble, that he might refine upon, himself, but who died eleven days after he was born. Things have never been the same between the Blooms since the death of this son; it is now more than ten years since Bloom has attempted complete intercourse with his wife—it is as if the birth of the sickly Rudy had discouraged him and made him doubt his virility. He is aware that his wife has lovers; but he does not complain or try to interfere—he is even resigned to her accepting money from them. He is a Ulysses with no Telemachus and cut off from his Penelope.

We now follow Bloom's adventures on the day of June 16, 1904 (the whole of "Ulysses" takes place within less than twenty-four hours). Lotus-eaters allure him; he is affrighted by Laestrygonians. He assists at the burial of an Elpenor and descends with him in imagination to the underworld; he suffers from the varying favor of an Æolus. He escapes by ruse from the ferocity of a Cyclops and he disengages himself through prudence from the maiden charms of a Nausicaa. And he emerges finally a man again from the brothel of a Circe who had transformed him into a swine.

The comings and goings of Stephen during the day are woven in and out among the wanderings of Bloom: the two encounter each other twice but do not recognize each other. Both men, we become aware, are constantly accompanied and oppressed by ideas which they have tried to dismiss from their minds: the family situation of each really lies back of and explains all that he does that day. In Stephen's case, it is only a few days from the anniversary of his mother's death, and he is haunted by the memory of it: she had begged him on her deathbed to kneel down and pray for her soul and, in rebellion against the Catholic education which had disciplined and maimed his spirit, jealous of the independence he had won and in fear of the past to which he had returned, he had cruelly refused and had allowed her to die without the comfort of believing that he had repented of his apostasy. But now that she is dead, this incident tortures him. He has in the early morning reproached Mulligan—accusing really himself—for something the latter had said about Stephen's mother at the time of her death which Stephen had overheard and resented; and, as he has looked out upon the bright morning sea, the

pathos and horror of her life have become suddenly vivid to
him—he has been dragged back to relive all that she had suffered. Then, "No, mother!" he has cried out within himself as
he thrust her memory down out of his mind, "let me be and
let me live!" But through his whole bitter and baffled day, it is
his helpless feeling of guilt toward his mother, his hopeless
discouragement and disgust with his father, which govern all
his thoughts and movements. When he teaches school, he
brings the class to a close by a hysterical joke about "the fox
burying his grandmother under a hollybush," and in a stupid
boy who cannot do his sums he can see now only his own
graceless youth which his mother had shielded from the world.
After school, he has gone to walk on the beach and has contemplated paying a visit to the family of a maternal uncle
whom he despises, as if he could do penance in this fashion for
his hardness to his mother and somehow make it up to her
now by kindness to her wretched relatives; but again the
counter-impulse which had proved too strong on the former
occasion comes into play to block his intention: his mind drifts
off to other things and he walks beyond where he should have
turned. The artist still conflicts with the son—the two are irreconcilable: he sets out to compose a poem, but the poem
itself breaks down and he is left gazing at a silent homing
ship.—Visiting the library later in the day, he improvises a
long, pretentious lecture on the relation of Shakespeare to his
father—a lecture which has little to do with Shakespeare, but a
good deal to do with Stephen himself.

And as Stephen is ridden by thoughts of his parents, so
Bloom is ridden by thoughts of his wife. He has seen Molly at
breakfast get a letter which he suspects—and suspects rightly —
to be from Blazes Boylan, a flashy buck about town who is
managing a concert tour for her and with whom she is having
a love affair. All day he has to change the subject when Boylan's name is mentioned—all day he avoids meeting him in the
street. In the afternoon, while Bloom is eating at the Ormond
Hotel, Boylan comes into the bar, gets a drink and sets off to
call on Mrs. Bloom, and when he has gone, Bloom hears the
men in the bar talking and laughing about Molly's easy favors.
And the conversation, later on in the pub, about Boylan's
having won money in a boxing-match—in spite of Bloom's

gently insistent efforts to induce the company to talk about tennis—is one of the incidents which give rise to an antagonism between Bloom and the rest of the company and eventually to the quarrel between the Cyclops-Citizen and Bloom. At the end of the Nausicaa episode, the voice of the cuckoo-clock from the priest's house tells Bloom that he is now a cuckold.

In the evening, Bloom goes to a maternity hospital to inquire after the wife of a friend who has been having a hard delivery: there he meets and recognizes Stephen, who is drinking with the medical students. In the "Odyssey," the final shipwreck of Ulysses and his subsequent misfortunes are the result of the impiety of his companions, who in defiance of all his warnings have killed and eaten the Oxen of the Sun. So Bloom is pained by the impiety of the medical students as they joke obscenely about childbirth and maternity. On the part of Stephen, whose mother died only a year ago, this levity seems especially shocking, but Stephen's very feeling of guilt about her makes him particularly blasphemous and brutal. Yet Bloom has himself in his own way offended against the principle of fertility by his recent prolonged neglect of Molly: the Calypso who has detained him since his shipwreck is the nymph who hangs in his bedroom and whom he makes the object of amorous fantasies. It is this sin against fertility which—at the hour when Mrs. Bloom is entertaining Boylan—has landed Bloom on the Phæacian strand indulging in further erotic daydreams in connection with little Gerty MacDowell, the Nausicaa of the Dublin beach.

When Mrs. Purefoy's child has finally been born, the party rushes out to a public house; and, later on—after a drunken altercation between Dedalus and Buck Mulligan at the tram station, in which Antinous and Telemachus apparently dispute over the key to the tower and Telemachus goes away homeless —Stephen, with one of his companions and with Bloom following some distance behind, proceed to a brothel. Both, by this time, are pretty drunk—though Bloom, with his invincible prudence, is not so drunk as Stephen. And in their drunkenness, in the sordid gaslight and to the tune of the mechanical piano of the brothel, their respective preoccupations emerge fully for the first time since the morning into their conscious minds: Bloom beholds himself, in a hideous vision, looking on

at Blazes Boylan and Molly, an abject cuckold, the laughing-
stock of the world; and there rises suddenly in Stephen's imagination the figure of his dead mother come back from the
grave to remind him of her bleak disheartened love and to implore him to pray for her soul. But again he will not, cannot,
acquiesce; in a desperate drunken gesture, intolerably torn by
his conflict of impulses, by his emotions which deadlock each
other, he lifts his stick and smashes the chandelier—then rushes
out into the street, where he gets embroiled with two English
Tommies and knocked down. Bloom has followed and, as he
bends over Stephen, beholds an apparition of his own dead
son, little Rudy, as Bloom would have had him live to be—
learned, cultivated, sensitive, refined: such a youth, in short, as
Stephen Dedalus. Ulysses and Telemachus are united.

Bloom picks Stephen up and takes him first to a coffee-
stand, then home to his own house. He tries to talk to him of
the arts and sciences, of the general ideas which interest him;
but Stephen is morose and exhausted and makes little response.
Bloom begs him to spend the night—to come and live with
them, but Stephen declines and presently takes his leave.
Bloom goes up, goes to bed with Molly, describes to her his
adventures of the day, and soon drops off to sleep.

But Bloom's encounter with Stephen is to affect both
Stephen's life and the relations between the Blooms. To have
rescued and talked with Stephen has somehow restored
Bloom's self-confidence. He has gotten into the habit in the
past of cooking breakfast for Molly in the morning and
bringing it to her in bed—it is the first thing we have seen him
doing at the beginning of the day; but to-night, before he goes
to sleep, he gives her to understand that he expects her to get
breakfast next morning herself and to bring it up to him. This
amazes and disconcerts Mrs. Bloom, and the rest of the book
is the record of her meditations as she lies awake thinking over
Bloom's homecoming. She has been mystified by his recent
behavior, and her attitude toward him now is at first a mixture
of jealousy and resentment. She congratulates herself upon the
fact that, if Bloom neglects her nowadays, her needs are ably
supplied by Blazes Boylan. But as she begins to ruminate on
the possibility of Stephen Dedalus's coming to live with them,
the idea of Blazes Boylan's coarseness becomes intolerable to

her: the thought of Stephen has made her fastidious, and, rapidly becoming very tender about him, she prefigures a relation between them of an ambiguous but intimate character, half-amorous, half-maternal. Yet it is Bloom himself who has primarily been the cause of this revolution in Molly's mind: in telling her about Stephen, he has imposed upon her again his own values; in staying away from the house all day and coming back very late at night, and in asking for his breakfast in bed, he has reasserted his own will. And she goes back in her mind over her experience of Bloom—their courtship, their married life. She remembers how, when she had promised to marry him, it had been his intelligence and his sympathetic nature, that touch of imagination which distinguished him from other men, which had influenced her in his favor—"because he understood or felt what a woman is and I knew I could always get around him"; and on the day when he had first kissed her, he had called her "a flower of the mountain." It is in the mind of his Penelope that this Ulysses has slain the suitors who have been disputing his place.

As for Stephen, unresponsive as he has seemed to Bloom's interest and cordiality, he has at last, none the less, found in Dublin someone sufficiently sympathetic to himself to give him the clew, to supply him with the subject, which will enable him to enter imaginatively—as an artist—into the common life of his race. It is possible that Molly and Bloom, as a result of Bloom's meeting with Stephen, will resume normal marital relations; but it is certain that Stephen, as a result of this meeting, will go away and write "Ulysses." Buck Mulligan has told us that the young poet says he is going "to write something in ten years": that was in 1904—"Ulysses" is dated at the end as having been begun in 1914.

II

This is the story of "Ulysses" in the light of its Homeric parallel; but to describe the book in such a way gives no idea of what it is really like—of its psychological and technical discoveries or of its magnificent poetry.

"Ulysses" is, I suppose, the most completely "written" novel since Flaubert. The example of the great prose poet of

Naturalism has profoundly influenced Joyce—in his attitude toward the modern bourgeois world and in the contrast implied by the Homeric parallel of "Ulysses" between our own and the ancient world, as well as in an ideal of rigorous objectivity and of adaptation of style to subject—as the influence of that other great Naturalistic poet, Ibsen, is obvious in Joyce's single play, "Exiles." But Flaubert had, in general, confined himself to fitting the cadence and the phrase precisely to the mood or object described; and even then it was the phrase rather than the cadence, and the object rather than the mood, with which he was occupied—for mood and cadence in Flaubert do not really vary much: he never embodies himself in his characters nor identifies his voice with theirs, and as a result, Flaubert's own characteristic tone of the sombre-pompous-ironic becomes, in the long run, a little monotonous. But Joyce has undertaken in "Ulysses" not merely to render, with the last accuracy and beauty, the actual sights and sounds among which his people move, but, showing us the world as his characters perceive it, to find the unique vocabulary and rhythm which will represent the thoughts of each. If Flaubert taught Maupassant to look for the definitive adjectives which would distinguish a given cab-driver from every other cab-driver at the Rouen station, so Joyce has set himself the task of finding the precise dialect which will distinguish the thoughts of a given Dubliner from those of every other Dubliner. Thus the mind of Stephen Dedalus is represented by a weaving of bright poetic images and fragmentary abstractions, of things remembered from books, on a rhythm sober, melancholy and proud; that of Bloom by a rapid staccato notation, prosaic but vivid and alert, jetting out in all directions in little ideas growing out of ideas; the thoughts of Father Conmee, the Rector of the Jesuit college, by a precise prose, perfectly colorless and orderly; those of Gerty-Nausicaa by a combination of school-girl colloquialisms with the jargon of cheap romance; and the ruminations of Mrs. Bloom by a long, unbroken rhythm of brogue, like the swell of some profound sea.

Joyce takes us thus directly into the consciousness of his characters, and in order to do so, he has availed himself of methods of which Flaubert never dreamed—of the methods of Symbolism. He has, in "Ulysses," exploited together, as no writer had thought to do before, the resources both of Symbolism and of Naturalism. Proust's novel, masterly as it is, does perhaps represent a falling over into decadence of psychological fiction: the subjective element is finally allowed to invade and to deteriorate even those aspects of the story which really ought to be kept strictly objective if one is to believe that it is actually happening. But Joyce's grasp on his objective world never slips: his work is unshakably established on Naturalistic foundations. Where "A la Recherche du Temps Perdu" leaves many things vague—the ages of the characters and sometimes the actual circumstances of their lives, and—what is worse—whether they may not be merely bad dreams that the hero has had; "Ulysses" has been logically thought out and accurately documented to the last detail: everything that happens is perfectly consistent, and we know precisely what the characters wore, how much they paid for things, where they were at different times of the day, what popular songs they sang and what events they read of in the papers, on June 16, 1904. Yet when we are admitted to the mind of any one of them, we are in a world as complex and special, a world sometimes as fantastic or obscure, as that of a Symbolist poet—and a world rendered by similar devices of language. We are more at home in the minds of Joyce's characters than we are likely to be, except after some study, in the mind of a Mallarmé or an Eliot, because we know more about the circumstances in which they find themselves; but we are confronted with the same sort of confusion between emotions, perceptions and reasonings, and we are likely to be disconcerted by the same sort of hiatuses of thought, when certain links in the association of ideas are dropped down into the unconscious mind so that we are obliged to divine them for ourselves.

But Joyce has carried the methods of Symbolism further than merely to set a Naturalistic scene and then, in that frame, to represent directly the minds of his different characters in Symbolistic monologues like "Mr. Prufrock" or "L'Après-midi d'un Faune." And it is the fact that he has not always stopped here which makes parts of "Ulysses" so puzzling when we read them for the first time. So long as we are dealing with internal monologues in realistic settings, we are dealing with familiar elements merely combined in a novel way—that is, instead of reading, "Bloom said to himself, 'I might manage to write a story to illustrate some proverb or other. I could sign it, Mr. and Mrs. L. M. Bloom,'" we read, "Might manage a sketch. By Mr. and Mrs. L. M. Bloom. Invent a story for some proverb which?" But as we get further along in "Ulysses," we find the realistic setting oddly distorting itself and deliquescing, and we are astonished at the introduction of voices which seem to belong neither to the characters nor to the author.

The point is that of each of his episodes Joyce has tried to make an independent unit which shall blend the different sets of elements of each—the minds of the characters, the place where they are, the atmosphere about them, the feeling of the time of day. Joyce had already, in "A Portrait of the Artist," experimented, as Proust had done, in varying the form and style of the different sections to fit the different ages and phases of his hero—from the infantile fragments of childhood impressions, through the ecstatic revelations and the terrifying nightmares of adolescence, to the self-possessed notations of young manhood. But in "A Portrait of the Artist," Joyce was presenting everything from the point of view of a single particular character, Dedalus; whereas in "Ulysses" he is occupied with a number of different personalities, of whom Dedalus is no longer the centre, and his method, furthermore, of enabling us to live in their world is not always merely a matter of making us shift from the point of view of one to the point of view of another. In order to understand what Joyce is doing here, one must conceive a set of Symbolistic poems, themselves involving characters whose minds are represented Symbolistically, depending not from the sensibility of the poet speaking in his own person, but from the poet's imagination playing a rôle absolutely impersonal and always imposing upon itself all the Naturalistic restrictions in regard to the story it is telling at the same time that it allows itself to exercise all the Symbolistic privileges in regard to the way it tells it. We are not likely to be prepared for this by the early episodes of "Ulysses": they are as sober and as clear as the morning light of the Irish coast in which they take place: the characters' perceptions of the external world are usually distinct from their thoughts and feelings about them. But in the newspaper office, for the first time, a general atmosphere begins to be created, beyond the specific minds of the characters, by a punctuation of the text with news-paper heads which announce the incidents in the narrative. And in the library scene, which takes place in the early afternoon, the setting and people external to Stephen begin to dissolve in his apprehension of them, heightened and blurred by some drinks at lunch-time and by the intellectual excitement of the conversation amid the dimness and tameness of the library—"Eglintoneyes, quick with pleasure, looked up shybrightly. Gladly glancing, a merry puritan, through the twisted eglan-tine." Here, however, we still see all through Stephen's eyes—through the eyes of a single character; but in the scene in the Ormond Hotel, which takes place a couple of hours later—our reveries absorb the world about us progressively as daylight fades and as the impressions of the day accumulate—the sights and sounds and the emotional vibrations and the appetites for food and drink of the late afternoon, the laughter, the gold-and-bronze hair of the barmaids, the jingling of Blazes Boy-lan's car on his way to visit Molly Bloom, the ringing of the hoofs of the horses of the viceregal cavalcade clanging in through the open window, the ballad sung by Simon Dedalus, the sound of the piano accompaniment and the comfortable supper of Bloom—though they are not all, from beginning to end, perceived by Bloom himself—all mingle quite un-Naturalistically in a harmony of bright sound, ringing color, poignant indistinct feeling and declining light. The scene in the brothel, where it is night and where Dedalus and Bloom are drunk, is like a slowed-up moving-picture, in which the in-tensified vision of reality is continually lapsing into phantas-magoric visions; and the let-down after the excitement of this, the lassitude and staleness of the cabmen's shelter where Bloom takes Stephen to get him some coffee, is rendered by a prose as flavorless, as weary and as banal as the incidents which it re-ports. Joyce has achieved here, by different methods, a rela-tivism like that of Proust: he is reproducing in literature the different aspects, the different proportions and textures, which things and people take on at different times and under differ-ent circumstances.

III

I do not think that Joyce has been equally successful with all these technical devices in "Ulysses"; but before it will be possible to discuss them further, we must approach the book from another point of view.

It has always been characteristic of Joyce to neglect action, narrative, drama, of the usual kind, even the direct impact on one another of the characters as we get it in the ordinary novel, for a sort of psychological portraiture. There is tremendous vitality in Joyce, but very little movement. Like Proust, he is symphonic rather than narrative. His fiction has its progressions, its developments, but they are musical rather than dramatic. The most elaborate and interesting piece in "Dubliners"—the story called "The Dead"—is simply a record of the modification brought about during a single evening in the relations of a husband and wife by the man's becoming aware, from the effect produced on the woman by a song which she has heard at a family party, that she has once been loved by another man; "A Portrait of the Artist as a Young Man" is simply a series of pictures of the author at successive stages of his development; the theme of "Exiles" is, like that of "The Dead," the modification in the relations of a husband and wife which follows the reappearance of a man who has been the wife's lover. And "Ulysses," again, for all its vast scale, is simply the story of another small but significant change in the relations of yet another married couple as a result of the impingement on their household of the personality of an only slightly known young man. Most of these stories cover a period of only a few hours, and they are never carried any further. When Joyce has explored one of these situations, when he has established the small gradual readjustment, he has done all that interests him.

All, that is, from the point of view of ordinary incident. But though Joyce almost entirely lacks appetite for violent conflict or vigorous action, his work is prodigiously rich and alive. His force, instead of following a line, expands itself in every dimension (including that of Time) about a single point. The world of "Ulysses" is animated by a complex inexhaustible life: we revisit it as we do a city, where we come more and more to recognize faces, to understand personalities, to grasp relations, currents and interests. Joyce has exercised considerable technical ingenuity in introducing us to the elements of his story in an order which will enable us to find our bearings: yet I doubt whether any human memory is capable, on a first reading, of meeting the demands of "Ulysses." And when we reread it, we start in at any point, as if it were indeed something solid like a city which actually existed in space and which could be entered from any direction—as Joyce is said, in composing his books, to work on the different parts simultaneously. More than any other work of fiction, unless perhaps the "Comédie Humaine," "Ulysses" creates the illusion of a living social organism. We see it only for twenty hours, yet we know its past as well as its present. We possess Dublin, seen, heard, smelt and felt, brooded over, imagined, remembered.

Joyce's handling of this immense material, his method of giving his book a shape, resembles nothing else in modern fiction. The first critics of "Ulysses" mistook the novel for a "slice of life" and objected that it was too fluid or too chaotic. They did not recognize a plot because they could not recognize a progression; and the title told them nothing. They could not even discover a pattern. It is now apparent, however, that "Ulysses" suffers from an excess of design rather than from a lack of it. Joyce has drawn up an outline of his novel, of which he has allowed certain of his commentators to avail themselves, but which he has not allowed them to publish in its entirety (though it is to be presumed that the book on "Ulysses" which Mr. Stuart Gilbert has announced will include all the information contained in it); and from this outline it appears that Joyce has set himself the task of fulfilling the requirements of a most complicated scheme—a scheme which we could scarcely have divined except in its more obvious features. For even if we had known about the Homeric parallel and had identified certain of the correspondences—if we had had no difficulty in recognizing the Cyclops in the ferocious professional Fenian or Circe in the brothel-keeper or Hades in the cemetery—we should never have suspected how closely and how subtly the parallel had been followed—we should never have guessed, for example, that when Bloom passes through the National Library while Stephen is having his discussion with the literary men, he is escaping, on the one hand, a

Scylla—that is, Aristotle, the rock of Dogma; and, on the other, a Charybdis—Plato, the whirlpool of Mysticism; nor that, when Stephen walks on the seashore, he is reënacting the combat with Proteus—in this case, primal matter, of whose continual transformations Stephen is reminded by the objects absorbed or washed up by the sea, but whose forms he is able to hold and fix, as the Homeric Proteus was held and vanquished, by power of the words which give him images for them. Nor should we have known that the series of phrases and onomato-poetic syllables placed at the beginning of the Sirens episode—the singing in the Ormond Hotel—and selected from the narrative which follows, are supposed to be musical themes and that the episode itself is a fugue; and though we may have felt the ironic effect of the specimens of inflated Irish journalism introduced at regular intervals in the conversation with the pa-triot in the pub—we should hardly have understood that these had been produced by a deliberate technique of "gigantism" —for, since the Citizen represents the Cyclops, and since the Cyclops was a giant, he must be rendered formidable by a pa-rade of all the banalities of his patriotic claptrap swollen to gi-gantic proportions. We should probably never have guessed all this, and we should certainly never have guessed at the inge-nuity which Joyce has expended in other ways. Not only, we learn from the outline, is there an elaborate Homeric parallel in "Ulysses," but there is also an organ of the human body and a human science or art featured in every episode. We look these up, a little incredulously, but there, we find, they all actually are—buried and disguised beneath the realistic surface, but carefully planted, unmistakably dwelt upon. And if we are tipped off, we are able further to discover all sorts of concealed ornaments and emblems: in the chapter of the Lotos-Eaters, for example, countless references to flowers; in the Laestrygo-nians, to eating; in the Sirens, puns on musical terms; and in Æolus, the newspaper office, not merely many references to wind but, according to Mr. Gilbert—the art featured in this episode being Rhetoric—some hundred different figures of speech.

Now the Homeric parallel in "Ulysses" is in general point-edly and charmingly carried out and justifies itself: it does help to give the story a universal significance and it enables Joyce to show us in the actions and the relations of his characters meanings which he perhaps could not easily have indicated in any other way—since the characters themselves must be largely unaware of these meanings and since Joyce has adopted the strict objective method, in which the author must not comment on the action. And we may even accept the arts and sciences and the organs of the human body as making the book complete and comprehensive, if a little laboriously systematic—the whole of man's experience in a day. But when we get all these things together and further complicated by the virtuosity of the technical devices, the result is sometimes baffling or confusing. We become aware, as we examine the outline, that when we went through "Ulysses" for the first time, it was these organs and arts and sciences and Homeric correspondences which sometimes so discouraged our interest. We had been climbing over these obstacles without knowing it, in our attempts to follow Dedalus and Bloom. The trouble was that, beyond the ostensible subject and, as it were, beneath the surface of the narrative, too many other subjects and too many different orders of subjects were being proposed to our attention.

It seems to me difficult, then, not to conclude that Joyce elaborated "Ulysses" too much—that he tried to put too many things into it. What is the value of all the references to flowers in the Lotos-Eaters chapter, for example? They do not create in the Dublin streets an atmosphere of lotus-eating—we are merely puzzled, if we have not been told to look for them, as to why Joyce has chosen to have Bloom think and see certain things, of which the final explanation is that they are pretexts for mentioning flowers. And do not the gigantic interpolations of the Cyclops episode defeat their object by making it impossible for us to follow the narrative? The interpolations are funny in themselves, the incident related is a masterpiece of language and humor, the idea of combining them seems happy, yet the effect is mechanical and annoying: in the end we have to read the whole thing through, skipping the interpolations, in order to find out what has happened. The worst example of the capacities for failure of this too synthetic, too systematic, method seems to me the scene in the maternity hospital. I have described above what actually takes place there as I have worked it out, after several readings and in the light of Joyce's outline. The Oxen of the Sun are "Fertility"—the crime committed against them is "Fraud." But, not content with this, Joyce has been at pains to fill the episode with references to real cattle and to include a long conversation about bulls. As for the special technique, it seems to me in this case not to have any real appropriateness to the situation, but to have been dictated by sheer fantastic pedantry: Joyce describes his method here as "embryonic," in conformity to the subject, maternity, and the chapter is written as a series of parodies of English literary styles from the bad Latin of the early chronicles up through Huxley and Carlyle, the development of the language corresponding to the growth of the child in the womb. Now something important takes place in this episode—the meeting between Dedalus and Bloom—and an important point is being made about it. But we miss the point because it is all we can do to follow what is happening at the drinking-party, itself rather a confused affair, through the medium of the language of the Morte d'Arthur, the seventeenth-century diaries, the eighteenth-century novels, and a great many other kinds of literature in which we are not prepared at the moment to be interested. If we pay attention to the parodies, we miss the story; and if we try to follow the story, we are unable to appreciate the parodies. The parodies have spoiled the story; and the necessity of telling the story through them has taken most of the life out of the parodies.

Joyce has as little respect as Proust for the capacities of the reader's attention; and one feels, in Joyce's case as in Proust's, that the *longueurs* which break our backs, the mechanical combinations of elements which fail to coalesce, are partly a result of the effort of a supernormally energetic mind to compensate by piling things up for an inability to make them move.

We have now arrived, in the maternity hospital, at the climactic scenes of the story, and Joyce has bogged us as he has never bogged us before. We shall forget the Oxen of the Sun in the wonderful night-town scene which follows it—but we shall be bogged afterwards worse than ever in the interminable let-down of the cabman's shelter and in the scientific question-and-answer chapter which undertakes to communicate to us through the most opaque and uninviting medium possible Dedalus's conversation with Bloom. The night-town episode itself and Mrs. Bloom's soliloquy, which closes the book, are, of course, among the best things in it—but the relative proportions of the other three latter chapters and the jarring effect of the pastiche style sandwiched in with the straight Naturalistic seem to me artistically absolutely indefensible. One can understand that Joyce may have intended the colorless and tiresome episodes to set off the rich and vivid ones, and also that it is of the essence of his point of view to represent the profoundest changes of our lives as beginning naturally between night and morning without the parties' appreciating their importance at the time; but a hundred and sixty-one more or less deliberately tedious pages are too heavy a dead weight for even the brilliant flights of the other hundred and ninety-nine pages to carry. Furthermore, Joyce has here half-buried his story under the virtuosity of his technical devices. It is almost as if he had elaborated it so much and worked over it so long that he had forgotten, in the amusement of writing parodies, the drama which he had originally intended to stage; or as if he were trying to divert and overwhelm us by irrelevant entertainments and feats in order that we might not be dissatisfied with the flatness—except for the drunken scene—of Dedalus's final meeting with Bloom; or even perhaps as if he did not, after all, quite want us to understand his story, as if he had, not quite conscious of what he was doing, ended by throwing up between us and it a fortification of solemn burlesque prose—as if he were shy and solicitous about it, and wanted to protect it from us.

IV

Yet even these episodes to which I have objected contribute something valuable to "Ulysses." In the chapter of parodies, for example, Joyce seems to be saying to us: "Here are specimens of the sort of thing that man has written about himself in the past—how naïve or pretentious they seem! I have broken through these assumptions and pretences and shown you how he must recognize himself to-day." And in the question-and-answer chapter, which is written entirely from the conventional point of view of science and where we are supplied with every possible physical, statistical, biographical and astronomical fact about Stephen's visit to Bloom: "This is all that the twentieth-century man thinks he knows about himself and his universe. Yet how mechanical and rigid this reasoning seems when we apply it to Molly and Bloom—how inadequate to explain them!"

For one of the most remarkable features of "Ulysses" is its interest as an investigation into the nature of human consciousness and behavior. Its importance from the point of view of psychology has never, it seems to me, been properly appreciated —though its influence on other books and, in consequence, upon our ideas about ourselves, has already been profound. Joyce has attempted in "Ulysses" to render as exhaustively, as precisely and as directly as it is possible in words to do, what our participation in life is like—or rather, what it seems to us like as from moment to moment we live. In order to make this record complete, he has been obliged to disregard a number of conventions of taste which, especially in English-speaking countries, have in modern times been pretty strictly observed, even by the writers who have aimed to be most scrupulously truthful. Joyce has studied what we are accustomed to consider the dirty, the trivial and the base elements in our lives with the relentlessness of a modern psychologist; and he has also— what the contemporary Naturalist has seldom been poet enough for—done justice to all those elements in our lives which we have been in the habit of describing by such names as love, nobility, truth and beauty. It is curious to reflect that a number of critics—including, curiously enough, Arnold Bennett—should have found Joyce misanthropic. Flaubert is misanthropic, if you like—and in reproducing his technique, Joyce sometimes suggests his acrid tone. But Stephen, Bloom and Mrs. Bloom are certainly not either unamiable or unattractive—and for all their misfortunes and shortcomings, they inspire us with considerable respect. Stephen and Bloom are played off a little against the duller and meaner people about them; but even these people can scarcely be said to be treated with bitterness, even when, as in the case of Buck Mulligan or the elder Dedalus, Stephen's feeling about them is bitter. Joyce is remarkable, rather, for equanimity: in spite of the nervous intensity of "Ulysses," there is a real serenity and detachment behind it—we are in the presence of a mind which has much in common with that of a certain type of philosopher, who in his effort to understand the causes of things, to interrelate the different elements of the universe, has reached a point where the ordinary values of good and bad, beautiful and ugly, have been lost in the excellence and beauty of transcendent understanding itself.

I believe that the first readers of "Ulysses" were shocked, not merely by Joyce's use of certain words ordinarily excluded to-day from English literature, but by his way of representing those aspects of human nature which we tend to consider incongruous as intimately, inextricably mingled. Yet the more we read "Ulysses," the more we are convinced of its psychological truth, and the more we are amazed at Joyce's genius in mastering and in presenting, not through analysis or generalization, but by the complete recreation of life in the process of being lived, the relations of human beings to their environment and to each other; the nature of their perception of what goes on about them and of what goes on within themselves; and the interdependence of their intellectual, their physical, their professional and their emotional lives. To have traced all these interdependences, to have given each of these elements its value, yet never to have lost sight of the moral through preoccupation with the physical, nor to have forgotten the general in the particular; to have exhibited ordinary humanity without either satirizing it or sentimentalizing it—this would already have been sufficiently remarkable; but to have subdued all this material to the uses of a supremely finished and disciplined work of art is a feat which has hardly been equalled in the literature of our time.

In Stephen's diary in "A Portrait of the Artist," we find this significant entry apropos of a poem by Yeats: "Michael Robartes remembers forgotten beauty and, when his arms wrap her round, he presses in his arms the loveliness which has long faded from the world. Not this. Not at all. I desire to press in my arms the loveliness which has not yet come into the world."

And with "Ulysses," Joyce has brought into literature a new and unknown beauty. Some readers have regretted the extinction in the later Joyce of the charming lyric poet of his two little books of poems and the *fin de siècle* prose writer of the *fin*

de siècle phases of "A Portrait of the Artist as a Young Man"
(both the prose and verse of the early Joyce showed the influence of Yeats). This poet is still present in "Ulysses": "Kind air
defined the coigns of houses in Kildare Street. No birds. Frail
from the housetops two plumes of smoke ascended, pluming,
and in a flaw of softness softly were blown." But the conventions of the romantic lyric, of "æsthetic" *fin de siècle* prose,
even of the æsthetic Naturalism of Flaubert, can no longer, for
Joyce, be made to accommodate the reality of experience. The
diverse elements of experience are perceived in different relations and they must be differently represented. Joyce has found
for this new vision a new language, but a language which, instead of diluting or doing violence to his poetic genius, enables
it to assimilate more materials, to readjust itself more completely and successfully than that of perhaps any other poet of
our age to the new self-consciousness of the modern world.
But in achieving this, Joyce has ceased to write verse. I have
suggested, in connection with Valéry and Eliot, that verse itself
as a literary medium is coming to be used for fewer and fewer
and for more and more special purposes, and that it may be
destined to fall into disuse. And it seems to me that Joyce's literary development is a striking corroboration of this view. His
prose works have an artistic intensity, a definitive beauty of surface and of form, which make him comparable to the great
poets rather than to most of the great novelists.

Joyce is indeed really the great poet of a new phase of the
human consciousness. Like Proust's or Whitehead's or Einstein's world, Joyce's world is always changing as it is perceived by different observers and by them at different times. It
is an organism made up of "events," which may be taken as infinitely inclusive or infinitely small and each of which involves
all the others; and each of these events is unique. Such a world
cannot be presented in terms of such artificial abstractions as
have been conventional in the past: solid institutions, groups,
individuals, which play the parts of distinct durable entities—
or even of solid psychological factors: dualisms of good and evil,
mind and matter, flesh and spirit, instinct and reason; clear
conflicts between passion and duty, between conscience and
interest. Not that these conceptions are left out of Joyce's

world: they are all there in the minds of the characters; and the realities they represent are there, too. But everything is reduced to terms of "events" like those of modern physics and philosophy—events which make up a "continuum," but which may be taken as infinitely small. Joyce has built out of these events a picture, amazingly lifelike and living, of the everyday world we know—and a picture which seems to allow us to see into it, to follow its variations and intricacies, as we have never been able to do before.

Nor are Joyce's characters merely the sum of the particles into which their experience has been dissociated: we come to imagine them as solidly, to feel their personalities as unmistakably, as we do with any characters in fiction; and we realize finally that they are also symbols. Bloom himself is in one of his aspects the typical modern man: Joyce has made him a Jew, one supposes, partly in order that he may be conceived equally well as an inhabitant of any provincial city of the European or Europeanized world. He makes a living by petty business, he leads the ordinary middle-class life—and he holds the conventional enlightened opinions of the time: he believes in science, social reform and internationalism. But Bloom is surpassed and illuminated from above by Stephen, who represents the intellect, the creative imagination; and he is upheld by Mrs. Bloom, who represents the body, the earth. Bloom leaves with us in the long run the impression that he is something both better and worse than either of them; for Stephen sins through pride, the sin of the intellect; and Molly is at the mercy of the flesh; but Bloom, though a less powerful personality than either, has the strength of humility. It is difficult to describe the character of Bloom as Joyce finally makes us feel it: it takes precisely the whole of "Ulysses" to put him before us. It is not merely that Bloom is mediocre, that he is clever, that he is commonplace—that he is comic, that he is pathetic—that he is, as Rebecca West says, a figure of abject "squatting" vulgarity, that he is at moments, as Foster Damon says, the Christ—he is all of these, he is all the possibilities of that ordinary humanity which is somehow not so ordinary after all; and it is the proof of Joyce's greatness that, though we recognize Bloom's perfect truth and typical character, we cannot pigeonhole him

in any familiar category, racial, social, moral, literary or even—
because he does really have, after all, a good deal in common
with the Greek Ulysses—historical.

Both Stephen and Molly are more easily describable because
they represent extremes. Both are capable of rising to heights
which Bloom can never reach. In Stephen's rhapsody on the
seashore, when he first realizes his artist's vocation, in "A Portrait of the Artist as a Young Man," we have had the ecstasy of
the creative mind. In the soliloquy of Mrs. Bloom, Joyce has
given us another ecstasy of creation, the rhapsody of the flesh.
Stephen's dream was conceived in loneliness, by a drawing
apart from his fellows. But Mrs. Bloom is like the earth, which
gives the same life to all: she feels a maternal kinship with all
living creatures. She pities the "poor donkeys slipping half
asleep" in the steep street of Gibraltar, as she does "the sentry
in front of the governor's house . . . half roasted" in the sun;
and she gives herself to the bootblack at the General Post Office as readily as to Professor Goodwin. But, none the less, she
will tend to breed from the highest type of life she knows: she
turns to Bloom, and, beyond him, toward Stephen. This gross
body, the body of humanity, upon which the whole structure
of "Ulysses" rests—still throbbing with so strong a rhythm
amid obscenity, commonness and squalor—is laboring to
throw up some knowledge and beauty by which it may transcend itself.

These two great flights of the mind carry off all the ignominies and trivialities through which Joyce has made us pass:
they seem to me—the soaring silver prose of the one, the deep
embedded pulse of the other—among the supreme expressions in literature of the creative powers of humanity: they are,
respectively, the justifications of the woman and the man.

V

Since finishing "Ulysses," Joyce has been engaged upon another work, about half of which has been published in the
transatlantic monthly, *Transition*. It is not possible to judge
this book properly in the imperfect form in which it has appeared. It is intended as a sort of complement to "Ulysses";

Joyce has explained that, as "Ulysses" deals with the day and with the conscious mind, so his new work is to deal with the night and with the subconscious. The whole book is apparently to occupy itself with the single night's sleep of a single character. Joyce has already exhibited in "Ulysses" a unique genius for the representation of special psychological states: I know of nothing else in literature, for example, like the drunken night-town scene, with its astounding recreation of all the deliriums, dazes, gibberings, exaltations and hallucinations of drunkenness. And Joyce's method of rendering the phases of sleep is similar to his methods in the Circe episode. But he is here attempting something even more difficult, and his way of doing it raises an important question in regard to all Joyce's later work. Joyce, as I have said, always nowadays represents the consciousness of his characters directly: but his method of representing consciousness is to let you overhear his characters talking to themselves. Joyce's people think and feel exclusively in terms of words, for Joyce himself thinks in terms of words. This is partly due, no doubt, to his defective eyesight, which of late years has become so serious as to make it difficult for him to work. There is an interesting passage in "A Portrait of the Artist" in which Joyce himself discusses this aspect of his writing:

"He drew forth a phrase from his treasure and spoke it softly to himself:

"—A day of dappled seaborne clouds.——

"The phrase and the day and the scene harmonized in a chord. Words. Was it their colors? He allowed them to glow and fade, hue after hue: sunrise gold, the russet and green of apple orchards, azure of waves, the greyfringed fleece of clouds. No, it was not their colors: it was the poise and balance of the period itself. Did he then love the rhythmic rise and fall of words better than their associations of legend and color? Or was it that, being as weak of sight as he was shy of mind, he drew less pleasure from the reflection of the glowing sensible world through the prism of a language many colored and richly storied than from the contemplation of an inner world of individual emotions mirrored perfectly in a lucid supple periodic prose."

And in "Ulysses" we hear the characters far more plainly than we see them: Joyce supplies us with descriptions of them in sparse, scrupulous phrases, one trait here, another there. But the Dublin of "Ulysses" is a city of voices. Who has a clear idea of how Bloom or Molly Bloom looks?—and should we have a clear idea of Stephen if we had never seen photographs of Joyce? But their eternally soliloquizing voices become our intimate companions and haunt us long afterwards.

Joyce already seems sometimes, in "Ulysses," to go a little beyond the probabilities in the vocabulary which he allows Bloom to command. When Bloom, in the drunken scene, for example, imagines himself giving birth to "eight male yellow and white children," all "with valuable metallic faces" and each with "his name printed in legible letters on his shirt-front: Nasodoro, Goldfinger, Chrysostomos, Maindorée, Silversmile, Silberselber, Vifargent, Panargyros"—we have difficulty in believing that he would have been learned enough for this. Yet I do not suppose that Joyce means us to think of Bloom as actually formulating these words in his mind: it is the author's way of conveying in words a vision which on the part of Bloom must have been a good deal less distinct, or at least a good deal less literary, than this. Now, in his new book, Joyce has tried to make his hero express directly in words, again, states of mind which do not usually in reality make use of words at all—for the subconscious has no language—the dreaming mind does not usually speak—and when it does, it is more likely to express itself in the looking-glass language of "Jabberwocky" than in anything resembling ordinary speech. Joyce's attempts to write the language of dreams have a good deal in common with those of Lewis Carroll; but the difference between his new novel and the Alice books is that, whereas in the Alice books it is the author who is supposed to be telling in straight English the adventures which his heroine thinks she is having and the literary language peculiar to dreams appears only in a poem which she reads, in Joyce's book he is plunging us directly into the consciousness of the dreamer itself, which is presented, without explanations by the author, entirely in the Jabberwocky language. The book is thus more easily comprehensible to literary people than to people who are not "word-minded," whose minds do not habitually breed words in response to sensations, emotions and thoughts. Yet it is worth making the effort to understand, because what Joyce is trying to do is both artistically and psychologically extremely interesting, and it may be that he will turn out to have written the most remarkable piece of dream-literature in existence.

The best way to understand Joyce's method is to note what goes on in one's own mind when one is just dropping off to sleep. Images—or words, if one thinks in words like Joyce—which were already in the conscious mind will suddenly acquire an ominous significance which has nothing to do with their ordinary functions; some vivid incident which may have taken place just before one went to bed will begin to swell with a meaning, an emotion, which at first we do not recognize because it has come up from the submerged part of the mind and is attempting to pass itself off in the clothes of an immediate experience—because it is dissociated from the situation out of which it originally arose. Or conversely, one may rid oneself of a troublesome abstract idea with which one has been preoccupied by allowing it to transform itself into some innocuous concrete image more easily dismissed from the attention: the page of a philosophical book, for example, where one had been continually stumbling over phrases and terms may vanish on the threshold of sleep in the guise of a spotted man, the spots having substituted themselves for the impenetrable words and phrases. And so the images which our waking mind would keep distinct from one another incongruously mix in our sleep with an effect of perfect congruity. A single one of Joyce's sentences, therefore, will combine two or three different meanings—two or three different sets of symbols; a single word may combine two or three. Joyce has profited, in inventing his dream-language, by Freud's researches into the principles which govern the language actually spoken in dreams: certain people, it appears, do make up "portmanteau-words" in their sleep; but we are not, I take it, to suppose that Joyce's hero necessarily frames all these sentences to himself. Except when he dreams he is reading something or carrying on a conversation, the language is merely a literary equivalent for sleeping states not even articulate in fancy. Nor are we to assume that Joyce's sleeper is actually master of all the languages or understands all the allusions of which Joyce makes him avail himself in his

dream. We are now at a level below particularized languages—
we are in the region whence all languages arise and where the
impulses to all acts have their origin.

The hero of the night's sleep in question is, we gather, a man
named H. C. Earwicker, a Norwegian or descendant of Nor-
wegians, living in Dublin. He seems to have attempted a number of occupations—to have been a postman, to have worked
in Guinness's Brewery, to have kept a hotel and a shop. He is
married and has children, but has apparently been carrying on
a flirtation with a girl named Anna Livia. This, along with
other lapses from respectability associated with it in his mind,
troubles his conscience and his repose. We are introduced, at
the very beginning, into Earwicker's drowsing consciousness,
and we have to make what we can of the names, the shapes, and
above all, of the voices, which fill that dim and shifting world—
they combine and recombine, they are always changing into
one another—but as we go on, we find the same themes recurring and we begin to be able to understand them in relation
to one another—we become familiar with the character of
Earwicker—we begin to guess at his condition and history. We
identify Maggie and the children, the house in which they live,
the four old men with the donkey, Earwicker's drunken misdemeanors and his fear of being caught by the police, the
washerwomen gathering up their washing, Anna Livia on the
bank of the Liffey, the Hill of Howth, the tree and the stone.
But none of these elements is seen clearly or objectively—they
are all aspects, the dramatic projection of aspects, of Earwicker
himself: men and women, old and young, stronger and weaker,
river and mountain, tree and stone—it is the dreamer who
speaks or is spoken to, who sees or is seen, in all of them. The
old men come to admire him as he is sleeping on the moun-
tainside, but in a moment it is Earwicker himself who is talking
about himself; or he splits up into two personalities, one of
whom bullies or accuses the other. He is coming out of a pub
into the street with a party of drunken companions, many
people are standing about but the revellers do not care how
much attention they attract: they egg on one of their number
to sing but the song turns out to be a recital of all Earwicker's
failures and sins—he has proved himself a fool and a swindler
to the derision of all Dublin, his wife is going to read him the

Riot Act. Or he sets out very sweetly to explain something by a fable of "the Mookse and the Gripes": the Mookse comes swaggering up to the Gripes, who is hanging on a tree—a sort of altercation takes place, and it turns into rather a painful reënactment of one of Earwicker's encounters with the police—but dusk falls and the washerwomen come out and carry off the Mookse and the Gripes, who are now merely two pieces of laundry.

One of the most remarkable parts which have so far appeared is the *allegro* conclusion to the first of the four long sections which are to make up the completed work. (Joyce has allowed it to be published separately in a little book called "Anna Livia Plurabelle.") Here the washerwomen have become identified with the stone and elm on the riverbank—we hear them gossiping about Anna Livia, who is both the girl with whom the hero is in love and the river Liffey; and their gossip is the voice of the river itself, light, rapid, incessant, almost metrical, now monotonously running on one note, now impeded and syncopated, but vivaciously, interminably babbling its indistinct rigmarole story, half-unearthly, half-vulgarly human, of a heroine half-legendary, half-real:

"Oh tell me all about Anna Livia! I want to hear all about Anna Livia. Well, you know Anna Livia? Yes, of course, we all know Anna Livia. Tell me all. Tell me now. You'll die when you hear. . . . Tell me, tell me, how cam she camlin through all her fellows, the neckar she was, the diveline? Linking one and knocking the next, tapting a flank and tipting a jutty and palling in and pietaring out and clyding by on her eastway. Waiwhou was the first thurever burst? . . . She says herself she hardly knows whuon the annals her graveller was, a dynast of Leinster, a wolf of the sea, or what he did or how blyth she played or how, when, why, where and who offon he jumnpad her. She was just a young thin pale soft shy slim slip of a thing then, sauntering, by silvamoonlake, and he was a heavy trudging lurching lieabroad of a Curraghman, making his hay for whose sun to shine on, as tough as the oaktrees (peats be with them!) used to rustle that time down by the dykes of killing Kildare, that forstfellfoss with a plash across her. She thought she's sankh neathe the ground with nymphant shame when he gave her the tigris eye!"

As darkness falls between stone and elm, the voices grow
husky and vague:

"And ho! Hey? What all men. Hot? His tittering daughters
of Whawk?

"Can't hear with the waters of. The chittering waters of.
Flittering bats, fieldmice, bawk talk. Ho! Are you not gone
ahome? What Tom Malone? Can't hear with bawk of bats, all
the liffeying waters of. Ho, talk save us. My foos won't moos.
I feel as old as yonder elm. A tale told of Shaun or Shem? All
Livia's daughtersons. Dark hawks hear us. Night! Night! My
ho head halls. I feel as heavy as yonder stone. Tell me of John
or Shaun? Who were Shem and Shaun the living sons or
daughters of? Night now! Tell me, tell me, tell me, elm! Night
night! Tell me tale of stem or stone. Beside the rivering waters
of, hitherandthithering waters of. Night!"

Night is just falling in this first section of the book, and the
shadow of the past, the memory presumably of the day before,
darkens the hero's sleep—the vulgarities of his waking life op-
press him and pursue him; but after midnight, as dawn approaches, as he becomes dimly aware of the first light, the
dream begins to brighten and to rise unencumbered. If I am
not mistaken, the middle-aged Earwicker reverts to the period
of his youth, once again he is carefree, attractive, well-liked—
his spirit turns refreshed to the new day. Are we to leave him
on the verge of waking or are we finally to see the fantasies of
the dream closed down into the commonplace fate which we
have already been able to divine?

This new production of Joyce's exaggerates the qualities
we have noted in "Ulysses." There is even less action than in
"Ulysses." Joyce has set out with certain definite themes and
the themes are evidently all to have their developments, but
these developments take a long time. We make progress—we
pass from night to morning—and no doubt, when the whole
book is before us, we shall see that some sort of psychological
drama has been played out in Earwicker's mind—but, as we
progress, we go round and round. And whereas in "Ulysses"
there is only one parallel, in this new book there are a whole
set: Adam and Eve, Tristan and Isolde, Swift and Vanessa, Cain
and Abel, Michael and Lucifer, Wellington and Napoleon. The
multiplication of references does, to be sure, deepen and

extend the significance of Earwicker: he and Anna Livia are the eternal woman and the eternal man, and during the early hours of heaviness and horror of Earwicker's dream, he is an Adam fallen from grace—to be redeemed, Joyce is said to have announced, with the renewal of the morning light. And it would seem that Joyce has provided plausible reasons for the appearance of all these personages in his hero's dream: Napoleon and Wellington have gotten in by way of the Wellington monument in the Phœnix Park, near which one of Earwicker's misdemeanors has been committed; and Michael and Lucifer—it appears from the last instalment published, in which Earwicker is partly waked up toward morning by the crying of one of his children—by a picture on the bedroom wall. Yet the effect of the superposition, one upon the other, of such a variety of parallels seems sometimes less to enrich the book than to give it a mere synthetic complication. Joyce is again, we come to the conclusion, trying to do too many things at once. The style he has invented for his purpose works on the principle of a palimpsest: one meaning, one set of images, is written over another. Now we can grasp a certain number of such suggestions simultaneously, but Joyce, with his characteristic disregard for the reader, apparently works over and over his pages, packing in allusions and puns. This appears clearly from the different versions which have been published in various places of the Anna Livia Pluribelle section (I have given in an appendix three stages of the same passage from this). Joyce has improved it in making the texture denser, but this enrichment also obscures the main outlines and somewhat oversolidifies and impedes the dim ambiguous fluidity of the dream—especially when it takes the form of introducing in the final version puns on the names of some five hundred rivers. And as soon as we are aware of Joyce himself systematically embroidering on his text, deliberately inventing puzzles, the illusion of the dream is lost.

Yet, on the whole, this illusion is created and kept up with extraordinary success. There is a curious fascination about becoming gradually acquainted with a character whom we know only from the inside and from his dreams. And without the complications of his vocabulary, Joyce would no doubt never be able to paint for us with so sensitive and sure a hand the turbid life of that mental half-world where the unconscious is merged with the conscious—as without his machinery of history and myth, he would not be able to give his subject any poetic freedom of significance beyond the realistic framework which holds it firm. We are to see in H. C. Earwicker Every-man (he imagines his initials standing for Here Comes Every-body). We are to find in his dream all human possibilities—for out of that human nature, that psychological plasm, which swims dark and deep beneath the surface of the meagre words, the limited acts, the special mask, of one man's actual daytime career, all history and myth have arisen—victim and con-queror, lover and beloved, childhood and old age—all the forms of human experience. And what humor, what imagina-tion, what poetry, what psychological wisdom, Joyce has put into Earwicker's dream! I have offered the criticisms above only tentatively and without assurance: when we come to think about what we take at first to be the defects in Joyce's work, we find them so closely involved with the depth of his thought and the originality of his conception that we are obliged to grant them a certain necessity. And whatever difficulties we may have with this book in its present fragmentary and incom-plete state, I feel confident that, when we read it as a whole, we shall find, not only that it is not unworthy—as the snappers at the heels of genius have been so eager and prompt to assert— of the great master of letters who wrote it, but that he is still at the height of his power.

VII. Gertrude Stein

GERTRUDE STEIN, born in Allegheny, Pennsylvania, a student of psychology and medicine who is said to have been considered by William James the most brilliant woman pupil he had ever had, published in 1909 a book of fiction called "Three Lives." It was brought out by a small and obscure publisher and at that time attracted little attention, but, loaned from hand to hand, it acquired a certain reputation. "Three Lives," which bore on its title-page a quotation from Jules Laforgue, was a work of what would at that time have been called realism, but it was realism of rather a novel kind. The book consisted of three long short stories—the histories of three women, two of them German servant-girls, the other a mulatto girl. What is most remarkable in these stories—especially if we compare them with such a typically Naturalistic production as Flaubert's "Un Cœur Simple," in which we feel that the old family servant has been seen from a great distance and documented with effort—is the closeness with which the author has been able to identify herself with her characters. In a style which appears to owe nothing to that of any other novelist, she seems to have caught the very rhythms and accents of the minds of her heroines: we find ourselves sharing the lives of the Good Anna and Gentle Lena so intimately that we forget about their position and see the world limited to their range, just as in Melanctha's case—and this is what makes her story one of the best as well as one of the earliest attempts of a white American novelist to understand the mind of the modern Americanized negro—we become so immersed in Melanctha's world that we quite forget its inhabitants are black. And we discover that these histories have a significance different from that of ordinary realistic fiction: Miss Stein is interested in her subjects, not from the point of view of the social conditions of which they might be taken as representative, but as three fundamental types of women: the self-sacrificing Anna, who combines devotion with domination; the dreamy and passive Lena, for whom it is natural to allow herself to be used and effaced from life by other lives; and the passionate and complex Melanctha, who "was always losing what she had in wanting all the things she saw." Behind the limpid and slightly monotonous simplicity of Gertrude Stein's sentences, one becomes aware of her masterly grasp of the organisms, contradictory and indissoluble, which human personalities are.

"Three Lives," though not widely circulated, exercised a considerable influence. Carl Van Vechten wrote about it; Eugene O'Neill and Sherwood Anderson read it with admiration. It is interesting to note that all three of these writers were to occupy themselves later with negro life, in regard to which Miss Stein had given an example of an attitude not complicated by race-consciousness. And Sherwood Anderson seems to have learned from her, in his own even less Naturalistic, even more dreamlike, fiction, both his recurrent repetitions with their effect of ballad refrains and his method of telling a story in a series of simple declarative sentences of almost primer-like baldness.

Gertrude Stein's next book was a long novel, "The Making of Americans," written between 1906 and 1908, but not published till 1925. I confess that I have not read this book all through, and I do not know whether it is possible to do so. "The Making of Americans" runs to almost a thousand large pages of small closely-printed type. The first chapters show the same remarkable qualities as "Three Lives," though in a somewhat diluted form. Miss Stein sets before us the men and women of her German-Jewish families with all the strong sense we have already admired for the various and irreducible entities of human character; and we are made, as we are in "Three Lives," to feel life as her people feel it, to take for granted just as they do the whole complex of conditions of which they are part. But already some ruminative self-hypnosis, some progressive slowing-up of the mind, has begun to show itself in Miss Stein's work as a sort of fatty degeneration of her imagination and style. In "Three Lives," the rhythmic repetitions were successful in conveying the recurrences, the gradual unwinding of life, and in the dialogue they produced the effect of the speech of slow-minded people: "I never did use to think I was so much on being real modest, Melanctha, but now I know really I am, when I hear you talking. I see all the time there are many people living just as good as I am, though they are a

little different to me. Now with you, Melanctha, if I understand you right what you are talking, you don't think that way
of no other one that you are ever knowing." But, though in
"The Making of Americans" this sort of thing is appropriate to
the patient and brooding repetitiousness of the German-
Jewish Americans of the first and second generations, it is here
carried to such immoderate lengths as finally to suggest some
technique of mesmerism. With sentences so regularly rhythmical, so needlessly prolix, so many times repeated and ending so
often in present participles, the reader is all too soon in a state,
not to follow the slow becoming of life, but simply to fall
asleep. And the further we get, the more difficult we find it to
keep our mind on what we are reading: Miss Stein abandons
altogether for long stretches any attempt to tell her story by
reporting what her characters do and say, and resorts to a curious abstract vein of generalization: "Some are needing themselves being a young one, an older one, a middle aged one, an
older one, an old one to be ones realizing what any one telling
about different ways of feeling anything, of thinking about
anything, of doing anything is meaning by what that one is
telling. Some are needing themselves being a young one, an
older one, a middle aged one, an older one, an old one to be
one being certain that it is a different thing inside in one being
a young one, from being an older one, from being a middle
aged one, from being an older one, from being an old one,"
etc., etc. The psychological truth is still there, no doubt, but it
is in a solution of about one percent to the total volume of the
dose, and the volume of the dose is enormous.

This repetitious and abstract vein of the last pages of "The
Making of Americans" persists still in the psychological portraits of Picasso and Matisse published in 1912: "One was quite
certain that for a long part of his being one being living he had
been trying to be certain that he was wrong in doing what he
was doing and then when he could not come to be certain that
he had been wrong in doing what he had been doing, when he
had completely convinced himself that he would not come to
be certain that he had been wrong in doing what he had been
doing he was really certain then that he was a great one and he
certainly was a great one. Certainly every one could be certain
of this thing that this one is a great one."

This is queer and very boring, like a good deal of "The Making of Americans," but it is still intelligible. A little later, however, Miss Stein published privately another "portrait" which represented something of a new departure. In the "Portrait of Mabel Dodge," she seems to be groping for the instinctive movements of the mind which underlie the factitious conventional logic of ordinary intercourse, and to be trying to convey their rhythms and reflexes through a language divested of its ordinary meaning.

"Tender Buttons," which appeared in 1914 and was the first of Miss Stein's books to attract attention, went even further than the "Portrait of Mabel Dodge" in the direction of dislocating words from their meanings. The pieces in "Tender Buttons" are in a different vein from anything she had published before: she has here given up her long rhythms and writes pungently, impressionistically, concisely. Miss Stein had by this time gone to live in Paris (where she has remained ever since) and had become interested in the modern French painting of the generation of Picasso and Matisse, which she was one of the first to appreciate and collect; and the pieces in "Tender Buttons"—the title was supposed to describe the contents— are said to have been intended as prose still-lifes to correspond to those of such painters as Picasso and Braque. A pattern of assorted words, though they might make nonsense from the traditional point of view, would be analogous to a Cubist canvas composed of unidentifiable fragments.

"*Red Roses*. A cool red rose and a pink cut pink, a collapse and a sold hole, a little less hot.

"*A Sound*. Elephant beaten with candy and little pops and chews all bolts and reckless rats, this is this.

"*Custard*. Custard is this. It has aches, aches when. Not to be. Not to be narrowly. This makes a whole little hill.

"It is better than a little thing that has mellow real mellow. It is better than lakes whole lakes, it is better than seeing.

"*Chicken*. Alas a dirty word, alas a dirty third, alas a dirty bird."

Gertrude Stein is said, at this period, to have made a practice of shutting herself up at night and trying utterly to banish from her mind all the words ordinarily associated with the ideas she had fixed upon. She had come to believe that words had other values than those inherent in their actual meanings, and she was attempting to produce a kind of literature which should work with these values exclusively.

In "Have They Attacked Mary He Giggled—A Political Satire" (1917), she developed, however, still another genre, which at least partially left to language its common meanings —a sort of splintered stenographic commentary made up of scraps of conversation as they reverberate in the mind and awaken unspoken responses. The volumes of miscellaneous pieces which have followed—"Geography and Plays" (1922) and "Useful Knowledge" (1928)—contain examples of all her previous styles as well as several variations, including a curious kind of "play" which consists simply of long lists of phrases divided into acts. Among these, some of the satires are funny, some of the portraits rather interesting and bits of the "abstract" impressionism charming, and there are one or two really excellent short stories such as "Miss Furr and Miss Skeene," in which the repetitive rigmarole manner is admirably suited to render the monotony and insipidity of the feminine lives which are being narrated. But most of what Miss Stein publishes nowadays must apparently remain absolutely unintelligible even to a sympathetic reader. She has outdistanced any of the Symbolists in using words for pure purposes of suggestion— she has gone so far that she no longer even suggests. We see the ripples expanding in her consciousness, but we are no longer supplied with any clew as to what kind of object has sunk there.

II

Sometimes these writings of Gertrude Stein make us laugh: her humor is perhaps the one of her qualities which comes through in her recent books most clearly; and I should describe them as amusing nonsense, if "nonsense" were not a word which had so often been used in derogation both of the original Symbolists and of the contemporary writers dealt with in this book. If I should say that Miss Stein wrote nonsense, I might be thought to be implying that she was not serious or that she was not artistically successful. As a matter of fact, one should not talk about "nonsense" until one has decided what "sense" consists of—and one cannot investigate this without becoming involved in questions which go to the bottom of the whole Symbolist theory and throw further light on the issues it raises.

The original Symbolists supposed themselves to be defending the value of suggestion in literature as against the documentation of Naturalism and the logic of rationalism—and both they and their opponents seemed to tend to take it for granted that the suggestion was all on one side and the sense all on the other. We have already noted this tendency in Valéry, in Eliot and in Yeats, and we have stumbled over the difficulties it leads to. Now, as a matter of fact, all literature, all writing, all speech, depends equally upon suggestion; the "meaning" of words is what they suggest. Speaking accurately, it is impossible to say that one kind of writing suggests, whereas another kind proves or states. Any literary work, if it accomplishes its purpose, must superinduce in the reader a whole complex of what we are accustomed to call thoughts, emotions and sensations — a state of consciousness, a state of mind; it depends for its effectiveness upon a web of associations as intricate and in the last analysis as mysterious as our minds and bodies themselves. Our words themselves are the prime symbols, and the only originality of the Symbolists consisted in reminding people of the true nature and function of words. It is of course possible to think of words abstractly so that they shall seem to have pure definite meanings, but the fact remains that as soon as we begin to use them, we cannot help pouring them full of suggestion by our inflections, our pauses, our tones or by their order and collocation on the page, and in any case by selecting them in such a way as to bring out certain previous associations.

Let us examine passages from various books, ranging from what we should call the most nonsensical to what we should call the most rational. Most people, I suppose, would grant today that it is the business of poetry to suggest and that it is possible to write very fine poetry which is neither logical in the ordinary sense nor true; and most people, I suppose, could be persuaded, after a moment or two of reflection, that there is really no difference in kind between poems like "Kubla Khan" and "Ulalume" and poems like "Jabberwocky," "The

Jumblies" and "The Owl and the Pussycat" (unless it constitutes a difference in kind that Lear and Carroll intend to be
amusing whereas Coleridge and Poe do not)—and even to admit that this realization should have the effect of making one
think more highly of Lear and Carroll rather than less highly of
Coleridge and Poe. But *prose* the ordinary reader might claim,
as we have seen that Paul Valéry does, ought to convey a
"sense." Yet there is a prose which, as anyone will recognize, is
extremely close to poetry. Take one of the passages I have
already quoted from Yeats:

"We make out of the quarrel with others, rhetoric, but of
the quarrel with ourselves, poetry. Unlike the rhetoricians, who
get a confident voice from remembering the crowd they have
won or may win, we sing amid our uncertainty, and, smitten
even in the presence of the most high beauty by the knowledge of our solitude, our rhythm shudders."

This appears a fairly reasonable statement, yet must we not
confess, when we come to examine it, that we are being moved
by beautiful words rather than convinced of a psychological
fact? And in Yeats's own mind there is a line unmistakably
drawn between this kind of prose and certain other kinds. In
"A Vision," he writes as follows of that phase of human personality in his Great Wheel to which he assigns Bernard Shaw:
"Style exists now but as a sign of work well done, a certain energy and precision of movement; in the artistic sense it is no
longer possible, for the tension of the will is too great to allow
of suggestion."

From Yeats's point of view, then, the prose of Shaw is devoid of suggestion, and, consequently, even of style. Yet let us
look at a typical passage from "The Intelligent Woman's
Guide to Socialism and Capitalism," a masterpiece of prose
exposition:

"Naturally the squires were not disposed to take this defeat
lying down. They revenged themselves by taking up Lord
Shaftesbury's agitation for the Factory Acts, and showing that
the employer's little finger was thicker than the country gentleman's loins; that the condition of the factory employees
was worse than that of the slaves on the American and West
Indian plantations; that the worst cottages of the worst landlords had at least fresher air than the overcrowded slums of the

manufacturing towns; that if the employers did not care whether their 'hands' were Church of England or Methodist, neither did they care whether they were Methodists or Atheists, because they had no God but Mammon; that if they did not persecute politically it was only because the hands had no votes; they persecuted industrially as hard as they could by imprisoning Trade Unionists; and that the personal and often kindly relations between the peasantry and the landlords, the training in good manners and decent housekeeping traditions learnt by the women in domestic service in the country houses, the kindnesses shown to the old and sick on the great estates, were all lost in the squalor and misery, the brutality and blasphemy, the incestuous overcrowding, and the terrible dirt epidemics in the mining and factory populations where English life was what the employer's greed had made it."

If we scrutinize this paragraph on industrial conditions, we see at once that it depends as much on suggestion as the passage on rhetoric and poetry which has just been quoted from Yeats. Yeats suggests a state of mind where we are preoccupied with solitude and introspection, whereas Shaw suggests a state of mind where we are preoccupied with our relation to society; but that is the only difference. Shaw wants to turn our attention out, whereas Yeats wants to turn it in; but both use words not merely to reason but to put a spell on us and excite our emotions. What makes the passage by Shaw effective is the belligerent sound of such homely figures as "showing that the employer's little finger was thicker than the country gentleman's loins" and "because they had no God but Mammon"; it is the rousing rhythm of the piled-up indictment. The whole passage is loaded with suggestion from beginning to end: the suggestion produced by calling harsh names, by violent antithesis, by shifting quickly from a picture of horrible conditions to a picture of attractive ones and then abruptly shifting back to another picture more horrible still.

Let us, however, take another passage from a work which makes no claim to be literature, in which in fact the utmost effort has been exerted to keep as far away from poetry and to make sense as plainly as possible—let us take a passage from the United States Courts-Martial Manual:

"The Army is an emergent arm of the public service which

the Nation holds ready for a time of great peril. Military service is an obligation which every citizen owes to the government. It is settled law that such service may be compelled, if necessary, by draft. Nor is the obligation of the soldier who volunteers for a fixed period different from that of the drafted soldier. By his act of volunteering he consecrates himself to the military service. His engagement, supported by an oath of allegiance, is that the nation may depend upon him for such service during the fixed period, whatever may be the emergency. When this engagement is breached a high obligation to the nation is disregarded, a solemn oath of allegiance is violated, and the government is defrauded in the amount of its outlay incident to inducting the soldier into the military service, training, clothing and caring for him while he remains in that service, and transporting him to the station from which he deserts. Desertion is thus seen to be, not simply a breach of contract for personal service, but a grave crime against the Government; in time of war perhaps the gravest that a soldier can commit, and at such times punishable with death."

It will be seen that the Courts-Martial Manual also deals in metaphors: "The Army is an emergent arm of the public service"; and its cumulative rhythms: "When this engagement is breached a high obligation to the nation is disregarded, a solemn oath of allegiance is violated, and the government is defrauded," etc. And the word "death" is made to dominate the paragraph by being placed at the end of the sentence. The author of the Courts-Martial Manual is trying like Bernard Shaw, but even more single-mindedly, to suggest a state of mind in which we shall be conscious of ourselves only in our relation to society.

Now let us turn to a recent piece of Gertrude Stein's:

A PATRIOTIC LEADING

Verse I
    Indeed indeed
    Can you see.
    The stars
    And regularly the precious treasure.
    What do we love without measure.
    We know.

Verse II
  We suspect the second man.

Verse III
  We are worthy of everything that happens.
  You mean weddings.
  Naturally I mean weddings.

Verse IV
  And then we are,
  Hail to the nation.

Verse V
  Do you think we believe it.

Verse VI
  It is that or bust.

Verse VII
  We cannot bust.

Verse VIII
  Thank you.

Verse IX
  Thank you so much.

Gertrude Stein is here attempting to convey an impression exactly the opposite of the impression which the author of the Courts-Martial Manual is aiming at: she and he diverge in the same directions as Yeats and Bernard Shaw, but they are even farther apart. Miss Stein is trying to superinduce a state of mind in which the idea of the nation will seem silly, in which we shall be conscious of ourselves as creatures who do not lend themselves to that conception. Yet the methods by which she accomplishes her ends are very similar to those of the author of the Manual. Like him, she proceeds by incantation. And "The Army is an emergent arm of the public service which the Nation holds ready," etc. is actually as metaphorical as Miss Stein's statement, in another recent piece of writing, that "toasted Susie is my ice-cream." The Army is not an emergent arm of anything: it is a collection of human beings. The difference between Gertrude Stein and the author of the Courts-

Martial Manual is entirely a technical one: it is a difference simply of syntax and of the order in which each evokes his or her selected group of images.

This discussion would, of course, lead us, if we pursued it, to the nature of language itself and hence to the mysteries of human psychology and what we mean when we talk about such things as "reason," "emotion," "sensation" and "imagination." And this must be left to the philosophers, who are largely in the dark about it themselves. But it is well to remember the mysteriousness of the states with which we respond to the stimulus of works of literature and the primarily suggestive character of the language in which these works are written, on any occasion when we may be tempted to characterize as "nonsense," "balderdash" or "gibberish" some new and outlandish-looking piece of writing to which we do not happen to respond. If other persons say they do respond, and derive from doing so pleasure or profit, we must take them at their word.

Gertrude Stein is a singular case in this respect. Widely ridiculed and seldom enjoyed, she has yet played an important rôle in connection with other writers who have become popular. I have spoken of her influence on Sherwood Anderson—and Ernest Hemingway, not only in such short stories as "Mr. and Mrs. Elliot" (who recall Miss Furr and Miss Skeene), but also in certain passages of "The Sun Also Rises" and "A Farewell to Arms," where he wants to catch the slow rhythm of time or the ominous banality of human behavior in situations of emotional strain, owes her a similar debt. Most of us balk at her soporific rigmaroles, her echolaliac incantations, her half-witted-sounding catalogues of numbers; most of us read her less and less. Yet, remembering especially her early work, we are still always aware of her presence in the background of contemporary literature—and we picture her as the great pyramidal Buddha of Jo Davidson's statue of her, eternally and placidly ruminating the gradual developments of the processes of being, registering the vibrations of a psychological country like some august human seismograph whose charts we haven't the training to read. And whenever we pick up her writings, however unintelligible we may find them, we are aware of a literary personality of unmistakable originality and distinction. Sherwood Anderson, who is so sensitive to her quality, has written of it admirably as follows:

"In the great kitchen of my fanciful world in which I [see] Miss Stein standing, there is a most sweet and gracious aroma. Along the walls are many shining pots and pans, and there are innumerable jars of fruits, jellies, and preserves. Something is going on in the great room, for Miss Stein is a worker in words with the same loving touch in her strong fingers that was characteristic of the women of the kitchens of the brick houses in the town of my boyhood. She is an American woman of the old sort, one who cares for the handmade goodies and who scorns the factory-made foods, and in her own great kitchen she is making something with her materials, something sweet to the tongue and fragrant to the nostrils."

III

This may be an appropriate place to mention the systematic comic nonsense called Dadaism. There is no need to describe it at length—I have given in an appendix an entertaining history of the Dadaist Movement written in 1922 by Tristan Tzara, a Rumanian poet, who was perhaps its chief promoter. Many of the jokes of the Dadaists were pretty bad: a piece of silliness, obscenity or bad taste should have spontaneity to carry it off, whereas the antics of the Dadaists seem too often deliberately and mechanically perpetrated by essentially rather humorless young men. But it was natural in the Paris of the years immediately after the War for the youngest writers to produce a literature—they intended it as a campaign against literature—which should aim to set people's teeth on edge. The Dadaists were both cynical and hysterical, and their work was one of the symptoms of the social, intellectual and moral chaos of Europe after the Armistice. The exhaustion of the resources of life had had the result of rendering desperate and sterile even the youngest generation of Frenchmen who had scarcely taken part in the fighting, but who had grown up in the atmosphere of the War.

Dadaism was a queer special development of Symbolism. The writings of the Dadaists grew directly out of the Symbol-

ist tradition, as their hoaxes and practical jokes recall the perverse *non sequitur* capers of Jules Laforgue's "Pierrot Fumiste"
and Tristan Corbière's stroll in Rome with a mitre, a dress-suit
and a pig. The writer, however, of the first Symbolist generation whom the Dadaists seem most to have admired was a man
named Isidore Ducasse, the author of the "Chants de Maldoror," who signed himself "Comte de Lautréamont." Ducasse
was a Frenchman born in Uruguay, who came to Paris in 1867
when he was twenty-one and, full of the literature of the Romantics from Byron to Baudelaire, composed an immature but
not unpromising book in which the expression of what had
become by that time the conventional attitudes of Romanticism was given a slightly new accent and handled in a slightly
new way. "Les Chants de Maldoror" is full of the familiar
ferocities and blasphemies, the familiar sombre confessions of
uncommon and magnificent sins, carried, however, to unprecedented lengths by a young writer who evidently felt that his
predecessors had set him a high standard to surpass; but the
images of his nightmares and tirades have that peculiar phan-
tasmagoric quality which was to be characteristic of Symbolism. Very little is known about Ducasse, but he has been
identified with considerable plausibility with a man of the same
surname, a particularly violent social-revolutionary orator who
attracted a certain amount of notice at the popular meetings
authorized by Napoleon III on the eve of the Franco-Prussian
War. Ducasse was found dead in his room one morning, three
years after he had come to Paris, and there are reasons for
believing that he was murdered by Napoleon's secret police.
At any rate, a legendary Ducasse, thin, catlike, small and dry,
with a shrill grating voice and a "tête de décapité," half-
buffoon but with a demon's energy, hushing crowds with his
bloodthirsty speeches and dashing down at top speed during
his solitary nights a book of sadistic and scandalous visions,
became the patron saint of Dadaism.

The Dadaists were themselves, as time went on, to turn
social-revolutionary: their savage spirit of opposition found a
new field in political journalism. And, discarding the name of
Dadaists though still intent on the destruction of conventional
literature, they took to automatic writing, which they called
"Surréalisme."

VIII. Axel and Rimbaud

THE six writers with whom I have here been concerned represent then a further development of the methods and ideals of the Symbolists. These æsthetic ideals of Symbolism implied, however, a general point of view which was also given a further development by this second set of writers.

"One's great objection to the Symbolist school," writes André Gide, "is its lack of curiosity about life. With perhaps the single exception of Vielé-Griffin (and it is this that gives his verse so special a savor), all were pessimists, renunciants, resignationists, 'tired of the sad hospital' which the earth seemed to them—our 'monotonous and unmerited fatherland,' as Laforgue called it. Poetry had become for them a refuge, the only escape from the hideous realities; they threw themselves into it with a desperate fervor.

"Divesting life as they did of everything which they considered mere vain delusion, doubting whether it were 'worth living,' it was not astonishing that they should have supplied no new ethic—contenting themselves with that of Vigny, which at most they dressed up in irony—but only an æsthetic."

This ideal of renunciation of the experience of the outside world for the experience of the imagination alone, this withdrawal of the individual from society, did, however, give rise to an attitude quite distinct from the stoicism of Vigny. It had already been indicated in England by Walter Pater:

"Those childish days of revery," he writes of "Marius the Epicurean" (1885), "when he played at priests, played in many another day dream, working his way from the actual present, as far as he might, with a delightful sense of escape in replacing the outer world of other people by an inward world as himself really cared to have it, had made him a kind of 'idealist.' He was become aware of the possibility of a large dissidence between an inward and somewhat exclusive world of vivid personal apprehension, and the unimproved, unheightened reality of the life of those about him. As a consequence, he was ready now to concede, somewhat more easily than others, the first point of his new lesson, that the individual is to himself the measure of all things, and to rely on the exclusive certainty to himself of his own impressions. To move afterwards in that outer world of other people, as though taking it at their estimate, would be possible henceforth only as a kind of irony."

But this doctrine had been preached to that generation perhaps most uncompromisingly and emphatically by a work of which Yeats has told us that he read it in his early manhood "slowly and laboriously as one reads a sacred book" and which Lalou, the author of the "Histoire de la Littérature Française Contemporaine," has described as "the 'Faust' of the later nineteenth century."

Villiers de l'Isle-Adam's "Axel," which was published in 1890, is a sort of long dramatic poem in prose, which, as it was the last thing Villiers wrote, sums up and gives final expression to his peculiar idealism. Count Axel of Auersburg is a young man "of an admirable virile beauty," with "a paleness almost radiant" and "an expression mysterious from thought." He inhabits, in an atmosphere half-Wagnerian, half-romantic-Gothic, an ancient and isolated castle in the depths of the Black Forest, where he has given himself up to the study of the hermetic philosophy of the alchemists and is being prepared by a Rosicrucian adept for the revelation of the ultimate mysteries. And this castle entombs its own secret: when Napoleon's armies had menaced Frankfort, the people from miles around had brought in gold, jewels and other valuables to be deposited in the Frankfort National Bank, and it had been decided to send the gigantic treasure, amounting to three hundred and fifty million thalers, under an escort headed by Axel's father to a secret place of safe-keeping. But certain villainous government officials had plotted to murder the Count and possess themselves of the treasure, making it appear that he had allowed himself to fall into the hands of the French. The Count, however, before succumbing to this treachery, has had the time to hide the treasure underground somewhere in his vast estate, imparting the secret to no one but his wife, who has died without divulging it.

Now, during the winter when the drama opens, a cousin of Axel's, the Commander Kaspar, has come to the castle and got wind of the treasure. The Commander, who declares "I am *real life!*," is represented as an insufferable vulgarian. Axel's life of pure reflection and imagination seems to him morbid, un-profitable and empty, and he tries to tempt his young cousin away by telling him of the glories of the court and the plea-sures of amorous conquest; but the fastidious and fiercely proud young Count brushes these suggestions politely aside. When, however, the Commander comes to touch upon the treasure, which he urges Axel to take steps to recover, the young man instantly summons a servant and orders two swords to be brought. He reveals now, in resounding language, his contempt for the Commander's conceptions of honor and pleasure; explains his defiance of and voluntary exile from a so-ciety which has betrayed and murdered his father; asserts his supremacy and his haughty independence in the forest fast-nesses where he has chosen to dwell; reviews at overpowering length the loyal forces he can call to his defence; describes im-pressively the enormous masked trenches in which he could cause the mightiest armies to be engulfed—and in a duel runs the Commander through.

In the meantime, however, the secret of the whereabouts of the treasure has been discovered in a Book of Hours formerly belonging to Axel's mother, by a young French noblewoman, who has been put in the convent to which the book has passed. This young girl makes a daring escape just as the nuns have almost compelled her to take the veil, and finds her way to Axel's castle, where he offers her a lodging for the night. Sara waits till she thinks everybody is asleep, then descends secretly to the family tombs in the crypt below the castle. Seeking out a certain heraldic death's-head, she presses with the point of a dagger a button between its eyes, and from behind a sliding panel the treasure comes pouring forth in cataracts of burning gold-pieces, cloud-bursts of pearls and diamonds. But in a mo-ment she has become aware that Axel has been watching her unnoticed, and whipping out two fine pistols of steel, fires them at him one after the other—only wounding him, how-ever, slightly in the chest. Axel seizes her and wrests away her dagger, with which she had been preparing to attack him, but she is as beautiful as Axel is handsome, and in a moment they have fallen in love.

Sara turns out to be a Rosicrucian, too: her escape from the convent has been signalized by the blooming of the mystic rose. She and Axel embrace in an ecstasy: for the first time, these two chaste and haughty spirits have found objects worthy of their passion. "Say, beloved," breathes Sara to Axel, speaking as if in a dream, "wouldst thou travel to those lands where the caravans pass in the shade of the palm-trees of Cashmir or Mysore? Wouldst to Bengal to choose in the bazaars roses, stuffs and Armenian maidens as white as the ermine's skin? Wouldst raise armies and, like a young Cyaxares, foment rebellion in northern Iran?—or shall we rather set sail for Ceylon, with its white elephants carrying vermilion towers, with its fiery macaws in the trees and with its dwellings all drenched in sun, where the rain of the fountains falls in the marble courts? . . . How delightful to fasten on our skates on the roads of pale Sweden! or in the region of Christiania, among the dazzling fjords and passes of the mountains of Norway!"— and so on for four solid pages. They are holding the whole world in their hands—they have love, youth, social position, power, the supernatural backing of the Rosicrucian spirits and three hundred and fifty million thalers' worth of treasure—"all the dreams to realize," says Sara.

But here Axel, "grave and impenetrable," strikes an unexpected note. "Why realize them?" he asks. "They are so beautiful!" And to her plea of "come and live!" he replies: "Live? No. Our existence is full—and its cup is running over! What hour-glass can count the hours of this night! The future? . . . Sara, believe me when I say it: we have just exhausted the future. All the realities, what will they be to-morrow in comparison with the mirages we have just lived? . . . The quality of our hope no longer allows us the earth. What can we ask from this miserable star where our melancholy lingers on save the pale reflections of such moments? The Earth, dost thou say? What has the Earth ever realized, that drop of frozen mud, whose Time is only a lie in the heavens? It is the Earth, dost thou not see? which has now become the illusion! Admit, Sara: we have destroyed, in our strange hearts, the love of life—and it is in REALITY indeed that ourselves have become our souls. To consent, after this, to live would be but sacrilege against ourselves. Live? our servants will do that for us. . . . Oh, the external world! Let us not be made dupes by the old slave, chained to our feet in broad daylight, who promises us the

keys to a palace of enchantments when it clutches only a handful of ashes in its clenched black fist! Just now, thou wast
speaking of Bagdad, of Palmyra, of—what was it?—Jerusalem?
If thou didst but know what a heap of uninhabitable stones,
what a sterile and burning soil, what dens of loathsome creatures, those wretched places in *reality* are—though they appear to thee all glamorous with memories far away in that
imaginary Orient which thou carriest within thyself! And what
sad weariness the mere sight of them would cause thee!"

He proposes that they shall kill themselves at once. Sara de-
murs: she suggests one night of love. But Axel begs her not to
be trivial. "Oh, my beloved," he tries to explain to her, "tomorrow I should be the prisoner of thy wondrous body! Its
delights would have enchained the chaste energy which animates me now!"—and then, their love could never endure:
some cursed day they would find it burnt out. She pleads still:
"But remember the human race!" "The example I leave it," he
answers, "is well worth those it has given me." "Those who
fight for Justice say that to kill oneself is to desert." "The verdict of beggars," he declares, "for whom God is but a way to
earn their bread." "It might be nobler to think of the general
good!" "The universe devours itself: at that price is the good
of all." And he finally succeeds in persuading her: they drink a
goblet of poison together and perish in a rapture.

It will easily be seen that this super-dreamer of Villiers's is
the type of all the heroes of the Symbolists, of our day as well
as of his: Pater's contemplative, inactive Marius, the exquisitely
sensitive young men of his "Imaginary Portraits"; Laforgue's
Lohengrin, who, the night of his wedding, shrinking from
union with his Elsa, turns his back on her and embraces his pil-
low begging it to carry him away—his Salome, "the victim of
having tried, like all of us, to live in the factitious instead of in
the honest everyday"; the Hamlet of Mallarmé's posthumous
drama, "Igitur," who is the only character in the play and does
nothing but soliloquize. And above all, Huysmans's Des Esseintes, who set the fashion for so many other personalities,
fictitious and real, of the end of the century: the neurotic
nobleman who arranges for himself an existence which will
completely insulate him from the world and facilitate the cultivation of refined and bizarre sensations; who sleeps by day and

stays up at night and whose favorite reading is Silver Latin and the Symbolists. Des Esseintes is living up to the ideal of Axel and Sara when, having set out to visit London—excited by the novels of Dickens—he turns back at the railroad station: he has already driven in a cab through a foggy day in Paris, visited Galignani's English book-store, dined at an English restaurant on oxtail soup, haddock, beefsteak and ale—and as he remembers that he has left his tooth-brush, it occurs to him that on a former occasion he had been sadly disappointed by a visit to Holland and that the real London cannot possibly come up to the one he has just been imagining. It is difficult to agree with M. Lalou as to the literary merits of "Axel," but it is certainly true that it is in a sense a *fin de siècle* "Faust." And if we compare Villiers's point of view with the point of view of the Romantics, we see plainly the fundamental difference between Symbolism and Romanticism.

The later movement, as I have already said, was an antidote to nineteenth-century Naturalism, as the earlier had been an antidote to the neo-classicism of the seventeenth and eighteenth centuries: Symbolism corresponds to Romanticism, and is in fact an outgrowth from it. But whereas it was characteristic of the Romantics to seek experience for its own sake—love, travel, politics—to try the possibilities of life; the Symbolists, though they also hate formulas, though they also discard conventions, carry on their experimentation in the field of literature alone; and though they, too, are essentially explorers, explore only the possibilities of imagination and thought. And whereas the Romantic, in his individualism, had usually revolted against or defied that society with which he felt himself at odds, the Symbolist has detached himself from society and schools himself in indifference to it: he will cultivate his unique personal sensibility even beyond the point to which the Romantics did, but he will not assert his individual will—he will end by shifting the field of literature altogether, as his spokesman Axel had done the arena of life, from an objective to a subjective world, from an experience shared with society to an experience savored in solitude.

The heroes of the Symbolists would rather drop out of the common life than have to struggle to make themselves a place in it—they forego their mistresses, preferring dreams. And the

heroes of the contemporary writers with whom I have been
dealing in this book are in general as uncompromising as
Axel—sometimes, indeed, the authors themselves seem almost
to have patterned their lives on the mythology of the earlier
generation: the Owen Aherne and Michael Robartes of Yeats,
with their lonely towers and mystic chambers, their addiction
to the hermetic philosophy—and Yeats himself, with his astrology and spiritualism, his own reiterated admonitions (in spite
of considerable public activity) of the inferiority of the life of
action to the life of solitary vision: Paul Valéry's M. Teste,
sunken also in solitary brooding so far below the level where
the mind is occupied in attacking particular practical problems
that it is no longer interested even in thoughts which have
for their objects particular fields of experience, but only in the
processes of thought itself—and Teste's inventor, the great
poet who can hardly bring himself to write poetry, who can
hardly even bring himself to explain why he cannot bring himself to write poetry; the ineffectual fragmentary imagination,
the impotence and resignation, of the poet of "Gerontion"
and "The Waste Land"; the supine and helpless hero of "A la
Recherche du Temps Perdu," with his application of prodigious intellectual energy to differentiating the emotions and
sensations which arise from his passive contacts with life and
with his preference for lying in bed by himself and worrying
about Albertine's absences to getting up and taking her out—
Proust himself, who put into practice the regime which Huysmans had invented for his hero, keeping his shutters closed by
day and exercising his sensibility by night, whose whole elaborate work might have been based on Axel's contention in regard to foreign travel that the reality never equals the dream;
Joyce's Bloom, with his animated consciousness and his inveterate ineptitude; Joyce's new hero who surpasses even the feats
of sleeping of Proust's narrator and M. Teste by remaining
asleep through an entire novel; and Gertrude Stein, who has
withdrawn into herself more completely, who has spun herself
a more impenetrable cocoon, than even Michael Robartes,
M. Teste, Gerontion, H. C. Earwicker or Albertine's asthmatic lover.

There is a difference between Proust's cork-lined bedroom
and Alfred de Vigny's ivory tower. Vigny was dealing, even in

his art, with that active life of the world in which he had participated, but the post-Romantic writer who sleeps by day has
lost touch with that world so completely that he no longer
knows precisely what it is like. We recognize in a Romantic like
Coleridge, with his mulling, metaphysics-weaving mind and
his drugs, much of the temperament and mentality of the author of "A la Recherche du Temps Perdu"; but even Coleridge
has more politics than Proust.

II

One of the principal causes, of course, for this withdrawal of
the *fin de siècle* poets from the general life of their time, was
the fact that in the utilitarian society which had been produced
by the industrial revolution and the rise of the middle class, the
poet seemed to have no place. For Gautier's generation, the
bourgeois had already become the enemy; but one took a
lively satisfaction in fighting him. By the end of the century,
however, the bourgeois's world was going so strong that, from
the point of view of the poet, it had come to seem hopeless to
oppose it. The artistic heroes of Thomas Mann with their abject "inferiority complex" in the presence of the good German
burgher are typical of the end of the century; but certain
writers with a strong Romantic strain like H. G. Wells and
Bernard Shaw tried to promote through the new social sciences, in the teeth of the bourgeois world, the realization of
those visions of universal happiness which had been cherished
by some of the most individualistic of the Romantics, such as
Shelley and Rousseau. But if one had no sociological interest
and no satirical bent and so no way of turning society to account, one did not try to struggle with it or to attract attention by publishing one's grievances against it: one simply did
one's best to ignore it, to keep one's imagination free of it
altogether.

The poets of the end of the century, when they happened to
be incapable of Naturalism or of social idealism like William
Morris's, were thus peculiarly maladjusted persons. We are less
conscious of this in the case of the early Symbolist writers I
have mentioned because they were men who either, not possessing particularly vigorous personalities, resigned themselves

easily to their special situation or, from illness or for some
other reason, were not able to rebel against it long. Pater and
Mallarmé were professors, living quietly and modestly among
their books; Verlaine drifted with every wind; Corbière and
Laforgue were dying of tuberculosis in their twenties; Ducasse
was dead at twenty-four, perhaps murdered for his alliance
with the Socialists; and for Villiers de l'Isle-Adam, a man of
distinguished family who had plumbed the depths of poverty
and misery in Paris to emerge finally, with health and disposition ruined, as a reputation of the literary cafés, it was easy to
reject, in the rôle of the haughty Axel, imaginary treasures and
honors. Yet both the characteristic tendency of the Symbolists
to intimate rather than speak plainly and their cult of the
unique personal point of view are symptomatic of the extent to
which they found themselves out of touch with their fellows
and thrown in upon their own private imaginations. Another
hero and pioneer of Symbolism, however, was both to struggle
with the world and survive—though to survive as something
other than a poet; and his career reveals the whole situation in
a dramatic burst of light.

Arthur Rimbaud was born in the north of France, the son
of a pious and strong-willed countrywoman and of an army
officer who, during the years of his campaigning, paid little attention to his family and finally abandoned them altogether. A
prize scholar at his provincial school, Rimbaud had run, by the
time he was nineteen, through the whole repertoire of modern
ideas: he had reacted against a strict religious training into romantic atheism and paganism; had flamed up, at the fall of the
Second Empire, with social-revolutionary idealism; and had
finally devoured Darwin and the other evolutionary writers—
as, in poems written between sixteen and nineteen (1870–73),
he had, as one of his biographers has said, "lived in three years
the literary evolution of modern times." Rimbaud's earliest
poetry was in a familiar Romantic vein, to which, however, he
soon brought fresh strong colors and new elements of irony
and invective. He had already, at seventeen, attempted, in a
letter to a friend, an original reëstimate of the Romantics, of
whom he asserted that they had never properly been judged,
and proposed at the same time a new theory of poetry which,

though more violent and apocalyptic than most expressions of Symbolist doctrine, prophesied the advent of Symbolism:

"I say that one must be a *visionary*—that one must make oneself a VISIONARY.

"The poet makes himself a *visionary* through a long, immense and reasoned *derangement of all the senses.* All forms of love, of suffering, of madness; he seeks himself, he exhausts all poisons in himself to keep only their quintessences. An indescribable torture in which he has need of all faith, all superhuman force, in which he becomes, among all, the great sick man, the great criminal, the great accursed—and the supreme Scholar!—for he arrives at the *unknown*— Because he has cultivated his soul, already rich, more than anyone else! He arrives at the unknown; and even if, driven insane, he should end by losing his grasp on his visions, he has seen them! Let him perish, in his plunging, by unheard-of unnamable things: other horrible workers will come; they will begin at those horizons where their predecessors sank! . . .

"The poet is a true Stealer of Fire.

"He is charged with humanity, with the animals themselves; he must make his inventions felt, handled, heard. If what he brings back from *beyond* has form, he gives form; if it is formless, he gives the formless. To find a language;

"—All speech, furthermore, being idea, the time of a universal language will come! One has to be an academician—deader than a fossil—to make a dictionary of any language at all. The weak-minded would begin *thinking* about the first letter of the alphabet and might quickly end by going mad!—

"This language will be of the soul for the soul, summing up all, perfumes, sounds, colors, catching hold of thought with thought and drawing it out. The poet would define the quantity of unknown awakening in his time in the universal soul: he would give more than the formula of his thought, more than the annotation of his march to *Progress!* An enormity becoming a norm absorbed by all, he would be a true *multiplier of progress!* . . .

"I habituated myself," he wrote later, "to simple hallucination: I would see quite honestly a mosque instead of a factory, a school of drummers composed of angels, calashes on the

roads of the sky, a drawing-room at the bottom of a lake: monsters, mysteries; the announcement of a musical comedy would
cause horrors to rise before me.

"Then I explained my magical sophistries by the hallucination of words!

"I ended by finding sacred the disorder of my intelligence. . . ."

Rimbaud had apparently arrived at the point of view set
forth in his letter independently of the influence of any other
French poet; and, in the productions described in the later
passage, had merely been giving expression to a unique personal way of seeing—though he was to know something of
English literature and had probably read Poe's poetry as early
as 1872. A few months after writing this letter, however, he had
made the acquaintance of Paul Verlaine. Verlaine, though he
published his poems in the collections of the Parnassians, was
already tending toward pure musical effects and taking unau-
thorized metrical liberties; and he had a special predisposition
toward the sort of poetry with which Rimbaud was beginning
to experiment boldly. He helped and encouraged the boy; took
him into his house in Paris and tried to put him in touch with
the Parisian literary world.

And Rimbaud in his turn was not only profoundly to influence Verlaine's poetry, but to play havoc with his life. Verlaine,
then twenty-seven, had just been married and his wife was
expecting a baby; but his impressionable feminine nature, at
once rakish and sentimental, was delighted and infatuated
by Rimbaud. Rimbaud, who, for all the boy's blue eyes and
apple-cheeks which were combined with his ungainly figure
and his large bumpkin's hands and feet, for all his unsteady adolescent's voice with its northern country accent, had already
his hard core and his harsh will; and he now brought to the
rôle of outlaw the moral force which he had inherited from his
mother, even though her narrowness and rigor, her merciless
domination of his childhood, had been driving him to take the
part of Satan. A provincial in Paris without a penny, as well as a
man of genius at an age when most boys are only just
beginning to indulge their first doubts and to hazard their first
original phrases, Rimbaud's position would by no means have
been easy even if his nature had not been intractable. He ran

amuck in the literary circles to which Verlaine introduced him, and, after disrupting Verlaine's household, carried him off on a vagabondage of adventure through Belgium and England. Verlaine had already, presumably, become rather discontented with his bourgeois domestic life—he was obliged to live with his wife's family—and Rimbaud had quickly infected him with his own ambition to become a supreme Visionary and a supreme outlaw against bourgeois society: "I had, indeed, in all sincerity of spirit," Rimbaud writes in one of his prose poems, "undertaken to restore him to his primitive condition of child of the Sun—and we wandered, fed with the wine of thieves' dens and the hard-tack of the road, I eager to find the place and the formula." But this programme was too much for Verlaine, whom Rimbaud ridiculed and bedevilled and who was made uneasy by memories of his wife: her child had been born in the meantime and she was now bringing an action for divorce. Rimbaud himself, in the abrupt ruthless confrontation of the realities of his situation which followed this hallucinated period, was aware of the extent to which he had made Verlaine a victim of his own special maladjustment—and of the extent to which he himself, in regard to that maladjustment, had been taking a line of least resistance: "Beside his dear sleeping body," he makes Verlaine say in "Une Saison en Enfer," "how many hours of the night I have watched, seeking why he should desire so furiously to escape from reality. Never before had man such an ambition. I recognized—without fearing for him—that he might be a serious danger to society. Has he perhaps secrets to change life?" Rimbaud had always been given to seeing himself in the rôle of a criminal: "Even as a child," he writes, "I used to admire the incorrigible convict on whom the jail is always closing again. . . . He had for me more strength than a saint, more good sense than a traveller—and himself, himself alone! for witness of his glory and his reason." And now he makes Verlaine play at this game with him: on one occasion, they both get arrested for discussing imaginary robberies and murders in the railway station at Arras.

The literary results of this expedition were Verlaine's "Romances sans Paroles" and Rimbaud's "Illuminations." Their titles indicate the wide difference between the temperaments and geniuses of the two men; yet the poems represent a sort of

collaboration which was to be as important as Mallarmé's cé-
nacle in making the new poetry self-conscious and in giving it
the courage of its convictions.

At last, after several quarrels and separations, Verlaine and
Rimbaud parted definitively—though not until Verlaine had
been sentenced to two years in prison at Brussels for shooting
Rimbaud in the wrist, and Rimbaud, meeting Verlaine at
Stuttgart after the latter's release and finding that he had while
in jail repented of his former errors and found repose in the
bosom of the Church, had first proceeded to get Verlaine
drunk and make him blaspheme his faith, "cause" as Rimbaud
wrote in a letter, "the ninety-eight wounds of Our Lord to
bleed," and then—according, at least, to the legend—as they
were walking through the Black Forest and another altercation arose, knocked him down with a club and left him unconscious.

In the meantime, while Verlaine was in jail, Rimbaud had returned to his mother's house in the Ardennes, where, during
the spring and summer of 1873, he composed that extraordinary masterpiece "Une Saison en Enfer," in which the hysteria
of the late nineteenth century in France, not very different
from that of our own time—an age recently deprived of religious faith, demoralized and embittered by war and already
becoming dissatisfied with social utopianism, science and the
cult of art as an end in itself—was crystallized in the sharp and
dazzling fragments of what Verlaine called a "diamond prose."
But now, not merely unreconciled to the bourgeois world and
at the centre of the conflict of its intellectual currents, but disillusioned at last with all these, disgusted with his own inco-
herence and even with the brilliant literature which he had
created to give it expression, he had planned an escape from
the European reality by a more effective means than self-
hallucination. Rimbaud had always thought of himself as a
peasant, as a member of "the inferior race," the blue-eyed
Gauls whom the Romans had conquered—and he had always
longed for some life that would take the place of the lost brutality and innocence of Europe, for the non-Christian, non-
middle-class life of the Orient, of Africa:

"Priests, professors, masters," he now writes, "you are
wrong to give me up to justice. I have never belonged to these

people; I have never been a Christian; I am of the race who sang in torture; I do not understand the laws; I haven't the moral sense, I am a brute; you are doing wrong. Yes, my eyes are closed to your light. I am a nigger, a beast. But I may be saved. You yourselves are false niggers, savage and grasping madmen. Tradesman, you are a nigger; magistrate, you are a nigger; general, you are a nigger; emperor, old itching palm, you are a nigger: you have drunk of a contraband liquor from Satan's distillery. This people is inspired by fever and cancer. Invalids and old men are so respectable that they ought to be boiled. The wisest course is to quit this continent, where madness prowls to provide these wretches with hostages. I am entering into the true kingdom of Shem.

"Do I know Nature? do I know myself?—*No more words.* I bury the dead in my belly. Shouts, drums, dance, dance, dance! I do not even foresee the hour when the white men will land among us and when I shall be nothing again.

"Hunger, thirst, shouts, dance, dance, dance, dance!"

Having finished his "pagan book, nigger book," as he called it before he gave it its final name, "A Season in Hell," he went down in the autumn to Paris, where the literary men in the cafés, who had heard of his escapades with Verlaine, received him with insulting coldness. He returned to his mother's house and burnt up all the copies of "Une Saison en Enfer" which he had just received from his publisher, as well as all the other manuscripts he had.

And now he proceeded to carry out the resolution which he had announced in the work he had burnt. Shutting himself up and studying continuously, sometimes for twenty-four hours at a time, he applies himself to learning the modern languages— he had always had a linguistic gift—which are most useful for travel and trade: English, German, Spanish, Italian, Russian, Arabic and Greek. And as a few years before, just out of school, without money and almost without friends, he had kept obstinately running away to Paris—so now, determined to turn his back on Europe, as moneyless and more friendless than before, he tries repeatedly to reach the East. First, after teaching for a year in Germany, he sells his trunk and makes his way to Italy, with the intention of joining a friend who has a soap-factory in the Cyclades; but, undertaking to travel to Brindisi on foot, he

gets a sunstroke and is repatriated by the French consul. At
Marseilles, he manages to live by unloading cargo and helping
truck-drivers, and then enlists in the Carlist army, but finally
returns to his mother's house. Next, in order to get passage to
Java, he enlists for six years in the Dutch army—lands at
Batavia, deserts, joins the crew of an English sailing-vessel,
goes back to France and home again. The next year, under the
pretext of wanting to go to Austria for the purpose of learning
German, he succeeds in getting some money out of his
mother; but immediately upon arriving in Vienna, he takes his
cabman out for a drink and in return is robbed of his coat with
all his money, and finds himself obliged to sell key-rings and
shoe-laces in the street till he gets into a row with the Austrian
police and is sent back again to France. Soon, however, he sets
out on foot for Hamburg, whence he hopes to find some way
of getting to the East, but where, instead, he falls in with a circus, with which he travels as interpreter and barker on a tour of
the Scandinavian countries, finally getting himself sent back by
the consul from Stockholm to Charleville again. On his next
attempt, after earning a little money unloading cargo at Marseilles, he buys passage to Alexandria, but on the ship develops
gastric fever from a rubbing of his ribs against his abdomen,
caused by too much walking—and goes back to Charleville.

Three months afterwards, however—in the spring of 1878
—by way of Switzerland, Italy and Egypt, he succeeds in
reaching the island of Cyprus and gets a job as foreman in one
of the quarries. But he catches typhoid and by the spring of
the next year is at home with his family once more. When a
friend asks him whether he is writing nowadays, he replies with
annoyance and scorn: "I don't do anything with that any
more"; and when, on the eve of his departure the next spring,
he hears one of his friends congratulate another on having just
bought some Lemerre editions—Lemerre had been the publisher of the Parnassians—he bursts out: "That's a lot of
money wasted. It's absolutely idiotic to buy books—and especially books like that. You've got a ball between your shoulders
that ought to take the place of books. When you put books on
your shelves, the only thing they do is cover up the leprosies of
the old walls." He looks for work in Cyprus, in Egypt, in
Abyssinia, in all the ports of the Red Sea, and finally finds a job

at Aden working at twelve francs a day for a firm of French coffee importers. This company presently sends him to Harrar, where it is starting a new branch, and later makes Rimbaud the director of all its expeditions into Galla and Somaliland. Rimbaud was the first European to penetrate into the country of Ogadain; and on his return from an extremely dangerous expedition to one of the native potentates, he traced for the first time the itinerary afterwards taken by the Ethiopian railway. At last, however, he quarrels with his employers and, after adventures of various kinds, sets up at Harrar a trading-post of his own, where he traffics in sugar, rice, silk, cotton-goods and arms, sending out his own caravans, intriguing with the local kings, entertaining European travellers with enchanting and cynical conversation and maintaining a harem of native women carefully selected as coming from different parts of the country so that they may teach him their different languages. During this period, he wrote to a friend on *Le Temps* asking to be sent as war correspondent to cover the Italo-Abyssinian campaign. This proposal was declined, but in answering his letter the friend informed him that his poems, preserved by Verlaine, were being published and read in Paris, and that, in the circles of the new Symbolist school, he had become a legendary figure, an attempt having even been made to found a new literary system on a sonnet in which he had assigned different colors to the vowels. But at this period, Rimbaud's only literary concern was to supply reports to the Geographical Society, and, when he refers to his poetry at all, it is to dismiss it as "absurd" or "disgusting." "I couldn't go on with it," he told his sister later. "I should have gone mad—and besides it was bad stuff." The only ambition he now admits is to make enough money to marry a French girl and retire from his present business— "to have at least one son whom I could spend the rest of my life bringing up according to my own ideas, cultivating and arming him with the completest education that one can get in this age, and whom I could see become a famous engineer, powerful and rich through science."

One winter, however, after Rimbaud had been twelve years in the East, he found himself suffering from what he took at first to be varicose veins; but he refused to go to a doctor, kept on walking and riding, as if he could dominate even disease by

his stubborn and brutal will—and presently found that his leg
was so swollen that he was obliged to direct his business from
bed. At last the pain had become so severe that he was compelled to give up altogether and have himself carried on a litter
to Aden, a terrible journey of twelve days, on the second of
which he spent sixteen hours without shelter under pouring
rain.

The English doctor at Aden told Rimbaud that he would be
unable to treat him properly, and shipped him back to France,
where, in the hospital at Marseilles, they amputated his leg.
For the last time Rimbaud returned to his mother's: he tried
to get about on a crutch, but the infection had spread through
his whole system. He spent an agonizing summer of pain and
fever, and then, with a fixed idea of returning to the East, had
himself sent back to Marseilles. There he died, attended only
by his sister. It was harvest-time on the family farm, and the
daughter's absence was bitterly resented by her mother, who
when Arthur had been away, had refused to get for him instruments and books which he had sent her the money to
buy. Isabelle, Rimbaud's sister, had never known till after her
brother's death, when she read about it in the papers, that
Arthur had been a poet, but she heard him "end his life in a
sort of continual dream, saying strange things very gently in a
voice that would have charmed me if it had not pierced my
heart. What he was saying was all dreams, yet it was not the
same thing at all as when he had had the fever. It was as if he
did it on purpose. . . . He mixed all sorts of things up, and
with art." But Rimbaud, in his final delirium, was still obsessed
by the idea of the East: on his death-bed, he insisted upon dictating a letter to a steamship company, asking how much the
passage would cost and when he should have himself carried
aboard.

One is likely to be guilty of over-simplification in using
people's personal careers to point the morals of general social
situations. Rimbaud, in his rôle of African trader, had obviously succeeded at last in emulating his father and his mother
both at once—repeating the career of the former, who had
campaigned in Italy, Algiers and the Crimea, by his wanderings
and his intolerant independence at the same time that, by his
sound character as a trader and his concentration upon making

money, he was achieving the only sort of success which his mother could understand. Yet Rimbaud's life has a typical significance: it moves us, it seems to put before us an acute phase of the human predicament, as if it were a great play. The other poets of whom I have been writing were as little at home in their nineteenth-century world as Rimbaud, and they were mostly as disillusioned with its enthusiasms; but they had remained in it and managed to hold their places in it by excreting, like patient molluscs, iridescent shells of literature—whereas Rimbaud, with genius equal to any's, with genius perhaps superior to any's, had rejected Europe altogether—not merely its society and ideas, but even the kind of sensibility which one cultivated when one tried to live at odds with it and the kind of literature this sensibility supplied—getting away to a life of pure action and a more primitive civilization.

And if actions can be compared with writings, Rimbaud's life seems more satisfactory than the works of his Symbolist contemporaries, than those even of most of his Symbolist successors, who stayed at home and stuck to literature. Rimbaud was far from finding in the East that ideal barbarous state he was seeking; even at Harrar during the days of his prosperity he was always steaming with anxieties and angers—but his career, with its violence, its moral interest and its tragic completeness, leaves us feeling that we have watched the human spirit, strained to its most resolute sincerity and in possession of its highest faculties, breaking itself in the effort to escape, first from humiliating compromise, and then from chaos equally humiliating. And when we turn back to consider even the masterpieces of that literature which Rimbaud had helped to found and which he had repudiated, we are oppressed by a sullenness, a lethargy, a sense of energies ingrown and sometimes festering. Even the poetry of the noble Yeats, still repining through middle age over the emotional miscarriages of youth, is dully weighted, for all its purity and candor, by a leaden acquiescence in defeat.

III

What then is to be the future of this literature? Will the poets become more and more esoteric as the world becomes more and more difficult for them, diverging further and further from the methods and the language of popular literature in proportion as popular literature approximates more and more closely to journalism? Will the sciences dominate the future, as Pierre de Massot has suggested in a book which traces the development of Symbolism from Mallarmé to Dadaism, "smothering the last works of the past, until the day when literature, music and painting have become the three principal branches of neurology"? Paul Valéry has recently predicted that as radio, moving picture and television come to take the place of books as means of affecting people's feelings and ideas, literature, as we have known it in the past, may become "as obsolete and as far removed from life and practice as geomancy, the heraldic art and the science of falconry." Literature, according to Valéry, has become "an art which is based on the *abuse of language*—that is, it is based on language as a creator of illusions, and not on language as a means of transmitting realities. Everything which makes a language more precise, everything which emphasizes its practical character, all the changes which it undergoes in the interests of a more rapid transmission and an easier diffusion, are contrary to its function as a poetic instrument." As language becomes more international and more technical, it will become also less capable of supplying the symbols of literature; and then, just as the development of mechanical devices has compelled us to resort to sports in order to exercise our muscles, so literature will survive as a game—as a series of specialized experiments in the domain of "symbolic expression and imaginative values attained through the free combination of the elements of language."

I agree with Valéry that "the development in Europe, since 1852, of literary works which are extremely difficult, subtle and refined, which are written in a complicated style, and which, for that reason, are forbidden to most readers, bears some relation to the increase in number of literates," and to the consequent "intensive production of mediocre or average works." But I am by no means sure that the future destiny of this difficult and subtle art is to be practised only as a sort of game and with no relation to other intellectual activities. The truth is, I believe, that Valéry's pessimism arises itself from the special point of view which, as I have said, has been associated from the beginning with the school of literature that Valéry represents.

The disillusion and weariness which we recognize as characteristic of the eighties and nineties were in reality the aspects of a philosophy which, implicit in the writings of the Symbolists, was to come to its full growth and exert its widest influence during the period that followed the War. I do not mean that Symbolism as an organized movement went on becoming more and more powerful until it triumphed over all rival movements: the eminence at this particular time of a set of writers—such writers as I have discussed in this book—all stemming more or less directly from Symbolism, was unexpected and rather sudden, and it was due largely to extra-literary accidents. The period immediately before the War had been characterized, on the whole, by a predominance of Naturalistic and social-idealistic literature—the great reputations in England and France had been those of writers like Shaw, Wells, and Bennett, Romain Rolland and Anatole France. But when the prodigious concerted efforts of the War had ended only in impoverishment and exhaustion for all the European peoples concerned, and in a general feeling of hopelessness about politics, about all attempts to organize men into social units—armies, parties, nations—in the service of some common ideal, for the accomplishment of some particular purpose, the Western mind became peculiarly hospitable to a literature indifferent to action and unconcerned with the group. Many of the socially-minded writers, besides, had been intellectually demoralized by the War and had irreparably lost credit in consequence; whereas these others—Yeats, Valéry, Joyce, Proust—had maintained an unassailable integrity and now fell heir to the prestige which had been sacrificed by other poets and novelists who had abandoned the detached study of human motives and the expression of those universal emotions which make all classes and peoples one, to become intolerant partisans. It had required a determined independence and an overmastering absorption in literature to remain unshaken by the passions and fears of that time—and in the masterpieces which these scattered and special writers had been producing in isolation, and, as it were, secretly, while pandemonium raged without, their justification was plain. These books revealed new discoveries, artistic, metaphysical, psychological: they mapped the labyrinths of human consciousness as they seemed never to have been mapped before, they made one conceive the world in a new way. What wonder that for those who survived the War these writers should have become heroes and leaders?

There are, as I have said, in our contemporary society, for writers who are unable to interest themselves in it either by studying it scientifically, by attempting to reform it or by satirizing it, only two alternative courses to follow—Axel's or Rimbaud's. If one chooses the first of these, the way of Axel, one shuts oneself up in one's own private world, cultivating one's private fantasies, encouraging one's private manias, ultimately preferring one's absurdest chimeras to the most astonishing contemporary realities, ultimately mistaking one's chimeras for realities. If one chooses the second, the way of Rimbaud, one tries to leave the twentieth century behind—to find the good life in some country where modern manufacturing methods and modern democratic institutions do not present any problems to the artist because they haven't yet arrived. In this book, I have been occupied with writers who have, in general, taken Axel's course; but the period since the War has furnished almost as many examples of writers who have gone the way of Rimbaud—without usually, however, like him, getting to the point of giving up literature altogether. All our cult, which Wyndham Lewis has denounced, of more primitive places and peoples is really the manifestation of an impulse similar to Rimbaud's—D. H. Lawrence's mornings in Mexico and his explorations of Santa Fé and Australia; Blaise Cendrars's negro anthology, the negro masks which bring such high prices in Paris, André Gide's lifelong passion for Africa which has finally led him to navigate the Congo, Sherwood Anderson's exhilaration at the "dark laughter" of the American South, and the fascination for white New Yorkers of Harlem; and even that strange infatuation with the infantile—because our children are more barbarous than we—which has allowed the term Expressionism to be applied at once to drawings done by the pupils in German schools and to the dramas of German playwrights, which caused Nathalia Crane to be taken seriously and made Daisy Ashford all the rage; that hysterical excitement over modern "primitives" which has led the generation of Jean Cocteau to talk about the douanier Rousseau as their fathers did about Degas—all this has followed in the wake of Rimbaud.

Yet Lawrence, for all his rovings, must come back to the collieries again; and for Anderson, though he may seek in New Orleans the leisure and ease of the old South, it is the factories of Ohio which still stick in his crop. The Congo masks in Paris are buried in galleries or in the houses of private collectors almost as completely as if they were sunk among the ruins of their vanished dynasties in the African wilderness; and when white New Yorkers, obstreperous and drunken, visit the Harlem cabarets at night, they find the negroes in American business suits, attempting modestly and drearily to conform to the requirements of Western civilization. Our shocking children soon grow up into adults as docile as their mothers and fathers. And as for those that choose Axel's course, the price paid by the man of imagination who, while remaining in the modern world, declines to participate in its activities and tries to keep his mind off its plight, is usually to succumb to some monstrosity or absurdity. We feel it in Proust's hypochondriac ailments and his fretting self-centred prolixities; in Yeats's astrology and spirit-tappings and in the seventeenth-century cadence which half puts to sleep his livest prose; in the meagreness of the poetic output of Paul Valéry and T. S. Eliot contrasted with their incessant speculations as to precisely what constitutes poetry, precisely what function it performs and whether there is any point in writing it; even in the mystifications by which Joyce, "forging," just behind that screen, "the uncreated consciousness" not merely of the Irish but of the western man of our time, has made his books rather difficult of access to a public for whom a few chapter headings or a word of explanation might have enabled them to recognize more readily a mirror for the study of their own minds. (The philosophical mathematicians and physicists whose work these novelists and poets parallel seem to have developed, no doubt from the same social and political causes, a similar metaphysical hypertrophy: consider the disproportionate size of the shadow-structure of speculation which such a writer as Eddington tries to base on some new modification of physical theory, itself suggested on most uncertain evidence.)

It is true of these later writers that they have not dissociated themselves from society so completely as the original group of Symbolists: they have supplied us, as a matter of fact, with a good deal of interesting social criticism; but it is usually a criticism which does not aim at anything, it is an exercise—Proust is the great example—of the pure intelligence playing luminously all about but not driven by the motor power of any hope and not directed by any creative imagination for the possibilities of human life. If these writers ever indicate a preference for any social order different from the present one, it is invariably for some society of the past as they have read of it in its most attractive authors—as Yeats likes to imagine himself in the rôle of some great lord and patron of arts of the Renaissance, or as Eliot dedicates his credo to a seventeenth-century Anglican bishop. And this tendency to look to the past, in spite of the revolutionary character of some of their methods, has sometimes given even to their most original work an odd Alexandrian aspect: the productions of Eliot, Proust and Joyce, for example, are sometimes veritable literary museums. It is not merely that these modern novelists and poets build upon their predecessors, as the greatest writers have done in all times, but that they have developed a weakness for recapitulating them in parodies.

When these writers do turn their attention to the contemporary world and its future, it is usually with strange, and even eerie, results. Eliot has recently—explaining by the way, in regard to causes in general, that "we fight rather to keep something alive than in the expectation that anything will triumph" —put forward, or announced his intention of putting forward, a programme of classicism, royalism and Anglo-Catholicism; and Yeats, in his astrological "Vision," has predicted the future of Europe as follows:

"A decadence will descend, by perpetual moral improvement, upon a community which may seem like some woman of New York or Paris who has renounced her rouge pot to lose her figure and grow coarse of skin and dull of brain, feeding her calves and babies somewhere upon the edge of the wilderness. The decadence of the Greco-Roman world with its violent soldiers and its mahogany dark young athletes was as great, but that suggested the bubbles of life turned into marbles, whereas what awaits us, being democratic and *primary*, may suggest bubbles in a frozen pond—mathematical Babylonian starlight. . . .

"It is possible that the ever increasing separation from the community as a whole of the cultivated classes, their increasing certainty, and that falling in two of the human mind which I have seen in certain works of art is preparation. During the period said to commence in 1927, with the 11th gyre, must arise a form of philosophy which will become religious and ethical in the 12th gyre and be in all things opposite of that vast plaster Herculean image, final *primary* thought. It will be concrete in expression, establish itself by immediate experience, seek no general agreement, make little of God or any exterior unity, and it will call that good which a man can contemplate himself as doing always and no other doing at all. It will make a cardinal truth of man's immortality that its virtue may not lack sanction, and of the soul's reëmbodiment that it may restore to virtue that long preparation none can give and hold death an interruption. The supreme experience, Plotinus's ecstasy of the Saint, will recede, for men—finding it difficult—substituted dogma and idol, abstractions of all sorts of things beyond experience; and man may be long content with those more trivial supernatural benedictions as when Athena took Achilles by his yellow hair. Men will no longer separate the idea of God from that of human genius, human productivity in all its forms."

I believe therefore that the time is at hand when these writers, who have largely dominated the literary world of the decade 1920–30, though we shall continue to admire them as masters, will no longer serve us as guides. Axel's world of the private imagination in isolation from the life of society seems to have been exploited and explored as far as for the present is possible. Who can imagine this sort of thing being carried further than Valéry and Proust have done? And who hereafter will be content to inhabit a corner, though fitted out with some choice things of one's own, in the shuttered house of one of

these writers—where we find ourselves, also, becoming conscious of a lack of ventilation? On the other hand, it seems
equally unsatisfactory, equally impossible, to imitate Rimbaud;
we carry with us in our own minds and habits the civilization
of machinery, trade, democratic education and standardiza-
tion to the Africas and Asias to which we flee, even if we do
not find them there before us. Nor can we keep ourselves up
very long at home by any of the current substitutes for Rimbaud's solution—by occupying ourselves exclusively with prize-
fighters or with thugs or by simply remaining drunk or making
love all the time. In the meantime, western Europe has been
recovering from the exhaustion and despair of the War; and in
America the comfortable enjoyment of what was supposed to
be American prosperity, which since the War has made it possible for Americans to accept with a certain complacency the
despondency as well as the resignation of European books, has
given way to a sudden disquiet. And Americans and Europeans
are both becoming more and more conscious of Russia, a
country where a central social-political idealism has been able
to use and to inspire the artist as well as the engineer. The
question begins to press us again as to whether it is possible to
make a practical success of human society, and whether, if we
continue to fail, a few masterpieces, however profound or
noble, will be able to make life worth living even for the few
people in a position to enjoy them.

The reaction against nineteenth-century Naturalism which
Symbolism originally represented has probably now run its full
course, and the oscillation which for at least three centuries has
been taking place between the poles of objectivity and subjectivity may return toward objectivity again: we may live to see
Valéry, Eliot and Proust displaced and treated with as much intolerance as those writers—Wells, France and Shaw—whom
they have themselves displaced. Yet as surely as Ibsen and
Flaubert brought to their Naturalistic plays and novels the sensibility and language of Romanticism, the writers of a new reaction in the direction of the study of man in his relation to his
neighbor and to society will profit by the new intelligence and
technique of Symbolism. Or—what would be preferable and is
perhaps more likely—this oscillation may finally cease. Our conceptions of objective and subjective have unquestionably been

based on false dualisms; our materialisms and idealisms alike
have been derived from mistaken conceptions of what the
researches of science implied—Classicism and Romanticism,
Naturalism and Symbolism are, in reality, therefore false alter-
natives. And so we may see Naturalism and Symbolism combine to provide us with a vision of human life and its universe,
richer, more subtle, more complex and more complete than
any that man has yet known—indeed, they have already so
combined, Symbolism has already rejoined Naturalism, in one
great work of literature, "Ulysses."

I cannot believe, then, with Paul Valéry that Symbolism is
doomed to become more and more highly specialized until it
has been reduced to the status of an intellectual pastime like
anagrams or chess. It seems to me far more likely that it
will be absorbed and assimilated by the general literature and
thought. All the exponents of Symbolism have insisted that
they were attempting to meet a need for a new language.
"To find a tongue!" Rimbaud had cried. "One has to be an
academician—deader than a fossil—to make a dictionary of
any language at all." And Valéry himself had followed Mallarmé in an effort to push to a kind of algebra the classical language of French poetry; Gertrude Stein has explained that her
later writings are intended to "restore its intrinsic meaning to
literature"; and Joyce, in his new novel, has been attempting
to create a tongue which shall go deeper than conscious spoken speech and follow the processes of the unconscious. It is
probably true, as Pater has suggested, that there is something
akin to the scientific instinct in the efforts of modern literature
to render the transitory phases of "a world of fine gradations
and subtly linked conditions, shifting intricately as we ourselves change." In any case, the experiments of men who in
their lifetimes have been either received with complete indifference or denounced as practical jokers or lunatics may perhaps prove of equal importance with those scattered researches
in mathematics and physics which seemed at first merely
whimsical exercises on the margins of their subjects, but which
have been laid under contribution by the great modern physical systems—without which these could scarcely have been
constructed. Mallarmé's poetry, in its time, seemed no more
gratuitous and abstruse than Gauss's fourth-dimensional

coördinates—yet it has been built upon by writers as considerable in their own field as Einstein is in his.

As I have pointed out in connection with Gertrude Stein,
our ideas about the "logic" of language are likely to be superficial. The relation of words to what they convey—that is, to
the processes behind them and the processes to which they
give rise in those who listen to or read them—is still a very mysterious one. We tend to assume that being *convinced* of things
is something quite different from having them *suggested* to us;
but the suggestive language of the Symbolist poet is really performing the same sort of function as the reasonable language
of the realistic novelist or even the severe technical languages
of science. The most, apparently, we can say of language is that
it indicates relations, and a Symbolist poem does this just
as much as a mathematical formula: both suggest imaginary
worlds made up of elements abstracted from our experience of
the real world and revealing relations which we acknowledge
to be valid within those fields of experience. The only difference between the language of Symbolism and the literary languages to which we are more accustomed is that the former
indicates relations which, recently perceived for the first time,
cut through or underlie those in terms of which we have been
in the habit of thinking; and that it deals with them by means
of what amounts, in comparison with conventional language,
to a literary shorthand which makes complex ideas more easily
manageable. This new language may actually have the effect of
revolutionizing our ideas of syntax, as modern philosophy
seems to be tending to discard the notion of cause and effect.
It is evidently working, like modern scientific theory, toward a
totally new conception of reality. This conception, as we find it
to-day in much Symbolist literature, seems, it is true, rather
formidably complicated and sometimes even rather mystical;
but this complexity may presently give rise to some new and
radical simplification, when the new ideas which really lie
behind these more and more elaborate attempts to recombine
and adapt the old have finally begun to be plain. And the result
may be, not, as Valéry predicts, an infinite specialization and
divergence of the sciences and arts, but their finally falling all
into one system. He himself suggests such a possibility by constantly reminding us of the single "method" common to all

departments of thought. And who can say that, as science and art look more and more deeply into experience and achieve a wider and wider range, and as they come to apply themselves more and more directly and expertly to the needs of human life, they may not arrive at a way of thinking, a technique of dealing with our perceptions, which will make art and science one?

The writers with whom I have here been concerned have not only, then, given us works of literature which, for intensity, brilliance and boldness as well as for an architectural genius, an intellectual mastery of their materials, rare among their Romantic predecessors, are probably comparable to the work of any time. Though it is true that they have tended to over-emphasize the importance of the individual, that they have been preoccupied with introspection sometimes almost to the point of insanity, that they have endeavored to discourage their readers, not only with politics, but with action of any kind—they have yet succeeded in effecting in literature a revolution analogous to that which has taken place in science and philosophy: they have broken out of the old mechanistic routine, they have disintegrated the old materialism, and they have revealed to the imagination a new flexibility and freedom. And though we are aware in them of things that are dying—the whole belle-lettristic tradition of Renaissance culture perhaps, compelled to specialize more and more, more and more driven in on itself, as industrialism and democratic education have come to press it closer and closer—they none the less break down the walls of the present and wake us to the hope and exaltation of the untried, unsuspected possibilities of human thought and art.

APPENDIX I

Three Versions of a Passage from James Joyce's New Novel

1. NAVIRE D'ARGENT: 1925.

Tell me, tell me, how could she cam through all her fellows, the daredevil? Linking one and knocking the next and polling in and petering out and clyding by in the eastway. Who was the first that ever burst? Someone it was, whoever you are. Tinker, tailor, soldier, sailor, Paul Pry or polishman. That's the thing I always want to know. She can't put her hand on him for the moment. It's a long long way, walking weary! Such a long way backwards to row! She says herself she hardly knows who her graveller was or what he did or how young she played or when or where or how often he jumped her. She was just a young thin pale soft shy slim slip of a thing then, sauntering, and he was a heavy trudging lurching lieabroad of a Curraghman, making his hay for the sun to shine on, as tough as the oaktrees (peats be with them!) used to rustle that time down by the dykes of killing Kildare, that forestfellfoss with a plash across her. She thought she'd sink under the ground with shame when he gave her the tiger's eye!

2. TRANSITION: 1927.

Tell me, tell me, how could she cam through all her fellows, the neckar she was, the diveline? Linking one and knocking the next, tapping a flank and tipping a jutty and palling in and petering out and clyding by on her eastway. Wai-whou was the first that ever burst? Someone he was, whoever they were, in a tactic attack or in single combat. Tinker, tailor, soldier, sailor, Paul Pry or polishman. That's the thing I always want to know. Push up and push upper and come to headquarters! Was it waterlows year, after Grattan or Flood, or when maids were in Arc or when three stood hosting? Faith will find where the Doubt arises like Nemo from Nirgends found the Nihil. Worry you sighin foh, Albern, O Anser? Untie the gemman's fistiknots, Qwic and Nuancee? She can't put her hand on him for the moment. It's a long long way, walking weary! Such a long way backwards to row! She says herself she hardly knows whuon the annals her graveller was, a dynast of Leinster, a wolf of the sea, or what he did or how young she played or when and where and how often he jumnped her. She was just a young thin pale soft shy slim slip of a thing then, sauntering, and he was a heavy trudging lurching lieabroad of a Curraghman, making his hay for the sun to shine on, as tough as the oaktrees (peats be with them!) used to rustle that time down by the dykes of killing Kildare, that forstfellfoss with a plash across her. She thought she'd sink under the ground with nymphant shame when he gave her the tigris eye!

3. "ANNA LIVIA PLURABELLE," a small book published in 1928.

Tell me, tell me, how cam she camlin through all her fellows, the neckar she was the diveline? Linking one and knocking the next, tapting a flank and tipting a jutty and palling in and pietaring out and clyding by on her eastway. Waiwhou was the first thurever burst? Someone he was, whuebra they were, in a tactic attack or in single combat. Tinker, tilar, souldrer, salor, Pieman Peace or Polistaman. That's the thing I always want to know. Push up and push upper and come to headquarters! Was it waterlows year, after Grattan or Flood, or when maids were in Arc or when three stood hosting? Fidaris will find where the Doubt arises like Nieman from Nirgends found the Nihil. Worry you sighin foh, Albern, O Anser? Untie the gemman's fistiknots, Qvic and Nuancee? She can't put her hand on him for the moment. Tez thelon langlo, walking weary! Such a loon way backwards to row! She says herself she hardly knows whuon the annals her graveller was, a dynast of Leinster, a wolf of the sea, or what he did or how blyth she played or how, when, why, where and who offon he jumnpad her. She was just a young thin pale soft shy slim slip of a thing then, sauntering, by silvamoonlake, and he was a heavy trudging lurching lieabroad of a Curraghman, making his hay for whose sun to shine on, as tough as the oaktrees (peats be with them!) used to rustle that time down by the dykes of killing Kildare, for forstfellfoss with a plash across her. She thought she's sankh neathe the ground with nymphant shame when he gave her the tigris eye!

APPENDIX II

Memoirs of Dadaism*

by Tristan Tzara

At the beginning of the year 1920, I arrived back in Paris, extremely glad to see my friends again. I took part in the demonstrations which aroused the rage of the Parisian public, in company with Aragon, Breton, Dermée, Eluard, Ribemont-Dessaignes, Picabia, Péret, Soupault, Rigaut, Marguerite Buffet and others. The début of Dadaism in Paris took place on the twenty-third of January, at the matinée organized by the Dadaist review *Littérature*. Louis Aragon, a slender young man with feminine features, A. Breton, whose behavior displays the stigmata of the religious sectarians, G. Ribemont-Dessaignes, a man whose simple appearance conceals the fiery temper of the great accusers of humanity, and Philippe Soupault, whose facility of expression flows forth in bizarre images, gave readings from their works. Picabia, who has undergone so many influences, particularly those of the clear and powerful mind of Marcel Duchamp, exhibited a number of pictures, one of which was a drawing done in chalk on a blackboard and erased on the stage; that is to say, the picture was valid for only two hours. As for me, announced as "Dada," I read aloud a newspaper article while an electric bell kept ringing so that no one could hear what I said. This was very badly received by the public, who became exasperated and shouted: "Enough! Enough!" An attempt was made to give a futuristic interpretation to this act, but all that I wanted to convey was simply that my presence on the stage, the sight of my face and my movements, ought to satisfy people's curiosity and that anything I might have said really had no importance.

At the Grand Palais des Champs Elysées, thousands of persons of all classes manifested very uproariously it is impossible to say exactly what—their joy or their disapproval, by unexpected cries and general laughter, which constituted a very pretty accompaniment to the manifestoes read by six people at once. The newspapers said that an old man in the audience gave himself up to behavior of a character more or less intimate, that somebody set off some flashlight powder and that a pregnant woman had to be taken out. It is true that the papers had also announced that Charlie Chaplin was going to deliver a lec-

*A partial translation of these appeared in *Vanity Fair*, to which I am indebted for permission to republish them.

ture on Dada. Although we denied the rumor, there was one reporter who followed me everywhere. He thought that the celebrated actor was up to some new stunt and was planning a surprise entrance. I remember with tenderness that Picabia, who was to have taken part in the demonstration, disappeared as soon as it began. For five hours it was impossible to find him. The séance ended with a speech by "The King of the Fakirs," M. Buisson, who has a curious occupation: he predicts the future every day to those who wish to listen to him, on the Boulevard de la Madeleine. In the evening he sells papers at the Metro exits.

Several days afterwards, there took place in a church which had been transformed into a cinema—premises of the Club du Faubourg—at the invitation of that association, which includes more than three thousand workers and intellectuals, an explanation of the Dadaist Movement. There were four of us on the stage: Ribemont-Dessaignes, Aragon and Breton; and I. M. Léo Poldès presided. On this occasion, the audience were more serious: they listened to us. Their disapproval was expressed in shrill cries. Raymond Duncan, the philosopher who walks about Paris in the costume of Socrates, was there with all his school. He came to our defense and quieted the audience. A debate followed. The very best Socialist orators took sides and spoke for or against us. We replied to the attacks and the audience boiled in unison. Aragon wrote a moving article on that memorable matinée in *Les Ecrits Nouveaux.*

A week later, a public debate on Dada took place at the Université Populaire. Eluard, Fraenkel, Dermée, Breton, Ribemont-Dessaignes, Soupault and I participated with all the force of our temperaments in a séance torn by political passions. All the manifestoes of the presidents appeared in the Dadaist review, *Littérature*—it is well known that the Dadaist Movement has three hundred and ninety-one presidents and that anyone can become a president without the slightest trouble.

391 was also the name of a review which several of us started; it expanded and became a periodical of world-wide reputation. People finally became afraid of it, because it described things as they really were without any attempt to soften them. How many critics came to regret having uttered so many imbecilities!

A scandal provoked by the hypocrisy of certain Cubists in the bosom of a modern art society brought on the complete schism between the Cubists and the Dadas—an event which gave great force of cohesion to the nineteen dissenting Dadaists.

Paul Eluard, whom we call the inventor of a new metal of darkness, began to publish his review *Proverbe* in which all the Dadaists collaborated and which contributed a vein of its own. It was chiefly a matter

of contradicting logic and language. This is how Soupault characterizes the collaborators of *Proverbe*:

> Louis Aragon, the Glass Syringe.
> Arp, Clean Wrinkles.
> André Breton, the Glass of Water in a Storm.
> Paul Eluard, the Nurse of the Stars.
> Th. Fraenkel, the Great Earth Serpent.
> Benjamin Péret, the Lemon Mandarin.
> G. Ribemont-Dessaignes, the Steam Man.
> Jacques Rigaut, the Hollow Plate.
> Philippe Soupault, the Musical Urinal.
> Tristan Tzara, the Man with the Pearl Head.

Dadaist hand-bills and books were spreading the agitation through
Paris and the whole world.

In the month of May, the demonstration at the Théâtre de
l'Œuvre, that courageous enterprise directed by Lugné-Poe, showed
the vitality of Dada at its height. Twelve hundred people were turned
away. There were three spectators for every seat; it was suffocating.
Enthusiastic members of the audience had brought musical instruments to interrupt us. The enemies of Dada threw down from the
balconies copies of an anti-Dada paper called *Non* in which we were
described as lunatics. The scandal reached proportions absolutely
unimaginable. Soupault proclaimed: "You are all idiots! You deserve
to be presidents of the Dadaist Movement!" Breton, with the house
completely dark, read in his thunderous voice a manifesto far from
gentle toward the audience. Then Ribemont-Dessaignes read a
soothing and complimentary manifesto. Paul Eluard presented some
"examples." I will give one: the curtain goes up; two people, one of
them with a letter in his hand, appear from opposite sides of the stage
and meet in the centre; the following dialogue takes place:

> *"Le bureau de poste est en face."*
> *"—Que voulez vous que ça me fasse?"*
> *"Pardon, je vous voyais une lettre à la main. Je croyais . . ."*
> *"—Il ne s'agit pas de croire, mais de savoir."*

After which, each goes his way, and the curtain falls. There were six of
these examples, very widely varied, in which the mixture of humanity,
idiocy and unexpectedness contrasted curiously with the brutality of
the other numbers. I invented on the occasion of this performance a
diabolical machine composed of a klaxon and three successive invisible echoes, for the purpose of impressing on the minds of the audience certain phrases describing the aims of Dada. The ones which
created the most sensation were: "Dada is against the high cost of

living," and "Dada is a virgin microbe." We also produced three short plays by Soupault, Breton and Ribemont-Dessaignes and "La Première Aventure Céleste de M. Antipyrine," which I had written in 1916. This play is a boxing match with words. The characters, confined in sacks and trunks, recite their parts without moving, and one can easily imagine the effect this produced—performed in a greenish light—on the already excited public. It was impossible to hear a single word of the play. Mlle. Hania Routchine was to have sung at the end of the play a sentimental song by Duparc. The audience either took this for a sacrilege or considered that a thing so simple—it was intended to produce a contrast—was out of place on this occasion; in any case, they did not restrain their language. Mlle. Routchine, who was accustomed to the great successes of the Vaudeville, did not understand the situation and, after exchanging some amenities with the public, refused to finish the song. For two hours we could hardly calm her, for she wept wildly.

At the Salle Gaveau, at the Dada Festival, the scandal was also great. For the first time in the history of the world, people threw at us, not only eggs, salads and pennies, but beefsteaks as well. It was a very great success. The audience were extremely Dadaist. We had already said that the true Dadaists were against Dada. Philippe Soupault appeared as a magician. As he called the names of the Pope, Clemenceau and Foch, children's balloons came out of a large box and floated up to the ceiling. Paul Souday in his notice in *Le Temps* said that really, at a certain distance, the faces of the summoned actually appeared on the surfaces of the balloons. The audience was so excited and the atmosphere so overcharged that a number of other ideas merely suggested took on the appearance of reality. Ribemont-Dessaignes did a motionless dance and Mlle. Buffet interpreted some Dadaist music. A flashlight taken by the newspaper *Comœdia* during a performance of a play by me shows everybody in the house waving their arms and with their mouths open shouting.

All the Paris celebrities were present. Mme. Rachilde had written an article in a newspaper inviting some *poilu* to shoot us with a revolver. This did not prevent her a year later from appearing on the stage and defending us. She no longer regarded us as a danger to the *esprit français*. They did not kill us in the Salle Gaveau, but all the journalists tried to do so in their notices. Columns were written declaring that Dada wasn't to be talked about any more—which suggested this observation to Jean Paulhan [the following is in English in the original]:

"If you must speak of Dada you must speak of Dada.

If you must not speak of Dada you must still speak of Dada."

Among the other Dadaist reviews, *Cannibale* had a great success:

it developed the absolutely anti-literary point of view which will be the relativist point of view of future generations. The super-abundance of life of these future generations will find its place in the movement, and they will forget the rigid conventions, the par-alyzed ideas, of a tradition which is nothing but laziness.

* * *

After France, the country tormented most by this impulse which knows no frontiers has been Germany. Already in 1918, Huelsenbeck, a vigorous and intelligent man and a poet of talent, who had assisted at the foundation of Dada in Zurich, brought the Dadaist verities into Germany with the zeal of a true apostle. He found there enthusiastic friends: George Grosz, who had lived in America, and who expressed in his drawings the tumultuous life of the great American cities, W. Heartfield, a sensitive poet, and Raoul Hausmann, who interests him-self only in life. They had long been convinced of the guilt of the Kaiser in bringing on the war, and their relations with Liebknecht, Professor Nicolai and the pacifists were a secret to no one. The many demonstrations which they organized had a great influence and they can boast of having helped to bring on the German revolution.

They have their newspapers, their publishing house and a Dada Club, which soon brought to light great talents—the song writer, W. Mehring, for example; the painter, Mlle. H. Hoech; the philosopher, Daimonides, etc., etc. They have organized international expositions, and tours of the principal German cities. These tours came to a very bad end: if it had not been for the intervention of the police, the Dadaists would have been killed by their audiences. At Hanover, where the crowd took possession of their baggage, they had to get out of town as fast as possible. At Dresden, their cash-box was confis-cated. When an opera singer who had nothing to do with Dada made an attempt to calm the audience, she was beaten up by the angry mob. At Prague, the scandal took on such proportions that the Czecho-Slovak government was forced to drive the Dadaists out and to forbid any Dadaist demonstration on Czecho-Slovakian territory.

I have not yet spoken of Baader, who is the head of the Dadaist re-ligion. He has had visions: Jesus Christ has appeared to him several times. The number of his adepts is enormous. He has also played a political rôle. At Weimar he threw proclamations into the parliament and interrupted the sitting by accusing the new revolutionary Ger-many of being inspired by the reactionary ideas of Goethe and Schiller. Baader, who calls himself the President of the World, is the father of three children. He has twice been locked up by mistake in a lunatic asylum. He is not an especially interesting man, but certainly a very genial one. On the occasion of the death of his wife, he delivered a long oration to the three thousand people at the funeral, contending that death is essentially a Dadaist affair. He was wearing a smile on his lips. He had, none the less, been very fond of his wife. The same day he cut off his beard, which had been that of a true apostle.

Huelsenbeck is at present a doctor and journalist at Danzig. He is a great lover of America, whose praises he has sung in three books: "Dada the Conqueror," "Forward Dada!" and "Germany Must Go." The last Dadaist exposition at Berlin came to a very bad end: the Minister of War brought an indictment against the men who had organized it for having insulted the German officers "by deformations and tendencious inscriptions." The defenses of some of the Dadaists are masterpieces of malice and irony.

Another group lives in Cologne, Dada W. 3. Max Ernst, painter and poet, has made a great many Dadaist discoveries. His paintings bear the same relation to painting that the moving-pictures do to photography—fresh and direct realizations of a mind which owes nothing to the researches of its predecessors. His intelligence is fine and distinguished; it is plain that he is an enthusiastic Alpine climber. We call him the inventor of the mystery on rollers. Baargeld, a young millionaire, was a Bolshevist before being converted to Dadaism. His specialty is methodology. He was brought up in the love of Stendhal, for whom his father has more than admiration. The "Rosa Bonheur of the Dadaists" has done some very amusing things in painting. Job Haubrich contributes to their efforts with a sincere enthusiasm. Their organ is called *Die Schammade*. They have obtained from the city of Cologne two very important concessions: they have been allowed to hold an exposition in a public urinal, with free admission; and the city has published at its own expense a handsome album of Dada lithographs by Max Ernst. Ernst has founded with Arp, of whom I shall speak in a moment, a society for the manufacture of "Fatagaga" pictures. The dissenting Dadaists have grouped themselves under the name of "Stupid" [sic]. K. Schwitters is not an absolutely pure Dadaist. He lives in Hanover—it seems that he has quite an original turn of mind. The publisher Stegemann at Hanover has sold more than four hundred thousand little Dada books.

Dada has no adepts in England, but it is very well known there. M. A. Binnyon has given a lecture on Dadaism and F. S. Flint has written a brochure about us.

In Russia, the Dadaists call themselves "41°": Zdanevitch, Krutchony and Terentiev. They are abstract and very productive. The first-mentioned is professor of Dadaism at the University of Tiflis.

In Holland, Dada has fervent adherents: J. K. Bonset at Leyden and Th. van Doesburg, who will come to the defense of Dada in a forthcoming book. Their review appears in several languages and is

called *Mécano*. P. Citroen and Bloomfield have made Amsterdam
their base of operations.

Dada has received much attention in Spain. Its promoters are
Jacques Edwards, Guillermo de Torre, Lasso de la Vega and Cansino
d'Assens.

In Rome, Dada is philosophical, distinguished, fastidious and skeptical with the Baron J. Evola; in Milan and Mantua, determined and
trenchant with Cantarelli, Fiozzi and Bacchi grouped about the *Blue
Review*. Tired of the single-track ideas of Marinetti, these young men
are getting away from Futurism and from the other artistic formulas.

Arp still lives in Switzerland, at Zurich: he is Alsatian, his mother is
French. He is one of my best friends. He has illustrated two books of
my poems. He is one of the most sympathetic men I have ever met.
He wears shoes specially made for him at Ascona. They look like hip-
popotamuses' feet and have a pretty design in leather. The stories that
he tells have an irresistible gaiety. The reliefs he has done represent
imaginary solidified vegetations, and his drawings: embroidery, rain
and the sleep of marine insects and crystal fingers. Mlle. Teuber has
made for a marionette theatre puppets representing Dadaists and psychoanalysts like Dr. Jung. The painter Augusto Giacometti is too old
to be a genuine Dadaist. He has declared that Dada is the sole joy of
his life. Dada is known throughout the world. I have been able to observe for myself in the course of a trip that Dada is as well known in
Switzerland as at Milan, Venice, Belgrade, Vincovtch, Bucharest,
Jassy, Constantinople, Athens, Messina, Naples and Rome. On the
Acropolis, a professor of theology was telling me, as he shook his fists
toward the Wingless Victory, that God would avenge himself on
Dada and all these newfangled ideas. I had good reason to know he
spoke truly: I caught a cold which made me miserable for three
weeks.

At Constantinople, I talked with a Greek doctor who had lived in
Paris, and who didn't know who I was. He told me that he knew Tristan Tzara very well. Calmly, in spite of my amazement, I asked him
what Tzara looked like. "He is tall and blond," he replied. I couldn't
keep from laughing, because I am small and dark.

UNCOLLECTED REVIEWS

H. L. Mencken

A MAN has withdrawn from the tumult of American life into the seclusion of a house in Baltimore. He is unmarried and has surrounded himself with three thousand books. From this point of vantage he watches the twentieth century with detached and ironic dismay. A not ungenial materialist, he reflects that all human activities are, after all, mainly physical in origin: inspiration is a function of metabolism; death is an acidosis; love is a biological phenomenon; idealism is insanity. But the body is capable of much enjoyment; why worry about its obvious supremacy? As long as there is Chicken à la Maryland and plenty of liquor from the boot-leggers, as long as it is possible to read Conrad and hear Bach and Beethoven occasionally, why should a man of aristocratic temperament be particularly disturbed about anything? Let the capitalist exploit the wage-slave and the wage-slave blow up the capitalist; let political charlatans and scoundrels pick the pockets of the Republic; let the women run the men to ground and the men break their hearts for the women; let the people go off to the wars and destroy each other by the billion. They can never rob Mencken of his sleep nor spoil a single dinner for him. Outside, it is all a question of Christianity and democracy, but Mencken does not believe in either, so why should he take part in the brawl? What has he to do with the mob except to be diverted by its idiocy? He may occasionally attend a political convention to gratify a "taste for the obscene" or entertain his speculative mind by predicting the next catastrophe, but, on the whole, the prodigious din and activity and confusion of the nation roars along without touching him particularly; it is all to him "but as the sound of lyres and flutes." . . .

Something like this is the comic portrait which Mencken has painted of himself; he has even pretended that it is the character in which he prefers to be accepted. But there is, behind this comic mask, a critic, an evangelist and an artist; there is a mind of extraordinary vigor and a temperament of extraordinary interest, and neither of these has ever yet been examined as seriously as it should have been. Mencken has been left far too

much to the rhapsodies of his disciples and the haughty sneers
of his opponents. Indeed, he has assumed such importance as
an influence in American thought that it is high time some one
subjected him to a drastic full-length analysis. The present
writer has only space for the briefest of suggestions.

II

The striking things about Mencken's mind are its ruthlessness and its rigidity. It has all the courage in the world in a
country where courage is rare. He has even had the fearless-
ness to avoid the respectable and the wholesome, those two
devils which so often betray in the end even the most intelligent of Americans. He fought outspokenly against optimism,
Puritanism and democratic ineptitude, at a time when they had
but few foes. It is well to remember, now that these qualities
have become stock reproaches among the intelligentsia, that it
was Mencken who began the crusade against them at a lonely
and disregarded post and that we owe to him much of the dis-
favor into which they have recently fallen,—and also that it was
Mencken who first championed the kind of American literary
activity of which we have now become proudest. But the activity of his mind is curiously cramped by its extreme inflexibility.
In the first place, as a critic, he is not what is called "sympathetic." His criticisms deal but little with people from their
own point of view: he simply brings the other man's statements and reactions to the bar of his own dogma and, having
judged them by that measure, proceeds to accept or reject
them. Though one of the fairest of critics, he is one of the least
pliant.

In the second place, in spite of his scepticism and his frequent exhortations to hold one's opinions lightly, he himself
has been conspicuous for seizing upon simple dogmas and
sticking to them with fierce tenacity. When he is arguing his
case against democracy or Christianity, he reminds one rather
of Bishop Manning or Dr. Straton than of Renan or Anatole
France. The true sceptics like Renan or France see both the
truth and weakness of every case; they put themselves in the
place of people who believe differently from themselves and
finally come to sympathize with them,—almost, to accept their

point of view. But Mencken, once having got his teeth into an idea, can never be induced to drop it, and will only shake his head and growl when somebody tries to tempt him with something else.

Thus, in 1908, when he published his admirable book on Nietzsche, he had reached a certain set of conclusions upon society and ethics. Humanity, he had come to believe, is divided into two classes: the masters and the slaves. The masters are able and courageous men who do whatever they like and are not restrained by any scruples save those that promote their own interest; the slaves are a race of wretched underlings, stupid, superstitious and untrustworthy, who have no rights and no raison d'être except to be exploited by the masters. To talk of equality and fraternity is the most fatuous of nonsense: there is as much difference in kind between the masters and the slaves as there is between men and animals.

Therefore, Christianity is false because it asserts that all souls are worth saving and democracy is a mistake because it emancipates the slaves and tries to make them the masters. It is absurd to try to correct the evolutionary process which would allow the fittest to survive and the weaklings and fools to go under. "I am," Mr. Mencken has said, "against the under dog every time." But things are getting more and more democratic and consequently worse and worse. What we need is an enlightened aristocracy to take charge of society. But there has never been any such aristocracy and we are certainly not going to produce one. In the meantime, one can but curse the mob and die at one's post.

I have not space here to criticize these views—to ask, for instance, when he says he thinks the strong should be allowed to survive at the expense of the weak, whether he means the strong like Jack Johnson or the strong like Nietzsche and Beethoven. I must assume that the confusion of thought is apparent to the reader and go on to point out that Mencken has been upholding these theories without modification since 1908 at least. He has cherished them through the European war and through the industrial war that has followed it. (Quite recently they have led him into the absurdity of asserting that it would have been a good thing for America if the war had continued longer, because this would have stamped out "hundreds of thousands of the relatively unfit." The men who were left at the end of the war in the French and German armies, were, he adds "very superior men.") And, in consequence, it seems to me that he has cut himself off in an intellectual cul-de-sac.

He has much to say to America that is of the first usefulness and importance: he has no peer in the brilliance and effectiveness of his onslaught upon political ignorance and corruption, upon Y.M.C.A.'ism and popular morality, upon the cheapness and sordidness of current ideals. But, though the moral strength which gives him courage is drawn partly from his Nietzschean principles, these principles so close his horizon as to render his social criticism rather sterile. In the matters of politics and society he can do nothing but denounce. He has taken up a position in which it is impossible that any development should please him. He detests the present state of affairs, but he disbelieves in liberalism and radicalism, and any change in their directions would presumably only make him detest the world more. He really hates repression and injustice, but he has long ago repudiated the idea of human rights to freedom and justice and he consequently cannot come out as their champion.

There have, however, been a few signs of late that he feels his old house too small: in his recent discussion of Mr. Chafee's book on free speech, he reached a pitch of righteous indignation at which he has scarcely been seen before. "In those two years," he cried, "all the laborious work of a century and a half —toward the free and honest administration of fair laws, the dealing of plain justice between man and man, the protection of the weak and helpless, the safeguarding of free assemblage and free speech—was ruthlessly undone." This is obviously in direct contradiction to the faith he has previously professed. What has one who is "against the under dog every time" to do with "the protection of the weak and helpless"? He has told us again and again that we should let the weak and helpless perish.

The truth is that in the last few years Mencken has entered so far into the national intellectual life that it has become impossible for him to maintain his old opinions quite intact: he has begun to worry and hope with the American people in the throes of their democratic experiment. I know that this is a terrible statement; it is as if one should say that the Pope had begun to worry and hope with the western world in its attempt to shake off creed; but I honestly believe it is true. This phenomenon seemed to make its appearance toward the last page of The American Language; and if it does not come to bulk yet larger we shall have one of our strongest men still fighting with one arm tied behind his back.

III

So much for the critic; but what of the evangelist and artist? For Mencken, in spite of all his professions of realistic resignation, is actually a militant idealist. Most Americans—even of fine standards—have long ago resigned themselves to the cheapness and ugliness of America, but Mencken has never resigned himself. He has never ceased to regard his native country with wounded and outraged eyes. The shabby politics, the childish books, the factories turning out wooden nut-megs have never lost their power to offend him. At this late date, he is, I suppose, almost the only man in the country who still expects American novelists to be artists and American politicians gentlemen.

And his expression of his resentment is by no means temperate or aloof. It is righteous indignation of the most violent sort. His denunciations are as ferocious as those of Tertullian or Billy Sunday. It is in purpose rather than in method that he differs from these great divines. (See especially his excommunication of the professors in the essay on The National Letters.) In his exhortations to disobey the rules of the current American morality he has shown himself as noisy and as bitter as any other Puritan preacher.

And this brings us to what is perhaps, after all, the most important thing about Mencken, the thing which gives him his enormous importance in American literature today: it is the fact that here we have a genuine artist and man of first-rate education and intelligence who is thoroughly familiar with, even thoroughly saturated with, the common life. The rule has been heretofore for men of superior intelligence, like Henry Adams and Henry James, to shrink so far from the common life that, in a country where there was practically nothing else, they had almost no material to work on, and for men who were part of the general society, like Mark Twain, to be handicapped by Philistinism and illiteracy; but in the case of Mencken we have Puritanism and American manners in a position to criticize itself. For in his attitude toward all the things with which Puritanism is supposed to deal Mencken is thoroughly American and thoroughly Puritan. If he were what he exhorts us to be in regard to the amenities and the pleasures he would never rage so much about them. His sermons would be unintelligible, I should think, to a Frenchman or an Italian. Nobody but a man steeped in Puritanism could have so much to say about love and yet never convey any idea of its beauties or delights; poor Aphrodite, usually identified in his pages with the whore and the bawdy-house, wears as unalluring a face as she does in the utterances of any Y.M.C.A. lecturer; no one else would confine himself to a harsh abuse, on principle, of the people who have outlawed love. Nobody else would express his enthusiasm for the innocent pleasures of alcohol in such a way that it sounded less like a eulogy than like an angry defiance. He is an unmistakable product of Puritan training and environment. Horace or Anatole France, who really represent the sort of civilization which Mencken admires, would never be so acutely conscious of the problems of love and art and wine; they would take them easily for granted and enjoy them as a matter of course. But Mencken, who was born an American, with the truculent argumentative mind of the Puritan, can never enjoy them as a matter of course, as even some Americans can do, but must call down all the dark thunders of logic to defend them, like any Milton or Luther.

And he is saturated with the thought and aspect of modern commercial America. He is, we feel, in spite of everything, in the long run most at home there; are we not told that once, when walking in Paris in the spring, he was annoyed by the absence of a first-class drug-store? Instead of taking refuge among remote literatures, like Mr. Cabell and Mr. Pound, he makes his poetry of the democratic life which absorbs and infuriates him. He takes the slang of the common man and makes fine prose of it. He has studied the habits and ideas and language of the common run of his countrymen with a close first-hand observation and an unflagging interest. And he has succeeded in doing with the common life what nobody else has done,—(at least with any authentic stamp of literary distinction): he has taken it in all its coarseness and angularity and compelled it to dance a ballet, in which the Odd Fellow, the stockbroker, the Y.M.C.A. Secretary, the Knight of Pythias, the academic critic, the Methodist evangelical, the lecturer at Chautauquas, the charlatan politician, the Vice Crusader, the Department of Justice, the star-spangled army officer,—and the man who reveres all these, with all his properties and settings: the derby hat, the cheap cigar, the shaving soap advertisement, the popular novel, the cuspidor, the stein of prohibition beer, the drug store, the patent medicine, the American Legion button,—join hands and perform, to the strains of a sombre but ribald music, which ranges from genial boisterousness to morose and cynical brooding.

Take the following passage, for example, from a sort of prose poem:

Pale druggists in remote towns of the hog and cotton belt, endlessly wrapping up Peruna. . . . Women hidden away in the damp kitchens of unpainted houses along the railroad tracks, frying tough beefsteaks. . . . Lime and cement dealers being initiated into the Knights of Pythias, the Redmen or the Woodmen of the World. . . . Watchmen at lonely railroad crossings in Iowa, hoping that they'll be able to get off to hear the United Brethren evangelist preach. . . . Ticket-choppers in the Subway, breathing sweat in its gaseous form. . . . Family doctors in poor neighborhoods, faithfully relying upon the therapeutics taught in their Eclectic Medical College in 1884. . . . Farmers plowing sterile fields behind sad meditative horses, both suffering from the bites of insects. . . . Greeks tending all-night coffee-joints in the suburban wildernesses where the trolley-cars stop. . . . Grocery clerks stealing prunes and gingersnaps and trying to make assignations with soapy servant-girls. . . . Women confined for the ninth or tenth time, wondering hopelessly what it is all about. . . . Methodist preachers retired after forty years of service in the trenches of God, upon pensions of $600 a year. . . . Wives and daughters of Middle Western country bankers, marooned in Los Angeles, going tremblingly to swami seances in dark smelly rooms. . . . Chauffeurs in huge fur coats waiting outside theatres filled with folks applauding Robert Edeson and Jane Cowl. . . . Decayed and hopeless men writing editorials at midnight for leading papers in Mississippi, Arkansas and Alabama. . . .

One recalls the enumeration of another set of visions:

The pure contralto sings in the organ loft,
The carpenter dresses his plank, the tongue of his foreplane whistles its wild ascending lisp,
The married and unmarried children ride home to their Thanksgiving dinner,
The pilot seizes the king-pin, he heaves down with a strong arm,
The mate stands braced in the whale-boat, lance and harpoon are ready,
The duck-shooter walks by silent and cautious stretches,
The deacons are ordained with cross'd hands at the altar,
The spinning girl retreats and advances to the hum of the big wheel,
The farmer stops by the bars as he walks on a First-day loaf and looks at the oats and rye, . . .
The young fellow drives the express-wagon (I love him, though I do not know him),
The half-breed straps on his light boots to compete in the race,
The Wolverine sets traps on the creek that helps fill the Huron,
The clean-hair'd Yankee girl works with her sewing machine or in the factory or mill,
The Missourian crosses the plains toting his wares and his cattle. . . .

This was the day before yesterday, and Mencken is today. Is not Mencken's gloomy catalogue as much the poetry of modern America as Walt Whitman's was of the early Republic? When the States were fresh and new and their people were hardy pioneers, we had a great poet, from whose pages the youth and wonder of that world can reach us forever; and now that that air is soured with industry and those pioneers have become respectable citizens dwelling in hideously ugly towns and devoted to sordid ideals, we have had a great satirist to arouse us against the tragic spectacle we have become. For Mencken is the civilized consciousness of modern America, its learning, its intelligence and its taste, realizing the grossness of its manners and mind and crying out in horror and chagrin.

The New Republic, June 1921

The Poetry of Drouth

The Waste Land, by T. S. Eliot

M R T. S. ELIOT'S first meagre volume of twenty-four poems was dropped into the waters of contemporary verse without stirring more than a few ripples. But when two or three years had passed, it was found to stain the whole sea. Or, to change the metaphor a little, it became evident that Mr Eliot had fished a murex up. His productions, which had originally been received as a sort of glorified *vers de société*, turned out to be unforgettable poems, which everyone was trying to rewrite. There might not be very much of him, but what there was had come somehow to seem precious and now the publication of his long poem, The Waste Land, confirms the opinion which we had begun gradually to cherish, that Mr Eliot, with all his limitations, is one of our only authentic poets. For this new poem—which presents itself as so far his most considerable claim to eminence—not only recapitulates all his earlier and already familiar motifs, but it sounds for the first time in all their intensity, untempered by irony or disguise, the hunger for beauty and the anguish at living which lie at the bottom of all his work.

Perhaps the best point of departure for a discussion of The Waste Land is an explanation of its title. Mr Eliot asserts that he derived this title, as well as the plan of the poem "and much of the incidental symbolism," from a book by Miss Jessie L. Weston called From Ritual to Romance. The Waste Land, it appears, is one of the many mysterious elements which have made of the Holy Grail legend a perennial puzzle of folk-lore; it is a desolate and sterile country, ruled over by an impotent king, in which not only have the crops ceased to grow and the animals to reproduce their kind, but the very human inhabitants have become unable to bear children. The renewal of the Waste Land and the healing of the "Fisher King's" wound depend somehow upon the success of the Knight who has come to find the Holy Grail.

Miss Weston, who has spent her whole life in the study of

the Arthurian legends, has at last propounded a new solution for the problems presented by this strange tale. Stimulated by Frazer's Golden Bough—of which this extraordinarily interesting book is a sort of offshoot—she has attempted to explain the Fisher King as a primitive vegetable god—one of those creatures who, like Attis and Adonis, is identified with Nature herself and in the temporary loss of whose virility the drouth or inclemency of the season is symbolized; and whose mock burial is a sort of earnest of his coming to life again. Such a cult, Miss Weston contends, became attached to the popular Persian religion of Mithraism and was brought north to Gaul and Britain by the Roman legionaries. When Christianity finally prevailed, Attis was driven underground and survived only as a secret cult, like the Venus of the Venusberg. The Grail legend, according to Miss Weston, had its origin in such a cult; the Lance and Grail are the sexual symbols appropriate to a fertility rite and the eerie adventure of the Chapel Perilous is the description of an initiation.

Now Mr Eliot uses the Waste Land as the concrete image of a spiritual drouth. His poem takes place half in the real world —the world of contemporary London, and half in a haunted wilderness—the Waste Land of the mediaeval legend; but the Waste Land is only the hero's arid soul and the intolerable world about him. The water which he longs for in the twilit desert is to quench his thirst which torments him in the London dusk.—And he exists not only upon these two planes, but as if throughout the whole of human history. Miss Weston's interpretation of the Grail legend lent itself with peculiar aptness to Mr Eliot's extraordinarily complex mind (which always finds itself looking out upon the present with the prouder eyes of the past and which loves to make its oracles as deep as the experience of the race itself by piling up stratum upon stratum of reference, as the Italian painters used to paint over one another); because she took pains to trace the Buried God not only to Attis and Adonis, but further back to the recently revealed Tammuz of the Sumerian-Babylonian civilization and to the god invited to loosen the waters in the abysmally ancient Vedic Hymns. So Mr Eliot hears in his own parched cry the voices of all the thirsty men of the past—of the author of Ecclesiastes in majestic bitterness at life's futility, of the Chil-

dren of Israel weeping for Zion by the unrefreshing rivers of
Babylon, of the disciples after the Crucifixion meeting the
phantom of Christ on their journey; of Buddha's renunciation
of life and Dante's astonishment at the weary hordes of Hell,
and of the sinister dirge with which Webster blessed the
"friendless bodies of unburied men." In the centre of his poem
he places the weary figure of the blind immortal prophet Tiresias, who, having been woman as well as man, has exhausted all
human experience and, having "sat by Thebes below the wall
and walked among the lowest of the dead," knows exactly
what will happen in the London flat between the typist and the
house-agent's clerk; and at its beginning the almost identical
figure of the Cumaean Sibyl mentioned in Petronius, who—
gifted also with extreme longevity and preserved as a sort of
living mummy—when asked by little boys what she wanted,
replied only "I want to die." Not only is life sterile and futile,
but men have tasted its sterility and futility a thousand times
before. T. S. Eliot, walking the desert or London, feels profoundly that the desert has always been there. Like Tiresias, he
has sat below the wall of Thebes; like Buddha, he has seen the
world as an arid conflagration; like the Sibyl, he has known
everything and known everything vain.

Yet something else, too, reaches him from the past: as he
wanders among the vulgarities which surround him, his soul is
haunted by heroic strains of an unfading music. Sometimes it
turns suddenly and shockingly into the jazz of the music-halls,
sometimes it breaks in the middle of a bar and leaves its hearer
with dry ears again, but still it sounds like the divine rumour of
some high destiny from which he has fallen, like indestructible
pride in the citizenship of some world which he never can
reach. In a London boudoir, where the air is stifling with a
dust of futility, he hears, as he approaches his hostess, an echo
of Anthony and Cleopatra and of Aeneas coming to the house
of Dido—and a painted panel above the mantel gives his mind
a moment's swift release by reminding him of Milton's Paradise and of the nightingale that sang there.—Yet though it is
most often things from books which refresh him, he has also a
slight spring of memory. He remembers someone who came
to him with wet hair and with hyacinths in her arms, and
before her he was stricken senseless and dumb—"looking into

the heart of light, the silence." There were rain and flowers
growing then. Nothing ever grows during the action of the
poem and no rain ever falls. The thunder of the final vision is
"dry sterile thunder without rain." But as Gerontion in his dry
rented house thinks wistfully of the young men who fought in
the rain, as Prufrock longs to ride green waves and linger in
the chambers of the sea, as Mr Apollinax is imagined drawing
strength from the deep sea-caves of coral islands, so in this new
poem Mr Eliot identifies water with all freedom and illumination of the soul. He drinks the rain that once fell on his youth
as—to use an analogy in Mr Eliot's own manner—Dante drank
at the river of Eunoë that the old joys he had known might be
remembered. But—to note also the tragic discrepancy, as Mr
Eliot always does—the draught, so far from renewing his soul
and leaving him pure to rise to the stars, is only a drop absorbed in the desert; to think of it is to register its death. The
memory is the dead god whom—as Hyacinth—he buries at
the beginning of the poem and which—unlike his ancient
prototype—is never to come to life again. Hereafter, fertility
will fail; we shall see women deliberately making themselves
sterile; we shall find that love has lost its life-giving power and
can bring nothing but an asceticism of disgust. He is travelling
in a country cracked by drouth in which he can only dream
feverishly of drowning or of hearing the song of the hermit-
thrush which has at least the music of water. The only reappearance of the god is as a phantom which walks beside him,
the delirious hallucination of a man who is dying of thirst. In
the end the dry-rotted world is crumbling about him—his own
soul is falling apart. There is nothing left to prop it up but
some dry stoic Sanskrit maxims and the broken sighs from the
past, of singers exiled or oppressed. Like de Nerval, he is disinherited; like the poet of the Pervigilium Veneris, he is dumb;
like Arnaut Daniel in Purgatory, he begs the world to raise a
prayer for his torment, as he disappears in the fire.

It will be seen from this brief description that the poem is
complicated; and it is actually even more complicated than I
have made it appear. It is sure to be objected that Mr Eliot has
written a puzzle rather than a poem and that his work can possess no higher interest than a full-rigged ship built in a bottle.
It will be said that he depends too much upon books and bor-

rows too much from other men and that there can be no room for original quality in a poem of little more than four hundred lines which contains allusions to, parodies of, or quotations from, the Vedic Hymns, Buddha, the Psalms, Ezekiel, Ecclesiastes, Luke, Sappho, Virgil, Ovid, Petronius, the Pervigilium Veneris, St Augustine, Dante, the Grail Legends, early English poetry, Kyd, Spenser, Shakespeare, John Day, Webster, Middleton, Milton, Goldsmith, Gérard de Nerval, Froude, Baudelaire, Verlaine, Swinburne, Wagner, The Golden Bough, Miss Weston's book, various popular ballads, and the author's own earlier poems. It has already been charged against Mr Eliot that he does not feel enough to be a poet and that the emotions of longing and disgust which he does have belong essentially to a delayed adolescence. It has already been suggested that his distaste for the celebrated Sweeney shows a superficial mind and that if he only looked more closely into poor Sweeney he would find Eugene O'Neill's Hairy Ape; and I suppose it will be felt in connexion with this new poem that if his vulgar London girls had only been studied by Sherwood Anderson they would have presented a very different appearance. At bottom, it is sure to be said, Mr Eliot is timid and prosaic like Mr Prufrock; he has no capacity for life, and nothing which happens to Mr Prufrock can be important.

Well: all these objections are founded on realities, but they are outweighed by one major fact—the fact that Mr Eliot is a poet. It is true his poems seem the products of a constricted emotional experience and that he appears to have drawn rather heavily on books for the heat he could not derive from life. There is a certain grudging margin, to be sure, about all that Mr Eliot writes—as if he were compensating himself for his limitations by a peevish assumption of superiority. But it is the very acuteness of his suffering from this starvation which gives such poignancy to his art. And, as I say, Mr Eliot is a poet—that is, he feels intensely and with distinction and speaks naturally in beautiful verse—so that, no matter within what walls he lives, he belongs to the divine company. His verse is sometimes much too scrappy—he does not dwell long enough upon one idea to give it its proportionate value before passing on to the next—but these drops, though they be wrung from flint, are none the less authentic crystals. They are broken and sometimes infinitely tiny, but they are worth all the rhine-stones on the market. I doubt whether there is a single other poem of equal length by a contemporary American which dis-plays so high and so varied a mastery of English verse. The poem is—in spite of its lack of structural unity—simply one tri-umph after another—from the white April light of the opening and the sweet wistfulness of the nightingale passage—one of the only successful pieces of contemporary blank verse—to the shabby sadness of the Thames Maidens, the cruel irony of Tiresias' vision, and the dry grim stony style of the descriptions of the Waste Land itself.

That is why Mr Eliot's trivialities are more valuable than other people's epics—why Mr Eliot's detestation of Sweeney is more precious than Mr Sandburg's sympathy for him, and Mr Prufrock's tea-table tragedy more important than all the pas-sions of the New Adam—sincere and carefully expressed as these latter emotions indubitably are. That is also why, for all its complicated correspondences and its recondite references and quotations, The Waste Land is intelligible at first reading. It is not necessary to know anything about the Grail Legend or any but the most obvious of Mr Eliot's allusions to feel the force of the intense emotion which the poem is intended to convey—as one cannot do, for example, with the extremely ill-focussed Eight Cantos of his imitator Mr Ezra Pound, who presents only a bewildering mosaic with no central emotion to provide a key. In Eliot the very images and the sound of the words—even when we do not know precisely why he has chosen them—are charged with a strange poignancy which seems to bring us into the heart of the singer. And sometimes we feel that he is speaking not only for a personal distress, but for the starvation of a whole civilization—for people grinding at barren office-routine in the cells of gigantic cities, drying up their souls in eternal toil whose products never bring them profit, where their pleasures are so vulgar and so feeble that they are almost sadder than their pains. It is our whole world of strained nerves and shattered institutions, in which "some infinitely gentle, infinitely suffering thing" is somehow being done to death—in which the maiden Philomel "by the bar-barous king so rudely, forced" can no longer even fill the desert "with inviolable voice." It is the world in which the pursuit of grace and beauty is something which is felt to be obsolete—the reflections which reach us from the past cannot illumine so dingy a scene; that heroic prelude has ironic echoes among the streets and the drawing-rooms where we live. Yet the race of the poets—though grown rarer—is not yet quite dead: there is at least one who, as Mr Pound says, has brought a new personal rhythm into the language and who has lent even to the words of his great predecessors a new music and a new meaning.

The Dial, December 1922

Edith Wharton

H AS Mrs. Wharton ever been given her rightful place as the foremost of living American novelists and one of the foremost living novelists of the world? I have seen very little intelligent criticism of her by American and none by English critics. The best discussion of her novels I have ever read was written by a Frenchman,—M. Régis Michaud, in his *Réalistes et Mystiques Anglo-Saxons*. In America she is commonly regarded as a sort of super-Robert W. Chambers, preoccupied exclusively with the lives of very smart and very rich people,— though *Ethan Frome* and *Summer* and *Bunner Sisters* are there to prove that she is interested in people of all sorts and though the four of her major novels which do deal with the rich cover entirely different areas of society.

But really she is the only one of our novelists whose work, for intensity and finish, stands comparison with the best fiction of England and France. She is the only one who combines thorough knowledge of a section of the national life with a brilliant and polished style and an expert mastery of form. Has Thomas Hardy ever done anything better than *Ethan Frome* or Anatole France any satire that was truer to France than *The Custom of the Country* is to America?

The hardness and insistence on material things that people object to in her novels are the hardness and materialism of New York and New England themselves. What could be more like New York than Mrs. Wharton's novels about it? Like New York, they are full of glitter and exasperated nerves, luxurious and unlovely appointments and unpicturesque sordidness. Was Thackeray more of London or Balzac of Paris? She has been accused of being snobbish; but in regard to money and social distinction, no one could be less snobbish. She is really a bitter intellectual snob toward both money and society. Her novels about New York are written with a corrosive scorn which sees the soul and intelligence of men ground down and finally destroyed by the weight of material possessions and the pressure of money-getting.

And in her most recently published novel, *The Age of Inno-*

cence, she has delivered an even more drastic judgment than she has ever done before. It is true that *The Age of Innocence* has not the intensity of her earlier work and that its style is feebler and less sharp; one suspects that her mastery of English has begun to disintegrate a little through her long residence in France. But as an intrepid examination of American manners and morals she has, I think, never equalled it. *The Custom of the Country* and *The House of Mirth* attack the *nouveau riche* America a little from the point of view of Washington Square, —from the point of view of the older class who had at least some education and taste. But *The Age of Innocence* attacks the tradition of the people of education and taste from the point of view of the artist and the citizen of the world.

In this severest of American novels, Mrs. Wharton makes no respectable assumptions, she begins by accepting no conventions. The old tradition, with its provincialism and prudery and hollowness, with its abject slavery to custom and its lack of intellectual curiosity is exhibited as no less cruel than the grosser world which supplanted it: in it every brave passion is smothered, every impulse toward beauty extinguished; the potentially superior man is strangled in an all-embracing mesh of idiotic conventions. There is nothing but respectability,—the fear of not being respectable.

And *The Age of Innocence* is not merely a picture of a world which is obsolete: we are all of us living to a great extent in the air of that inherited tradition. By showing it in its pure state, when nothing else had broken in on it, Mrs. Wharton is able to make it so monstrous that the most conventional of readers cannot help but shudder at it. But it is really, in a cruder form, our master and tyrant still. Newland Archer, the extraordinary man who always does the ordinary thing, is still an American figure: the universities are full of him; he hears echoes from strange lands of freedom and romance and for a moment or two catches in his eyes the reflected splendour of their light; then he marries some stupid woman and decides to make a great deal of money and lives and dies as a supporter of our commercial civilization. Mrs. Wharton should have written at the end of her novel: *De te, fabula!*

Vanity Fair, March 1923

A Guide to Gertrude Stein

T HERE is, perhaps, no other American writer of impor- tance who has been so badly underestimated as Gertrude Stein. And this critical neglect would seem chiefly to be due to an unfortunate accident. The earlier half of Miss Stein's liter- ary work has never really had a fair chance of recognition: it was one of her most advanced and most daring experiments which first attracted public attention. The first most of us heard of Gertrude Stein was when *Tender Buttons* was pub- lished in 1914 and was greeted with raucous guffaws as an example of exotic Greenwich Villagism. Yet Miss Stein had already published at this time, besides two curious and inter- esting brochures, one of the most distinguished works of fic- tion by any living American author—a book which had far more claim to serious recognition than the works of most of the Hergesheimers and the Cathers which followed it and which were raised to the dignity of masters by the eagerness of the new literary generation to discover authentic American tal- ent. It was a little as if Henry James had first attracted atten- tion with *The Wings of the Dove* or George Meredith with *One of Our Conquerors.* No one realized that the strange looking stuff which diverted him as a form of literary lunacy was really only a comparatively late phase of a genius extraordinarily con- scientious and sane, which had been working steadily for many years to express itself in prose.

Gertrude Stein's first book, *Three Lives,* appeared, in 1909, at a time when there was little audience, either popular or critical, for serious American fiction. If *Three Lives* were published to- day we should probably hear much more about it. Indeed, have we not done honor to Sherwood Anderson, who is essen- tially a disciple of Miss Stein and whose very best stories, I think, are no better than *Three Lives?*

Three Lives was a work of realism but realism of rather a novel kind. There had come to be a sort of realistic formula for writing about domestic servants, invented perhaps by Flaubert and fostered, I suppose, by the Goncourts. But Miss Stein, though she shared with these writers their ironic sense and their detachment, had discovered a technique of her own. When we read *Un Coeur Simple* of Flaubert we are continually thinking about Flaubert—of his technical virtuosity, of his *tour de force* of the imagination in being able to put before us so lowly a creature at all—his researches into her simple heart are like a last triumph of sophistication. But Gertrude Stein, in her treatment of her servant girls, occupies no such acrid literary altitudes. Her portraits, though no less ruthless than Flaubert's, are far closer to the originals. Indeed they are not dazzling feats of ingenuity like Flaubert's, at all, but rather the projection of three actual human beings as complex and as complete as life. The style itself, which seems to owe nothing to that of any other novelist, takes on the very accents and the rhythms of the minds whose adventures it is recording. We have ceased to see the nurse-girl as an insect to be examined at arm's length; we find ourselves living in her own world and watching it through her own eyes. And far from proving sordid or boring, it becomes extraordinarily beautiful and noble.

In *Three Lives* the style, though extremely individual, is not yet especially eccentric—though some of the author's characteristic tricks have already begun to appear. You have the rhythmic repetitions, like the refrain of a ballad, which we find imitated in Sherwood Anderson, and you have the strange stringing together of present participles which seems at first merely an attempt to reproduce some mannerism of Negro conversation, but which was afterwards to grow on Miss Stein as a mannerism of her own. "I never did use to think I was so much on being real modest, Melanctha, but now I know really I am, when I hear you talking. I see all the time there are many people living just as good as I am, though they are a little different to me. Now with you, Melanctha, if I understand you right what you are talking, you don't think that way of no other one that you are ever knowing."

Three Lives and the gigantic *History of a Family* constitute Miss Stein's first period. The latter found no publisher when it was first written and has remained in obscurity ever since, though those who have read it in manuscript consider it her most important work and, with the example of Proust and

Ulysses, it is to be hoped that some publisher will undertake it. Her middle manner—a logical elaboration of the earlier style of *Three Lives*—first appears in 1912 in the portraits of Matisse and Picasso, published by Mr. Stieglitz in *Camera Work*, and in a sketch of the Galeries Lafayette, in a defunct magazine called *Rogue*. I shall quote the beginning of the portrait of Matisse: "One was quite certain that for a long part of his being one being living he had been trying to be certain that he was wrong in doing what he was doing and then when he could not come to be certain that he had been wrong in doing what he had been doing, when he had completely convinced himself that he would not come to be certain that he had been wrong in doing what he had been doing he was really certain then that he was a great one and he certainly was a great one. Certainly every one could be certain of this thing that this one is a great one." This was a little queer but still intelligible; but, about this time another "portrait" appeared which presented far greater difficulties. It suddenly became evident that Gertrude Stein had abandoned the intelligible altogether.

The *Portrait of Mabel Dodge of the Villa Curonia*, printed privately in Florence, retained the flowing manner of the other portraits but had begun speaking in a strange and disturbing language, rather like Mallarmé's language of Symbolism; and finally, in *Tender Buttons* Miss Stein abandoned even her long limpid sentences and began expressing herself in fantastic strings of words without syntax or connection. This was the sort of thing that astonished the world in 1914:

Red Roses. A cool red rose and a pink cut pink, a collapse and a sold hole, a little less hot.

A Sound. Elephant beaten with candy and little pops and chews all bolts and reckless reckless rats, this is this.

Custard. Custard is this. It has aches, aches when. Not to be. Not to be narrowly. This makes a whole little hill.

It is better than a little thing that has mellow real mellow. It is better than lakes whole lakes, it is better than seeing.

Chicken. Alas a dirty word, alas a dirty third alas a dirty third, alas a dirty bird.

It appeared that Miss Stein had decided to try using words for the values which she believed them to possess apart from those inherent in their actual meanings. We are told that she used to shut herself up at night and try utterly to banish from her brain all the words ordinarily associated with the ideas she had fixed upon. Concentrating upon the given image she would make her mind a blank to its ordinary vocabulary, invoking other, more subtly relevant words to render it anew.

But the real key to understanding *Tender Buttons* is to be found in Miss Stein's preoccupation with modern painting. Long a friend of Matisse and Picasso, and one of the earliest of their admirers, she has for many years been living in Paris in the full excitement of the new movement and has accumulated a collection of modern paintings, which is one of the most remarkable in Europe. It is not surprising that she should have come to wonder whether analogous effects might not be produced in literature. We are all more or less familiar by this time with the theory of cubism and its sister genres—that violent reaction from naturalism, which holds that by splitting up or distorting an object you can give a far truer impression of its effect on the beholder than by any literal representation—and it is not difficult to see how Miss Stein's later work attempts the same fresh rendering in prose.

The *Portrait of Mabel Dodge* was merely a portrait in the manner of Picasso, and the sketches in *Tender Buttons*, of which the subtitle was *Objects, Food, Rooms* were simply a series of cubist still-lifes in the manner of Gleize or Braque. She had cut down her long repetitive ruminations to telegraphic economic strokes; instead of turning the object over and over, like the ocean lapping a pebble, she had begun dropping the pebble in a well and recording only the ripples on the surface, when the pebble itself had disappeared and sunk many yards out of sight. It is not the object which we see but the vibrations caused by the object—not a focussing of something outside the artist, but the consciousness of the artist herself.

Her next publication, a small pamphlet called, felicitously, *Have They Attacked Mary. He Giggled—A Political Satire* (1917), and her most recent book, *Geography and Plays* (1922) which contains also specimens of almost all her other manners, seem to apply the method of the still-lifes in *Tender Buttons* to more complicated subjects. You have travel, anecdotes, conversations, all splintered up and reduced to their essentials, a queer selective stenography of life. Some of this is recognizable and amusing; more is completely incomprehensible; and all is tantalizing with the suggestion of a fine artist just out of reach. For the chief strength of Miss Stein's genius still appears to be her grasp of character. In spite of her excursions into still-life, she has always been preoccupied with portraits. The three women of *Three Lives*, besides being three accurately reported individuals, achieved an almost Shakespearean significance as the representatives of certain salient human types; and the essays on the modern painters seemed excellent criticism of artistic personality. Now, in her latest writings—though with a lighter irony—we have the portrait painter again: Miss Furr and Miss Skeene are plain—and incomparable—but what of Tourtebattre and Johnny Grey? We have the feeling that we have somehow been cheated out of the masterpieces of a first-rate writer of fiction.

And is it right that we should lose Gertrude Stein? That is a difficult question to answer; but I am inclined to think we should not. It is not that I object to experiments—however bold—with language and form, nor that I deny Miss Stein's partial success—it may well be, as Mr. Anderson suggests, that she has made a contribution of importance to modern prose; but that I believe her complete literary success has been prevented by her unfortunate analogy with the plastic arts. I am told by her friends that for many years she has seen almost no literary people but only sculptors and painters; and it is a fact that there is scarcely a literary reference to be found in any of her works. It would seem that Miss Stein has cut herself off so completely from the tradition and experience of other writers that she has ceased not only to recognize the limitations of literature but even to understand its aim. I admit as much as you please that in the plastic arts one need not be representational, that one should avoid especially being "literary", as the modern painters say; but, though painting ought not to be literary, I do not see why literature should not. In painting, though you may have eliminated everything else, you have at least a shape or a pattern and this is no doubt all you need; but it seems to me that literature is inevitably founded on ideas. Human speech is a tissue of ideas—however forms and colors may not be—and it seems more or less impossible for a work of literature to be anything but an arrangement of ideas.

Compare the scene in the "pub" in *Ulysses*, in which a somewhat similar use of language is made, with one of Gertrude Stein's "plays": in the former the queer devices are effective because we know what the author is trying to describe; but in the latter they go for nothing because we do not know what the "play" is all about. Miss Stein no longer understands the conditions under which literary effects have to be produced. There is sometimes a genuine music in the most baffling of her works, but there are rarely any communicated emotions. When Gertrude Stein succeeds in her new manner it is as any other poet succeeds, through coining an idea miraculously into words. But it is not, in the long run, I believe, as a painter of cubist still-lifes after Braque. And, in any case, it is in her *thought* that we are chiefly interested, and it is precisely her thought which we now rarely get. We figure her as the great pyramidal Buddha of Mr. Jo Davidson's statue, ruminating eternally on the ebb and flood of life, registering impressions like some august seismograph. And we cannot but regret that the results of her meditations are communicated to us in oracles.

Vanity Fair, September 1923

Bernard Shaw Since the War

Saint Joan, by Bernard Shaw

No one was ever more perturbed than Bernard Shaw by the disgraces and the failures of humanity; they have indeed been his chief preoccupation; but no one has ever been clearer than he as to exactly what is causing the trouble and exactly what is necessary to prevent it. His plays, though they have constituted exceedingly complex presentations of the conflicting prejudices and interests of society, have almost invariably ended cheerfully enough with a precise indication of the solution—and the preface has usually supplied an even more explicit analysis concluding with a clause by clause program for action.

In Major Barbara, for example, we have at the end a sort of allegorical group of Religion wedded to Culture taking over Industry; in Androcles and the Lion, Brute Force and Humanitarianism defying Tyranny; and in Getting Married the unknown spiritual quantity which will satisfy the whole set of ill-balanced marital equations is definitely discovered, just before the curtain, to be that of "Christian fellowship." A constructive critic was precisely what Mr. Shaw was—constructive almost to excess.

In Mr. Shaw's world before the war there were no insoluble problems. Political and economic salvation—which implied all the other kinds—were unarguably to be effected by Socialism and Socialism was to be effected through the orderly process of education and penetration undertaken by the Fabian Society. There was much indignation in Shaw but no real pessimism. And it was impossible for him to take other dramatists seriously when they wrote in scepticism or despair: Shakespeare's tragedies, for all their genius, he has always regarded as fundamentally unsatisfactory because they offer no constructive criticism of life and Molière's masterpiece, Le Misanthrope, he has characterized as the author's "dullest and worst play" because, like Hamlet or Antony and Cleopatra, it presents a desperate impasse of character which is obviously insusceptible of being resolved by the application of a Shavian formula. For all his intelligence, the tendency of Shaw has always been to simplify too much—to substitute a sort of Puritan morality having its sanction in Socialism, for the Puritan morality having its sanction in the Bible, which he was reacting against.

All this does still, of course, to some extent hold true. In the preface to Back to Methuselah, for example, he seems to suppose that the "Life Force" presented in that "Metabiological Pentateuch" somehow constitutes a substitute for that religion which he finds so disastrously lacking in the modern world. But, on the whole, he has unmistakably since the War shown signs both of a longer view of human affairs and of a deeper feeling for human nature. His latest plays do fall short, to be sure, of the electricity and vividness of the old ones, but on the other hand, if they are somewhat less sharp they are also somewhat less cocky and, in any case, present a relief from the sterile formula of such comedies as Misalliance and Overruled which no amount of intellectual energy could make either convincing as life or acceptable as art. For one thing, both in Heartbreak House and the last section of Back to Methuselah there appears, however unwinningly conveyed, some genuine feeling for the disappointments and enthusiasms of lovers—a subject which, with scarcely even an exception in the instance of Candida, he has insisted upon regarding as a lot of romantic nonsense intended to stultify what at its best could be conceded as hardly more than an agreeable biological necessity. Heartbreak House is perhaps the first play of Shaw's which actually has any heartbreak in it, and it differs also from almost all its predecessors in failing to end with quite the neat Q. E. D. which has usually closed his demonstrations. Just as in some of his political speeches after the War and his published lecture on Ruskin's Politics he seemed finally to have become capable of doubting the ultimate efficacy of the methods of the Fabians—so in Back to Methuselah he takes us for the first time beyond the best that Socialism may be expected to do, through the regression of European society to a sort of unorganized Arcadia and to the final enfranchisement of the human spirit as a set of vortices in space—a solution which disposes of the problem of life only by announcing it all to begin over again and a triumph which must be admitted to give rise to feelings of horror and despair.

Now in Saint Joan we get no such ultimate victory of the saint as we did in Androcles and the Lion: on the contrary, what is unexpected in Shaw, we find the forces of tradition and authority represented as equally intelligent and morally admirable with the heretic and the rebel and, instead of being left with the reassuring inference that the catastrophe of Joan—like the disillusionment of Major Barbara or the embitterment of Vivie Warren—is merely a sacrifice which will immediately bear fruit in a more intelligent program of social reconstruction, we are left with the moral that the same thing may happen again. "My God! my God! why hast thou forsaken me?" cries Major Barbara in her hour of anguish; but immediately afterwards she readjusts her ideas of God in such a way as still to find Him at the helm of her readjusted world. "How long, O Lord, how long?" cries Saint Joan; but they are her last words in the play.

Not that Shaw has been seduced from his rôle of social critic by the purely pathetic possibilities of Joan. He has managed one or two capital dramatic moments, of a kind rather rare with him, in which it is predominantly the personality of Joan which holds us—such as the scene in which she rouses the Dauphin and his partisans to follow her lead against the English. But primarily Saint Joan, like Shaw's other plays, is a criticism of society—only longer-sighted and less hopeful than has been his wont. Most of the really thrilling passages are those in which we feel the great forces of human history at work—the scene in the tent between Warwick and Cauchon in which the Bishop prophesies the downfall of Europe as the result of the disruption of the Catholic Church and the later scenes in which we realize Joan's predicament caught between the institution to which she is dangerous and the nation which she has helped to defeat. I do not see how those critics who have objected to the Epilogue can really understand what the play is about: if the Epilogue were to go, the tent scene would have to go, too—as would also the Inquisitor's speech and a great deal more; we should, in fact, have to have a different play built on different lines, and with Joan's individual tragedy and not human history as its theme.

Saint Joan, like Shaw's other plays, however—though in a somewhat less degree than many of them—is not free from the characteristic over-rationalizations of the social historian turned dramatist. Shaw is reported to have said that every time he saw a play of Tchekov's he felt like throwing all his own into the fire and it is quite easy to see why: Tchekov is able to have his characters convey to us their aims, their prejudices and their places in society not only with an incomparable economy which is no less telling than Shaw's prolixity, but also without ever doing violence to the likelihood of the way in which they are made to reveal themselves: whereas Shaw has been largely restricted to having his characters make out logically reasoned cases for them and defend them with debaters' skill. This is true even in the case of Saint Joan, who sometimes seems disconcertingly out of key with the naive faith of the middle ages. In one passage particularly she is allowed to rationalize her point of view beyond all bounds of probability or dramatic propriety. When Baudricourt assures her that her divine Voices are the products of her imagination, she replies all too sensibly, "Of course. That is how the messages of God come to us." And Shaw has over-explained not only in the case of Joan but also to some extent even in the cases of those other characters who may more reasonably be supposed to have understood what they were doing: the Bishop of Beauvais and the Earl of Warwick are made perfectly aware both of the functions they fill in contemporary civilization and of their subsequent places in history and even designate the tendencies they are discussing and which were then in their infancy with names like Protestantism and Nationalism which could only have existed when these were mature. Shaw says in this connection:

It is the business of the stage to make its figures more intelligible to themselves than they would be in real life; for by no other means can they be made intelligible to the audience . . . the play would be unintelligible if I had not endowed them (the Earl of Warwick, the Inquisitor and Bishop) with enough of this consciousness to enable them to explain their attitude to the twentieth century . . . beyond this neither drama nor history can go in my hands.

This last sentence, though evidently not intended for one, reads like a confession of limitation and I believe, in fact, that this over-explicitness marks Shaw's worst weakness as a dramatic artist—his imperfect grasp of "character in action." The business of the dramatist should be precisely, as Tchekov does, to find a means of making things intelligible without suggesting to the audience that it is hearing a book read instead of witnessing a real event. To have kept out the language of written history would have been to heighten the illusion of reality, and to have heightened the illusion of reality would have been to intensify the drama.

But even if Saint Joan—like Back to Methuselah—had never been intended by its author to be acted, it would still be a work of extraordinary interest. What these later plays of Shaw's remind one of rather than of any other acted drama are the series of Drames Philosophiques which Renan wrote in his old age; these two bodies of work present some striking resemblances and it is interesting to compare them: both are dramas of ideas and in some cases of the same ideas but, beside Renan, who has traveled in his life-time over the whole geography of ideas of humanity and who has learned a polite hesitation about preferring one to another, Shaw even in his later and more tolerant phases shows a little provincial and harshly Protestant: such historical values as the point of view of the mediæval church with which Renan was familiar from boyhood are brought to our attention by Shaw at this late date with something of an air of excitement and surprise and the scepticism of all politics and politicians at which Renan had arrived before the end of the last century comes to Shaw in Back to Methuselah as the last disillusion of old age. Yet beside Renan, Shaw shows a kind of fire which sometimes gives a superiority to limited ideas over more learned and wiser ones. Shaw's demonstrations and programs and systems are probably much less important than he thinks and their defects consequently less important than his critics think them. What is important is the imagination with which they are illustrated and the intensity with which they are expressed. It is these which have really spoken to us in Shaw and which continue to speak to us even now that his brand-new, one-hundred-percent-efficient social system has begun to lose credit not only with us but with the inventor himself.

W. B. Yeats

THE twentieth century, though it has turned out a great deal of verse, has so far produced very little poetry of the first order. It would seem that the conditions under which we live are not favorable to the kind of emotions appropriate to poetry. A great poet must take himself seriously; he must believe in his own dignity and the nobility of his emotions; he must be willing to identify himself with the god with whom he was formerly supposed to be inspired. But today that is rather difficult. For one thing, we have learned to see ourselves scientifically: we are conscious of our kinship with the other animals and of our subjection to physical laws, rather than of our relation to the gods. Our great men of imagination seem often to occupy themselves with scientific theory rather than with poetry. And for another thing, we are living in the first phases of democratic society—a period when the distinction of the poet—or any other kind—is more difficult than it was at a time when fewer people were educated, but those who were had to meet a higher standard and when the dominating ideals of civilization were less completely identified with commercial enterprise. Instead of poetry, we have the novel, which has become the characteristic modern literary form because it admits more easily of the point of view of science, with which it has always been closely allied, and because by its looser form it lends itself to the journalism and by its more familiar tone to the less distinguished events, of a democratic society. Flaubert and his followers or those who were under the influence of the French novel of the time—Turgeniev and James and Joyce—have succeeded in bringing to the novel the sort of concentration and artistic integrity which had hitherto chiefly been found in the poem or poetic play; but a poem would scarcely have been an equally appropriate vehicle for the tone of irony which in these writers arises both from the scientific point of view and from the phenomena of a middle-class society. In the meantime, on the other hand, from Byron's Don Juan, through Browning, to the "novels in verse" of Mr. E. A. Robinson, the long poem has shown a tendency to assimilate itself to the novel and in

proportion as it has done so has fallen short of succeeding as
poetry.

Now Mr. W. B. Yeats is one of the only men living who, in
spite of these unfavorable influences, has taken poetry with
thorough-going seriousness and achieved success of the highest order. In an age when writers of verse have as a rule either
been content to drop the grand manner and adopt the language and point of view of the newspapers or, if they try to
sustain a noble mien, do so with self-consciousness and with a
patent artificiality, Mr. Yeats has worn his robe and wreath as if
they were a legitimate inheritance. The dignity of the poet sits
naturally upon him and not like a deliberately assumed disguise.
Yet it is interesting to see, in connection with the present situation of poetry, what comprehensive and resolute rejections
Mr. Yeats has been obliged to make in order to preserve this
rôle. He has had to turn his back on the whole scientific democratic world, and stand apart from the questions which agi-
tate it. That he has been distinctly conscious of taking up a
position appears from his autobiographical writings: he tells
for example, in The Trembling of the Veil, of the vital issue
which seemed to be raised for him in his youth by the then
popular and novel "realism" of Bastien-Lepage as against the
mysticism of the pre-Raphaelite painters. The Joan of Arc of
Bastien-Lepage already to the young Yeats meant the scientific
vision which contradicted and destroyed his own.

The passages in which he discusses Bernard Shaw are particularly illuminating. Shaw—an Irishman come to London like
himself and a man of equal imaginative force and intellectual
ability—chose the opposite road from Yeats and took on the
whole unwieldy cargo of the modern world—sociology, economics, physical science and journalism. Shaw heroically
shouldered it all; but Yeats as systematically eschewed it, and
says that, with all admiration for Shaw, he was sometimes appalled by the aspect of his work, which had taken on the character of the materials with which it dealt and become "so
much metropolitan lead and solder." The only sciences which
Yeats pursued were those which, with poetry, were sinking to
decay—astrology, clairvoyancy and magic. While Mr. Shaw
was grappling with Marx, Mr. Yeats was editing Blake: and it is
significant that Mr. Yeats, whose sense of reality is not inferior

to that of any scientist or realist living, should seem to feel a
belief in the supernatural to be somehow bound up with the
faith in the poet's vision. Yet the comparative difficulty of this
belief, even for Mr. Yeats himself, indicates the profound gulf
which science has fixed between the present and the past. It
does not seem ridiculous for Dante to have believed in his visions; nor even for Blake to have believed in his. But it does
somehow seem ridiculous for Mr. Yeats to believe in Madame
Blavatsky's. He himself, as I say, appears unsatisfied: one feels,
in his narration of his supernatural experiences, a margin of
scientific doubt. Like Huysmans, he betrays an instinct to scrutinize and check them up that is disastrous to genuine mysticism. Yet I do not want to suggest that Mr. Yeats would have
got any further if he had occupied himself with legitimate science. His writings on mysticism are full of great intelligence and
great imaginative insight and his theories—such as that which
postulates a sea of racial images rolling to and fro through the
mind of humanity—are often impressive, despite the fact that
they have been arrived at mystically instead of through the
methods of modern psychology.

None the less, for all his isolation and his occultism, Mr.
Yeats has in another direction been closely related to the contemporary consciousness. He is the greatest representative in
English of the modern literary movement originally known as
Symbolism, which constitutes perhaps the only important
poetic development since the beginning of the seventies—that
is, the only successful attempt to adapt poetry to the changing
mentality of the western world. The later Yeats does, to be
sure, present striking differences from most of the later practitioners of Symbolism: one of the most popular discoveries of
the movement has come to be that tragi-comic vein originally
worked by Corbière and Laforgue and recently imported into
English by Mr. T. S. Eliot. This has provided a vehicle in verse
for the ironic tone of which I have spoken in Flaubert and
Joyce and has turned it to real poetic account. The poignancy
of these writers results from the conflict in them between the
poet's conviction of nobility and the universal banality of the
modern man. Like Flaubert in Trois Contes, like Joyce in
Ulysses, they are contrasting their own lives unfavorably with
some other kind of life of which they believe men once to have

been capable. But Yeats has never exploited this vein because he has never been infected by that banality. The dreary summer resort closing for the winter which discouraged Jules Laforgue, the afternoon teas which inhibit Mr. Eliot, do not disconcert Mr. Yeats; he does not feel life in terms of these things; his temperament stands as far removed from them as his round tower in Ireland does. Another popular development of Symbolism has been in the direction of obscurity. The Symbolists, coasting down the slope of romanticism away from objective description and universal emotions, arrived at a highly special subjective language for unique individual sensations. The danger was, as appeared from the beginning in Mallarmé, that either on account of insufficiently vivid sensations or insufficient skill in suggesting them, the poet would become unintelligible. The formula of Symbolism, which admits such a confusion of images and ideas, has always enabled a great deal of nonsense to pass for poetry. It has also encouraged a great deal of arid ingenuity, such as we find in much of the work of Miss Edith Sitwell, Mr. Wallace Stevens and M. Tristan Tzara.

Mr. Yeats has escaped all these tendencies but he derives essentially from the same school as these other writers. The images of symbolistic poetry stand in a somewhat different relation to the sensations they are supposed to convey than the metaphors of more classical poetry to the things they are supposed to describe: it has been suggested that the characteristic of Symbolism was to allow the subconscious to possess itself of the waking mind and to put together what images it chose with a minimum of rational scrutiny; and certainly the successful poetry of Symbolism has something of the significance in irrelevance of dreams. Now a great deal of Yeats answers to this description as well as Mallarmé or Rimbaud. As Mr. Padraic Colum has pointed out, much of Mr. Yeats's Irish mythology —the Danaan children, the Shadowy Horses and Fergus with his brazen cars—has no more exact meaning than Verlaine's "guêpe ivre de son vol fou" or Rimbaud's angels and unearthly coaches and apocalyptic landscapes. They are simply the shadows by which he hopes to suggest certain complexes of feelings and ideas. His symbolistic affinities become especially plain in such a poem as the recently published Black

Centaur, which makes no use of Irish mythology and which resembles exactly certain things of Rimbaud. In all this, Mr. Yeats differs from the general stream of contemporary English poetry, as distinguished from American and Irish. The Modern Georgians, of whom I suppose Mr. Masefield is the chief, have never been Symbolists—nor has Mr. A. E. Housman.

So much for Mr. Yeats in relation to the ideas and influences of his time: any further account of him must concern itself with the development of his individual genius. This genius first manifested itself in the iridescent brilliance of his early poetry, which stained a sort of Shelleyan fluidity with a sort of Keatsian richness of color: The Wanderings of Oisin may be taken indeed as Mr. Yeats's Endymion. If he had never written anything else but this long poem and such lyrics as The Lake-Isle of Innisfree and The Man Who Dreamed of Fairyland, he would still, as the creator of a new sort of strangeness, have been a considerable poet. And indeed many people seem to suppose that Mr. Yeats's career began and ended with these early rainbows. Yet they have proved scarcely more than a romantic prelude to his more important poetry. Some time about the beginning of the century, Mr. Yeats tells us in his autobiography, he became dissatisfied with this early work and resolved to eliminate rigorously from his style both romantic rhetoric and symbolistic vagueness. He would reduce it to something definite and hard; something both severer and more intense. In a poem which is at once an example of this later style and a description of it, he says that—

> Maybe a twelvemonth since
> Suddenly I began,
> In scorn of this audience
> Imagining a man,
> And his sun-freckled face,
> And grey Connemara cloth,
> Climbing up to a place
> Where stone is dark under froth,
> And the down turn of his wrist
> When the flies drop in the stream:
> A man who does not exist,

> A man who is but a dream;
> And cried, "Before I am old
> I shall have written him one
> Poem maybe as cold
> And passionate as the dawn."

The change to this new style is seen very clearly in the collected volume of Later Poems* which has just been published in America. The first pieces in the collection—those originally included in The Wind Among the Reeds and dating from 1899 —are still ornamented with "the flaming lute-thronged angelic door" and "the heaven's embroidered cloths—enwrought with golden and silver light" of the younger Yeats. But by 1912 these pre-Raphaelite growths have been completely rooted out. He has worked into a soberer and solider style from which the soap-bubble colors have vanished and left only the clear aspect of "cold Clare rock and Galway rock and thorn."

He has become less prodigal of symbols and names and those symbols which he does employ have acquired a new austerity —a new purity and precision—

> I call to the eye of the mind
> A well long choked up and dry
> And boughs long stripped by the wind,
> And I call to the mind's eye
> Pallor of an ivory face,
> Its lofty dissolute air,
> A man climbing up to a place
> The salt sea wind has swept bare.

When he revisits the heroic world of Irish mythology it is seen with a new homeliness of detail. And more and more he fixes upon the imperfect world in which he actually finds himself. He desires, as he says in another part of the poem about the fisherman, "To write for my own race And for the reality." And again—

*Later Poems, Plays, Plays and Controversies, Essays, by W. B. Yeats. New York: the Macmillan Company. $2.50 each. The first four volumes of a new collected edition of Yeats, to be complete in six volumes. The last two volumes—Early Poems and Stories, and Autobiography—are announced for early publication.

> Through all the lying days of my youth
> I swayed my leaves and flowers in the sun;
> Now I may wither into the truth.

With a boldness rewarded by a success unequalled among his English contemporaries, he undertakes to intensify into poetry the circumstances of his own life and the events of the life about him. And this he does, not by vulgarizing his style, but by dignifying his subjects—at the same time that he does not cease to deal with them in the plainest language. He can even challenge comparison with Dante—whom he now describes as "the chief imagination of Christendom"—in his ability to achieve a grand manner by sheer intensity without rhetoric.

How he suggests the sharpness of Dante's allusions, for example, in the following passage:

> Traders or soldiers who have left me blood
> That has not passed through any huxter's loin,
> Pardon, and you that did not weigh the cost,
> Old Butlers when you took to horse and stood
> Beside the brackish waters of the Boyne
> Till your bad master blenched and all was lost.

And Dante's scorn in the following—

> Why should I blame her that she filled my days
> With misery, or that she would of late
> Have taught to ignorant men most violent ways,
> Or hurled the little streets against the great,
> Had they but courage equal to desire?

Mr. Yeats has assumed a Dantesque mask of pride—but has a Dantesque exaltation as well as bitterness—

> And what of her that took
> All till my youth was gone
> With scarce a pitying look?
> How should I praise that one?
> When day begins to break
> I count my good and bad,
> Being wakeful for her sake,

> Remembering what she had,
> What eagle look still shows,
> While up from my heart's root
> So great a sweetness flows
> I shake from head to foot.

Yet the development of this later style seems to coincide with a disillusion which first definitely appears in the poetry of about fifteen years ago. He had made the fairies in one of his earliest poems tell the child whom they were leading away that "the world is more full of weeping than you can understand"; but he can no longer escape to fairyland like the heroes of his early poems. He cannot evade the frustrations of life and in general the ecstasies with which he offsets them are such as life actually offers within its own limits. The acute consciousness of these limits has brought his art to a sharper focus. The unbinding of "youth's dreamy load" has made him a better poet. It is as if, no longer hoping much from anything but poetry, he had applied to it as never before all the diligence of his mind and the energy of his passion. One almost fears that the occasional tendency of his very latest work to run to a new sort of rhetoric of its own may be the unavoidable result of his recent re-entry into Irish politics. But it would make little difference if it were: the bulk of poetry contained in this collected volume—with which should be reckoned the Four Plays for Dancers*—constitutes a contribution to literature not only quite outranking any but two or three even possible others by living writers in English but probably comparable only to the very greatest in its kind in the world.

Mr. Yeats is one of the few genuine masters alive—perhaps the only poet of the first magnitude. And it is to be hoped that the publication of this new volume—which includes some matter hitherto inaccessible—will give his later work a wider audience. As I have suggested, the popular conception of Mr. Yeats seems hitherto to have limited itself to the cliché of an agreeable but innocuous "mystic" identified with "the Lake of Innisfree" and the Celtic Twilight.

*Plays and Controversies, by W. B. Yeats, New York: the Macmillan Co. $2.50.

Bernard Shaw once predicted that when the contemporaries of Eugène Brieux died and went to Heaven they would be almost as much ashamed to acknowledge they did not know anything about his plays as the dead Elizabethans would have been to confess they had never heard of Shakespeare. If this were to be said today of Mr. Yeats, it would be a great deal more appropriate and calculated, I should say, to avert a more considerable danger. Three years ago, the volume of Plays for Dancers, which showed the later Yeats at his very best, took second place or third place or no place in the columns of the literary reviews, while Mr. Cabell, Mr. Hergesheimer and Mr. Huxley got their liberal front pages.

> A woman's beauty is like a white
> Frail bird, like a white sea-bird alone
> At daybreak after a stormy night
> Between two furrows upon the ploughed land;
> A sudden storm and it was thrown
> Between dark furrows upon the ploughed land.
> How many centuries spent
> The sedentary soul
> In toils of measurement
> Beyond eagle or mole,
> Beyond hearing or seeing,
> Or Archimedes' guess,
> To raise into being that loveliness?
>
> A strange unserviceable thing,
> A fragile, exquisite, pale shell,
> That the vast troubled waters bring
> To the loud sands before day has broken.
> The storm arose and suddenly fell
> Amid the dark before day had broken.
> What death? what discipline?
> What bonds no man could unbind
> Being imagined within
> The labyrinth of the mind,
> What pursuing or fleeing,
> What wounds, what bloody press
> Dragged into being
> This loveliness.

The book which contained this lyric and much else had little to say to our critics in general and aroused no excitement or awe among them. But, unlike most of the works which took precedence to it, it could afford to wait and lie idle: it was written for a long life.

CHRONOLOGY

NOTE ON THE TEXTS

NOTES

INDEX

Chronology

1895   Born Edmund Wilson Jr. on May 8 in Red Bank, New Jersey, the only child of Edmund Wilson and Helen Mather Kimball, after a difficult delivery during which his mother was injured by his large head. (Father, son of a Presbyterian minister, was born in Shrewsbury, New Jersey, in 1863. After attending Princeton and Columbia Law School, he began a successful civil and criminal trial practice in 1891. Mother, daughter of a homeopathic physician, was born in Eatontown, New Jersey, in 1865 and attended Abbot Academy in Andover, Massachusetts. She married Edmund Wilson Sr. in 1892. She was interested in outdoor sports and gardening.) Mother calls him "Bunny," since he looks "just like a plum-bun."

1899–1907 Father begins to suffer from morbid hypochondria after his brother dies from Bright's disease. Mother loses much of her hearing. Edmund enters Shrewsbury Academy. Takes nature walks with aunt Laura Kimball; looks up to his uncle Reuel Kimball, pillar of the family and father of his cousin Sandy (Reuel Kimball Jr.), who becomes his inseparable companion. His Wilson grandmother reads him the Old Testament stories that had molded his father. Loves summer family reunions in upstate New York—the old stone house in Talcottville (bought by his father from his mother's relatives), the open countryside with its hills and lofty skies, large dairy farms, and dark rivers: "We fished and swam in the rivers, had all sorts of excursions and games." Develops a lifelong interest in performing magic tricks.

1908   Visits Europe with his family, traveling to Italy, Austria, Bohemia, Germany, France, and England.

1908–10   Father is appointed Attorney General of New Jersey by Republican governor John Franklin Fort and serves until 1914; he will impress Democratic governor Woodrow Wilson (no relation) by his successful prosecution of the corrupt Republican political machine in Atlantic City.

1909–12   Wilson attends the Hill School in Pottstown, Pennsylva-
            nia, where he makes literary friends and begins to think of
            himself as a writer and critic. John A. Lester, an English
            teacher from the Lake District, impresses on him the
            rhetorical trinity of "Lucidity, Force, and Ease"; in a trib-
            ute in *The Triple Thinkers*, Wilson will describe Alfred
            Rolfe, his Greek master, as "the perfect Hellenist" who
            made him feel "that there was . . . something exhilarat-
            ing in the air of the classroom, human, heroic, and shin-
            ing." Writes fiction, satire, and literary essays, for school
            literary magazine. Reads with enthusiasm Hippolyte
            Taine's *History of English Literature* (which he discovers
            in his father's library), Shaw, and Mencken; rejects the
            evangelical Christianity inculcated at Hill.

1912–16   Attends Princeton University. Discovers the American
            classics, including Emerson, Whitman, Mark Twain, and
            Henry James. Serves on the editorial board of the *Nassau
            Literary Magazine* and contributes poems, stories, re-
            views, and editorials. Deeply influenced by professors
            Norman Kemp Smith, a Scottish philosopher who inter-
            prets Kant and Hume, and Christian Gauss, who teaches
            Dante and French literature, seeking to reconcile Neo-
            Classical aesthetic with history and biography. Reads and
            admires the criticism of Sainte-Beuve. Forms friendships
            with John Peale Bishop and F. Scott Fitzgerald. Spends
            summer of 1914 in England, where he begins the series of
            notebooks and journals that he will continue to keep for
            almost six decades, and is in London when war is declared
            on August 4. With Fitzgerald collaborates on *The Evil
            Eye*, a musical comedy presented by Princeton's Triangle
            Club in 1915.

1916–17   After graduation attends summer military camp at Platts-
            burgh, New York, and decides he cannot participate in
            killing "in cold blood." When his father, who has told him
            he will have to support himself, asks about his plans, he
            proposes "to learn something about all the main depart-
            ments of human thought." With help from his father, gets
            job as reporter for the *New York Evening Sun*. Lives at 15
            West 8th Street, New York City. Enlists in U.S. Army Med-
            ical Corps in June, and is sent to France in November 1917.

1918   Serves as an orderly at base hospital in Vittel. After period
            of relative inactivity in which he has time to read and

write ("I have decided to begin the writing of my subsequent books, war or no war," he informs Fitzgerald), begins treating wounded men in June, including burned victims of mustard gas. Treats victims of the flu epidemic; patrols halls to keep crazed patients from jumping out of windows; attends deathbeds and assists an elderly undertaker on his rounds, sometimes piling bodies up "like logs." Shortly before the Armistice, his father gets him transferred to intelligence section at U.S. General Headquarters at Chaumont. Enjoys the company of cynical reporters doing propaganda work.

1919   Reads reports on European political crises, the Allies' rival ambitions, and affairs in revolutionary Russia. Returns to New York in July. Shocked to learn his cousin Sandy has been institutionalized after a nervous breakdown and diagnosed as schizophrenic. Gratified that his father shares his outrage at mass arrests of radicals ordered by U.S. attorney general Mitchell Palmer. Moves into an apartment on West 12th St. Writes steadily and submits work to magazines. Submits a parody to *Vanity Fair*, which attracts the favorable attention of Dorothy Parker; as a result of her recommendation, he is hired to read manuscripts at the magazine. When Parker and Robert Benchley leave the staff in quick succession, Wilson replaces Benchley as managing editor (he will fill the post off and on until 1923). John Peale Bishop joins staff as Wilson's assistant.

1920   Writes a literary column in *Vanity Fair* as well as reviews and essays for *The Dial*, *The New Republic*, and others. Meets John Dos Passos, later to become a close friend, and Edna St. Vincent Millay, whose poetry he promotes in *Vanity Fair*. Writes essay appraising H. L. Mencken. Has first sexual experience with Millay in July 1920 and writes impassioned letters to her: "I suppose all this is pretty casual to you, but it's not to me, as you know." Proposes marriage to Millay during a visit to her in Provincetown; she rejects the offer.

1921   Begins affair with actress Mary Blair, whom he first sees onstage in Eugene O'Neill's *Diff'rent* in February. Has started to drink heavily. Spends summer in France and Italy. Meets Jean Cocteau and Djuna Barnes in Paris.

Writes to Fitzgerald of his hopes "for New York as a cultural center just now—America seems to be actually beginning to express herself in something like an idiom of her own," although "the intellectual and aesthetic manifestations have to crowd their way up and out from between the crevices left by the factories, the office buildings, the apartment houses, and the banks."

1922   *The Undertaker's Garland*, a collection of verse and prose by Wilson and Bishop, is published by Alfred A. Knopf. Writes scores of reviews; topics include *The Waste Land*, *Ulysses*, W. B. Yeats, Edith Wharton, Fitzgerald, and others; also writes sketches of popular culture and the New York scene. Becomes close friend of poet Elinor Wylie, who joins staff of *Vanity Fair*. Lives with Hill classmate and occasional *Vanity Fair* contributor Ted Paramore. Moves in November into a corner room with bath in the same apartment building on University Place where Wylie lives.

1923   Marries Mary Blair, who is pregnant, on February 14. Leaves *Vanity Fair*. Father dies of pneumonia in May. Father's will, made decades earlier, leaves his mother in charge of his estate, so Wilson will be dependent on her to supplement his earnings as editor, critic, and journalist, a situation that leads to strains in their relationship. Lives in Brookhaven, Long Island, with Mary, before they move first to Brooklyn and then to the University Place building, where he rents half a floor. Meets D. H. Lawrence in August and writes an essay on Gertrude Stein in September. Daughter Rosalind Baker Wilson born September 19, 1923.

1924   Wilson's *The Crime in the Whistler Room* is produced by the Provincetown Players in New York, with Mary Blair in the lead role. Travels to California in an unsuccessful effort to persuade to Charlie Chaplin to act in his ballet "Chronkite's Clocks"; during his stay Ted Paramore introduces him to an unhappily married friend, Margaret Canby. Literary friends include E. E. Cummings, Louise Bogan, and Paul Rosenfeld. Wilson writes first American review of Ernest Hemingway's *In Our Time*.

1925   Hired as reviewer and reporter for *The New Republic* (where he will serve as literary editor, 1926–31). Covers New York night-life—theater, vaudeville, movies, music—

as well as literature; publishes essays on Yeats and Henry James; will solicit material for the magazine from writers including E. E. Cummings, Louise Bogan, Allen Tate, Malcolm Cowley, and Ernest Hemingway.

1926   Vacations in New Orleans, where he meets Sherwood Anderson. Separates from Mary Blair; moves to a sparsely furnished room on West 13th Street that will remain his base for several years. Rosalind is by now under the care of Wilson's mother in Red Bank, where he spends weekends. *Discordant Encounters: Plays and Dialogues* published by Albert and Charles Boni.

1927   Begins affair with Frances Minihan, a Ukrainian-American waitress and taxi-dancer whom he meets at the Tango Gardens on 14th Street in February (at a time when her husband is in prison for car theft). Contracts gonorrhea but is cured. Becomes deeply involved with Frances, in a sexual relationship complicated by class differences. Begins to write detailed accounts of their lovemaking in his journals. Responds to execution of anarchists Sacco and Vanzetti in short story "The Men from Rumplemayer's."

1928   Writes essay on Proust for *The New Republic*. Completes a draft of *I Thought of Daisy*, a novel set in Greenwich Village. Becomes a drinking companion of Margaret Canby, who has moved to New York after her divorce, and in April they begin an affair. While Canby is in Paris during the spring, Wilson seduces the poet Léonie Adams, but this affair goes no further. Continues to see Frances Minihan. Takes leave from *The New Republic* in the fall to stay at a beach house near Canby's home in Santa Barbara, where he revises *I Thought of Daisy*. During same period, works on critical study *Axel's Castle*; assures Max Perkins of Scribner's that "popular accounts" of the modernist writers whom he views as emerging from French Symbolism will "persuade people to read them." Shocked by death from a stroke of Elinor Wylie at age 43 in December.

1929   In February, after finishing *I Thought of Daisy*, suffers a nervous collapse marked by acute anxiety and indecision. Spends three and a half weeks at the Clifton Springs Sanitarium in upstate New York; while there begins assembling a collection of his poems, *Poets, Farewell!*, and resumes work on *Axel's Castle*. Scribner's publishes *I Thought of Daisy* in August. Chapters from *Axel's Castle* are serialized in *The New Republic* in the fall and winter. Breaks off affair with Frances Minihan; asks Canby to come east for the winter.

1930 Obtains divorce from Mary Blair in February. Marries Margaret Canby on May 8. Spends summer on Cape Cod with Margaret, Rosalind, and Margaret's son Jimmy in house belonging to Eugene O'Neill. Reads Marx; discusses politics with John Dos Passos, his neighbor on the Cape. In the fall moves with Margaret into a residential hotel on Fifth Avenue. Begins to write political journalism on a regular basis.

1931 *Axel's Castle: A Study in the Imaginative Literature of 1870–1930* published by Scribner's. Publishes "Appeal to Progressives" to "take Communism away from the Communists" in *The New Republic*. Reports on demonstrations, suicides, and other signs of social tension in New York City. Gives up editor's job to crisscross the country as a reporter. Publishes "Detroit Motors," a portrait of the Ford assembly line. Reports on independent radical unions and the case of the Scottsboro Boys; visits with Allen Tate in Tennessee. In the summer Margaret, who has been left behind on these travels, meets him in New Mexico and they go on to Santa Barbara. In "The Jumping-Off Place," he contrasts a luxury hotel in San Diego with a catalog of recent suicides in the city. When he returns east, Margaret remains in California for several months, where she is sometimes despondent.

1932 In February, with Malcolm Cowley, Mary Heaton Vorse, and others, participates in delivery of food and clothing to striking miners in Kentucky. *The American Jitters: A Year of the Slump* published by Scribner's in the spring. Supports Communist presidential candidate William Z. Foster as a protest vote. Drinks heavily and quarrels with Margaret; she goes to California for the summer without him. He works on a play, drinks bathtub gin, and writes political and historical essays; stays on Cape Cod with Rosalind. On two occasions he sees Frances, who wants to be his lover again. Learns on returning to New York in late September that Margaret has died after falling down a flight of stone stairs in Santa Barbara while leaving a party. Flies to California for funeral; wonders if her death could have been a suicide. In lengthy notes begun immediately afterward, remarks: "After she was dead, I loved her." Rents house at 314 East 53rd Street for $50 a month. Visits Jane Addams at Hull House in November and writes an account of Chicago slums.

1933–34   Records impressions of Roosevelt and early New Deal. Spends drunken evening with Fitzgerald and Hemingway in January 1933. Receives visit from T. S. Eliot in May. Resumes affair with Frances. Begins affair with old friend Louise Fort Connor, who is now unhappily married, meeting her occasionally in Chicago, Massachusetts, and New York. Enjoys close literary friendships with Louise Bogan, with whom he reads poetry and studies German, and John Dos Passos, with whom he argues about literature and politics, including developments in the Soviet Union. In 1934 joins editorial board of radical *Modern Monthly*. Conceives a history of revolutionary socialism to be told in terms of personalities. Plans trip to the Soviet Union, funded by a Guggenheim fellowship. Dos Passos enlists the aid of Maxim Gorki to help Wilson obtain a visa, and warns him to avoid political indiscretions in Moscow.

1935   Makes final break with Frances. Leaves for Europe in May; from London sails to Leningrad on Soviet ship, *Berengaria*. After five days in Leningrad, travels to Moscow. Since he is not a member of the Communist Party and is known to associate with American Trotskyites, he is denied permission to work in the Marx-Engels-Lenin Institute. Attends Soviet theatrical productions. Tours collective farm in early June. Meets literary critic D. S. Mirsky (who will be arrested in 1937 and die in the Gulag in 1939). Troubled by cult of Stalin ("This glorification of Stalin is undoubtedly one of the things which affects an American most unpleasantly") and notes: "The atmosphere of fear and suspicion does really become oppressive." Visits Lenin's home in Ulyanovsk, as well as Stalingrad, Rostov-on-Don, Kiev, and Odessa. Becomes ill with scarlet fever while traveling, and is hospitalized for six weeks in chaotic and filthy Odessa hospital, where he is impressed by efficiency and modernity of the Communist Party nurse on the hospital staff and by the dedication of a doctor from the old nobility. Suffers acute kidney attack toward end of stay. Begins studying Russian in order to read Pushkin. Returns to U.S. in October by way of Paris, where he meets André Malraux and James Joyce.

1936   *Travels in Two Democracies*, a collection of reports on the
        United States and the Soviet Union, published by Har-
        court, Brace. To protect Soviet friends he leaves out
        darker aspects of his experience, but his account nonethe-
        less angers the Communists. Stays at rented rooms and in
        Red Bank. Moves in the fall from New York to "Trees,"
        a country house near Stamford, Connecticut, lent to him
        by a literary friend, the heiress Margaret de Silver.

1937   Dismayed by Moscow purge trials and critical of acquain-
        tances who attempt to defend them. Researches early
        utopian socialists for *To the Finland Station*. Publishes a
        play, *This Room and This Gin and These Sandwiches*. In
        September breaks off affair with Louise Connor and an-
        other with Elizabeth Waugh, a married friend on the
        Cape. At a lunch with editors of *Partisan Review* in the
        fall, meets Mary McCarthy (b. 1912), and within a few days
        they become lovers.

1938   Gives lecture at Harvard in January. Wilson and Mc-
        Carthy are married on February 10. He encourages her
        writing. *The Triple Thinkers: Ten Studies of Literature*
        published by Harcourt, Brace in the spring. In June,
        when Mary is two months pregnant, a violent episode (of
        which each will subsequently give very different accounts)
        leads her to spend three weeks in the Payne Whitney Psy-
        chiatric Clinic in New York, diagnosed as suffering from
        anxiety. They move from "Trees" to a house in Stamford.
        Mary enters therapy and resumes writing stories. Visited
        in November by Fitzgerald ("sober, industrious, com-
        pletely transformed") and Sheilah Graham. Son Reuel
        Kimball Wilson born on Christmas Day.

1939   Teaches summer courses at the University of Chicago on
        Dickens and on "Taine and the Marxist texts." Writes two
        long essays on Dickens that will be integrated in *The
        Wound and the Bow*. Meets Saul Bellow in Chicago. Wil-
        son and Mary spend the winter at Truro on Cape Cod.
        She works on her story collection *The Company She Keeps*
        and he on *To the Finland Station*.

1940   *To the Finland Station: A Study in the Writing and Acting
        of History* published in September by Harcourt, Brace.
        Works during the summer at Truro on *The Wound and
        the Bow*; in the fall returns to *The New Republic* as an
        editor. Vladimir Nabokov, newly arrived in the United

States, seeks him out and they begin a long association. Severs ties with *The New Republic* after the magazine's English owner abrogates the editors' independence to urge American intervention in World War II, which Wilson opposes. Fitzgerald, who has been corresponding with Wilson about *To the Finland Station* and his own Hollywood novel, dies on December 21.

1941   Buys a house on Cape Cod, in Wellfleet, with a bank loan and money borrowed from his mother, and moves in with Mary and Reuel during the summer. *The Boys in the Back Room: Notes on California Novelists*, series of essays on writers including John Steinbeck and Nathanael West, is published as a chapbook by Colt Press of San Francisco. *The Wound and the Bow: Seven Studies in Literature* is published by Houghton Mifflin. Edits Fitzgerald's unfinished novel *The Last Tycoon* for publication in October.

1942–43   *Note-Books of Night*, a collection containing memoirs along with romantic and satirical verse, is published by Colt Press in the fall of 1942. Marriage becomes increasingly strained. McCarthy has come to hate Wilson's drinking and spends long periods in New York undergoing psychoanalysis. Wilson helps Nabokov's American career, introducing him to editors and recommending him for reviewing assignments, teaching jobs, and a Guggenheim fellowship. Begins long friendship with Dawn Powell. *The Shock of Recognition*, his anthology documenting the responses of American writers to one another's work, is published by Doubleday in 1943. Works on a novel to be titled "The Story of the Three Wishes" (the only completed segment published in 1998 as *The Higher Jazz*) and on the stories eventually published in *Memoirs of Hecate County*.

1944   In January assumes position as a weekly book reviewer at *The New Yorker*, where most of his work of the next 25 years will first appear. Job enables him to move with Mary to an apartment on Gramercy Park. Their final summer together in Wellfleet is marked by a violent quarrel, after which Wilson promises to stop drinking and for a time keeps his promise. Friendship with Dawn Powell is momentarily chilled when he writes a critical review of her most recent novel, *My Home Is Far Away*, in November. Appalled by wartime propaganda and by Allied bombing campaigns, writes in his journal: "We have arrived now at the same state in which the Germans have been. We are bombing Berlin to cinders, but nobody talks about it."

1945   *The Crack-Up*, a collection of uncollected writings by Fitzgerald, edited by Wilson, is published by New Directions. After quarreling with Wilson in New York, Mary sues for separation and sole custody of Reuel. *New Yorker* editor William Shawn sends Wilson to Europe to survey conditions at the end of the war. Arrives in London in April, and meets many British literary figures, including Graham Greene, George Orwell, Cyril Connolly, Henry Green, and Evelyn Waugh. Is infatuated with young English woman, Mamaine Paget, who becomes a close friend. Visits Italy, where he reports on conditions in Naples, Milan, and Rome. Writes to Nabokov: "The ruined parts of Italy affect me with more repugnance than anything else, I think, that I have ever seen." Meets Ignazio Silone, Alberto Moravia, and George Santayana. Travels to Greece and Crete. After returning home, has brief affair with Anaïs Nin. Custody case comes to trial in September and judge orders a settlement, awarding Mary custody during the school year and Wilson during the summer.

1946   *Memoirs of Hecate County* published by Doubleday. Prosecuted as pornography, the book briefly becomes a bestseller (before being banned in New York and Massachusetts); it earns Wilson $35,000. Meets and falls in love with Elena Mumm Thornton. (Born in France in 1906 to aristocratic German and Russian parents, she is now unhappily married to a Canadian businessman.) After an exhilarating seven-month courtship of letters and irregular meetings, they go to Nevada to obtain divorces, are married on December 10, and then return to the Cape, where she will make a home for him.

1947   *Europe Without Baedeker: Sketches in the Ruins of Italy, France, and England* published by Doubleday. Contracts with Oxford University Press to write a book on American literature "between the Civil War and about 1910," and starts developing materials for it in *The New Yorker*. Enjoys what will become close friendships with W. H. Auden and Isaiah Berlin. Enthusiastically disputes tastes and ideas with Nabokov, exchanging long letters when they are unable to meet. Sends Nabokov a case study from

Havelock Ellis's *Psychology of Sex* of a Ukrainian who despairs of overcoming his love of young girls. Meets Haitian writer Phito Toby-Marcelin, whose fiction he has admired. In September visits Dos Passos in hospital after the car accident in which his wife, Katy, was killed. Mary Blair dies. Visits Zuñi pueblo in New Mexico at the winter solstice and writes detailed account of what he observes there.

1948   Daughter Helen Miranda born February 17. He is disturbed by a visit to Edna Millay at Steepletop, the farm in Austerlitz, New York, where she and Eugen Boissevain have isolated themselves for 20 years: "I reflected in dismay . . . on the tendency of the writers of my generation to burn themselves out or break down."

1949   Spends six weeks in Haiti, November–December, on assignment for *The Reporter*.

1950   *Classics and Commercials: A Literary Chronicle of the Forties*, a collection of book reviews and essays, is published in the fall by Farrar, Straus. Roger Straus becomes his primary publisher; Wilson will no longer have to struggle to get his books into print, and Straus, making loans against Wilson's work, provides a financial arrangement more satisfactory for him than were his mother's sometimes grudging contributions. Edna Millay dies in October.

1951   Wilson's mother dies on February 3, and he inherits the stone house in Talcottville, New York, along with her New Jersey home and a trust fund income of $8,000 a year. His play *The Little Blue Light* is produced in Cambridge, Massachusetts, with Jessica Tandy and Hume Cronyn; the subsequent New York production fails. Christian Gauss dies in November.

1952–53   *The Shores of Light: A Literary Chronicle of the Twenties and Thirties* reintroduces Wilson's earlier reviews to a new generation. Writes essays on Russian classics. In 1952 he spends his first summer at Talcottville since inheriting the house, then goes to Princeton for the winter. Delivers papers on Civil War figures in a seminar established in Gauss's memory (those attending include John Berryman, Saul Bellow, and Leon Edel). Begins studying Hebrew at Princeton Theological Seminary. Jason Epstein, an editor at Doubleday, includes *To the Finland Station* among the initial titles in the new Doubleday Anchor series of paperbacks, to be followed by three more Wilson volumes over the next five years.

1954   *Eight Essays* appears in Anchor Books. *Five Plays* published. Sails to Europe in January; fellow passengers include Jason and Barbara Epstein and Buster Keaton. Spends a week in Paris where he sees Malraux, as he will again later in the year. Teaches American literature at Salzburg seminar in February. In England meets with Cyril Connolly, Angus Wilson, E. M. Forster; travels to Edinburgh where he meets novelist Compton Mackenzie. Visits Max Beerbohm in Italy. Travels to Israel in April for *The New Yorker*. Reads manuscript of *Lolita*, but writes to Nabokov: "I like it less than anything else of yours I have read."

1955   Wilson's account of the Dead Sea Scrolls appears in *The New Yorker*; an expanded version of the *New Yorker* essay is published by Oxford as *The Scrolls from the Dead Sea* and sells well. (Will continue to revise and update the book for the next 12 years.) Immerses himself in Turgenev. Talcottville has become a home to him but not to Elena, who will limit her visits to two weeks in August.

1956   *Red, Black, Blond and Olive: Studies in Four Civilizations: Zuñi, Haiti, Soviet Russia, and Israel*, travel writing that verges on cultural anthropology, is published by Oxford. Publishes a memoir of his father ("The Author at Sixty") in *A Piece of My Mind: Reflections at Sixty*. Anchor Books publishes *A Literary Chronicle* (a selection from *The Shores of Light* and *Classics and Commercials*). Travels to England in July and early August; has second honeymoon in Paris with Elena.

1957   Spends the first of four winters working on the literature of the Civil War era in Harvard's Widener Library. Suffers from gout, a condition he first developed in the early 1940s; has adverse reactions to sulfa drugs when he drinks. Visits the Nabokovs in Ithaca and succeeds in repairing relations with Vladimir, despite tension with Vera Nabokov. "Turgenev and the Life-Giving Drop," his longest literary portrait since his studies of Marx and Dickens, appears in *The New Yorker* in October. Begins a study of the New York Iroquois.

1958   *The American Earthquake: A Documentary of the Twenties and Thirties*, a collection incorporating *The American Jitters* along with other journalistic writings, is published by Anchor Books. Praises Boris Pasternak's *Doctor Zhivago* in "Doctor Life and his Guardian Angel." Visits the Tonawanda and Seneca reservations and becomes a journalistic spokesman on behalf of Indian land rights threatened by development projects. The Internal Revenue Service discovers he has paid no federal income tax between 1946 and 1955, although payments had been withheld by *The New Yorker*, Princeton, and Farrar, Straus; Elena begins sorting through decades of canceled checks and bank statements. Wilson is tried for tax evasion in Utica in November, and is ordered to pay $68,500 in back taxes, penalties, and interest.

1959   Needing money to pay the I.R.S., takes one-year position as Lowell professor at Harvard, lecturing from his Civil War manuscript and giving a seminar on onomatopoeia from the *Aeneid* to Proust and Joyce. Enjoys interacting with visiting writers and intellectuals, including Isaac Bashevis Singer and George F. Kennan.

1960   *Apologies to the Iroquois* published. When a Hungarian translation of his plays arrives at Talcottville from Budapest, begins study of the language with Mary Pcolar, who works in the local drugstore and becomes his driver, typist, and companion. He now polishes his journal as he writes, believing there will be no time to revise it.

1961   *Night Thoughts*, a volume of his collected poems, published. Signs protest against the Bay of Pigs invasion. Attacks both Soviet and American imperialism in the introduction to *Patriotic Gore*, writing: "Whenever we engage in a war or move in on some other country, it is always to liberate somebody." Mortgages Talcottville house and sells his papers to Yale to pay off debts incurred as a result of tax problems.

1962   *Patriotic Gore: Studies in the Literature of the American Civil War* published. *Life* magazine criticizes Wilson's sweeping analogies between Lincoln's historical role and those of Lenin and Bismarck. The book is widely admired by critics and historians; its portraits of Grant, Sherman, Lincoln, Harriet Beecher Stowe, and Justice Holmes are likened by Robert Lowell and Alfred Kazin to Plutarch.

I.R.S. attempts to cut off Wilson's sources of income. Attends a White House dinner for Malraux in May, and has several exchanges with Kennedy; questioned by the President about the view of American wars in *Patriotic Gore*, he suggests that he buy the book. Has what seems a severe heart attack (angina). Writes the first of two self-interviews, dialogues outlining his intellectual world. In September goes to Toronto and Montreal for a study of Canadian literature.

1963   Dispute with the I.R.S. is settled after intervention by Arthur M. Schlesinger, Jr. (then serving as a White House adviser), although Wilson owes collateral payments against future earnings. Publishes *The Cold War and the Income Tax: A Protest*, an account of his experience in which he objects to the use of tax money for nuclear, biological, and chemical weapons. Kennedy adds Wilson's name to the list for his first Medals of Freedom. (When officials from the I.R.S. object, he comments, "This is not an award for good conduct but for literary merit.") Kennedy also expresses interest in Wilson's project, outlined in a 1962 letter to Jason Epstein, to reprint American classics in a series modeled on the French Pléiade. Contributes a second self-interview detailing his tastes in music and the arts to the first issue of *The New York Review of Books*; it is followed by "My Fifty Years with Dictionaries and Grammars." Spends summer in Talcottville, then visits London before going to Paris with Elena and Helen for the late autumn and winter.

1964–65   Visits Rome and Budapest in the spring. Spends a year as a Fellow at the Center for Advanced Studies at Wesleyan. (When an English Department critic pronounces that literature is dead, comments: "How much less, then, should we need criticism?") Publishes *O Canada: An American's Notes on Canadian Culture* and *The Bit Between My Teeth: A Literary Chronicle of 1950–1965*. Criticizes Nabokov's literal translation of Pushkin's *Eugene Onegin* in *The New York Review of Books*; Nabokov in turn dismisses Wilson's critique by ridiculing his grasp of Russian, beginning a series of bitter public exchanges.

1966   *Europe Without Baedeker* reissued, with the addition of "Notes from a European Diary, 1963–1964." Awarded the Emerson-Thoreau Medal of the American Academy of Arts and Letters and the National Medal for Literature.

1967 Publishes *A Prelude: Characters and Conversations from the Early Years of My Life*. Makes cuts in *The Twenties* and interpolates passages of new writing. (Will intermittently work on *The Thirties* until his death. *The Twenties*, *The Thirties*, *The Forties*, *The Fifties*, and *The Sixties* will be posthumously published between 1975 and 1993.) Visits Israel and Jordan, April–May. By now suffers a range of symptoms attributable to emphysema, diabetes, arthritis, shingles, and a disease resembling malaria, caught in Haiti.

1968 "The Fruits of the M.L.A.," a satirical attack on the heavily annotated texts of American classics endorsed by the Modern Language Association, published in *The New York Review of Books*. Receives award of the Aspen Institute of Humanistic Studies ($30,000) at the Waldorf-Astoria (his heart condition prevents him from traveling to the Colorado mountains). In his acceptance speech speaks of Taine's influence in his boyhood, and again attacks the "disgraceful" Vietnam War. Turns from the public world in his journal to chronicle illnesses and recoveries as his health declines.

1969 Publishes *The Dead Sea Scrolls, 1947–1969* (an expanded version of his 1955 book) and *The Duke of Palermo and Other Plays* (with an "Open Letter to Mike Nichols" in which he lists American plays he believes should be revived).

1970 Has a coronary occlusion in New York in March; refuses a pacemaker. Suffers a slight stroke around Christmas.

1971 Publishes *Upstate: Records and Recollections of Northern New York*, which sells unexpectedly well. Exchanges friendly letters with Nabokov, but their reconciliation ends when Nabokov is angered by the account in *Upstate* of Wilson's visit to Ithaca in 1957. Mary McCarthy, with help from James Baldwin, arranges for Wilson to receive the Golden Eagle Award from the International Festival of Books in Nice; he is also awarded the bi-annual Jerusalem Prize, but the prize is transferred to Jorge Luis Borges when Wilson is unable to fulfill the condition of receiving it in person in Jerusalem.

1972 For new edition of *To the Finland Station*, revises portrait of Lenin. Last essays on Russian literature published in *A Window on Russia*. Assembles essays published in *The*

Devils and Canon Barham: Ten Essays on Poets, Novelists and Monsters (1973). Spends winter at Naples, Florida. Has another stroke at Cape Cod in May. Is promised by Roger Straus that his journals will not be censored after his death. Goes to upstate New York for what he reassures Elena will be two weeks. Dictates a last letter to Auden. On June 11 brings the journal up to date after not writing for five months. Dies in the old stone house at Talcottville from a coronary occlusion on the morning of June 12. Buried at Wellfleet June 15.

Note on the Texts

This volume contains two works by Edmund Wilson—*The Shores of Light: A Literary Chronicle of the Twenties and Thirties* (1952) and *Axel's Castle: A Study in the Imaginative Literature of 1870–1930* (1931) —along with six reviews not collected by Wilson.

The Shores of Light was conceived by Wilson as a companion to his previously published collection of book reviews, *Classics and Commercials: A Literary Chronicle of the Forties* (1950). As he notes in his introduction, the scope of *The Shores of Light* was expanded to include, among its 97 pieces, "dialogues, jeux d'esprit, satires, short sketches and personal letters." In preparing the book, Wilson interpolated passages of new writing that introduce, enlarge upon, and update the earlier material, explaining in a prepatory note: "I have thoroughly revised almost everything, sometimes trimming and toning down what I originally wrote and sometimes expanding it with material taken from my old notes." *The Shores of Light* was originally published by Farrar, Straus and Young in 1952. The text printed here is taken from the 1961 Vintage paperback printing of the book, which contains the text of the first printing but also includes short postscripts added to two essays written after the book was first published.

Axel's Castle was Wilson's fourth published book, preceded by two miscellaneous collections—*The Undertaker's Garland* (1922), in collaboration with John Peale Bishop, and *Discordant Encounters: Plays and Dialogues* (1926)—encompassing essays, stories, poems, and a play, and his novel *I Thought of Daisy* (1929). Wilson had already begun work on the book when he sent a tentative outline to the editor Maxwell Perkins in 1928. While Wilson had written in previously published essays about a number of the figures discussed in *Axel's Castle*, and used some of the material from those essays, everything was subjected to a thoroughgoing revision. The text published here is that of the first edition, published by Charles Scribner's Sons in 1931.

The six uncollected reviews included in this volume were published between 1921 and 1925 in the following periodicals:

H. L. Mencken: *The New Republic*, June 1921.

The Poetry of Drouth: *The Dial*, December 1922.

Edith Wharton: *Vanity Fair*, March 1923.

A Guide to Gertrude Stein: *Vanity Fair*, September 1923.

Bernard Shaw Since the War: *The New Republic*, August 1924.

W. B. Yeats: *The New Republic*, June 1925.

Some passages in "The Poetry of Drouth," "A Guide to Gertrude Stein," and "W. B. Yeats" were reworked by Wilson for *Axel's Castle*.

The texts of the original printings chosen for inclusion here are presented without change, except for the correction of typographical errors. Spelling, punctuation, and capitalization are often expressive features and are not altered, even when inconsistent or irregular. The following errors have been corrected: 14.30, le; 23.31, and it; 32.34, characters,; 52.19, lose; 57.22, Stendahl; 62.30, conciousnes; 65.17, *Grey*; 67.30, Ranier; 85.19, stories he; 145.20, *dell' arte*; 158.10, *Eleanora*; 173.33, Ivor; 204.31–32, polygot; 211.4, revised; 264.4, grad-/ate; 305.14, Saint-Beuve 313.14, Akin; 361.12, ascetism; 386.12, *Coloneus*; 396.4, East.; 429.15, allies:; 443.36, *Parti-cle*; 453.33, Guadenzio; 456.9, as first; 487.8, then that; 492.15, Thorton; 585.26, of; 604.31, *de*; 605.21, Kennerleys; 671.12, Lake of; 675.13, others rhetoric; 699.22, to be; 709.31, peach!; 710.6, L'automme, l'au-tomme!; 745.6, ostracisim; 800.8, Guiness's; 847.5, PLURIBELLE; 890.2, cried!; 890.32, fisherman.; 892.12, frustations.

Notes

In the notes below, the reference numbers denote page and line of this volume (the line count includes headings). No note is made for material included in standard desk-reference books. Biographical information beyond that included in the Chronology may be found in Lewis M. Dabney, *Edmund Wilson: A Life in Literature* (Farrar, Straus & Giroux, 2005); Jeffrey Meyers, *Edmund Wilson: A Biography* (Houghton Mifflin, 1995); Edmund Wilson, *The Twenties* (1975), Edmund Wilson, *The Thirties* (1980), *The Forties* (1983), and *The Fifties* (1986, all ed. Leon Edel, Farrar, Straus & Giroux); Edmund Wilson, *The Sixties* (ed. Lewis M. Dabney, Farrar, Straus & Giroux, 1993); Edmund Wilson, *Red, Black, Blond, and Olive: Studies in Four Civilizations* (Oxford University Press, 1956); Edmund Wilson, *A Prelude: Landscapes, Characters and Conversations from the Earlier Years of My Life* (Allen and Unwin, 1967); Elena Wilson, ed., *Letters on Literature and Politics* (Farrar, Straus & Giroux, 1977); Simon Karlinsky, ed., *The Nabokov-Wilson Letters, 1940–1971* (Harper & Row, 1979, 2001); David Castonovo and Janet Groth, *Edmund Wilson: The Man in Letters* (Ohio University Press, 2003).

THE SHORES OF LIGHT

8.2–3   Nathan . . . *World*] H. L. Mencken and George Jean Nathan were co-editors of *The Smart Set* from 1914 to 1923; the New York *World* regularly published criticism by Alexander Woollcott (1925–28) and Heywood Broun (1921–28).

11.20–21   Irving Babbitt] Literary scholar (1865–1933), professor of French literature at Harvard, and a founder with Paul Elmer More of the New Humanist movement; see "Notes on Babbitt and More," on page 367 in this volume.

12.38   Joseph Henry house] Official residence of the dean of Princeton College, designed by the scientist Joseph Henry and built in 1837.

13.39   Taine's] Hippolyte Taine (1828–1893), French historian and literary critic noted for his dramatic skills and for approaching writers through their historical background, of whom Wilson wrote: "My whole point of view about literature was affected by Taine's methods of presentation and interpretation." See "A Modest Self-Tribute" in *The Bit Between My Teeth* (1965).

14.22   *'d'une façon civile'*] In a cordial way.

14.22–23   *'Entrez, brave home,'*] Come in, good man.

14.25–26   *'tout mangé des vers, et jadis bleu'*] Eaten by worms, and formerly blue.

14.29–33   Et, pendant qu'il séchait . . . des constellations.] And while
he dried this wretched rag / From which streamed the rain and the water of
the quagmires, / I dreamt that this man was full of prayers. / And, deaf to
what we were saying, I looked at / His rough garment where I saw constellations.

15.37   André Chénier] French poet (1762–1794), guillotined during the
Revolution.

16.20   M. de Malesherbes] Chrétien-Guillaume de Malesherbes (1721–
1794), reformist French political figure who helped defend Louis XVI and
was subsequently executed.

16.21   Saintsbury] George Saintsbury, English literary critic and journalist (1845–1933) whose works included *A History of English Prose Rhythm* (1912)
and *A History of the French Novel to the Close of the Nineteenth Century* (1917–
19). Wilson called him "the sole English literary critic of the late-nineteenth
early-twentieth centuries . . . who is really of first-rate stature" ("George
Saintsbury's Centenary," *Classics and Commercials*, 1950).

17.23   Bibi-La-Purée] A frequenter of Montmartre and the Latin Quarter in Paris in the late 19th and early 20th centuries, he was known as "The
King of Bohemia."

17.34   More] Paul Elmer More (1864–1937), critical ally of Irving Babbitt
and author of *The Shelburne Essays*; see "Notes on Babbitt and More," on
pages 367–80 in this volume.

18.26–27   *"Il est intelligent tout de même?"*] He is nonetheless intelligent?

19.11   Leopardi] Giacomo Leopardi (1798–1837), Italian poet, essayist,
and aphorist.

19.12   *"con isdegnoso occhio."*] With disdainful eye.

20.20   John Peale Bishop] Poet (1892–1944), close friend of Wilson, a
contemporary at Princeton.

21.33–34   prison of Chillon] The Château de Chillon, located near Mon-
treux, Switzerland, setting of Byron's poem "The Prisoner of Chillon."

22.8   Werner Sombart] German economist (1863–1941) who incorporated Marxist principles in his work.

26.34   *"il ben del intelletto."*] The good of intellect. See Dante, *Inferno*,
Canto 3, lines 16–18: "We have come to the place where I have told you you
will see the wretched people who have lost the good of intellect."

29.30–33   Chè in la mente . . . l'uom s'eterna. . . .] Cf. Dante, *Inferno*, Canto 15, lines 82–85: "For in my memory is fixed, and now saddens my heart, your dear, kind, paternal image, when in the world hour by hour you taught me how man makes himself eternal." The lines are addressed to Dante's teacher Brunetto Latini.

32.3–7   Agib, who could readily . . . Pantechnicon all night.] W. S. Gilbert, "The Story of Prince Agib," *Bab Ballads* (1869–73).

44.33   Tanagra statuette] Greek terracotta figure of a young woman.

45.31   Pratinas . . . Gaudier-Brzeska] Pratinas, Athenian tragic poet, a contemporary of Aeschylus; Henri Gaudier-Brzeska (1891–1915), French sculptor associated with Vorticism.

46.19   Lorenzaccio] Lorenzo di Medici (1514–1548), assassin of his cousin Alessandro di Medici in 1537; subject of Alfred de Musset's play *Lorenzaccio* (1833).

46.28   Arnaut Daniel] Provençal poet of the late 12th century.

47.3–4   Van Wyck Brooks] Critic and literary historian (1886–1963) whose early works included *America's Coming-of-Age* (1915) and *The Ordeal of Mark Twain* (1920). See "The Pilgrimage of Henry James" on pages 182–90 in this volume and "Van Wyck Brooks's Second Phase," "A Picture to Hang in the Library: Brooks's Age of Irving," and "Van Wyck Brooks on the Civil War Period" in *Classics and Commercials* (1950).

52.28–29   *"L'espoir luit . . . dans l'étable,"*] Hope gleams like a sprig of straw in the stable.

52.29–30   *"Que crains-tu de la guêpe . . . son vol fou?"*] What do you fear from the wasp, drunk with its mad flight?

57.25–26   Burbank . . . Bleistein with his cigar] Cf. "Burbank with a Baedeker: Bleistein with a Cigar," T. S. Eliot, *Poems* (1920).

63.5   *La Révolte des Anges*] *The Revolt of the Angels*, novel (1914) by Anatole France.

63.29   Floyd Dell] Writer (1887–1969) and editor of *The Masses* and *The Liberator*.

63.30   Till Eulenspiegel] German prankster of folklore and literature.

64.30   *Yellow Book*] *The Yellow Book*, periodical (1894–97) edited by Henry Harland, with Aubrey Beardsley as art editor; its contributors included Max Beerbohm, Henry James, and W. B. Yeats.

65.17   *À Rebours*] *Against the Grain* (1884), novel by J. K. Huysmans.

68.26   E. P. Roe] Edward Payson Roe (1838–1888), a Presbyterian minister and popular American novelist.

72.23   Haeckel]   Ernst Haeckel (1834–1919), German biologist who was
an early advocate of Darwinism.

72.25   Michael Arlen]   British novelist (1895–1956) of Armenian extrac-
tion, author of the tremendously popular *The Green Hat* (1924).

85.7   Bill Nye]   American humorist (1850–1896) known for his writings
about the West.

85.9   John Held]   John Held Jr. (1889–1958), cartoonist who helped create the image of 1920s Jazz Age youth.

87.24–25   George Ade]   Humorist (1866–1944) best known for *Fables in
Slang* (1899).

88.6   Stephen   Leacock's . . . Irvin   Cobb's]   Leacock   (1869–1944),
Canadian humorist whose books include *Nonsense Novels* (1911); Cobb (1876–
1944), popular American writer, author of *Old Judge Priest* (1916).

90.34–35   Stanley Houghton]   English playwright (1881–1913) whose plays
included the very successful *Hindle Wakes* (1912).

91.21   Stark Young]   Drama critic and playwright (1881–1963); he was on
the staff of *The New Republic* from 1921 to 1957.

94.2–3   *It Pays to Advertise*]   Comedy (1914) by Roi Cooper Magrue.

94.5   *Turn to the Right*]   Comedy (1916) by Winchell Smith and John E.
Hazzard.

99.27   Richard Watson Gilder]   Poet (1844–1909) and influential editor
of *The Century* from 1881 until his death.

100.5   James Gordon Bennett]   Newspaper publisher (1841–1918) who
succeeded his father as publisher of the *New York Herald*.

100.13–14   Clyde Fitch and Lillian Russell]   Fitch (1865–1909), popular
playwright, author of *Captain Jinks of the Horse Marines* (1901); Russell
(1861–1922), singer and actress who became famous in the 1880s.

100.34   Walter Besant]   English novelist (1836–1901) and proponent of
social reform in books such as *All Sorts and Conditions of Men* (1882).

102.2–3   Burton Rascoe]   Literary critic (1892–1957), a friend of Wilson;
see "Burton Rascoe," pages 326–30 in this volume.

103.18   McAlmon]   Robert McAlmon (1896–1956), expatriate American
writer and publisher.

103.19   Mina Loy]   English-born poet (1882–1966) associated with modernist circles in New York after 1916; her poetry collection *Lunar Baedeker*
appeared in 1923.

107.30   Don Stewart]   Donald Ogden Stewart (1894–1980), playwright, humorist, and screenwriter, later blacklisted after he was named as a Communist before the House Un-American Activities Committee.

109.3   *Paul Rosenfeld . . . Matthew Josephson*] Paul Rosenfeld (1890–1946), critic of music and the arts, friend of Wilson (see "Paul Rosenfeld: Three Phases" in *Classics and Commercials*); Matthew Josephson (1899–1978), popularizer of Dada and other European artistic trends in the 1920s, later a biographer and historian.

109.5   *Broom*] *Broom: An International Magazine of the Arts* (published 1921–24) was initially edited by Harold Loeb and Alfred Kreymborg, with Malcolm Cowley and Matthew Josephson assuming greater control in later issues.

109.19   Bugs Baer] Arthur Baer (1886–1969), syndicated sports writer.

112.9   Klingsor] In Wagner's opera *Parsifal*, magician who covets the Holy Spear and the Holy Grail after being rejected as a Grail knight.

112.13   Tzara] Tristan Tzara (1896–1963), a resident of Paris from 1920; a founder of the Dada movement and later a Surrealist; see Appendix II of *Axel's Castle*, pages 848–54 in this volume.

118.10   Landru] Henri-Désiré Landru (1869–1922) was convicted in Paris of murdering ten women who had answered his matrimonial advertisements, as well as the 17-year-old son of one of his victims. He was sentenced to death and guillotined.

118.11   Léon Daudet] French journalist (1867–1942), a co-founder of the extreme royalist journal *L'Action Française* in 1907; his son Philippe died under mysterious circumstances of a gunshot wound while riding in a taxi in 1923. After the death was ruled a suicide by authorities, Daudet wrote a series of articles claiming that his son was the victim of an anarchist assassination plot, and was in turn sued for defamation by the taxi driver, whom he had implicated in the plot. Daudet was fined and imprisoned; he escaped from prison, fled to Belgium, and was eventually pardoned in 1929.

118.12–13 Morris Gest . . . Reinhardt's *Miracle*] The impresario Gest (1875–1942) organized the American opening of Max Reinhardt's lavish production *The Miracle* in 1924.

118.13–14 The Oil Scandal] The corruption scandal in the Harding administration involving the leasing of federal oil reserves at Elk Hills, California, and Teapot Dome, Wyoming.

120.12   Leo Ornstein . . . Roger Sessions] Leo Ornstein (1892–2003), Russian-born American composer whom Wilson wanted, but did not get, to compose the music for his ballet "Cronkhite's Clocks" (published in *Discordant Encounters*, 1926); Roger Sessions (1896–1985), American composer influenced by European modernism.

120.13   Lopez . . . Whiteman]   Popular bandleaders Vincent Lopez (1895–1975) and Paul Whiteman (1880–1967).

126.7   Jeffries]   Richard Jefferies (1848–1887), English naturalist and writer whose books include *Life of the Fields* (1884) and *The Open Air* (1885).

127.7–8   Marie Bashkirtseff]   Marya Konstantinovna Baskirtseva (1860–1884), painter and diarist.

131.2   Harriman . . . Hill]   Edward Henry Harriman (1848–1909), financier and railroad magnate; James Jerome Hill (1838–1916), financier who battled Harriman for control of the Northern Pacific Railroad.

131.27   Marc Connelly]   Playwright (1890–1980) whose early successes included *Dulcy* (1921) and *Merton of the Movies* (1922), both co-written with George S. Kaufman; he won the Pulitzer Prize for *The Green Pastures* (1930).

131.28   Rube Goldberg]   Syndicated cartoonist (1883–1970) known for cartoons featuring elaborately impractical inventions.

134.7   Marguerite Clark]   Movie actress (1883–1940) of the silent era, whose films included *Uncle Tom's Cabin* (1918) and *Mrs. Wiggs of the Cabbage Patch* (1919).

134.22   Christopher Morley]   Popular writer (1890–1957), author of *Parnassus on Wheels* (1917) and other books.

134.28   the Fratellini clowns]   Family of circus performers who in the 1920s became a star attraction at the Cirque Medrano in Paris.

135.5   Mr. Dooley]   Irish-American saloon-keeper, a character created by the Chicago journalist Finley Peter Dunne (1867–1936).

136.18–19   Guitry . . . *Le Rire*]   Sacha Guitry (1885–1957), actor, playwright, and filmmaker, known for light comedies such as *Faisons un rêve* (1916); Georges Rip, French writer for stage and film; *Le Rire*, humor magazine founded in 1894.

137.4   Opper]   Frederick Burr Opper (1857–1937), illustrator and cartoonist best known for creating the comic strip characters Happy Hooligan and Alphonse and Gaston.

137.5–6   Weber and Fields]   Joe Weber (1867–1942) and Lew Fields (1867–1941), team of comedians and later theatrical managers; their many successful shows included *Helter Skelter* (1899) and *Whoop-dee-doo* (1903).

138.5   Frank Tinney]   Blackface comedian (1878–1940) who appeared in such shows as *Tickle Me* (1920) and *Daffy Dill* (1922).

138.7   F.P.A.]   Franklin P. Adams (1881–1960), journalist and humorist whose column "The Conning Tower" often presented work by promising young writers. Wilson appeared in the column in 1911, when he was a student at the Hill School.

138.8–9   James J. Morton] Vaudeville comedian (1862–1938) known as "first master of ceremonies" for his on-stage commentaries on other performers.

138.16–17   the Jimmy Powerses . . . McIntyres and Heaths] James T. Powers (1862–1943), vaudeville and circus comedian who later starred in such musicals as *The Geisha* (1897) and *Havana* (1909); Nat M. Wills (1873–1917), comedian known as "The Happy Tramp"; James McIntyre (1857–1937) and Thomas Heath (1852–1938), blackface comedy team who appeared in *In Hayti* (1909) and *The Show of Wonders* (1916).

138.37–38   Cocteau's . . . *Mariés de la Tour Eiffel*] *Le Potomak* (1919), a prose fantasy; *Les Mariés de la Tour Eiffel* (1921), a ballet with music by five composers, among them Darius Milhaud and Francis Poulenc.

140.22   Edith Sitwell] English poet (1887–1964) noted for flamboyant eccentricity.

145.19   Jacques Callot] French painter and engraver (c. 1592–1635).

152.24–25   James Huneker] American critic (1860–1921), author of *Overtones* (1904), *Iconoclasts* (1905), *Ivory Apes and Peacocks* (1915), and other books that introduced Americans to innovative trends in European literature, art, and music.

152.27   Thomas Holley Chivers] Poet (1809–1858), an acquaintance of Poe; his works include *Eonchs of Ruby* (1851).

154.28   Waldo Frank] Novelist and critic (1889–1967), a founder of the magazine *The Seven Arts*.

155.17   Maurice de Guérin] French poet (1810–1839).

156.5–6   Rolla . . . René . . . Childe Harold, Manfred and Cain] Protagonists of *Rolla* (1833) by Alfred de Musset, *René* (1805) by François-René de Chateaubriand, and *Childe Harold's Pilgrimage* (1812–18), *Manfred* (1817), and *Cain* (1821) by Lord Byron.

163.10   Laura Riding] Poet (1901–1991) originally associated with the magazine *The Fugitive*. Born Laura Reichenthal, she briefly published under her married name Laura Gottschalk.

163.10   Donald Davidson] Poet (1893–1968) who was a co-founder of *The Fugitive*.

167.18   Mr. Fletcher] John Gould Fletcher (1886–1950), poet associated with the Imagist movement.

173.13   Laura Gottschalk] See note 163.10.

180.10   Richard Harding Davis] Journalist and popular novelist (1864–1916), famous as a war correspondent.

185.26–27   Titus and Bérénice, Alceste and Célimène] The protagonists respectively of Jean Racine's *Bérénice* and Molière's *Le Misanthrope*.

192.2   Stuart P. Sherman] Literary critic (1881–1926) influenced by the New Humanism of Irving Babbitt; author of *On Contemporary Literature* (1917) and *The Genius of America* (1923).

192.36   Joseph Hergesheimer] Novelist (1880–1954) whose many books, widely popular and in their time often critically acclaimed, included *The Three Black Pennys* (1917) and *Java Head* (1919).

193.9   Poictesme] Imaginary medieval domain in which James Branch Cabell set many of his novels.

195.29   John H. Lawson] John Howard Lawson (1895–1977), playwright whose plays included *Processional* (1925) and *The International* (1928). Later a screenwriter, he was blacklisted as one of the "Hollywood Ten" in the late 1940s.

195.39   Lord Dunsany] Irish writer (1878–1957), born Edward John Moreton Drax Plunkett, known for fiction, poetry, and drama, often in a vein of fantasy.

197.11   A. B. Walkley] Long-time drama critic of the London *Times*.

197.14–15   Willard Huntington Wright] Critic (1888–1939) of literature and art, at one time editor in chief of *The Smart Set*; as S. S. Van Dine he wrote the Philo Vance mystery novels.

209.35   *Kalevala*] Finnish epic constructed from surviving oral traditions by Elias Lönnrot (1802–1884) and published in 1835.

214.12–13   Les faux beaux jours . . . aux cuivres du couchant.] The false fine days have shone all day, my poor soul, / And now they vibrate in the copper tints of the setting sun.

217.27–29   Indignatur item privatis . . . sortita decentum.] Cf. Horace, *Ars Poetica*, lines 90–92: Likewise such themes as Thyestes' banquet rebel at portrayals couched in an everyday idiom or stated in comedy's language.

220.12–13   E. V. Lucas, Robert Hichens and Clutton-Brock] E. V. Lucas (1868–1938), English essayist; Robert Hichens (1864–1950), English novelist, author of bestsellers *The Green Carnation* (1894) and *The Garden of Allah* (1904); Arthur Clutton-Brock (1868–1924), English critic, literary editor of *The Speaker*.

223.37   Casaubon] Isaac Casaubon (1559–1614), French Huguenot theologian and scholar who settled in England in 1610.

225.1   *"O curas hominum! O quantum est in rebus inane!"*] Oh the cares of man! Oh how much emptiness there is in things!

225.16   *callida junctura*] Skillful joining.

256.33 Walter Bagehot] British journalist (1826–1877) and political thinker, author of *The English Constitution* (1867).

269.1–2 Teasing Tom song in *Patience*] Poem recited by Archibald Grosvenor in Act II of Gilbert and Sullivan's *Patience* (1881), beginning with the lines: "Teasing Tom was a very bad boy, / A great big squirt was his favorite toy. / He put live shrimps in his father's boots, / And sewed up the sleeves of his Sunday suits."

289.34 Nast] Thomas Nast (1840–1902), American political cartoonist famous for his role in exposing the Tweed Ring in New York City.

290.8 Callot] See note 145.19.

297.31 *Simplicissimus*] German satirical weekly, published from 1896 to 1944; artists who contributed work to it included George Grosz, Käthe Kollwitz, and John Heartfield.

298.6 The *Liberator*] A successor of *The Masses* published between 1918 and 1924; its editors included Max Eastman and Floyd Dell.

299.9 Robert Chanler] Artist and designer (1872–1930), a specialist in mural painting.

302.21 the Playwright's Theater] The New Playwrights' Theatre, organized in 1926 by Lawson, Dos Passos, and Gold, among others.

305.13–14 Renan, Taine, Sainte-Beuve, Leslie Stephen and Brandes] Ernest Renan (1823–1892), philosopher, author of *Life of Jesus*; Taine, see note 13.39; Charles-Augustin Sainte-Beuve (1804–1869), French literary historian and critic known for his weekly articles; Leslie Stephen (1832–1904), English critic and biographer (father of Virginia Woolf); George Morris Brandes (1842–1927), Danish literary historian and critic.

309.1–2 *"Longtemps, je me suis couché de bonne heure,"*] For a long time I went to bed early.

315.24 Sacheverell Sitwell] Poet and essayist (1897–1988), brother of Edith and Osbert Sitwell.

316.16 *"la pluie et le beau temps"*] The rain and the fine weather.

317.11 Mme. de Sévigné] Marquise de Sévigné (1626–1696), celebrated for her prolific correspondence with her daughter, first published in 1725.

317.31–35 *"Toutes ces obligations . . . peut-être d'y retourner. . . ."*] "All those obligations which are not sanctioned in present-day life seem to belong to a different world, founded on goodness, scrupulousness, sacrifice, a world entirely different from this one, and which we left in order to be born on this earth, perhaps before returning there. . . ." Wilson comments on this passage in "Letter to the Russians About Hemingway," 508.10–26 in this volume.

318.25 Dunsanys] See note 195.39.

319.18   *Vathek*]   Gothic novel (1782) by William Beckford, originally written in French.

320.12   *Appearance and Reality*]   Philosophical work (1893) by F. H. Bradley.

320.13   Spengler]   Oswald Spengler (1880–1936), German historian whose massive work *The Decline of the West* (1918–22) made him internationally famous.

322.26   Variorum Edition of Shakespeare]   Fourteen volumes of the *New Variorum Shakespeare*, edited by Horace Howard Furness, were published between 1871 and 1913.

331.11   R.A.]   A member of the Royal Academy.

333.33   Octave Mirbeau]   French journalist and novelist, author of *The Torture Garden* (1898), *The Diary of a Chambermaid* (1900), and other works. See "In Memory of Octave Mirbeau" in *Classics and Commercials.*

335.15   Baron Wrangel]   Piotr Nikolayevich Wrangel (1878–1928), Russian general who served in the Russo-Japanese War, World War I, and in the White Army in southern Russia; his evacuation of the Crimea in November 1920 ended the Civil War in Russia.

335.17   Sonia Kovalevsky]   Sofya Vasilyevna Kovalevskaya (1850–1891), Russian mathematician, who became the first European woman to obtain a doctorate in the subject.

339.2   Watson's behaviorism]   John Broadus Watson (1878–1958), influential behavioral psychologist.

340.13   John Jay Chapman]   American essayist (1862–1933) whose books included *Emerson and Other Essays* (1898) and *Practical Agitation* (1900). See "John Jay Chapman" in *The Triple Thinkers* (1938, revised 1948).

341.23   Myrtle Reed]   Popular American writer (1874–1911) whose books included *Lavendar and Old Lace* (1902) and *Old Rose and Silver* (1909).

341.36–37   William Wetmore Story]   American sculptor (1819–1895); his statue of a discreetly robed Cleopatra typifies the gentility of American Victorian art.

347.34   William Barnes]   English poet (1801–1886), much of whose verse is written in the Dorsetshire dialect.

353.16   Michael Gold]   Marxist writer (1893–1967), author of the novel *Jews Without Money* (1930) and an editor of *The Liberator.* See "The Literary Class War," pages 434–38 in this volume.

355.4   F. H. Bradley]   English philosopher (1846–1924).

367.19   Jebb and Jowett]   R. C. Jebb (1841–1905), editor and translator of

Sophocles and author of *The Growth and Influence of Greek Poetry* (1893); Benjamin Jowett (1817–1893), Oxford professor renowned for translations of Plato, Thucydides, and Aristotle.

368.9–10   ὅτι . . . δίκαιον,]   Aristotle, *Rhetoric*, 1373b10–11: that it is right, although forbidden by law, to bury Polyneices, because this is right according to nature.

368.29–30   σοί . . . ὀφλισκάνω.]   Sophocles, *Antigone*, 469–70: If I seem to you to be doing foolish things, you could almost say that I am being charged with foolishness by a fool.

370.17–19   Cromwell's, "My brethren . . . you may be mistaken!"]   In August 1650 Oliver Cromwell appealed to the General Assembly of the Church of Scotland: "I beseech you in the bowels of Christ, think it possible you may be mistaken."

373.5   Entsagung]   Renunciation; self-denial.

376.17   Apollonius Rhodius]   Apollonius of Rhodes, Alexandrian poet (3rd century BCE), author of the *Argonautica*.

382.22   ὕβρις]   Hubris.

384.18   Eckermann]   Johann Peter Eckermann (1792–1854), Goethe's literary assistant, who published *Conversations with Goethe* in 1832–33.

388.2   Herbert Croly]   Editor (1869–1930), founder of *The New Republic*; author of the influential Progressive manifesto *The Promise of American Life* (1909).

398.9   the Greek anthology]   A collection of short poems dating as far back as the 3rd century BCE, compiled in the 10th century in Byzantium.

400.29   Dwight W. Morrow and Owen D. Young]   Morrow (1873–1931), lawyer and banker, American ambassador to Mexico, senator, father-in-law of Charles Lindbergh; Young (1874–1962), lawyer with General Electric who negotiated a plan for German reparation payments, 1929–30.

401.33   Gurdjieff]   Georges Gurdjieff (c. 1866–1949), Armenian-born teacher of mystical philosophy who settled in France after the Russian Revolution.

402.5   A. R. Orage]   Alfred Richard Orage (1873–1934), editor of *The New Age* and later *The New English Weekly*; proponent of Social Credit and a disciple of George Gurdjieff.

404.14   Gastonia strike]   Millworkers' strike in Gastonia, North Carolina, which began in April 1929 and was brutally suppressed by forces including the National Guard, resulting in a number of deaths. Five men were tried and acquitted for the murder of Ella May Wiggins. There were no gains for the National Textile Workers Union. Seven strikers were convicted in the fall of 1929 of second-degree murder in the killing of Gastonia police chief Orville Aderholt. After their appeal was denied they all jumped bail, and five of them went to the Soviet Union. Their leader, Fred Neal, returned in 1933 and eventually served four years of his sentence. His memoir, *Proletarian Journey* (1937), detailed his disillusionment with Communism.

404.25–26   Mary Heaton Vorse] Journalist and radical activist (1874–1966).

411.32   Clyde Fitch] See note 100.13–14.

424.8   the Factory Acts] Legislation passed in Great Britain limiting the number of hours women and children could work.

425.5–6   Lawrence Dennis] After working in the State Department and for the Seligman banking firm, Dennis (1893–1977) wrote *Is Capitalism Doomed?* (1932) and *The Coming American Fascism* (1936). An opponent of American participation in World War II, he was indicted for sedition in 1944 and tried along with 29 other right-wing activists; the case ended in a mistrial.

429.19–20   Lippmann] Walter Lippmann (1889–1974), liberal political columnist, associated with *The New Republic* from its founding through the early 1920s.

431.25   NEP] The New Economic Policy, introduced by Lenin in 1921 as a temporary measure, ended forced food requisitions, instituted a tax in kind on agricultural production while allowing peasants to sell surplus produce, and restored private retail trade and small-scale private enterprise; under the NEP, the Soviet state retained control of heavy industry, transportation, banking, and foreign trade. Stalin ended the NEP in 1928 and instituted the first Five-Year Plan, which called for rapid industrialization and the forced collectivization of agriculture.

432.8   Edward L. Bernays] American public relations consultant (1891–1995) of the 1920s and 1930s.

433.5   Ivy Lee] Consultant (1870–1934) regarded as the originator of modern public relations.

433.16   Senator Norris] George W. Norris (1861–1944), progressive Republican senator from Nebraska who was reelected in 1936 as an independent.

436.6–7   shirtwaist makers' strike . . . Triangle fire] In 1909, women workers in the New York shirtwaist industry, led by the Women's Trade Union League, struck for improved wages and working conditions, and were ultimately successful; on March 25, 1911, a fire at the Triangle Waist Company in New York took the lives of 146 employees, most of them women.

440.16   Dr. Watts . . . Jane Taylor] Isaac Watts (1674–1748), theologian and writer of hymns including "O God, Our Help in Ages Past"; Jane Taylor (1783–1824), writer of poems for children including "Twinkle, Twinkle, Little Star."

446.25   Julia Margaret Cameron]   Photographer (1815–1879) whose subjects included Tennyson, Carlyle, and Ellen Terry.

447.14–15   Ellen Terry]   English actress (1847–1928).

448.8–9   "Je n'impose rien . . . j'expose,"]   I impose nothing; I propose nothing: I expose.

449.30   Mme. du Deffand]   Marquise du Deffand (1697–1780) held an influential salon; her close acquaintances included Turgot and d'Alembert.

456.10   *Analogy* of . . . Butler]   *Analogy of Religion, Natural and Revealed, to the Constitution and Course of Nature* (1736) by Bishop Joseph Butler (1692–1752).

458.17–18   Jonas Chuzzlewits, the Bounderbys, the Smallweeds and the Grides]   Jonas Chuzzlewit, murderous miser in *Martin Chuzzlewit*; Mr. Bounderby, successful businessman in *Hard Times*; Joshua Smallweed, discounter of bills and eventual blackmailer in *Bleak House*; Arthur Gride, money lender in *Nicholas Nickleby*.

460.1   *André Malraux*]   See also "Malraux and Silone" in *Europe Without Baedeker* (1947) and "André Malraux: The Museum Without Walls" in *The Bit Between My Teeth* (1965).

461.7   Jules Romains]   Novelist (1885–1972) best known for his long series of novels *Men of Good Will*, published between 1932 and 1947.

461.24   René or Manfred]   See note 156.5–6.

462.29   Conrad's Marlow]   Narrator of many works of fiction by Conrad, including "Heart of Darkness" (1899) and *Lord Jim* (1900).

463.11   Paul Morand]   Diplomat and novelist (1888–1975) whose works included *Tendres Stocks* (1921) and *Ouvert la nuit* (1922).

465.22–466.19   Le 2 oct. . . . la *New Republic*.]   A translation of the letter:

October 2

Sir: On returning to Paris I have found the article you were so kind as to devote to me.

Since I write to you in response to this article, allow me first to make a few clarifications. In addition to the books you cited I have published only one book and one chapbook (which I am sending you)—the remainder is very brief and of no importance. For the rest, my father was not an official in Indochina. I went to Asia at 23, as an assistant on an archeological mission. Subsequently I gave up archeology, organized the Young Annam movement, and then became a commissioner of the Kuomintang in Indochina and finally in Canton.

There is some truth in what Trotsky said about Garine, and in what you yourself have said. Nonetheless perhaps a certain objectivity should be taken into account. This character is no Marxist. Perhaps he was in the wrong, but that is the way it was. In Canton in 1927 (things were very different in 1927) there were many more revolutionary adventurers than Marxists. And when Borodine conversed with Sun-Yat-Sen, the subject was never the class struggle.—I do not want to raise that as an argument, but as a nuance. For it is entirely true that the role of objectivity in my novels is not predominant, and that *The Conquerors* is an "expressionist" novel, like (making all necessary allowances) *Wuthering Heights* or *The Brothers Karamazov*.

You say very correctly that *Man's Fate* develops certain ideas implicit in *The Conquerors*. And also that it is a better book (at least, to tell the truth, it the only one I like). My construction, indeed, could not be compared to that of a writer like Morand: his fictional types are based on ironic observation, mine on a need to translate through characters a certain order of ethical values.

Don't see this attempt at a discussion as anything but a way of thanking at greater length the first critic in America who has taken an interest in what I write and please believe, my dear sir, in my artistic sympathy, for I have been following for some time what *The New Republic* has been doing.

André Malraux

468.10   Marie Laurencin] French painter (1885–1956) known for her depictions of young girls and for her theatrical designs.

468.28   Glenway Wescott] American novelist (1901–1987) long resident in France, author of *The Grandmothers* (1927). See "Glenway Westcott's War Work" in *Classics and Commercials*.

469.15–16   Jacques-Emile Blanche] French painter (1861–1942) known primarily for portraits.

472.16   *Adolphe . . . de Clèves*] *Adolphe* (1816), by Benjamin Constant; *La Princesse de Clèves* (1678), by Mme. de La Fayette.

480.36–37   A. J. Muste] Social activist (1885–1967), a proponent of nonviolence.

491.10–12   Granville Hicks . . . Haakon Chevalier] Granville Hicks (1901–1982), Marxist literary critic; Newton Arvin (1900–1963), literary critic and professor at Smith College; Haakon Chevalier (1901–1985), scholar and French translator.

496.11   Max Eastman] Political journalist (1883–1969), a founder of *The Masses* and *The Liberator*, and associated in the 1930s with the anti-Stalinist left.

496.17   D. S. Mirsky] Literary historian (1890–1939), author of the English-language *History of Russian Literature* (1927). Mirsky was arrested by the NKVD in 1937 and died in a forced labor camp.

497.1   Meyerhold's] Vsevolod Meyerhold (1874–1940), leading figure of Russian avant-garde theater. Meyerhold was arrested by the NKVD on June 20, 1939, brutally tortured, and then shot on February 2, 1940.

497.18   Taïrov]   Alexander Taïrov (1885–1950), founder of the Moscow Chamber Theater in 1914.

497.34–35   Ostrovsky's *Talents and Admirers*]   Play (1882) by Alexander Ostrovsky (1823–1886).

498.19   Komsomol]   Communist Union of Youth, a Soviet organization for young people aged 14 to 28; many Komsomol activists later became Party members.

499.7   Colley Cibber]   Actor, playwright, and poet (1671–1757); his version of *Richard III*, dating from 1700, continued to be performed well into the 19th century.

499.20   murder of Kirov]   Sergei Kirov (1886–1934), Leningrad Party chief and Politburo member, whose assassination on December 1, 1934, was used by Stalin as a pretext to heighten repression through false claims that Kirov's murder was the result of conspiracy involving Trotsky and several other Old Bolshevik leaders. (The allegation that Stalin was complicit in the assassination himself remains unproven.)

501.4   VOKS]   All-Soviet Society for Cultural Relations Overseas.

501.4   Sergei Tretyakov]   Constructivist playwright (1892–1937). He was arrested on false charges of espionage in July 1937 and either committed suicide in prison or was shot.

501.12   LEF]   Avant-garde Soviet literary magazine, *The Left Front of Art*, founded in 1923 by Vladimir Mayakovsky and Osip Brik.

502.10   valuta]   Foreign currency.

513.16   *Riders to the Sea*]   One-act play (1904) by J. M. Synge.

515.7   C. K. Ogden]   Psychologist and linguist (1889–1957) who, with I. A. Richards, developed Basic English.

515.9   Richard Grant White]   Literary and cultural critic (1821–1885), author of *Handbook of Christian Art* (1853) and *Studies in Shakespeare* (1885).

520.5   Belinsky]   Vissarion Belinsky (1811–1848), preeminent Russian literary critic of his era.

520.35–521.1   Lord Beaconsfield]   Benjamin Disraeli, 1st Earl of Beaconsfield (1804–1881), novelist and Conservative prime minister.

521.1   Mr. Morley . . . Lord Acton]   John Morley (1838–1923), Liberal member of Parliament and government minister, a close associate of Gladstone; Lord Acton (1834–1902), historian and Liberal statesman.

522.40   Zinoviev and Kamenev]   Grigory Zinoviev (1883–1936) and Lev Kamenev (1883–1936), prominent Old Bolsheviks who had led the unsuccessful "Left Opposition" to Stalin, 1925–27. In August 1936 they were shot after a public trial in which they falsely confessed to conspiring with Trotsky to assassinate Kirov and overthrow the Soviet government.

523.2   Radek]   Karl Radek (1885–1939), a Polish-born Bolshevik active in the Comintern. He was arrested in 1936 and publicly confessed in late January 1937 to conspiring with Trotsky to commit espionage, sabotage, and terrorism against the Soviet Union. Radek received a ten-year sentence and was killed in prison, reportedly by another inmate.

523.36   Krylov's]   Ivan Krylov (1768–1844), author of nine collections of fables published between 1809 and 1843.

524.18–19   Lovestonite]   Jay Lovestone (1897–1990) was a founder of one branch of what became the Communist Party USA; in 1929 he was expelled from the party for supporting Nikolai Bukharin and became the head of a splinter group commonly known as Lovestonites. After World War II Lovestone worked with the AFL-CIO and the CIA to promote anti-Communist unions in the international labor movement.

525.4   Vernon L. Parrington]   Liberal historian and literary scholar (1871–1929), a professor at the University of Washington; best known for *Main Currents in American Thought* (1927–30).

525.12   RAPP]   The Russian Association of Proletarian Writers, founded in 1928, sought to impose a dogmatic "proletarian" style on Soviet literature and severely criticized Boris Pilnyak, Vladimir Mayakovsky, Yevgeny Zamyatin, and other nonconformist writers.

525.14   the Shostakovich incident]   In January 1936 Stalin walked out of a Moscow performance of Shostakovich's opera *Lady Macbeth of Mtensk*, and the composer was subsequently denounced in *Pravda* for "petit-bourgeois formalism."

530.13   King Charles's head]   Mr. Dick, in Charles Dickens' *David Copperfield* (1850), reverts to the subject of King Charles's head under all circumstances.

531.25   Leopardi]   See note 19.11 above.

532.22   Fannie Hurst]   Author (1889–1968) of bestselling novels, including *Imitation of Life* (1933), which were often adapted into films.

533.17   *Caleb Catlum's America*]   Satirical novel (1936) by Vincent McHugh.

539.9   Emil Jannings]   German actor (1884–1950) who became internationally famous for his roles in such films as *The Last Laugh* (1924) and *Variety* (1925). On his brief period in Hollywood see Wilson's review of his film *The Way of All Flesh* in *The American Earthquake* (1958). He then returned to Germany, starring in *The Blue Angel* (1930) and later appearing in Nazi propaganda films.

539.36   Lubitsch]   Ernst Lubitsch (1892–1947), German film director who began working in the United States in 1924, specializing in sophisticated comedies such as *The Marriage Circle* (1924), *So This Is Paris* (1926), and *Trouble in Paradise* (1932).

541.11   Schulberg]   B. P. Schulberg (1892–1957), studio executive at Paramount Pictures (father of novelist and screenwriter Budd Schulberg).

544.34   Colonel Lawrence]   T. E. Lawrence (1888–1935), known as Lawrence of Arabia.

546.13   V. F. Calverton]   Marxist critic (1900–1940), founder in 1923 of *Modern Quarterly* (later *Modern Monthly*).

546.25   Em Jo Basshe's *The Centuries*]   *The Centuries: Portrait of a Tenement House*, produced in 1927 by the New Playwrights' Theatre.

548.30   Stephen Phillips . . . Arthur Symons]   Phillips (1864–1915), English poet, author of verse plays including *Paolo and Francesca* (1900); Symons (1865–1945), poet and author of *The Symbolist Movement in Literature* (1899).

548.36   Jim Tully's *Beggars of Life*]   Tully (1891–1947) published his *Beggars of Life: A Hobo Autobiography* in 1924.

554.12–13   G. Lowes Dickinson's *A Modern Symposium*]   *A Modern Symposium: Basic Political Viewpoints Debated*, published by Dickinson (1862–1932) in 1905.

560.18   Arthur Quiller-Couch]   English critic (1863–1944) and professor at Cambridge University; editor of *The Oxford Book of English Verse* (1900).

561.1   bouts rimés]   A game in which lines of verse are written to fit rhymed words.

568.29   Callot]   See note 145.19.

572.13–14   *Les Chants de Maldoror*]   Series of apocalyptic prose poems by Comte de Lautréamont (1846–1870, pen name of Isidore-Lucien Ducasse), published four years after his death.

575.9   "lily on lily, that o'erlace the sea"]   See Robert Browning, "Cleon."

575.17   George Borrow]   English writer (1803–1881) noted for his depictions of Gypsy life in *Lavengro* (1851) and *The Romany Rye* (1857).

576.8   "in a fine frenzy rolling,"]   See *A Midsummer Night's Dream*, V.i.12–13: "The poet's eye, in a fine frenzy rolling, / Doth glance from heaven to earth, from earth to heaven."

577.3   James Huneker]   See note 152.24–25.

577.21   Orson Welles's *Julius Caesar*]   Welles's modern-dress production for the Mercury Theatre, designed to suggest a parallel with Fascism, opened in 1937.

582.6   Young Hegelian movement in Germany] A group of academics at the University of Berlin in the 1830s and 1840s, whose members included David Strauss, Ludwig Feuerbach, and Bruno Bauer; Karl Marx and Friedrich Engels were younger members but later attacked the group.

587.11   Stakhanovist methods] In 1935 the Soviet government began a campaign to speed up industrial production, taking as its inspiration the exceptional productivity attributed to Alexei Stakhanov, a coal miner in the Donets Basin.

601.16   Maxine Elliott] American stage actress (1868–1940) who enjoyed great success in the late 19th and early 20th century.

602.28   Rolfe Humphries] Poet and classical scholar (1894–1969).

603.25   Ruth Pickering's] Later a journalist for *The New Republic* and *The Nation.*

603.27   Miss Reese . . . Miss Teasdale] Poets Lizette Woodworth Reese (1856–1935) and Sara Teasdale (1883–1933).

603.35   A.E.F.] American Expeditionary Force.

614.3   Susan Glaspell] Playwright (1882–1948), a founder of the Provincetown Players.

618.18   Hutchins Hapgood] Radical journalist (1869–1944), author of *The Autobiography of a Thief* (1903) and *The Spirit of Labor* (1907).

621.35   *"On en parle toujours, mais on ne le fait jamais."*] They keep talking about it, but they never do it.

624.13   Mary Carolyn Davies] Poet whose books included *Songs* (1914) and *The Drums in Our Street* (1918), and who contributed to the *Others* anthologies edited by Alfred Kreymborg.

634.31–32   *Si qua recordanti . . . ora voluptas*] Catullus 76: If a man can take any pleasure in remembering the good things he has done.

634.33–34   Ipse valere . . . pietate mea!] I want myself well, to be rid of this sickness. / Do this for me, O gods, in reward for my piety.

637.29   George Dillon] Poet (1906–1968) who collaborated with Edna St. Vincent Millay on translation of Baudelaire's *Flowers of Evil*, published in 1936. His affair with Millay is the subject of her sonnet sequence *Fatal Interview.*

AXEL'S CASTLE

647.4–7   "The atoms of Democritus . . . shine so bright!"] Cf. William Blake, "Mock on Mock on Voltaire Rousseau," lines 9–12.

649.29–35   "Nor wilt thou snare him . . . yelp alone."] Cf. *The Princess*, Canto 7.

650.1–2   "The silver eel . . . with gold."] "Windsor Forest." See page 212 in this volume.

650.19   "Bouvard et Pécuchet" or "L'Education Sentimentale."] Novels by Gustave Flaubert, published respectively in 1881 and 1869.

653.4–8   "I *know* . . . of spiritual *effect*."] In "Marginalia."

653.14–15   "Comme de longs échos . . . se répondent,"] Like long echoes which at a distance mix together . . . / Scents, colors, and sounds correspond: *Les Fleurs du Mal*, "Correspondances," lines 5 and 8.

653.19–26   "Night arrived . . . melodious monotone."] In "The Colloquy of Monos and Una."

654.38   "J'ai perdu ma force et ma vie."] I have lost my strength and my life.

655.24–25   Thomas Bailey Aldrich] Boston-based editor and author (1836–1907), best known for *The Story of a Bad Boy* (1870).

656.36   Moréas] Jean Moreas, name adopted by Iannis Pappadiamantopoulos (1856–1910), a Greek poet who wrote in French.

656.37   Henri de Régnier] Poet and novelist (1864–1936), a proponent of *vers libre*.

657.4–5   "Donner un sens . . .de la tribu."] To give a purer meaning to the words of the tribe: "Le Tombeau d'Edgar Poe," line 6.

660.3–4   Lockhart's attack on Keats and Byron's attack on Jeffrey] John Lockhart savagely criticized Keats' *Endymion* in *Blackwood's Magazine* in 1818; Byron satirized Francis Jeffrey, editor of *The Edinburgh Review*, in the poem "English Bards and Scotch Reviewers."

663.7–20   "Le vierge, le vivace . . . inutile le Cygne."] The virgin, vigorous, and beautiful today / Will it cleave for us with a drunken wingbeat / This hard forgotten lake haunted beneath the frost / By the transparent glacier of flights that have not flown? / A swan of a former time remembers it is he / Magnificent but who without hope frees himself / For not having sung the region to be lived in / When the tedium of the sterile winter has shone. / His whole neck will shake off that white agony / Inflicted by space on the bird who denies it, / But not the horror of the ground where the plumage is taken. / Phantom who is assigned to that place by his pure brilliance, / He goes motionless at the cold dream of contempt / With which the Swan robes himself in his useless exile.

672.22   Bastien-Lepage . . . Carolus Durand] Jules Bastien-Lepage

(1848–1884), French genre painter; Emile Auguste Carolus-Durand (1837–1917), French portrait painter and teacher whose students included John Singer Sargent.

676.17   Walton's "Lives"]   Brief biographies by Izaak Walton (1593–1683) of John Donne, Sir Henry Wotton, Richard Hooker, George Herbert, and Bishop Robert Sanderson.

677.14   Madame Blavatsky]   Helena Petrovna Blavatsky (1831–1891), born in Russia, came to the U.S. in 1873 and founded the Theosophical Society; author of *The Secret Doctrine* (1888).

678.15   Charcot's]   Jean-Martin Charcot (1825–1893), French neurologist who studied hysteria. Sigmund Freud was a student in his Paris clinic from October 1885 to February 1886.

683.19–20   John Stuart Mill's attack upon Sir William Hamilton]   In *An Examination of Sir William Hamilton's Philosophy* (1865).

683.24   Boehme]   Jakob Boehme (1575–1624), German mystic, author of treatises including *Aurora* (1612) and *Mysterium Magnum* (1623).

689.40   Valéry Larbaud]   Poet and novelist (1881–1957).

694.12–15   "Que si ta bouche . . . Eve!"]   So that if your mouth makes a dream, / This thirst that dreams of the envigorating sap, / This deliciousness half in the future / Is eternity that is melting, Eve!

694.29   "L'insecte net gratte la sécheresse"]   The insect, distinct, scratches at drought.

694.31   "Où tant de marbre est tremblant sur tant d'ombres"]   Where so much marble trembles over so many shadows.

694.32–33   "une tendre lueur . . . existe"]   A tender gleam of an ambiguous time of day exists.

694.35–36   "Onde déserte . . . d'un cygne"]   Deserted wave, and worthy, by its luster, of the glossy disappearance of a swan.

695.2–6   "Si l'âme intense . . . Sur ce roc"]   If the intense soul blows, and furiously swells / The abrupt wave on top of the wave beaten down, and if the wave / Thunders against the cape, immolating a monstrous candor, / And comes from the high seas to spew the depths / Upon this rock . . .

695.10–14   "Calme, claire . . . de ton mouvement!"]   Calm, clear, heavy with charms, / I dominated furtively, / My eye in the glowing gold of your fleece, / The nape of your neck, enigmatic and charged / With the secrets of your movement!

695.16–18   "Le marbre aspire . . . du mouvement!"]   The marble aspires, the gold draws itself up! / Those blonde foundations of shadow and amber / Tremble on the edge of movement!

695.21   "Ta forme au ventre pur qu'un bras fluide drape."]   Your form
with its pure belly that a fluid arm drapes.

699.24   Alain] Pen name of Émile-Auguste Chartier (1868–1951), philosopher and essayist whose works included *Les Idées et les âges* (1927).

702.35   Mme. de Caillavet] Mme. Arman de Caillavet (1844–1910),
whose literary salon was highly influential.

708.26   "L'espoir luit comme un brin de paille dans l'étable"]   See note
52.28–29.

710.4–23   "Hier l'orchestra attaqua . . . qu'une fois"]   Yesterday the orchestra attacked / Its last polka / Oh! Autumn, autumn! / The casinos /
Abandoned / Put their pianos in storage! . . . / Phrases, glassware / Clots
of memories. / Oh! how thin she's gotten! / What will become of me? . . .
/ Farewell! The daughters of the yew trees in the gray mist / Resemble
mourners at funerals / In the black stormy wind that wants everything to go
away. / Enough, enough, / You're the one who started it. / Go, it's no
longer the odor of your furs. / Go, your slightest winks are perjuries. / Shut
up, with your kind nothing lasts. / Shut up, shut up / One only loves
once.

717.16   "Pervigilium Veneris"] Poem of unknown authorship, dating
possibly from the 3rd century, describing the eve of the festival of Venus.

717.18   Arnaut Daniel] See note 46.28.

717.28   May Sinclair] Novelist (1863–1946), author of *The Three Sisters*
(1914) and *Mary Olivier: A Life* (1919); a literary reviewer interested in psychoanalysis.

719.1–2   "O Nature . . . en âge"]   O nature, give me the strength and
the courage to believe myself of age.

721.14   "Wanna Go Home, Baby"] Published in book form as *Sweeney
Agonistes: Fragments of an Aristophanic Melodrama.*

721.31   Wyndham Lewis] Painter, novelist, and essayist (1882–1957) associated with Vorticism; founder of *Blast* (1914–15) with Ezra Pound.

721.34–35   Aldington, Nancy Cunard] Richard Aldington (1892–1962),
poet and novelist, author of *Death of a Hero*; Nancy Cunard (1896–1965), English writer and editor.

723.38   the Fratellinis] See note 134.28.

724.18–19   "Les plus désespérés . . . de purs sanglots."]   The most desperate songs are the most beautiful, / And I know some immortal ones that
are pure sobs.

726.1–2   "Georgics," . . . "Ars Poetica" . . . Manilius] *Georgics* (29
BCE), poem on agriculture by Virgil; *Ars Poetica*, poem on aesthetic principles

by Horace; Marcus Manilius, poet of the 1st century, author of *Astronomica*, a long poem on astrology.

728.29   Shenstone] William Shenstone (1714–1763), minor English poet who often wrote on pastoral themes.

734.19–20   *"Longtemps, je me suis couché de bonne heure,"*] See note 309.1–2.

738.28–30   Lady Dedlock . . . Mr. Merdle] Lady Dedlock, young wife of Sir Leicester Dedlock in *Bleak House*; Mr. Merdle, bankrupted financier in *Little Dorrit*.

747.19–20   *jeune fille à marier*] Marriageable girl.

756.16   those dialogues of Leopardi] *Operette morali*, published posthumously in 1845.

774.25–26   the Edward Ponderevos, the Clayhangers, the Jacob Stahls, the Michael Fanes] Protagonists of, respectively, *Tono-Bungay* (1909) by H. G. Wells; *Clayhanger* (1910) and three subsequent novels by Arnold Bennett; *The Early History of Jacob Stahl* (1911) by J. D. Beresford; and *Sinister Street* (1913–14) by Compton Mackenzie.

787.26–27   the book on "Ulysses" which Mr. Stuart Gilbert has announced] Published as *James Joyce's Ulysses* (1932).

796.33–34   another work] *Finnegans Wake*, published in 1939.

796.35   *Transition*] Literary magazine—properly *transition*—established in 1927 by Eugene Jolas; his co-editor was Elliot Paul. The last issue appeared in 1938.

817.6–7   "Chants de Maldoror"] See note 572.13–14.

819.12   Villiers de l'Isle-Adam's] Philippe-Auguste, comte de Villiers de l'Isle-Adam (1838–1889), novelist and playwright, an impoverished descendant of Breton nobility; in addition to *Axel* (1890) he wrote the dramas *Elen* (1865) and *Morgane* (1866), the novel *L'Ève Future* (1886), and the stories collected in *Contes cruels* (1883).

838.32–33   Blaise Cendrars's negro anthology] *Anthologie nègre* (1921), a groundbreaking anthology of African myths, tales, poems, and other materials.

839.2–3   Nathalia Crane . . . Daisy Ashford] Nathalia Crane (b. 1913) published her first poetry collection at the age of 11; Daisy Ashford (1881–1972) wrote *The Young Visiters* at the age of nine.

850.31–34   *"Le bureau de poste . . . mais de savoir."*] "The post office is just opposite." "—And what difference is that supposed to make to me?" "Excuse me, I saw you had a letter in your hand. I thought . . ." "—It's not a matter of thinking, but of knowing."

858.34   Bishop Manning . . . Dr. Straton] William Thomas Manning (1866–1949), Episcopal bishop at the Cathedral of St. John the Divine; the Rev. John Roach Straton (1875–1929), pastor of Calvary Baptist Church in New York, known for his public attacks on immorality and atheism.

859.32   Jack Johnson] African-American boxer (1878–1946) who became heavyweight champion of the world in 1908; he lost the title to Jess Willard in 1915.

861.23–24   Tertullian or Billy Sunday] Tertullian (c. 160–225), Christian theologian whose treatises included *The Apology* and *The Prescription of Heretics*; Billy Sunday (1862–1935), American evangelical preacher.

872.9   Robert W. Chambers] Prolific popular novelist, author of *The Fighting Chance* (1906), among other books.

873.38   *De te, fabula!*] Cf. Horace, Satires, I.i.69: "de te fabula narratur" (the story applies to you). It was used by Karl Marx as an epigraph for *Das Kapital*.

880.27   the Fabian Society] English socialist organization advocating gradual reform, founded in 1885; leading members included Sidney and Beatrice Webb as well as George Bernard Shaw.

888.35   "guêpe ivre de son vol fou"] See note 52.29–30.

892.29–30   perhaps the only poet of the first magnitude] Wilson was apparently the first outside the poet's circle to acknowledge Yeats as the preeminent modern poet.

893.2   Eugène Brieux] Realist playwright (1858–1932) whose plays included *The Red Robe* (1900).

Index

THE LIBRARY OF AMERICA SERIES

The Library of America fosters appreciation and pride in America's literary heritage by publishing, and keeping permanently in print, authoritative editions of America's best and most significant writing. An independent nonprofit organization, it was founded in 1979 with seed money from the National Endowment for the Humanities and the Ford Foundation.

This book is set in 10 point Linotron Galliard,
a face designed for photocomposition by Matthew Carter
and based on the sixteenth-century face Granjon. The paper
is acid-free lightweight opaque and meets the requirements
for permanence of the American National Standards Institute.
The binding material is Brillianta, a woven rayon cloth made
by Van Heek-Scholco Textielfabrieken, Holland. Compo-
sition by Dedicated Business Services. Printing by
Malloy Incorporated. Binding by Dekker Book-
binding. Designed by Bruce Campbell.

—